P

Se

SELECTED J … S

John James Audubc … Audubon and his mistress, Jeanne Rabin, was born on April 26, 1785, in Les Cayes, Santo Domingo, where his father, a French trader and sea captain, owned a plantation. Jeanne Rabin died six months later. When he was three years old, Audubon was sent to Nantes, France, to be raised by his stepmother, Anne Moynet Audubon. In 1803 Audubon left France for the United States, where his father owned a large farm in Pennsylvania. In 1808 he married Lucy Bakewell, daughter of an English neighbor, and set out to earn his fortune as a trader and a storekeeper in Kentucky. In 1820, discouraged by a number of financial setbacks, Audubon turned exclusively to his art, determined to become America's foremost painter of birds. After a lengthy stay in Louisiana, where his wife had found a job as a private schoolteacher on a prosperous plantation near Saint Francisville, Audubon sailed for England, where he eventually found an engraver, Robert Havell, to prepare the plates for *Birds of America*. In 1838 the fourth and final volume of the great work was published. It stands today as one of the monumental achievements in the entire history of naturalistic art. As a companion volume to the engraved paintings, Audubon (with the help of William MacGillivray of Edinburgh) wrote a detailed commentary on the individual birds, the *Ornithological Biography*. It was completed, in five volumes, in 1839. In 1840, with his good friend the Reverend John Bachman of Charleston, South Carolina, Audubon began work on *Viviparous Quadrupeds of North America*. Before he could complete it, he died at his home in New York, on January 27, 1851.

Ben Forkner is a professor of English and American literature at the University of Angers in France. He has published essays on writers from Ireland and from the American South, and has edited two anthologies of Irish short stories, *Modern Irish Short Stories* (Penguin) and *A New Book of Dubliners*. He has also edited a pair of companion anthologies, *Louisiana Stories* and *Georgia Stories*, devoted to the two major historical sources of the modern Southern short story, and with Patrick Samway, S.J., he has co-edited four other anthologies of Southern literature: *Stories of the Modern South* (Penguin), *Stories of the Old South* (Penguin), *A Modern Southern Reader*, and *A New Reader of the Old South*. Recently, he has written the text for *Cajun*, an album featuring the photography of Fonville Winans. His latest work is a monograph, *The Boethius of Crawfordville*, on the prison diary of Alexander Stephens, the anti-secessionist vice president of the Confederacy. Forkner's two-volume French edition of John James Audubon's journals and essays, *Journaux et Récits*, appeared in 1992.

SELECTED JOURNALS AND OTHER WRITINGS

JOHN JAMES AUDUBON

EDITED
WITH AN INTRODUCTION BY
BEN FORKNER

PENGUIN BOOKS

PENGUIN BOOKS
Published by the Penguin Group
Penguin Books USA Inc., 375 Hudson Street, New York, New York 10014, U.S.A.
Penguin Books Ltd, 27 Wrights Lane, London W8 5TZ, England
Penguin Books Australia Ltd, Ringwood, Victoria, Australia
Penguin Books Canada Ltd, 10 Alcorn Avenue, Toronto, Ontario, Canada M4V 3B2
Penguin Books (N.Z.) Ltd, 182–190 Wairau Road, Auckland 10, New Zealand

Penguin Books Ltd, Registered Offices: Harmondsworth, Middlesex, England

This collection first published in Penguin Books 1996

1 3 5 7 9 10 8 6 4 2

Library of Congress Cataloging-in-Publication Data
Audubon, John James, 1785–1851.
[Selections. 1996]
Selected journals and other writings / John James Audubon ;
edited with an introduction by Ben Forkner.
p. cm. — (Penguin nature classics)
ISBN 0 14 02.4126 4 (pbk.)
1. Audubon, John James, 1785–1851—Diaries. 2. Naturalists—United States—Diaries.
3. Audubon, John James, 1785–1851—Journeys—North America.
4. North America—Description and travel. 5. Natural history—North America.
I. Forkner, Ben. II. Title.
III. Series.
QL31.A9A3 1996
598'.092—dc20
[B] 95-40325

Printed in the United States of America
Set in Postscript Sabon

PENGUIN NATURE CLASSICS

Nature is our widest home. It includes the oceans that provide our rain, the trees that give us air to breathe, the ancestral habitats we shared with countless kinds of animals that now exist only by our sufferance or under our heel.

Until quite recently, indeed (as such things go), the whole world was a wilderness in which mankind lived as cannily as deer, overmastering with spears or snares even their woodsmanship and that of other creatures, finding a path wherever wildlife could go. Nature was the central theater of life for everybody's ancestors, not a hideaway where people went to rest and recharge after a hard stint in an urban or suburban arena. Many of us still do hike, swim, fish, birdwatch, sleep on the ground, or paddle a boat on vacation, and will loll like a lizard in the sun any other chance we have. We can't help grinning for at least a moment at the sight of surf, or sunlight on a river meadow, as if remembering in our mind's eye paleolithic pleasures in a home before memories officially began.

It is a thoughtless grin because nature predates "thought." Aristotle was a naturalist, and nearer to our own time Darwin made of the close observation of bits of nature a lever to examine life in many ways on a large scale. Yet nature writing, despite its basis in science, usually rings with rhapsody as well—a belief that nature is an expression of God.

In this series we are presenting some nature writers of the past century or so, though leaving out great novelists like Turgenev, Melville, Conrad, and Faulkner, who were masters of natural description, and poets, beginning with Homer (who was perhaps the first nature writer, once his words had been transcribed). Nature writing now combines rhapsody with science and connects science with rhapsody, and for that reason it is a very special and a nourishing genre.

Edward Hoagland

ACKNOWLEDGMENTS

I am grateful to a number of good people who have helped in the making of this book. Pierre Michaut, genial founder of Atalante in Nantes, France, kindly granted me permission to print part of my preface to *Journaux et Récits* (Atalante and the Bibliothèque Municipale de Nantes, 1992) in its original, unpublished English version. Pierre, together with Mireille Rivalland and Patrick Couton, were indulgent and generous supporters from the beginning. Nadine (my Brittany songbird), Benjamin, Olive, Pete, and John were, as usual, unsparing in their love and encouragement. My friends Pat Samway of New York, and John Paine of Nashville, supplied me several times with vital information from American libraries. Finally, I would like to thank my editor, Michael Millman, for going far beyond the call of editorial duty in bringing Audubon back to life as a Penguin. This volume, including the choice of illustrations, has been immeasurably improved by Michael's attentions. He and his assistant, Kristine Puopolo, deserve all my praise and gratitude.

CONTENTS

LIST OF ILLUSTRATIONS

INTRODUCTION

Writing the American Woods
The Journals and Essays of John James Audubon

MISSISSIPPI RIVER JOURNAL

"Without any money my talents are to be my support and my enthusiasm my guide. . . ." Thus begins, on October 12, 1820, one of the opening entries in a weather-scarred but neatly penned journal kept by John James Audubon. Most of his many journals have been lost or destroyed; the *Mississippi River Journal* of 1820–21 is one of the rare survivals. Saved by his son Victor, for whom it was written, it is surely one of the remarkable documents to come out of the entire early American experience, and one of the most compelling portraits we have of an unproved artist's single-minded ambition. At the time, the author of these rather innocent-sounding romantic vows was thirty-five years old, a husband, and father of two young boys. He had failed in every business venture he had undertaken. He was leaving behind not only his wife and sons until he could support them, but also a twisted trail of doubts and debts that reached from his French father's home near Nantes to his wife's English relatives in Pennsylvania to the various American friends and associates he had met during the past twelve years trying to establish himself in the tough frontier settlements of Kentucky. He was now traveling down the Ohio River on his way to New Orleans, camping out on the damp deck of a very functional flatboat, fighting the mosquitoes by day and the cold weather by night, hunting wild game on the shore to help pay for his passage, and eating sweet potatoes out of his hand when the wind and rain forced him to stay on the boat.

And yet Audubon was not a man to be easily dispirited by hard times and poor prospects. Those first lines reveal a strong steady quality of stubborn will in what was otherwise a rather carefree and restless personality. Even as he set out on this last-ditch effort to restore his pride and make his fortune, Audubon, the self-made naturalist and artist, was convinced he had made the right decision. He planned to search out, observe, shoot down, study, sketch, and paint specimens of every known and unknown bird within his range. This trip south down the Ohio and the Mississippi would be the first step, to be followed by as many more as necessary, west, north, east, and farther south, each time increasing his scientific knowledge and artistic skill, and each time adding to the growing pile of paintings. When the time was right, he would then gather together his best work and present it to the unsuspecting world at large as the finest, most complete collection of native American birds ever painted by a single individual. After years of false starts and second thoughts, he was now fully determined to do what was necessary to accomplish his aim. If it meant months of privation, wandering, and absence from his family, he was prepared. He had brought along as a talisman a miniature portrait of his wife, Lucy. And as a reminder that his purpose was not entirely a question of lofty self-ambition he had drawn on a single sheet of paper a straight line representing the length of Lucy's feet. Once he had the money, he would buy her a pair of new shoes.

THE BIRDS OF AMERICA

Audubon did experience some brief moments of panic and loss of sleep on the flatboat journey, especially when he carelessly left his portfolio on the wharf in Natchez. Even this did not shake his determination. And I doubt if he would have been in the least surprised had he been granted a glimpse into the last years of his life, and discovered that his astonishing one-man project had been completed, and successfully published as *Birds of America*, to almost universal acclaim. This monumental work had appeared in two different editions, the immense life-size double elephant folio published in London between 1827 and 1838, and the smaller octavo version published in New York and Philadelphia between 1840 and 1844. And the same Audubon who had been jailed for debts in Louisville a year before setting out on the cold flatboat down the Ohio was now, twenty years later, comfortably surrounded by his wife and family on a substantial estate in New York, busily painting away on his new work of native American mammals, the *Viviparous Quadrupeds of North America*, and acknowledged as a great original artist in every major capital of the Western world.

Audubon's fame in our times continues to be based, as it should be, on *Birds of America*, and on his reputation as one of the revolutionary figures in the history of ornithological art. His skill at combining exact detail with dramatic lifelike visions of the individual bird's actual behavior in the outside world had a far-reaching influence, not only on future wildlife artists, but also on the vital perception that the wild bird or beast is most fully seen and appreciated in its natural habitat. Then there is the odd quirky imaginative touch in Audubon's brilliant compositions. Once seen, it is difficult to forget the stiff blustery military pomp of the American white pelican, the outraged comic stare of the purple martin, or the precise piercing oriental beauty of his smaller songbirds. The *Birds of America* has never been out of print for long, and can be found without trouble today in large luxurious editions from New York to London to Paris. Over the years, however, especially as lost journals have come to light and have been deposited in libraries, there has been increasing recognition among scientists, historians, men of letters, and the curious layman, that the brightness of his painted birds has somewhat obscured another side of Audubon's importance; and by that I refer to the rich record of his life and times presented in the mass of miscellaneous writing he left behind him after his death.

THE ORNITHOLOGICAL BIOGRAPHY

Of course, much of this writing had been published during his lifetime. This was the case for the five-volume *Ornithological Biography*, which he began in 1830 and finished in 1839. Conceived at first as a straightforward descriptive text to supplement the engravings of the *Birds of America*, the *Biography* turned out to be a considerably more complex and intriguing enterprise. It finally reflected, as did almost everything else Audubon put his mind to, an unwillingness to limit himself to a single subject, and a powerful desire to gratify the multiple selves his singular personality contained: romantic adventurer, gifted artist, loyal family man, inspired storyteller, methodical taker of notes, and ambitious would-be scientist.

To begin with, the *Ornithological Biography* collected, as the title announced, a number of so-called "bird biographies," dense, carefully written essays describing the various birds he had painted. They are conscientiously packed with physical facts and measurements, close-up observations about how each bird hunted for food, chose its roosting place, fought, sang, played, courted, nested, and nursed its young. Audubon included as well all manner of far-ranging information he had noted down during his trips, much of it still valuable today, concerning the vegetation, climate, and general geographical situation, anything that could help define the bird's particular pattern of existence. For the self-taught Audubon, who worried all his life about not having a university education, and was constantly on the defensive as far as his scientific knowledge was concerned, the rigorous commentary of the bird biographies was aimed primarily at establishing his credibility as a serious naturalist. Even given these scientific parameters, however, he could not completely repress a natural exuberance, a tendency to pepper his descriptions with personal anecdotes and eccentric reflections, and a self-dramatizing urge to thrust himself forward as a subject of interest at least on an equal footing with his birds. Only when we turn to the numerous nonbird biographies, however, the strange collection of short sketches and reminiscences Audubon called "episodes," and which he scattered throughout the *Ornithological Biography*, in between the official documentation, does this impulse bloom out in all its egocentric glory.

THE EPISODES

Audubon was conscious that the episodes were probably not in their proper place when they were first published. He realized, rightly, that their appeal was more historical than scientific, and slightly more literary than either. When he reprinted the bird biographies in the smaller octavo edition of the *Birds of America*, the episodes were deliberately left out. A group of them was later translated into French by Eugène Bazin in 1868, in his anthology of Audubon's writings, *Scènes de la Nature dans les Etats-Unis et le Nord de l'Amérique*, but they were not republished again in English until Maria Audubon's two-volume edition, *Audubon and His Journals*, appeared in 1897, forty-six years after her grandfather's death. It is fascinating to speculate on the process by which Audubon arrived at his original version of the episodic form, a compressed mixture of diverse elements roughly made up of part recollection, part direct report, part hearsay, part invention, part theater, and part the imperial imagination's demand for the completed pattern.

To a certain extent, Audubon was writing well within the tradition of the personal travel essay, a genre with a respectable history, especially in France and England, and a staple of the nineteenth-century magazine and newspaper. But to a certain extent, too, he was influenced by two developments in American fiction that were just then beginning to make an impact on the reading public: the birth of the modern short story, and the popular urban taste for backwoods humor and the frontier sketch. Audubon himself loved to read, and along with his fiddle and flute and sketch pad and gun, he carried his favorite books deep into the swamps and big woods. His journals are filled with references to poems and novels, and to the writers he admired: Byron, Scott, Edgeworth, Thompson, Smollet, La Fontaine. One of these was Washington Irving, widely celebrated for such stories as "Rip Van Winkle" and "The Legend of Sleepy Hollow," and considered by the time Audubon began publishing his own literary efforts as the founder of the new short story and the living father of an independent American literature. Audubon took the trouble of searching him out on a visit to Washington in 1833, and received from Irving a generous offer to help him secure a government boat for his expedition to Florida. Irving's literary skills were beyond Audubon's reach or ambition, but the dramatic unified effect of the short story form definitely made an impact on his imagination. It is hard to think that Audubon could have written his best episodes, such as "The Prairie" or "Death of a Pirate," without the inspiration of the early American short story writers glimmering somewhere in the back of his mind.

Whatever Audubon may have learned from the formal requirements of the short story in terms of dramatic technique and concentrated focus, much of the energy and exotic choice of subject in the episodes points straight to the magazine sketches of frontier life that had suddenly become the fashion in the big eastern cities in the 1830s. Many of these were published in the New York journal *Spirit of the Times*, edited between 1831 and 1856 by a westward-looking enthusiast, William T. Porter, who did more than anyone else to encourage the mode. He compiled two best-selling anthologies that not only sold fast and furiously in New York City but were carried by travelers and booksellers all across the eastern seaboard; they became standard reading fare in every tavern and hotel that cared about keeping its reputation up to snuff. Enterprising innkeepers made their own collections; they would rip out the best sketches from newspapers and paste them into homemade books to be read out loud around the dinner table at night.

Written primarily by southern writers in Georgia, Tennessee, Alabama, and Louisiana, these sketches were meant to bring back news of the wild unsettled territories lying just west of civilization. Full of outrageous boasts and improbable exploits, the stories of Augustus Baldwin Longstreet, Johnson Jones Hooper, and Thomas Bangs Thorpe did not aim very high; they were extremely popular, but they were usually labeled as subliterary entertainments by intellectual readers who happened to take a look. This did not overly disturb their authors, most of whom were not professional writers but lawyers, doctors, and newspaper men who liked to play hard jokes, tell tall tales, and who genuinely admired the fierce independence of the frontier trapper and hunter. Davy Crockett and Daniel Boone were among their heroes, and the fantastic "bear story" their favorite test of storytelling skill. Audubon could write a good Daniel Boone story himself. The episode "Colonel Boone" purports to be a faithful account of what Boone told Audubon "in his own words," and the episode "Kentucky Sports" uses Boone as the best example of the Kentucky hunter's prowess with the rifle. As for bear stories, Audubon provides several of these as well, including the episode "Scipio and the Bear," and the *Missouri River Journal* account of the hunter whose life was miraculously saved when he was caught in a tree after being mauled to the bone and tossed six feet in the air by a wounded grizzly.

Audubon borrowed freely from these literary sources when composing the episodes, but he had a flair for the vivid emphatic incident that was all his own, and he had the great advantage of setting down on paper, for the most part, scenes he had witnessed himself. Even while the *Ornithological Biography* was being published, his veracity on several occasions was attacked by jealous naturalists and travel writers such as George Ord, biographer and editor of Alexander Wilson, and Charles Waterton, author of *Wanderings in South America*, both of whom had their own books and authority to sell. But there was very little absolute invention in Audubon's stories. He confused dates, blended separate events into a single tale, and perhaps overdramatized his friendships with brilliant men and obscure women, but there is too much corroborative evidence from other sources to doubt the fundamental accuracy of the events he described. What he sometimes lacked in convincing literary style, he usually made up in compelling detail. The fine description of his frightened horse in "The Earthquake," during the great earthquake of 1813, spreading out his four legs to keep from falling, and groaning with fear, cannot be dismissed even if Audubon did heighten the effect with an extra flourish or two. And in "The Hurricane," the yellow smudge in the sky before the storm, and the strong smell of sulfur afterward, are both telling perceptions that anyone who has ever lived through a hurricane out-of-doors can readily confirm.

The picture Audubon presents of himself in such episodes as "The Earthquake" and "The Hurricane," the solitary traveler absorbed by the natural world, juxtaposed alone against the elemental earth and sky, is exactly what seduced readers in the nineteenth century, and exactly what continues to strike the imagination of readers and writers today. From these episodes, and from his various journals, modern poets and novelists such as Robert Penn Warren and Eudora Welty have discovered in Audubon a powerful symbol of the individual visionary struggling against time and, to some extent, against the destructive impulse of civilization. Aside from all the other reasons for collecting a large number of the episodes along with the two American journals, this may be the most attractive: the image of Audubon the free-spirited woodsman, his hair shoulder-length, the way he liked it all his life, walking and riding as instinct and desire directed him, chasing a single rare hawk for days at a time, rambling at his ease down countless Indian and animal trails, camping beneath thousand-year-old live oaks in a primeval forest that seemed to have no end: the self-made American Frenchman, passionately attached to the idea of hope and promise, plunging deeper and deeper into the timeless reality of a vast green land, yet at the same time stalked by a desperate feeling that he would not be able to record everything he saw before it disappeared.

Throughout his letters and journals, particularly in Europe where he missed America to such an extent that even wide awake at his desk he could distinctly hear the sound of birds flying in the Mississippi forest, he frequently remarks that it may very soon be too late, and that his own unsophisticated literary powers are too weak for the task. When asked one December day in 1826 in Edinburgh why he doesn't write a "little book" about America, Audubon ironically exclaims, in the privacy of his journal, "I cannot write at all, but if I could how could I make a *little* book, when I have seen enough to make a dozen *large* books? I will not write at all." He wished he could somehow bring himself to speak about all this to the contemporary writer he revered over all others, Sir Walter Scott, to persuade him to visit Louisiana and set the vision down in the language it deserved: "Without Sir Walter Scott these beauties must perish unknown to the world."

It should be emphasized that many of the most interesting episodes look back toward the earlier period of Audubon's life along the Ohio and Mississippi rivers. For the most part they are rewritten versions of journal entries, a reassuring fact considering that most of the original journals no longer exist. Audubon apparently kept journals sporadically from the time he left his father's unprospering farm Mill Grove in Pennsylvania in the spring of 1808 and migrated to Kentucky with his young bride, Lucy. Intended for Lucy and later for his sons as well, these journals were written while he was traveling away from his family, often for months, and, in the case of the European journals, for three years. But to return to Audubon's portrait of America in his episodes, journals, letters, and other writings, it is well to remember that he had the good fortune (for himself and his readers) to be in the right place at the right time, and that his initiation into a frontier existence at the age of twenty-three occurred when great stretches of the territory west of the Appalachian Mountains were still in a state of nearly pristine wilderness.

AUDUBON'S INDIANS

The southern Indians up and down the Mississippi Valley had not yet been pushed completely out of their ancestral hunting grounds into the western territories, although this would happen all too quickly in the next twenty years. Audubon thus witnessed the last vestiges of aboriginal Indian life before the accumulated pressures of 300 years of forced contact with European-Americans finally condemned it forever. He was in England, in the midst of completing *Birds of America*, when in 1838 the last of the Cherokees in Georgia and North Carolina were made to take all the belongings they could carry and to walk over a thousand miles in the shameful "trail of tears" removal, thus following the Creeks, the Chickasaws, and the Chocktaws across the Mississippi River.

During Audubon's Kentucky period, he often met Indians on his path, and almost invariably joined them for a hunt or a meal or an improvised dance. Near the mouth of the Ohio during the winter of 1810 and 1811, held up by ice on a trip with his French business partner, he helped a band of Shawnees kill wild swans for the feathers they sold to traders buying on behalf of European hatmakers. He was struck by the independence and strength of a squaw at their camp. The day after giving birth to twins, she made them a swinging cradle from the vines and bark of two opposite trees, and pushed it back and forth while she went about her work tanning deer hides.

In fact, for most of his life Audubon admired and to some degree envied the freedom and seasonal rhythms of the Indian world. He was once mistaken for an Indian by a customs officer in France and did nothing to correct the error. Audubon was under no spell concerning the high-minded nobility of the Indian character, and criticized painters and writers like George Catlin, who, he felt, had romantically filtered out the cruelty and harshness of their existence. But he observed them carefully, and compared himself to them again and again. One of the unforgettable features of his American journals is the haunting motif of the Indians' tragic fate. There is nothing surprising in the fact that Audubon's attitude toward Indians shifted and turned throughout the twenty years the journals cover. His reflections understandably depended on the circumstances of his trips, including of course his own relative youth and experience, and the particular Indian or tribe he met. But in whatever mood or disposition, he is always capable of a sensitive insight or a pungent revelation of Indian life and culture.

Toward the beginning of the *Mississippi River Journal*, just as he left the Ohio River and entered the Mississippi, he frankly expressed the wish that he were an Indian himself, instead of a destitute passenger on a flatboat: "I saw here two Indians in a canoe. They spoke some French, had bear traps, uncommonly clean kept. [They] had a few venison hams, a gun, and looked so independent, free and unconcerned with the world that I gazed on them, admired their spirits, and wished for their condition." Later on that same trip he spotted several Indians reduced to selling wild game in the streets of Natchez. Audubon knew the history of the Natchez tribe, since his own birthplace, Santo Domingo, was part of the story. For centuries the Natchez had been the most advanced of the Indians in the lower Mississippi, up until 1731 when they were thoroughly wiped out in a war with the French and their chiefs sold into slavery in Santo Domingo. Thirteen years later, in his Labrador journal, after having discussed the plight of the local Indians with some British navy officers one evening, Audubon did not hesitate to place the blame on the white man's deadly greed: "We are often told rum kills the Indian; I think not; it is oftener the want of food, the loss of hope as he loses sight of all that was once abundant, before the white man intruded on his land and killed off the wild quadrupeds and birds with which he has fed and clothed himself since his creation. Nature herself seems perishing."

MISSOURI RIVER JOURNAL

Another ten years later, on the expedition up the Missouri to gather specimens and sketches for his last great project, the *Viviparous Quadrupeds of North America*, the decline of the Indians had accelerated beyond control. Tens of thousands had recently succumbed to the terrible 1837 epidemic of smallpox, committing individual and collective suicide rather than watch themselves fall like flies and writhe on the ground before they died. The Indians who had been driven westward into alien territory were at war off and on with the local tribes, and all of them seemed on the verge of starvation. They were so hungry that they ate drowned buffalo, covered with flies and rotting on the river banks. Audubon at this stage does not know quite what to think. He pities them, but laments the fact that they have lost their independence and pride and have accepted the roles of beggars and thieves. The once haughty Crows huddle around Fort Clark like vultures waiting for scraps: "The appearance of these poor, miserable devils, as we approached the shore, was wretched enough. There they stood in the pelting rain and keen wind, covered with Buffalo robes, red blankets, and the like, some partially and most curiously besmeared with mud."

The one Indian he could not help but admire, a magnificent Blackfoot princess who rode and swam like a legend, ended by spoiling the image with her choice of dinner. Audubon had wanted to sketch the head of a slain bull buffalo, but "the princess had its skull broken open to enjoy its brains. Handsome, and really courteous and refined in many ways, I cannot reconcile to myself the fact that she partakes of raw animal food with such evident relish." As a final spectacle of the once mighty native American people humbled and humiliated there is something sadly symbolic in Audubon himself gravehunting for the head of an Indian chief to paint. Actually, the coffin he was searching for was not in a grave but, as was the custom, above ground in the branches of a tree: "The coffin was lowered, or rather tumbled, down, and the cover was soon hammered off. . . . Worms innumerable were all about it; the feet were naked, shrunk, and dried up. The head had still the hair on, but was twisted off in a moment, under jaw and all."

THE PASSENGER PIGEON

Alongside the changing frontier's human exhibition of Indian, settler, planter, squatter, riverman, trapper, slave, and soldier, the greatest appeal of Audubon's American scenes may lie in the account he gives of lush, oversized, and largely unspoiled landscapes. The abundance of the wildlife and the immensity of the vegetable world dazzled Audubon wherever he went. The *Ornithological Biography* in particular is full of descriptions that have since become classic set pieces in the history of nature writing. One of the best known concerns the massive flocks of passenger pigeons so dense and numerous that their migrations blackened the sky for hours, even days at a time. Farmers would beat them down from the trees by the thousands and fatten their hogs on the dead and wounded scattered on the ground. Audubon estimated that one flock he watched contained over a billion birds. Since the last passenger pigeon in America died in the Cincinnati zoo in 1914, this is a number that seems wholly miraculous, another brazen exaggeration in the frontier spirit. But another pioneer painter of American birds, Audubon's rival and immediate predecessor, the Scottish expatriate Alexander Wilson, saw in Kentucky a flock of over 2 billion, and it is generally agreed by specialists today that the passenger pigeon in the early nineteenth century outnumbered all the other species of American birds combined.

THE CHIMNEY SWIFT

My favorite Audubon story of this sort occurred not long after he arrived in Louisville in 1807 just before his marriage to set himself up as a trader and shopkeeper. A friend took him to see a huge hollow sycamore tree that had become a local landmark. As the sun went down Audubon watched thousands of chimney swifts race through a hole in the trunk, going to roost "like bees hurrying into their hive." The next morning he returned and placed himself next to the tree, pressing his ear against the bark: "All was silent within when suddenly I thought the great tree was giving way. The swallows were now pouring out in a black continued stream. I listened with amazement to the noise within which I could compare to nothing else than the sound of a large wheel revolving under a powerful stream." Audubon calculated that 9,000 swifts roosted at night in the single tree.

A reader today, turning from these brimming scenes of natural plenty to all the passages in which Audubon listed without the slightest sign of guilt the great number of birds he killed for his research and drawings, might be tempted to take a rather cynical view of his constantly professed love of the world he painted. Yet Audubon obviously had to kill in order to paint accurately, and the missionary urge itself to collect and preserve was a form of homage to the mysterious world that man did not create. He used his writings to cry out against and condemn the senseless waste of professional hunting, such as the large-scale massacre of seals in Labrador. And as he grew older he came to bitterly mourn killing for mere sport: the insane target shooting of buffalo grazing on the western plains, or the shotgun slaughter of pelicans roosting in mangrove trees in the Florida Keys. It is not for nothing that so many societies and organizations today use his name as a symbol of conservation, or that, in the United States, the initial development of the national park system was largely the work of a man, John Muir, who as a boy in his native Scotland had been inspired by that same famous Audubon description of the skies blackened by passenger pigeons, and of the farmers feeding mounds of dead and half-dead pigeons to their pigs.

AUDUBON'S AMERICA

During his three years in England and France, from 1826 to 1829, the period of the European journals and of the launching of the *Birds of America*, Audubon was often tormented by memories of the American woods he had left behind. He daydreamed of Louisiana, where his wife was working on a plantation as a teacher and governess, and he missed to the point of tears the lonely bayou vistas and the southern trees thick with singing birds. Hard at work on his new paintings in Edinburgh, he writes regretfully that the American forest was "the only place in which I truly *live*." Not long before Christmas that same year he thinks to himself that he had never longed so much "for a glimpse of our rich magnolia woods." He hears a bugle one morning in Newcastle-upon-Tyne, and his first thought is that the music would sound better in America: "I often, even before this, have had a wish to be a performer on this instrument, so sure I am that our grand forests and rivers would re-echo its sonorous sounds with fine effect." The hospitality of his Scottish friends, generous as they are, cannot dissuade him of the idea that he had enjoyed his meals far more on the frontier. For one thing, the dinners in high society last too long: "I recall briefer meals that I have had, with much more enjoyment than I eat the bountiful fare before me. This is not a *goûter* with friend Bourgeat on the Flat Lake, roasting the orange-fleshed Ibis, and a few Sun-perch; neither is it on the heated banks of Thompson's Creek, on the Fourth of July, swallowing the roasted eggs of a large soft-shelled Turtle; neither was I at Henderson, at good Dr. Rankin's, listening to the howlings of the Wolves, while sitting in security, eating well roasted and jellied venison."

By that time he had become completely attached to his adopted country, and leaped to its defense with such exuberance and good-natured conviction that he usually won his listeners over by the sheer charm of his enthusiasm. He apparently began promoting the virtues of America as soon as he stepped off the boat in Liverpool in 1826. It was in Liverpool where he was welcomed as a guest by the Rathbone family, and where Mrs. Rathbone, whom he affectionately called "The Queen Bee" because of her maternal care and concern, presented him with a personal seal engraved with a miniature of a wild turkey he had drawn for her, and marked underneath with the motto "America, my country." He used the seal for the rest of his life. Audubon praised America so frequently, and so unstintingly, that a reader might wonder at times if he had forgotten or repressed his French origins for good. And yet a page or two farther on the reader finds Audubon recalling his boyhood summers on the banks of the Loire near Couëron, or setting down his memories of Nantes during the unruly days of revolution and the reign of terror at the turn of the century. This is in fact one of the revelations of his writings: his wonderful ability to negotiate all the divergent elements in his background into an amiable unity, his sense that a dual nationality could be a gift instead of a liability, a power instead of a poison.

There can be no question that Audubon deliberately concealed his illegitimacy, and was often reluctant to mention Santo Domingo as the place of his birth. We know now, however, that his father had pledged him at an early age, for legal reasons, not to disclose the name of his real mother, whose family and kin still lived around Nantes. He thus had good reasons to fabulate and pretend when a discussion turned to the exact circumstances of his birth. But as far as the rest of his French youth was concerned, he was more than willing to talk, and he talked with affection and pride. And perhaps too with some playful cunning, but this is again part of his basic human appeal.

Surely it did not hurt his efforts to attract attention for his paintings when in England he called himself the American woodsman, and continued to use strong-smelling bear grease on his hair for months after his arrival. And in America there was nothing like a little deliberate mystery added to a strong French accent to make heads turn and to set him apart as a special case. When rumors circulated, as they did off and on all during his life, that he was almost exactly the age of Louis XVI's son, who was said by some to have disappeared suddenly after his father's death, Audubon slyly did nothing to disavow the suggestion. There was, however, especially in the years before the *Birds of America* had brought him fame and security, a more immediate pragmatic reason that explained why Audubon liked to dwell on his upbringing in Nantes. France was known as the center of culture and the social arts, and Audubon's skill at dancing, fencing, painting, and music made him a perfect choice when the wealthier families of Kentucky and Louisiana needed a portrait for the mantelpiece or a tutor for their children. Just before setting sail from New Orleans to England, he conducted a final dance class in the village near the plantation of Beech Woods where Lucy was working: "With my fiddle under my arm, I entered the ballroom. I placed the gentlemen in line. How I toiled before I could get one graceful step or motion. I broke my bow and nearly my violin in my impatience. Next I had the ladies alone. Then I tried both together—pushed one here, another there—all the while singing to myself. At the close I was asked to dance to my own music."

Audubon formally requested American citizenship when he was twenty-one, and for all his good memories and boyhood attachments he never really considered returning to France to live. France was the country he had been given, but America was the country he had chosen. Both had their virtues, but for Audubon, after he married Lucy in Pennsylvania, France was the finished past and America the unlimited present and future. When he visited France to round up subscriptions for the *Birds of America* in 1828, he commented that the countryside seemed more desolate than what he remembered, and he put off going to Nantes to see his stepmother, whom he did not know had been dead for seven years. Perhaps he did not wish to stir up old feelings; more likely he simply did not want to risk turning up out of the blue and complicating the long-standing lawsuits and legal problems surrounding his father's estate. At any rate, though he returned to France once again, and though he eventually sent his son Victor as an emissary to explore the situation of the Audubon inheritance and to visit Audubon's half sister Rose and her husband in Couëron, he never went back himself.

AUDUBON'S ORIGINS

Thanks to the monumental pioneering biography of Francis Hobbart Herrick, *Audubon the Naturalist* (1917), particularly the revised second edition of 1938, and the subsequent researches of Alice Ford, whose more recent biography, *John James Audubon* (1964, 1988), is useful but not half as well-organized or as readable as Herrick's, the once-murky beginnings of Audubon's existence are now relatively clear, and it is easy enough to summarize the bare facts.

He was born on April 26, 1785, on his father's plantation in Les Cayes, Santo Domingo. The young twenty-five-year-old woman who became his mother, Jeanne Rabin, had come to Santo Domingo from Nantes as a passenger on the same ship Audubon's father, Jean Audubon, had sailed on in October of the previous year. So as a matter of record, both of Audubon's natural parents link him ancestrally to western France. His father, born in Les Sables d'Olonne in 1744, had set up household in Nantes after his marriage in 1772 to Anne Moynet, daughter of a local wine merchant. Jeanne Rabin owed her presence in Santo Domingo to the fact that she had been employed as a chambermaid by a wealthy French family returning to their estate after several years in Nantes. She died only a few months after her son's birth, the following November. For the next three and a half years, young Audubon (at that time called Jean Rabin) lived on his father's plantation, unbaptized and unknown to his future stepmother back in Nantes. He was cared for by the domestic slaves, who lived in the plantation house, and he learned to take his first steps and to speak his first words in the midst of the growing family his father had established with his permanent island mistress, Sanitte, a mixed-blood daughter of a fellow French planter.

Almost nothing is known of Jeanne Rabin, aside from her name and nationality and the not overly surprising appreciation of Audubon's father, who described her as "extraordinarily beautiful." Of Jean Audubon himself, however, the official record is more ample, due largely to the fact that he spent many years of his life on active service in the French navy and merchant marine. He began his long seafaring career as a cabin boy of thirteen on a cod-fishing voyage to Cape Breton with his father. By the time of his marriage to Anne Moynet, he had decided to reduce his activities as a merchant seaman and to set himself up as a planter and slave trader in Santo Domingo. For the next seventeen years, from 1772 to 1789, most of his financial interests were concentrated in the French West Indies. For many of those years, aside from his various voyages to France and to America, he lived almost exclusively on the plantation he had purchased. And he was well on his way to realizing a large fortune in land and slaves when the revolutionary fires of the period flamed up in Santo Domingo with one of the fiercest and longest slave revolts in history. In a few years almost every plantation house and its effects had been burned to the ground or seized, and almost every planter and his family killed or forced to flee. French newspapers that had been used to advertising Santo Domingo as a prosperous tropical paradise for European speculators now spoke of the "smoking bath of blood," and published periodic lists of the terror's victims.

Like most of the other planters, Audubon sold out as best he could and left Santo Domingo for good in 1790. He had arranged for his small son, Jean, to be taken back to France in the summer of 1788. Three years later, in 1791, when the massacre of whites on the island had reached a fever peak, Jean's half sister Rose followed, accompanied by one of Audubon's planter neighbors. In Nantes, Jean was quickly accepted by his stepmother as her own son. She had inherited several townhouses in the heart of the old city where the Audubon family lived during the winters. During the summers they stayed at La Gerbetière, a solid spacious country villa not far from the Loire on the outskirts of Couëron. Audubon's father had purchased it back in 1781 shortly after having returned home from his tour of duty with the French fleet that had assisted the Americans during the War of Independence.

In his journals and letters, Audubon does not dwell much on his memories of life in the city. His father, now called Citizen Audubon, had cast his lot with the republican forces and had volunteered for service as a leading member of the Committee of Public Safety, a local branch of the National Guard. For most of the next ten years he was often away from his Nantes household on dangerous missions in the outlying districts. Nantes seems to have been associated in Audubon's mind primarily with school and the violence of the revolution, both of them painful experiences he preferred not to think about. As the largest city near the Vendée, Nantes of course was a raging hotbed of revolutionary and counterrevolutionary struggle. Life became so uncertain, especially after Carrier's indiscriminate slaughter of royalist sympathizers early in 1794, that Audubon and Rose were formally adopted by his father and stepmother in March of that same year, and given the revolutionary names Fougère and Muguet, just in case. Audubon, looking back on Nantes in his journal thirty years later, remembered the constant civic disruption, the angry crowds in the streets, and Charette being shot in the Place Viarme in 1797. Though he later recalled with some fondness his private tutors in fencing and music, he reserved most of his praise for the marshy low-lying countryside around La Gerbetière, well away from the clamor and commotion of the city center. Here he was allowed to wander at his leisure, along the winding river paths and next to the old hedgerows in the fields. He carried a basket and collected eggs and nests and rocks, which his indulgent stepmother allowed him to store in his room. And he also tried his hand at sketching birds.

This pastoral existence ended abruptly for Audubon one day in the summer of 1796 when his father, now stationed at Rochefort-sur-Mer doing coastal duty with the republican navy, returned to Couëron for a short visit and decided that his son's extended vacation was certain to be the ruin of his future. He enrolled Audubon as a naval student in the training academy at Rochefort, where he remained under the watchful eye of his father for the next three and a half years. Given to bouts of seasickness, a problem he suffered from all his life, and not the type to adapt well to the strict discipline of military life, the best one can say is that Audubon did not shine as a career-bound cadet. He became an accomplished swimmer, and improved his fencing skills, but boredom seems to have been his prevailing impression of the period. Many years later, on one of the most depressing New Year's days of his life, he wrote in his journal that he was reminded of another New Year in Rochefort when he also had very little to celebrate: "This day twenty-one years since I was at Rochefort in France. I spent most of the day at copying letters of my father to the Minister of the Navy. What has happened to me since would fill a volume. . . . This day, January first, 1821, I am on a keel boat going down to New Orleans, the poorest man on it."

Young Audubon did not have to wait long after the dull New Year's day of 1800 to escape a career he had never sought. His father finally realized his son was not cut out for the navy, nor for military life in general, and sent him back in March to his stepmother in Nantes. As an ardent Catholic, she was the one who insisted that he be baptized six months later, *le premier brumaire, an neuf,* at the only church still functioning in Nantes, Saint Similien. From this date until the time he left Nantes for America in the summer of 1803, there are very few reliable records of his activities. It is certain that he lived with the rest of the Audubon family in La Gerbetière, where he would have continued his studies at home with the occasional private tutor, and where he would have no doubt grasped every occasion to distract himself from his textbooks by resuming the long pleasant walks in the Loire countryside that Rochefort and the navy had coldly interrupted. We do know that his father had definitely changed his mind about military service for his son. He admired Napoleon—his gift for command, his instinct for taking control of impossible situations—but admiration or not, he was determined to keep his only son safe from the awful maw of Napoleon's devouring war machine. By 1803, retired from active service, Audubon *père* was weary of Europe's wars and troubles, and ready to turn his mind again toward America.

He already had a foothold there, a large secluded farm with house and mill and outbuildings called Mill Grove, a little over twenty miles northwest of Philadelphia, set in the midst of a hardwood forest and overlooking a wide flourishing creek. Like many other fleeing planters from Santo Domingo, he had considered the United States the safest place to invest in when he bought the property in 1789, and had thought about moving there permanently himself. Most of the Santo Domingo families had chosen to settle in the southern states, where they could legally bring their slaves, at least the ones they had managed to keep. By the end of the century there were several sizable refugee communities in South Carolina, Georgia, and Louisiana, and not a few newly acquired southern plantations where the sounds of Caribbean French could be heard shouted out in the cotton and sugarcane fields.

AUDUBON'S EARLY LIFE IN AMERICA

Audubon's father, however, purchased his American plantation in the free state of Pennsylvania, still under the influence of the peace-loving Quakers who had founded it a hundred years earlier. In 1802 he heard that a promising lead mine had been discovered on his land by his tenant. This news, along with the sale of Louisiana to the United States in April of the following year, gave him the plan he had been searching for. After sending over a Nantes native named Francis Dacosta to scout out the mining possibilities, he placed his son on a New England ship that sailed from France in August. On Audubon's passport his name was Anglicized, or Americanized, from Jean Jacques to John James, and the site of his birth was marked Louisiana, not that far from the truth since both Louisiana and Santo Domingo had originally been American colonies belonging to France. Now that Louisiana was an American possession, Audubon would be able to apply for American citizenship with a good chance of success. Actually, he eventually made his way to Louisiana, spent several years there, and from then on patriotically claimed he preferred it to all other American regions. Audubon was never reluctant to make fate bend to a personal fiction, especially if a higher reality, such as a spiritual homeland, were at stake. It was no accident that Louisiana furnished him with more specimens for *Birds of America* than any other state. When he first arrived there, in 1820, he drew as if possessed by sudden new powers, as if it had finally been revealed to him who he was and what he could do. On one plantation alone, Oakley, near the small river community of Bayou Sarah, where he was tutor for a time in 1821, he produced one quick masterpiece after another: the pine creeping warbler, the mockingbird, the Mississippi kite, the yellow-throated vireo, the red-cockaded woodpecker, the American redstart, the summer redbird, the prairie warbler, the Tennessee warbler.

In 1803, however, Louisiana was just a sonorous name on a convincing false passport. At the age of eighteen, with an allowance to be paid to him by his father's tenants, Mr. and Mrs. Thomas, a tolerant Quaker couple, Audubon found himself alone and free and well provided for in the midst of the rich woodlands of Pennsylvania. It proved to be a year of almost pure contentment and self-discovery, and the turning point of his life. He arrived, as he said himself, somewhat of a spoiled dandy, fond of society and fine clothes. After a few months he was calling himself an American woodsman, and had developed into a skillful hunter and one of the best shots with a rifle in the region. It was characteristic of Audubon even then that the dandy and the woodsman need not cancel each other out: "Not a ball, a skating match, a house or riding party took place without me." He met his wife-to-be, Lucy Bakewell, the attractive sixteen-year-old daughter of an English family recently settled across the woods from Mill Grove. Lucy's love of nature had been nurtured back in England by the Bakewell's family doctor, Erasmus Darwin, poet, botanist, and grandfather of Charles. Audubon courted her by taking her into a cave near Perkiomen Creek and showing her the nest-building skills of the phoebes, who had paired off to start their families. Lucy was impressed, and so was her younger brother, William, when he was taken to see the room at Mill Grove that Audubon had converted into a sort of improvised museum. William wrote that the walls "were festooned with all kinds of birds' eggs, carefully blown out and strung on a thread. The chimney piece was covered with stuffed squirrels, raccoons and opossums; the shelves were crowded with fishes, frogs, snakes, lizards. Paintings were arrayed on the walls, chiefly of birds."

Audubon spent more time with Lucy, and with his birds and paintings, than he did with his father's affairs. He experimented with taxidermy, and with other methods of giving his models lifelike attitudes, but nothing satisfied him until he hit upon the discovery of skeletal wiring he later described in his episode "My Style of Drawing Birds." After an especially bad day, he woke up before daylight the next morning and went to town for wire: "I shot the first kingfisher I met, pierced the body with a wire, fixed it to the board, another wire held the head, smaller ones fixed the feet. The last wire proved a delightful elevator to the bird's tail and at last—there stood before me the real kingfisher." Audubon's carefree American baptism ended after a year and a half when he quarreled with Dacosta, who was not an easy man to deal with and who had been writing treacherous letters back to Audubon's father about Lucy and the Bakewells in terms calculated to put a stop to the courtship. Audubon decided to return to Nantes to settle matters face to face and to secure his father's permission to marry Lucy. By that time Lucy was sending notes to him addressed "Laforest," a French/English coinage that pleased him enormously. He answered them with his own notes in which he used the familiar Quaker second-person forms "thee" and "thou." As his journals and letters indicate, and as later reports of his distinctive spoken English confirm, he continued this practice long after leaving Pennsylvania.

He left for France in March 1805, and remained there over a year, staying close to La Gerbetière for fear of being scented out by Napoleon's conscription agents, more desperate than ever for fresh bodies now that Napoleon had crowned himself emperor, with new international ambitions. He wrote to Lucy's father that he was determined to stay clear of the "snares of the eagle." Strictly speaking, this last year in France was no less important for his long-term career than the time spent at Mill Grove. Under the guidance of his father's physician, Charles-Marie D'Orbigny, a well-read naturalist who carried his learning and enthusiasm lightly, and who lent Audubon a copy of Buffon to read, he sharpened his scientific knowledge of ornithology and made a careful study of the birds around Couëron. The earliest drawings of Audubon still in existence, a few sketches from the small French portfolio he had promised Lucy, date from this period. Buffon had an irritating effect on Audubon that the kindly D'Orbigny could not very well have anticipated. Along with some other rather foolish proclamations, such as the call for razing what was left of French forests and turning them into large well-groomed lawns, Buffon had pontificated disparagingly on American birds he had never seen. Audubon dedicated himself then and there to setting the great Buffon right, and made the claim years later that *Birds of America* owed at least a spark of its initial inspiration to a simple act of revenge.

In April 1806, Audubon returned to Pennsylvania, this time accompanied by Ferdinand Rozier, son of a local Nantes friend of the family. By now he had adopted Lucy's playful name of affection, and signed himself, somewhat awkwardly, John Laforest James Audubon. On his passport, his birthplace was still listed as Louisiana. Rozier and Audubon planned to go into business together, either on the property at Mill Grove, where Rozier's father had bought a half interest, or elsewhere if necessary. It did not take them long to decide they were not suited for farming, or for sitting still, and they soon sold most of Mill Grove to Dacosta. After a short unhappy training spell as big city clerks, Audubon in New York with Benjamin Bakewell, Lucy's uncle, and Rozier in Philadelphia, they left together for Kentucky. They worked as partners in trade for almost three years, first in Louisville, then in the much smaller hamlet of Henderson. In the winter of 1810 the more merchant-minded Rozier opened a new store by himself in upper Missouri. Audubon remained in Henderson, built a house next to his log-cabin store, and entered into partnership with his brother-in-law, Thomas Bakewell. For fourteen years, in fact, from 1806 until his momentous decision of 1820, when he set out on the New Orleans-bound flatboat to make his fortune as America's foremost painter of birds, Audubon tried one inconclusive venture after another: clerk, storekeeper, trader, mill owner, speculator, taxidermist, portrait painter. He had married Lucy on April 5, 1808. They spent their honeymoon crowded together on a boat with other westward-moving families and their livestock until they arrived in Louisville, where he and Rozier had already lived the better part of the preceding year prospecting for a good place to begin business. Audubon and Lucy recovered from the poultry and cattle on the boat by choosing as a semipermanent home the town's best inn, the Indian Queen, where their first son, Victor, was born a year later.

As many of the early episodes clearly demonstrate, Audubon's twelve-year Kentucky period was not an unrelieved disaster. He did seem to lose money wherever he turned, but his financial failures were due primarily to the fact that he sought every opportunity to go hunting for birds in the forest and to continue his drawings. He became an expert at observing wildlife. He watched the snowy owl lying "flat and lengthwise with its head down near the water. One might have supposed the bird sound asleep. The instant a fish rose to the surface, the owl thrust out the claw that was next to the water, seized it and drew it out like lightning." He and Lucy, who loved the out-of-doors as much as her husband did, slipped easily into the communal rhythms and habits of Kentucky, bought some real estate and a few slaves, and, by Audubon's own account years later, made many loyal lifelong friends. They also made a rather improbable enemy in the person of John Keats's younger brother, George, who had come fortune-hunting to America with his sixteen-year-old bride, Georgiana, at the urging of his brother. The hospitable Audubons had welcomed the English couple in their Henderson cabin, but unfortunately Audubon talked George into investing in a bad note on a sunken steamboat, and they both lost their money. The poet back in London was furious: "I cannot help thinking Mr Audubon a dishonest man," he wrote Georgiana. "Tell Audubon he's a fool."

All of the Kentucky episodes have their interest, but two of them are worth mentioning here as having a special biographical and historical significance. They reveal an Audubon looking back at a time when he was slowly gaining confidence in his own skills as a painter and student of nature. Written some twenty years after the events they describe, and narrated with a now-habitual blend of irony, amusement, and self-justification, they describe a youthful Audubon measuring himself against two other struggling American naturalists still hard at work in the field, but right on the very threshold of professional fame: Alexander Wilson and Constantine Rafinesque. Both of these strange solitary men were every bit as determined and single-minded as Audubon. And they both were pioneer figures whose work preceeded his by several years. By writing about them the way he did, familiarly and without the slightest sense of inferiority, he suggested rather emphatically, of course, that twenty years later he was now ready to take his own place amid their illustrious company.

CONSTANTINE RAFINESQUE

Audubon's humorous episode "The Eccentric Naturalist" concerns the visit he received in 1818 from surely one of the oddest and most brilliant men in the annals of early American science, Constantine Samuel Rafinesque, evolutionist, poet, botanist, and as indefatigable a walker of the woods as Audubon. Rafinesque had been born in Constantinople of a French father and a German mother and brought up in France. He emigrated to America in 1802 at the age of twenty, returned to Europe to spend ten years in Sicily, and then made his way back to America to become a well-known professor at Transylvania University in Lexington, Kentucky, not far from Audubon. His masterpiece was *Ichthyologia Ohiensis, or the Natural History of the Fishes Inhabiting the River Ohio and Its Tributary Streams.*

Audubon's comic portrait of Rafinesque must be understood partially in terms of the raw and rough humor expected in the standard frontier sketch. But there is more than a hint that Audubon recognized something of himself in Rafinesque's fierce quixotic indifference to the world's conventions. This recognition did not, however, stop Audubon from playing on his visitor the oldest joke known in the backwoods South, the staged hunt that leaves the innocent victim lost, bewildered, and exhausted. Audubon begins his story by noting a certain physical resemblance between guest and host on the first evening of the visit. "His beard was as long as I have known mine to be during some of my peregrinations, and his lank black hair hung loosely over his shoulders." After a long conversation in and out of the house, during which Audubon listened to Rafinesque "with as much delight as Telemachus could have listened to Mentor," they both retired for the night. Before too long a loud uproar was heard from the visitor's room. Audubon "opened the door [and] saw my guest running about the room naked, holding the handle of my favorite violin, the body of which he had battered to pieces in attempting to kill the bats which had entered by the open window." Rafinesque explained that he was certain the bats belonged to "a new species." Audubon as a good host dutifully took up the bow of his destroyed instrument and "soon got specimens enough."

A few days later, inspired by mischief, and no doubt a bit piqued as well by the loss of his prized violin, Audubon led Rafinesque into the midst of an enormous thicket, or canebrake, and the fun began. "Heavy rain drenched us. Briars had scratched us, nettles stung us. Rafinseque threw away all his plants, emptied his pockets of fungi, lichens and mosses. I led him first one way, then another until I myself, though well acquainted with the brake, was all but lost in it. I kept him stumbling and crawling until long after midday." Unfortunately for Rafinesque, the joke does not end there. Audubon also described several local fish, all imaginary, which Rafinesque carefully noted down in his ledger without verifying for himself. Was the self-taught Audubon somehow wryly fixing forever in his memory the lesson that he had better always trust personal observation over secondhand testimony if he were going to be accepted one day by his peers as a serious scientist? At any rate, in the middle of the otherwise erudite *Icthyologia Ohiensis*, university students all over America could read about the strange Devil-Jack Diamond Fish that Professor Rafinesque had seen, he admitted, "only at a distance." "Wonderful stories are related concerning this fish but I have principally relied upon the description and figures given me by Mr Audubon. Its length is 4 to 10 feet. The whole body is covered with large stone scales half an inch to one inch in diameter. They strike fire with steel! and are ballproof!"

ALEXANDER WILSON

Audubon's meeting with Alexander Wilson occurred some eight years before the Rafinesque episode, in March 1810 while Audubon was tending his store in the small town of Shippingport, a few miles above Louisville on the Ohio River. Unknown to Audubon, Wilson two years earlier had just finished the first volume of his *American Ornithology*, a projected ten-volume collection of paintings and life histories of every known American bird. This was the book that gave Audubon the idea and the form of his own *Birds of America*, and from 1810 on Wilson's *Ornithology* was his model, his guide, and, to some degree, his nemesis. If he were going to establish himself as a recognized authority and expert, and as America's finest ornithological artist, Wilson was the man he had to challenge and surpass. This was not an easy accomplishment, and for years after he had obtained the recognition he had searched for, Audubon was harrassed by Wilson's jealous defenders. The most furious attacks came from Wilson's biographer and editor, George Ord, who after Wilson's death in the summer of 1813 accused Audubon of using every possible device of artistic chicanery and self-promotion to steal the limelight from Wilson. Ord was one of the prime movers, along with Charles Waterton, in orchestrating the highly publicized newspaper campaign calling into question the rattlesnake in the tree Audubon had placed in one of his most celebrated paintings, that of the mockingbirds in Louisiana trying to protect their nest. The campaign did not have much effect on Audubon's overall reputation, but it did succeed in stinging his pride, and it did force him to spend valuable time soliciting testimonies and letters from reliable southern natives who were ready to claim they had also seen rattlesnakes climb trees and fences.

Audubon's portrait of Wilson appears in his first episode, the one titled "Louisville in Kentucky." Again, in order to understand the tone of Audubon's remarks, the reader must realize that Audubon is looking back over a period of more than two decades. He has already been long at work on the series of prints to be collected in the finished version of *Birds of America*, and he is in the midst of preparing, with the able assistance of the young Scottish naturalist William MacGillivray, the text of his five-volume *Ornithological Biography*. His reputation at this point is secure enough for him to take the noble role in not treating the deceased Wilson too harshly, but even Audubon's deliberate display of serenity and good nature in the affair cannot hide his offense at having been snubbed in the ninth volume of Wilson's *Ornithology*. When Wilson arrived in Shippingport, he was traveling in a sad-looking skiff named the "Ornithologist," combing towns and cities east and west for likely subscribers. He had been born in Scotland in 1766, and had emigrated to America in 1794 after having worked most of his life as a weaver, unpaid poet, and militant socialist. After several years of teaching school in America, he was befriended by the famous naturalist and travel writer William Bartram of Philadelphia, and by 1808 he had launched his project. He was in fact carrying a sample copy of the first volume in his bag when he met Audubon.

As Audubon's version explains, he had taken up his pen and was on the point of signing his name to Wilson's list of subscribers when Audubon's partner, Rozier, interrupted him in French and told him not to sign, saying that Audubon's own work was far better. Wilson understood Rozier's French, and asked to be shown the drawings. "Mr Wilson now examined my drawings with care, asked if I should have any objections to lending him a few during his stay, to which I replied I had none." At the end of the visit a few days later, during which Audubon showed Wilson around the countryside and helped him hunt the specimens he wanted, Wilson left for New Orleans. Audubon records that Wilson silently refused his host's offer of corresponding in the future, and went away "little knowing how much his talents were appreciated in our little town, at least by myself and my friends." After describing a final meeting with Wilson in Philadelphia where Audubon was made to feel that his "company was not agreeable," he makes his final ironic thrust by citing Wilson's own ill-tempered words on the famous Kentucky visit: "I neither received one act of civility from those to whom I was recommended, one subscriber nor one new bird. . . . Science or literature has not one friend in this place." This, Audubon seems to be saying with a hopeless shrug of shoulders, is how one great naturalist returns a favor from another.

AUDUBON'S LITERARY TESTAMENT

All Audubon's episodes, it must be remembered, appeared in the first three volumes of his *Ornithological Biography*. Although the text was written, or rather rewritten, with the help of Lucy and MacGillivray, for the general public, the effort involved in preparing it for publication against a self-imposed deadline was enormous. Audubon wrote to his good friend John Bachman in Charleston that "for my part I would rather go without a shirt or any inexpressibles through the whole of Florida swamps in mosquito time than labor as I have hitherto done with the pen." The result of such labor, however, had the advantage of producing some of Audubon's most accomplished prose. As far as his published writing was concerned, there is no question that Audubon himself would have wanted to be judged first and foremost as the author of the bird biographies, and a dozen or so of the more substantial episodes.

As opposed to the biographies and the episodes, Audubon's journals seem to have been written primarily for the eyes of his family alone, as an intimate record of his various voyages and expeditions. He also used them (and prized them) as a private archive richly stored with notes, commentary, and random observations to be "ransacked" (his own expression) when he needed material for his public writings. Some of them were lost or destroyed during his lifetime. The few that did survive were published only many years after his death. Several of the original manuscripts were destroyed by his granddaughter Maria Audubon after she had revised and reshaped them to conform to her rather stiff Victorian tastes for her 1897 edition of *Audubon and His Journals*. This was the case for the *Labrador Journal*, the *Missouri River Journal*, and most of the *European Journals*. The first section of the *European Journals* (the section that covers 1826, the decisive year of his voyage to England) does exist, however, in a manuscript that was saved and preserved by Audubon's descendants. Transcribed by Alice Ford and published as *The 1826 Journal of John James Audubon* in 1967, it allows us to judge with some exactitude the nature and range of Maria Audubon's revisions. It must be said that her hand was almost always heavy, and could be ruthless, especially when it came to cutting out passages in which Audubon is playful or extreme in his judgments. Still, though she did suppress much of Audubon's spontaneity in the manuscript (the comic stories, the bouts of depression, the delight in female company, the lonely late-night endearments to Lucy), she could not suppress or reinvent the larger presence of Audubon, and the *European Journals* remain an invaluable biographical source.

Fortunately, when we turn to Audubon's major American journals, the editorial problems are less troublesome. The essential work is of course the *Mississippi River Journal*, untouched and untampered with, transcribed by Howard Corning in 1929 from the original manuscript exactly as it was written by Audubon in 1820 and 1821. Here we have, along with certain letters to his wife and friends, the best evidence of Audubon's actual voice: direct, alert, vibrating with the urgency of the situation, and completely unaffected. The rawness of his written English (it would improve rapidly over the next few years) increases rather than lessens the effect of absolute immediacy. As a companion to the *Mississippi River Journal*, Audubon's first American journal, I have chosen to include his last, the *Missouri River Journal* of 1843. The only version of this journal we now possess is the one printed by Maria Audubon in 1897. My own feeling, however, leads me to believe she interfered with it far less than with the other journals. She may have added or cut out a passage here and there, but the main narrative is pure Audubon: kinetic, curious, entertaining, and highly skilled in his perception of the crucial detail. By the time Audubon wrote it, his English had become fluent, and I have no doubt that he intended to have at least parts of it published exactly the way he had written it down in his ledgers.

Compared with the *Mississippi River Journal* of 1820–21, the *Missouri River Journal* of 1843 shows no dimming of insight or excitement in writing down late at night what he has seen or done during the day. As usual, Audubon's day begins several hours before anyone else's. By this time, of course, Audubon realizes he is on his last long trip; significantly it will take him deeper than he has ever been before into the American wilderness, where he had always felt more himself and more at home. By the middle of his journal he confesses that he regrets having promised Lucy that he would come back in the fall. He had set out on the Missouri excursion with no teeth, and hesitated at first to join the younger men on their longer hunting forays. But the energizing days out of doors, on the river and around the blazing campfires of dried buffalo dung, do their work, and before too long the almost sixty-year-old toothless celebrity is lying on his back on the ground trying to stimulate the curiosity of a wary antelope: "We determined to stop and try to bring him to us; I lay on my back and threw my legs up, kicking first one and then the other foot, and sure enough the Antelope walked towards us, slowly and carefully."

The old woodsman dancing on his back on the western plains: one more arresting image in a life that paradoxically was never at rest, and a good place to stop and reflect on the elemental exuberance and resourcefulness of spirit that can be found in everything Audubon set his mind to, including the remarkable succession of self-portraits he committed to the written page. Audubon admitted that he was not a professional writer, and proclaimed that everything he wrote was intended to serve his higher mission as a painter of birds. And yet his writing stands today as an astounding achievement by a man who did not think of himself as a writer. Among his many gifts, the most striking was surely that of remaining undivided, resolutely self-completing, through all the multifarious interests and far-flung wanderings. He is able to project in his journals and essays an independent voice that invariably pierces through the occasional borrowed mannerisms and improprieties of an untrained style. As a child of the early nineteenth century, Audubon saw no reason not to rhapsodize in ink when he felt in the mood, and he could never quite immunize himself against a romantic overemphasis or two when he began to evoke the big woods and the wild open spaces.

But there is more realism than romanticism in his vision of the natural world, and far less mistiness than light.

Above all else, he aspired to see things clearly, and fretted sorely when he could not get close enough to study what he wanted to reveal. I have no doubt that readers coming to Audubon's autobiographies in the following pages will immediately recognize their affinities with the more celebrated watercolors. Almost every paragraph manages to radiate the single powerful purpose, and to convey in keeping with the mind behind the great painted birds the same awe at the fact of earthly existence. Audubon, who at various times in his life saw reflections of himself in almost every bird he painted, from eagle to barn swallow, affirms in all his work, on the page and on the canvas, at least two vital verities: the artistic credo that there is as much mystery to be contemplated in the visible world as there is in the invisible, and the conviction (once more we have the antelope to consider) that man has more grace to gain than to lose by recognizing his eternal kinship with the birds and beasts of the only world he can genuinely call his own.

Ben Forkner
Angers, France

CHRONOLOGY

1785

April 26 Audubon (under name of Jean Rabine) is born in Les Cayes, Santo Domingo, where his father, Jean Audubon, a French trader and sea captain, owns a plantation.

November 10 Audubon's mother, Jeanne Rabine, mistress of Jean Audubon, dies in Les Cayes.

1788

August 26 Audubon (as protection against first stirrings of the French slave revolt) is sent to Nantes to live with his father's wife, Anne Moynet.

1789

Spring Audubon's father purchases Mill Grove, a large farm in Pennsylvania.

1794

March 7 Audubon and his half sister, Rose Buffard, are officially adopted by their father and stepmother in Nantes.

1796–1800

Audubon is enrolled as cadet in naval training school in Rochefort-sur-Mer.

1800

October 23 Audubon, back in Nantes, is baptized under the name Jean Jacques Fougère Audubon.

1800–3

Audubon divides his time between Nantes and the family villa, La Gerbetière, in Couëron, a small river town on the Loire just west of Nantes.

1803

Summer Audubon is sent by his father to the United States to live at Mill Grove and to learn a trade. He begins to study American wildlife and to draw the local birds.

1804

Winter Audubon becomes engaged to Lucy Bakewell, his future wife.

1805

March Audubon returns to Nantes to seek his father's approval of marriage.

1806

Summer After over a year in France, mainly at Couëron, where he continues his study of birds under the guidance of a family friend, Dr. Charles Marie D'Orbigny, Audubon returns to Mill Grove.

Autumn Audubon works as clerk for Lucy's uncle in New York City.

1807

Summer Audubon makes trip to Louisville, Kentucky, accompanied by his French partner, Ferdinand Rozier, to scout out opportunities in trade and to open a store.

1808

April Audubon marries Lucy and sets out for Louisville. Kentucky will be their home for the next eleven years.

1809

June 12 Victor Gifford, their first child, is born at the Indian Queen inn in Louisville.

1810

March Alexander Wilson passes through Kentucky and spends several days with Audubon.

Summer Audubon and family move to Henderson, Kentucky.

1811

Spring Audubon dissolves partnership with Rozier and sets up in trading business with Lucy's brother, Thomas Bakewell. He continues to operate his store in Henderson.

1812

July 3 American citizenship is granted to Audubon. He had applied for it six years earlier.

November 30 Audubon's second son, John Woodhouse, is born.

1816

Spring Audubon joins Thomas Bakewell in new venture to build and operate a sawmill in Henderson.

1818

February 19 Audubon's father dies in Nantes.

Summer Constantine Samuel Rafinesque pays Audubon a visit. George Keats (the brother of poet John Keats) and his wife rent rooms from the Audubons.

1819

Summer The sawmill venture collapses. Audubon is briefly jailed for debts and forced to declare bankruptcy.

1819–20

Audubon tries to make a new start making portraits in Louisville and in Cincinnati, where he also works for several months as a taxidermist in the Western Museum.

1820

Autumn Audubon leaves family behind and sets off with a young assistant, Joseph Mason (both without funds), on a trip to Louisiana down the Ohio and Mississippi rivers, determined to make a name for himself as a great painter of American birds.

1821

Audubon lives in New Orleans, and later in the year spends five months as a tutor to the daughter of Mr. and Mrs. Pirrie, wealthy owners of the Oakley Plantation near Saint Francisville, a small village on the Mississippi River just north of Baton Rouge. Some of his finest drawings are made at this time. Lucy and sons arrive in New Orleans in December.

1822

Audubon resides and paints for several months in Natchez, and is later joined there by Lucy and sons.

1823

Audubon uses Natchez as base for several short painting tours around the area. Lucy begins a private school at Beech Woods (on Bayou Sarah), the vast Percy plantation near Saint Francisville. She remains there for almost four years, before moving her school to another plantation, nearby Beech Grove, where she will remain until January 1830.

1824

Audubon travels to Philadelphia with his bird portfolio, seeking patrons and a publisher. He meets Charles Bonaparte and visits New York, Albany, Rochester, Niagara Falls, and Pittsburgh. He returns to Louisiana and to Lucy in November.

1825

Audubon teaches at Saint Francisville and makes preparations to go to Europe.

1826

May 27 Audubon sails for England from New Orleans on the cotton schooner *Delos*.

July 21 Audubon arrives in Liverpool and begins three-year tour of England and France.

November Audubon signs contract with Edinburgh engraver W. H. Lizars to prepare plates for the *Birds of America*.

1827

Spring Audubon publishes the *Prospectus* for *Birds of America*. He travels to London and engages a new engraver, Robert Havell, to replace Lizars. By the end of the year, twenty-five plates of *Birds of America* have been completed. Eleven years later, in 1838, the fourth and final folio volume of the great work will be published.

1828
Audubon continues to seek subscribers for *Birds of America*. He travels to France for same purpose in September and is praised by Cuvier.

1829
April 1 Audubon sets sail for the United States.
May 5 Audubon arrives in the United States and spends several months traveling and painting in New Jersey before returning in October to Lucy in Louisiana.

1830
April 1 Audubon and Lucy set sail for England.
October Audubon, with the help of William MacGillivray of Edinburgh, begins work on the *Ornithological Biography*.

1831
March The first volume (of five) of *Ornithological Biography* is published.
May Audubon and Lucy spend a month in Paris.
August 2 Audubon and Lucy set sail for the United States, arriving on September 3.

1831–34
Audubon travels up and down the Atlantic coast of the United States, painting new birds, and signing up new subscribers to *Birds of America*.

1832
Spring Audubon explores Florida and Florida Keys.

1833
Summer Audubon makes an expedition to Labrador with his son John.
October Audubon's son Victor sails to England as business manager for his father.

1834
April 1 Audubon, Lucy, and John set sail for England. They eventually settle in Edinburgh, where Audubon continues to work on *Ornithological Biography*.

1836
August Audubon and John return to the United States.

1837
Spring Audubon makes trip along coast of Gulf of Mexico.
July 17 Audubon and John leave for England. They are accompanied by John's wife, Maria Bachman, daughter of Audubon's friend, John Bachman of Charleston. Victor will marry Maria's sister, Eliza, two years later.

1838
June 20 The last engraving of *Birds of America* is completed.

1839

May The fifth and final volume of *Ornithological Biography* is published.

September Audubon and Lucy return to the United States for good.

1840

October Audubon begins work on the octavo edition of *Birds of America.* With John Bachman he makes plans for *Viviparous Quadrupeds of North America.*

1841

Spring Audubon purchases land on the Hudson River for his New York estate, Minnie's Land.

1842

April Audubon and family make permanent move to Minnie's Land.

September Audubon travels to Canada and later throughout New England to seek subscribers.

October 20 The *Prospectus* for *Viviparous Quadrupeds of North America* is published.

1843

March 11 Audubon leaves for Saint Louis to make expedition up the Missouri River into Indian territory.

November Audubon returns to Minnie's Land.

1845

First folio volume of the *Quadrupeds* is published.

1846

Audubon's health begins to fail, and he is forced to abandon work on the *Quadrupeds* after publication of the second folio volume. Audubon's son John takes over his father's work on the *Quadrupeds.*

1847

Audubon suffers stroke and becomes increasingly helpless.

1851

January 27 Audubon dies at Minnie's Land.

SELECTED JOURNALS AND OTHER WRITINGS

MYSELF

This autobiographical sketch (written for his sons) is the longest and most complete of several more or less fragmentary versions of Audubon's early life he left scattered throughout his journals and other writings. In this collection, it can be compared with the much shorter account Audubon wrote for his son Victor in the Mississippi River Journal. *"Myself" was first written in 1835 but was not published until March 1893, over forty years after Audubon's death, in* Scribner's Magazine. *It was made available to* Scribner's *by Audubon's granddaughter, Maria Audubon, who later included it in her edition of* Audubon and His Journals, *first published in 1897. It is difficult to know how much of the original text was subsequently amended by Audubon's wife, Lucy, or by Maria Audubon. Maria, of course, is well known for having rewritten or deleted long passages in the journals when her grandfather's literary style did not quite reflect the parlor polish her own Victorian tastes required. Still, aside from the misinformation concerning Audubon's mother, a confusion that Audubon himself often encouraged, the details of the narrative stick very close to the known facts, and can be readily confirmed by other sources.*

The precise period of my birth is yet an enigma to me, and I can only say what I have often heard my father repeat to me on this subject, which is as follows: It seems that my father had large properties in Santo Domingo, and was in the habit of visiting frequently that portion of our Southern States called, and known by the name of, Louisiana, then owned by the French Government.

During one of these excursions he married a lady of Spanish extraction, whom I have been led to understand was as beautiful as she was wealthy, and otherwise attractive, and who bore my father three sons and a daughter,—I being the youngest of the sons and the only one who survived extreme youth. My mother, soon after my birth, accompanied my father to the estate of Aux Cayes, on the island of Santo Domingo, and she was one of the victims during the ever-to-be-lamented period of the negro insurrection of that island.

My father, through the intervention of some faithful servants, escaped from Aux Cayes with a good portion of his plate and money, and with me and these humble friends reached New Orleans in safety. From this place he took me to France, where, having married the only mother I have ever known, he left me under her charge and returned to the United States in the employ of the French Government, acting as an officer under Admiral Rochambeau. Shortly afterward, however, he landed in the United States and became attached to the army under La Fayette.

The first of my recollective powers placed me in the central portion of the city of Nantes, on the Loire River, in France, where I still recollect particularly that I was much cherished by my dear stepmother, who had no children of her own, and that I was constantly attended by one or two black servants, who had followed my father from Santo Domingo to New Orleans and afterward to Nantes.

One incident which is as perfect in my memory as if it had occurred this very day, I have thought of thousands of times since, and will now put on paper as one of the curious things which perhaps did lead me in after times to love birds, and to finally study them with pleasure infinite. My mother had several beautiful parrots and some monkeys; one of the latter was a full-grown male of a very large species. One morning, while the servants were engaged in arranging the room I was in, "Pretty Polly" asking for her breakfast as usual, *"Du pain au lait pour le perroquet Mignonne,"* the man of the woods probably thought the bird presuming upon his rights in the scale of nature; be this as it may, he certainly showed his supremacy in strength over the denizen of the air, for, walking deliberately and uprightly toward the poor bird, he at once killed it, with unnatural composure. The sensations of my infant heart at this cruel sight were agony to me. I prayed the servant to beat the monkey, but he, who for some reason preferred the monkey to the parrot, refused. I uttered long and piercing cries, my mother rushed into the room, I was tranquillized, the monkey was forever afterward chained, and Mignonne buried with all the pomp of a cherished lost one.

This made, as I have said, a very deep impression on my youthful mind. But now, my dear children, I must tell you somewhat of *my* father, and of his parentage.

John Audubon, my grandfather, was born and lived at the small village of Sable d'Olhonne, and was by trade a very humble fisherman. He appears to have made up for the want of wealth by the number of his children, twenty-one of whom he actually raised to man and womanhood. All were sons, with one exception; my aunt, one uncle, and my father, who was the twentieth son, being the only members of that extraordinary numerous family who lived to old age. In subsequent years, when I visited Sable d'Olhonne, the old residents assured me that they had seen the whole family, including both parents, at church many times.

When my father had reached the age of twelve years, his father presented him with a shirt, a dress of coarse material, a stick, and his blessing, and urged him to go and seek means for his future support and sustenance.

Some *kind* whaler or cod-fisherman took him on board as a "Boy." Of his life during his early voyages it would be useless to trouble you; let it suffice for me to say that they were of the usual most uncomfortable nature. How many trips he made I cannot say, but he told me that by the time he was seventeen he had become an able seaman before the mast; when twenty-one he commanded a fishing-smack, and went to the great Newfoundland Banks; at twenty-five he owned several small crafts, all fishermen, and at twenty-eight sailed for Santo Domingo with his little flotilla heavily loaded with the produce of the deep. "Fortune," said he to me one day, "now began to smile upon me. I did well in this enterprise, and after a few more voyages of the same sort gave up the sea, and purchased a small estate on the Isle à Vaches; the prosperity of Santo Domingo was at its zenith, and in the course of ten years I had realized something very considerable. The then Governor gave me an appointment which called me to France, and having received some favors there, I became once more a seafaring man, the government having granted me the command of a small vessel of war."

How long my father remained in the service, it is impossible for me to say. The different changes occurring at the time of the American Revolution, and afterward during that in France, seem to have sent him from one place to another as if a foot-ball; his property in Santo Domingo augmenting, however, the while, and indeed till the liberation of the black slaves there.

During a visit he paid to Pennsylvania when suffering from the effects of a sunstroke, he purchased the beautiful farm of Mill Grove, on the Schuylkill and Perkiomen streams. At this place, and a few days only before the memorable battle (*sic*) of Valley Forge, General Washington presented him with his portrait, now in my possession; and highly do I value it as a memento of that noble man and the glories of those days. At the conclusion of the war between England and her child of the West, my father returned to France and continued in the employ of the naval department of that country, being at one time sent to Plymouth, England, in a seventy-five-gun ship to exchange prisoners. This was, I think, in the short peace that took place between England and France in 1801. He returned to Rochefort, where he lived for several years, still in the employ of government. He finally sent in his resignation and returned to Nantes and La Gerbétière. He had many severe trials and afflictions before his death, having lost my two older brothers early in the French Revolution; both were officers in the army. His only sister was killed by the Chouans of La Vendée, and the only brother he had was not on good terms with him. This brother resided at Bayonne, and, I believe, had a large family, none of whom I have ever seen or known.

In personal appearance my father and I were of the same height and stature, say about five feet ten inches, erect, and with muscles of steel; his manners were those of a most polished gentleman, for those and his natural understanding had been carefully improved both by observation and by self-education. In temper we much resembled each other also, being warm, irascible, and at times violent; but it was like the blast of a hurricane, dreadful for a time, when calm almost instantly returned. He greatly approved of the change in France during the time of Napoleon, whom he almost idolized. My father died in 1818, regretted most deservedly on account of his simplicity, truth, and perfect sense of honesty. Now I must return to myself.

My stepmother, who was devotedly attached to me, far too much so for my good, was desirous that I should be brought up to live and die "like a gentleman," thinking that fine clothes and filled pockets were the only requisites needful to attain this end. She therefore completely spoiled me, hid my faults, boasted to every one of my youthful merits, and, worse than all, said frequently in my presence that I was the handsomest boy in France. All my wishes and idle notions were at once gratified; she went so far as actually to grant me *carte blanche* at all the confectionery shops in the town, and also of the village of Couëron, where during the summer we lived, as it were, in the country.

My father was quite of another, and much more valuable description of mind as regarded my future welfare; he believed not in the power of gold coins as efficient means to render a man happy. He spoke of the stores of the mind, and having suffered much himself through the want of education, he ordered that I should be put to school, and have teachers at home. "Revolutions," he was wont to say, "too often take place in the lives of individuals, and they are apt to lose in one day the fortune they before possessed; but talents and knowledge, added to sound mental training, assisted by honest industry, can never fail, nor be taken from any one once the possessor of such valuable means." Therefore, notwithstanding all my mother's entreaties and her tears, off to a school I was sent. Excepting only, perhaps, military schools, none were good in France at this period; the thunders of the Revolution still roared over the land, the Revolutionists covered the earth with the blood of man, woman, and child. But let me forever drop the curtain over the frightful aspect of this dire picture. To think of these dreadful days is too terrible, and would be too horrible and painful for me to relate to you, my dear sons.

The school I went to was none of the best; my private teachers were the only means through which I acquired the least benefit. My father, who had been for so long a seaman, and who was then in the French navy, wished me to follow in his steps, or else to become an engineer. For this reason I studied drawing, geography, mathematics, fencing, etc., as well as music, for which I had considerable talent. I had a good fencing-master, and a first-rate teacher of the violin; mathematics was hard, dull work, I thought; geography pleased me more. For my other studies, as well as for dancing, I was quite enthusiastic; and I well recollect how anxious I was then to become the commander of a corps of dragoons.

My father being mostly absent on duty, my mother suffered me to do much as I pleased; it was therefore not to be wondered at that, instead of applying closely to my studies, I preferred associating with boys of my own age and disposition, who were more fond of going in search of birds' nests, fishing, or shooting, than of better studies. Thus almost every day, instead of going to school when I ought to have gone, I usually made for the fields, where I spent the day; my little basket went with me, filled with good eatables, and when I returned home, during either winter or summer, it was replenished with what I called curiosities, such as birds' nests, birds' eggs, curious lichens, flowers of all sorts, and even pebbles gathered along the shore of some rivulet.

The first time my father returned from sea after this my room exhibited quite a show, and on entering it he was so pleased to see my various collections that he complimented me on my taste for such things: but when he inquired what else I had done, and I, like a culprit, hung my head, he left me without saying another word. Dinner over he asked my sister for some music, and, on her playing for him, he was so pleased with her improvement that he presented her with a beautiful book. I was next asked to play on my violin, but alas! for nearly a month I had not touched it, it was stringless; not a word was said on that subject. "Had I any drawings to show?" Only a few, and those not good. My good father looked at his wife, kissed my sister, and humming a tune left the room. The next morning at dawn of day my father and I were under way in a private carriage; my trunk, etc., were fastened to it, my violin-case was under my feet, the postilion was ordered to proceed, my father took a book from his pocket, and while he silently read I was left entirely to my own thoughts.

After some days' travelling we entered the gates of Rochefort. My father had scarcely spoken to me, yet there was no anger exhibited in his countenance; nay, as we reached the house where we alighted, and approached the door, near which a sentinel stopped his walk and presented arms, I saw him smile as he raised his hat and said a few words to the man, but so low that not a syllable reached my ears.

The house was furnished with servants, and everything seemed to go on as if the owner had not left it. My father bade me sit by his side, and taking one of my hands calmly said to me: "My beloved boy, thou art now safe. I have brought thee here that I may be able to pay constant attention to thy studies; thou shalt have ample time for pleasures, but the remainder *must* be employed with industry and care. This day is entirely thine own, and as I must attend to my duties, if thou wishest to see the docks, the fine ships-of-war, and walk round the wall, thou may'st accompany me." I accepted, and off together we went; I was presented to every officer we met, and they noticing me more or less, I saw much that day, yet still I perceived that I was like a prisoner-of-war on parole in the city of Rochefort.

My best and most amiable companion was the son of Admiral, or

Vice-Admiral (I do not precisely recollect his rank) Vivien, who lived nearly opposite to the house where my father and I then resided; his company I much enjoyed, and with him all my leisure hours were spent. About this time my father was sent to England in a corvette with a view to exchange prisoners, and he sailed on board the man-of-war "L'Institution" for Plymouth. Previous to his sailing he placed me under the charge of his secretary, Gabriel Loyen Dupuy Gaudeau, the son of a fallen nobleman. Now this gentleman was of no pleasing nature to me; he was, in fact, more than too strict and severe in all his prescriptions to me, and well do I recollect that one morning, after having been set to a very arduous task in mathematical problems, I gave him the slip, jumped from the window, and ran off through the gardens attached to the Marine Secrétariat. The unfledged bird may stand for a while on the border of its nest, and perhaps open its winglets and attempt to soar away, but his youthful imprudence may, and indeed often does, prove inimical to his prowess, as some more wary and older bird, that has kept an eye toward him, pounces relentlessly upon the young adventurer and secures him within the grasp of his more powerful talons. This was the case with me in this instance. I had leaped from the door of my cage and thought myself quite safe, while I rambled thoughtlessly beneath the shadow of the trees in the garden and grounds in which I found myself; but the secretary, with a side glance, had watched my escape, and, ere many minutes had elapsed, I saw coming toward me a corporal with whom, in fact, I was well acquainted. On nearing me, and I did not attempt to escape, our past familiarity was, I found, quite evaporated; he bid me, in a severe voice, to follow him, and on my being presented to my father's secretary I was at once ordered on board the pontoon in port. All remonstrances proved fruitless, and on board the pontoon I was conducted, and there left amid such a medley of culprits as I cannot describe, and of whom, indeed, I have but little recollection, save that I felt vile myself in their vile company. My father returned in due course, and released me from these floating and most disagreeable lodgings, but not without a rather severe reprimand.

Shortly after this we returned to Nantes, and later to La Gerbétière. My stay here was short, and I went to Nantes to study mathematics anew, and there spent about one year, the remembrance of which has flown from my memory, with the exception of one incident, of which, when I happen to pass my hand over the left side of my head, I am ever and anon reminded. 'T is this: one morning, while playing with boys of my own age, a quarrel arose among us, a battle ensued, in the course of which I was knocked down by a round stone, that brought the blood from that part of my skull, and for a time I lay on the ground unconscious, but soon rallying, experienced no lasting effects but the scar.

During all these years there existed within me a tendency to follow Nature in her walks. Perhaps not an hour of leisure was spent elsewhere than in woods and fields, and to examine either the eggs, nest, young, or parents of any species of birds constituted my delight. It was about this period that I commenced a series of drawings of the birds of France, which I continued until I had upward of two hundred drawings, all bad enough, my dear sons, yet they were representations of birds, and I felt pleased with them. Hundreds of anecdotes respecting my life at this time might prove interesting to you, but as they are not in my mind at this moment I will leave them, though you may find some of them in the course of the following pages.

I was within a few months of being seventeen years old, when my stepmother, who was an earnest Catholic, took into her head that I should be confirmed; my father agreed. I was surprised and indifferent, but yet as I loved her as if she had been my own mother,—and well did she merit my deepest affection,—I took to the catechism, studied it and other matters pertaining to the ceremony, and all was performed to her liking. Not long after this, my father, anxious as he was that I should be enrolled in Napoleon's army as a Frenchman, found it necessary to send me back to my own beloved country, the United States of America, and I came with intense and indescribable pleasure.

On landing at New York I caught the yellow fever by walking to the bank at Greenwich to get the money to which my father's letter of credit entitled me. The kind man who commanded the ship that brought me from France, whose name was a common one, John Smith, took particular charge of me, removed me to Morristown, N. J., and placed me under the care of two Quaker ladies who kept a boarding-house. To their skilful and untiring ministrations I may safely say I owe the prolongation of my life. Letters were forwarded by them to my father's agent, Miers Fisher of Philadelphia, of whom I have more to say hereafter. He came for me in his carriage and removed me to his villa, at a short distance from Philadelphia and on the road toward Trenton. There I would have found myself quite comfortable had not incidents taken place which are so connected with the change in my life as to call immediate attention to them.

Miers Fisher had been my father's trusted agent for about eighteen years, and the old gentlemen entertained great mutual friendship; indeed it would seem that Mr. Fisher was actually desirous that I should become a member of his family, and this was evinced within a few days by the manner in which the good Quaker presented me to a daughter of no mean appearance, but toward whom I happened to take an unconquerable dislike. Then he was opposed to music of all descriptions, as well as to dancing, could not bear me to carry a gun, or fishing-rod, and, indeed, condemned most of my amusements. All these things were difficulties toward accomplishing a plan which, for aught I know to the contrary, had been premeditated between him and my father, and rankled the heart of the kindly, if somewhat strict Quaker. They troubled me much also; at times I wished myself anywhere but under the roof of Mr. Fisher, and at last I reminded him that it was his duty to install me on the estate to which my father had sent me.

One morning, therefore, I was told that the carriage was ready to carry me there, and toward my future home he and I went. You are too well acquainted with the position of Mill Grove for me to allude to that now; suffice it to say that we reached the former abode of my father about sunset. I was presented to our tenant, William Thomas, who also was a Quaker, and took possession under certain restrictions, which amounted to my not receiving more than enough money per quarter than was considered sufficient for the expenditure of a young gentleman.

Miers Fisher left me the next morning, and after him went my blessings, for I thought his departure a true deliverance; yet this was only because our tastes and educations were so different, for he certainly was a good and learned man. Mill Grove was ever to me a blessed spot; in my daily walks I thought I perceived the traces left by my father as I looked on the even fences round the fields, or on the regular manner with which avenues of trees, as well as the orchards, had been planted by his hand. The mill was also a source of joy to me, and in the cave, which you too remember, where the Pewees were wont to build, I never failed to find quietude and delight.

Hunting, fishing, drawing, and music occupied my every moment; cares I knew not, and cared naught about them. I purchased excellent and beautiful horses, visited all such neighbors as I found congenial spirits, and was as happy as happy could be. A few months after my arrival at Mill Grove, I was informed one day that an English family had purchased the plantation next to mine, that the name of the owner was Bakewell, and moreover that he had several very handsome and interesting daughters, and beautiful pointer dogs. I listened, but cared not a jot about them at the time. The place was within sight of Mill Grove, and Fatland Ford, as it was called, was merely divided from my estate by a road leading to the Schuylkill River. Mr. William Bakewell, the father of the family, had called on me one day, but, finding I was rambling in the woods in search of birds, left a card and an invitation to go shooting with him. Now this gentleman was an Englishman, and I such a foolish boy that, entertaining the greatest prejudices against all of his nationality, I did not return his visit for many weeks, which was as absurd as it was ungentlemanly and impolite.

Mrs. Thomas, good soul, more than once spoke to me on the subject, as well as her worthy husband, but all to no import; English was English with me, my poor childish mind was settled on that, and as I wished to know none of the race the call remained unacknowledged.

Frosty weather, however, came, and anon was the ground covered with the deep snow. Grouse were abundant along the fir-covered ground near the creek, and as I was in pursuit of game one frosty morning I chanced to meet Mr. Bakewell in the woods. I was struck with the kind politeness of his manner, and found him an expert marksman. Entering into conversation, I admired the beauty of his well-trained dogs, and, apologizing for my discourtesy, finally promised to call upon him and his family.

Well do I recollect the morning, and may it please God that I may never forget it, when for the first time I entered Mr. Bakewell's dwelling. It happened that he was absent from home, and I was shown into a parlor where only one young lady was snugly seated at her work by the fire. She rose on my entrance, offered me a seat, and assured me of the gratification her father would feel on his return, which, she added, would be in a few moments, as she would despatch a servant for him. Other ruddy cheeks and bright eyes made their transient appearance, but, like spirits gay, soon vanished from my sight; and there I sat, my gaze riveted, as it were, on the young girl before me, who, half working, half talking, essayed to make the time pleasant to me. Oh! may God bless her! It was she, my dear sons, who afterward became my beloved wife, and your mother. Mr. Bakewell soon made his appearance, and received me with the manner and hospitality of a true English gentleman. The other members of the family were soon introduced to me, and "Lucy" was told to have luncheon produced. She now arose from her seat a second time, and her form, to which I had previously paid but partial attention, showed both grace and beauty; and my heart followed every one of her steps. The repast over, guns and dogs were made ready.

Lucy, I was pleased to believe, looked upon me with some favor, and I turned more especially to her on leaving. I felt that certain *"je ne sais quoi"* which intimated that, at least, she was not indifferent to me.

To speak of the many shooting parties that took place with Mr. Bakewell would be quite useless, and I shall merely say that he was a most excellent man, a great shot, and possessed of extraordinary learning—aye, far beyond my comprehension. A few days after this first interview with the family the Perkiomen chanced to be bound with ice, and many a one from the neighborhood was playing pranks on the glassy surface of that lovely stream. Being somewhat of a skater myself, I sent a note to the inhabitants of Fatland Ford, inviting them to come and partake of the simple hospitality of Mill Grove farm, and the invitation was kindly received and accepted. My own landlady bestirred herself to the utmost in the procuring of as many pheasants and partridges as her group of sons could entrap, and now under my own roof was seen the whole of the Bakewell family, seated round the table which has never ceased to be one of simplicity and hospitality.

After dinner we all repaired to the ice on the creek, and there in comfortable sledges, each fair one was propelled by an ardent skater. Tales of love may be extremely stupid to the majority, so that I will not expatiate on these days, but to me, my dear sons, and under such circumstances as then, and, thank God, now exist, every moment was to me one of delight.

But let me interrupt my tale to tell you somewhat of other companions whom I have heretofore neglected to mention. These are two Frenchmen, by name Da Costa and Colmesnil. A lead mine had been discovered by my tenant, William Thomas, to which, besides the raising of fowls, I paid considerable attention; but I knew nothing of mineralogy or mining, and my father, to whom I communicated the discovery of the mine, sent Mr. Da Costa as a partner and partial guardian from France. This fellow was intended to teach me mineralogy and mining engineering, but, in fact, knew nothing of either; besides which he was a covetous wretch, who did all he could to ruin my father, and indeed swindled both of us to a large amount. I had to go to France and expose him to my father to get rid of him, which I fortunately accomplished at first sight of my kind parent. A greater scoundrel than Da Costa never probably existed, but peace be with his soul.

The other, Colmesnil, was a very interesting young Frenchman with whom I became acquainted. He was very poor, and I invited him to come and reside under my roof. This he did, remaining for many months, much to my delight. His appearance was typical of what he was, a perfect gentleman; he was handsome in form, and possessed of talents far above my own. When introduced to your mother's family he was much thought of, and at one time he thought himself welcome to my Lucy; but it was only a dream, and when once undeceived by her whom I too loved, he told me he must part with me. This we did with mutual regret, and he returned to France, where, though I have lost sight of him, I believe he is still living.

During the winter connected with this event your uncle Thomas Bakewell, now residing in Cincinnati, was one morning skating with me on the Perkiomen, when he challenged me to shoot at his hat as he tossed it in the air, which challenge I accepted with great pleasure. I was to pass by at full speed, within about twenty-five feet of where he stood, and to shoot only when he gave the word. Off I went like lightning, up and down, as if anxious to boast of my own prowess while on the glittering surface beneath my feet; coming, however, within the agreed distance the signal was given, the trigger pulled, off went the load, and down on the ice came the hat of my future brother-in-law, as completely perforated as if a sieve. He repented, alas! too late, and was afterward severely reprimanded by Mr. Bakewell.

Another anecdote I must relate to you on paper, which I have probably too often repeated in words, concerning my skating in those early days of happiness; but, as the world knows nothing of it, I shall give it to you at some length. It was arranged one morning between your young uncle, myself, and several other friends of the same age, that we should proceed on a duck-shooting excursion up the creek, and, accordingly, off we went after an early breakfast. The ice was in capital order wherever no air-holes existed, but of these a great number interrupted our course, all of which were, however, avoided as we proceeded upward along the glittering, frozen bosom of the stream. The day was spent in much pleasure, and the game collected was not inconsiderable.

On our return, in the early dusk of the evening, I was bid to lead the way; I fastened a white handkerchief to a stick, held it up, and we all proceeded toward home as a flock of wild ducks to their roosting-grounds. Many a mile had already been passed, and, as gayly as ever, we were skating swiftly along when darkness came on, and now our speed was increased. Unconsciously I happened to draw so very near a large air-hole that to check my headway became quite impossible, and down it I went, and soon felt the power of a most chilling bath. My senses must, for aught I know, have left me for a while; be this as it may, I must have glided with the stream some thirty or forty yards, when, as God would have it, up I popped at another air-hole, and here I did, in some way or another, manage to crawl out. My companions, who in the gloom had seen my form so suddenly disappear, escaped the danger, and were around me when I emerged from the greatest peril I have ever encountered, not excepting my escape from being murdered on the prairie, or by the hands of that wretch S—— B——, of Henderson. I was helped to a shirt from one, a pair of dry breeches from another, and completely dressed anew in a few minutes, if in motley and ill-fitting garments; our line of march was continued, with, however, much more circumspection. Let the reader, whoever he may be, think as he may like on this singular and, in truth, most extraordinary escape from death; it is the truth, and as such I have written it down as a wonderful act of Providence.

Mr. Da Costa, my tutor, took it into his head that my affection for your mother was rash and inconsiderate. He spoke triflingly of her and of her parents, and one day said to me that for a man of my rank and expectations to marry Lucy Bakewell was out of the question. If I laughed at him or not I cannot tell you, but of this I am certain, that my answers to his talks on this subject so exasperated him that he immediately afterward curtailed my usual income, made some arrangements to send me to India, and wrote to my father accordingly. Understanding from many of my friends that his plans were fixed, and finally hearing from Philadelphia, whither Da Costa had gone, that he had taken my passage from Philadelphia to Canton, I walked to Philadelphia, entered his room quite unexpectedly, and asked him for such an amount of money as would enable me at once to sail for France and there see my father.

The cunning wretch, for I cannot call him by any other name, smiled, and said: "Certainly, my dear sir," and afterward gave me a letter of credit on a Mr. Kauman, a half-agent, half-banker, then residing at New York. I returned to Mill Grove, made all preparatory plans for my departure, bid a sad adieu to my Lucy and her family, and walked to New York. But never mind the journey; it was winter, the country lay under a covering of snow, but withal I reached New York on the third day, late in the evening.

Once there, I made for the house of a Mrs. Palmer, a lady of excellent qualities, who received me with the utmost kindness, and later on the same evening I went to the house of your grand-uncle, Benjamin Bakewell, then a rich merchant of New York, managing the concerns of the house of Guelt, bankers, of London. I was the bearer of a letter from Mr. Bakewell, of Fatland Ford, to this brother of his, and there I was again most kindly received and housed.

The next day I called on Mr. Kauman; he read Da Costa's letter, smiled, and after a while told me he had nothing to give me, and in plain terms said that instead of a letter of credit, Da Costa—that rascal!—had written and advised him to have me arrested and shipped to Canton. The blood rose to my temples, and well it was that I had no weapon about me, for I feel even now quite assured that his heart must have received the result of my wrath. I left him half bewildered, half mad, and went to Mrs. Palmer, and spoke to her of my purpose of returning at once to Philadelphia and there certainly murdering Da Costa. Women have great power over me at any time, and perhaps under all circumstances. Mrs. Palmer quieted me, spoke religiously of the cruel sin I thought of committing, and, at last, persuaded me to relinquish the direful plan. I returned to Mr. Bakewell's low-spirited and mournful, but said not a word about all that had passed. The next morning my sad visage showed something was wrong, and I at last gave vent to my outraged feelings.

Benjamin Bakewell was a *friend* of his brother (may you ever be so toward each other). He comforted me much, went with me to the docks to seek a vessel bound to France, and offered me any sum of money I might require to convey me to my father's house. My passage was taken on board the brig "Hope," of New Bedford, and I sailed in her, leaving Da Costa and Kauman in a most exasperated state of mind. The fact is, these rascals intended to cheat both me and my father. The brig was bound direct for Nantes. We left the Hook under a very fair breeze, and proceeded at a good rate till we reached the latitude of New Bedford, in Massachusetts, when my captain came to me as if in despair, and said he must run into port, as the vessel was so leaky as to force him to have her unloaded and repaired before he proceeded across the Atlantic. Now this was only a trick; my captain was newly married, and was merely anxious to land at New Bedford to spend a few days with his bride, and had actually caused several holes to be bored below water-mark, which leaked enough to keep the men at the pumps. We came to anchor close to the town of New Bedford; the captain went on shore, entered a protest, the vessel was unloaded, the apertures bunged up, and after a week, which I spent in being rowed about the beautiful harbor, we sailed for La Belle France. A few days after having lost sight of land we were overtaken by a violent gale, coming fairly on our quarter, and before it we scudded at an extraordinary rate, and during the dark night had the misfortune to lose a fine young sailor overboard. At one part of the sea we passed through an immensity of dead fish floating on the surface of the water, and, after nineteen days from New Bedford, we had entered the Loire, and anchored off Painbœuf, the lower harbor of Nantes.

On sending my name to the principal officer of the customs, he came on board, and afterward sent me to my father's villa, La Gerbétière, in his barge, and with his own men, and late that evening I was in the arms of my beloved parents. Although I had written to them previous to leaving America, the rapidity of my voyage had prevented them hearing of my intentions, and to them my appearance was sudden and unexpected. Most welcome, however, I was; I found my father hale and hearty, and *chère maman* as fair and good as ever. Adored *maman*, peace be with thee!

I cannot trouble you with minute accounts of my life in France for the following two years, but will merely tell you that my first object being that of having Da Costa disposed of, this was first effected; the next was my father's consent to my marriage, and this was acceded to as soon as my good father had received answers to letters written to your grandfather, William Bakewell. In the very lap of comfort my time was happily spent; I went out shooting and hunting, drew every bird I procured, as well as many other objects of natural history and zoölogy, though these were not the subjects I had studied under the instruction of the celebrated David.

It was during this visit that my sister Rosa was married to Gabriel Dupuy Gaudeau, and I now also became acquainted with Ferdinand Rozier, whom you well know. Between Rozier and myself my father formed a partnership to stand good for nine years in America.

France was at that time in a great state of convulsion; the republic had, as it were, dwindled into a half monarchical, half democratic era. Bonaparte was at the height of success, overflowing the country as the mountain torrent overflows the plains in its course. Levies, or conscriptions, were the order of the day, and my name being French my father felt uneasy lest I should be forced to take part in the political strife of those days.

I underwent a mockery of an examination, and was received as midshipman in the navy, went to Rochefort, was placed on board a man-of-war, and ran a short cruise. On my return, my father had, in some way, obtained passports for Rozier and me, and we sailed for New York. Never can I forget the day when, at St. Nazaire, an officer came on board to examine the papers of the many passengers. On looking at mine he said: "My dear Mr. Audubon, I wish you joy; would to God that I had such papers; how thankful I should be to leave unhappy France under the same passport."

About a fortnight after leaving France a vessel gave us chase. We were running before the wind under all sail, but the unknown gained on us at a great rate, and after a while stood to the windward of our ship, about half a mile off. She fired a gun, the ball passed within a few yards of our bows; our captain heeded not, but kept on his course, with the United States flag displayed and floating in the breeze. Another and another shot was fired at us; the enemy closed upon us; all the passengers expected to receive her broadside. Our commander hove to: a boat was almost instantaneously lowered and alongside our vessel; two officers leaped on board, with about a dozen mariners; the first asked for the captain's papers, while the latter with his men kept guard over the whole.

The vessel which had pursued us was the "Rattlesnake" and was what I believe is generally called a privateer, which means nothing but a pirate; every one of the papers proved to be in perfect accordance with the laws existing between England and America, therefore we were not touched nor molested, but the English officers who had come on board robbed the ship of almost everything that was nice in the way of provisions, took our pigs and sheep, coffee and wines, and carried off our two best sailors despite all the remonstrances made by one of our members of Congress, I think from Virginia, who was accompanied by a charming young daughter. The "Rattlesnake" kept us under her lee, and almost within pistol-shot, for a whole day and night, ransacking the ship for money, of which we had a good deal in the run beneath a ballast of stone. Although this was partially removed they did not find the treasure. I may here tell you that I placed the gold belonging to Rozier and myself, wrapped in some clothing, under a cable in the bow of the ship, and there it remained snug till the "Rattlesnake" had given us leave to depart, which you may be sure we did without thanks to her commander or crew; we were afterward told the former had his wife with him.

After this rencontre we sailed on till we came to within about thirty miles of the entrance to the bay of New York, when we passed a fishing-boat, from which we were hailed and told that two British frigates lay off the entrance of the Hook, had fired an American ship, shot a man, and impressed so many of our seamen that to attempt reaching New York might prove to be both unsafe and unsuccessful. Our captain, on hearing this, put about immediately, and sailed for the east end of Long Island Sound, which we entered uninterrupted by any other enemy than a dreadful gale, which drove us on a sand-bar in the Sound, but from which we made off unhurt during the height of the tide and finally reached New York.

I at once called on your uncle Benjamin Bakewell, stayed with him a day, and proceeded at as swift a rate as possible to Fatland Ford, accompanied by Ferdinand Rozier. Mr. Da Costa was at once dismissed from his charge. I saw my dear Lucy, and was again my own master.

Perhaps it would be well for me to give you some slight information respecting my mode of life in those days of my youth, and I shall do so without gloves. I was what in plain terms may be called extremely extravagant. I had no vices, it is true, neither had I any high aims. I was ever fond of shooting, fishing, and riding on horseback; the raising of fowls of every sort was one of my hobbies, and to reach the maximum of my desires in those different things filled every one of my thoughts. I was ridiculously fond of dress. To have seen me going shooting in black satin smallclothes, or breeches, with silk stockings, and the finest ruffled shirt Philadelphia could afford, was, as I now realize, an absurd spectacle, but it was one of my many foibles, and I shall not conceal it. I purchased the best horses in the country, and rode well, and felt proud of it; my guns and fishing-tackle were equally good, always expensive and richly ornamented, often with silver. Indeed, though in America, I cut as many foolish pranks as a young dandy in Bond Street or Piccadilly.

I was extremely fond of music, dancing, and drawing; in all I had been well instructed, and not an opportunity was lost to confirm my propensities in those accomplishments. I was, like most young men, filled with the love of amusement, and not a ball, a skating-match, a house or riding party took place without me. Withal, and fortunately for me, I was not addicted to gambling; cards I disliked, and I had no other evil practices. I was, besides, temperate to an *intemperate* degree. I lived, until the day of my union with your mother, on milk, fruits, and vegetables, with the addition of game and fish at times, but never had I swallowed a single glass of wine or spirits until the day of my wedding. The result has been my uncommon, indeed iron, constitution. This was my constant mode of life ever since my earliest recollection, and while in France it was extremely annoying to all those round me. Indeed, so much did it influence me that I never went to dinners, merely because when so situated my peculiarities in my choice of food occasioned comment, and also because often not a single dish was to my taste or fancy, and I could eat nothing from the sumptuous tables before me. Pies, puddings, eggs, milk, or cream was all I cared for in the way of food, and many a time have I robbed my tenant's wife, Mrs. Thomas, of the cream intended to make butter for the Philadelphia market. All this time I was as fair and as rosy as a girl, though as strong, indeed stronger than most young men, and as active as a buck. And why, have I thought a thousand times, should I not have kept to that delicious mode of living? and why should not mankind in general be more abstemious than mankind is?

Before I sailed for France I had begun a series of drawings of the birds of America, and had also begun a study of their habits. I at first drew my subjects dead, by which I mean to say that, after procuring a specimen, I hung it up either by the head, wing, or foot, and copied it as closely as I possibly could.

In my drawing of birds only did I interest Mr. Da Costa. He always commended my efforts, nay he even went farther, for one morning, while I was drawing a figure of the *Ardea herodias,* he assured me the time might come when I should be a great American naturalist. However curious it may seem to the scientific world that these sayings from the lips of such a man should affect me, I assure you they had great weight with me, and I felt a certain degree of pride in these words even then.

Too young and too useless to be married, your grandfather William Bakewell advised me to study the mercantile business; my father approved, and to insure this training under the best auspices I went to New York, where I entered as a clerk for your great-uncle Benjamin Bakewell, while Rozier went to a French house at Philadelphia.

The mercantile business did not suit me. The very first venture which I undertook was in indigo; it cost me several hundred pounds, the whole of which was lost. Rozier was no more fortunate than I, for he shipped a cargo of hams to the West Indies, and not more than one-fifth of the cost was returned. Yet I suppose we both obtained a smattering of business.

Time passed, and at last, on April 8th, 1808, your mother and I were married by the Rev. Dr. Latimer, of Philadelphia, and the next morning left Fatland Ford and Mill Grove for Louisville, Ky. For some two years previous to this, Rozier and I had visited the country from time to time as merchants, had thought well of it, and liked it exceedingly. Its fertility and abundance, the hospitality and kindness of the people were sufficiently winning things to entice any one to go there with a view to comfort and happiness.

We had marked Louisville as a spot designed by nature to become a place of great importance, and, had we been as wise as we now are, I might never have published the "Birds of America;" for a few hundred dollars laid out at that period, in lands or town lots near Louisville, would, if left to grow over with grass to a date ten years past (this being 1835), have become an immense fortune. But young heads are on young shoulders; it was not to be, and who cares?

On our way to Pittsburg, we met with a sad accident, that nearly cost the life of your mother. The coach upset on the mountains, and she was severely, but fortunately not fatally hurt. We floated down the Ohio in a flatboat, in company with several other young families; we had many goods, and opened a large store at Louisville, which went on prosperously when I attended to it; but birds were birds then as now, and my thoughts were ever and anon turning toward them as the objects of my greatest delight. I shot, I drew, I looked on nature only; my days were happy beyond human conception, and beyond this I really cared not.

Victor was born June 12, 1809, at Gwathway's Hotel of the Indian Queen. We had by this time formed the acquaintance of many persons in and about Louisville; the country was settled by planters and farmers of the most benevolent and hospitable nature; and my young wife, who possessed talents far above par, was regarded as a gem, and received by them all with the greatest pleasure. All the sportsmen and hunters were fond of me, and I became their companion; my fondness for fine horses was well kept up, and I had as good as the country—and the country was Kentucky—could afford. Our most intimate friends were the Tarascons and the Berthouds, at Louisville and Shippingport. The simplicity and whole-heartedness of those days I cannot describe; man was man, and each, one to another, a brother.

I seldom passed a day without drawing a bird, or noting something respecting its habits, Rozier meantime attending the counter. I could relate many curious anecdotes about him, but never mind them; he made out to grow rich, and what more could *he* wish for?

In 1810 Alexander Wilson the naturalist—not the *American* naturalist—called upon me. About 1812 your uncle Thomas W. Bakewell sailed from New York or Philadelphia, as a partner of mine, and took with him all the disposable money which I had at that time, and there [New Orleans] opened a mercantile house under the name of "Audubon & Bakewell."

Merchants crowded to Louisville from all our Eastern cities. None of them were, as I was, intent on the study of birds, but all were deeply impressed with the value of dollars. Louisville did not give us up, but we gave up Louisville. I could not bear to give the attention required by my business, and which, indeed, every business calls for, and, therefore, my business abandoned me. Indeed, I never thought of it beyond the ever-engaging journeys which I was in the habit of taking to Philadelphia or New York to purchase goods; these journeys I greatly enjoyed, as they afforded me ample means to study birds and their habits as I travelled through the beautiful, the darling forests of Ohio, Kentucky, and Pennsylvania.

Were I here to tell you that once, when travelling, and driving several horses before me laden with goods and dollars, I lost sight of the pack-saddles, and the cash they bore, to watch the motions of a warbler, I should only repeat occurrences that happened a hundred times and more in those days. To an ordinary reader this may appear very odd, but it is as true, my dear sons, as it is that I am now scratching this poor book of mine with a miserable iron pen. Rozier and myself still had some business together, but we became discouraged at Louisville, and I longed to have a wilder range; this made us remove to Henderson, one hundred and twenty-five miles farther down the fair Ohio. We took there the remainder of our stock on hand, but found the country so very new, and so thinly populated that the commonest goods only were called for. I may say our guns and fishing-lines were the principal means of our support, as regards food.

John Pope, our clerk, who was a Kentuckian, was a good shot and an excellent fisherman, and he and I attended to the procuring of game and fish, while Rozier again stood behind the counter.

Your beloved mother and I were as happy as possible, the people round loved us, and we them in return; our profits were enormous, but our sales small, and my partner, who spoke English but badly, suggested that we remove to St. Geneviève, on the Mississippi River. I acceded to his request to go there, but determined to leave your mother and Victor at Henderson, not being quite sure that our adventure would succeed as we hoped. I therefore placed her and the children under the care of Dr. Rankin and his wife, who had a fine farm about three miles from Henderson, and having arranged our goods on board a large flatboat, my partner and I left Henderson in the month of December, 1810, in a heavy snow-storm. This change in my plans prevented me from going, as I had intended, on a long expedition. In Louisville we had formed the acquaintance of Major Croghan (an old friend of my father's), and of General Jonathan Clark, the brother of General William Clark, the first white man who ever crossed the Rocky Mountains. I had engaged to go with him, but was, as I have said, unfortunately prevented. To return to our journey. When we reached Cash Creek we were bound by ice for a few weeks; we then attempted to ascend the Mississippi, but were again stopped in the great bend called Tawapatee Bottom, where we again planted our camp till a thaw broke the ice. In less than six weeks, however, we reached the village of St. Geneviève. I found at once it was not the place for me; its population was then composed of low French Canadians, uneducated and uncouth, and the ever-longing wish to be with my beloved wife and children drew my thoughts to Henderson, to which I decided to return almost immediately. Scarcely any communication existed between the two places, and I felt cut off from all dearest to me. Rozier, on the contrary, liked it; he found plenty of French with whom to converse. I proposed selling out to him, a bargain was made, he paid me a certain amount in cash, and gave me bills for the residue. This accomplished, I purchased a beauty of a horse, for which I paid dear enough, and bid Rozier farewell. On my return trip to Henderson I was obliged to stop at a humble cabin, where I so nearly ran the chance of losing my life, at the hands of a woman and her two desperate sons, that I have thought fit since to introduce this passage in a sketch called "The Prairie," which is to be found in the first volume of my "Ornithological Biography."

Winter was just bursting into spring when I left the land of lead mines. Nature leaped with joy, as it were, at her own new-born marvels, the prairies began to be dotted with beauteous flowers, abounded with deer, and my own heart was filled with happiness at the sights before me. I must not forget to tell you that I crossed those prairies on foot at another time, for the purpose of collecting the money due to me from Rozier, and that I walked one hundred and sixty-five miles in a little over three days, much of the time nearly ankle deep in mud and water, from which I suffered much afterward by swollen feet. I reached Henderson in early March, and a few weeks later the lower portions of Kentucky and the shores of the Mississippi suffered severely by earthquakes. I felt their effects between Louisville and Henderson, and also at Dr. Rankin's. I have omitted to say that my second son, John Woodhouse, was born under Dr. Rankin's roof on November 30, 1812; he was an extremely delicate boy till about a twelvemonth old, when he suddenly acquired strength and grew to be a lusty child.

Your uncle, Thomas W. Bakewell, had been all this time in New Orleans, and thither I had sent him almost all the money I could raise; but notwithstanding this, the firm could not stand, and one day, while I was making a drawing of an otter, he suddenly appeared. He remained at Dr. Rankin's a few days, talked much to me about our misfortunes in trade, and left us for Fatland Ford.

My pecuniary means were now much reduced. I continued to draw birds and quadrupeds, it is true, but only now and then thought of making any money. I bought a wild horse, and on its back travelled over Tennessee and a portion of Georgia, and so round till I finally reached Philadelphia, and then to your grandfather's at Fatland Ford. He had sold my plantation of Mill Grove to Samuel Wetherell, of Philadelphia, for a good round sum, and with this I returned through Kentucky and at last reached Henderson once more. Your mother was well, both of you were lovely darlings of our hearts, and the effects of poverty troubled us not. Your uncle T. W. Bakewell was again in New Orleans and doing rather better, but this was a mere transient clearing of that sky which had been obscured for many a long day.

Determined to do something for myself, I took to horse, rode to Louisville with a few hundred dollars in my pockets, and there purchased, half cash, half credit, a small stock, which I brought to Henderson. *Chemin faisant,* I came in contact with, and was accompanied by, General Toledo, then on his way as a revolutionist to South America. As our flatboats were floating one clear moonshiny night lashed together, this individual opened his views to me, promising me wonders of wealth should I decide to accompany him, and he went so far as to offer me a colonelcy on what he was pleased to call "his Safe Guard." I listened, it is true, but looked more at the heavens than on his face, and in the former found so much more of peace than of war that I concluded not to accompany him.

When our boats arrived at Henderson, he landed with me, purchased many horses, hired some men, and coaxed others, to accompany him, purchased a young negro from me, presented me with a splendid Spanish dagger and my wife with a ring, and went off overland toward Natchez, with a view of there gathering recruits.

I now purchased a ground lot of four acres, and a meadow of four more at the back of the first. On the latter stood several buildings, an excellent orchard, etc., lately the property of an English doctor, who had died on the premises, and left the whole to a servant woman as a gift, from whom it came to me as a freehold. The pleasures which I have felt at Henderson, and under the roof of that log cabin, can never be effaced from my heart until after death. The little stock of goods brought from Louisville answered perfectly, and in less than twelve months I had again risen in the world. I purchased adjoining land, and was doing extremely well when Thomas Bakewell came once more on the tapis, and joined me in commerce. We prospered at a round rate for a while, but unfortunately for me, he took it into his brain to persuade me to erect a steam-mill at Henderson, and to join to our partnership an Englishman of the name of Thomas Pears, now dead.

Well, up went the steam-mill at an enormous expense, in a country then as unfit for such a thing as it would be now for me to attempt to settle in the moon. Thomas Pears came to Henderson with his wife and family of children, the mill was raised, and worked very badly. Thomas Pears lost his money and we lost ours.

It was now our misfortune to add other partners and petty agents to our concern; suffice it for me to tell you, nay, to assure you, that I was gulled by all these men. The new-born Kentucky banks nearly all broke in quick succession; and again we started with a new set of partners; these were your present uncle N. Berthoud and Benjamin Page of Pittsburg. Matters, however, grew worse every day; the times were what men called "bad," but I am fully persuaded the great fault was ours, and the building of that accursed steam-mill was, of all the follies of man, one of the greatest, and to your uncle and me the worst of all our pecuniary misfortunes. How I labored at that infernal mill! from dawn to dark, nay, at times all night. But it is over now; I am old, and try to forget as fast as possible all the different trials of those sad days. We also took it into our heads to have a steamboat, in partnership with the engineer who had come from Philadelphia to fix the engine of that mill. This also proved an entire failure, and misfortune after misfortune came down upon us like so many avalanches, both fearful and destructive.

About this time I went to New Orleans, at the suggestion of your uncle, to arrest T—— B——, who had purchased a steamer from us, but whose bills were worthless, and who owed us for the whole amount. I travelled down to New Orleans in an open skiff, accompanied by two negroes of mine; I reached New Orleans one day too late; Mr. B—— had been compelled to surrender the steamer to a prior claimant. I returned to Henderson, travelling part way on the steamer "Paragon," walked from the mouth of the Ohio to Shawnee, and rode the rest of the distance. On my arrival old Mr. Berthoud told me that Mr. B—— had arrived before me, and had sworn to kill me. My affrighted Lucy forced me to wear a dagger. Mr. B—— walked about the streets and before my house as if watching for me, and the continued reports of our neighbors prepared me for an encounter with this man, whose violent and ungovernable temper was only too well known. As I was walking toward the steam-mill one morning, I heard myself hailed from behind; on turning, I observed Mr. B—— marching toward me with a heavy club in his hand. I stood still, and he soon reached me. He complained of my conduct to him at New Orleans, and suddenly raising his bludgeon laid it about me. Though white with wrath, I spoke nor moved not till he had given me twelve severe blows, then, drawing my dagger with my left hand (unfortunately my right was disabled and in a sling, having been caught and much injured in the wheels of the steam-engine), I stabbed him and he instantly fell. Old Mr. Berthoud and others, who were hastening to the spot, now came up, and carried him home on a plank. Thank God, his wound was not mortal, but his friends were all up in arms and as hot-headed as himself. Some walked through my premises armed with guns; my dagger was once more at my side, Mr. Berthoud had his gun, our servants were variously armed, and our carpenter took my gun "Long Tom." Thus protected, I walked into the Judiciary Court, that was then sitting, and was blamed, *only,*—for not having killed the scoundrel who attacked me.

The "bad establishment," as I called the steam-mill, worked worse and worse every day. Thomas Bakewell, who possessed more brains than I, sold his town lots and removed to Cincinnati, where he has made a large fortune, and glad I am of it.

From this date my pecuniary difficulties daily increased; I had heavy bills to pay which I could not meet or take up. The moment this became known to the world around me, that moment I was assailed with thousands of invectives; the once wealthy man was now nothing. I parted with every particle of property I held to my creditors, keeping only the clothes I wore on that day, my original drawings, and my gun.

Your mother held in her arms your baby sister Rosa, named thus on account of her extreme loveliness, and after my own sister Rosa. *She* felt the pangs of our misfortunes perhaps more heavily than I, but never for an hour lost her courage; her brave and cheerful spirit accepted all, and no reproaches from her beloved lips ever wounded my heart. With her was I not always rich?

Finally I paid every bill, and at last left Henderson, probably forever, without a dollar in my pocket, walked to Louisville alone, by no means comfortable in mind, there went to Mr. Berthoud's, where I was kindly received; they were indeed good friends.

My plantation in Pennsylvania had been sold, and, in a word, nothing was left to me but my humble talents. Were those talents to remain dormant under such exigencies? Was I to see my beloved Lucy and children suffer and want bread, in the abundant State of Kentucky? Was I to repine because I had acted like an honest man? Was I inclined to cut my throat in foolish despair? No!! I *had* talents, and to them I instantly resorted.

To be a good draughtsman in those days was to me a blessing; to any other man, be it a thousand years hence, it will be a blessing also. I at once undertook to take portraits of the human "head divine," in black chalk, and, thanks to my master, David, succeeded admirably. I commenced at exceedingly low prices, but raised these prices as I became more known in this capacity. Your mother and yourselves were sent up from Henderson to our friend Isham Talbot, then Senator for Kentucky; this was done without a cent of expense to me, and I can never be grateful enough for his kind generosity.

In the course of a few weeks I had as much work to do as I could possibly wish, so much that I was able to rent a house in a retired part of Louisville. I was sent for four miles in the country, to take likenesses of persons on their death-beds, and so high did my reputation suddenly rise, as the best delineator of heads in that vicinity, that a clergyman residing at Louisville (I would give much now to recall and write down his name) had his dead child disinterred, to procure a fac-simile of his face, which, by the way, I gave to the parents as if still alive, to their intense satisfaction.

My drawings of birds were not neglected meantime; in this particular there seemed to hover round me almost a mania, and I would even give up doing a head, the profits of which would have supplied our wants for a week or more, to represent a little citizen of the feathered tribe. Nay, my dear sons, I thought that I now drew birds far better than I had ever done before misfortune intensified, or at least developed, my abilities. I received an invitation to go to Cincinnati, a flourishing place, and which you now well know to be a thriving town in the State of Ohio. I was presented to the president of the Cincinnati College, Dr. Drake, and immediately formed an engagement to stuff birds for the museum there, in concert with Mr. Robert Best, an Englishman of great talent. My salary was large, and I at once sent for your mother to come to me, and bring you. Your dearly beloved sister Rosa died shortly afterward. I now established a large drawing-school at Cincinnati, to which I attended thrice per week, and at good prices.

The expedition of Major Long passed through the city soon after, and well do I recollect how he, Messrs. T. Peale, Thomas Say, and others stared at my drawings of birds at that time.

So industrious were Mr. Best and I that in about six months we had augmented, arranged, and finished all we could do for the museum. I returned to my portraits, and made a great number of them, without which we must have once more been on the starving list, as Mr. Best and I found, sadly too late, that the members of the College museum were splendid promisers and very bad paymasters.

In October of 1820 I left your mother and yourselves at Cincinnati, and went to New Orleans on board a flat-boat commanded and owned by a Mr. Haromack. From this date my journals are kept with fair regularity, and if you read them you will easily find all that followed afterward.

In glancing over these pages, I see that in my hurried and broken manner of laying before you this very imperfect (but perfectly correct) account of my early life I have omitted to tell you that, before the birth of your sister Rosa, a daughter was born at Henderson, who was called, of course, Lucy. Alas! the poor, dear little one was unkindly born, she was always ill and suffering; two years did your kind and unwearied mother nurse her with all imaginable care, but notwithstanding this loving devotion she died, in the arms which had held her so long, and so tenderly. This infant daughter we buried in our garden at Henderson, but after removed her to the Holly burying-ground in the same place.

Hundreds of anecdotes I could relate to you, my dear sons, about those times, and it may happen that the pages that I am now scribbling over may hereafter, through your own medium, or that of some one else be published. I shall try, should God Almighty grant me life, to return to these less important portions of my history, and delineate them all with the same faithfulness with which I have written the ornithological biographies of the birds of my beloved country.

Only one event, however, which possesses in itself a lesson to mankind, I will here relate. After our dismal removal from Henderson to Louisville, one morning, while all of us were sadly desponding, I took you both, Victor and John, from Shippingport to Louisville. I had purchased a loaf of bread and some apples; before we reached Louisville you were all hungry, and by the river side we sat down and ate our scanty meal. On that day the world was with me as a blank, and my heart was sorely heavy, for scarcely had I enough to keep my dear ones alive; and yet through these dark ways I was being led to the development of the talents I loved, and which have brought so much enjoyment to us *all,* for it is with deep thankfulness that I record that you, my sons, have passed your lives almost continuously with your dear mother and myself. But I will here stop with one remark.

One of the most extraordinary things among all these adverse circumstances was that I never for a day gave up listening to the songs of our birds, or watching their peculiar habits, or delineating them in the best way that I could; nay, during my deepest troubles I frequently would wrench myself from the persons around me, and retire to some secluded part of our noble forests; and many a time, at the sound of the wood-thrush's melodies have I fallen on my knees, and there prayed earnestly to our God.

This never failed to bring me the most valuable of thoughts and always comfort, and, strange as it may seem to you, it was often necessary for me to exert my will, and compel myself to return to my fellow-beings.

MISSISSIPPI RIVER JOURNAL

One of three surviving original manuscripts of Audubon's journals, the Mississippi River Journal *was given by Colonel John E. Thayer in 1913 to the Museum of Comparative Zoölogy of Harvard University. In 1929 Howard Corning's painstaking transcription of the entire journal, followed by the slighter 1840–43 journal in a separate volume, was published (under the title* Journal of John James Audubon: Made During His Trip to New Orleans in 1820–21) *by the Club of Odd Volumes in Cambridge, Massachusetts. Words enclosed in brackets here were crossed out (and replaced with substitute words) by Audubon himself in the original manuscript.*

This is an intense, vital document of Audubon's early career, and one of the most remarkable diaries in the annals of American natural history. By the middle of 1820, with his wife Lucy's approval and support, Audubon had finally determined to break out of the downward spiral his life and fortunes had taken. He had lost almost all he possessed in a series of business failures and bad investments; he had suffered the humiliation of having been jailed for debt; he had been forced to declare bankruptcy; and he had toiled with little conviction through several ill-paid months as a taxidermist in the new Western Museum in Cincinnati. Leaving Lucy and their two sons behind, he set off with a young assistant, Joseph Mason, down the Ohio and the Mississippi with the sole aim of becoming nothing less than America's greatest painter of birds.

Though he was tormented at times by solitude, depression, and fears of failure, by the end of the journal his resolution was, if anything, stronger than ever. His faith in his skill and ultimate success had been revived, and his career as an independent artist with a sovereign mission was now launched for good. He had daily increased his already formidable knowledge of animals and birds in their natural habitat, storing up a fund of firsthand observations he could draw on the rest of his life. And he had painted some of his finest watercolors, especially during his stay at the Oakley Plantation near Saint Francisville, Louisiana. The journal ends, as if announcing the beginning of a new life, on the last day of December 1821, just two weeks after his wife and sons had finally arrived to join him in New Orleans, and over fourteen months after he had left them behind in Cincinnati.

Thursday—Ohio River Oct—12th 1820. I left Cincinnati [today at] this afternoon at half past 4 o'clock, on Board of Mr. Jacob Aumack's flat Boat—bound to New Orleans—the feeling of a Husband and a Father, were My Lot when I kissed My Beloved Wife & Children with an expectation of being absent for Seven Months—

I took with me Joseph Mason a Young Man of about 18 years of age of good familly and naturally an aimiable Youth, he is intended to be a Companion, & a Friend; and if God will grant us a safe return to our famillies our Wishes will be [most Likely] congenial to our present feelings Leaving Home with a Determined Mind to fulfill our Object =

Without any Money My Talents are to be My Support and My enthusiasm my Guide in My Dificulties, the whole of which I am ready to exert to [meet] keep, and to surmount.

The Watter is Low, although a Little froth, sailed the River a few days since, about $4\frac{1}{8}$ feet. We only floated 14 Miles by the Break of the 13th of Oct*re* the Day was fine, [and] I prayed for the health of My familly—prepared Our Guns and went on shore [on the] in Kentucky [Side]—Cap^{e} Saml Cummings who left Cincinnati with an Intention of Noting the Channels of this River and the Mississipi accompanied us—We shot thirty Partridges—1 Wood Cock—27 Grey Squirrels—a Barn Owl—a Young Turkey Buzzard and an Autumnal Warbler as Mr. A. Willson as being pleased to denominate the Young of the Yellow Rump Warbler—this was a Young Male in beautifull plumage for the season and I Drew it—as I feel perfectly Convinced that Mr. Willson has made an Error in presenting this Bird as a New Specie I shall only recommend You to Examine attentively My Drawing of Each and his Description—its Stomach was filled with the remaines of Small Winged Insects and 3 Seeds of Some Berries, the names of which I could not determine—

Early in the morning the wind rose and we came to on the Ohio side by G^{l} Wm Harrisons' Plantation—and remained untill nine o'clock *PM*—

I saw several flocks of Ducks in the morning before we had cleaned our Guns—hundreds of Meadow Lark Alanda Magna seen travelling Southwest—

[the Night became] the Wind Rose and brought us to shore, it raind and blowed Violantly untill the Next Day—

Saturday Oct 14TH 1820 After an early Breakfast We took to the Woods I say *We* because Joseph Mason, Cap*e* Cummings & myself I believe are allways [—] together—

I shot a *Fish Hawk Falco Aliaetos* at the mouth of the Big Miami River a handsom Male in good Plumage. he was wingd only and in attempting to Seize Joseph's hand, he ran one of his Claws through the Lower Mandille of his Bill and exibited a very Ludicrous object—these Birds walk with great dificulty and Like all of the Falco and Strix Young throw themselves on their backs to defend themselves—

We returned to our Boat with a Wild Turkey 7 Partriges a Tall Tale Godwit and a *Hermit* Thrush which was too much torn to make a drawing of it this was the first time I had met with this Bird and felt particularly Mortified at the Situation—

We passd the Small Towns of [Madi] Laurenceburgh—in Indiana—Petersbugh in K^{y}.—, We Walked in the afternoon to *Bellevue* the former residence of a *Far Famed* Lady of our acquaintance Mrs Bruce; Saw Thomas Newell and old Cap^{e} Green—if My Eyes did not err I saw my suspicions of her conduct that Evening Justified. We Killed 4 Small Grebes at one Shot from a Flock of about 30 We approached them with ease to within about 40 yards, they were chassing each other and quite Merry when the Destructive fire through the Whole in consternation. the Many Wounded escaped by Diving the rest flew off—this is the second time I have seen this Kind, and they must be extremely rare [Bird] in this part of America—

About Three Miles above Bellevue in Kentucky we walked through a Fissure of Rocks really romantic the Passage in [that] form of a half Moon is about 6 feet Wide, the rocks are composed of Large Round pebles cimented with Coarse Sand about 100 feet High on one Side and Sixty on the other—I made a Sketch of it for [my] your future Pleasure—We walked this day about 40 miles Saw one Deer crossing the River

Sunday Oct. 15, 1820— there was this morning as heavy a white frost as I Ever Saw, the Wind blew cold and heavy from the North Shott 2 *Tell Tale Godwits*—and chased a Deer in the River for some considerable time, but a Canoe with Two Indianna Men had the advantage of us and caught it as I rose to shoot it—the Wind being fair We floated tolerably well, killed 5 *Teal* One Blue Wingd Teal, [a young Malard] 2 Doves 3 Partriges and fortunately another Hermit Thrush Turdus Solitarius—We met and went on Board the Steam Boat *Velocipede* Saw Col. Oldham, Mr. Bruce, Mr. Talcut & Lady [on Board] Passengers besides a Consider Number of Strangers, Opend a Letter directed to Your Mother by Your Uncle W^am^ B— Mr [—] Aumack Killed a Young Malard Duck—the Contents of the [—] Gizard of one of the 4 Grebes I open was Nothing else than a solid mass of fine hair apparently belonging to some very Small quadrupeds—(feathers)

Saw a Chimney Swallow; the Number of Ducks Increasing—and an Appearance of a Cold Nights—Killed a Great Carolina Wren the Grebes were cooked and eat but extremely Fishy rancid and fat—

at 10 'oclock We were roused from sound sleep by the Boats having ran on Rocks—the hands had to go in the Watter to take them off, it was cold and Windy—

Monday Oct 16th 1820 the frost much as yesterday; Turkey, being heard close by we took a walk after them unsuccessfully, they answered to my calls but kept off—

I did not feel well; took some Medicine and Drew the *Hermit Thrush Turdus Solitarius* that I killed yesterday—this Bird can easily be known from the Turdus Auracapillus being about $\frac{1}{3}$ Larger, and from the Tawny Thrush, by Looking at the inner part of its Wings which exhibit a handsome light Band of Buff—its stomach contained the remains of insects and the Seed of the Winter Grape—was very fat and [and] delicate eating—these Birds are scarce and not generally known their note a plaintive soft one—Seldom more than 2 are seen together—Some of the Country we saw [to] is extremely high, hilly and broken—saw a wood grouse—many ducks Several *Northern Divers* or Loons—Some Cormorants, Many Crows—Several flocks of Cow Buntings moving Southward—Killed two Partriges and One Turkey—

the Boats ran ashore sandbar at Seven o'clock, with great Exercising one was brought off it was the one I was living in the other stayed fast all night, the hands suffered much from the cold—

Tuesday Oct 17th 1820 The weather disagreably Cold, but Clear, the other Boat still fast We went early on Shore,—in Kentucky—a Long Walk through the woods was fruitless, I saw 4 Ravens—Many Winter Hawks—some Red breasted Thrushes or Robins—the Wood full of Grey & Black Squirrels returned to the Boats the *other* having joined us with Two Turkeys & One Wood Grouse or Pheasant—

The Turkeys extremely plenty and Crossing the River hourly from the North Side, great Number destroyed [there] falling in the Stream from want of strength—the Partrige when Crossing also, and in fact, all the Game that Cannot propery be called Migratorius =

Saw a Great Number of Chimney Swallows going Southwest—this Bird travells much more advantageously than most all others being able to feed without halting—Killed a fine *American Buzard Falco Leverianus* he was feeding on a Grey Squirel on a stump tree, he fell to the ground and Raised again without loosing his praise—his stomack was filled with that Last Prey—a Large Turkey Cock was stolen from us by some travellers—killed today 17. partridges—One *wood grouse* 4 Turkeys I Killed 2 at one shot—One Hare—One Robin and the American Buzzard—We put some fish Lines out having Landed for the Night all hands being very much fatigued—

Could My Wishes be fulfilled I would have [the] you well fed on that game as the rich calls it richest—the thermometre down at 36—

Wednesday Oct 18th 1820 Jacob Aumack went hunting with us saw some fine Turkeys, Killed a Common Crow Corvus [—] Americanus which I Drew; many Robins in the woods and thousand of Snow Buntings Emberiza Nivalis—several Rose Breasted Gross Beaks—We killed 2 Pheasants, 15 Partridges—1 Teal, 1 T. T. Godwit—1 Small Grebe all of these I have seen precisely alike in all parts—and one Barred Owl that is undoutedly the most plentifull of his Genus—I felt poorly all day and Drawing in a Boat were a man cannot stand erect gave me a Violent headache—The Watter raising a little gave me some Hopes of reaching Louisville before Sunday—anxious to know my Fate—I am confortably situated and would be sorry to be obliged to part with them—the Weather Milde & Cloudy—Caught No Fish Last night—

Thursday Oct.^{R}—19th 1820 Cap^{e} Cummings Mr Aumack and Joseph after a Long Walk return to Dinner with only 7 Partridges and 1 Pheasant—Mr Shaw Shot 1 Pheasant—I finished my Drawing of the *Common Crow* and after Dinner Went a Shore with the Company—saw Many Cedar Birds killed a Young Blackburnian Warbler—a Young Carolina Cuckow so much reduce by the Hard Weather that he could scarcely fly—killed 5 pheasants 14 Partridges 1 Squirel and 3 Turkeys, Shot *at once* by *Joseph* who was not a little proud when he heard 3 Chears given him from the Boats this was his first essay on Turkeys—

[in the] While absent the boats having put too to make Sweeps. a flock of Turkeys came among^{t} them and in tring to kill some with Aumack's pistols one was bustted and the other wounded Joseph's Scull pretty severely—saw an astonishing number of Gray Squirels—the Country being extremely hilly opposite *Wells Point* the hunting Was Laborious and fatiguing.

The Stomack of the Cuckoo Contained 2 entire Grass Hopers one Large Green *Kid diddid* and the remainder of remains of Diferents colopterous Insects.

WEDNESDAY NOVEMB[R] 1ST 1820 Weather drizly and windy Landed a few hundred yards below *Evansville* in Indianna on a/c of M[r] Aumack Who had some money to Collect—he brought on Board only a french Double Barrel Gun and a Gold Watch the man made for Sale —I Wrote to my Beloved *Wife & Mr H. W. Wheeler* Saw Large flocks of Snow Geese but only one in perfect Plumage.

Not so stupid as mentioned in Linne. Left Evansville at 2 o'clock, P.M.—Cap[t] Cummings & Joseph parted in the Skiff for Henderson to Get *Dash* a slut I had Left in the Charge of M[r] Brigs—about 3 Miles down We Saw 3 of these Birds that I have considered as being the Brown Pelican they made a noise somewhat like a raven—they alighted on a Red Maple Tree—after many [fruitless] hard trials:—We landed below them and Went a Shore with great expectation of Procuring one—M[r] Aumack drew near them but Missed 2 that Were together and that I expected and hoped to see fall—the wind raising it was Concluded We Should remain—rather sorry that the Cap[e] & Joseph were absent—as we had expected to go Within 2 Miles of Henderson & meet them [them] on their return—

The people at Evansville very Sickly, could not see M[r] D[d] Negley as it was my wish, he being at his House 4 Miles up Pigeon Creek—

Extremely tired of my Indolent Way of Living not having procured any thing to draw since Louisville—

THURSDAY NOVEMBER 2ND, 1820 Cap[e] Cummings Joseph & Dash arrived at one o'clock this morning having a severe rowing match of it We started about 5 and floated down slowly within 2 miles of Henderson when We experienced quite a *Gale* and Put to on the Indianna Shore opposite Henderson—The Wind Blew so violently that I could only make a very rough Drawing of that Place—I can scarcely Conceive that I staid there 8 Years and Passed them Comfortably for it undoutedly is one the poorest Spots in the Western Country according to My present opinion =

Saw some Large Sea Gulls—[a]: Larus argentatus Some Geese, Ducks, &c. So Warm to night that Bats are flying near the Boats—extremely anxious to be doing something in the Drawing Way—

[a]: they are Pale blue above, Tail & Belly White—a few of the outer Primaries Black and about the size of a Raven—

Friday Novemb[r] 3rd, 1820 We left our harbour at day Break and passed Henderson about sun raise, I Looked on the Mill perhaps for the Last Time, and with thoughts that made my Blood almost Cold bid it an eternal farewell—

Here one of the hands left us a Poor Sickly Devil who had been acting as Cook, called Luke a Shoe Maker of Cincinnati—

The *Indian Summer* that extraordinary Phenomenon of North America, is now in all its Splendor, the Blood Red Raising Sun—and the Constant *Smoky* atmosphere, is undoutedly not easily to be accounted for—it has been often supposed that the Indians, firing the Prairies of the West were the Cause, but since We have Left C. the Eastwardly Winds have prevailed without diminishing in any degree the Smoke—it is extremely bad to Most Eyes and particularly so to Mine—

Cap[e] Cummings, M[r] Shaw & Joseph took a Long Walk [for] but saw nothing, killed 4 Squirels—one Butcher Bird, and a Swamp Blackbird—Large flocks of them seen travelling Southwest—I shot a Turkey Buzard, *Vulture Aura* about 120 yards off with a ball—Saw When We Landed at the foot of Diamond Island a fine *Snow Goose* [but] a Young One—Saw several N. Divers, Some Geese, a few Sand Hill Cranes—& some Ducks—

Saturday Novemb[r] 4th, 1820 Landed Last evening opposite the Middle of Diamond Island lately the property of Walter Alves Deceased of Henderson—about 9 o'clock the Wind Rose & Blowed a tremendous Gale which continued all Night, fortunately for us We Were under the Lee of the Land—

This Morning the Wind had abated alitle, but We could not go, the River making immediatly below us a Turn Southwest[d]—5 of us took guns and Went to the Island, We Walked almost all over it—Saw great many Turkeys—and Many Dears—I killed a Large Buck that died in the Cane, and Lost it—We Brought Nothing on Board, if 2 of us only had been there, probably We could have Made a good hunt—I Shot a *Winter Wren* but cut it so much that it could not be drawn [it]—

Returned to our Boats about 5 o'clock the Wind still Blowing, but rounding to the Northwest and Weather very Cold.

Watter falling—

I Remarked this morning that the Turkey Buzzards that had roosted over a dead Hog Last Night, Took a Long flight eastwardly this Morning as if to excite their appetite and returned to Consume their filthy Meal about 2 o'clock the number considerably Increased—While sailing high several Hawks for the Sake of amusement Chased them and sailed Many of them almost to the ground—

My Slut Dash apparently good for nothing for the want of Employment—

Now & Then We see a Blue Crane—Saw Many Wood Groos on the Island

Sunday November 5th, 1820 The Weather fair this morning, the Thermoter down at 30—the sun rose beautifull and reflected through the Trees on the Placid Stream much like a Column of Lively fire—the frost was heavy on the decks and when the Sun Shun of it it Looked beautifull beyond expression—

We floated tolerably well the river being here contracted by Large Sand Barrs—

Gayly we were overtaken by a Skiff containing a Couple of Gentill Young Men, Bound to New Orleans they had Matrasses, Trunks, a Gun & Provisions—

Saw about the same time a fine Brown Eagle—Shot at it without effect—

Many Dears where Merely Gamboling on the Sand Barrs and [much] excited us [to]

We passed *Mount Vernon* a Small Village in Indianna about one mile above the upper end of Slim Island—Mr Shaw & Cap^{e} Cummings went to the Island but returned without any thing—this part of the River rather Dificult—

We Landed about 3 Miles above the Mouth of *High Land Creek* in the *Mississipi* Bend—

Saw Many Geese, some Sand Hill Cranes—a few Loons some *Red Breasted Thrushes,* many Sparrows & parokets.

Killed only one Winter Hawk, & Shot at one Wood Cock.

as I promised You a Picture of the Caracters We have on Board of Both Boats I will attempt to Copy them, [Was my Talent in writting anything] Could my Pen Act as a Black Chalk by the help of my fingers you might rely on the Exibition of the figures—Yet I undertake it with pleasure, knowing how sweet this May be to you & Myself some Years hence, while sitting together by the fireside Looking at Your Dear Mother reading to us—

being on Board of Boats Much in the situation of Passengers I am of Course Bound to give the preference to those who are termed Capitains and Mr Aumack is the First that I will bring to your attention—

You have seen him and of Course I have not much to say the acquaintance of Man When unconnected by Interest is *plain* [and] easily *understood* & Seldom Deviates.—

he is a good Strong, Young Man, Generously Inclined rather Timorous on the River, Yet Brave and accustomed to hardships—he Commands the Boat where I am—

Mr Loveless is a good Natured Natured, rough fellow brought up to Work without pride, rather anxious to Make Money—Playfull & fond of Jokes & Women—

Mr Shaw the owner of Most of the Cargo puts me in mind of some Jews, who are all Intent on their Interest & Wellfare; of a keen Visage & Manners; a Bostonian—Weak of Constitution but strong of Stomack—Would Live Well if at any one else' Expense. =

The Crew is Composed as follows

Ned Kelly a Wag of 21. Stout Well Made, handsome if Clean, possessed of Much Low Wit, produces Mirth to the Whole even in his Braggardism—Sings, dances and fiels always happy—he is Baltimorian—

2 Men from Pennsylvania although not brothers, are possessed of a great sameness of Caracters—these are *Anthony P. Bodley* & *Henry Sesler*—they Work Work Well, talk but litle and are Carpenters by Trade.

The Last is Much Like the Last of every thing, the Worst Part—Joseph Seeg, Lazy, fond of Grog, says nothing because it cannot help himself, sleeps Sound, for he burns all his Cloths, while in the ashes

Cap^e Cummings Joseph & Myself form the Rear at Times and at Times the Van—You have seen the Life and there Likeness could not give you a better Impression than that you have formed—We agree Well, and are Likely to agree Still—

Monday Novemb^r 6th 1820 The thermometer this morning was down at 28 and it felt very disagreable—Took to the Shore and walked 9 miles to the Mouth of the Wabash, but saw nothing to Shoot at—about one Mile below that the Wind springing ahead Brought us to on the Illinois Shore and 5 Guns went hunting, I shot 6 Dear!—

the people here have a dreadfull sickly aspect and their Deportment not the Most Inticing—

the Caves plenty—

Our Boats started about One Hour before sun down, & Cap^e Cummings having extended his hunt up the Wabash had a Long Walk for nothing—

We landed for the Night about 6 miles above Shawaney Town on the Kentucky Shore—

Weather appearance of rain, and blowing, Much Warmer—

Saw Some Robins, a few Blue Jays, a few Blue Birds, Geese, S. H. Cranes, Ducks—Buzzards & the [general] usual number of W. Peckers common at this season—

Tuesday Novembr 7th 1820 Weather at 50 this morning, rainy & Desagreable, Landed at Shawaney Town where we staid six hours—I staid snugg on Board Mr Aumack having naild up the only accessible hole to our Boat.—

I Wrote to My Wife & Directed it to Mr Wheeler—We left Shawaney town at half 5 & went only to the Lower end of it, the Wind raising again with an appearance of a Very Boisterous Night—

Jacob Aumack killed a *Rusty Grakle* a beautifull Male and as these Birds are scarce I intend Drawing it tomorrow = it is but seldom that Many of these Birds are seen together, they Walk with great Statliness and Elegance, are swifter of flight than the Swamp Blackbirds.

I felt very anxious during all the time of our stay to be off from this Place.

This Evening Ned Kelly & his Companion Joe Seeg having Drank rather freely of Grog, they had a Litle Scrape at the Expense of Mr Seeg's Eyes & Nose—

The People of Shawney Complaining of Sickness, the place improved but Litle

Wednesday Novembr 8th, 1820 the Weather Calm & beautifull this Morning [and] We started with a good prospect and our Landing within Two Miles of the famous *Rock in Cave* to night prove it—

I Drew this Morning My *Rusty Grakle, Gracula Ferruginea,* and made a handsome piece of it.

Cape Cummings hunted all day but saw nothing—since 3 Days we have been particularly unfortunate in our Hunts.

Near our Landing Place We Went on Shore to procure some Venaison Hams—Mr Shaw bought 4 prs for 2$ remarkably fine—the young man who sold them had Killed 3 Dear to day and had hung one Large Buck for his Dogs to feed on—

Killed to day One Grey Squirel & 3 Tell Tale Godwits these Birds Wade so deep that one would suppose they are swimming, fly a few Yards into Shallower Watter, holding their wings up untill perfectly satisfied of their being on the Bottom—then run about briskly & ketch small fishes with great dexterity—

Saw one Sea Gull a Large one—a few Gold Finches Many Cardinals—some Divers—but neither Ducks or Geese—The Weather has become Cloudy & raining by Intervalls is Now beautifull with an appearance of Frost

about Two hours before sun sett a *Barred Owl* teased by four Crows and Chased from the tree where he was Lit raised up in the manner of a Hawk in the air so high that We Lost Entire sight of him, he acted as if Lost—now & then making very short Circles and flapping his Wings quickly, then zig zag lines—this was quite a new Sight and I expect take place but seldom—I felt anxious to see his Descent to the Earth but Could not—

The Trees here have Lost all their foliage, the Cane & a few Green Briars is all that animate the Woods—the Shores are thickly sett with Cotton Wood Trees.

THURSDAY NOVEMB[R] 9TH 1820 The Wind blowed nearly all day a head, the Weather cold—Saw no Game although We Walked a great deal in the Woods the Country extremely poor here—

We Landed at Sun Set at the *Rockin Cave* having Come only about 2 Miles—

I began My Sketch of it immediately, regretting that We had not reached this place Last Night.

We Purchased a Skiff from a flat Boat—Ducks & Geese very numerous flying down the Stream—Shot 2 Ducks of the flocking Fowl Kind —& 3 Squirels—the Thermometer in the Watter at sun set was down to 27, appearance of a Very Cold Night—

a Man on the Shore told me that Last Winter he had Caught a Large Number of Malard Ducks with a Trap set with a figure of 4 & shaped Like a Partridge trap

The Tell Tales we eat to Day were very fat but very fishy—I eat the purple Grakle it tasted well—

FRIDAY NOVEMB[R] 10TH 1820 as soon as Day Light permitted me this morning—I Took Joseph on Shore and Lighted a good fire—took also My Drawing Book etc with a Skiff—the Morning pleasant and the Thermometer raised to 50° While I was taking My Sketch of the *Rockin Cave* Cap[e] Cummings took a Good Walk through the Woods—at 9 My Drawing was compleat—this Cave is one of the Curiosities that attract the attention of allmost every Traveler on the Ohio and thousands of

Names & Dates ornament the sides & Cealing—there is a small upper room dificult of access imediatly above & through the Cealing of the Ground floord one, Large enough to Contain 4 or 5 persons when sitted on their hams—this place is said to have been for Many Years the *rendez Vous* of a noted Robber of the name of Mason it is about 20 Miles below Shawaney town on the same side; had our Boats spent a Day there, I would have been pleased to take several Diferent Views of it—the Rocks are Blue Lime Stone containing in Many Parts Round Masses of a fine flinty appearance Darker than the main Body—

at Nine o'clock it became Cloudy & Cold, We left for our Boats, but before We reached them, it snowed & Hailed & Wetted us Compitly—Our Boats had parted to Cross & Run through the *Walker's Barr* and *Hurricane Island*—We Landed only about One Mile below the Latter, the rain Increasing and the Weather extremely Disagreable—Never have seen so much snow at this season in this Latitude—

Saw a fine Black Hawk Falco Niger—& Black Gull,—Shot Two Ducks—

Saturday Novembr 11th, 1820 It rained hard during the whole of the Night and this day floated only about 7 Miles—

Saw a few Turkeys,—

A Flock of *Carrion Crows* made us go to the shore but they were so exceedingly shy that they would fly several hundred Yards off—while the Turkey Buzzards that [when] accompanied them would suffer us to Walk under the trees on which they alighted—the Carrion Crows are very scarce in this Part of the Country and keep Generally Lower to the South—their flight is heavy and their appearance while on the Wing awkward

We Landed for the Night a Golconda a small Town of the Illinois—Titles disputed of course the place not Improving—Court was sitting—

Sunday Novembr 12th 1820 The Wind Blowed this Morning and We did Not Leave the Shore untill 9 o'clock—Wind fair—Weather raw & Cloudy—Mr. Aumack Killed a Duck [Ruddy Duck] out of a Flock of 5 that proved to be a Nondescript—and also a *Imber Diver*—the Wind rendered our Cabin smoky I could Not begin to Draw untill after Dinner—I had the pleasure of Seing Two of the same Ducks Swimming Deep, with their Tail *erect*, and Diving for food—having never seen these Birds before, it was highly satisfactorily to Me—Tomorrow I will give a thorough Description of it

The *Imber Diver* was Shot Dead and proved a beautifull specimen—of Cours I will give You a Drawing of it—for Some time before I procured one of them; they Were Called *Northern Divers,* the Moment I Saw this, the size and Coloring Made Me Sure of it being an *Imber Diver*—

Saw a Large flock of Turkeys fly across from an Island to the Main, killed None—

We are Landed about half a Mile above the *Cumberland Island* the weather not so cold as it feels the Thermometer at 38—had some spits of snow in the forenoon—

Vast flocks of Ducks & Geese flying Southwardly

MONDAY NOVEMBR 13TH, 1820 a Beautifull Morning enable[d] me to go on with my Drawing very early—a Light frost embelished the raising of the Sun

We Landed at the Middle of Cumberland Island to dispatch a Skiff to take Soundings—

finished My Duck by Dinner Time and Was Lucky enough to kill another of the same kind, precisely a Like but rather Less in Size, it is with apparent Dificulty or a Sluggish disposition that these Birds rise out of the Watter & yet will not dive at the flash of a Gun—while on the Wing are very Swift

this afternoon I Begun the Drawing of the Imber Diver had Two Long Chases after a Couple of others, that out Managed our Skill—they would Dive as if Going down the Stream and raised from One to Two hundred Yards above us—they frequently Dipp their Bill in the Watter, and I think have the power of judging in that Way if the place Contains Fish—One I shot at; dove & raised again Imediatly as if to see Where I was or What Was the Matter—

I Saw Several of the *Fin Tail Ducks,* all acting the Same Way i.e. Swimming Deep & the Tail Erect—No Doubt this appendage is very usefull to them when under the Watter—

Saw a Bear on a Sand Barr, had a great run after it—to no purpose—

Saw 2 of those Birds I take for Black Pelicans—Many Loose flocks of Blackbirds Ducks & Geese—Mr *Aumack* saw an *Eagle* with a White head and *Brown Body & Tail,* this Corroborates with the Idea of Willson of its being the same Bird with the *Brown* Eagle

Landed about the Middle of Tenessee Island Weather Much Milder—

Joseph Made a *Faux Pas* this day—the Whole of our Folks not in the best humour—Killed 7 Partridges 1 G. Squirel & One Duck

Tuesday Novemb[r] 14th 1820 Drawing this Morning as soon as the Light would permit me—Started early—

Went out in the Skiff to try to Shoot the *Largest* White *Crane*, with Black tips, but he walk[d] off from the Shore and I return[d] knowing that it would be vain to attempt to follow him on a Large naked Sand Barr —felt great anxiety to procure such for he appeared Beautifull—

Saw several Eagles, Brown & White headed—Although I drew nearly the whole of this day I did finished My *Imber Diver;*

Cap[e] Cummings killed 26 Starlings, Sturnus Pradetorius all young—eat them at our Supper, good & Delicate—1 golden Plover & Two Squirels—

Mr. Shaw killed an Owl that unfortunately he did not fetch; = We passed this Day *Fort Massacre* here the Ohio is Magnificent, the river about one & $\frac{1}{4}$ mile Wide affords a view of 14 or 15 Miles, and this afternoon being Calm with one of those *Whimsical* sunsetts that only belong to America rendered the Scene extremely interesting.

We landed about One Mile below what is called the Little Chain an partial obstruction to the Navigation of this Queen of Rivers.—

Saw several *Swans* flying very high—Geese are in Constant View but have so far outwited us, these Birds are Wilder on the Rivers than when in the Ponds or small Lake that in Many places run Parralel with the Ohio at a Small distance in Land—

Cap[e] C. Brought an Oppossum, Dash after having broke I thought all its bones left it—it was thrown over Board as if dead, yet the moment he toucht the Watter he swam for the Boats—so tenacious of Life are these animals that it tooked a heavy blow of the Axe to finish him—Tomorrow We Hope to Pass the Last Dificulty & Two Days More May take us to the Mississipi.

Total Length of the Fin Tailed Duck 15$\frac{1}{2}$ Inches—$\frac{3}{4}$ [— —] to [—] of Tail Bill Dark Blue, Broad for the size of the Bird—& sharply hook at the point—Legs & feet L. Blue the palms Black, Tung fleshy—upper Part of the Head [Dark Brown,] Back Wings—& Tail Dark Brown Zig Zags with transversal Bars—of Light D[o]—Sides Dark Chestnut Eye rather small Neck Breast & Belly Light Brown with transversal Black drops—A Triangular White spot forms the under Tail Coverts—

Tail composed of 18 Feathers rounding each feather narrow Sharp & Terminating in Spoon Like Shape Points—this is White—the Head & Neck Short & Thick—Swims Deep with part of the Belly Silvery white

Breadth 22 Inches—Wings Brown not reaching the Tail by $\frac{1}{2}$ Inch—No Wing Stripe—

When I saw these Birds the Weather was Boisterous since fair have not seen one—

Imber Diver Weighes 6 lbs
Total Length 2 8/12 feet—
to end of Tail 2 4½/12— " —
Weidth tip to tip 4 "
Length of the Gut 5 8/12 "

Contents of gut & Gizzard Small Fish, Bones & Scales and Large Gravel———Body extremely fat

rancid—Belly & Vest White but not silvery as in the Grebes—

Wednesday 15th 1820 November— At Work again this morning as early as could be, a beautiful day—finished My Drawing to my liking having Sketch[d] our Boats in the View of this Magnificient Part of the Ohio = Saw more than a Dozen of Eagles and one I had a good view of had a White Tail & a Brown head, Again [Yet] I remark[d] that the *Brown Eagles In Ohio* Esp. were at Least ¼ Larger than the White headed ones

Saw a Large flock of Large White Gulls with Black Wing Tips very shy while on the Wing but not at all so when swimming fired two guns Without affect

Passed the famous Chain of Rocks, Much diversion to see M[r] Aumack's Movements—

having seen Steam Boats allmost every day fast on Sand Barrs I have taken no particular notice of any of their Names & Positions—have Passed this day 3 flat Boats belonging to W[m] Noble of Cincinnati that left that Place early in August—3 out of 6 are lost

Landed about 2 Miles above New America on the Illinois Shore—Broken Land, fine Timber of Oak & Poplar = Killed an Oppossum—

Our People Much MELOWED; Saw Winter & Shore Larks Many Geese & Ducks 2 Swans—

Thursday November 16th, 1820 We floated only about Two Miles & Landed at *America*—to sell some *Articles*; people very sickly, a miserable place altogether—took a long Walk this Morning—[and] this afternoon Cap[e] C. Joseph & I took a Skiff and spent the afternoon hunting, but killed nothing—Saw Two Black Hawks =

At our Return at Night found M[r] Aumack in Bad humor, and after We had retired to our Cabin for the Night, Received a *Humorous Lesson* that I shall Never forget—

My Dear Children if Ever you read these trifling remarks pay your attention to what follows—

Never be under what is Called obligations to Men not Aware of the Value or the Meaness of their *Conduct*

Never take a passage in any State or Vessel without a well understood agreement between you & the owners or Clerks & of all things Never go for Nothing if you Wish to save Mental Troubles & Body Viscisitude

Well aware that I shall never forget this Night as Long as I live, I close [here]

The old *Washington* Steam Boat came along side of us Took 70 barrels of salt rais[d] steam and made herself fast about 2 miles Below—

FRIDAY NOVEMBER 17TH 1820 We left early—I took the Skiff and Went to the Mouth of the Ohio, and round the point up the Misisipi—

Eleven Years ago on the 2 of January I ascended that Stream to St. Genevieve Ferdinand Rozier of *Nantes* my partner in a Large Keel Boat Loaded with Sundries to a Large Amount *our* property

The 10th of May 1819 I passed this place in an open Skiff Bound to New Orleans with two of My Slaves—

Now I enter it *poor* in fact *Destitute* of all things and reliing only on that providential Hope the Comforter of this Wearied Mind—in a flat Boat a Passenger—

The meeting of the Two Streams reminds me a little of the [Young,] Gentle, [man] Youth who Comes in the World, spotles he presents himself, he is gradually drawn in to thousands of Dificulties that Makes him wish to keep [to himself] apart, but at Last he is over done [and] mixed, and lost in the Vortex—

The Beautifull & Transparent Watter of the Ohio when first entering the Misisipi is taken in small Drafts and Looks the More aquable to the Eye as it goes down surrounded by the Muddy Current, it keeps off as much as possible by running down on the Kentucky side for several miles but reduced to a narrow strip & is lost—I saw here two Indians in a Canoe they spoke some French, had Bear traps, uncomonly clean kept, a few Venaison hams a gun and Looked so Independent, free & unconcerned with the World that I Gazed on them, admired their Spirits, & wished for their Condition = here the Traveller enters a New World, the current of the stream about 4 miles per hour, puts the steersman on the alert and awakes him to troubles and difficulties unknown on the Ohio, the Passenger feels a different atmosphere, a very diferent prospect—the Curling stream & its hue are the first objects—the caving in of the Banks and the Thick Set Growth of the Young Cotton Wood is the next = the Watter's dencity reduced the thermoter from 62 to 20 degrees = We

Landed Very Early, Cap[e] C & I Walked Through the Woods, and remark[d] the Great Diference of Temperature so suddenly felt—

I bid my farewell to the Ohio at 2 o'clock P.M. and felt a fear gathering involuntarily, every moment draws me from all that is Dear to Me My Beloved Wife & Children—

The Boats separated on Entering the Mississipi, as being safer to navigate it singly—We felt the better for this and Hope good Cheer will revive again—

Although I hunted a good Deal this Day I saw but Little and Nothing New, a few King Fishers, some Divers, Geese Ducks—some Gold Finches the Notes of Which reminded Me of the *Canary Birds*, a few Blue Geays, Now & then the Plaintive farewell note of the *Blue Bird*: rather sorry that the Strong Current we are in Will Not permit Me to go a Shore unless Landed by the force of Contrary winds—

The Mississipi is a good Midle Stage at present

Saturday November 18th 1820 floated within about 2 miles of the Iron Banks and Land in Kentucky at about ½ past 3 oclock—

I took a sketch of the River below us comprehending on our Left the Iron Banks, the Chalk Bank on our Right in the Back ground Wolff Island and Part of the Missoury shore.

My drawing finished took a Walk in the Woods, the Country full of Ponds of Stagnant Watters, Shot 2 Malards While Dash was bringing out the Last one a White headed Eagle *Dashed* at the Duck the Bitch brought it—

Killed an Oppossum Many Blackbirds the Thermometer at 64. Bats in the Evening and Butterflies seen to day in quantity as well as many other Insects—

The Game Not so plenty as on the Ohio and Much Shier—

Sunday 19th November 1820 When We Left Cincinnati, we agreed to shave & Clean completely every Sunday = and often have been anxious to see the day come for certainly a shirt worn one week, hunting every day and sleeping in Buffalo robes at night soon becomes soiled and Desagreable. We pass this morning the famous Wolf Island, the history of which is amply given in the Ohio Navigator—here said Mr. Lovelace a Man [of] called *White* having become a Lunatic as I was going up the River, jumped over Board in the Night made the shore although he could not swim and I was then at anchor in 7 feet of watter and never seen afterward, I sent several *hands* to Look for him, his tracks only Led to the Top of the Bank—the Muskitoes being then remarkly

Bad—he must have Died in the Same Bend of the River found 2 dead men shot through the head could not burrie them their stench was too great—

We floated to day almost 20 Miles Killed Nothing—saw Mr *James Asler* who told Me that Mr *Thomas Litton* & himself Lived with a Mile of *Chalk Banks*—

Ivory Billed Wood Peckers are Now Plenty, Bears, Wolf, &c but the Country extremely Difficult of Access, the *caves* Extending in Many Places several Miles from the River—

On Sundays I look at My Drawings and particularly at that of My Beloved Wife—& like to spend about one hour in thoughts devoted to My family—

Landed opposit the Head of N° 8. at the foot of N° 7—in Missoury—put out our Lines caught a Cat fish—Weather agreable,

Saw Many Gulls—unknown—

the Woods deserted almost by small Birds—Saw four Partriges—

The Wild Geese here sits on the Banks Many feet above Watter and feed on the seeds of a small grape somewhat resembling *Fol Avoine*—but are extremely shy—

Monday 20th November 1820 The winds on this River are Contrary to our Wishes as that of an Ole Rich *Maid* to the wishes of a Lover of Wealth, We are anxious to Make progress on account of our Situation—but it is disposed off Diferently by a *Superior Power*

We Came but a few Miles and Landed about Noon in Such a Dreary place that Neither the Woods Nor the Stream would afford us any benefit—it rain^d in the evening—

Killed to day a *Red Tailed Awk* a great distance with a Ball—a Red Owl *Strix Asio*—one goose—Nothing in the Woods that are rendered almost Impenitrab by the Caves—being on a Very Loose Muddy Ground caught no fish—

Tuesday November 21st 1820 The Wind High all Day Landed at New Madrid at 3 o'clock P.M.—

This allmost deserted Village is one of the poorest that is seen on this River having a Name; the Country Back was represented to us as being good, but the Looks of the Inhabitants contradicted strongly their assertions—they are Clad in Bukskin pantaloons and a sort of Shirt of the same, this is seldom put aside unless so ragged or so Blooded & Greased, that it will become disagreable even to the poor Wrecks that have it on—

The Indian is More decent, better off, and a thousand time more happy—here familly dicensions are at their Zenith, and to Kill a [man] Neighbour is but More than a Kill Deer or a Racoon—

A M[rs] Maddis formerly the Lawfull Wife of M[r] Reignier of St. *Genevieve* resides and keeps a small store in Company with a French Gentleman. We where told that the Partnership was rendered agreable to both by a mutual wish of Nature—Went to this Lady's house who knew me first and exibited much of the french Manners

Felt dull, this evening for every object that brings *forward* the *Background* of My Life's Picture shew too often with poignancy the diference of situation—

Made some inquiries about the regulations of the Post office, now suficiently encouraging to enable my writing a few Lines to My Beloved Wife & Son—

Saw some geese, Killed one, & Golden Plovers and tw Shore Larks —Caught No Fish—

A Black Hawk passed within a few Yards of me to day when I had a Rifle and could Not kill it on the Wing, these Birds become more aboundant as we descend; a few swans are now & then seen very High,

All our Hands Playing Cards untill bed Tim about 9. oclock = The *Swamp Sparrows* and Snow Birds are plenty in the High Dry Grass that Lines the Banks of this River, but the Woods have Nothing in More than the *Pait Pait Pait* of the Monogamous—Wood Peckers—

Wednesday November 22[d] 1820 We Left New Madrid at day Break. We had gone but a very Short Distance when The Wind Rose, yet we made as the Best days' run since in this River and Landed after Dark 3 Miles above the *Little* Prairie on the Missoury Shore—

Joseph & Myself floated before the Boats almost all day in hunt of a White headed Eagle, in Vain, I shot at & Missed a Beautifull *Black Hawk* and a *Brown Eagle* having a very Long *Bend* to run through, We helped Mr. Lovelac's; While We when rowing, a White headed Eagle Dashed off from the Top of a High Cypress Tree, after a Little *Duck* the *Spirit* and was on the point of being in Possession of it—when I sent him Two heavy Loads from My Gun that Wounded him badly—

I called this Morning at *Belle Vue* Wood Yard to see M[r] Dela Roderic, he was absent to a Cypress Swamp, I saw his Wife & Sister, and Left my Respects

the Weather quite Pleasant, although We have Light White frosts every Night—

Some minutes after Landed, Dash started an oppossum that took

Every Man to Shore thinking it was a Bear, the Poor Oppossum came on Board with us—

fishing lines all out lost one, and a large *Cat Fish* in tringig to hawl him in—Geese, Sandy Hill Cranes Plentifull on the Sand Barr opposite us, they regularly resort to these for roost.

THURSDAY NOVEMBER 23 1820 As soon as we had eat our *Common Breakfast* fried Bacon and Soaked Biscuits—Joseph went to his station and I to Mine, i.e., he rowed the skiff and I steering it—Went to the *Little Prairie* shot at a Brown Eagle probably 250 yards and yet cut one of its legs—

at this Place We Saw a great number of Birds, Mostly *Red Breasted Thrushes*—the sungs of Which revived our Spirits and Imparted within us the Sweet sensation that Spring brings to Minds of *our Kind.*

the Rusty Grakles extremely Plenty—Snow Birds—& Many Sparows

I shot a Beautifull *White headed Eagle Falco Leucocephalus*—probably 150 yards off, My Ball Went through its body—

Returned to our Boats immediately and began My Drawings—it is a Handsome Male—

Many Shots at Geese, but We find them so shy that We Loose Much Ammunition in Contending With them—

Floated 23 miles Landed opposite Island No. 20 according to the Old Navigator, some Indians camped on it, Made us Load all our pieces—

I saw Two Eagles Nest, One of them I remembered seeing as I went to New Orleans 18 months ago it had being worked upon and no doubt young Where raised in it, it is in a Large Cypress Tree, Not very high, Made of Very Large Dead sticks and about 8 feet in Diameter—

Since I killed the one before me I am Convinced that the *Bald Eagle* and the *Brown Eagle* are Two Diferent Species—

FRIDAY NOVEMBER 24TH 1820 high Winds, remained at Our Last Night's harbour all day—at Day Break saw a Deer crossing the River below us, ran him down and Brought him to the Boats; Cleaned, it Weighed 1/12 td had 9 points to its horns and so much run down that its Neck Was swolen ½ the Size of its Body—

I spent the greater part of the day drawing; All hands hunting—Killed Two Geese, 1 Racoon & 1 Oppossum—

the Woods here are so Dreadfully tangled with *Bull rushes,* Green Briars and Canes that the Travelling through them is extremely Irksome =

Saw some *Carrion Crows* and some *Turkey Buzards* that were attracted by the scent?? of the Deer We had hung in the Woods??

Immediately below us is a family of Three people in Two Skiffs a Woman & 2 men; they are Too Lazy to Make themselves Comfortable, and Lie on the Damp Earth, near the Edge of the Watter, have *Racoons* to Eat and Muddy Watter to help that food down, are from the Mouth of Cumberland and moving to a Worst Part of the Worst Without Doubt—

Saw some Ivory Billed Wood Peckers, these Birds allways go in Paires and when they Leave a Tree to fly to another they Sail and Look Not unlike a *Raven.* I shot and Killed a Turkey Buzzard a great Distance, Mistaking it for a Carrion Crow—unfortunately we are in bad part of the River for Fish—

SATURDAY NOVEMBER 25TH 1820 I spent the whole of this day drawing the *White* headed *Eagle,* the Weather exceedingly Warm, the thermometer rose to 70°. The wind Blowing Strong a head We remained still; in the Course of the Afternoon a small Steam Boat, the *Independence* passed us, I saw with the spy glass old Cap^{e} Nasson of Louisville; Butterflies, Wasps & Bees plenty all day about us—the Skiff family of yesterday a few hundred yards below us, the Woman washed for us

At Sunset the Wind Shifted, A heavy Clouds came over us and Made a great difference in the atmosphere—

Killed 2 Geese and Two Racoons—Saw a few *Carrion Crows* attracted by the Scent of the Deer We Caught yesterday

Our Hands sailing all day

SUNDAY NOVEMBER 26TH 1820 Drawed all day, floated 18 Miles —the family in the Skiffs came on Board this Morning. Nearly frozen, the Thermometer down at 22—the ground very hard, and my being without a Shirt—Made Me feel rather unpleasant.

the Woman of the Skiffs Mending My Good Brown Breeches—

to Look on those people, and consider cooly their Condition, then; compare it to mine; they certainly are more Miserable to Common Eyes—but, it is all a Mistaken Idea, for poverty & Independance are the only friend that will travel together through this World.

Shot at an Eagle With a White head and Brown Tail.

Ducks, Geese, Swans, & other Birds all going southwardly—

MONDAY NOVEMBER 27TH 1820 the weather raw and Cloudy. Finished my drawing of the White headed Eagle, having been 4 days at it—

That Noble Bird weighed $8\frac{1}{2}^{lb}$, Measured 6 feet 7/2/12 his Total Length 2:7/2/12—it proved a Male, the heart extremely large, My Ball having passed through his Gizzard I could not see any of the Contents—

Those Birds are becoming very Numerous, hunt in pairs, and roost on the Tall trees above their Nests—One this morning took up the head of a Wild Goose thrown over board, with as much ease as a man could with the hand—they chase Ducks and if they force one from the Flock he is undoubtedly taken, carried on a Sand Bank and eat by Both Eagles—they are more shy in the afternoon than in the morning—they seldom sail High at this season, Watch from the tops of trees and Dash at any thing that comes near them—to secure a Goose, the Male & Femelle, Dive alternatively after it and give it so little time to breath that the poor fellow is forced in a few Minutes.

We are all unwell having eat too freely of the Buck. Mr Shaw went off this morning to Mr Lovelace's boat—Made a good run—saw a Large Flock of White Gulls—but not a Land Bird—Much to My surprise I have not yet seen a Pelican, nor a Swan on the Barrs or in the River—Malards are the only Ducks we now see—No Game, to be procured Not able to hunt on the shores—We are Landed at the foot of Flour Island, opposite the first Chicasaw Bluff—the First High Ground since the Chalk banks—

While Looking at My Beloved Wife's Likeness this day I thought it was altered and Looked sorrowfull, it produced an Immediate sensation of Dread of her being in Want—yet I cannot hear from her for Weeks to Come—but Hope she and our Children are Well—

The Eagles along the Banks of this River, retire in bad weather to the Inner parts of High Cypress Woods and remain on Low Limbs for whole day, I had an opportunity of seeing several from our Landing place, with my spy glass.—

Tuesday November 28th 1820 As it is a rainy morning, I cannot, hunt, and will take this opportunity to retaling to you such incidents relative to my Life as I think you may at some future period be glad to know—

My Father John Audubon, was born at *Sables D'Olorme* in France; the son of a man who had a very Large familly, being 20 males & one femelle. his Father started him at a very early age *Cabin Boy* on Board a Whaleing Ship—of course [his youth his] by education he was [no more than what is call here w] nothing; but he naturally was quick, Industrious and soberly Inclined; his voyage was a hard one but he often assured me that he never regretted it—it rendered him Robust, active and fit to go through the World's rugged paths. He soon became able to command a Fishing Smack, to purchase it, and so rapidly did he proceed on the road of Fortune, that when of Age, he commanded a small Vessel belonging to him, trading to St. Domingo—

A Man of Such Natural Talents and enterprise could not be confined to the common drudgery of the Money Making Annimal, and entered an officer in the French Navy's Service under Louis the 16th was fortunate and Employed an Agent at St. Domingo to Carry the trade—Every movement was a Happy hit, he became Wealthy = the American Revolution brought him to this Country Commander of a Frigate under the Count Rochambeau, he had the honor of being presented to the Great Washington, and Major Croghan of Kentucky who has told me often that he then Looked Much Like me was particularly well acquainted with him. My Father was in several Engagements in the American service and at the taking of Lord Cornwallis—

Before his Return to Europe he purchased a Beautifull Farm on the *Schuillkill* and *Perkioming* Creek in Pennsylvania; the Civil Wars of France and St. Domingo, brought such heavy ravages of Fortune on his head, that it was with the utmost Dificulty that his Life Was Spared—

he along with thousands now saw his Wealth Torn from him, and had Little More left than was Necessary to Live and Educate Two Children Left out of five—having 3 older Brothers killed in the Wars—

he remained in France reentered in the Service under Bonaparte; but the French Navy prospered not and he retired to a Small [but] beautifull Country Seat, Three Leagues from *Nantes* in Sight of the Loire and ended his Life happy = Most Men have faults, he had one that never Left him untill sobered by a Long Life common to Many Individual, but this was Counter balanced by Many qualities—his Generosity was often too great—as a Father I never complained of him and the many Durable Friends he had prove him to have been a *good* Man—

[Two lines blotted out here]

My Mother, who I have been told was an Extraordinary beautifull Woman, died shortly after my Birth and My Father having remaried in France I was removed thereto when only Two Years Old and receive by that Best of Women, raised and cherished [by her] to the utmost of her Means—My Father gave me and My Sister *Rosa* an education appropriate to his purse. I studied Mathematicks at an early Age, and had many Teachers of Agreable Talents. I perhaps would have much stored up, if the Continual Wars in Which France Was engaged had not forced me away when only Fourteen Years Old = I entered in the Navy and was Rec^{d} a Midshipman at Rochefort Much against my Inclinations—the

Short Peace of 1802 between England & France ended My Military Carreer [—]. & [but] the Conscription determined My Father on sending me to *America* and Live on the *Mill Grove* Farm I have mentoned above—he sent me to the care of *Miers Fisher,* Esqr a rich and honest Quaker of Philadelphia who had been his agent for many years, and who received me so Politelly that I was sure he Esteemed My Name—

A Young Man of *Seventeen* sent to America to *Make Money* (for such was My Father's Wish) brought up in France in easy Circumstance who had never thought on the Want of an article I had had at Discretion, was but ill fitted for it—

I spent much Money and One Year of My as Happy as the Young Bird; that having Left the Parents sight carolls Merily, While Hawks of All Species are Watching him for an easy prey

I had a Partner with whom I did not agreed, he [— — — —] [tried] waited his opportunity [— — — —] [that] We parted forever.

Here it is well I should Mentioned, that I Landed in *New York,* took the Yellow Fever and did not reach Philadelphia for Three Months—

Shortly after My Arrival on My Farm, Your Mother *Lucy Bakewell* came with her Father's Familly to a Farm Called *Fatland Ford* and divided from mine only by the [road going from] Philadelphia Road.

We soon became acquainted and *I* attached to her. I went to France to Obtain My Father's Consent to Marry her, and returned with a Partner, Ferdinand Rozier of Nantes entered in Business for the thoughts of Marriage brought Ideas so new to me that I [entered] began with pleasure in the [Business] War to secure my Future Wife and Familly the Comforts We had both been used to—I travelled through the Western Country and Made Louisville my Choice for a residence—On my return and being of age I married your Beloved Mother on the 5th of April 1808 and removed to Kentucky—Louisville did not suit our Plans and we left that place with a View to Visit St. Louis on the Mississipi; but it is so seldom that our Wishes are favored that we did not reach that Place, for My Partner not being on good Terms with My Wife, I left her and You *Victor* at Henderson, you when there a babe, having reached St. Genevieve through Many Dificulties, Ice, &c I parted from Mr Rozier and Walked to Henderson in Four Days 165 Miles.

Your present Uncle T. W. Bakewell Joined me in opening a House at New Orleans that the War with England Made us Remove to Henderson.—

This Place saw My best days, My Happiest, My Wife having blessed me with Your Brother Woodhouse and a sweet Daughter I Calculated, to Live and died in Comfort, Our Business Was good of course We agreed. but I was intended to meet Many Events of a Disagreable Nature; A Third Partner Was taken in and the Building of a Large Steam Mill, the Purchasing of Too Many goods sold on Credit of course Lost. reduced us—Divided us—

Your Uncle who had maried a Short time previous removed to Louisville—Men with whom I had Long been connected offered me a Partnership. I accepted and a small ray of Light reappeared in My Business but a *Revolution* occassioned by a Numberless quantities of Failures, put all to an end; the Loss of My Darling Daughter affected Me Much; My Wife apparently had Lost her spirits. I felt no wish to try the Mercantile Business. I paid all I could and Left Henderson, Poor & Miserable of thoughts.

My Intention to go to France to see My Mother and Sister was frustrated, and at Last I resorted to My Poor Talents to Maintain, You and Your Dear Mother, who fortunately [now] apparently became easy at her Change of Condition, and gave me a Spirit such as I really Needed, to Meet the surly Looks and Cold receptions of those Who so shortly before where pleased to Call me Their Friend.

in Attempting the Likeness of James Berthoud, Esqr a Particularly good Man and I believed the Only *Sincere* Friend of Myself and Wife We ever had—to please his Son & Lady I discovered such Talents that I was engaged to proceed and succeeded in a Few Weeks beyond my Expectations.

Your Mother who had remained at Henderson to come by Watter, was at Last obliged to come in a Carriage, and for the second time You had a sweet sister born. How I have dwelt on her Lovely features, when sucking the nutritious food from her Dear Mother—Yet she was torn away from us when only 7 months old = having taken all the likeness Louisville could afford I removed to Cincinnati, leaving you all behind untill satisfied of some Means of Making something for a Maintanance —Through Talents in stuffing Fishes I entered in the service of the Western Museum at One hundred and Twenty five Dollars per Month, and raised a Drawing School of 25 Pupils, Made some Likeness, and had You around Me Once More—but small towns do not afford a support for any time.

Ever since a Boy I have had an astonishing desire to see Much of the World & particularly to Acquire a true Knowledge of the Birds of North America, consequently, I hunted when Ever I had an Opportunity, and Drew every New Speciman as I could, or dared *steel time* from my Business and having a tolerably Large Number of Drawings that have been generally admired, I Concluded that perhaps I Could Not do better than to Travel, and finish My Collection or so nearly [so] that it would be a Valuable Acquisition—My Wife Hoped it might do Well, and I Left her Once More with an intention of returning in Seven or Eight Months; I wrote to Henry Clay Esq[r] with Whom I Was acquainted and he Enclosed Me in a Very Polite & Friendly Letter One of General Introduction = I received Many from Others—General Harrison, &c—

from the day I left Cincinnati untill the present My Journal gives you a rough Idea of My Way of Spending the tedious Passage in a Flat Boat to New Orleans—

We moved from our Landing of Last Night and only crossed the River for the rain Lowered the *Smoake* so Much that it was impossible to see, beyond 20 or 30 Yards; played great deal on the flutes, Looked at My Drawings, read as Much as I Could and yet found the day very Long and heavy for Although I am Naturally of light spirits and have often tried to Keep [my spirits] these good, when off from my Home, I have often dull Moments of Anguish—[it stopped] the rain abated for a few Minutes. Cap[e] C. Joseph & I took a Walk to a Sand Barr Where Joseph Killed a Large blue Crane, unfortunately a Young one—saw few Geese, many *Cardinals,* some *Carolina Wrens*—We are better to day—[fortunately] Luckily our Boat does not Leek—Saw a few Purple Finches =

Wednesday November 29th 1820 the rain that begun two days since, accompanied us the whole of this day, yet We Left our Harbour at about 7 this morning and removed 20 miles—We passed the second Chicasaw Bluff, raining so much that I could not draw them; they are Much More Interesting than the Chalk Banks indeed they Look grand and Imposing. they are from 150 to 200 feet High Irregularly Caving down and Variegated in stratas of Red, Yellow, Black, and deep Lead Colors, the Whole of Such Soapy and Washing Nature as to give an interesting contrast by the Dashing of the Wash down to the edge of the Watter which here is very deep the upper Strata (the whole run horizontal) is perferated with Thousands of holes, the Nests of the *Bank Swallow*—these Bluffs are about two Miles ½ Long, the Country back, Barren & Poor—

Confined to the Inside of the Boat nearly the day, saw but a few Gulls, apparently all White, some White headed Eagles, & a few Cranes—a Large flock of Gold Finches—a few Blue Geays, & *Cardinals*, the Ivory Bill Wood Peckers heard from time to time,—

We are Landed at the foot of N° 35 a few miles above what the

Navigators call the Devil's Raceground—but the whole of the Mississipi being so much of the same nature, it feels quite immatereal to follow the Devil's tracks any where along its Muddy Course—

THURSDAY NOVEMB[R] *30*[TH] *1820* We found the race path of the Devil well cleared and beaten, and went through it with great Ease, Many places on this River are rendered More terrible in Idea by their Extraordinary Names than real dificulties—

We run a Race with M[r] Lovelace's Boat of several miles that was well nigh terminating in a dispute—it reminded me of Gamblers that although playing for Nothing are allways grieved by Lossing—

We came 25 Miles and Landed a little below the Twelve Outlets, passed the third Chicasaw Bluffs, the view of those was intercepted by our Running on the Right of an Island—the Weather Cold, & very Disagreable, Wind blowing all day mostly ahead = Some Men came on Board M[r] L. Boat who said had Killed Three Bears a few days' before—saw a few Indians at a Small Encampment—this morning I remarked Two Flocks of *American Teals* flying up the River; the Parokeets Numerous in the Woods—a Large flock of Sand Hill Cranes Sailed over us for some time, sounding & Elevating themselves to a Considerable Hight took a southwardly course—One Swan was seen on a Barr, but so shy that he flew several times at shore as he perceived the Boat. Whenever We Land a Number of *Swamp Sparrows* are seen [Sku] Scullking through the High Grass that borders the Banks, the seeds of Which are the heath or more properly Mud; the Geese feed freely on these Whilst the Grass affords them an agreable place during the day—Saw a few Gulls, a Large flock of Sprig Tail Ducks going all southwardly—the Cedar Birds Ampellis Americana fly northeast.

We passed this afternoon 19 Flat Boats Lying at the Shore, some of which had Left the Falls 10 days previous to our Departure—

I saw to day 2 Common Crows the only I have seen on the Mississipi—

FRIDAY DECEMBER 1ST *1820* This Morning was Cold and Cloudy, Flocks of Ducks Geese, &[c] flying High plentifully, all bound to the Southwest—I remarked Large Flocks of Merganzers, I Mean, The Large. These Birds seldom Leave, the Clear Ohio or its tributary streams untill Compell[d] by the Ice Closing most parts of them; their passing southwardly so early indicates a severe winter above us—*A* their Flight is Direct, regularly formed in Acute Angles and so swift that one might suppose the noise over head as proceeded from a violent storm of

Wind—Saw Early to day several Hundreds of Gull, playing over a Large Barr—When We attempted to Close on them, they rose high and off South—4 White headed Eagles where at the same time regalling themselves on the Carcass of a Deer—The sworms of Grakles that are passing us is astonishing—the Purple Finches also very Numerous saw several hundreds in one flock—Where the Weather is Intensely Cold, scarcely a Fowl is to be seen along the Banks, the ponds offering themselves at that time food & Shelter Passed a Large Settlement of Wood Cutters—Mr Shaw killed 5 Geese 4 at one shot saw two *Slate Colored Hawks, Falco Pennsylvanicus* and a *Winter Hawk*. I went a shore to a House about 5 Miles above *Wolf River* in a sharp running Bend, saw 2 beautifull Trees the *Pride of China* here the High Land is within 2 miles of the River and the spot on which the Plantation stands never overflows, these are remarkable spots—

We are Landed immediately at the foot of Old *Fort Pickering*. We Walked up to it through a very narrow crooked path, and found in a very decayed situation; the Position a Beautifull one the Land Rich about it—and were told that the Spaniards own it it was an agreable spot to Live at—about 2 Miles above this, the Mouth of Wolf river came in from the East, and is the Landing place of a Town Called *Memphis* = have runned 24 miles—Saw some Towe Buntings and Many Sparrows —[The following paragraph is written across page]

At New Orleans on the 25th of February same year saw an a/c in a New York Paper saying that the Weather had been Intensely severe that the Mercury had been so Low as 24 Degrees below 0 = that the Port of New York was completely closed by Ice and that all the Streams in that state & Pennsylvania where closed—Much pleased to see that particularly the Migrations of a swift Moving Bird such as the Merganser can so truly be considered as the herald of Weather in its Movements when going Northward & Southwardly

at the Watter Edge (then about midle Stage) there is a Bed of Coals running Orisontally about 2 feet Deep above the surface—this and the Eligeability of the Situation May become Valuable—

I saw this afternoon Two Eagles Coatiting—the femelle was on a Very high Limb of a Tree and squated at the approach of the Male, who came Like a Torrent, alighted on her and quakled shrill untill he sailed off the femelle following him and zig zaging herself through the air—this is a scarce proof I have had the pleasure of witnessing of these and all of the *Falco Genus* breeding much Earlier than any Other Land Birds—

We lost one of our Fishing Lines, a Large Fish Must have Carried it, its being very Strong and Well fastened to a Strong Willow Pole—

The Beard of the Turkey shews about one Inch Long the 1st Year, and one of the Male in full growth and plumage must be 3 Years old =

So well exercised are the Geese at extricating themselves from danger when a Flat Boat Comes Near them that they will Walk off from the Edge of the Watter out, into the Young Willows & Cotton Wood several 100 yards—but when in a Bend where the Shore is Steep they May be reached With more Ease.

Saturday December 2D 1820 Cloudy & Cold, took the Skiff and went ahead of the Boats, the only way I have now of hunting, and when any game is on Sight Lay down in the Bow and float untill distance—Shot at a Large W. H. Eagle and a *Black Hawk* Missed both, this Latter in going off *flapped* his Wings Like a Pigeon, they more Swifter than any bird in their Common flight. I could Not Well account My Missing these Birds, they were not More than 100 yds off—I shot 3 Turkeys at 2 shots—their Crops completely filled with *winter Grapes* [their] Gizzards of the seeds of the same and large gravel. They were extremely gentle [and] I floated immediately to them and Came within 25 yds. Cold days force the geese away from shore—the Woods Literally filled with Parokeets great Many Squirels—and Many *Snow Birds*—begun raining at about one—Now & then a Wood Cutter's Hut is seen in a Small Parcel of cleard Land between Two Thick Cane Brakes—

The Lights or *Pulmon* of the Turkeys I Examined This Day, had much the appearance of *Waddles* connected by a Thin Skin, the *Wadles* about ½ Inch Long = the Thin Skin about ¼ of an Inch—

Many *Golden Wings* Woodpeckers—a few Sparrow Hawks

We Landed on What is Named a *Tow head* a little above the Island No 51—a Tow head is a small Willow Island overflown in High Watter—

in was Not Dark and We Walk Round it—Saw Many Geese, and a Young *Bear*, but its being so late & dark Was Called out, and gave it up.—

Raining & very Disagreable—Many Gulls flew about us to day and Picked up the Lights & fat of the Turkey, & Geese that Were thrown over Board

Sunday December 3D 1820 It rained Heavy all night, this morning it was concluded the boats would not Leave, yet our Captains went hunting the Wind Blowing at Intervals and then ceasing, made some diference of the force of the rain = Saw several Crows Many *Brown*

Larks, Many Geese, and Malards = Killed to day 3 Geese, 2 Malards and 2 Mergansers, both femelles measuring 25 Inches—the Bill & Legs Not so bright a cealing Wax Color as usual—tongues sharp Triangular and Toothed—think them young—one of them had Caught a Fish about 9 Inches of the *Sucker* Kind and had only partly down its throat when Killed—there was 5 together we drove them several times out of a Pond in the inner part of an Island and at Last Shot these on the Wing = the Geese very Shy—Three Keel Boats passed us about 2 o'clock P.M.—they had left the Falls of Ohio 3 weeks ago—Left our Harbour and floated about 4 Miles to the foot of Buck Island—here I saw with the setting sun hundreds of Malards travelling *South* and the *Finest* rainbow I ever beheld, the Clouds were also beautifull apposite it = Looked at my Beloved Wife's Likeness Shaved and Cleaned One of the few enjoyments Flat Boats Can afford—the Goose we eat at Dinner extremely fishy.

Joseph who now is obliged to officiate as Cook does not appear to relish the thing—the more I see Cap[e] C the more I Like him = Wish that we could say the same of all the World—

The Towhead on Little Island on Which Laid Last Night and to day had *Vast Many dry* Nests of Thrushes on the small Willow Trees—the Tall Grass with many Sparows—Saw 2 Flocks of Partridges, Many Parokeets.

Saw a Blue Crane.

MONDAY DECEMBER 4TH 1820 We had a dreadfull night of Wind, the hands obliged to move the boats. I did not sleep, the Knocking of the Boats against the Sand Barr very desagreable—This Morning the Wind still blowing hard. Went to a Small Lake to Shoot—there I saw a *Killdeer plover,* a *King Fisher;* Many Geese & Ducks—but no *Swans* as we had been led to expect from reports of a Squater—Killed 3 Geese, and 3—*American Teals*—Saw a few Turkeys—this Lake about 2 Miles from the River, contains some of the Largest Muscles I ever saw, and Vast Many perewinkles that appear to be of a Peculiar Species and I put some in My pockets—I found these in round Parcels of about 20 to 30 close together—My Slut Dash brought out of the Watter very well—When returned to our Boats, 9 of the Boats we had passed some days previous went by, and we pushed off immediately—We floated only about 4 miles—and Landed on the Tennessee Shore—

Saw to day great Many *Autumnal Warblers,* the first I have seen since on the Mississippi, a few *Crows* some *Winter* Wren, some *Eagles W. H[d]—it is very Seldom that brown Eagles are seen;—the others are now courting* seeing them every day chasing off the Batchelors—

I doubt not that the Migrations of the *Autumnal Warblers* is the latest of all that Genus—

I was taken off Suddenly a few Minutes ago to take a Cat Fish of our Line. I had some trouble for a few minutes but having drowned him put my Left hand in his Geels and hauled it in the Skiff—it weighed $64\frac{1}{2}^{lb}$ and Looked fat—Killed it by stabbing it about the Center of its head, this was so Effectual that in a few Second it was quite Motionless—

I would be Inclined that, from *Shape, Size, Color* & Habits so diferent to that of the Cat Fish Caught in the River Ohio the present one is a diferent *Species.*

Tuesday December 5th 1820 Skinning the Cat Fish was the first Job this morning—this was done by cutting through the Skin (which is very Tough) in Narrow Long Strips and tearing those off with a Strong Pair of Pincers—While at this saw Several hundred of those Black Birds yet unknown to me that I denominate *Black Pelicans* flying South forming a very obtuse Angle, without uttering any Noise—have some Hopes therefore to see some of them on the Watters of Red River or Washita—Sand Hill Cranes were also fling and We saw More Geese than usual—Joseph Killed 4 American Teals—those fly up stream—saw 3 Swans—While Geese are flying in a Travelling order the Young or Smallest are about the center of the *Lines* and the Larger Gander Lead the Van, the Oldest Goose Drives the Rear—the Weather beautifull but cold, and No Doubt that the Frogs that Wistled so merily Yesterday are well buried in the Mud this Morning—

We made an Awkward Landing, Lodged in the Mud for about $\frac{1}{2}$ an hour, and our Commander had a good opportunity of Exercising his Powers at Swearing—More particularly when Anthony broke his Sweep Oar. this Took Place about 30 Miles from our starting place of this Morning, [at the foot of No] opposite the head of 57 & 58—"fine Weather but No Fish" says Cap^e^ Cummings—

Wednesday December 6th 1821 Light frost, Rich Clouds of Purple & Light Green Indicates Wind—extremely anxious to overtake the fleet ahead our Commanders have yesterday and this morning exerted themselves more than usual and have left our harbours as soon as Day Light would permit—how beneficial a fleet constantly a head Would be!—

Saw 2 Large White Cranes with Black Tips—too Shy to get in floating distance;—Many A^n^ Teals and as Many Geese as Ever—

Passed the *St. Francis River* the mouth of which at this time appeared

Closed by a Mud Barr—but the people who Lived on the Point formed by that stream and the Mississippi told us that there was plenty, and that Keel Boats go up it 400 Miles, many settlements on the banks the first about 15 miles—the Same people told us that they had seen many *Pelicans* a few days previous in Passing—saw some *Old Blue Cranes* on the Trees but could not go within 150 *yds* of any of them—a Little before we passed the Place called the *Big Prairie* shot a Monstrous Turkey Cock, I think the Largest I every saw; it appears considerably Larger than one I weighed that was over 31 *lb*—My anxiety to have it Made Me Miss—the *Big Prairie* is a Tolerable sized Plantation rather higher than usual on this River, about $\frac{1}{4}$ of a Mile Back—the Land rises in Gentle Hills, and when told is extremely Rich there, I first saw the *Mississippi Kites*[a]: ascending in the Steam Boat Paragon in June 1819—Bought some Delicious *Sweet Potatoes* at $\frac{1}{2}$ Dollar p*r* Bushel the Squater assured me that a few Weeks previous, the Pelicans were so numerous that Hundreds where often in sight on a Barr below this Place—people very sickly—Landed on the Tennessee Shore about 7 Miles from the *Settlement of the Hills.* the Wonderfull fleet still about 4 miles a head, our Comodores had a Meeting, the result was that We should *Start* one hour before day and run down the D*d* Rascals—

[The following lines in the diary are put on a blank space of the preceding page as an explanation.]

[a]The Mississippi Kite Were Busily Employed in Catching small Lizards off the Bark of Dead Cypress Trees, this effected by Sliding beautifully by the Trees and suddenly Turning on their Side and Graple the prey—having At that time no Crayons or Paper, did not Draw one, and determined Never to Draw from a Stuffed Specimen, Carried No Skins—

Thursday December 7th 1820 Caught a Nice *Cat Fish* weighing 29 lb. at 3 o'clock this Morning—stabd him as we had the former but it did not die for One Hour—at Day Break the Wind stiff a head, a Couple of Light Showers Lulled it, and we put off—Mr Aumack Winged a *White headed Eagle,* brought it a live on board, the Noble Fellow Looked at his Ennemies with a Contemptible Eye. I tied a String on one of its Legs this Made him Jump over Board. My Surprise at Seeing it Swim well Was very great, it used its Wings with great Effect and Would have Made the Shore distant there about 200 *yds* Dragging a Pole Weighing at Least 15*lbs*—Joseph went after it with a Skiff, the Eagle Defended itself—I am glad to find that its Eyes were Coresponding with My Drawing—this Specimen rather less than the one I draw—the femelle hovered over us and shrieked for some time, exibiting the *true sorrow* of the *Constant Mate*—Prepared a Bed for My Slut *Dash* expecting her to be delivered from her Burthen every Day—

Our Eagle Eat of Fish freely about one hour after we had him, by fixing a piece on a stick and puting it to its Mouth—however while I was friendly Indian toward it it Lanced one of its feet and caught hold of My right thum, made it feel very sore—

Went to an Eagle's Nest; busily Employed Building Shot at the femelle, which is at all times distinguished by her size, the Male was also asitting—Killd *One* Goose—as We Reachd the head of the Sand Barr close to Island No 62 We passed the *Fleet* at anchor but they all pushed off when they saw us go through this Place—One Boat suffered Much, by being runned down by another in Landing—Came 25 Miles—the Evening Looking Stormy, the Current strong as our Landing Could not put out our Lines—Our Comodores Much Elated—

FRIDAY DECEMBER 8TH 1820 Not satisfied about our Landing in a strong Current I slept but little, Whenever I walk*d* on the deck the Eagle Hissed at Me, and ruffed itself in the Manner that Owls do generally—the Weather Warm, Cloudy, & Windy—put off late and only run about 3½ miles forced by the storm to land at the foot of what I supposed the Island No 63—leaving all the fleet behind us—

with Some Hopes of Shortly being at the Arkansas Fork I feel Inclined to Copy a few of the Letters I had for that Place Particularly those of Generals *Harrison* & Lytle.

Cincinnati Sept 7th 1820

Dear General

Mr. Audubon who will have the honor to hand you this, is upon a Tour through the Extensive forests of *Western America* for a Scientific Purpose—that of Completing a Collection of American Birds—I beg leave to Introduce him to you & to request your aid and [assistance] Countenance in the [highly] accomplishment of his highly laudable project—

Mrs Harrison is well & my daughter Lucy & Son Syomms both Maried since you were at my House, the latter to a Daughter of Genl Pikes—

Your Friend
W. H. Harrison

Governor I. Miller
Arkansas T—y.—

Cincinnati Ohio Octr 9th 1820

Dear Sir—

Permit me to Introduce to your Acquaintance John J. Audubon es*qr* who is on a Visit to the Territory of Arkansas and the Norwest as an ornithologist—for the taking drawings of Birds—Fowls &c—for a Work he has on hand. Any facilities You May have it in Your Power to offer him toward promoting the Object in view will be thankfully received by him and duly appreciated by

Yours friend and Hble Servt
Wam Lytle

Cincinnati Octr 10th 1820

Revr Gentlemen—

Permit me to Introduce to your Kind regards John J. Audubon Es*qr* who proposes traversing Louisiana for the purpose of Compleating a Collection of Drawings of the Birds of the U. States which he proposes to publish at some Future Period—he has been engaged in our Museum for 3 or 4 Months & his performances do honor to his Pencil—

I regreat to hear that you have been visited by Sickness. I Hope you May get Safe to your journey end, & be prospered in the great & glorious work on Which you have Entered—I should be Pleased to hear from you frequently

I Remain Your Sincere Friend & Brother in the *Lord*
Elijah *Slack*

Reverend Veil & Chapman—

Elijah Slack was then President of the Cincinnati College

Cess des the above I received several Letters from Docr *Drake* Directed to the Reverend Mr *Chapman* Osage Mission—*Coll Breasly* Indian agent & *Governor Miller*—

I Will give You here the Copy of the Letters I Received from the Honorable Henry Clay to the one I Wrote from Cincinnati the Copy of Which is annexed at the Beginning of the Part of My Journal

Sir—

I received your letter of the 12th inst and now do myself the pleasure to transmit to you inclosed such a letter as I presume you want—I suppose a general letter would answer all the purposes of special introduction, which I should have been at a loss to give as I do not know the particular points which you may Visit—and even if I did, I might not have there any personal acquaintances—

Will it not be well for you before you commit yourself to any great Expense in the preperation and publication of your Contemplated Work to ascertain the success which attended a similar undertaking of Mr Wilson?

With Great Respect
I am Yours
H. Clay

Lexington—25 Augt 1820

I have had the satisfaction of a personal acquaintance with Mr. John J. Audubon; and I have learnd from others who have Known him longer and better, that his Character and Conduct have been uniformly good: being about to take a Journey, through the Southwestern portion of our Country with a laudable object connected with its Natural History, I take great Pleasure in recommending him to the Kind Offices of the Officers, and Agents of Government and other Citizens whom he may meet, as a Gentleman of amiable and Excellent qualities, well qualified, as I believe, to execute the object which he has undertaken

H. Clay

H. Clay Was then the Speaker of the House of Representatives, and I Hope to rec*e* some benefits from this Letter—

M*r* Aumack killed a Goose and Joseph an *Intrepid Hawk,* Swans extremely Plenty fired at them Many Times with Balls without Success—

Drifted at 3 o'clock P. M.—about 4 Miles and Landed at foot of No 64—

I began a letter to My Beloved Lucy with some Hopes of reaching the Fort of Arkansas Tomorrow, but Hopes are Shy Birds fling at a great Distance [and it is] seldom [that] reached by the best of Guns [can reach them]

SATURDAY 9TH DECEMBER 1820 I have nothing to say for this day. I drew a little [today,] seeing a Green Briar with seeds on—Wrote to My Lucy and Lived on Sweet Potatoes—how Surly the Looks of Ill fortune are to the poor. I Hope to see the fort of Arkansas tomorrow and Hope to Leave the Boat I am now in if there is What the Kentuckians Term a *"half Chance"*. Our Commanders Looks and acting are so strange that I have become quite Sickened—

the Weather quite rough, all day, cleared at night, the Flat Boats passed us this evening—We have made a bad Landing according to my Ideals—

SUNDAY 10TH DECEMBER 1820 We floated down to the *Caledonian point* or Petite Landing about 4 Mile above the *real* mouth of *White River*

here it was Concluded that Mr Aumack should *walk* to the old *Post of Arkansas* of course I & Joseph prepared and having made Enquiries concerning the road we determined to go by Watter to the mouth of the *Cut off* and then walk the remainder; Anthony joined us, and the Skiff doubled oared was taken; We left at 10 o'clock with Light hearts, Small Bottle of Whiskey a few Biscuits, and the determination of Reaching the Post that Night—

At the Entrance of White River we discovered that that stream Was full and Run Violently, the Watter a Dull Red Clay Color; We soon found ourselves forced to Land to Make a Natural Cordel of several *Grape Vines* and pull up by it—the distance to the Cutt off is Seven Miles that appeared at Least 10 to us: here We Met 2 Canoes of Indians from the *Osage Nation,* Landed our Skiff on the opposite side of White River Which we here found a *beautifull Clear Stream* and Backed by the Watters of Arkansas running through the Cut off; We Walked through a *Narrow Path* often so thickly beset with green Briars that We Would be forced to give back and go round—this followed through *Cypress Swamps* and round *Pounds* and Cane Breaks untill We reached the first Settlement owned by a Frenchman Called Monsr Duval. this friendly Man about going to bed offered us his assistance put on shoes & clothing and Lead us 7 Miles through Mud & Watter to the Post; and at 9 o'clock P. M. We Entered the Only Tavern in the Country—*Wearied,* Muddy, Wet, & hungry—the Supper Was soon calld for, and soon served, and to see 4 Wolfs taring an old Carcass would not give you a bad Idea of our Manners while helping *Ourselves* the *Bright Staring Eyes* of the Land Ladies Notwithstanding

however I found Mrs Montgomery a handsome Woman of good Manners and rather superior to those in her rank of Life—to Bed and to sleep sound was the next Wish for 32 Miles in such a Country May be Calculated as a full dose for any *Pedestrian per day*—Led into a Large Building that formerly perhaps saw the great *Concils of Spanish Dons* we saw 3 Beds containing 5 men, Yet, all was arrangd in a few moments and as the Breaches were Coming off our Legs, Mr Aumack & Anthony slided by into one and Joseph & myself into Another, to force Acquaintance with the strangers being of course necessary a Conversation ensued that Lulled Me a Sleep, and Nothing but the Want of *Blankets* Kept Me. from Resting Well, for I soon found a Place between the *Tugs* that Supported about 10 lbs of Wild Turkey Feathers to save (?), My roundest Parts from the Sharp Edges of An Homespun Bedstead—

The Morning broke and with it, Mirth *all about us,* the *Cardinals,* the Iowa Buntings, the Meadow Larks and Many Spcies of Sparrows, chearing the approach of a Benevolent sun Shining day—dressed and about to take a View of *all things* in this Place, Met a Mr *Thomas* known formerly when in the Paragon Steam Boat—he introduced Me generally to the Medley Circle, around, and from thence took Me to a Keel Boat to receive the Information I Wanted about the Upper Countries through Which this Noble Stream Meanders—think of My Surprise at seeing here a Man who 13 years ago gave me Letters of Introduction at Pittsburgh (Penn) for Men in Kentucky—this Was Mr. *Barbour* the former Partner of Cromwell—he Met Me with great Cordiality, told me of the absence of the *Governor,* the Indian agent and also that the Osage Missionaries had proceeded about 150 miles up to a Place called the *Rocky* Point. the Cadsaw is [hi] beyond that where a New town, the seat of Govornt was expected to be situated.

disapointed to the utmost in Not Meeting those who I supposed Would of Course give me the best Information I requested of Mr Thomas to give the Governor My Letters and beg of him to Write Me a few Lines at New Orleans to the Care of Governor Robertson—[the Gentleman—] Mr Barbour told Me that he had for Several years past gone up to the Osage Nation about 900 Miles and that his Last Voyage he fell in with *Nutall* the *Botanist* and had him on board for 4 Months—that Many species of *Birds* were in that Country unknown in this and that the Navigation Was an agreable One, at the same time that it was rendered profitable by the enormous profits derived from the Trade with the Indians, whom he represented as friendly and Honorouble in all there dealings—that he would be extremely Happy of My Company and that of My Companions and that if I did not go with him at present that he Hoped I would Meet him when coming down the Arkansas Next Spring or Summer for he is about 6 Months employd each Voyage—The Post of Arkansas is Now a poor, Nearly deserted Village, it flourished in the time that the Spaniards & French kept it, and One 100 years passed it could have been called and agreable Small Town—at present, the decripid Visages of the Worn out Indian Traders and a few American famillies are all that gives it Life, the Natural situation is a handsome One, on a high Bank formerly the Edge of a *Prairie,* but rendered extremely sickly by the Back Neighborhood of Many Overflowing Lakes & Swamps.—

I was assured that only Two frosts had been felt here this Season and that the Ice in the River never Stopped the Navigation—

the Town now Prospering at *Point Rock* is high healthy and in the Center of a Rich tract of [Land] Wood & Prairie Lands—and probably may flourish—the *Arkansas River* flows a Thick Current of red Clay & Sand, and if not for its coloring would have much of the appearance of the Mississippi—Cotton is raised here With some advantage—Corn grows Well, game & Fish are plenty—

I here feel Inclined to tell you that an oportunit of Good; Fresh Flour Whiskey, Candles, Cheese, Apples, Porter, Cider, Butter Onions, Tow Linen and Blankets would meet with advantageous Sales during Winter, accompanied by *Powder Lead, Flint,* [and] Butchers Knives, Rifles, and *blue Shrouds* for the Indians.

After Breakfast We Left the Post of Arkansas with a Wish to see the Country above, and so *Strong* is My Anthusiasm to Enlarge the Ornithological Knowledge of My Country that I felt as if I wish Myself *Rich again* and thereby able to Leave My familly for a Couple of Years—here I saw a French Gentleman who but a few Weeks passed had Killed a *Hawk* of a Large size *perfectly White* except the Tail Which Was a *bright red.* Unfortunately, no remains of its Skin Legs or Bill were to be found—We travelled fast—reachd the Cutt off and Landd our Skiff, having Killed 5 *Crows* for their *Quills,* Never before did I see these Birds so easily approachd and in fact all the Birds We saw, 2 Hawks I did not know hovered high over us—the Indians still at their Canoes, We Hailed, and gave them a Drachem of Whiskey, and as they could not speak either french or English, I *Drew* a *Deer* with a stroke across its hind parts, [—] and thereby Made them Know our Wants of Venaison hams—

they brought 2 We gave them 50^{cts} and a Couple Loads of Gun Powder to each, brought out smiles, and a Cordial Shaking of Hands—a Squaw with them a *Handsome Woman* waded to us as Well as the Men and drank freely—[Never do I] Whenever I meet *Indians* I feel the greatness of our Creator in all its Splendor, for there I see the Man Naked from his Hand and yet free from Acquired Sorrow =

in White River We saw a great number of Geese Malards and Some Blue Cranes—also Two Large Flocks of these *unknown Divers* or *Pelicans*—

reached our Boats about 6 in the afternoon fatigued but Contented a good Supper, Merry Chat—and good Looks all round—Went to bed all Well—

before I leave the Trip to the *Arkansas Post* I think I will give you More of it—We saw there a *Velocipede* Judge how fast the Arts & Sciences Improved in this Southwestern Country—I want also to tell you that the Squaw on White River While Wading out to us Craked a Large *Louse* taken from under her arm—

The *Intrepid Hawks* are extremely plenty along the Banks of the Mississipi where the feed aboundantly on the *Swamp Sparrows* as also on the *Sturnus depradatorius*; some of these are so strong and daring that they Will attack some Ducks on the Wing and often carry them off several hundreds of yards to the Sand Bars—

The Brown Eagles that were so plenty on the Ohio have entirely disapeared and nothing by White Headed Ones are to be seen—

The Lakes found in the Interior are stored with the finest of Fishes Such as Pikes, Salmons—Rock, Bass Sun Perches &c[c] and the bottom covered with Thousands of Muskle Shells and Perrywinkles of many species—those Latter of Course find their Way while the Spring floods are so so general—the Bottom of Most of these Lakes is firm and Level—

Tuesday Decemb[r] 12th 1820 This day M[r] *Shaw* and *Anthony* Walked off to the Post and We floated down to the Mouth of that River, this We reached and Landed. I was so fortunate as to Meet the *Steam Boat* the Maid of [New] *Orleans* on board of Which I put a Letter for My Dearest Friend My Wife—with orders to put it in the St. *Louis* Post Office—Saw to Day Many Crows Mergansers and Geese, some *Dun Divers*—and a Large flock of My unknown Divers—

the Blue Jeays are now & then seen—the great *Carolina Wrens* are very Aboundant—but the Snow Birds have disappeared, the weather is so Warm that *Buterflies, Bats, Bees,* & Many Insects are flying about us and at the Arkansa I was assured that they had had but *Two* Light frosts—

M[r] Shaw is Expected Tomorrow Night and perhaps Will Leave us here to Proceed up that River, for we are told the Orleans Market is Extremely dull—Killed a Gull precisely Such as I shot at *New Port Kentucky,* rather Fatter

The Wild Geese we now Shoot have Eggs swollen to the size of N[o] 3 Britt Shots—

An Indian Chief at the Mouth of the Arkansas Killed *Three Swans* one of which I was told Measured 9 feet from Tip to Tip—Those Indians had Left when We arrived,—a View of Such Noble Specimen Would have been very agreable—

The *Prairie Hawk* that I see here is not the *Marsh Hawk* of Willson it is Much Less-Lighter Color, the Tip of the Wings Black and only One Large Bend of Dark ending the Tail—they fly Much Like the *Night Hawk* and Catch Small Birds on the Grass Without Stopping their course—

Wednesday Decemb^{R} 13TH 1820 A Beautifull day, Walked up the Arkansas in Search of a Lake but the Cane so thick that we give it up —Killed Two Geese. Mr Aumack Shot at a *Prairie Hawk* but did not Kill it—I wrote Governor Miller the Copy of which is here annexed—

To his Excellency Govr Miller of the Arkansas—Sir—having had the Honor to receive several letters of recommandation to your Excellency, from Genl *Harrison,* Genl *Lyttle* and other Gentlemen, I felicated myself with the pleasure of an Interview with you—I Reached the Post of Arkansas but was foiled by your absence; having only a few Moments to remain at that place I begged of Mr Thomas to present you the Letters I was the Bearer of—these I even was not able to seal—

My ardent Wish to Compleat a collection of drawings of the *Birds* of our Country, from *Nature,* all of Natural *Size,* begun about 15 years since, and to Acquire either by *occular,* or reliable observations of others the Knowledge of their Habits & residence; makes me wish to travel as far at Least as the Osage Nations on the Arkansas as also along the Whole of our Frontiers—

Should your arduous avocations admit—I would Consider myself very Highly honored and under great obligations to receive from your Excellency a few lines of Information respecting the *Time,* the Manner of travelling and what might be necessary to render such a Journey fruitfull to my Views—as well as your Personal Information of the discoveries you have made in Ornithology, in that part of America—My Intention is to Visit the country around New Orleans as far East as the Florida Keys, then ascend Red River, and to go to the Hot Springs—thence across to the Arkansas and Come down [it] to its Mouth where on My return to Cincinnati at present My familly Residence—yet My Plans are alterable as advised by Gentlemen of more Experienced

Should your Excellency contemplate any expedition upon Your River and I was sufered to Join it, I would be anxious to Meet any Wishes my Humble talents Could afford at any time—

With Hopes that your [Excellency] will not be displeased at the liberty I have here taken

I remain with high respect
Your V. H. St
J. J. A.

P. S. if agreeable please
Direct to Governor
Robertson

Saw some Turkey Buzzard
Some Merganzers and Sand Hill Cranes—
Malards—Crows—Some Buntings—
Winter Wrens—Meadow Larks—Partridges
Red Winged Starlings—and a Vast Number of
Swamp Sparrows in the High Mississipi grass
Parokeets—Golden Crowned Wrens—

Mr Shaw & Anthony [not] returned [yet] at eleven o'clock, but did not effect their Business, They returned in a canoe, 30 Miles down the Arkansas to the *cut off* through that about 6 (miles) down White River 7 and down the Mississipi 15—this makes 58 and the Distance from Arkansas Post to the Mouth of that River is 60—

about One Mile below the Mouth of Arkansas in a Thick patch of *Cane* are Two *Women* the remainder of a party of Wandering Vagarounds that about 2 years ago Left some part of the Eastern State to proceed to the *Promised Land*—these Two Wretches, Never Wash Comb or Scarcely clad themselves, and subsist from the Scant generosity of the Neighbours—Now and then doing a little Sawing and Washing—

Thursday Decembr 14th 1820 After Long consideration, our Gentlemen determined to do *Nothing,* and [Left our Landin] We *Cutt Loose* about 10 this Morning, the Weather quite Warm, Distant frequent Clapps of Thunder announcing a change—it soon begain to Rain, the Fog raised and We Landed again about 2 o'clock—saw here 5 Ivory Bill Wood Peckers feeding on the Berries of Some Creeper they were gentle —Keeping a Constant Cry of *Pet Pet Pet*—Killed a Crow on the Drift wood it was not untill then that I discovered that a Crow Killed by Mr Shaw while I was at the Arkansas was a *Fish Crow*—it rained all Night Watter raising fast—

Friday Decemb^r^ 15th 1820 Rainy & Cold, floated about 6 Miles —at One o'clock the Steam Boat, *James Ross* passed us—in the afternoon I had the good fortune to Kill a Beautifull *Marsh Hawk Falco Eulginosus* feeding on a Swamp Sparrow that I saw him Catch—When I approach him before I Shot he saw me first and flew a few yards where he sat tearing at his prey untill death reached him—the *Prairie Hawk* seen Yesterday is entirely different, in Size, Color, & Manner of flying and [h]as it is a Nondescript I Hope I may meet it again—Killed 4 Teals and 2 Geese—the Watter rose 20 Inches this day—

I have seen the Marsh Hawks about September flying down the Ohio River, and several times about that season I have seen *flocks* of them travelling high and southwesterly—finding them Now plenty on these Shores Where great deal of rich food is afforded them by the Numerous quantity of Swamp Sparrows the mildness of the Weather, no doubt assures them a good Winter Residence—

the One I Killed Was a Male, in good order, Weighing Only $\frac{3}{4}$ lb— Measured 18 Inches full Length, breadth $3\frac{1}{2}$ feet—the Insides of the Mouth Black—

Saturday December 16th 1820 the weather much the same, heard this Morning that the Ohio has raised Immensely—Spent the day Drawing my Hawk but so dark and disagreable that I could not finish it—having Landed for 3 or 4 hours at the Head of the *Cypress Bend* We floated but a Short Distance—

Vast Many Geese seen to day—Joseph Killed a *Pewee fly catcher* close by the Boat—the little fellow Was very active, and in very good order —a femelle—

this Evening about *100 Pelicans* were in view on a Sand Barr, and although I had no expectations of reaching them We put off in the Skiff, when about 300 yards off from them, they flew and I sent them My Ball, without effect—these are the first I have seen this Journey. I Hope I will have one to draw before I reach N. Orleans—

The generality of the geese We Kill are very poor—and scarcely fit to eat—the Steam Boat *Govr Shelby* pass^d^ us heavily Laden—

When I was trying to approach the Pelicans, they rose from their slumber one at a time, and Shook their Wings as if to try if able to fly in Case of need—the Nearer We Came the faster they gethered and walked off untill they all flew without uttering any Noise—

Sunday December 17th 1820 Raining all day. I finished my Drawing—Landed at *Pointe Chico* a few Miles before this the *Spanish*

Beard is seen—Pointe Chico is a handsome spot on this river that never overflows—and answers well for the Growth of Cotton Corn &c[c]—Peach & Aple Trees flourish well here, but Sugar will not grow—

a Man of good Manner assured me that the *Marsh Hawks* were very plenty here all winter, but not to be seen in Summer—and that the *Pelicans* disapear at this season for the South and return early in April with young—Many Red Winged Starlings—and Many *Bleu Birds* these were pleasing to me, the poorest note of these is allways wellcome to Mine ears—

the Watter raising very fast—

Last Night M[r] Aumack who was *rather Merry*—Went to Shoot a Pelican about 10 o'clock P. M. to Cool himself return[d] without a Shot—

Saw Winter Wrens and a beautifull plant in full Bloom—*Ivory Billed Wood Peckers* becoming more plenty—

Monday Dec[r] 18th 1820 Raining all day, floated but a few Miles —Landed at a Place where Geese & Ducks abounded—Killed a Crow, a *Great Horned Owl*, and a Winter *Falcon.*

Tuesday Decemb[r] 19th 1820 Rain and fog all day—Landed within 7 Miles of Last Nights—Killed a *Carrion Crow*, a *Winter Wren* and *16 Parokeets,* I heard and saw once a *Thrush* unknown to me but could not get a Shot at it—Immense flocks of Parokeets and Swamp *Blackbirds*—the *Carrion Crow* I shot at Would Not suffer us to go near than about 100 yards and forced me to draw My Shot and Put in a Ball this brought him down Lifeless—

This Morning I Shot at a Bird unknown to Me and no doubt a Non Descript—it was of the Sparrow Genus—

Saw several Thrushes, very Shy. they sung Sweetly and also Constantly. Took for the Golden *Crown[d] Thrush Turdus Auracapillus;* Also a *French Mocking Bird Turdus Rufus*—the Trees in Many places in the Thick Canes full of Leaves—and during this Rainy *Spell* the Weather as felt Much Like the Beginning of May—

Wednesday Decemb[r] 20th 1820 The Weather as desagreable as one could wish it—Raining and so foggy that we could not see 50 yards—drawing all day—in the Morning the *Winter Wren Sylvia troglodites* and afterwards the *Carrion Crow, Vultur Atratus*—at Twelve o'clock a Short Clearing taking place We floated about 4 Miles and Landed opposite side of the River—Cap[e] Cummings Shot at an *Ivory*

Billed Wood Pecker Picus Principallis broke his Wing and When he Went to take it up it Jump up and claimed a tree, as fast as a Squirel to the Very Top, he gave it up having but a few Loads of Shot—Joseph Came and saw it—Shot at it and brought him down—

We Boiled 10 Parokeets to night for Dash who has had 10 Welps—purposely to try the effect of the Poisoning effect of their hearts on animals. Yesterday We Were told that 7 Cats had been Killed Last Summer by Eating as Many Parokeets—Killed Two Geese—Several Boats Landed along us to night

THURSDAY DECEMB^R 21TH 1820 We at last had fine weather, floated about 35 miles this brought us to the upper Part of *Stack Island* Now only a Barr the former having being sunk by the Earthquakes—Drawing nearly all day I finished the Carion Crow, it stunk so intolerably, and Looked so disgusting that I was very glad when I through it over Board—

Saw in the afternoon a *Black Hawk,* a flock of *Pelicans* at which I shot at about 200 yards as near as I could approach, Without effect. the Sand Barr where they were was Literally covered with excrements and their Feathers. Vast Many Geese seen all day, these Birds Now *Pairing.* Spanish Moss very aboundant on all the Cypress trees—Large flocks of *American Teals* and the constant Cry of Ivory Billed Wood Peckers about us—scarcely any other except a few *Peleated* & Golden Wings—have not seen a red head Wood Pecker for some time—the *Carolina* Wrens and *Cardinals* exercising their Vocal powers all day—

We received the visits of 2 Men, Wood Cutters from the Shore—they assured me that *Pelicans* were here at all seasons but that when the Weather is bad they keep in the Lakes in Great Flocks along with the Geese, Swans, Ducks, Cranes—and there find an aboundance of food—they spoke of a *Black Hawk* that Lives on Fish but I could not ascertain Much about size of anything else concerning it—

they reported that a few Weeks passed a Youth of about 12 Years having Met a Large *Brown Tiger,* or *Cougar* called here a *Painter* was so frightened that he died after reaching his Parents' house—those animals are now scarce, but Dear, Bears and Wolfs are plenty—Anxious to Know if Alligators were seen during this season, they answered in the affirmative. They could be seen every few days—some Keeping in Small ponds too Shallow to cover their backs and there Catch the *Garr Fishes,* root for frogs &^c that one Killed Lately had a Large Quantity of Black Walnut and Hickorys—they are Killed here for the Skin, that when tanned gives a fine Leather preserving the Lozanges of the Scales. One of the men said he owed them a Grudge for Killing An Excellent hunting Dog—while following a wounded Deer across a Lake, and that he retaliats on the Whole Species Whenever an opportunity offers—a Boy told us that one that had dugged a hole about 20 feet under the ground to resort to, in bad weather, was taken a few days ago; the earth having fallen on him during a heavy Dash of rain—they are easily Killed with a Clubb—the usual way of destroying them—they Move slow on the ground—but swiftly in the Watter—this is all hear say and put it here to Compare it with My Own future Observations

Friday December 22[D] 1820 Started at 5 o'clock this Morning, and certainly deserves Noting—after breakfast Joseph & I push off as usual in the Skiff in which we remained untill near Sun Down—Saw *Three Black Hawks,* Shot at this Twice, but these Birds are So Shy that I dared not advance nearer than Rifle Shot and Missed them—Went to a house, to Warm our fingers, the wind blowing rather Sharp this morning—found a Handsome familly of Young Brats who as well as their Mamma Looked Clean and healthy—here We saw the *Pameta Plants* along the Fences—

in the afternoon the sun Shown Warm, the Geese where in Thousands on the Willow Bar, fighting and Mating. Malards, Teals and Wood Ducks aboundant—Killed One Malard and Two Wood Ducks—saw One Swan—One Redtailed *Hawk,* several *Sparrow Hawks*—Many Crested Titmouse—Autumnal Warblers all through the Shaggy *Beards* —The *Carrion Crow* plenty, and their relation the Buzzard.

the *Pewee Fly Catchers* very busy diving at Insects and Singing Merely—saw several Bald Eagles that I Might have Shot at—

a little before Sun down a Steam Boat Called the *Mars* passed us, a poor running Machine—apparently an Old Barge—

Our Commanders spoke of *Cutting a Stick* at 12 o'clock, but the Axes were dull and We did not get up untill 3.—

Saturday Decemb[R] 23[D] 1820 the Moon shining beautifully Clear, the Weather, calm a heavy White frost—started at 3 o'clock—

as soon as the fog disapeared, J. & I putt off for the Mouth of the *Yazoo River,* seeing some Geese Made for them and Killed One—in the Mouth of that River I perceived a Large flock of My unknown *Blackbirds* that I suppose Brown Pelicans—Landed below them, and after crawling on My belly for about 300 yards I arrived within about 45 yards I fired at 3 that were perched Close together on a dead Stick about 7 feet above the Watter, at my shot they all fell as so many stones. I expected them to be all dead but to My surprise, those and about 20 swimming under them had dove, they soon rose and took Wing after running on the Watter about 50 Y^ds^ at the exception of the One I had taken aim on—it would not raise, the Skiff brought up We rowed after it, diving below us up the Yazoo Nearly one Mile, Yet I could not give it up, it became Warier, & remained Less under Watter the Nearer We approach when at Last Joseph Shot at its *head* [the] & Neck (the only part in view Looking much Like a Snake) and Keeled it over—I took it up with great pleasure and anxiety—but I could Not ascertain its Genus—for I could not Make it an [d] *Albatros* the only Bird I can discover any relation to—

We had to exert ourselves to reach our Boats—this done, I began Drawing—We passed to day the *Walnut Hills* a handsome situation on the Mississipi covered with Cotton plantations—We also passed the Small Village of *Warren* commonly Called "Warington" opposite this place (Not Improving) Met the St. *Elca S.—B.*

The *Yazoo River* flowed a Beautifull Stream of transparent Watter, Covered with 1000^ds^ of Geese & Ducks and filled With Fish—the Entrance Low Willows & Cotton Trees—We run to day 49 Miles—the Weather rather too Warm—

MONDAY DECEMBER 25TH 1820 CHRISMAS DAY We passed, the Petit Gulf—early this morning—the Steam Boat Comet passed by from Louisville 9 Days—

I had the pleasure of seeing Mr Aumack Killed a *Great Footed Hawk,* the *Bird* Alexander Willson heard so Many wonderfull Tales of—these Birds are plenty on this River at this season every Year according to all the accounts I have Collected but allways extremely Shy, and I Believe few Men Can Boast of having Killed Many of them, for 15 years, that I have hunted and seen probably one hundred [of] I Never had the satisfaction of bringing one to the Ground—I often have seen them after hearing their Canon Ball Like wissling Noise through the Air seize their Prey on the Wing particularly at *Henderson* Kentucky, where I watched for Weeks near a Pigeon House, that furnished one of those daring Robbers, with food & Exercise—No doubt that the Clouds Ducks of some many Species as are found on this River, renders it a pleasant and fruitfull Winter Residence—

We have seen about 50 since a few Weeks—they fly fast, with quick motions of their Wings, seldom Sailing except when about alighting:—the Specimen before me is a very Old Bird and a beautifull one, When on the Wing they appear Black and are often Mistaken for the *Falco Niger*—Killed 3 Geese;—

Saw a *Tell Tale Godwit,* the Only one seen since I Left the Ohio—but understanding that that River is now considerably raised, I expect they are forced to abandon it—

Cap^{e} Cummings saw 4 Deer this Evening—

We are Now Landed about 15 Miles above Natchez, and if No head Wind takes place Must reach that City To morrow

I Hope that My Familly wishes me as good a Christmas as I do them—Could I have spent it with My Beloved Wife & Children, the exchange of situation would have been most Agreable—I hope to have some tidings of them Tomorrow = the Shores are now Lined with Green Willows the Weather much Like May—at *Henderson*—The Thermometer is allmost every day from 60 to 65—

TUESDAY DECEMB^{R} 26TH 1820 Beautifull Morning, Light frost—I began my drawing as soon as I could see—drawing all day—

We saw to day probably *Millions* of those *Irish Geese* or Cormorants, flying Southwest—they flew in Single Lines for several Hours extremely high—

At half Past 11 o'clock The Boats Landed at the Natchez Bluffs amongst about 100 More, several S.B.^{ts} were also at this place = the Carrion Crows first attracted my Attention, hundreds of them flying constantly Low over the Shores and alighting on the Houses—

I Rec^{d} Two Letters from my Beloved Wife, dated 7th & 14th of Novr the Last date contained one from My Brother *G. Loyen Dupuygandeau* dated July 24 1820

So Busy I have been all day drawing, that I did not even go to the Shore—a Little before Dusk I saw from our Boat Roof the Magnolia & Pines that ornement the Hills above this Place—

I Wrote a Long Letter to My Lucy with Hopes that it would be in time for the Mail of Tomorrow—

Our Commanders and Mr Shaw found every article of Produce Low, perhaps too Low to resound themselves—

I found the Stomack of the Great footed Hawk filled With Bones, feathers, and the Gizzard of a Teal, also the Eyes of a Fish and Many Scales—it was a femelle Egg numerous and 4 of them the size of Green Peas—

As we approach Natchez I [saw] remarked in several places—Saw Mills, placed over ditches cut from the River and running to the Swamps which in time of floods afford a Good Current—these ditches also serve to furnish the Mills with timbers floated through them from the Interior =

We have also seen very Large Rafts of Long Logs Intended for M[r] Livingston's Warf at New Orleans—a Rafter assured us of having rec[d] 6000$ for the Last Parcel he stole rom the Government's Land—

WEDNESDAY DECEMB[R] 27TH 1820 As soon as my drawing was finished, I cleaned and Went to Natchez properly speaking—there to my uttmost surprise I met Nicholas Berthoud, who accosted Me Kindly, and ask[d] me to go to New Orleans in his Boat—I accepted his offer—

from the River opposite Natchez, that place presents a Most Romantick scenery, the Shore Lined by Steam vessels [and f] Barges & flat Boats, seconded by the Lower town, consisting of Ware Houses, Grogg, Chops, Decayed Boats proper for the uses of Washer Women, and the sidling Road raising along the Caving Hills [about 200] on an [Inclinat] oblique of a quarter of a Mile and about 200 feet High covered with Goats feeding peaceally on its declivities, while hundreds of Carts, Horses and foot travellers are constantly, meeting and Crossing each Other reduced to Miniature by the distance renders the whole really picturesque [the Carrion Crows Looking on the Whole with Wistfull Eye]; on the Top of this the Traveller comes in sight of the town as he enters [and] avenues of regularly planted Trees Leading to the diferent Streets running at right Angles towards the River; on the left the *Theater* a poor framed Building and a New and Elegant Mansion the property of M[r] Postlewait attract the Anxious eye—on the right the rollings of the hearth [and left in the St] thinly diversified by poor habitations soon close the prospect—advancing, [Two feet] he is Led into Main Street; this as well as the generality of the place [is] too Narrow to be Handsome, is rendered Less Interesting by the poorness & Iregularity of the Houses, few [Built] of which are Bricks—and at this season very much encumbered by Bales of Cotton—the Jail, Court House are New and tolerable in their form the Lower part of the former [is] a Boarding House of some Note. there are Two Miserable Looking Churches; [and already the] I dare not say unattended but [I] think so—

the Natchez's Hotel is a good House built on the Spanish plan, i.e. with Large Piazas and Many Doors and Windows—Well Kept by M[r] John Garnier and is the rendez vous of all Gentile Travellers and Boarders—Several Large tavern which I did not Visit furnish Amply the Wants of the Strangers that at all times abound from [all] different parts of the Union—this place now Contain about 2000—inhabitants and Houses, has a Bank in good Credit—a Post Office receiving the Diferent Mails Thrice per Week, a Public reading Room and 2 printing offices—

the Naturalist will immediatly remark the general Mildness of the temperature on seeing at this season the [Vegitation in] premature Growth of Lettuces, Radishes and other vegetables that in our Eastern Latitudes are Carefully nursed in April and sometimes in May—

the *Pewee* fly Catcher, the Notable Mocking Bird, constant residents [often] assure him that if frosts are few they must be of short duration, and the Numberless prostrated Carrion Crows in the less frequented Streets [and Yards] prove to him the unhalhiness of the atmosphere—those certainly may be considered as necessary Evils, for no Birds are more disagreable at the same time that few are More Valuable in Climates Like this—

I saw here a Gentleman with Whom I travelled some distance down the Mississipi My first Voyage but as he did not or Would Not recognize my features I spoke not to him—

the Country back of Natchez was represented as Good and fitted by rich planters who once raised a Large [annual] quantity of Cotton the principal article of Export—Opposite this the Lands are extremely Low and overflow to a great Extent and Depth the Mail in Times of flood goes by Watter through the Woods nearly 40 Miles Toward Natchitoches on Red River.

Indians are Daily seen here with diferent sorts of of Game—for which they receive high Prices, I saw Small Wild Turkey sold by them for One Dollar each, Malards at 50*cts*

Although the Weather is Comparatively Mild, the Orange trees will not bear the Winters in open air = and sometimes the frosts for a day or two are severely felt—the remains of an Ancient Spanish fort are perceivable, the Center is now Honored by the Gallows and the Ditch serves as buriing ground for Slaves—the Cemetiere Lies at the extremity of the Town—about 2 Years ago a Large part of the Hill gave Way, Sunk probably 150 feet and Carried Many Houses into the River—this was occasioned by the quick Sand Running Springs that flows into the Strata of Clay and pebles of Which the Hill is Composed—

this sunken part is Now used as the depot of Dead Carcasses, and often times during the Summer emits such Exalaisons as attract hundreds, Nay I was told Thousands of Carrion Crows = an Engine is now Nearly in Operation Intended to raise the Watter of one of the springs or *ecoulement* or drains to suply the City—This indeed is much wanted, Watter hauled from the River is sold at 50cts pr Barrel [and] taken out of the Eddy very impure = I found few Men Interested towards Ornithology except those who had heard or pleased to Invent Wonderfull Stories respecting a few Species—

M[r] Garnier on whom I can rely told me that he had given Liberty to a Mocking Bird after several Years confinement and that for several Years afterward the Bird came daily in the House as if to thank him for his Generosity and Past Kind Attentions = M[r] James Willkins to whom A. Willson had Letters of Introduction assured me that his Work was far from Completed, that through his Mere transient observations he had discovered several New Specimens but being a *Man of Business* he Never had Noted any

a Bird Much resembling the femelle humming Bird is often seen (it is said) during Summer, feeding by Suction amongst the Magnolias She is about Twice the Size of a Wren—

The Carrion Crows Never breed in or Near the Town—having Not one Cent when I Landed here I imediatly Looked for something to do in the Likeness Way for our Support ([for] unfortunately Naturalists are Obliged to eat and have some sort of Garb) I entered the room of a Portrait Painter Naming himself *Cook* but I assure you he was scarcely fit for a Scullion, Yet the *Gentleman* had some politeness and procured me the drawing of two Sketches for 5$ each, this was fine sauce to our empty stomacks

One was imediately paid for, the other a very excellent resemblance of M[r] *Mathewson* probably never will be, for that Gentleman absented the same Evening and never Left orders to any body to pay—I merely put this down to give you the Best advice a Father Can present you with. Never to Sell or Buy without imediately paying for the same—a constant adherence of this Maxim will Keep your Mind and person all times free, & Happy

M[r] Cook much pleased with My Drawings and quickness of performance, desired to travel with us if suitable Mutual arrangements could be Made. I Asked him to pay me Two Dollars per day Monthly in advance and furnish besides, One Third of the Whole Expenses, [furnishing] providing himself with Whatever Materials might be necessary—

He spoke of Joining us in a Couple of Weeks; I thought it very uncertain—the awkwardness I felt when I sat to Dinner at the Hotel was really justified to me; having not used a fork and Scarcely even a Plate since I left Louisville, I involuntarily took Meet and Vegetables with My fingers several times; on Board the flat Boats We seldom eat together and very often the hungry Cooked, this I perform[d] [often] when in need by Plucking & Cleaning a Duck, or a Partridge and throwing it on the Hot embers; few Men have eat a Teal with better appetite than I have dressed in this manner—

Others prefering Bacon would Cut a Slice from the *Side* that hung by the Chimney and Chew that raw with a hard Biscuit—Such Life is well intended to drill men Gradually to hardships to go to Sleep with Wet Muddy Clothing on a Buffalo skin stretch on a Board—to hunt through Woods filled with fallen trees, Entengled with Vines, Briars, Canes, high Rushes and at the same time giving under foot; produces heavy sweats [and] strong Appetite, & Keeps the Imagination free from Worldly thoughts, [and] I Would advise Many *Citisens* particularly our Eastern *Dandys* to try the experiment—leaving their high heeled Boots, but not their *Corsets,* for, this would no doubt [would] be Serviceable whenever food giving way, they might wish to depress their stomacks for the occasion—

Thursday December 28th 1820 Weather sultry. Saw some Mocking Birds and was assured that they remained during the Winter here—

Nicholas having invited me to stay at his Lodgings I Breakfasted at the Hotel of Mr Garnier a French Gentleman of Agreable Manners who kindly procured me Willson's Ornithology from Mr James Wilkins to whom I was introduced to by Nicholas.

Friday December 29th 1820 The weather this Morning had taken a remarquable Change, the Thermometer had fallen from 72 to 36—it snowed and blew hard from the Northwest—last night the Musquitoes, were quite troublesome

I made Two Sketches to day for 5$ each; after Many Inquiries for the 9th Volume of Willson I was disapointed in my wish of examining it none of the subscribers have recd it—

Joseph and Cape Cummings still remaining on Board of Mr Aumack's Boat—I had the satisfaction of ransacking the *Fables* of Lafontaine, with Engravings—Wrote to Dr. Drake and Mr. Robt Best—

Saturday Decembr 30th 1820 the Weather very Cold, the Thermometer a 25—Spent all day Writting the Name and Such Descriptions of the Watter [s] Birds in Willson as would enable me to Judge whenever a New Specimen falls my Praise—

Mr Aumack Left this Morning in our Boat taking with him Cape Cummings—I felt Sorry at parting With that really agreable Compagnion [and the More so When I thought that Like Me he had to meet all the—.] I Wrote to My Beloved Wife—

Sunday Decemb[r] 31th 1820 Early this Morning We prepared for our Departure, our things were Collected, and Carried to the Keel Boat—however it Was not untill One o'clock that the Steam Boat Columbus hauled off the Landing—

We Made fast to her Stern with Two Ropes and went very Swiftly the Moment She was under full headway—

I drew this afternoon—and here I have to tell a sad Misfortune that took place this Morning—having Carried under My Arm My Smallest Port Folio and Some other articles I Laid the Whole on the Ground and ordered M[r] Berthow's Servant to take them on Board

I unfortunately Went off to Natchez again to breakfast the Servant forgot My Folio on the Shore and Now I am Without, any Silver paper, to preserve my Drawings, have Lost some very Valuable Drawings, and My Beloved Wife's Likeness = the greatest Exercions I now Must Make to try to find it again, but so dull do I feel about it that I am nearly Made Sick

I Wrote to M[r] John Garnier, requesting him to advertise and procure some one to try to find My Port Folio [for] but no Hopes can I have of ever seeing it when Lost amongst 150 or 160 flat Boats and Houses filled with the Lowest of Caracters—No doubt My Drawings will serve to ornement their Parlours or will be Nailed on Some of The Steering Oars—

We passed to day A Long Line of Bluffs exquisiting grand to the sight—

My Port Folio Contained 15 Drawings Three of Which were Non Descripts—One a Duck extremely Curious and rare that I had Named the *Fintail:* Should I not get it again, it may retard My return home very Considerable—

Monday January 1st 1821 This day 21 Years since I was at *Rochefort* in France. I spent most of that day at Copying Letters of My Father to the Minister of the Navy—

What I have seen, and felt since, would fill a Large Volume—the Whole of Which Would end at *this Day January 1st 1821. I am on Board a Keel Boat going down to New Orleans the poorest Man on it*—& What I have seen and felt has brought some very dearly purchased Experience, and Yet Yesterday I forgot that No servant could do for Me What I might do Myself; had I acted accordingly; My Port Folio Would now have been safe in my possession—

Not Willing to dwell on Ideal futurity, I do not at present attempt to forsee where My Poor Body may be this day 12 Months at 12 o'clock to day the *Columbus* Came too at Bayou *Sarah*—a Small Village at the Mouth of that Inlet—Many flat Boats the Steam Boat and 2 Briggs waiting for Cotton—the Steam Boat *Alabama* put off as we came to, and about half an hour after; the Columbus Left us to ourselves to try to reach *Baton Rouge* before her, to procure the freight there—promissing to wait 3 hours.

The Lands are flatening fast—the Orange trees are now and then seen near the Rich Planter's habitation—and the Verdure along all the shore is very Luxuriant and agreeable—the Thermometer at—68 at 12 o'clock in the Shade, the Day Beautifully fair—Expected to see some Alligators = Many *Irish Geese* in the Eddys—Malards but few geese = at half past 6 o'clock P.M. we came opposite *Baton Rouge* but the Steam Boat had left and of Course we proceeded on our Way floating—this Last place is a Thrifty Villege on the New Orleans State—from some distance above *Levees* have made their appearance—I saw a Negro Man fishing by deeping a Scoup Net [constantly] every moment in the Watter immediately at a point Where the current ran swift forming an eddy below, he had taken several tolerably Large Cat Fishes—

TUESDAY JANUARY 2D 1821 We floated all night without accidents, the river since Natchez is much deeper, and free of Sawers and Snaggs—at day breake found ourselves about 50 Miles below Baton Rouge; the day Cloudy, raw, and some Wind a head—

the Plantations increase in number, and the Shores have Much the Appearance of those on Some of the Large rivers of France, their Lowness Excepted, the points are quite diferent to those on the River above, One May see the River below them by Looking across in Many places—and from the Boat we can only have a View of the upper windows, Roofs and Tops of the Trees about them. the Whole is backed by a dark Curtain of Thickly Moss covered Cypresses—flat Boats are Landed at nearly every Plantation, this being a Sure method of disposing of their produce to a better profit, travellers on horse Back or Gigg go by us full Gallop as if their Life depended on the accelerity of their movements—I have Seen More Common Crows since Natchez than I ever saw in My Whole Life before, the Shores and Trees are Covered with them but yet very few fish Crows have been Seen—saw some Pelicans, Many Gulls, Buzzards & C. Crows—

our Situation in this Boat is quite Comfortable—We have a good Servant to wait on us, are served with regular Meals, Clean and in Plates—Move much faster than With Messrs Aumack & Lovelace, having here 8 Roaers who dare not contradict orders—

it rained and blowed hard a head, about One Mile below *Bayou Lafourche*. We Came to—the weather did not stop Joseph and Myself from taking a walk to the Swamp back of Plantation in front of which the Boat was moored—after Chasing the Note of What I supposed a New Bird for a considerable time, I found the deceiving Mocking Bird close by me and Exulting with the Towe Bunting's *cheep*—Joseph was more fortunate he Killed Two Warblers, one the *Red Poll* (of this We saw about a dozen) the other I have Not yet ascertained—although in Beautiful plumage; Both Male—how Sweet for me to find Myself the 1st of January in a Country where the woods are filled with Warblers, Thrushes, and at the same time see the Rivers and Lakes covered with all Kinds of Watter Birds—

the Pewees are quite gaily, I have seen this day 3 Cat Birds—if this is not the winter retreat of all our Summer Birds it is at all Events that of very many—how happy would I feel to see some future January surrounded by the diferent species of Swallows Skeeping about, with the Whippoorwill & Night Hawk

—I drew the Likeness of Mr Dickerson the Master of the Boat—he paid me in Gold—took the Outlines of Both *the Warblers by Candle Light to afford Me time to morow to finish both*—

3D Raining & Blowing hard all Night the weather cooled Considerably. much Like some of our April day at Henderson—took a Walk Early, while waiting for the Light to Increase and enable Me to Work—passed through a Large Cotton Plantation yet unpicked Looked Like if a Heavy Snow had fell and frose on every Pod—

the great regularity with which this is [Planted] sowed and raised attracts the Eye imediatly; it Lays in rows I believe allways runing at right Angle to the River, about 6 feet distant from each other and the plants about 3 and so straight that your Eye is Carried to the farthest extremity of the field without the Lease obstruction—even at this time that the Cotton has Ceased to be attended for Many weeks, it is quite free from Weeds of any sort—

the Woods here have a new and very romantic appearance—the Plant Called Pamitta raises promiscuously through them the Moss on every tree darkens the under growth and affords to the [Mind] melancholy [fashioned] Mind a retreat thooted by the Chirpings of hundreds of [—] Beautifully Plumed inhabitants—

the flocks of *Blackbirds* taking the Species En Masse, feel the air, they pass Southwest constantly; forming a Line Like disbanded Soldiers all anxious to reach the point of destination each hurring to pass the companion before him—

Doves are plenty, the Cardinal Gros Beaks very numerous and all Species of Sparrow inabiting the Interior are here—I remark[d] great Many *Brown Larks* busy feeding on the Drift Wood that feels Many Eddys—

I drew both My Birds, the first on a plant in full bloom that I plucked Near the Boat—saw about 50 Mocking Birds some of them extremely Gentle, and holding their tail Leaning back allmost over their Heads—

We were Visited by several *french Creoles* this is a Breed of animals that Neither speak French English nor Spanish correctly but have a Jargon composed of the Impure parts of these three—

they Stared at My Drawing, and when a litle Composed Gazed and Complimented Me very Highly—on asking them the names of about a dozen diferent Birds then lying on the Table they Made at once and without hesitating a Solid Mass of *Yellow Birds* of the Whole—One of them a young Man told Me that he could procure 3 or 4 dozen of them every Night by hunting the Orange trees with a Lantern—I can said he "see the Rascalls White belies and Knok them down with a Stick very handy"—few of these good Natured Souls could answer any valuable account of the Country—

Some toads were hoping about this evening, and on turning a Dead Tree over, we found several Lizards, who moved with great Vigour—at Sunset the Wind Lulled, the Captain, Sailors and passingers all anxious to reach New Orleans, it was determined that after a that after a good supper the oars would be used untill day break tomorow,. if so We May see the City early

I Shot this Evening at a *Sparrow Hawk* that being badly Wounded sailed directly for a hole (probably that a Wood pecker) and [escaped us] no doubt died there—a few moments previous he Was teazing an American Buzzard—

Joseph Killed One Teal—with several Goldfinches and Warblers, some Sparrows, but Nothing New—

THURSDAY JANUARY 4TH 1821 at 4 o'clock this morning the wind was so high, that it forced us to Come to a litle above *Bonne Care's* Church—the weather was rather cold, as soon as day broke walk[d] over to the Swamp

Saw some Birds that I took for Large non described *Cukoos* as they flew high over us, they had a new Note to me—Many Warblers, Robins, blue Birds, Cardinals, Grakles, Sparows Goldfinches, doves, Golden

Wing Woodpeckers, One Red headed one, Many, Carolina & Winter Wrens—Sparrow Hawks, and a Large one unknown, on our return to the boat we Started with Hopes that We could make *some* headway—but were forced to about a Mile below the Church—I paid my Respects to the Pastor, to make some Inquiries respecting M[r] *Lecorgne, George Crogham,* and the country; but I found only a tall thin dirty Creole who could not say much besides the prayer for the prosperity of the Brick Church now erecting—from this pennsionary of Bigots I went to a School House; there I had the pleasure of meeting an Old, Polite, and well Instructed French Gentleman in charge of about a dozen of Pupils of Both Sexes—he told me that *George Crogham* resided about 3 Miles from this Place across the Mississipi, that he was not acquainted with Lecorgne's name—that this Country was a fine field for my Wishes; [he] walked to the Boats, examined attentively My Drawings and told Me that having Left Europe and the World of Talents for so many Years such a Sight was very gratifying—We hunted again and Saw more of the *Cuckoos* these [by] this time I saw on the Ground and Knew them at once for some of the same Birds I had Shot my preceeding Voyage and had taken for *Boat Tailed Grakles*—I Killed 3, Two femelles and one Male and had the pleasure of examinng their Manners very Closely—their Voice is Loud and Sweet and their Movements elegantly airy—a Beautifull male was very busily Engage[d] in carying some straws to a Large Live Oak, but loosing the Bird every time through the Spanish Moss, I Could Not see any appearance of Nest, and so early in the season could not presume it was for the purpose of building one—I Shot him—and Joseph Killed another femelle—these Birds are considerably More Shy than any other Grakle—fly very Loosely when in flocks, uttering constantly a Chuck [very] diferent to that of the *purple Grakle—Gracula quiscula*—and their flight resembles that of our Cuckoos and that of the Cukoo of Europe—While on the ground their walk is Elegant and Stately carrying their Long concave tails rather high—feed Closer to each other than Swamp Black Birds: Turton speaks of their Shortish Bills and gives for total length 13 Inches—this was taken no doubt from a Young femelle—the Male now before me Measures 15¾ Inches—my drawing Shews you Male & femelle, and tomorow it being finished I will give you a description—the French here call them starlings but on all questions respecting them or any other birds their answer is a constant *Oh Oui*—the country is here richly adorned by handsome dwelling Houses, Many Sugar and Cotton Plantations running about One Mile and half to the Swamp, free from Old trees and Stumps—every house a *L'Espagnole*—orange trees, now hanging with their golden fruits forming avenues and Edges—the fields Well fenced in and dreaned by ditches running to the Swamps—

the Mocking Birds are so Gentle that I followed one along a fence this morning for nearly one Mile Keeping only one panel between us the whole of the distance—I have Not heard one sing yet; but imitating Many Birds—

about 5 o'clock we again ventured off and again the Wind drove us in Shore and now we are Landed on a point where our Boat rolls merily—raining hard—thermometer to day at 52—this morning the french Gentlemen Wrap[d] up in their Cloaks Kept their Handerkerchiefs to their Noses—What would become of them on the Rocky Mountains at this Season—our Captain Exchanged some Apples for Oranges receiving 2 for 1—

Friday January 5th 1821 We had some Light Snow this morning, drawing nearly all day, the wind blowing violently—Shortly after Breakfast I saw some *Terns Winowing* in the Eddy below us. Killed Two on the Wing—on the Falling of the first, the Second approach[d] as if to see What was the Matter. I shot it dead, when the remaining Two that where coming fast wheeled and flew out of our Sight imediatly—these Birds flew Lightly with their Bills perpendicular over the Watter on which they appeared to Keep a close attention, Now & then falling to it and taking up Small fragments of Buiscuits thrown from our Boat—I finished my *Gracula Barita* but not the drawing; the rocking of the Boat quite disagreable—took a Long Walk towards Evening, saw Many Warblers particularly the *Maryland Yellow throat.* Shot an *Hermit Thrush;* paid a Visit to a Cottager a French Creole, handsome Children who were all afraid of me—the Lady *remarkably handsome* their Little Garden was adorned with a few orange Trees some fine Lettuces filled the Borders; Gren Peas nearly in bloom, Artichaux, reminding me of the Happy days spent in France—bought some delightfull radishes, and Enquired of Birds of Course; One League distant is a fine Lake, now the rendez vous of Ducks, Geese, &[c] but could not obtain Valuable remarks—the transient Cool Weather as rendered the Mocking Birds so gentle that they Scarcely would move out of the Way—

at Night I drew the Outline of the Tern I had shot and ransacked Turton's but all without effect. Yet I do not Consider this as a New Speci[men], untill I See Willson's 9th Volume—the Gracule Male I draw Measured in Breadth 22 Inches—Tongue bifid—and I found to day that the Carrying Straws up in the Trees was simply to pick the rice contained in the heads—I saw this day thousands of them—particularly found of

Catle pens, alighting close to them and hunting in the fresh Dung in the manner of the Uropean Starling

Saturday January 6th 1821 the Thermother fell by Sun rise to 30. We had some ice on the running Boards; after So much Warm weather experienced since the Latitude 33 this felt very uncomfortable, and our Litle Stove was good Company, the Wind blew hard ahead Yet—I drew slowly, the Tern I Killed Yesterday; Joseph Made his first attempt from Nature on the femelle—I was very much pleased with his assay—the wind falling aloft at 8 o'clock We push^{d} off—and rowed 12 Miles with much Dificulty, I did not expect our Commander would Leave our harbour with as dull a prospect—We were blowed a Shore opposite *Monsieur St Armand's* Sugar Plantation—

Out on Shore with Guns imediately—the Swamps about 3 Miles back we gave up going to them fearing the departure of our boat while absent that far—here Was the finest Plantations we have seen Mr S. A^{d} own 70 Negroes and Makes about 400 Hogshead of Sugar—besides raising, Corn Hay, Rice &^{c}—this Gentleman, apparently Young was Shooting Red Winged Starlings, on the Wing for his amusement, had a richly ornemented Doubled Barelled Gun of which he Made excellent use—the Slaves employed at Cutting the Sugar Cane—this they perform with Large heavy Knifes not unlike those used by Butchers to Chop—some cutting the Head of the plants and others the Cane itself—tying the Last in small fagots with the Tops. Carts with Entire Wooden Wheels drawn by 4 oxen haul it to the House where it is, bruised, pressed [and] Boiled & Made into Sugar—the Miserable Wretches at Work begged a Winter Falcon We had Killed, saying *it Was a great treat for them;* the Overseer a Good Looking Black Man, told us of his being in the same Employ for 8 Years and had obtain so much of his Master's Confidence, as to have the Entire Care of the Plantation—he Spoke roughly to his under servants but had a good indulgent Eye, and no doubt does what he Can to Accomodate, Master and All—those Immense Sugar Plantations Looked Like Prairies early in Summer for Scarce a Tree is to be seen, and particularly here where the Horizon was bounded by Cleared Land—

We saw Many Catle, Horses, and Sheep, but all poor and Slack, the Latters have but Litle Wool and that only on the back the Rams wear a Long Kind of hairy beard Like Goats—

the Gardens were beautifull. Roses in full bloom revive the Eye of the Traveller—who for lengthy Days has been Confined to the Smoky inside of a Dark flat Bottomed Boat—the Wind entirely Lulled away at Sun

Set—the Moon's Disk assured us of a fine Night and We Left our Station to drop within a few Miles of the City—Tomorow perhaps May take us there, yet so uncertain is this World that I should not be Surprised if I never Was to reach it—the further removed, the Stronger My anxiety to see My familly again presses on My Mind—and Nothing but the astonishing desire I have of Compleating my work Keeps My Spirits at par—

saw a few Fish Crows; a Marsh Hawk—a Red Shouldered Hawk, one the Boatman Killed a *Barred Owl,* this and the Winter Falcon Much Lighter Colored than usual—

Several Steam Boats passed us going up & down Length of the Tern 13 Inches—to the end of the tail—Wings extending 2 Inches beyond, tail 12 feathers—tongue Longue Slender and bifid. Mouth orange Color—Breadth 2:7$\frac{1}{4}$/12—Eye dark brown—Legs & feet red Orange—

Sunday January 7th 1821 at New Orleans at Last—We arrived here about 8 o'clock this Morning; hundreds of Fish Crows hovering near the shipping and dashing down to the Watter Like Gulls for food—uttering a cry very much like the young of the *Common crow* when they first Leave the Nests—I saw Mr Prentice, who directed me to the House of Messrs *Gordon & Grant* where he told me N. Berthoud Was; I saw him and was Introduced to Mr Gordon of whom I shall have opportunity of speaking probably frequently hereafter and the *British Consul* Mr Davisson I heard that my familly Was Well, and saw a Note from My Wife to N. Berthoud, that accompanied a p^{re} of Gloves made by her for him—

We walked out, Met Col^{l} George Croghan, our former acquaintance saw Many of the Louisville Gentry too tedious to mention names—

Arrived at the House of Mr Arnauld an old friend of N. B^{ds} father. we were invited to take dinner, and although we had engaged previously to Mr Gordon we staid, We had a good dinner and great deal of Mirth that I call *french Gayety* that really sickened me. I thought Myself in Bedlam, every body talk^{d} Loud at once and the topics dry Jokes—Yet every one appeared good, well disposed, Gentlemen, and were very polite to us—a Monkey amused the Company a good deal by his Gambols and pranks—formerly I would have been able as well as anxious to go to the Theatre but now I can only partake of the Last, and after having paid a Short Visit to Mr Gordon I retired to the Keel Boat; with a bad head Hake occasioned by drinking some Wine—and very sorry that I probably Could not have Letters from the Post Office untill Tuesday,

Tomorow being a grand French Fete the aniversary of the Memorable Batle of Orleans

Joseph had spent his day visiting the Town and was not prepossessed in its favor—

I saw at Mr Arnauld 2 American Doves who have been Caged for Two Years, they *Layd* Eggs Last Spring, and incubated them for four days, but they were broke by Accident—

MONDAY JANUARY 8TH 1821 at Day breake, went to Market having received information that Much and great variety of game was brought to it—We found Vast Many Malards, some teals, some American widgeons, Canada Geese Snow Geese, Mergansers, Robins; Blue Birds; Red wing Starlings—Tell Tale Godwits—every thing selling extremely high $1.25 for one pare of Ducks, 1.50 for a Goose &c Much surprised and diverted on finding a *Barred Owl* Cleand and Exposed for sale Value 25cts—some fine Fish; Indiferent Meat—some Vegetables both of this Country and West Indies = these Latters are put up in Small parcels on the ground opposite the owner, who has fixed prices for each Lot—I went to the review and will remember it and the 8th of January forever —My Pocket was rifled of my pocket Book taken in this Morning with an intention of going to the Governor with the Letters I had received for him, and to Mr Wheeler's brother in Law—when I mentiond My Loss to N. Berthoud he called me a *Green Horn,* I do not Know the Color of My Horns but well, *those* of some Neighbours of Mine—

Not blaming fortune as is generally the Case I peaceably pack the whole to Myself and will try to grow Wiser if possible—I think the Knave who took it is now good deal disapointed and probably wishes I had it—the Parade was only tolerable I had a view of the Governor that is now no doubt all I May expect, he Looked about 60 a french face of good Countenance—We Walked to Bayou St John absolutly to Kill the time, the whole City taken with the festivals of the day—Joseph recd a Letter from his Parents—

this evening one of our Men Called *Smith* fell over board drunk and Would have drowned if Providence had not interfered a Women heard the Noise and the Yawl of the S. Bt U. States saw him—

—— *9TH* —— Breakfasted with J. B. Gilly. Recd a letter from My Wife—My Spirits very Low—Weather Cloudy & Sultry—begun raining paid a Visit to Jarvis the P. Painter—Saw Wam Croghan,—Wrote to My Wife—Wished I had remained at Natchez—having found No Work to do remained on Board the Keel Boat opposite the Market, the Dirtiest place in all the Cities of the United States—Wrote to John Garnier about My Port Folio—

WEDNESDAY JAN^{Y} 10TH 1821 Raining hard all day wrote My Brother G. L. Dupuygandeau and to My Mother—in the afternoon Cap^{n} Cummings arrived and dined with us—his appearance much Worst—the Weather so bad that I had no opportunity of doing any thing toward procuring Work—Strong thoughts of returning to Natchez Saw Cap^{n} Penniston who rec^{d} me very Politely

—— *11* —— Spent the Day Walking about trying to find some work Shewed My Drawings to Mr Gordon & the British Consul Mr Davisson—spoke good of the Publication—the former raised My Expectations of their value—

Remarked in Market, Blue Cranes, great Many Coots Caldwall Ducks, some Geese, Keeldeers—1 White Crane—or Herons and one Sand Hill Crane—

Was sometime with Mr Prentice who gave me a letter to Doctor Hunter, whom I wished to see, to procure the Information I so much Need about the Red River, What life &^{c}—Joseph Employed in Making Enquiries about the Lost Port Folio from every Boat Landing from Natchez—No Work yet—rain, Warm, the Frogs all piping—

—— *12TH* —— Early this Morning I Met an Italian, painter at the Theatre. I took him to N. B^{d} Room and Shewed me the Drawing of the White Headed Eagle, he was much pleased, took me to his painting appartement at the Theatre, then to the Directors who very roughly offered me 100$ per Month to paint with Mons L'Italian.

I believe really now that my talents must be poor or the Country—Dined with Mr Gordon, conversation Birds & Drawings, Must exibit some again and again as New Guests came in—

I Rec^{d} to day a Letter from My Beloved Wife Dated Novr 28th 1820—gave My Letter for Mr Garnier to the Columbus—No work yet—paid a Visit to Monsieur *Pamar* but Audubon was poor to day and he Knew it when I made my bow—

Wrote this Evening to Henry Clay Es^{qr} for another Letter of Recommandation—

Weather, Warm, rainy, foggy, and altogether Disagreable Saw One Wood Cock in Market—

SATURDAY 13TH JANUARY 1821 I rose early tormented by many disagreable thoughts, nearly again without a cent, in a Busling City where no one cares a fig for a Man in my situation—I walked to *Jarvis* the Painter and shewed him some of my Drawings—he overlooked [at] them, said nothing then Leaned down and examined them minutely but never said they Were good or bad—Merely that when he drew an Eagle for Instance, he made it resemble a Lyon, and covered it with Yellow hair and not Feathers—some fools who entered the room, were so pleased at seeing my Eagle that theh prised it, and Jarvis wistled—I called him aside, While Joseph Rolled up our Papers and asked him if he needed assistance to finish his Portraits i.e. the Clothing and Grounds—he stared, I repeated my question and told him I would not turn my Back to any one for Such employment and that I had received good Lessons from good Masters—he then asked me to come the following day and Would think about it—

in following N. B. through the street while nothing better could be done, We entered the Warehouse of Mr Pamar and at once was surprised to hear *him* ask what I Charged for my Drawings of Faces; 25$;—but said he I have 3 Children and you May put them all on one piece; then I must have 100$—

N. Bd requested me to make a Sketch of the Litle Girl then present; a sheet of Paper was procured, My Pencil Sharped and Sitting on a Crate was soon at Work and soon finished; the Likeness was Striking; the Father Smiled, the Clerks stared me emased and the servant was dispatched to shew My Success (as it Was Called) to Mistress—Monsieur Pamar *Civilly* told me that I Must do my Best for him and Left it to Myself as to the Price—I would have Liked to earn the half of the Money that day, but the Eldest Daughter could not be ready perhaps for several Days—Yet here is found Hopes—how I Calculated on 100 Dollars; What relief to My Dear Wife and Children for Said I if I get this, I may send it her and no doubt I will soon procure some more Work—

I spent the remainder of this day in better Spirits took a Long Walk With Joseph toward the Lake—Saw an Aligator—

Wrote this Evening to Doctr Dl Drake—and read some Interesting tales, borrowed from Mr Prentice—

SUNDAY 14TH JANUARY 1821 I dispatch Joseph and *Simon* (N. B. Servant) across the river for some Life Oak to draw, brought some not fit—

Dressed I Went to Jarvis—he took me immediately in his painting room, and asked me many questions, until *I thought* that he *feared* my assistance [might become troublesome to him]; he very Simply told me he could not believe that I might help him in the Least—I rose, bowed, and Walk[d] out without one Word, and No doubt he Looked on Me as I did on him as an Original, and a Craked Man—

The Levee early was Crowded by people of all Sorts as well as Colors, the Market, very aboundant the Church Bell ringing [and] the Billiard Balls Knocking, the Guns heard all around. What a Display this is for a Steady Quaker of Philad[a] or Cincinnati—the day was beautifull and the crowd Increased considerably—I saw however no handsome Woman and the Citron hue of allmost all is very disgusting to one who Likes the [—] rosy Yankee or English Cheeks—

I took My Gun, rowed out to the edge of the Eddy and Killed a Fish Crow, these Birds are plenty on the River every fair day—(when otherwise, the food is plenty in the Swamps, the Crabs, Young Frogs, Watter Snakes, &[c] Shewing out in great Numbers)—When the one I Killed fell, hundreds flew to him and appeared as if about to Carry him off, but they soon found it their Interest to let me have him. I drew Near and Loaded for another; they all rose in Circling Like Hawks extremely High and then flew down the Stream, out of sight calling aloud all the times they suffer their Legs & feet to hang down as if broken—

I brought it on Board and began to Work imediately—at Dark took a Walk to M[r] Gordon, from there on to M[r] *Laville* where We saw some *White Ladies* and Good Looking ones—returning on Board the Quartroon Ball attracted My View but as it cost 1$ Entrance I Merely Listened a Short time to the Noise and came Home as We are pleased to Call it—

Monday 15th January 1821
Tuesday 16th " "
Wednesday 17th " "
Thursday 18th " "

This is a Way of Cutting Matter Short, but indeed the time has been so Long and dull during these days that I think it a good ridince to use them thus [— — — —] [I was sad when they passed heavily by] I spent them running about to procure Work, being sadly disapointed by M[r] Pamar who said the Lady Wanted Oil Colors—

Yesterday I Made My Long Acquaintance's Likeness John B. Gilly purposely to expose it to the Public—it is considered by every one who Knows him to be perfect—and to shew it this Morning (for I made it in a few hours) to Pamar procured Me the Making of that of his heldest

Daughter; by the time We receive the pay for it, We will be penny Less—

to day I rec[d] a letter from My Beloved Wife who rufled My Spirits Sadly it Was dated Cincinnati Dec[r] 31. 1820 I answered it. [— — — — — —]

Saw in Market—2 White Herons—one New Species of Snipe, but could not Draw any of them, being partly pluck[d]—Joseph Who hunted all day Yesterday, Killed Nothing New—saw Many Warblers—

		British Consul's Likeness	$ 25.00
19th	Friday—	Euphraim Pamar's Likeness	25.00
20	Saturday—	Another Sister "	25.00
21	Sunday		
22	Monday	M[rs] Pamar	25.00
23	Tuesday	Litle Daughter of D[o]	25.00
24	Wednesday	M[r] Forestall D[o]	25.00
25	Thursday	Young Lucin D[o]	25.00
26	Friday	M[rs] Lucin D[o]	20.00
27	Saturday	Mr [—] Carabie D[o]	25.00
			$200.00
28	SUNDAY	Drawing a Brown Pelican—	

fatigued, Wearied of Body but in good Spirits having plenty to do at good Prices, and my Work much admired—only sorry that the Sun Sets—

MONDAY JANUARY 29TH 1821 Drawing all day the Brown Pelican, Collected My Earnings purchased a Crate of queens Ware for My Beloved Wife, Wrote to her, W*m* Bakewell and Charles Briggs forwarding her by Letter and Parcel care of M*r* Buckamain of Louisville 270 Dollars—the Crate Cost 36: 33$—

TUESDAY 30TH Mr Duchamp's Likeness 25$

WEDNESDAY 31 Nothing disapointed by M. Laville

[*THURSDAY* " Drew a common gull]

Thursday—February 1st 1821— Began a Likeness of M*r* Louallier and Drew a Common Gull—

Friday 2d Mr Smith began hunting for Me at 25$ per Month stopped Thursday Morning—and the Girl *Began Cooking for us at 10$ per Month with washing*
Saturday 3d Wrote to My Beloved Wife—

Sunday 4th Disapointed again by M. Laville, returned to the Boat and Drew a *Grey Snipe*—
Joseph & M*r* Smith out hunting all day, brought a few Red Breasted Thrushes. some Pewee fly Catchers and Many Swamp Sparrows and Savanah Finches—Complaining very Much of the Hardships of hunting in the Cypress Swamps—Remarked in the Market many *Purple Galinules* but all so Mangled that I could not see one fit to draw—Saw also several *Rails or Soras*

Monday February 5th 1821 Running about pretty much all day trying to procure some More Work and also Enquiring about Willson's Ornithology, but in Vain—the high Value set on that work now particularly Lately as rendered it extremely rare, and the few who possess it will not Lend it—the Weather extremely sultry and Damp heavy Rains and thunder—saw to day at Mr Pamar, where I often Breakfast or Dine Mr Delaroderie

having been so extremely engaged the Two Days that I Drew the *Brown Pelican* I had not time to make such Memoranda as I wished—it was given me by Mr Aumack, the Bird was Killed on a Lake in this Vicinity and are rare—it was a Male, in tolerable order—Mr Gordon who before he had seen My Drawing thought it a Pelican Common in some of the West Indies, was much pleased at finding it a diferent Species—I was assured that these Birds were seen in Immense flocks in the Neighbourhood of *Buenos-Aires* by a Scotch Gentleman, of respectability—here the hunters call them *Grand Gozier* and say that seldom more than two are seen together—and only for Short Periods after heavy Gales from the Sea—

the Common Gulls pay us regular Visits With their usual Companions the Fish Crows every Morning about Sun Rise—Comming across the Land from the Lakes Barataria where I am told they resort to Roost—I was not a litle surprised at finding the Stomack of several We Killed a few days since filled with *Beetles* of different Kinds; Joseph examined the River and found Vast Many of these Last floating dead on the surface, the Crows also feed freely on the Same—the Gulls often chase the Crows for some Considerable distance but Never Successfully, the Crow being much Swifter on the Wing—the quantity of Robins or Red breasted Thrushes Killed here is astonishing, the Market abound with them and yet they bring 6 $\frac{1}{4}$ cents each—they are at present the principal Game to be found. Birds of all description are destroyed and eat, our Men Cooked the Gulls and found them excellent food—

I saw 12 of the Grey Snipes Similar to the one I Made My Drawing from, all alike in size and Marking, but the Stupid Ass who sold me one Knew Nothing, Not even where *he* had Killed them—

February 9th—1821— In walking this morning about a mile below this city I had the pleasure of remarking thousands of purple martins travelling eastwardly they flew high and circling feeding on [incectes] insects as they went they moved onwardly about $\frac{1}{4}$ miles an hour Thermometer at 68 weather Drisly.
Hundreds of Coots where in the market this morning

February 15th 1821 Wrote to My Beloved Wife this Day per N. Berthoud List of Drawings Sent My Beloved Wife February 17th by Nicholas Berthoud of Shipping port Esq*re*

1 Common gallinule—Not Described by Willson
2 Do—Gull— Do Do Do
3 Marsh Hawk
4 Boat Tailed Grakles Male & femelle—Not Describd by Willson
5 Common Crow
6 Fish Crow
7 Rail or Sora
8 Marsh Tern—
9 Snipe Not Described by Willson
10 Hermit Thrush
11 Yellow Red Pole Warbler
12 Savannah Finch
13 Bath Ground Warbler Not Described by Willson
14 Brown Pelican Not Described by Willson
15 Great footed Hawk
16 Turkey Hen—Not Described by Willson
17 Cormorant— Do Do Do

18 Carrion Crow or Black Vulture
19 Imber Diver
20 White Headed or Bald Eagle

May I have the Satisfaction of Looking at these and Many More in good Order on My return the fruits of a Long Journey—

Monday 19th February 1821 the Weather beautifull, Clear & Warm, the Wind having blown hard from the Southwest for 2 days & nights—

Saw this Morning Three Immense flocks of *Bank Swallows* that past over Me with the Rapidity of a Storm, going Northeast, their Cry was heard distinctly, and I knew them first by the Noise they made in the air coming from behind Me; the falling of their Dung resembled a heavy but thinly falling Snow; No appearance of any feeding While in our Sight—Which Lasted but a few Minutes—

I was much pleased to see these arbingers of Spring but Where could they be moving so rapidly at this early Season I am quite at a Loss to think & yet their Passage here was about as long after the Purple Martins that Went By on the 9th Instant as is their arrival in Kentucky a Month hence—perhaps Were they forced by the last Winds and now Enticed to proceed by the Mildness of the Weather the Thermometer being at 68—

how far More south Must I go Next January & February to see these Millions of Swallows Spending their Winter as Thousands of Warblers, fly Catchers, Thrushes and Myriads of Ducks, Geese, Snipes &c Do here?

the Market is regularly furnished with the *English Snipe* Which the french Call *Cache Cache*. Robins Blue Wingd Teals, Common Teals, Spoon Bill Ducks, Malards, Snow Geese, Canada Geese, Many Cormorants. Coots, Watter Hens, Tell Tale (Godwits, calld here *Clou Clou*) Yellow Shank Snipes, Some Sand Hill Cranes, Strings of Bleu Warblers, Cardinal Grosbeaks, Common Turtle Doves, Golden Wingd Wood Peckers &c

Wednesday 21st February 1821 I Met this morning with one of those slight discouraging Incidents connected with the life of the artists; I had a Likeness [—] Spoken of in very rude terms by the fair Lady it was Made for, and perhaps will Loose My time and the reward expected for My Labour,—Mrs *Andre* I here mention the Name as I May Speak More of the Likeness as the occasion Will require—

Saw Many Green Baked White Belied Swallows to day and Also four

Martins Hiroundo Purpurea—All of them very Lively and not exibiting much of the Muddy Appearance that immersion in the Swamps about this City would undoubtedly give them, [if they] had they remained buried in it since Last December at Which time late in that Month they were plenty and remarked passing by [and] ariving from North & East [Courses(?)] moving South Weswardly—here they Must Make a Long Pause or Move Eastwardly very Slowly as Seldom do they arrive in Pennsylvania before the 25 of [April] March and more frequently in the first days of [May] April—they find nowhere an abondance of Insects, and the Millions of Musquitoes that raise from the Swamps Would Sufice to feed the Swallows of all the World—

Saw Many Brown Larks.

the Fish Crows are remarkably fond of alighting in flocks on some Pacan trees about 12 Mile below this City about 9 o'clock in the Morning when they retire on these to rest from their Fishing excursions and remain Croaking untill the Midle of the day—

Thursday New Orleans February 22d 1821 We at Last have the Keel Boat off and have moved on the hearth again—Our present situation is quite a Curious one to Me, the room we are in and for which We pay $10 per Month is situated in Barraks Street near the Corner of that & Royal Street—between Two Shops of Grocers and divided from them and our Yellow Landlady by Mere Board Partitions, receiving at once all the new Matter that Issues from the thundering Mouths of all these groupes—the *Honest Woman* spoke much of honesty in Strangers and required one Month paid in Advance, this however I could not do, and satisfied her with one half Not taking a Receipt although She appeared very urgent—

I walked a good deal about the City in search of Work & Willson's Ornithology but was not favored with any success—extremely anxious to receive some news from My familly—am very much fatigued of New Orleans Where I cannot *Shoot Two Birds with one Stone* I retired to our Lodgings at Dusk—

Saw Cap*e* Barton's of Henderson who said he would Not have known me if I had not Spoke within his hearing [one half page blotted out]

Saturday 24th February 1821 Idle, and the weather fair, took a *Wade* in the Woods the vegetation forwarded beyond my expectations. Saw some handsome Plants in Bloom that made me regret of having sent My Drawings home—Birds extremely Shy and nothing New;—in the afternoon Paid a Visit to M*r* John F. Miller from Whom (I was told) I might expect an uncommon Share of Politeness, perhaps I walked in at a bad time but be this as it May, I Was received and Dispatched as promptly as the case would permit; the subject of Course During the few Moments I Left then rolled on Birds. I was asked if Many Ducks such as the *Canvas Back* &c (fine food) where residents of this Part of America, had I put those queries I might have expected a No from One that had resided 10 Years here, and yet this No I Was obliged to give—No doubt for want of True Knowledge for the Birds in question are said to be plenty here during Winter—and are Most Likely are the Sheldrakes Dun Divers and Mergansers having Many of these latters offered for Sale [— — — —]

This Morning the Market was well Stocked with Green Backed Swallows *Hiroundo Veridis,* the Whole very fat and in beautifull plumage; if these Dear Litle Cherubs have preferred their coats and these flesh so fresh during the pretended Torpor Occasioned by Winter' frost how much more fortunate they are than the Pork Beef & Butter of Kentucky that sowers however well Salted.

but I have been assured by Men on whom I can rely that some Winters are so Mild that Swallows are seen from time to time during every Months—

the Swallows in Markets Were caught in the holes about houses their resorting places during the Nights—this Morning the Weather is Quite Cold, and yet the Swallows are flying about the Street, over the River &c twitering very Lively—

Sunday 25th February 1821 Killed Some Green backed White bellied Swallows *Hirondo Veridis*—extremely fat, the Gizards completely filled with the remains of Wingd Insects—could not perceive any outward diference between the sexes, the femelles however were well Stored With eggs and the Males strongly marked—the Brother of Mr Pamar Killed a Beautifull White Robin, but his Dog Mangled it so much that I did not draw it—this extraordinary change of Color appeared as the Cause of old age, the Bill of the Bird much worn and the Legs were cicatrised in Several parts, the Bird however was very fat as well as Nearly all the others he killed this Day—

Saw a few Partridges these Birds are here much Sought and hunted down without Mercy, not even do the Sportsmen permit a few Paires to remain untouch & thereby the race in nearly extinguished Near the City—We Waded to day through an extensive Swamp with hopes of Meeting Some New Species, but Saw Nothing of the Kind to my astounishment—

March Saturday 10th 1821 Sent My Letter to My Lucy, Victor; Wam Bakewell & N. Berthoud by the steam Boat Car of Commerce—

Saw in Market this Morning some *Ampellis Americana* Vast Number of *Common Snipes* but the Robbins have nearly disapeared and are not even to be seen in the Woods—Was assured to Day that the *Baltimore Oriole* Wintered on the Island of *Cuba* and that the south west side of this island was the resort of Millions of Swallows during November, December & January; So strongly was this afirmed that it has determined me to go there Next Winter and to the bay of hondurass, where it is said they also are plenty during these Months Only—

Recd this Morning a Letter from My Beloved Wife dated Shippingport written a few days previous to the one I re*d* by the S. B. James Ross—

This Evening Cap*n* Cummings saw a Night Hawk or a *Chuck Will's Widow* flying about the Street Near our Lodgings—I presume it was the Latter Bird having been assured that in the first days of April they are seen in numbers at the Bay of St. Louis—

Sunday March 11th 1821 Walkd out this Morning with Joseph to try my Souvenir Gun and found it an excellent One. Shot Many Green Backed Swallows on the Wing—Some red Wing Starlings, Savannah Finches, one fish Crow, & c—but Nothing New Yet in the Woods, which unfortunately are Now very deep with Watter, the River being about 4 or 5 feet higher than the ground behind the *Levee*—

During a Walk this afternoon a Beautifull Mississipi Kite sailed by me, unfortunately I had no Gun.

Near our House a Mocking Bird regularly resorts to the South Angle of a Chimney top and salutes us with Sweetest Notes from the rising of the Moon untill about Midnight, and every Morning from about 8 o'clock untill 11, when it flys to the Convent Garden to feed—I have remarked that Bird allways in the Same Spot and Same Position, and have been particularly pleased at hearing him [try to] Imitate the Watchman's Cry of *All's Well* that Issues from the fort about 3 Squares Distant, and so well, has he sometimes performed that I Would have been mistaken if he had not repeated too often in the Space of a 10 minutes

March 15th Thursday 1821 Wrote to My Beloved Wife and Mr Rob Best Last Night—Saw Many *Chuck Will's Widow* flying about the streets and some *Night Hawks*

I Made a Likeness to day for a Lady's Sadle a thing I had not the Leass use for, but the Man I had Made a portrait for, Wanted his Wife's Very

Much and Could not Spare Money, and Not to disapoint him I sufered Myself to be Sadled—

While at Dinner We were all surprised at the astounishing Leaps that Some *Maggots* took about our Table.

they Issued out of a Very good piece of Cheese to perform this I remarked them drawing up their heads toward the Tail untill Nearly runing both half of the Body Parell and The Suddenly striking one of the ends Could Not see Which they through themselves about 50 or 60 Times their Length some time One Way sometimes another apparently in Search of the Cheese—

MARCH 16TH FRIDAY 1821 I had the pleasure of receiving a Letter this Morning from Mr. A. P. Bodley dated Natchez 8th Inst Informing me of my Port Folio having been found and Deposited at the office of the *Mississippi Republican* and that I could have it by writing—

I Acknowledge with a very sensible pleasure the Kindness of Mr. P. who worked his Passage down in Mr Aumack Boats—and at the same time cannot Conceive how the Book had escaped the researches of Mr Garnier—

Mr Gordon had the goodness to write to a friend to have it forwarded imediately and pay whatever charges there might be, the Politeness of that Gentleman is remarkable to a Man who is no more than a Stranger to him, but No doubt it would be impossible for a Good heart to act otherwise—

I took a Walk with my Gun this afternoon to see the Passage of Millions of *Golden Plovers* Coming from the North Est and going Nearly South—the distruction of these innocent fugitives from a Winter Storm above us was really astonishing—the Sportsmen are here more numerous and at the same time more expert at shooting on the Wing than any where in the U. States [and] on the first sight of these birds Early this Morning assembled in Parties of from 20 to 100 at Diferent places where they Knew by experience they told me the birds pass and arranged themselves at equal distances squatted on their hams, as a flock Came Near every man Called in a Masterly astonishing Manner, the Birds Imediately Lowered and Wheeled and coming about 40 or 50 yards run the Gantlet every Gun goes off in Rotation, and so well aimed that I saw several times a flock of 100 or More Plovers destroyed at the exception of 5 or 6—the Dogs after each Voleys While the Shooters charged their Pieces brought the Same to each Individuals—this continued all day, When I Left One of those Lines of Sharp Shooters then the

Sun Setting, they appeared as Intent on Killing More as when I arrived at the spot at 4 o'clock—

a Man Near [me] where I was seated had Killed 63 dozens—from the firing before & behind us I would suppose that 400 Gunners where out. Supposing each Man to have Killed 30 Dozen that day 144,000 must have been destroyed—On Enquiring if these Passages where frequent I was told that Six Years ago there was about such an Instance, imediatly after 2 or 3 days of Very Warm Weather a blow from the Northeast brought them, Which Was Nearly the Same to day—some few Were fat but the Greatest Number Lean, and all that I opened showed no food —the femelles Eggs extremely small

Saturday 17th March 1821 This Morning the Market Was plentifully suplied with Golden Plovers and *Pures*—I also saw a White Crane. Spent the day Walking about at the exception of an hour Drawing at a Likeness—

Sunday March 18th 1821 This Morning I was Witness and in some measure contributed to the presserving of a Tara of a new Kind at Least to Me.—Walking along the Levee to Mr Pamar Where I had an Appointment for a Likeness. I Was Invited to breakfast by Mr A. Liautaud—I Walked in and Met a Large Party, Well engaged round an old Gentleman at Pleasing him by the most extravagant round of praises—I understood the Caracter was rather Moony, and very gay When well managed, productive of Much Mirth to his hearers—During the Breakfast that Certainly Was a good one & on Which One *Prince Guest* touched heavily, We were several times struck by unexpected Voleys of Verses, composed for the Occasion, and that could not Indeed have had a better Effect that that produced—Every One enjoyed himself Very Much, particularly the Compositors who were highly Clapped, sometimes to be sure to put an end to his Loquacity.

Breakfast over I was told to remain and see the best part. Mr Liautaud the Learned Guest Was about being recd a *Mason* and My being a Brother entitled me at once to a seat—this was conducted in the most Ludicrous Manner any one can conceive, and I really pitied the Newly Initiated When all Ceremonies Were over the Man Was Burned in several parts, baptised in a Large Bucket of Watter, Tossed in a Blanket, and Make to Crawl Over about 50 Casks of Wine, on his belly and Knees, and When at Last given up for want of Invention, the Poor Devils Who had being praying for Mercy during all this was Left in the Necessary—

To this Man this Might be done perhaps again, but few could bear such treatment and I expected several times that his Cries or a Change of sensation from Cowardice to Courage would shew a very diferent scene but all however was Ended as Intended and the poor fellow took it for Granted that he [was] really Was a Mason—

I left and Made Mr Doucillier, Guesnore Likeness—

We purchased this Morning in Market a Beautifull *Blue Crane* the choice of 5 that were nearly alike—those I was told were come earlier than usual. Are extremely dificult of access

I Drew it and its coresponding so well with A. Willson Description stop*d* me from writing it Myself—

Total Length 30½ Inches
to end of tail 23½ "
Breadth 39¼ "
Tail Feathers 12 "
Weight 10 Onces—Midle Claw Serrate inwardly The Cotony Substance on the Breast followed the Breast Bones only—and reapeared on each side of the rump—I was assured it was beautifull Male—

WEDNESDAY MARCH 21ST 1821 In reading the Papers this morning at Mr Pamar, I saw the Treaty between Spain and our Country.

the 4th Article Speaking of an expedition to run the Line of Division formed by both Parties and to leave Natchitoches during the Course of this Year; I imediatly went to Mr Gordon to know from him What steps Would be necessary to procure an Appointment as Draftsman for this So Long Wished for Journey—he advised me to see Mr Hawkins Who would introduce me to Governor Robinson—

I saw Mr Hawkins who very politly promised to See the Governor and Mention to him my Wishes and to Call at his office on the 23d

to Join in Such an enterprise and to leave all I am attachd to, perhaps for ever, produced Many diferent sensations & thought, but all are Counterbalanced When persuaded as I am that My Labours [will all be of use to them] are all for their use & benefit.

I did not wait late on the 23d but My Spirits were sadly dampened when Mr Hawkins told Me that it was the Governor's opinion that nothing more [than common] would be done than to run the Line in question and that none but the surveyors would be Necessary;

Disapointed but not less anxious to try further I Calld on Mr Gordon, he Joined me in the Idea of My Adressing the President Directly and that he could Not think that a Journey so Interesting Would be performd only to say that Men had gone & Come back—in leaving this truly Kind Gentleman, I Met Mr Grayson of Louisville spoke to him to my thoughts and Wishes.

"I Can render a Service I believe Mr A and I Will do it. I will give you some Letters to diferent Members of Congress With whom I am Well acquainted and that will be glad to Meet Your Views, but Write to the President—

This sounded better to my Ears—

full of My plans I went home & Wrote to N Berthoud to request his Imediate Assistance—Walkd out in the afternoon seeing Nothing but hundreds of New Birds, in Imagination and supposed Myself often on the Journey—

on the 24th I called again on Mr Hawkins. Mr Gordon had spoke of me to him and the former again to the Governor, I spoke of adressing the President, he acquiestd and promissed to give a Letter for the same and procure one from the Governor—

going through the Street Not unlike I dare say a Wild Man thinking too much to think at all My Eyes Were attracted by a handsome faced Man. I Knew him it was My Old Acquaintance & friend George Croghan. We Met freely and I was eased. he Knew what I was going to say having dined the day previous at the Governor's with Mr Hawkins. he said he had spoke of Me but Would do more and promised to find Some Letters to Mr Hawkins for my use, and Invited Me with such forcible Kindness to go and spend Some time at his Plantation that I Accepted his offer—see me again Walking fast and Looking Wild, but recollecting the high price of time I hunted Mr D^{d} Prentice, and asked him if he would form a letter for Me—he answered Yes but told Me that I would do better by writing Myself and that he would freely give his advice and help if Needed—I Was then reduced to My poor thoughts to Express My Wishes—[but] Anxious, and Determined to leave no power of Mine untried, I sat to the Paper & Wrote in as Great a Hurry as I am Now doing, a Letter, that Mr Prentice to My utmost astonishment pronounced *all suficient*—he spoke much about the Journey and anticipated he said the pleasure of reading My Journal on My return—feeling a great Weight off My Shoulders I returned to My Room, took Gun Ammunition & Joseph & to the Woods Went in Search of New Species—

My Life has been strewed with Many thorns but could I see Myself & the fruits of my Labour safe, with My Beloved familly *all Well* on a return from Such an expedition, how gratefull Would I feel to My Country and [Thank]full of the Greatness of My Author—

In Market this Morning I saw Three of What Willson *Calls Bar-*

trams's Snipes, they Where very fat—are called here *Papacots*—Saw a Beautifull White Crane but without legs—Vast Many Green Wing[d] & blue winged Teals—hundreds of Snipes, *pures*, Solitary Snipes—Green back[d] Swallows—but robbins have disapeared—

The Migration of Birds does Not go a pace with the Vegetable Kingdom in this Part of America When, The Trees are as much in Leaves in Pensylvania, or Ohio, or Kentucky or even the upper Part of Tennessee [Birds] (*and this is about the Midle of May*) Birds back to the 25 of April have reach[d] these Parts and are preparing to answer the Calls of Nature—

to My Astonishment, the Many Species of Warblers, Thrushes &[c] that Were numerous during the Winter have all Moved on Eastwardly and None of the Species that resort this Part have yet reach[d] at the exception of Swallows and a Few Watter Birds—

this Would tempt me to believe that Most of Our Migratory Birds Leave their Winter resort [When Influenced by their Natural habits] with such Certainty [in the Weather] of Knowledge about the Weather and Such Swiftness of Movement over the Country as does not give us even the opportunity of remarking their Passage and the greater number [all] at once at the time appointed by the Strength of Passion—

Sunday 25th March 1821 Bought a beautifull Specimen of the *Great White Heron* [grus Americana] in perfect order it had been sent me by a hunter with Whom I had formed acquaintance a few days ago —Worked on it the Whole day and found it the most dificult to Imitate of any bird I have yet undertaken—Took a Walk in the afternoon and heard the Voice of a Warbler new to Me, but could Not reach it—

Monday 26th Walked early this Morning in search of Plants to form the back ground of My Drawing—Left Joseph out who Killed a beautifull, *Blue Yellow back Warbler Male Sylvia Pusilla*. I had seen some in the Swamp but the litle fellows where so Nimble and brisk that they had all escaped Me—Worked Nearly all Day Not having time to go and Purchase some articles I wanted to send My Lucy—

Saw M[r] Gordon, who on reading My adress to the President Tura told Me he would Make some Alternation to its form—I left it with him—

Tuesday 27th March 1821 Drawing at My Heron yet, it Smelt so dreadfully bad that When I opened it I could only take time to See *how plainly it proved a Male*—the Cottony Substance Was round the breast bone, on each Side of the Vent and on each Side the romp—the Midle Claws very pectinated

I Drew to Day Male & femelle of the *Blue Yellow back Warbler Sylvia Pusilla*—and in a Short Walk taken this Evening saw perhaps thousands of the same Species Killed several all alike in their sexes—

forwarded My Beloved Lucy pr Mr Prentice who left at 12 o'clock in the James Ross a piece of Linen, some Stockings, a piece of goods for our Boys and the Woman's Sadle I was almost forced to take some time since—

Gave Mr Forettale who also went in the same boat an order to get My Port Folio at Natchez and begged of him to forward it to Mr Gordon—

Saturday March 31st 1821 I spent my time these 3 Last Days More at thinking than any thing else—and often indeed have I thought My Head very heavy—

This Morning I Waited on Mr Gordon with a Wish to receive from him an amendment to my Letter to the President, for all in my head is the Pacific Expedition he Wrote, I read it, but was Not altogether Satisfied—I Called on Mr Vanderlyn the Historical Painter With my Port Folio—to shew him some of my Birds with a View to Ask him for a few Lines of recommandation—he examined them attentively and *Called* them *handsomely* done, but being *far* from possessing any Knowledge of Ornithology or Natural History, I was quite satisfied *he* Was No Judge but of their being better or Worst *Shaded* Yet he spoke of the beautifull Coloring and Good Positions and told Me that he would With pleasure give me a Certificate of his having *Inspected* them—Are all Men of Talents fools and Rude purposely or Naturally? I cannot assert, but have often thought that they were one or the other.

When I arrived at M^r^ V's Room, he spoke to me as if I had been an abject slave, and told Me in Walking Away to Lay my Drawings down *there the Dirty* [—] that he would return *presently* and Look them over.—I felt so vexed that My first Intention Was to *Pack* off, but the Expedition Was in View, I thought how Long Kempbell the Actor Waitted Once at the theatre in England, and stood patiently *although* not Laying My Drawing *Down there*

About 30 Minutes Elapsed, he returned with an officer and with an air More becoming a Man Who *Once Was Much* in My situation ask me in his private room. Yet I could plainly see in his Eye that selfish Confidence that allways destroy in some degree the Greatest Man's Worth.

the Swet ran down My face as I hastily open^d^ My Drawings and Laid them on the floor; I Look^d^ up to him. he Was looking at them, the officer's *By God* that's handsome, struck my eyars Vanderlyn took up a

Bird Look[d] at it closely put it down and said they Were *handsomely done.*

I breathed, Not because I thought him a Man of the Most Superior Talents, for to come to such a pitch one Must have no faults, and I With My Eyes *half Closed* (as you know the pretended Juges of our Day Look at Painting [Look]) saw a great Deffect in One of his figures of Women (the deffect that had being Corrected by the Lady I drew Lately.) but because this Gentleman had *some Talents,* that he Was Look[d] on as a Very Excellent Judge and that I had been Told that a few Words from him Might be serviceable—of My Likeness he spoke very diferently, the one I had Was fair, hard, and Without Effect, although he Acknowledged it Must have been a Strong one—

he sat, he Wrote, and I, thinking More of Journeying to the Pacific Ocean, than of Likenesses, Cared Not [Not] a *Pecayon* about these Later Observations—

as I Was Walking away from his house corner of S[t] Louis and Royal Streets—the *Corner of Events* the officer who had followed me, ask[d] me, the price of My *Black Chalk* Likeness and where I resided—all answered; I thought how Strange it was that a poor Devil Like me Could Steal the Custom of the Great Vanderlein—but fortune if not *blind* certainly Most have his Lunatic Moments—the officer said he would Call on Me Liking My Style Very Much—

M[r] Hawkings saw this afternoon some of My Drawings and I gave him My Letter to the President. he was apparently Much pleased With both—and told me he Would do all in his Power for Me—

I Put My Letters to My Beloved Wife—N. Berthoud & Judge Fowles in the [Office] Mail that Leaves every Sunday at 8 o'clock, and return[d] to our Lodging with a compound of Ideas Not Easily to be described—

I had Shot during a Short Walk I took Yesterday afternoon a *White Eyed fly Catcher* that the Rats having eat Last Night I could Not of course draw to day—Joseph to day [Drew] Shot a *Tyrant* Fly *Catcher* and a *Yellow belied Wood Pecker*

The Politeness of M[r] Vanderlyn Will be remembered—a long time by me; and When ever I Look over these Scrawls it will do me good to have a Litle of the same feelings—the following is the Copy of the Lines he handed me—

M[r] John J. Audubon has shewed me several Specimens of his Drawings in Natural History—such as Birds, with their Natural Colors, & other Drawings in plain Black & White Which Appear to be done With great [accuracy] truth & Accuracy of representation as much so as any I have seen in any Country—the Above Gentleman wishes Me to give this as My Opinion in Writting believing it may Serve as a recommendation to his being employed as a Draftsman in any Expedition to the interiors of our Country.

J. Vanderlyn

NEW ORLEANS 20th March 1821

APRIL 5TH 1821 I have just now recovered My Lost Port Folio Mr Garnier sent it me a fortnight ago to the Care of his son the trouble this gave me I will mention hereafter—I have to thank Mr Garnier but More *he* that found it on the River Bank and took Such very remarkable good Care of it—for on opening it I found the Contents in as good order as the day it Was Lost and *Only* One Plate Missing—

Blue Yellow Back Warblers

Orchard Orioles
Cardinal Grosbeaks
Yellow Eyed Cuckoos
Large Crested Fly Catchers
White Eyed — " — "
Night Hawks at Dawn of Day Plenty
Turkey Buzards
Carrion Crows
Common Gulls
Carolina Wrens by Vast Number
Partridges a few Very Shy
to see these in hunt of others I Was out since half past 2 o'clock this Morning untill 4 this afternoon Wading often to our Midles through the Swamps and then Walking through the Thickest Woods I believe I had yet seen—

Cape Cummings Left us on the 10th for Philadelphia the Poor Man had Not *One Cent* with him—saw Mr Hoyteura who arrived in the Columbus—Recd by that Vessel Letters from Lucy William Bakewell, Charles Briggs, N. Berthoud—Car of Commerce brought another from My Wife and one from Mr Mataleon the great flute player—answered

PAINTED BUNTING

Although these Birds are taken now and quite tamed in a few days, so much so as to sing as if at Large, when Caught Next Month they Die in a few hours, and shew dejection from the Instant they are caged—they are fond of Nesting in Live Oaks, Wild plum trees, Briars, Orange

Groves—when domesticated are fed on Rice—*Breed Twice*—femelle opened on the 15 April had Eggs the size of N° 5 Shot—

I had from reliable source that One Made his Escape from a Cage and returned Thirty odd Days after to the house, went to the Cage, and remained Many Years—a femelle Was seen in Cage to carry and Arrange the Material given her to form a Nest and Compleated it—but Never Laid—

Saw Some Young Mocking Birds in Market this Morning able to fly—these Birds are said by People here to breed as often as 4 Times during one season—I also was told that Young Ones sufered to be approach[d] by the Parents after a separation of Several days are often Poisonned by them, this *unatural* conduct demands [more] *Self* Confirmation—

Monday April 16th 1821 having received a Visit from D[r] heermann and Lady While hunting Last Saturday, I called on him at his House, he wished I would give a few Lessons of Drawing to M[rs] H—I acquiested and am to begin tomorow;—Joseph Hunting nearly all day Killed a Red Headed Wood Pecker, a Red bellied one—[Baltimore] Orchard Orioles, Black headed Titmouse—Green Painted Buntings—drew one With a blue head—Joseph Saw a *Yellow Breasted Chat* and some Baltimore Orioles—

Spent part of the Day with M[r] Hoyteura & *Young Towns* of Henderson on Board—

Was sorry as well as Surprised Not to have a Word by the S.B[t] Manattan from My Beloved Lucy—

Thursday 19th—April 1821 Low in funds again Left home with my *Port Folio* My *My Best friends* as to Introduction and travelled as far as D[rs] *Hunter* the renowned *Man* of Jefferson—We Came on him rather *unaware* the good Man Was P X X X g We Waited and I gave him My Letter of D[d] *Prentice*—

This *Phisician* May have been a Great *Doctor formerly* but Now deprived of all that I Call Mind I found it *Necessary* to leave to his Mill's Drudgery—

Called on a New Phenomena in Painting M[r] *Earl* I believe & there Saw M[r] *Earl Jackson*—*Great God* forgive Me if My Jugment is Erroneous—I Never Saw A Worst painted Sign *in the Street of Paris*—

April Sunday 22d 1821 Rec[d] Yesterday a letter from My Beloved Lucy, answered it Last Night and this Morning Wrote to N. Berthoud

& W[an] Bakewell sent Home One Box & 1 One Bag the Whole by the Steam Boat Car *of Commerce* that Left at 9 o'clock P.M.

Dinned at M[r] Pamar as I usually do on Sundays. My Pupils all religiously inclined did not give them Lessons—the great Ease and of Course Comfort that I find in the Company of M[rs] Pamar's familly renders my visits at that house quite what I wish and often need for a relief of exersions—Finished to day a Drawing of a *Snowy Heron Ardea Candidissima* a beautifull Male—Joseph Drawing Flowers all day—

MONDAY 23[D] found in Market a Gallinule that differs much from What I call the *Purple* one—the Yellow Legs & feet, their Stoutness—the Blue baby Top—& all Coloring—the hunters assured me they Never saw *One* with red Legs—but I cannot depend on their Memory—We also found another Male of Blue Grosbeak *Loxia Purpurea*—

Saw My Old Acquaintance John Gwathway of Louisville, he was *a la guettée* on the Levée the appearance of My Clothes, did Not please him we talk but Litle together.

TUESDAY APRIL 24[D] *1821* Much in want of Cash Walked to the Columbus Steam Boat and Made *Baxter Town's* Portrait for 25$—gave My Likeness and Drew the *Black Poll* Warbler Male—*Sylvia Striata,* pleased with my days Work, rec[d] a letter from My Son Victor.—Much pleased also at his improved hand write—

WEDNESDAY 25— Went again on board Columbus rec[d] My Pay from Towns—Made M[r] Hall's *Portrait* one of the best I believe I ever have taken—Met Gwathway & Thompson from Louisville—Dined at M[r] Pamar had a great Wish to see General Jackson but no time to spare yet —Paid our Board Rent & Washing to day—15$ for the 2 first Items and 5 for the Latter—raining hard—M[r] Hoyteura still in the Columbus—HIS THOUGHTS—

I am forced here to Complain of the bad figure that My friend Willson has given of the Warbler I drew yesterday, in the Bill only the length exceed that of Nature $\frac{1}{8}$ of an Inch—an enormous diference—and he has runned a broad White line round over the Eye that does not exist—

APRIL FRIDAY 27TH *1821* Walked on Board of the Columbus at 6 o'clock this Morning. Made John De Hart's Portrait M[r] Hoyteura came a litle before breakfast, had been absent all Night. Much taken by the other passengers

General Jackson Left the City about Twelve I saw him *thrice* found Vanderlyn's Likeness the Only good One I have seen, *Tully's* Plate *Miserable*—John De Hart's Likeness being Intended for Mrs Hall took it there. Spent a few Hours with her extremely agreably—Wrote to Charles Briggs—

Saturday 28th 1821 Rose early and went on Board the Heda to take Mr Bossien Portrait. Made it good Young *Guesnore* and Hetchberger the Painter spent the Evening with Me, Joseph Sick Wrote to My Beloved Lucy

Sunday 29th 1821 Rose purposely to go and collect some Money to forward home, received 105$ sent 100 in a U. S. Note N° 152 Mark A dated Philad^{a} April 5th 1817, payable at N. O. to B. Morgan's order—I gave it to John De Hart in an open^{d} Letter to remit to My Wife—Columbus left at 12 o'clock—Dined at Hetchberger Made his Lady's Likeness—coming home Walked in *Painter of Feathers'* room, very Civil, asked for My Card—Hoyteura p^{d} me a Short Visit Joseph better

Monday April 30th 1821 Steam Boat Paragon arrived No Letter for me—Mr Gordon had one from Mr Berthoud—sadly disapointed almost sicken, could not do any thing—

May 1st Tuesday 1821 Walked some, Wrote to My Wife but the boat I Intended for, not going—extremely uneasy about My Wife's health or her Children—done Nothing—

May 2 Wednesday— Wrote again to Lucy give the Letter to Baxter Towns [Give Lesson to] drew a Long Legged Plover—Contents Shrimpes & Insects and at the Diference of Size only found it nearly coresponding to Bewick's description—it was a Male I received it from Mr Duval the Miniature Painter who assured Me that he had Killed 6 or 7 he leaves here, all alike no diference whatever in the size or Coloring—they are often seen on Lake *Borgne* during the Summer Months—Was pleased with the Position in my drawing—

Thursday 3^{d} Bought 15 y^{ds} Nankeen for Summer Clothes—found M^{rs} H more aimiable if Possible than usual, talked freely to Me—became acquainted With an other Sister—Work^{d} at Mrs Hechburgers Portrait—

Weather fine Monday Morning Very Disagreably Hot—Thermoter, at 88–89—and to day at 3 o'clock in the Shade at 90—

Cases of Yellow fever in the City I was told—

May Sunday 1821 Rec^{d} a Letter by the Cincinnati from My Wife. Not Very agreable to My feelings, surprised at having Nothing from N. Berthoud—appraised *Joseph* of his Father's Death. Bore it well—Saw Mr Jesse Embrie of the Cincinnati Museum = Spent all day very Dull dined at *Hetchberger*

Monday —Counfounded Hot—Young *Guesnore* afronted and Ceased Speaking to me—

Tuesday 7th Wrote to My Wife but did not Close my Letter—Mr Hoyteura paid us a Short Visit—Much esasperated against Mr Gordon —Mr Gordon sent to England for Me for 10^{lb} *Italian Chalk,* 6 doz Black Lead Pencils, 2 Grosses Pastels—but did Not advance the Money—

Wednesday 8th finished My Letter to My Lucy and Wrote a Short One to N. Berthoud—put them on Board the Fayette, the Rose, the one I expected to Leave first Not being ready—*thought* to day that a Certain Gentleman to Whom I go to dayly felt *uncomfortable* While I was present, seldom before My coming to New Orleans did I think that I was Looked on so favorably by the *fair* sex as I have *Discovered* Lately—

Saw Hoyteura at Mr Hawkins in a High State of Spirits I dare not Call it Intoxication—he sailed this Evening for Liverpool—paid a Visit to the Amiable Vanderlyn, this Gentleman Like all substantial Men gained on acquaintance saw his Portrait of My Fair Pupil M^{rs} H—the Likeness good but roughly painted—he complimented me on My Drawings I thought too Much to be true—saw Gilly about settling for our Passage to Missingsat should I determine on going there—

Wrote to My Wife, N. Berthoud, Henry Clay, D^{l} Drake, on the 16th forwarded all by S.B.^{t} Paragon—

Dined at Governor Robertson, Polite reception, promessed Me a recommendatory letter to Mr Monroe

No news from Mr Berthoud yet.—

17th May 1821

begun lessons with Young Mr Bollin @ 1.50 per Lesson
" " " Miss Perry 2.00 " "
" " " Miss Dimitry 2.00 " "

New Orleans May 20th 1821 Sent a few lines to My Wife by the S.B.[t] Tamerlane—Last Week I Rec[d] a letter from M[r] J. Hawkins and one from M[r] Robertson the Governor for the President of the U. States—favors from Men of High Stations are favors indeed—

The Governor a Man of Strong Information extremely Polite—

Since So long without any news from my familly, My Spirits have failed me, and it is With Dificulty that I sit to Write at all—My Journal Suffers through the same Cause that affects me—attention—

June 16th New Orleans—1821 Left this City at about ½ past 12 o'clock—in the Steam Boat Columbus Cap[e] John de Hart—bound to Shippingport Kentucky—

pressed by much work on hand within some weeks passed, during every day, and too much incommodated by Musquitoes at evenings My poor Journal as been put a side [but] events and a wish not to discontinue to put down incidents that are of some Note and agreable to My Mind I come again to it—

a personnage who had some week ago boasted of his Interest towards me, and who on one occasion carried his attention quite too far and awkwardly must first take my attention—and here I will [take the Liberty] give you a Lesson, should you ever be Employed as a Teacher to any ostantatious oppolent person—*flatter,* Keep flattering and end in flattery or else expect No pay—

My Misfortunes often occur through a want of attention to that Maxim in similar Cases after having with assiduity attended on a Gentleman's Lady (Whose Name I will not at present Mention) for forty Days, I received the rudest of dismisal and My pride would not admit me to the House—to even ask any compensation—how agreable the first Lessons were I shall allways remember. *She thought* herself endowed with superior talents, and her Looking glass pleasing her Vanity I dare say made her believe She was a Star dropped from the heavens to ornament this Hearth—but dificulties augmented and of Course drawing seased to please, I could not well find time to finish every piece that I had began for her, and Constancy the Lady said was [not belonging] never to be found the Companion of Genius—toward the Last she Would be unwell when I walk[d] in, Yawn[d] and postponed to the morrow—I believe the Husband saw her Weakness, but the good Man Like *one* or *Two* More of My Acquaintances Was Weaker still—

I Knew well that My conduct had been correct and I felt a great pleasure in Leaving them, and, the One hundred Dollars I had hearned *with them*

The *Dimitry* familly on Whose's Daughters I had the pleasure of *at-*

tending as a Drawing Master—had become peculiarly agreable and I left them with anxiety for their wellfare and the pleasure that anticipation produces, having some Hopes of seeing them Next Winter,—Young Dimitry I never will forget a Youth of More genuine Natural Ability I never have Met—his sarcastism had much the turn of Dr Walcot's I Rec^d^ from the Young Ladies Miss Aimee & Euphrosine Two handsome Plants for My Beloved Lucy that I forward^d^ under the Care of Cap^e^ De Hart—

My True friend R. Pamar and his most amiable and Kind Wife I have to thank for all that I can Call the pleasures I felt Wilss at New Orleans—I Eat there whenever I could find time, and I was so Loved by the Children that I felt as if I parted from Mine when I left them—I had found^d^ a very slight acquaintance with Mr P. some years ago as he descended the Ohio on his way home—I had [he said] been Polite to him when he called at My Poor Log House at Henderson and he said often that Kindness had not been profuted to him that he was Well able to remember the Instances and that if I did Not please to Make free with his house he Would be Sorry for it—

I Rec^d^ Many Attentions from Mr Laville and Lady—Mr Hollander the Partner of My old but too rich Acquaintance Vincent Notte I had the pleasure of seing—he I believe saw that I had No wish to disgrace the Handsome Rich furniture of the Wealthy with My Intrusions when reduced to My Grey Breeches, and taking Me by both Hands One day as I was trying to Make Way from him, he said My Dear Mr Audubon Come and see me. I promise you I shall Not have any one at table and I will try to Raise your Spirits. I have some fine Paintings, and please bring Your Birds that I am Anxious to see—then You see that although I lived extremely retired and general show^d^ those that I thought I Would Incomodate I now & then stumbled on an Less Indiferent Member of this Life toward his fellows Who like Me have been rich and poor alternatly—

I had attended a Miss Perrie to Enhance her Natural tallen for Drawing, for some days When her Mother Whom I intend Noticing in due time, asked Me to Think about My Spending the summer and fall at their farm Near Bayou Sarah; I Was glad of such an overture, but would have greatly prefered her Living in the Floridas—We Concluded the Bargain promissing Me 60 Dollars per Month for One half of My time to teach Miss Eliza all I could in Drawing Music Dancing &^c^ &^c^ [and the] furnishing us with a Room &^c^ for Joseph & Myself—so that after the One hundred Diferent Plans I had form^d^ as Opposite as Could be to this, I found Myself bound for several Months on a Farm in Louisiana.

We left our abode in Quartier Street and Old Miss Louise without the Least regret, the filthiness of her Manners, did not agree with our feeling; and by this time We had fully discovered that a Clean Sweet HouseKeeper is quite Necessary to a Naturalist—

Our Good Spanish Neighbour Mr Taek We Loved, His Nieces sung Well, and his own Jokes now and then amusing us—

We Came to our Landing at the Mouth of Bayou Sarah of a hot sultry day without any accidents; bid farewell to Mr Gordon and after Mounting the Hill at St Francis Ville Rested ourselves some Moments at a Mr Semple dinner Was set, but Not My Heart for it. I wished Myself on Board the Columbus, I Wished for My Beloved Lucy, My Dear Boys—I felt that I would be Awkward at table and a good opportunity having offered to go to Mr Perrie place, We Walked slowly on, guided by some of their servants dispatch^{d} with the News of our Coming and some Light Baggage—

the Aspect of the Country entirely New to us distracted My Mind from those objects that are the occupation of My Life—the Rich Magnolia covered with its Odoriferous Blossoms, the Holy, the Beech, the Tall Yellow Poplar, the Hilly ground, even the Red Clay I Looked at with amazement [and] such entire change in so Short a time appears often supernatural, and surrounded once More by thousands of Warblers & Thrushes, I enjoy^{d} Nature

My Eyes soon Met hovering over us the Long Wished for, Mississipi Kite and Swallow Tailed Hawk, but our Guns Were pack^{d} and We could only then anticipate the pleasure of procuring them shortly—the 5 Miles We Walked appear^{d} Short We Arrived and Met Mr Perrie at his House Anxious to Know him I Inspected his features by Lavaters directions,—*We Were received Kindly*—

JULY 4TH 1821 during the diferent excursions We have made through the Woods here, and from Report of Such persons as we thought proper to Lessen to on the subject, I have made the following remarks—Viz—

The Blue Jeay Corvus Cristatus is seen in Lower Louisiana during the summer, not having met with More than a dozen Individuals in All our rambles—last April Immense Numbers of these Birds, so annoyed the Corn rows in this Neighborhood as to force the planters to Poison them with Corn boiled with Arsenic which had a great Effect—Killed the Thiefs often instantly—

YELLOW BIRD FRINGILLA TRISTIS

Saw a very few during Last Winter Near N. Orleans None at present—Kite do not breed here—

Baltimore Oriole, Oriolus Baltimore

Not an Individual to be met with at any season—

Wood Thrush Turdus Melodus—

Extremely plenty, in its usual haunts, i.e. deep Shady Woods—the first bird that Sings at the dawn of day—Never Killed one Coresponding with Willson's figure—

Robin—Turdus Migratorius—

Resorts here during Winter in vast Numbers, and becomes very fat—the sport to all the Gunners—leaves early in March—

White Breasted Black CapD Nuthatch Sitta Carolinensis—

Scarce, have Killed a few, Nestle here—Young quite Grown Midle of June, first brood—

Sitta Varia Red bellied Nutatch—

Not found—

Gold WingD Wood Pecker—Picus Auratus—

Pentifull—

Black Throated Bunting, Emberiza Americana

Not an Individual Met With

Blue Bird Sylvia Sialis,

Scarce, about one pair to each Plantation—Yet Nesting in holes of Peach & Apple Trees—

Orchard Oriole, Oriolus Nutatus—

Very aboundant, this Country appears to be chosen by them I found seventeen Nests on Mr Perrie's Plantation With Eggs or Young, during Two days Looking for them—the Young of Many already flying about Midle June—first brood—Was deceived one day by one imitating the Cry of the Loggerhead Shrieke and followed it a great distance before I found My Mistake; it Keptd on the tops of high trees in the forest, a very unusual circumstance, the figure of Willson has the bill Much too Large & Long, the figure of the Egg is also too large

GREAT AMERICAN SHRIEKE, LANIUS EXUBITOR—
a few seen during Winter—

RUBY CROWNED WREN—SYLVIA CALENDULA
a few during Winter seen Near N. Orleans—

SHORE LARK ALAUDA APESTRIS—
None at any season—

PINE GROS BEAK—LOXIA ENUCLEATOR
None—

MARYLAND YELLOW THROAT. SYLVIA MARILANDICA
Great Numbers during the Winter, Leaves early in March

YELLOW BREASTED CHAT. PIPRA POLIGLOTTA
As many here as I have met in any other state—that is, One about each Plantation, Never have seen a femelle—

SUMMER RED BIRD, TANAGRA AESTIVA
Tolerably plenty—

INDIGO BUNTING, FRINGILLA CYANEA
Tolerably plenty Not so much as in Kentucky or Pennsylvania, but more so than in Ohio—

AMERICAN RED START, MUSCICAPA RUTICILLA
Very plenty, Young quite grown Midle of June

CEDAR BIRD AMPELLIS AMERICANA—
Was remarked this Spring feeding on the Holy berries and remained to reap the fruit of the Wild Cherries—in Immense flocks, extremely fat—disappeared at once—

RED BELLIED WOOD PECKER, PICUS CAROLINUS
pleantifull as any where else

YELLOW THROATED FLY CATCHER MUSCICAPA SYLVICOLA—
Never Met With—

PURPLE FINCH—FRINGILLA PURPUREA

a few during Winter seen Near N. Orleans—allways in litle flocks of 4 to 6—

BROWN CREEPER—CERTHIA FAMILIARIS—

Not seen—

HOUSE WREN—

Not seen—

BLACK CAP^D TITMOUSE, PARUS ATRICAPILLUS

Very plenty—Young quite grown Midle of June—

CRESTED TITMOUSE—PARUS BICOLOR

the same—

WINTER WREN—SYLVIA TROGLODITIS—

during Winter, Numerous in the Cypress swamps—

RED HEADED WOOD PECKER, PICUS ERYTHROCEPHALUS

plenty—Young quite Grown 15 June—

YELLOW BELLIED [BELLIED] WOOD PECKER—

a [few] during Winter

HAIRY WOOD PECKER—

Not seen—

DOWNY WOOD PECKER, P. PUBESCENS

Scarce,—

MOCKING BIRD—TURDUS POLYGLOTTUS

Extremely plenty—Nestles in all sorts of situations having found Nest in the higher parts of Tall trees in, Small Bushes and even between fence rails garded only by the rail imediately over the Nest—the Egg represented by Willson very Litle Like any of the great Number I examined —these Birds Mock indiscriminately every Note of Birds—are very gentle With every thing but the Bird of Prey, these they give chase to and follow a great distance with much apparent Courage—here during Winter—

HUMMING BIRD. TROCHILUS COLUBRIS—

Plentifull—Was assured of their existence of Two Species by Many—represented as Much Larger—have Not Met with any individual yet and fear it to be a Mistake—these Birds are easily Caught by pouring sweetened Wine in the Calices of flowers—they fall intoxicated.
Willson erroneously says that this sweet Bird does not sing—I have many times lissened to its Low toned Melody with great pleasure and can assure you that if its Voice was as sonorous as it is varried and Musical it would be considered as surpassed by few other Species—

TOWEE BUNTING—EMBERIZA ERYTHROPTHALMA

Saw a very few Near New Orleans during Winter Not One found at present—

CARDINAL GROS BEAK. LOXIA CARDINALIS

Extremely plenty—during the Whole season increasing still by vast Numbers that come from the Eastward to spend their Winter here, very depradatory to Corn Cribs—Young very Large 15 June, Second brood Hatching—

SCARLET TANAGER, TANAGRA RUBRA

Plentifull—but do not find them by any Means confined to the Interior of the forests, but to the contrary found on the bordering Tall trees of Plantations—

RICE BUNTING—EMBERIZA ORYZIVORA

passes early in spring from further Southern parts going eastwardly, remarked some Last february and March—

Red Eyed Fly Catchers, Sylvia Olivacea [Muscicapa] plentifull—Young quite grown early in June

MARSH WREN—CERTHIA PALUSTRIS

Never saw one Like Willson's drawing—but have Killed Many Individual of the Marking & Shape of My Drawings—some of them a few Miles Above New Orleans in April—but never imediatly Near Rivers—

GREAT CAROLINA WREN—CERTHIA CAROLINIANA—

[to be seen] almost constantly in sight or hearing about the field or the forest—young full grown now found of damp places—

YELLOW THROAT WARBLER—SYLVIA FLAVICOLLIS
Never Met With—

TYRANT FLY CATCHER, LANIUS TIRANNUS
plentifull—young full grown now—

GREAT GREASTED FLY CATCHER—MUSCICAPA CRINITA—
Very Common—young full grown, very Timorous & Shy—

SMALL GREEN CRESTED FLY CATCHER. MUSCICAPA QUERULA
Extremely plenty—found of the road sides from where it dashes at flies from Low Bushes—

PEWIT FLY CATCHER—MUSCICAPA NONCIALA—
Plentifull during winter Near N. Orleans, a few remains in the Hilly parts of Louisiana during summer—

WOOD PEWEE—MUSCICAPA RAPAX—
Plentifull in the Woods—this bird hunts latter than any of its Genus. I have heard it uttering its Note Long after Dark—

FERUGINOUS THRUSH. TURDUS RUFUS—
have a very few Individuals, that had more the appearance of Lost Strangers, than of happy residents, rarely seeing more than one at a time—

GOLDEN CROWN THRUSH. TURDUS AUROCAPILLA—
Not Met [Lower than] at all during summer many seen during the Winter Months—

CAT BIRD, TURDUS LIVIDUS
Not One seen Since Last March When one Evening I saw Many on the Canal row of Willows, the public Walk Near N. Orleans—

BAY BREASTED WARBLER—SYLVIA CASTANEA
None Seen—

CHESTNUT SIDED WARBLER. SYLVIA PENSYLVA[A]
None seen—

MOURNING WARBLERS. SYLVIA PHILADELPHIA—
Never Met with—

RED COCKADED W. PECKER. P. QUERULUS
have seen and Killed one Only, but it Lodged and I Lost it—Not seen Near plantations, unless the weather be very Cold—Mostly in Pine Woods—

BROWN HEADED NUTHATCH—SITTA PUSILLA—
Never seen—

PIGEON HAWK FALCO COLUMBARIUS—
Never Met with—

BLUE WING[D] YELLOW WARBLER SYLVIA SOLITARIA—
Not Met with here

BLUE EYED YELLOW WARBLER SYLVIA CITRINELLA—
So many of these about New Orleans early in March Nimbly hunting for insects amongst the willows—but could not find one in the month of May, having past I suppose Eastwardly where it is so common in all our orchards—

GOLDEN WINGED WARBLERS SYLVIA CHRYSOPTERA—
Not seen here, a plentiuss bird in the Lower parts of Kentucky—

BLACK THROATED BLUE WARBLER—SYLVIA CANADENSIS—
Never have seen these Birds since I left Pensylvania Very Numerous in the Lower part of that state in April and May—

AMERICAN SPARROW HAWK FALCO SPARVERIUS
very Common, Nestle allways in hole, mostly that of the Wood Peckers—Young quite grown, Midle of June here—

FIELD SPARROW FRINGILLA PUSILLA
Not here—

Not a single Species of Sparrow to be met with at this season—

YELLOW RUMP WARBLER SYLVIA CORONATA—
remains here during the whole winter, in aboundance—saw them every day every where there was a Tree even in the City of N. Orleans—in May Not one to be found—

MARYLAND YELLOW THROAT—SYLVIA MARILANDICA
plenty during Winter, and very Gentle—

BLUE SMALL GREY FLY CATCHER MUSCICAPA COERULEA—
plenty during summer Nestles in Willows, Keeps in Small parties of 6 or 7—has much the manner of the Long Tailed Titmouse of Europe—

WHITE EYED FLY CATCHER—MUSCICAPA CANTATRIX—
the Commonest of all the Birds in our Woods—the young of which Two brood are raised in the season full grown [grown] Midle of July—

Saw 3 Red Ibisses pass over the plantation Yesterday—

CHUCK-WILL'S WIDOW
CAPRIMULGUS CAROLINENSIS FEMELLE

Yesterday the 25TH of July 1821 an Indian of the Choctaw Nation, who habitually hunts for Mr Perrie—brought me a femelle of the Chuck Will's Widow in full and handsome plumage. it Measured One foot in length, 25 Inches in breadth, the tail composed of Ten Feathers is rounded, but has not the White in any degree that Willson Mentions on the inner vanes of the 2 exterior feathers—the Craw of this was filled with the heads of Many of that Kind of bugs commonly called *pinching* Bugs, One of them a very Curious Large One Armed with Two equal paires of Pincers—

these Birds generally aboundant in this part of Louisiana, and at present very scarce, Not having been able to Meet one in any of our Excursions that often are of Twenty Miles—a few Weeks previous to our arrival they where heard from all parts of the adjacent Woods loud during the day—a few have been seen and a few heard since, all of which have eluded My [attempts at seeing and killing then] pursuits—they remain here untill Late in September. I suppose them at this time so occupied in search of food for their young that it has put an end to their Crying—Many of the Planters think that this bird has the Power and Judment of removing its eggs when discovered sometimes several hundred yards—these are usually laid on the bare earth under a Small bush or by the side of a Log—

Saw 3 of these birds on the 20th of August one Evening while I was Watching the arrival of some Wood Ibisses—they flew Lightly in the manner of the Night Hawk but Close to the Cotton plant tops, passing & repassing by me untill I could see No more—Not one of this Birds have I heard since Early in June—

On the 22d a beautifull femelle of this Bird was brought to me by Mr Perrie's Overseer who had Shot it the preceding evening on a Small dead Tree, Where the Chuck Will's Widow had taken a stand to Watch Beatles & Seizd on them as they passed by, he saw it raise several times and Catch them in the Manner that Mocking Birds often do While enchanting the observer of his Melodies—this Man's Wife had seen it for Several evenings previous at the same Spot and sport—These Birds differ Much in plumage particularly in being darker or Lighter as they are Older or younger, this had [several] Many Winter eggs; very fat—finding [generally] Birds of Migratory habits generally in good order during this season it May be concluded that it is a preparatory occasion Incident to them to Make them to bear the fatigues and probably the unavoidable wants of foods during their travels—the Stomack of this had entire Locusts—Green Wood Lice, Ground Crikets and 2 of these Long Beetles Called usually by the french *Scarabees*—as Most Birds at present Many of the Tail & Wing feathers were tender from the Moult—

July 26th 1821 Recd yesterday from New Orleans a Packet of Letters, 4 from My Wife, One from Benj. Bakewell & one from Mr N. Berthoud. much afraid that My Wife has not recd My Packet for the President forwarded her by the Cape of the Steam boat Car of Commerce—

Remarked to day that a Male of the *Orchard* Oriole, that I had wounded in the tip of the Wing and Caged had Violent fits of Convultions, that lasted for as much as ten Minutes each, this I atributed to the uncommon exertions he Made to escape through the Wire of the upper part of the Cage—

Yet he eat freely of Fruits and Also rice—

Saw Yesterday an unknown Awk of a Large Size, that at first appearance I took for an *Ash Colored Awk,* but at a dash he Made at some Pigeons I was able to see him Well and could not recognize it for any of the 22 Species I am acquainted with—our pieces not being Loaded, I Lost him—

The Martins have for about Two Weeks Every day followed a Course of Conduct quite New to me & very remarkable, they are seen Every

Morning about 50 in Number, the Whole of Which were inabitants of the Boxes put up for them, assembled on the top of a Dead tree Close by the House, from 8 o'clock until dinner time about 2 P.M. they amuse themselves over the Yard, after this the Whole disapear and Spends the Night, I know not where—going every turn they Leave due West—and returning from that point about sun rise—every Morning—do they spend their Night in Large trees at a great distance? or do they fly to & fro that While to try their power is uncertain; however, I suppose the first Case the true One—

Carrion Crows are extremely attached to their roosting Dead Trees and will spend the Whole of the Summer nights on the Same—Leaving it very late every morning When flying on a long Course they much resemble the True Turkey—flapping their wings 8 or 10 times then sailing about 50 yards, & again flap—

Allmost every Genius of Migratory Birds begain to depart as soon as the Young are fully able—saw to day large flock of the Tyrant fly Catchers going due south—

July 29th 1821 I had the pleasure of Meeting with Several Red Cockaded Wood Peckers yesterday during a Walk We took to the Pine Woods and [to] procured Two beautifull Males, both alive, being Slightly wounded each in the Wing—the particular & very remarkable cry of this Bird can be heard at a very considerable distance of a Still day, in articulation which resembles that of the Hairy Wood Pecker, but is much more Shrill *& Loud*. the Tall pine trees are its Chosen haunts and seldom does it alight on any other Kind of Timber—its Motions are quick, gracefull and easy, its Move in all directions either on the Trunk or Limbs, Looking often very cunningly under the Loose pieces of bark for Insects: is more Shy than any of its Genus. Watching attentively all our Movements below, they Kept allways on the opposite side—peeping carefully at us—The second one Shot did not Loose a Moment to think of its Misfortune, the Moment it fell to the ground it Hoped briskly to the Nearest tree and Would soon have reach its top had I not secured it—it defended itself With courage and so powerfully did it peck at my fingers that I was forced to let him go—

Confined in My Hat on my head, they remained still and stubborn. I looked at them several times, when I found them trying to hide their Heads as if ashamed to have lost their Liberty—the report of my Gun alarmed them every time I shot when they both uttered a Plaintive Cry—

through pain of the Wound or the heat felt in My hat one died before

We reachd Mr Perrie's house—the other I put in a Cage,—he imediatly reviewd the premises hoping about and hunting for a place to Work through, and used his chisel bill with great adroitness finding the Small Chips he cut to the right & left and having made his way to the floor, run to the Wall and Climbd up it as easily as if the back of his favorite Pine [bark]—had been his post hold, picking between the Bricks and Swallowing every Insect he found—remarking often his looking under Craks and the litle Shelves in the rough wall, I drew him in that position—Sorry I am to have to say that Mr Willson's Drawing could not have been Made from the *Bird fresh Killed* or if so it was in very bad order about the head; he having put the Small striek of red feathers of the head imediatly over the Eye While there is a White Line, the red being placed far back of the [h]ear—and the whole of the wing not at all Marked Like that of the Bird—the sides of the breast is also badly represented, the Lines in Nature are Longitudinal only, and Show more of a body—the appearance of this Bird when on the pine trees Would Make one suppose it to be Black all over and the Red Line is often covered by the Crown feathers in the living Bird—I first Met with this Species a few Miles from Nashville, when on My Way to Philadelphia in 1806 seeing them from time to time untill I left the first range of Mountains Called the Cumberland—of the Nest or time of Incubation I Cannot speak. I am told that during severe winters they will leave the pine Woods and approach Plantations—

the Length of Both those I attentively examined Was $8\frac{1}{4}$ Inches, Breadth $14\frac{1}{2}$—

the Gizzard filled with heads of Small Ants and a few Minute Insects—the birds smells strongly of Pine; as I Hope to be soon able to procure the femelle, I May probably with her portrait give More information—

Shot also a Young of the Great White Heron, entirely destitute of the Pendant silky feathers of the Shoulders, but so well grown that it Might easily in that stage be taken for another Species—Killed Two Young of the Snowy Heron, that Where with an old One, Neither of these had the recumbent feathers of the back and their Legs & feet were all of a Yellowish Green instead of the former Black and feet bright Yellow—Saw some Killdeer plovers. Kind fisher, Green Heron, and a ferruginous Thrush—Low Land bordering Watter courses are usually preferred by these—

The Martins Hiroundo Purpurea—that leave this place daily, Congregate with a parcel raised Near Thompson's Creek, about 5 Miles from this and I have no doubt will take their flight from thence, for their Winter resort—

This afternoon having finished My Drawing of the Red Cockaded Wood pecker and satisfied of its Correctness by a Close comparison to the living original I gave it its Liberty, and was glad to think that it must Likely Would do well as it flew 40 to 50 Yards at times and seemed Much refreshed by its return to Liberty—

Wednesday August 1st 1821 We were awakened Last night by a servant desiring that I should rise & Dress to accompany Mrs P. to a Dying Neighbour's house, about one Mile,—We Went, but arrived rather late for Mr James O'Conner Was Dead. I had the displeasure of Keeping his body's Company the remainder of the Night. On such Occasions time flys very slow indeed, so much so that it looked as if it Stood Still like the Hawk that Poises in the air over its prey—the Poor Man had drink himself Literally to an everlasting Sleep; peace to his Soul I Made a good Sketch of his head and Left the House and the Ladies engaged at preparing the ceremonial Dinner—the weather Sultry Thermometer at 93—it has Not raised yet this Season here above 96—

Our Sparrow Hawk Was Killed to day by a Hen engaged in guarding her Brood—Nero had become extremely Temeraire, Would Fall on a Grown duck as if thinking all Must answer his Wishes when hungry—he flew at liberty about the Place, caught Grasshopers with great ease and Would Catch in the Air any of the unfortunate Small birds Killed in our dayly walks when thrown toward him for food—he regularly refused all putrid flesh, Never Would touch [a] Woodpeckers, but dearly received Bats & Mice—he had grown handsome from an apparent parcel of Moving Cotton—sailed with the Wild Birds of his Species, returning every Night to the Inner upper part of a Sash in Mr P.'s Room—he seldom made use of the Note of the Old Birds but allmost constantly uttered his Cree, Cree, Cree—

Our Orchard Oriole I gave Liberty to seing that the Departure of every number of his tribe, had rendered him melancholy to excess; I have No doubt that that specie could be Kept in cages Without much trouble, and its Sprightly Songs certainly would well repay for the care employed to furnish them with food & Drink—

August 4th 1821—Saturday Louisianna Warbler. Sylvia Ludovicianna. I Shot this morning the same Bird or one of the same Kind that I pursued yesterday [with such anxiety] so eagerly and then without success—and Was Much pleased to discover in it a New Species—during My Chase of yesterday it flew briskly from one tree or small bush to another Not as if afraid of me, but as if anxious for food, hanging its Wings very much like the Hooded fly Catcher and constantly Keeping its tail much spread like the American Red Start the Only Note it repeated every time it left a place for another Was a simple soft single *Tweet,* all its Movements extremely quick gave Me much trouble to Shot it—this Bird I Never have Met before, and of Course I Consider it as a Very Scarce One, its Note attracted me as that of all New species do; More of its habit I would Like to Know—Total Length 5 Inches Breadth 8—Whole upper part of a rich Olive Yellow—deeper on the shoulders & back, Wing feathers Black edged with bright Olive—tail Much rounded, composed of 12 Feathers the 3 first exterior on each side Outwarding edged with brownish black and Yellow inwardly these edges broadening more as they goes to the Midle feathers that are of a dark brown nearly black edged with Olive—Under wing Coverts rich yellow—under tail Coverts the same, very long—

Eyes, full, Irises deep brown, bill the true Warbler horn col[d] above and Clay below, very Sharp with a few black bristle tongue forked & slender—Legs feet & Claws Yellowish Clay—it proved on dissection a Male, extremely fat—Gizzard containing, remains of Caterpillars, Small beetles and diferent Kinds of Small flies with a few fine Clean Sands—

August 29th* saw Two of those Birds to day a Male & femelle that I approached and Examined very attentively for some Minutes they were in a Low damp & Shady part of the wood. I Killed the femelle & have joined it to my drawing of a Male—I was anxious to procure her Mate but the discharge of my Gun so alarmed it that it flew off and I could not see it more—those Birds resemble the young of the Blue eyed Warbler of Willson in much of their plumage but not in Manners and are a scarce species—

[This entry under August 29th is written across the entry of August 4th in a different ink.]

Sunday August 12th 1821 We left this morning after an early breakfast to go and explore a Famous Lake about 5½ Miles from this where we were to find (as told) great many Very fine Birds—the walk to it was pleasant being mostly through rich Magnolia Woods, We Killed Two Wood Ducks in a Small pond that we had to leave on a/c of the depth of the Hole, but that were excellently wellcome to Two *Red Shouldered Hawks* that Carried them off in our Sight—these Last are the only Birds of this Kind I have seen at this season in this part of Louisianna —We saw a singularly rich col[d] spider that finding a Horse fly just entangled in her Net move to it and covered it in a Moment with the silk of her bag, Shooting it out in a stream and at the same time rolling the fly untill the whole Likened the appearance of a Small oblong ball of White Silk, the Spider then return[d] to the center of its Net—No doubt this is a Way of preserving the flies when the Spider is Not hungry;—

When we left the ridges We at Once saw a diferent Country in aspect, the Tall White & Red Cypress being the principal Trees in Sight with their thousand Knees raising Like so Many Loafs of Sugar—Our eagerness to see the Lake engage us to force Our Way through Deep stiff Mud & Watter—We came to it and saw several Large Alligators Sluggishly Moving on the Surface, Not in the Least disturb[d] by our Approach—

Saw a White Ibis on a Log where it sat a Long time arranging its feathers using its scythe Shape[d] bill very dexterously; Could have Killed it but having No boat and afraid of Sending a Dog in the Lake Left it Setting peaceably—

Saw a great Number of Prothonotary Warblers on the Low Bushes of the Swamp—Many *Yellow throated Warblers* these have all the habits of a Creeper, Moving quickly round, up and down the Limbs and trunks of the Cypress trees, fly swiftly in the Manner of the brown Creeper alighting generally low on the truck assending it searching nimbly for small Insects; these birds [*I* have] have so much the appearance of the *White & Black Creeper* that had I not seen one fly directly toward me and discovering then the beautifull & Rich Yellow Throat I would not have shot one—This however I effected and found Myself in possession of a Beautifull Male that Measured $5\frac{1}{2}$ Inches in Length & $8\frac{1}{4}$ in extent answering Willson Description, on Dissection the Bird Was very fat as all the Warblers We Shot Now Are, and had its Gizard filled with shells of Minute Insects—so found of the Cypress trees is this beautifull spirited litle bird that I Was Tempted to Call it the Cypress Swamp Warbler, where it is only to be Met in this part of the Country—

I Was also fortunate in Shooting a Male of the *Green blue Warbler* —One Week ago I had shot one but Never could find it, there was at this time five in Company, and Within only a few feet of Me M[r] Willson shot a femelle on the Cumberland River, and Never any more; about Two Months since I Discovered One in a small swamp Nearer M[r] Perrie—these birds sing sweetly, and No doubt breed here. Look Much like the *blue Yellow Back* Warblers and hang downwards by the feet like these and the Titmouse. Saw only the One I shot to day and having as much as I Know I could Well draw before they would be Spoiled by the heat of the Wheather returned to the House.

This Male Measured 5 Inches in Length and and $7\frac{3}{4}$ in breadth—All the Colors brighter & stronger than Willson's femelle, every Tail feather having White on their inner Vane except the Two Midle Ones—so fat was this bird and of so solid a Nature was that [grease][?] fat that it Cut like Mutton fat; its gizard Was filled entirely with some Small brown Shelly Insects and the remains of the same Kind that are extremely plenty in the Cypresses of these Swamps—

Shot a Watter Thrush, have found Many here.

Went to the Lake that We Visited Last Sunday and in Going there, I Was much pleased to observe that the *sound* that We heard on Sunday and had taken for the Plaintive Note of the *Wood Peewee* was in fact that of a Young Mississipi Kite, While waitting for the return of the Parents with food—this Young it seems had Actually remained [it appears] on the same tree Where we had heard it before but could not then discover it—this Morning perceiving that a long Vine reach[d] near to the Top of the Tree and hearing the Noise without Knowing it nor where it actually issued from, I Walked toward it still looking up to the Topmost branches When I perceived something Like a dead stick Lodged Cross ways in a limb—I Eyed it particularly and saw it Moved, I Shot at it and the Noise stop[d] but the Young M. Kite Closed her wings and destroyed the Dead Stik like appearance it had before my fire—I Waited for it to fall, it cried again shortly and I then saw the Old Bird bringing food and alight Close to the young with one of those Large Grass hopers that abound in the Mississipy flats—but the young was too far gone to relish food the Mother exibited much distress and after several trials to Make the young Bird take it it dropt it and taking old of her offspring by the feathers of the back carried it off with ease for about 25 yards to another tree where I follow[d] and Killed both at One Shot—the Young instead of having the head of a Light blue ash color like its Mother, had it of a handsome buff and remainder of the body Was Nearly black. I intended drawing Both and I purposely hided them under a Log, but on my return some quadrupedes had discovered them and eat them both—I regret much the Loss the young Bird was nearly full grown [but probably the want of Knowledge to procure food] Saw several paires of Ivory Bill *Wood Peckers* Killed a handsome Male.—Louisianna affords all the *Picus Genus* of the U. States—

Arrived at the Swamp and there saw a great Number of Small Birds. Shot a beautifull *new* Species of Fly Catcher Muscicapa, which I Will give you Tomorow when my Drawing of it Will be finished. I had the pleasure of seing Two that appeared Much alike, they were quarelling when I shot at them but fell only One—cannot say any More of this truly handsome bird having never seen any thing of them before to Day—

Saw within a few feet a beautifull *Mourning Warbler* but Was so situated Knee deep in the Mud that I could Not retrograde without alarming it I preferred gazing at it as it innocently gazed at Me hoping it would fly at a Short distance, but it Moved with a *Tweet* and out of sight in an instant. Much disapointed at My having lost the only oppr[y] I Ever have had of procuring this rare Bird.

Shot several of the *Yellow Throated Warbler* all alike and all Males the woods were full of them and yet Not a femelle could I Shot—they Move sideways on the small limbs of the Cypress in a Hoping Manner extremely quickly hang often to the ends of Limbs like the titmouse and run up or down the Large Trunks much like the Nuthatches—Killed Many *Blue Yellow back Warblers.* Saw Many *Prothonotarys,* several *Watter Thrushes* that I consider More Like Warblers the Habits of Which genus they exhibit to a very great degree and the Bill of Which they [co] have—Alligators as numerous as before basking in the Sun that this day was more than ordinarily uncomfortable—saw several Ibiss at respectful Distances in their common dull postures—

My Litle fly Catcher had only one wing touch[d] When I presented Myself to pick it up, it spread its Tail & open its Wings and Snap its bill [20 or] about 20 times in the [—] Manner that Many of this Genus do when they seize a fly, particularly those that are Nearest the Standard of the Genus.—I seldom have seen a bird of Such Small size With so Large & beautifull an Eye. I took it home to James Perrie's Es[qr] and had the pleasure of drawing it While a live and full of Spirit, it often Made off from My fingers by starting Suddenly and unexpectedly, and then would hop round the room as quick as a Carolina or Winter Wren would have done, uttering its tweet tweet tweet all the while, and Snapping every time I took it up. I put it in a Cage for a few Moments but it obstinatly forced the fore part of its head through the Lower part of the Wires and I relieved it by Confining it in My hat for the Night anxious to see More of its Movements—

Joseph unwell With a sick head Hacke—Length of the *Cypress Swamp Fly Catcher Muscicapa Rara,* $5\frac{1}{4}$ Inches—breadth $7\frac{3}{4}$ Inches [upp] Whole upper parts handsome ash Color appearing blue at a distance, the front of the Head mixed with Yellow, a Yellow Line Surround the Eye that is very Large Iriss deep brown, pupil Black, between the eye & Bill & under the eye shaded with darker ash Tail Coverts lighter than the back, tail slightly forked of 12 Feathers all plain bronish ash shafts deep brown as well as those of the wings under tail Coverts Long & White—the Throat breast belly & Vent Rich citron Yellow without intermission of Shade in any of these parts. Breast spotted with black [spots] forming small chains fallin to the beginning of the spurious wings—Bill, hooked at the Tip and broad at the base. Legs feet & Claws horn Colors the last Long & Sharp Nostrils very prominent, Tongue much Jagged, Mouth flesh color[d] & furnish outwardly With many Long black bristles—it proved a Male. Gizzard fleshy filled with wings of different Insects—Cheeks also ash col[d] My Drawing a very excellent one —finding this Bird very Weak in the Morning Killed it and put it in Whiskey—

Monday 20th August—1821 I spent the Night Nearly in pursuit of the Wood Ibiss and although I Killed One I could never find it this Morning. some Fox or Racoon had No doubt a good Repast of it—I saw 4 Coming, sailing & flapping alternatly; their Necks & Legs strached out a little over the tops of the Trees a few Moments after sun Setting. No Note, they alighted on the Largest Top Branches of the dead trees in a Large Cotton Plantation, drew their Necks & Heads on their shouldiers, Standing perpendicularly. Now & then arranging the feathers of their breast as if to put their Immense bill at Rest on it—I approach[d] them untill they Were immediatly over My head, but they never minded Me, its growing Dusky I shot at the Largest, it open its Wings and sailed to the hearth without a groan, the others raised and Sailed on Some other trees, the Darkness of the Night then prevented My seing them any More and Also forced Me to Look for the One I had undoubtedly Killed—After a Long Search this Morning begun with the dawn of Day I had to return, fatigued & Much Disapointed—the Planter and Negroes assured Me that for Many Years these Birds some time as Many as 60 & 70 in Numbers, and at other times only a few had resorted to these Dead Trees to roost Nearly said they the round Year, Missing a few Weeks only early in Spring and in Winter. Could Not ascertain the Months—About 2 Weeks since 3 had been Killed the Negroes pronounced their flesh Excellent food—

While sitting waiting for the arrival of these curious Birds saw Several flocks of the White Ibiss and bleu Herons, Moving from the Lake to this rendez-vousing place of Rest to a Large Sand Barr, at the Mouth of Thompson's Creek that empty a few Miles below Bayou Sarah—the first flew in [Waving] single Waving Lines silently—the bleu Herons in acute Angles passing the Word of March from the first to the Last in a Simply *Qua,* these are easily Known by their drawn in Necks and Notes, the others allways Keeping their Necks at its full Length

these passages take place every Evening from about one hour before Sunset untill Dark When the Noises of the One and the Pure Whiteness of the others are the only evidence of [their] Straglers still being going over—

—*August 25*— Finished drawing a very fine Specimen of a Rattle Snake—that measured 5 7/12 feet Weight 6 1/4 lb had 10 Rattles—

Anxious to give it such a Position as I thought would render it most interesting to Naturalist, I put it in that which that Reptile generally takes when on point to Inflict a Most severe wound—I have examined the Fangs of Many before and their position along the Superior Jaw Bones, but had never seen one Shewing the Whole exposed at the same time having before this thought that the probability was that those Laying Inclosed below the Upper one in Most Specimen Were to Replace these upper ones Which I thought [also] might drop periodically as the Animal Changes its Skin and Rattles—however on Dissection of these from the Ligament by Which they are fixed to the Jaw bones I found them Strongly and I think [with a] permanently [tendency to be] attached & as follows—Two Superior Next the upper Like (I speak of one side of the Jaw only) connected Well together at the bases & running parrallel their Whole Length. They had appartures on the upper & Lower side of their bases to receive the Venom connectivly and the discharging one a short distance from the Sharp points on the inner part of the fangs—the Two next Fangs about one quarter of an Inch below connected and running in the same Manner, but with only one base apperture on the Lower Side of each and the one at the point that issues the venom to the Wound—the 5th rather smaller is also about a quarter of an Inch below, Lonely appertures as in the Secondarius the scales of the belly to the Under part of the Mouth where they finished Numbered 170 and 22 from the vent to the tail—My Drawing I Hope Will give you a good Idea of a Rattle Snake although the Heat of the weather Would not permit me to Spend More than 16 hours at it—My amiable Pupil Miss Eliza Perrie also drew the same Snake; it is With Much pleasure that I now Mention her Name expecting to remember often her sweet disposition and the Happy Days spent near her—

Octr 10th sent 100$ to M^rs A—

Octr 20th 1821 This Morning about 6 o'clock We Left Mr *Perrie's* Plantation for New Orleans, Which Place we Reach^d on Monday the 21st at 2 o'clock but before I alight in that City, I Must Poise Myself and give you a short a/c of the Most Remarkable Incident that have taken

Place With us during our Stay at Oakley the Name of James P. Plantation—

Three Months out of the 4 we lived there Were Spent in peaceable tranquility; giving regular Daily Lessons to Miss P. of Drawing, Music, Dancing, Arithmetick, and Some trifling acquirements such as Working Hair &^{c} Hunting and Drawing My Cherished Birds of America; Seldom troublesome of Disposition, and not Caring for or Scarcely ever partaking or Mixing with the constant Transient Visitors at the House, *We* Were Called *good Men* and Now & then received a Chearing Look from the Mistress of the House and *sometimes* also one Glance of Approbation of the More Circumspect Miss Eliza—Governor Robertson visited us and then I formed a Still Stronger Opinion of that Man agreableness and Strength of Mind than I had before & Consider him as a really true Philosopher of the Age—Amongst our other Visitors the Brother of Henry *Clay* Mr John Clay of this City I found a good agreable Man to all appearance a Rather Singular Caracter Rich W^{am} Brand also spent some days at the House and Married in the Neighbourhood—All Kindly Polite to us;

Miss P. had No Particular admirers of her beauties but several very anxious for her fortune amongst Which a Certain Mr Colt a Young Lawer Who appeared quite Pressing although Very uncivilly Received at First—

Mr P. a Man of Strong Mind but extremely Weak of Habit and degenerating sometimes into a State of Intoxication, remarkable in its Kind, Never associating With any body on such occasions and Exibiting all the Madman's Actions With under its Paroxism—When Sober; truly a good Man a *Free Mason,* generous and Entertaining—his wife Raised to opulence by Dint of Industry an Extraordinary Woman—Generous I believe but giving Way for Want of understanding at times to the Whole force of her Violent Passions—found of quizing her husband and Idolatring her Daugher Eliza—

This Daughter Eliza of age 15 Years of a good form of *body,* not Handsome of face, proud of her Wealth and of herself cannot well be too Much fed on Praise—and God Knows how hard I tryed to Please her in Vain—and God Knows also that I have vowed Never to try as much again for any Pupil of Mine—as usual *I* had to do 2/3 of all *her* Work of Course her progresses Were Rapid to the Eyes of every body and truly astonishing to the eyes of some good observers—

a Sister Mrs Smith I cannot say that I Knew or rather I never did Wish to Know; of Temper Much like her Mother, of Heart Not so good Yet God forgive her the Injuries She did me—

her Husband a good, Honest Man and Citizen Viewed all the faults of her he Wedded With Patient Kindness and felt his reward through his own Correctness of Conduct—I admire him Much—

I saw there a Mrs Harwood of London England a *good* Little Woman [and] Very Kind to us in Mending our Linen &^{c}—her Little Daugher a sweet Child about 5 Years Old, Hated by Mrs P.—a Certain Miss Throgmorton Was also good deal Disliked, the poor Girl was nearly drove off as We Were by the Ladies—although she had been Invited there to Spend the Summer—

about a Month before We Left Miss P was taken seriously Ill, and as she was the only remaining Child unmaried and the 2^{d} of 7, 5 of which had died in the Course of a very few years, Much fears were entertained of the Survival of this One, and No doubt Much too Much Care Was taken of her; Kept in bed Long after She was convalescent and Not permitted to leave her room for a Long time She became, Low of flesh and Crabed of Speech; every thing Must have gone on the Smoothest way to hurt her feelings her Phisician the *Man she Loved* Would not permit her reassuming her Avavocations near Me and told the Mother that it would be highly Improper Miss Eliza Should Draw, Write &^{c} untill some Months; but that She Might Eat any thing Pleasing to her fancy—this fancy Was not Confined into small bounds. She Eat so plentifully of evering that could be procured that she had several Relapses of fevers—I saw her during this Illness at appointed hours as if I was an Extraordinary ambassador to some Distant Court—had to Keep the utmost Decorum of Manners and I believe Never Laughed Once With her the Whole 4 Months I was there—

Mrs P. on the 10th of Octr Dismissed me—Not anxious to revisit New Orleans so soon, I begged of her that We Should remain 8 or 10 Days Longer if the familly Would please to Consider us as Visitors, this agreed on, I Continued My Close Application to My Ornithology Writting every day from Morning untill Night, Correcting, arranging from My Scattered Notes All My Ideas and posted up partially all My Land Birds—the great Many Errors I found in the Work of Willson astonished Me I tried to speak of them With Care and as seldom as Possible; Knowing the good Wish of that Man [and] and the Hurry he was in and the Vast Many hear say he depended on—

We perceived however during all this While that a remarkable Coolness had taken place from the Ladies toward us, seldom seing any of them except at table and then With Looks far from Chearing My Spirits that Were during the Whole of My Stay there unfortunatly very Low—Mrs Smith took an utter dislike to Me and one day While I was engaged in finish a Portrait of Mrs P. begun by her Daughter Eliza, M^{rs} S addressed the Work and Me in the grossest Words of Insult, and afterwards Never Looked Directly at Me—

She Busted at another time in a ridiculous Laugh at table, When her good Husband Interfered and told her She ought to Make Me some Amends for her Conduct—I Left the table unwilling to hear any More of this—Saturday Came and a Settlement of Money Matter Was Necessary I charged for 10 days of Miss E. Ill time My Bill Was 204$ and Mrs P. in a perfect Rage fit told me that I Cheated her out of 20$—My Coolness sufered all her Vociferations to flow, I simply told her our former mutual Engagements on that score—I figured the Bill and sent it to M^{r} P Who Was then Labouring under one of his unfortunate fits of antoxication—

he Came to see Me, apologized in the Kindest Manner for his Lady's Conduct; Ordered his Son in Law Mr Smith to pay Me, and shewed Me all the Politeness he his possessed of—Mr Smith Congratulated My Firmness of Acting—and All Went on pretty Well that Day—

the Ladies early that Morning Left for St. Francisville Without bidding us any adieu, and expected that on their Return at Night We would be gone; this however was a disapointment for Mr *Perrie* requested We should Stay, representing how easily We could reach the Steam Boat the Next Morning before her time of departure in the Course of this Afternoon M^{rs} P sent for Joseph and presented him with a full suit of fine clothes of her Deceased son—to the acceptation of Which I positively refused to acquiesce, Knowing too Well how far some gifts are talked of—and Not Willing that My Companion should diminish the Self Respect I think Necessary for every Man to Keep towards himself however poor, when able by *Talents,* Health and Industry to Procure his own Necessities—

unfortunately there was Much Company in the evening [and] sometimes after supper We Left our Room were Mr Pirrie and Mr Smith had Joined us on leaving the Table to go and bid our farewell to the female Part of the familly—My Entry before the Circle posessed none of that Life and Spirit I formerly Enjoyed on Such Occasion, I would gladly have wished to be excused from the fatiguing Ceremonies yet I Walk^{d} in followed by Joseph and [Walking] approaching to Mrs P. bid her good bye as simply as ever any Honest Quaker Did, touch^{d} Slightly Mrs Smith's Hand as I boughed to her—My Pupil Raised from the Sopha and Expected a Kiss from Me—but None Were to be disposed off, I pressed her Hand and With a general Salute to the Whole Made My Retreat No doubt Much to the great Surprise of Every one Present Who had heard those very Women Speak Constantly before of Me in Highest Terms of

Respects, scarcely Deigning to Look at me Now—as Joseph Was following me he received a Voley of farewells from the 3 Ladies of the House put after him Ridiculously to Affect Me, but the Effect Was lost and it Raised a Smile on My Lips [and]—We Joined again the Two good Husbands in our Lodging Chamber—they remained with us untill bed time; Cordially parted With us, retired to repose Without Joining the Company—

Day Light of Sunday Saw us Loading our Trunks and Drawing Table. Vaulted our Sadles and Left this abode of unfortunate Opulence without a single Sigh of regret—

Not so with the sweet Woods around us, to leave them was painfull, for in them We allways enjoyed Peace and the sweetest pleasures of admiring the greatest of the Creator in all his unrivalled Works. I often felt as if anxious to retain the fill of My lungs with the purer air that Circulate through them. Looked With pleasure and sorrow on the few Virgin blooming Magnolias—the 3 Colored Vines and as We descended the Hills of St Francisville bid that farewell to the Country, that under diferent Circumstances We Would have Willingly divided With the Ladies of Oakley—

We Left the Mouth of Bayou Sarah at 10 o'clock in the Morning in the Steam Boat Ramaso with a Medley of Passengers and with a few Stoppages to Land and take occasional Travellers Reached the City on Monday—

the Weather Cool and Rainy, I left the Boat and Walked to My good acquaintance R. Pamar—I had perceived that My Long flowing buckled hair was Looked on with astonishment by the Passengers on board and saw that the effect Was stronger in town—My Large Loose Dress of Whitened Yellow Nankeen and the unfortunate *Cut* of My features Made me decide to be dressed as soon as Possible Like other folks and I had My Chevelure parted from My head the Reception of Mr Pamar's familly was very gratefull to My Spirits. I Was Looked upon as of a Son returned from a Long Painfull Voyage, the Children, the Parents the servants all hung about Me; What Pleasures for the Whole of us—

I dined there, afterwards Visiting the famous hunter Lewis Adam—and the Dimitry familly who also Received Me very Kindly

Rented une Chamber garnie in Rue St Anne No 29 for 16$ per Month and removed our baggage thereto from the boat—

We Spent Tuesday Wednesday & Thursday, Looking over the City for a Suitable House for My Litle Familly—this appeared a very dificult task and I nearly Concluded to take one we visited in Dauphine Street—

My Clothes being extremely Shabby and forced against My Will to provide some New ones, I bought some clothes and Now Wait very impatiently on the Gentleman Taylor for them that I May go and Procure some Pupils with a better grace—

having renewed our early Morning Visits to the Market to Look at all there—We found it allmost as well suplied of Vegetables, fruits, fish, Meats, flowers, &c as in the Spring—delightfull radishes Letuce &c plenty—Wrote to My Wife yesterday—per Mail it is Now 15 days since I forwarded her a Draft on Mr Gordon Which May probably have reach to day—

I found at Messrs Gordon Grant & Co a Box of Oil Colors and a Letter from Mr Briggs, I was sorry to See both, the first did not Contain What I Wish, and I Cannot say that I felt any pleasure in Reading the Latter—

I answered Mr Briggs's Letter this Evening—the 25th of Octr—

Octr 25th 1821 Raining hard the Whole of the day spent the greater part of it at R. Pamar and his Relation *Lewis Adam the hunter;* Rented a House in Dauphine Street for 17$ Per Month—

Joseph found the time rather Lost to himself Not a Thing to be found to Draw—

26th Wrote a few Lines to James Pirrie Esqr to Inform him that Messrs D. & G. Flower had not Paid the House of Gordon & Co One hundred Dollars according to Promise—Wrote a few Words to My Lucy and forwarded it by Mail Covering Brigg's Letter;

Walked a good Deal, Visited the familly Dimitry, Spend Much of the Day at Pamar's—in the evening Went some distance down the Levee, the Sky beautifull & serene—Miss Pamar Much Improved in Music and Manners—Many Men formerly *My Friend* passed *Me* without uttering a Word to me and *I as Willing* to Shun those Rascalls—

fatigued of being *Idle* so powerfull are habits of all Kinds that to spend a Month thus would render me sick of Life—

Hetchberger Visited us Much Pleased at My addition of Drawings since I Left Cincinnati Octr 12th 1820 I have finished 62 Drawings of *Birds & Plants,* 3 quadrupeds, 2 Snakes, 50 Portraits of all sorts and My Father *Don Antonio* have Made out to Live in humble Comfort with Only My Talents and Industry, Without *One Cent* to begin on at My Departure—

I have Now 42 Dollars, health, and as much anxiety to pursue My Plans of Accomplishing My Collection as Ever I had and Hope God Will Grant Me the same Powers to Proceed

My Present Prospects to Procure Birds this Winter are More Ample than ever being now Well Known by the Principal hunters on Lake Borgne, Barataria—Pontchartrain, and the Country of Terre a Boeuf—

OCT^R^ 27TH SUNDAY Dressed all new, Hair Cut, my appearance altered beyond My expectations, fully as much as a handsome Bird is when robbed of all its feathering, the Poor thing Looks, Bashfull dejected and is either entirely Neglected or Look^d^ upon With Contempt; such was my situation Last Week—but When the Bird is Well fed, taken care of, sufered to Enjoy Life and dress himself; he is cherished again, Nai admired—Such my situation this day—Good God that 40 Dollars should thus be *enough* to Make a *Gentleman*—ah My Beloved Country When will thy Sons value more Intrinsectly each Brother's Worth? Never!!

Exibited My Drawings at My good acquaintance Pamar's—received much valuable Intelligence coroborating With My own observations on these things that trully pleases My feelings—Dined there—

Payd a Visit to Mrs Clay and the young Ladies there, with My Portfolio—unknown, Passed for a *German* untill the latter part of My Stay—the Company Much Pleased With My Work—but no pupil as I expected to have—

took a Long Walk to the Canal, talked Much With My Hunter *Gilbert* Who Leaves for Barataria Tomorrow—Weather Beautifull and very warm, good Deal of Game in Market this Morning—

Green Back Swallows Gamboling over the City and the River the Whole day have great Hopes of ascertaining their Winter quarters Not far from this

OCT^R^ 29TH 1821 Spent this unfructuously in search of Employ^mt^ Visited several Public Institutions where I cannot say that I Was very politely received; in one or Two Notable ones (Not Willing to Mention Names) I was invited to Walk in and then out in very quick order—Dined at Pamar; Was Visited by John Gwathway of Louisville K^y^—Wrote to J^d^ Rozier to Procure my Drawing of the *Male Grous* or Prairie Hen—Determined on Exibiting some of My Drawings at Public Places for I Well recollect the effect of *Lafontaine* Fable that says that *"a l'oeuvre on connoit L'Artizan"*—unknown by most people here, I am like Many others who appear as advanturors look^d^ on with Care, and Suspicion—but so Moves the World, and no doubt it is *Wright* it should be so—

Visited Rich Mrs *Braud* was then very Politely received, "Must Call again"—Mrs Braud Married a Large fortune, the Honey Moon is not yet *Set* and she Looks well even on her Decline, promising full fullness bye & Bye—

Rec^{d} a Letter from My Beloved Friend My Lucy unfortunately of old Date, and the one also sent by Mr Ecard dated Nearly 2 Months—

Octr 30th 1821 New Orleans Returned to W^{am} Braud and Procured his Son for a Pupil at 2$ per Leson of one hour, and have some Hopes of having Mrs B. a pupil of *French* and Painting—

Visited another College. Politly Received by the Ladies Who examined My Port Folio with apparent siaisfaction. No Pupils however, a Certain Mr *Torain* having antecedented Me every Where—

Dined at Pamar and Drew My American Hare—to Exibit to the Public—Joseph at Work Preparing Father Antoine Coat

the Market Well suplied With game & Vegetables have resumed our Habit of taking a Walk there as soon as the Day Dawns—

The day Warm, Swallows Plenty and quite as gay in their flight as in June—

to find here those Birds in aboundance 3 Months after they have left the Midle States, and to Know that they Winter Within 40 Miles in Multitudes is one of the Gratifications the Most Exquisite I ever Wish^{d} to feel in Ornithological Subjects and that Puts [an] compleat *Dash* over *all* the Nonsense Wrote about their Torpidity during Cold Weather; No Man could ever have enjoyed the Study of Nature in her all Femine Bosomy Wild and err^{d} so Wide—

Octr 31st 1821 New Orleans Begun giving Lessons of Drawing to Mrs Braud and Young Master W^{am} Braud this Day at 3 Dollars per Lesson—

Spent some time at Work on Father Antoine and My Drawing of My American Hare—

Received a Visit of Mr Pamar, Mr Dimitry and Dumatras

Weather Warm in the Morning, Much fish Condemned in the Market—also some Game—Excellent regulations—the Wind Shifted to the Northwest and I premidited Cold Weather by the Swallows flying South about noon at Night quite Cool—What Knowledge these Litle Creatures possess and how true they are in their Movements—

November 1st 1821 Weather beautifull—gave Lessons at W^{am} Brauds—Dined at My Good Pamar's House—

Very unwell at Night with Violent Cholicks and was forced to My bed at seven o'clock a thing I have not done for Very Many Years—Visited M. Basteros, Painter—

at 12 o'clock Disturbed by the Cries of Fire—but as it Was Not in our imediate Neighbourhood did not Suffer *Joseph* to go—

November 2^{D}—Friday— felt Well at day light and Went to see the Market Much Game, but nothing for Me—

gave My Lessons at W^{am} Braud's—Much pleased to find his Lady possessed of a *Natural* talent, for Painting W^{am} Braud extremely Kind and Polite, very anxious to give his Son a good Education—

Rec^{d} the Visit of *Brutter* the Painter, the good Man Very sorry to see My *Father* Antonio—fearing an Engraving after it—

I determined to have My Drawing framed although it Cost Me about 30$ having some Hopes that it Would procure Me some Pupils of Note—

Saturday 3^{D} November give My Lessons—John Gwathwey announced me the Death of My *Constant* Enemy Mrs Bakewell My Wife's Mother's in Law—God forgive her faults—Etchberger the Painter spent the evening With us—Mr Hails borowed My Shot Bag at 10 o'clock P.M.—sufered some Mortifications this Morning in a House Were I showed My Birds—Weather Cloudy & Raw—

Sunday 4TH November N. Orleans Breakfasted at Pamar's saw a School Mistress there who requested that I should Call at her House to shew My Drawings—Did so at 11 o'clock Tolerable reception there, the Lady Drawing Well herself anxious to acquire My Style but Complaining Much of the extraordinary price I asked her—expect there several Pupils but Nothing very Certain—

Dined at Pamar's, Steam Boat Ramapo arrived Without *James Pirrie* Es^{qr} Much Disapointed on a/c of the 100$ that he was to Pay Messrs Gordon Grant & Co on the 20th ultimo—

took a Long Walk Down the River Shore and out to the Swamps—Swallows More Plenty than yesterday, generally Moving Eastwardly to the Lakes—Weather Delightfull, Much such that is felt in May in Kentucky—Many of the trees having a beautifull set of New foliage, Vast Many Plants in Bloom—Particularly the *Elder*—No Lessons at W^{am} Braud to day—

Monday 5TH give My Lecons at W. Braud—Drawing at My F. Antoine—Paid Mr Forestal 100$

Tuesday 6th gave My Lecons at W^am^ Braud—Swallows plenty—Appearance of *Indian Summer* Took a Long Walk and Much Work Done at My Drawing

Wednesday 7th Gave My Lecon to Mrs Braud & Son—Procured Two Pupils to begin Next Monday—Drew an American Avoset—Weather Beautifull—

BROWN PELICAN—

Length 4 feet 2½ Inches from the Tip of the Bill to the end of the Toes, which extend about 1½ Inches beyong the Tail—The Bill Measured 12½ Inches the upper Mandible armed with a strong Hooked Point projecting beyond the blade of the upper Mandible ½ Inch—and fitting the Lower one in its Whole Length to the Nail [the] Which runs to the forehead in Two furrows and Contains the Nostrils that are Extremely small, Linear, within ½ an Inch of the forehead and scarce perceivable—the outer edges of this Mandible as Well as that of the Lower and Sharp Cutting edges—3 Process edges are contained in the inner part of the upper Mandible also Sharp edged—the whole of this upper Part long stiff & Strong substance—of a Greyish Blue edging in Yellow—the edges of the Lower Mandible are the same Color averaging in Width about ½ an Inch truncated at the end and Capable of distention from their Natural [weigdth] depth of 1⅜ of an Inch to 6 Inches and furnished with a tail or pouch of a Bluish Distending Skin begaining at the under point of the Lower Mandible and Loosing itself along the Neck about 9½ Inches below the Junction of the Mandible from Which part to its utmost stratch point with the hand it Measured a foot—the Tongue is a Mere Knot about 12 Inches from the Tip of the Lower Mandible fast to this Bag—the Eye is Brown pretty Large and situated in the Skin that [so] covers the Cheeks and Jaws of the Bill—the upper of the Head and side of the Neck running along the Pouch of a Mole Cole Color, the hind head ornemented with a Crest of slender feathers of 1½ Inch in Length—the upper Plumage of the Neck, assuming a Silky appearance and Much Worn by resting on the back and Shoulders of the Bird—Shoulders & Back Covered With pointed, Small feathers the former Light ash in their Centers edged With Rufous & Some with brown—the Latter silvery in the Center edge With deep black to the Rump Where the Plumage is Larger yet Pointed ash & Rufous—the Tail Rounded Composed of 18 feathers quills Black shaded Silvery Ash—the Wings Extended Measured 7½ feet—the second Joint 9 Inches Closing on the Body reaching to the begainging of the Neck—and When closed the Tips reach the end of the Tail—the first 9 Primary quills White to their points below and about $\frac{1}{2}$ above; the feathering [dark] brownish black cast secondaries Much the same—Tertials Broad falling over the back part of the body to the root of the Tail; feathers of the Shoulders of a Light Ash some edged With brown, others With Black, quills very slender and Black—Whole under part White and in some Specimen Silvery—Legs Strong and Muscular far behind—4 Toes Webbed in Connection—the Whole of a Bluish greenish Yellow—Claws blunt, Much Hooked the Longest Pectinated Inwardly—the Bird emitting a Strong disagreable fishy Smell Weighed $6\frac{1}{2}^{lb}$ femorals Much as the Shoulders—on dissection it was a Male—the Stomack Very Long and slender, fleshy—Containing only about 50 slender Blue Worm all alive about $2\frac{1}{2}$ Inches Long—the Gut Measured 10 feet about the size of a Moderate Swans quill—the Bird Was Killed on Lake Barataria by Mr. Hunter Gilbert—the rump and the root of the Tail Was Covered With a Thin Coating of Oily Yellow fat extremely rancid, and Much air Was Contained between the Whole of the Skin and flesh of the body; the Bones of the Wings & Legs although Extremely hard and dificult to Breake, were very thin [and] Light and perfectly empty—

THURSDAY 8TH gave My Lecons at Mrs Braud's—Weather extremely sultry—Anxious to hear from My Wife—

NEW ORLEANS NOVEMBER, FRIDAY 9TH 1821 Weather quite Cool a diference in the atmosphere of 22 Degrees from that of yesterday and the Swallows that Were Numerous Last Evening are all gone for the Present—gave My Lecons at Mrs Braud's—

Carried My Port follio to Mrs Dimitry this morning to Show Miss Euphrosine the Progress of Joseph—Dined and Breakfasted at Good *Pamar's*—

Visited this afternoon Miss *Bornet's* academy of Young Ladies and shew^{d} some Drawings—but all to No purpose the Ladies there entirely in favor of Mr Torane Talents—

Mr Hawkins during My absence brought an Engraving of Vanderling's head of Adriane for Me to Copy and requested Joseph to tell Me Not to spare My Time on it—Mr Bartrop also Called While I was out—My feelings Much harrassed about My Beloved Wife from Whom I have Not heard for 2 Weeks—

SATURDAY 10TH Gave My Lecons at Mrs Braud—Called on Mr Hawkins who visited me to see father Antoines Drawing—Concluded to have the Engraving he Wished Me to Copy for not exceeding 50$ wishing it could be done as soon as possible—Saw Mr John Clay—very Polite to Me—

Weather Very beautifull but Cold Drew a female of the *Gadwall Duck* a remarkably fine Specimen—sent Me by My Hunter Gilbert—

Mr Basterop at My Lodgings—Wished that I should Join him in a Painting of a Panorama of this City—but My Birds My Beloved Birds of America feel all my time and nearly My thoughts I do not Wish to See any other *Perspective* than the Last Specimen of them Drawed—No News from My Beloved Lucy nor Children, Very uneasy on their Silence—Mississipi falling fast—

New Orleans Sunday November 11th 1821 Saw John Gwathway early this Morning, who told me that My Wife Intended Leaving Louisville about the first Instant in a Small Steam Boat for this Place—and this News Kept me Nearly Wild all day. Yet No Boat arrived No Wife No Friend yet near—

The Weather Beautifull & Warm Dined at Pamar—Drew a good Deal. Visited Basterop—Joseph hunting all day With Young Dimitry. Killed Nothing—Swallows Very plenty and as gay as could be—Saw some Common Gull, but Not a *Fish Crow* come yet—Mr Bermudas Visited Me a short time this Evening—The Nearer the Moment that I Expect to see My Beloved Lucy Approaches the greater My Impatience, my disapointment Dayly When evening draws on—

Monday 12th 1821 Began Given Lessons to Miss Delafosse and Miss at 2 Dollars per hour for both—

Gave My Lecon also at Mrs Braud—Saw Eliza Throgmorton there—Weather Beautifull but *No Ducks*—Drew a good Deal—Dined at Pamar—had a Conversation Mr John Clay Respecting M^r P—Mr Bermudas brought Me a *Green Winged* Teal as a great Rarity—No News from My Wife yet—

Tuesday 13th Gave Lecons at Mrs Braud but Miss Lafosse Wishes only to receive them 3 times per Week—Drew a Wild Goose Not represented by Willson—Weather quite Cool—Very Busy all day (The white fronted)

Wednesday New Orleans November 14th 1821 Wednesday—gave My Lecons at Mrs Braud's and Miss Delafosse's

Work Constantly the whole day—Drew a female of the *White Nun* or *Smew Merganser*—Weather Rainy & Raw—Dined on Bread & Cheese—Rec^{d} a Letter from Mrs A. the purport of Which Lower My Spirits very Considerably—alas were does Comfort Keep herself now; retired certainly on a Desolate Rock unwilling to Cast even a Look on our Wretched Species—

Mr E. Fiske formerly our Agent in this City presented Me this morning with a bill of Fellows & Rugles—I Spoke to him on that subject in Terms that astonished him, but My determination is bent and I Shall Philosophise Now on all things—Little Expectations of seing My familly before the Latter Part of Winter—

Thursday 15th Gave Lesson at Mrs Braud's—

Drew Closely all day finishing 3 Drawings of Birds and Continued after sun set by Candle light untill 10 at Vanderlyn's Head—

Weather fair but Cool—Very Low of Spirits Wished Myself off this Miserable Stage—

16th

Friday Gave Lesson to Mrs Braud—but Miss Delafosse Was unwell and Postponed taking untill tomorow—Sent a Bill to Dr Heermann—it was accepted and Promised Joseph Payment for Next Week

17th

Saturday Gave Lessons at Mrs Braud's & Miss Delafosse also—her Mother Knew My father—Drew Much to day and late this Evening—[Gilbert the Hunter Return^{d}]

November Sunday 18th 1821 Drawing all day; Dined at Mr Pamar Rec^{d} a Visit of Philip Guesnore—also one from the famous Hunter Louis Adams Who however had No Knowledge of the Small Merganzer I had drawn

19th Monday Gave Lessons at Mrs Braud, and Miss Dellfosse—these Latters have conetracted to have one every day Much to My satisfaction—Needing this acumulation of Income very Much—

Drew a Black Bellied Darter Male a Superb Specimen—

Was Visited by Mr Hawkins, an agreable Man Possessing Taste, Information & Judgment—

20th Tuesday Gave Lessons at Mrs Braud & Miss Dellfosse Drew Much and finished both My Black Bellied Darter and the Vanderlyn's Head—

Shabbily used by Dr Heermann—Who refused Paying My Well earned Bill—Visited by My good acquaintance Pamar—Basterop the Painter, Much Talk With My good Hunter Gilbert Who Procured Me a Superb Specimen of the *Great Sand Hill Crane*—
Sufering Much from Sore Eyes and Violent Headache the Whole Day—

Wednesday 21st Gave Lessons at Mrs Braud & Miss Delfose—Drawing all Day at My Whooping Crane—Weather Extremely Sultry—

November Thursday 22^{d} 1821 Gave Lessons at Mrs Braud—My fair Pupill Miss Delfosse engaged otherwise—Rec^{d} 40$ on a/c from Mr Hawkins who appeared to be Much Pleased With the Drawing I give him of *Arianne*—Weather Summer Heat—Swallows Plenty—Rec^{d} a Letter from My Wife. My Spirits yet very Low—Drew Much to day—received 100$ from Mr Forestal as Mr Gordon had Not Paid any Money to My Wife at Louisville—

23^{d} Friday—Gave My Lessons to Mrs Braud and Miss Dellfosse—Rainy and Warm—drawing all day—bought a Portfollio from Vigny for 8$—

24th Gave My Lessons at Mrs Braud and Miss Dellfosse and also at Pamar to his Daugher Who exibited the brightest Genius I believe I ever Met With—Miss Dellfosse beautifull and extremely agreable—

Wrote to My Wife and W^{am} Bakewell and forwarded to cash a Check on the U. S. Bank of Philadelphia Received by Mr Bermudas for me and for Which I Paid ten per cent—of 100$ Weather extremely changed Cold and Windy—

25th
Sunday Weather Very Cold and raw—Gave Two Lessons of Drawing to Euphemie Pamar—

26 Gave My Lessons to Mrs Braud. Miss Dellfosse and Euphemie Pamar—Weather rather Mild—Swallows plenty—Ship Fulton arrived 120 Passengers on Board

November Tuesday 27th 1821 Gave My Lessons at Both Places —Visited the Maire's Lady Mrs Rosignol Who had evinced a desire to see some of My Pencil Productions—Expect her Daughter for a Pupil Weather Charming—Drew 2 Ducks. Called by Willson the *Tufted Duck* Male & female the Clerk of the Steam Boat Ramapo Called on us Mr *Laurent* an agreable Man

28TH Wednesday Gave My Lessons at Both Houses Weather fine Rec^d^ a Visit from Mr Braud & his Lady—Basterop Not Much Pleased at this; Drew a good deal

29TH Thursday—Gave Lessons to Mrs Braud's only Rec^d^ a Letter from My Wife of an older date than the former one—Weather beautifull—Painted Joseph Likeness—

30TH Friday—Gave My Lessons to Mrs Braud's and at Miss Dellfosse—

NEW ORLEANS DEC^R^ 1ST 1820 (1821) [Friday] Saturday Gave My Lessons to both houses and Miss Pamar—Rec^d^ a Letter from My Beloved Wife—Expect her in a few Days U. S. Steam Boat arrived—feather uncommonly pleasant Rec^d^ this Evening a Non Descript Hawk—

*SUNDAY 2^D^* Gave 2 Lessons to Euphemie Pamar and One to Miss Dellfosse *only*—Weather beautifull finished My Drawings of the *Crested Hawk* Which proved a femalle with Many Minute Eggs how Rare this bird is I Need Not Say being the Only specimen I Ever have Met with—although I once before found some Tail feathers of another Killed by a Squatter on the Ohio—Which Tail feathers having Kept—Corespond exactly With those of the present bird—

Regret Much that I Cannot Save the Skin but the Weather being Warm and My Drawing having taken Nearly Two Days it was not possible to skin it—

*MONDAY 3^D^* Gave Lesson to E. Pamar at Mrs Braud and Miss Delfosse—saw Mr Wheeler who arrived this day—how little I Expected to have Ever Met with him—Weather quite Warm—

TUESDAY 4 Gave Lessons to Mrs Braud at Miss Delfosse also Rec^d^ 40$ from the former and paid the rent of the house in Dauphine Street Weather very Warm drew an American Bitern—

New Orleans Decemb[r] *5*[th] *1821* ½ quire of Paper to Miss Josephine

Wednesday—Gave Lessons at M[rs] Brauds and Miss Delfosse—Weather Cool and Rainy—Visited Basterop and Was Introduced to M[r] Sell another of the Trade—another day of Disapointment My Lucy Not arrived—Thursday Begun taking & Giving Lesson to M[r] Lombar Gave My Lessons at M[rs] Brauds and today Miss Delfosse—Mr. Pirrie Arrived to day

7th Friday Gave Lessons at M[r] Braud's & Miss Delfosse—M[r] Lombar Give Me Lesson on the Violin & I to his Son of Drawing in Exchange —Rainy Cold all day

8th Saturday—Gave Lessons at M[rs] Braud's and gave her 1 doz[n] Black Chalks Making 1½ 6 Pencil handles at Miss Delfosse and Miss Pamar—at Night Music & Drawing With young Lombard had the Pleasure of seing M[r] *Harwood* from London and Rec[d] by him My Bitch *Belle*—Weather Rain & Cloudy

9th Sunday Weather Extremely Disagreable the Steam Boat Hero arrived from Louisville but No Regular Information about My familly by it—Gave 2 Lessons at M[rs] Pamar where I spent the greater part of the Day—Young Lombar Drawing at my House the Whole Day—

10th Gave Lessons 2 to Miss Pamar, M[rs] Braud's house and Miss Delfosse—Received a Visit from M[r] Selle & Mr. Jany Painters—

New Orleans Dec 11th *Tuesday 1821* I have but little time to spare at present to write the Many Incidents connected with the Life I am forced to follow for My Maintainance and of Course hundreds of them are passed and forgotten although I am well assured that a Rearsal would at future period amuse My thoughts. *One* however so curious appeared Me this day that I Cannot let it escape—May you My Dear Sons reap some benefit from the details

I am a Teacher of Drawing and have some Pupils My Style of giving Lessons and the high rate I charge for My Tuition have proved Me the Ill will of Every other artist in the City who Knows me or has heard of My Maxims—I Called on a *Bastard* of *Appollon* this Day to see his *Labours* I was unknown, tolerably well received and had the pleasure of seing the *Animal in* action—I also heard his *Barkings* and saw his Eyes gladening at the sight produced on the canvass before them—a Third unfortunate Dauber came in who it appeared Was an old acquaintance that Criticised at once with ease on all that Was around us—as Every day arrivals by Sea and Land bring New hands to the bellows the Names of Many Were Called forth and Mine amongst them—I Kept Myself and Waited & the following Picture was given Me Without any Varnishing I assure You—"That Man Came No one knows from Whence —he goes throu the streets Like the Devil I am told that he has as Many Pupils as he Wishes for and Makes a Wonderfull quantity of What he Calls Portraits and Assures the good folks who employ him that in a few Months by his Method any One May become able Painter—and yet from What I am told the Man Never Drew [but] has bought a set of handsome Drawings of Beasts Birds Flowers, &c Which he Shews and Says are his own—all this a Lye and take in While I Who Was Naturally Intended to Paint Teach &c am Without a Pupil or Portrait."—

here I Took My Hat told the Gentleman where I resided and that I Would be happy to See him giving him the [Two firsts] Initials of My Name only for a Guide—from this Eloquent Member of the *Sans Culottes of the Trade*, I Moved pretty briskly to Mr Basterop's Room were in a few Minutes I had the Satisfaction of Seing Messrs Jelle & Janin—all artists and agreable Men. Not Well setled about the a/c of Myself I had so lately heard but thinking how strangely the good Man Will feel when *he* Calls on Me—if ever he does—

I Gave My Lessons first to Miss Pamar—Mrs Braud at Miss Dellfosse and then according to Promise Went to a Pensionnat (were My Young Friend Miss Pamar receives the *Larger* portion of her Education) to give her regular Lessons of Drawing—When I Entered the Room, I saw a Degree of Coolness in the appearance of the *Lady* of the Institution that along With My unfortunate or foolish Natural awkwardness in similar Cases rendered My stay extremely disagreable; My Pupil who is generally Lively and full of Confidence in her actions Was at this time so astonishingly astray from her Work that not a line was properly Copied—I perceived the sarcastic Looks of the Diferent Teachers who Were present going the round and Was highly relieved When the Clock struck My Departure—a few Expressions uttered on My Entering, Joined to a few that reachd My Ears (that burned all this while) as I was Making My Escape Made Me take the resolution Never again to trespass on that Threshold or any other Without first Knowing Well how it May agree with the Will of the first Caracters attached to them [It seems that there are good and bad (—) for everybody]

My Lovely Miss Pirrie of Oackley Passed by Me this Morning, but did not remember how beautifull I had rendered her face once by Painting it at her Request with Pastelles; She Knew not the Man Who with the utmost patience and in fact attention *Waitted* on her Motions to please her—but thanks to My humble talents I can run the gantlet throu this World without her help

Wednesday 12th Gave My Lessons at M[rs] Braud's—Miss Delfosse absent to day—gave Lesson also to E. Pamar having taken all in Consideration I put aside the Shadow and hang to the bone—and with a *White Lye* arranged the Matter quite Well With M[rs] Pamar to Whom I had said that I should Not return there any more—

December Thursday 13th 1821 Gave Lessons at M[rs] Braud and E. Pamar Miss Dellfosse finding the Weather Too Cold—So Anxious Am I during the Whole of My present days to see My familly that My head is scarce at right With My Movements and yet I Must feel My sad Disapointments and retire to rest without the comfort of her so much Wanted Company

I saw to day a Work on Natural History with Colored Plates rather better than usual—

14 Friday Gave Lessons to all this afternoon—but Miss Dellfosse appeared dejected and Work but Indiferently—

It is Now 26 days since the Last Letter I have from My Wife is dated. Three Steam Boats have arrived since from Louisville and No News of her departure have reached Me—My anxiety renders every Moment painfull and Irksome—

I Met quite unexpectedly My Pupil Miss Pirrie at M[rs] Brauds, the interview was Short more friendly than I expected and We parted as if We Might see each other again With some Pleasure at some future Period—

15th Saturday Gave My Lessons to All this afternoon Weather Cool & Clear; feeling much relieved from My Anxiety about My Familly having heard that the Steam Boat the Rocket by Which they are to Come had not Left on the 28th ultimo and that Probably they would Not arrive for 4 or 5 Days yet—

M[r] Jany Visited us this Evening and stayed Very Late—

DECEMBER 16TH 1821 SUNDAY—Gave 2 Lessons to E. Pamar & 2 to Miss Delfosse only—Weather fine but Cool begun Drawing a Young *Swan* Sent me by My Hunter Gilbert from Barataria—

Young Lombar at Work all Day in My Room Drawing—

17TH Monday Gave My Lessons all round—I Drew at My *Swan* Mr Jarviss paid me a Visit and I returned it imeditly—Gave him 3 pieces of Canvas—Weather very Dark & Rainy

18TH TUESDAY—Gave a Lesson to Miss Pamar and One to Mrs Braud—My Wife & My Two sons arrived at 12 o'clock all in good health—I took them to Mr Pamar Where We all dined and then Moved to our Lodgings in Dauphine Street after 14 Months absence the Meeting of all that renders Life agreable to Me, was gratefully wellcomed and I thanked My Maker for this Mark of Mercy

19TH WEDNESDAY I only gave Lesson to Mrs Braud having much to do arranging My familly—Examined My Drawings & found them not so good as I Expected them to be; When compared With those Drawn since Last Winter—Bonaparte's Service Was performed this Day here—

20TH THURSDAY—Gave My Lessons all round—Weather Extremely Warm—Recd a *Nondescript Rail*

21ST FRIDAY Gave Lessons at Mrs Braud's & Miss Delfosse but so Wet and Damp that I declined going to see E. Pamar—Drew a Streaked Rail

NEW ORLEANS DECEMBER 22D 1821 SATURDAY—Gave My Lessons all round—Weather very Disagreable—Recd 20$ on a/c from R. Pamar—Young Lombar Resumed his Lessons this Evening having Missed Coming Whilst I was arranging My familly at home—

23D SUNDAY Gave 2 Lessons to E. Pamar and 1 to Miss Delfosse—Weather Extremely Cold—having seen Ice this Morning Nearly one Inch Thick

24 MONDAY Gave a Lesson to E. Pamar Young Braud and 2 to Miss Delfosse—

Weather very Cold—Mr Rozier Came to Pay us a Visit—it is Eleven Years since he [and], I, and My Familly, Were all together—

25 Tuesday—Gave 2 Lessons to Miss Delfosse but not any were else—
Snowed from Day Light untill Twelve o'clock and afterwards froze hard—

26 Wednesday—Gave 2 Lessons to Miss Delfosse and 1 to Miss Pamar—M[r] Gordon Visited us this Morning and M[r] Colas the Miniature Painter this Evening to see My Birds—

27 Thursday—Gave 2 Lessons to E. Pamar 2 to Miss Delfosse and One at M[rs] Braud—Weather beautifull—Paid our Rent this Morning—

28 Friday Gave My Lessons all round 2 to Miss D.

29th Saturday—Gave My Lessons all round—

Dec[r] Sunday—30th 1821 Gave 1 Lessons to E. Pamar and 1 to Miss Delfosse—M[r] Pamar Dined with us—I Drew this Day a Ferruginous Thrush and am to Draw 99 Birds in that Number of Days for Which I am to Pay One Dollar for each to *Robert* the Hunter—Who is to furnish Me With One hundred Specimen of Diferent Kinds Should he Not fullil the Contracts, he is to have only 50[cts] for each furnished

31 Monday—Gave 2 Lessons to Miss Pamar 1 to M[rs] Braud and 1 at Miss Delfosses & Drew an *ampellis Americana*.

The following material appears at the back of the journal and is written in from the back cover as a first page. It has no apparent connection with the regularly kept journal.

Copy of a Letter Written to the Honorable Henry Clay, Speaker of the House of Representatives, Lexington, Kentucky—

Sir

After having Spent the greater part of Fifteen Years in Procuring and Drawing the Birds of the United States with a view of Publishing them; I find Myself possessed of a Large Number of such Specimen as usually resort to the Midle States Only, having a desire to complete the Collection before I present it to My Country in perfect Order, I intend to Explore the Territories Southwest of the Mississipi.

I Shall leave this place about the midle of Sep^{t} for the purpose of Visiting the Red River, Arkansas and the Countries adjacent, and Well aware of the good Reception that a few lines from one on Whom our Country looks up with respectfull Admiration, would procure me; I have taken the liberty of requesting such Introductory Aid, as you, May deem Necessary to a Naturalist, While at the Frontier forts and Agencies of the United States

I Remain
Respectfully
Your Ob^{t} Servt
J. J. A.

Cincinnati Ohio Augt 12th 1820

Descriptions of the Water Birds of the United States, with their Generic [arrangement] characters according to the arrangement of Latham as Described by Alexander Willson—the Species discovered by Myself are Marked with My Initials

SPOON BILL

Bill Long, thin, the tip dilated, Orbicular, flat, nostrils Small, placed near the base of the Bill, tongue Short, pointed; feet four toed, Semipalmate

Roseate Spoonbill, Platalea ajaja. 7.123

La Spatule couleur de Rose de Brisson—

I sent Willson from Natchez, Measured 2 feet 6/12 and 4 feet in extent, Bill 6 $\frac{1}{2}$ Inches Long from the Corner of the Mouth 7 from its upper lap, 2 Inches its greatest Width $\frac{3}{4}$ Inches Narowest place—$\frac{1}{2}$ Black covered with Scaly protuberances like the edge of oister shells—waitish stained with red—Nostrils oblong in the Midle of the upper Mandible—a deep groove runs along the Mandible about $\frac{1}{4}$ Inch from the edge—Crown & Chin bare covered with a greenish Skin; that below the Lower Mandible dilatable as in Pelicans—orange round the eye, Irides blood red; cheeks & hind head bare black Skin; Neck Long covered with Short White feathers, tipt on the Neck with Crimson; breast White its Sides burnt brown Color, a Long tuft of hair Like plumage proceeds from the breast pale rose Color back White Slightly tinged with brownish, Wings pale rose Color, Shafts of same Lake; Shoulders of the Wings covered with Long hairy plumage deep & splendid Carmine; upper & Lower tail Coverts Same; belly rosy; rump paler; tail equal at the end 12 bright brownish orange feathers, Shalf redish; Legs and Naked part of the thigh dark dirty red; feet $\frac{1}{2}$ Webbed—toes Very long particularly hind one, inside of the Wing richer than Outside

List of the Watter Birds of North America taken from Turton's Linne

American Avoset, head, Neck & Breast rufous—Bill Black, Legs pale blue—

Blue Crane, Head, & Neck dark purple—3 Long narrow pendant feathers 6 Inches beyond Eye—Length—23 Inches extent 3 feet

Snowy Heron—2 $\frac{1}{12}$ feet—extent 3 $\frac{2}{12}$ —orange yellow round the Eye—Irids vivid Orange—Whole plumage White—(Head Largely Crested—4 Inches) breast Do upper back feathers recumbent and Loose—

Night Heron, Bill Blk 4$\frac{1}{4}$ Inch Skin about eye Blue, Irids Red, Cap^{d} deep Blue—3 White feathers Issuing—Back deep blue—Vent & belly White, Legs & feet Light Buff—Length 2$\frac{4}{12}$ —extent 4 feet

Great White Heron Bill yellow, Legs & feet claws Blk; Whole body White, Back feathers falling far over tail—Length 3 feet 6 to end of tail, 7 or 8 Inches Long to extremities of back feathers—

Stormy Petrel—

Great Tern, Bill & feet red, Black Cap^{d} tail very forked, upper parts, Light Bluish Ash—Belly white

Lesser Tern, Bill & Leg Yellow, Blk Cap^{d} tail very forked—

Short Tail Tern, Bill & Legs Black, Cap & Cheek Blk, Tail Shorter than Wings—

Black Skimmer—

Spotted Sand Piper; Bartram, Sand Snipe, ring plover, Sanderling plover, Golden P. Kildeer P—

Red Breasted Snipe—Long Legged Avoset Bill Blk Red purpleish red, Eye red, whole upper part, Deep Olive, Solitary Sand piper, Yellow Shank Snipe—Tell tail D^{o}

[HERONS]

Turn Stone, Bill Black Leg deep Orange—Breast Side of Neck and Spot under the Eye Black; Much of Brick Color on the Wings—belly White—4 Toes

Ash Colored Sandpiper Legs dull Yellow—4 Toes

Pure—Bill Black, Legs & feet D^{o} 4 Toes

Black Bellied Plover—4 Toes the Hind one small and very high

Red Breasted Sandpiper—Bill Short Vent White, Bell breast and under Neck Deep Rufous—

Esquimaux Corlew—Legs Greenish Blue—4 Toes

Red Backed Snipe—Bill Much Curved Blk belied Bend

Semi Palmated Snipe—have this

Marbled Godwit—Bill Long rather inclined upwards—

Louisianna Heron, Legs Yellow Bill blue—upper head Purpled, Crest White, Back Feathers very Long Light Buff—Tail, Wing & Back Deep Blue—

Pin Oister Catcher—

Hooping Crane—Black Tips—Bill yellow

Long Bill Curlew, Legs Bluish—

Yellow Crowned Heron Bill dark Blue, Legs Yellow White Crested Very Long, throat and Head black with an Oval White Spot—

Great Heron, thigh Deep Rufous, under Crest Long Blk, upper White—Breast, & Back fathers Long & Loose

American Bittern, Dirty Yellow Oakre, Zig Zaged with dark Brown —a Black Triangular Line runs from the Mouth to the Back of Neck

Least Bittern—

Wood Ibis Gros Beak

Scarlet Ibis

Flamingo

White Ibis

Black Surf Duck Singular Bill—3 White Marks about the head— Legs Red—

Buffel Headed Duck—the Spirit—

Canada Goose

TUFTED DUCK Bill Blue—Head Neck and breast Blk a Rufous bend on the Lower part of Neck

GOLDEN EYE DUCK

SHOVELLER DUCK

GOOSANDER, Head Changeable Green

PIN TAIL DUCK Sprigg Tail

BLUE WING[D] TEAL

SNOW GOOSE

PIED DUCK Legs & feet Light Ockre, Ring round the Neck Connected with Back, Back Tail Belly and Line over the Eye Black, primaries also Black, the Remainder White

RED BREASTED MERGANSER—have this

AMERICAN WIDGEON, Bald Pate

BLUE BILL—head Neck & Breast Dark Brown—Back Canvassed—Rump Tail & Tail Coverts Blk

HOODED or CRESTED MERGANSER

LONG TAIL DUCK—Old Wife

SUMMER DUCK

GREEN WINGED TEAL

CANVAS BACK DUCK

RED HEADED DUCK—Head and neck half way—Bright Rufous—Lower part of Neck & Breast Blk. Back Canvassed—

MALARD

CADWALL DUCK

EIDER DUCK Male & femelle

the SMEW, the BLACK SPECTACLED GOOSANDER

RUDDY DUCK, Blue Bill, Legs Rosy—upper head Black, Neck & whole upper part Brick Color—Cheeks, Chin, & side of Head White—femelle Dark olive all upper Part—sides of Head Dusty Yellow—Breast transversally Barred with Brick Colored Lines—Belly & Vent dirty Yellow—

Brant

Scotter Duck Wholy Black, upper Mandible Yellow—Lower & Nails Blk—Protuberances Red—Legs Red

Velvet Duck—have it Large Blk Sea Duck

Harlequin Duck a Narrow regular White ring around the Lower part of Neck—

A Black Duck A Dusky Duck

Marsh Tern Black Cap[d] Wings, Back & Tail Light Ash or Blue—the first Very Long the Latter Slightly forked—Legs & palmate feet Lead—

Sooty Tern—Bill Black, front and whole under part White, upper Blk tail Much forked, the Tips White edged inwardly with Blk

The 9th Volume I believe Contains—the Loon = Purple Galinulle = Coot = Darter = Black Headed Gull = Great Footed Hawk, &[c] =

LETTERS

Audubon was a compulsive letter writer, often writing two or three letters a day in addition to the regular evening entry in his journal. Fortunately, a large number of these letters survive, though many have never been collected. They are the best place to discover Audubon's natural voice (uninhibited, humorous, and direct), and they are the best place to examine the inner history of his working life. Audubon could be urgent when the occasion demanded, but the main quality the letters reveal is an unhurried delight in using the written page as a form of familiar conversation. He is generous with details of what he has seen and done during the day, and he loves to embroider an anecdote, especially when writing to his wife, Lucy, or to a good friend like John Bachman.

The first series of letters was written to Lucy during his trip to Florida in the fall and winter of 1831–32. By this time the publication of the Birds of America *(1827–38) was well under way. Audubon's engraver in London, Robert Havell, had printed over one hundred plates, distributed to subscribers in bound "numbers" of five plate-prints apiece. In order to provide Havell with new paintings to engrave, and in order to make sure the finished book would be as complete and as accurate a compilation as possible, Audubon spent the next few years traveling, often in remote areas of North America, searching out new specimens. On his trip to Florida he was accompanied by George Lehman, a young Swiss artist Audubon had hired to do backgrounds, and by Henry Ward, an English taxidermist who had been sent to the United States under Audubon's supervision to prepare bird skins for two English ornithologists, William Swainson, a writer, and John Gould, the gifted artist who has since been called the English Audubon. Audubon carried with him letters from federal officials giving him permission to request help and transportation from all military vessels he encountered on his way.*

A key episode in this first series of letters narrates the meeting and growing friendship of Audubon with the Reverend John Bachman, a minister who lived in Charleston, South Carolina. Bachman and his family would become deeply involved with Audubon over the years. Bachman himself became one of Audubon's dearest friends (adviser and confidant combined). A superb naturalist, he later collaborated with Audubon on the Viviparous Quadrupeds of North America *(1845–54). Two of Bachman's daughters married Audubon's two sons, and Bachman's sister-in-law, Maria Martin, painted several backgrounds for Audubon.*

The second series of letters was written to Bachman (a letter to Lucy is also included) during Audubon's trip to the Gulf of Mexico in 1837. On this trip Audubon was accompanied by his good friend Edward Harris, and by Audubon's younger son, John. Both packets of letters are taken from the Letters of John James Audubon, 1826–1840, *edited by Howard Corning, and published in two volumes in 1930 by the Club of Odd Volumes.*

Letters to Audubon's Wife, Lucy, Written During His Trip to Florida in the Fall and Winter of 1831–32

To M*rs* AUDUBON
Louisville, Kentucky—

Richmond Sunday afternoon Oct*r* 9*th* 1831—

MY DEAREST FRIEND.—

We are at Richmond and if thou hast been favored thou, by this time, are at Wheeling—I sincerely hope it is so and that thou art *well* yet—I will write our Journey from our departure and do thou keep my letters as duplicates of my Journal—

We reached the Steam Boat (Po[h]chohontas) at about 8 of the morning after an early breakfast and our bill paid—The morning was fair & calm and we progressed down the Cheasapeek Bay with a motley cargo of passengers at a fair rate untill the evening—The Bay itself is truly beautiful and I enjoyed the scenery very much for I was without thee, without our Dear Sons and once more as if alone in the World. Towards night the wind rose—the waves also became boisterous—the Vessel worked heavily and we all were glad to retire to our matresses for rest—however little comfort could we have amidst more than one hundred passengers old & young and indeed for my part so full was I of the want of thy Company that my eyes closed only at intervals and at last the head ache brought me to the Deck again—We reached Norfolk at 5 of the morning distant from Baltimore *180 Miles* and it is only through accident that we came up to this place for we had no sooner landed than I went up to the Coach Office and took our places for Charleston S. C. but the man at the Bar could not change a 100 Dollars note and we concluded to come over the James River to Petersburgh.—We did so on board the *Richmond Steamer* and enjoyed the view of the Latter Stream very much; it is at first broad and finely shored; gradually diminishing in breadth to Cedar Point where to my surprise I saw several fine *Ships* loading in Tobacco—There we were told we had to go by the Stage to Petersburg 12 Miles and that it would cost us more than to ascend the River in the same boat we were in. Therefore we concluded to push for the place where we now are and reached at 7 last evening after running through the constantly narrowing Stream—It was pitch dark and rainy when we landed and the *Union Hotel* a good half mile distant—Lehman & I walked through the dark to Search for the Mighty Hotel and left Henry in charge of the baggage—he was clever for once at least, for he procured a cart for our baggage for 75*cts* which we his Elders could not do so for less than one Dollar and fifty cents—The Union Tavern is Large, dirty and but tolerably kept otherwise—We were all put into one room at No. 35 much as Victor & I were at Browns at Washington—however we have been without bugs or muschitoes and have managed to fill our stomachs in one way or another—

The Rain poured down all night yet this morning has been pretty fair—Out of the 4 letters I had for this place only one could I deliver the other persons being absent—The Governor *John Floyd*, the Brother of George Floyd formerly of Louisville but since dead, received us expremely politely—indeed he remembered me well having seen him at old Taratan (?) and at Doc*r* Scott—I showed him the Birds of America notwithstanding this is Sunday—*he has promised* to propose to the Legislature to Subscribe and the Secretary or Librarian of the College has done the same as soon as their respective Committees meet, when they are to write to Harlan—the Governor accompanied us to the Capitol or State House, shewed us every part of it—There we saw a *Splendid Statue* of Washington and a good portrait of Jefferson—he promised me some letters for the Governors of North & South Carolina and we parted—Richmond consists of a Long undulating street supported by a few others running parralel but in which the houses are less compact—The situation of the State House is elevated—the building Simple and in bad repair but will be soon retouched with Lime & Mortar—The General view of the Country from that spot is vast and rather interesting for our Country—the River going off meandering for 7 or 8 miles in the distance through a rather flat Country bounded as is always in America by Woods, Woods, Woods!—

The Governor assured me that beyond *the State* and the State's Library or that of the College no names could be procured unless I chose to ramble over the Country from one house to another—This I cannot do therefore we push off tomorrow morning at Eleven for *Columbia College* about 200 miles on our way to Charleston by the Mail—

The Negro disturbances are quite at an end and the famous *Genl. Nat* is supposed to have drowned himself for all the tales we have read of his having been made a prisoner are quite unfounded—

I am told that the rains have settled the Roads and that we may expect a *tolerable* ride—

I will write from the first place I stop at sufficiently long to enable me to do so—

Remember me kindly to William and his wife and to our dear Sons —Write often to S*t* Augustine Florida and try to spend thy time comfortably—God bless thee my Dearest Friend

thine for ever

J. J. Audubon

To M*rs* AUDUBON
Louisville, Kentucky

Fayetteville N. C. Thursday noon Octr 13*th* 1831

We are thus far my beloved Friend and here we are to stay untill a chance for us takes place in the Coach having arrived four hours too late last evening when the Mail which was to have taken us forward had left.—

We left Richmond from where I wrote to thee, on Monday morning 12 o'clock with 10 Inside and Two outside, reached Petersburgh at 3 dined and proceeded—There I met with Rob*t* Sully who came to the Coach Just as we were going off—plenty of talk but no cash.—I was forced to pay at that place 5$ for *extra baggage!*—The rain poured all that day and that night. The Roads most horrible and at last at 1/2 past 2 of the night our vehicle being on the point of upsettng we all got out and had to work for 2 & 1/4 hours in the mud knee deep and wet to the skin to get it out.—This was effected by pure main force—The next day cleared off, we left many of our Passengers and were congratuling ourselves when lo we were transferred to the Worst sort of a Wagon with mail bags & baggage with which we trundled for about 100 Miles—et pour comble de malheur 36 Miles back of this we had to take in 2 Ladies—3 Children and a *Man*—Thou may suppose how we we were cramed—however we arrived here safely—

from Richmond untill we crossed the Roanoke River the Country is a worn out one and the Laziness of the Virginians well proved & The Roanoke was very full we crossed it in a flat Ferry boat—after which the Pine Woods of *this State* became more & more plentiful untill scarcely anything else in the way of Timber was to be seen except when we crossed a water course when Magnolias and other shrubs exhibited themselves.—No game of any sort did we see—Scarcely a wood-peally. We crossed the Cape Fear River on a good wooden bridge which being very much closed in prevented us from seeing the stream.—Steam boats are here which go to Wilmington N. C*n*—Fayetteville is a ruined place at present almost every house having been burnt last July—the noise of the hammers &*c* fill my ears and 40 or more houses are raising from over the ashes and debris of the Ruins—Living is dearer than ever and apparently everything scarce.—Butter no more—corn bread and Sweet Potatoes the staple of the Table-d'hote &*c* &*c*

We have just returned from a walk and find that we have already overtaken the Birds—the Mocking birds and Robbins are in full song and had we wished to destroy them might have killed a good number, but as I hope we have a chance to proceed this afternoon at 4 we only brought a few rare birds which are now under the hand of the operator

Henry Ward.—we have collected a few fine Insects and that is all.—

We have had for compagnon de Voyage a Colonel Preston the nephew of the Large Colonel Preston which we knew at Louisville—an aimiable Gentleman who resides at Columbia S. C. and whom we will see there for he hired a Gig last evening and pushed for home having no baggage except a carpet bag—

I shall stay at Columbia 2 days as Co*l* Preston thinks that the College *at least* will Subscribe.—Our baggage is all in good order as far as can Judge by the outside—I will write from Columbia—I am extremely anxious to hear of thine & Dear Victor's safe arrival at Louisville and hope to hear from thee at Savannah—Love to all around thee—Tell John to skin all he can and collect everything possible—and Dearest best Friend once more *fare thee well*

God bless thee and our Sons—

Thine for ever JOHN J. AUDUBON.

To M*rs* AUDUBON
Louisville, Kentucky

Charleston S. C. 23d Oct*r* 1831—

MY DEAREST FRIEND—

I have just finished a drawing which I began this morning of a very rare species of Heron and I am determined ere another day passes or another Drawing is begun to write to thee and give thee an account of our proceedings since Fayetteville from whence I wrote my last—

We left the latter place on the day I wrote in a cramped Coach and passed over a flat level and dreary Country crossing at every half mile or so Swamps all of which might be termed truly dismal—no birds, no quadrupeds no prospect (save that of being Jostled)—The waters were all high—it took us 3 hours to cross the Pedee River in a Canoe &*c* &*c* but at last on Sunday last (a week this day) we arrived at Charleston—put up at a boarding house to the owner of which I paid 10 1/2 Dollars for 3 meals and 2 nights rest—I delivered my letters to M*r* Lowndes who received me as all strangers are when they present a letter of that kind and we parted.—I pushed almost out of town to deliver another to the Rev*d* Mr. Gilman—There I found a man of learning, of sound heart and willing to bear the "American Woodsman" a hand—he walked with me and had already contrived to procure us cheaper Lodgings &*c* when he presented me in the street to the Rev*d* M*r* Bachman!—M*r* Bachman!! why my Lucy M*r* Bachman would have us all to stay at his house—he would have us to make free there as if we were at our own encampment at the head waters of Some unknown Rivers—he would not suffer us to proceed farther South for 3 weeks—he talked—he looked as if his heart had been purposely made of the most benevolent materials granted to man by the Creator to render all about him most happy—Could I have refused his kind invitation? No!—It would have pained him as much as if grossly insulted. We removed to his house in a crack—found a room already arranged for Henry to skin our Birds—another for me & Lehman to Draw and a third for thy Husband to rest his bones in on an excellent bed! An amiable Wife and Sister-in-Law, Two fine young Daughters and 3 paires more of Cherubs all of whom I already look upon as if brought up among them—

Out shooting every Day—Skinning, Drawing, Talking Ornithology The whole evening, noon, and morning—in a word my Lucy had I thee and our Dear Boys along I certainly would be as happy a mortal as Mr. Bachman himself is at this present moment, when he has just returned from his Congregation—congratulated me on my days work and now sets amid his family in a room above me enjoying the results of his days work. This my Dearest Friend is the situation of thy husband at Charleston South Carolina—Some hopes of one or two Subscribers are afloat and time will enable me to let thee know the result—

Charleston is less in size than Baltimore—it lays flat in front of the Bay—The population is about 30,000—Politics run high with the Tariff men. I have become acquainted with several amiable characters and further I know not—

I have 3 Drawings under way—about 80 Skins—some insects &*c* Lehman and Henry behave well—Our expenses since Richmond Virginia have been very great—I have heard news from no one and that is I can say at present.—

I hope thou didst reach home safely and Victor also—that our Dear John is well and Brother William coining Dollars or Doubloons as fast as he may wish to do so—remember me to all—Write to me at S*t* Augustine Florida after this reaches thee as often as thou may please—write often to England and to Nicholas—to Doc[—] Harlan also and believe me thine Friend and husband for ever

John J. Audubon.

To M*rs* Audubon
Louisville, Kentucky

Charleston South Ca Octr 30*th* 1831—

My Dearest Friend.—

I received thy kind letter dated at Wheeling on Tuesday last and I was heartily glad to hear of thy having reached there safely—I will not forget the Friend of 25 Years standing I think—neither will I forget her precept for I am also aware that the World has an eye upon me and was the World blind I feel that it is more suitable to become wise if possible than to become a poor & useless being.—

I certainly have met with more kindness in this place than anywhere else in the United States—here I am the very pet of every body and had I time or Inclination to visit the great folk I might be in dinner parties from now untill Jan*y* next.—however I have other Fish to fry—I am positively busy—I have drawn 9 Birds since here which make 5 Drawings when finished—M*r* Bachman is more kind every day, and as I hope my letter of last Sunday (this day week) has reached thee I will not repeat any more the generous conduct which he has assumed towards us all—

I visited Sullivan's Island 3 days ago in the Company of Doc*r* Henry Ravenell of this place and hunted all day—had a splendid breakfast Dinner and was conveyed to & fro in a 6 oars boat all free gratis.—Doc*r* Ravenell is a great Conchologist and *will* give me a fine mess of shells—I wish in return that Victor should ship to him by way of Orleans a box of Ohio shells as soon as possible.

I am going to write to Doc*r* Harlan and to Havell—also to Lord Stanley—to the latter my Friend Bachman is about forwarding 3 Beautiful Deer, and I will ask of the Lord to forward some Pheasants, Partridges and a couple of hares to the good man of Charleston—

I have no Subscribers yet but a good deal of talk on the subject the all of which I hope may soon be realized—It is my intention to write to Savannah for our things letters &*c* to be forwarded to S*t* Augustine Florida direct & as soon as possible and to Sail for that Peninsula from this place—The weather is *now* rather cooler but we have had it *tremendously* hot—Lehman is at work—Henry has prepared 157 Skins amongst which are upwards of 20 Carion Crows & Turkey Buzzards—the ground Dove of which I have drawn 5 on a Wild Orange branch is one of the sweetest birds I have ever seen—I have just finished a Drawing of 2 Large Curlews—Tomorrow we are going with Friend Bachman and Doc*r* Samuel Wilson in Cariages 9 Miles shooting—The Doc*r* has made me a present of a New Foundland Dog that is as good as beautiful—

I have not a letter from any one as yet except thine from Wheeling mentioned here—I fear much that I will be at times much puzled to know what is going on abroad but I am determined to push ahead and will write to thee every Sunday at Least.—God bless my Dearest Wife and may God bless thee for ever—Kindest remembrances to our Dear boys—To Wiliam and his Dear Wife—Little John &*c* As we start at 5 tomorrow morning I am rather in a hurry and will bid thee take care of thy Sweet Self and believe ever thine

Husband
& Friend
JOHN J. AUDUBON.

To M*rs* AUDUBON
Louisville, Kentucky

Charleston S. C. Novembr 7th 1831—

Well my Dearest Friend we are spending another Sunday under the hospitable roof of my most excellent Friend the Reverend John Bachman. We have been here just three weeks and I have drawn 15 Birds which make 5 Drawings all of which are finished by Lehman with views Plants &*c* Henry has skinned and preserved 220 Specimens of 60 different species of Birds—we contemplated going off further South a week ago but my Friend here strongly advised me not untill a Frost takes place.—We have had the weather extremely hot and in all excursions the sand flies have tormented us at a round rate.—in consequence of the heat and the Insects Henry's Face and Legs have been rendered so sore that the poor Fellow could hardly walk and his Skin is now coming off from all over him—he was fairly frightened and thought he was going to die: he is now much better, indeed he went out shooting yesterday—

Tomorrow at 8 o'clock we go to Cole's Island about 25 miles down the bay to the South and will spend a night and return the next morning when the tide will serve.—we go there in the boat of a Friend called Connart who although no Sportsman is anxious for the progression of the Birds of America and gives us his boat—4 negroes to row and his clerk to Pilote us under my orders. M*r* Bachman always goes with us, is an excellent shot and full of Life & Spirits: we Laugh & talk as if we had known each other for Twenty Years—

Doc*r* Henry Ravenell, the person to whom I wish thee to forward some Ohio shells came yesterday to invite me to go to his Plantation 40 miles off to spend some weeks, but I declined for I am very anxious to see what sort of Country the Florida is.

In consequence of my remaining here so long I have received but one letter from thee dated Wheeling, but yesterday I wrote to M*r* W*am* Gaston of Savannah to forward me whatever he had of mine—Last Sunday I wrote to thee, to Havell, to Lord Stanley and to Doc*r* Harlan—I have not heard from any one as yet.—

My Friend Bachman has six Subscription papers distributed among his acquaintances each to be filled with twelve names at 5 Dollars per annum and 19 Dollars cash to pay for the first Volume—he expects by that means to procure half a dozen Subscribers, Companies, to the Work—Some of the lists which were delivered only a few days ago have already 4 or 5 names and he thinks that in the course of next week they will all be filled.—Should this take place my visit to Charleston will prove a most valuable one indeed. I must confess that no where in America have I met with so much attention, Kindness or hospitality as here. —Doc*r* Sam*l* Wilson a friend of Doc*r* Harlan gave me an excellent & beautiful Newfound Land Dog for which in my present Situation I would not take 100 Dollars and a few days afterward he called to see how we were coming on and presented me with a handsome Silver Snuff Box.—The Ladies have brought us 1/2 a dozen of bottles of Snuff and Mr. Connart six bottles.—The Papers here have *blown me up* sky high The Society of Natural Sciences of Philadelphia has *at last* elected me one of their members, the Papers say *Unanimously* I dare say my Friend Lea was not in the way.—My Friend Bachman was well acquainted with Alex*r* Wilson and *Friend Ord* and relates some Capital anecdotes—*he* has furnished me with a great deal of good Information on many birds and *Stories* for Tale pieces to my next Volume—do thee try to procure some thyself—I wish to God thou wert with me to See the kindness of the whole of this Family it would do thy own heart good I am sure.—

Henry has skinned as many as 42 Birds in a day Large and Small and *works well*, but is quite a [———] in everything else—he shoots well—he and his bed fellow Lehman did not very well agree at first but I Settled the matter at once and them in good order, respectful to each other and now in good terms—They are invited were ever I go and when not engaged they go with me—Many Gentlemen come and spend hours with him to see him work which he does not admire unless well dressed for he is a great beau when he can—

My Love to our Dear Sons, Brother William and his Wife—Write often to S*t* Augustine untill I say otherwise—take great care of thy Dear Self both as to regards health and *Intellect*, remember the Friend of Twenty Five years and believe me thy

Sincere Husband

JOHN J. AUDUBON.

To M*rs* AUDUBON
Louisville
Kentucky—

Charleston S. C. Novr 1831 *the* 13*th*

MY DEAREST FRIEND.—

We will leave this hospitable place on the day after tomorrow at 8 o'clock of the morning for S*t* Augustine Florida.—

I am induced to do so because first I have been Idle for a full week and again because I begain to feel ashamed of the trouble we must inevitably have given to the kind Family under whose roof we have resided for one month.—

I regret very much that I am forced to leave Charleston without receiving 6 letters that according to Mr. Wam. Gaston are at Savannah. —I wrote to that Gentleman and requested him to forward all he had for me to this place, but the *good natured man* answered that he was afraid the postage would prove enormous. I wish he knew how much postage I am in the habit of paying in Europe.—

I leave my most excellent Friend the Rev*d* John Bachman my agent for my Work and to his care the charge of my first Volume of Plates.— I know him so well and know him to be so uprightly good that I feel quite assured that all will go on well with him—

I have written this day to W*am* Rathbone, Rich*d* Harlan, Lemuel Goddard and my Friend M*r* Children—

I will pack a certain portion of my Bird Skins and leave the rest to be packed when dry by my good Friend Bachman—who will also forward them to Doc*r* Harlan—had I known what I now know I would certainly have followed Doc*r* Tideman's advice and would have remained in Pennsylvania one month or six weeks longer—we have passed the Birds of the North and not overtaken those of the South therefore I have lost time both ways.—

I am told that living at S*t* Augustine is extremely extravagant and it is therefore my intention to push either for the Plantation of General Hernandez or for Cape Carnaval, yet as no true knowledge is acquired without experience will leave everything to itself untill we reach the Land of Promise.—

Do my Dearest Lucy write to me at least as often as I do to thee i. e. every Sunday—I feel as if it were an age since I pressed thee to my breast and every moment brings to my recollection the remembrances of the many blessings I have enjoyed at thy own Dear hands—God bless thee Dearest Friend—do take great care of thy Dear Self and of *thy Intellect!* remember me most kindly to W*am* and his wife—to Brother Thomas if thou seest him and to all concerned towards the welfare of thy Sincere Friend and Husband

JOHN J. AUDUBON.

I have not mentioned our Dear Sons but nevertheless do I hope & wish them well & Happy—Still write to S*t* Augustine untill I write to the contrary as the United State's Commandant there will attend to the forwarding of all letters that may come—I have here two Subscriptions Insured and may be 2 or 3 more!—I have sent my Book to Columbia College care of a Professor Gibbs to whom Ward has sold his English bird skins for 50 Dollars. Doc*r* Cooper the President of that College is the son of M*r* Cooper who came to England with thy Father and Doc*r* Priestly who knows thee well—After the book returns here it will be sent to W*am* Gaston of Savannah who writes that he can get 5 or 6 Subscribers there after which it will return to my Friend Bachman who will forward it according to my orders.—

The name of the Schooner that takes us to S*t* Augustine is the Agnes, a regular Packet from here thence—

Again God bless thee Dearest Friend—write, collect and do all thou canst in our behalf and that of Science and once more for ever believe me thine Husband—

J. J. A.

To M*rs* AUDUBON
Louisville, Kentucky

St Augustine East Florida 23*d Novr* 1831

MY DEAREST FRIEND—

We arrived here on Sunday last in the morning after a passage of 5 days from Charleston on Board a Schooner called the Agnes, Cap*n* Sweazey.—

The winds were contrary and so was the Cap*n* as poor a "shoat" as ever I have seen—Our company consisted of 8 or 9 Ladies, some *overseers* a Cap*n* of the Army from New York named Dehart and some negroes, in all 23.—during the night of the 2*d*—24 hours the wind dead ahead and a stiff breeze our Cap*n* put back to S*t* Simmons Island on the Coast of Georgia.—There I landed and proceeded to the house of a M*r* Thos Arthur King to whom I gave my card—he knew of my name Invited me to dinner, had me shaved, shewed me his beautiful Garden and grounds and made me write an Invitation to my Lads and Cap*n* Dehart to Join us at Dinner—This was done.—The Dinner was prepared, nay the table was set—it was nearly 4 o'clock when all of a sudden Henry came running to the House and told me that the Agnes was under way —I jumped up took my cloak, and shook hands with M*r* King who on accompanying me to the shore, gave me *his card* and bid me put his name on my List of Subscribers.—M*r* King was anxious to keep us for a month or so with him being fond of shooting, Drawing &*c* and I now wish I had accepted of his generous offer.—However we left, passed S*t* Simon's Barr and again had head wind. it vered in the night blew like great Guns and at day light we were in view of this famous City. The entrance of the Port here is shocking we spent the whole of Saturday and part of the night coming over the different Barrs not exceeding 4 Miles &*c*—

Landed looked for Lodgings, ransacked the *four* Taverns that are here and at Last concluded to put up at a M*r* Fleshman for four and half Dollars per week each.—Hare, fish and venaison three times per day!—

S*t* Augustine resembles some old French Village and is doubtless the poorest village I have seen in America—The Inhabitants principally poor Fishermen although excellent Fishers—The streets about 10 feet wide and deeply sanded—backed by some thousands of orange Trees loaded with fruit at 2 cents apiece—A Garrison of one Company—and an old Spanish Castle once the Pride of this Peninsula but now decaying fast. —it is built of *Shell Stone* or a concrete of shells which hardens by exposure to the Air and is curious to the Geologist.—*no back Country* for after one leaves this would be a City no house is to be met with for 30 miles—The whole Country sandy, Timber, Pine, Live oak and different species of Mirtles and Magnolias—Whilst our Schooner was at anchor we went on S*t* Anastasia's Island and collected some hundreds of shells—in some places we could have taken them up (Live ones) by the shovel full—Saw great number of Water Fowls, Pelicans &*c* The weather was *then* very hot thermometer at 82, killed 2 large Snakes, Butterflies abundant—&*c* of course *some* flowers—To day the wind has been at Northwest and the glass has fallen down to 49.—have hunted a great deal but have shot only 2 birds to draw—one a beautiful Heron, the other a Sandpiper. have found only 2 acquaintances as yet—will give more of my letters in a few days—this morning received a letter from Doc*r* Harlan which has relieved me of much anxiety for by it I know thy safe arrival at Louisville and of the Subscription of M*r* Hancock, his having received thy letter demanding a volume for that Gentleman to whom do present my best wishes and thanks—Harlan says that he has forwarded many letters to Savannah to W*am* Gaston for me but not one have I received yet through the unfortunate management of M*r* Gaston who retained them fearing the postage and expecting me there.—Then we left Charleston without my large trunk which with the other articles will come here in about 3 weeks, letters and all, I am sorry for this for Harlan says one is desired outside to be forwarded with great dispatch —it is from England and I have been fretting myself with the Idea that Havell might be Dead. Such an event would stop my Journey at once and force me back to Europe in a very unprepared state.—I hope to God it is not so.—When I leave this (in about one month) I will have to forego the receiving of letters for a long time as I find that no mail goes further South than 30 miles—*write here* untill to the contrary as I will make arrangements with the Commandant of the Garrison to forward wherever I may be by Indian Runners—

Thou ought to write every week and at great length—I do the same as much as my work will possibly allow me—I am told that *Tallahassee is a miserable place for Merchants* having no back Country, that all is sold at long credit &*c*—

I directed my Friend John Bachman of Charleston to write to thee as often as he heard of me to give thee all kind of chances.—Lehman and Henry are quite well—and we have begun to work all hands since here—I wish thee to forward me *at New Orleans* to be kept for me some good socks as mine will be all worn out—the salt marshes through which I am forced to wade *every day* are the ruin of everything—

I have not shot but have seen a Hawk of great size entirely *new*—may perhaps kill him tomorrow—

I do not think it would be advisable for our Dear Son John to meet me in the Floridas, the expenses are too great but think that when I am about to go into Texas &*c* would be better time—I will write accordingly should I think it proper for him to come at that period—I will close my letter tomorrow God bless Thee Dearest Friend Good Night. —by the way, *know ye* all men that Rattlesnake *do clime Trees!!!* See Featherstonhaugh Journal—Wert thou here thou wouldst collect if willing a Ship load of Shells some truly beautiful—Doc*r* Ravenell gave me Two boxes of them at Charleston—Again Sweet Wife Good Night.

Novr 24th I have just returned from shooting up the North River so called here and have as much as will keep me very busy for two days—nothing else new—God bless thee my most and dearly beloved Wife and Friend—Would to God that I had thee to comfort me this night.—do thou write often God forever bless thee—remembrances to William, his wife; and Dear Sons &*c*—Thine for ever

JOHN J. AUDUBON.

To M*rs* AUDUBON
Louisville, Kentucky.

St. Augustine E. F. Novemb'r 29th 1831

MY DEAREST FRIEND—

Only one letter have I received from thee since we parted at Baltimore.—The one I received as I have often said before was dated Wheeling, and fortunately I have received a letter from Friend Harlan who mentions having received one from thee saying that thou had a Subscriber at Louisville.—

We have been here since 10 days having arrived last Sunday week—We have been uncommonly busy Shooting & Drawing—have drawn 13 different Species amongst which a *new one* which proves to be a *new Genera* for the United States—a kind of Exotic Bird probably very common in South America but quite unknown to me or to anyone else in this place—it is a mixture of Buzzard and Hawk and I have decided to call it *Catharses Floridaniis.*—I have written to Doc*r* Harlan about it and its description will be published in the transactions of the A. S. S. of Phila*a*—The transition of Idleness to hard Labour has operated upon me as if the electric fluid and I was very nearly *knocked up* last Sunday when I certainly drew faster than ever I have done in my Life.

The Weather here is uncommonly changeable—We have had alternately very hot & sultry Weather followed by what I call very cold although without Ice but a smart Frost.—in my last I gave thee an a/c of S*t* Augustine but all descriptions fall short of the reality as much as my own poor Drawings fall short of Nature's superior & Inimitable softness and beauty of Coloring.—I will therefore not attempt to say more on the Subject.—We are *tolerably* comfortable for 4 1/2 Dollars each per Week—feed principally on Fish and Venaison and have little more in sight than the Breaking Sea Surf in our Front and extensive Orange Groves in our rear—As far as I have been in the Interior of this place the Country is wretchedly sterile, Sandy and covered with almost impenetrable Spanish Sword plants (a species of Palmita) called in Louisiana The Bear Plant.—Birds are aboundant but to my extreme surprise wonderfully Shy therefore although we procure *Species* and make Drawings from morning untill night *Henry* is kept almost Idle.—

We have had 3 Invitations to 3 diferent Plantations on our way South and I have accepted of one laying about 46 miles near a place on the Sea board called Pulmira at the House of a Doc*r* Pocher who is in Partnership with a M*r* McCraigh to both of whom I had letters—

General Hernandez for whom I had several letters both from England and this Country has received me *rather* cooly and I daresay is not likely to be troubled with our Company—here we have received all possible civilities—The Authorities have called upon me I mean the Judges and several officers of the Army and all have proffered as much as in their power—

Our next move will be 46 Miles South to M*c*Craigh's plantation or as it is called Smirna but will remain here 3 weeks longer as we are doing well in the way of Water Birds.—Write here untill I say to the contrary and write often I do beg of thee for I am on thorns when without news from thee—I will leave instructions to have my letters forwared to wherever I may be—

I have not received my large trunk yet and I am almost out of clothes—My gray suit is quite gone and my good shirts are fairing roughly I assure thee.—I hope however that next week I will have the all of my Luggage and will be able to have plenty to change.—

I would give all in the World to talk to thee and to hear from Havell—I am constantly fretting about the Continuation of *our* Work in England—and yet I work now harder than ever I have done in my Life and so do my Young Men.—Lehman is as ever a most excellent industrious and Worthy Fellow—Henry is rather inclined to be Lazy but I pull him and have him out of his resting place as early as I do myself —I hope he will do better by and by—I expect a great batch of letters with my trunk &*c*., and long to read them—Should Havell die Victor must go to England and make arrangements for the Continuation of the Engraving and Coloring &*c* with Havell's assistant *Mr Blake* from whom I have understood and do know that equally good work may be expected—I cannot think of returning untill *my Journey* is compleated —and with me it is *Neck or Nothing!*—

At the exception of a letter from Doct*r* Harlan and the one from thee which I have mentioned, not a word have I heard from any soul.—

I have written several times to Havell—Rathbone, Cuthbertson, Kidd,—McGillivray—Children and Lemuel Goddard.—

Should we have the good luck of procuring Specimens as fast as we have done and the same opportunities of observing their Habits for a twelve month longer this Journey will prove as fruitfull to Science and to us as we could possibly desire it.—

The people of S*t* Augustine are *principaly Minorkas* (?) without any Intelligence and as lazy as Spaniards *our days* are wont to be. *Fishing* when hungry is their avocation—a few oranges—6 1/4 *cts* of Lard to fry their fish and some Rice is their usual food—My own camp will afford much better fare—

The Climate is the most changeable I ever saw—we have in 24 hours the Thermometer at 89—down to 45 and then a smart frost after which the southerly winds have made us all sweat at our Drawings.

I certainly do wish much that I had our Dear John but I find my expenses already very great, so much so indeed that I do not indulge in any thing like what I would call comfort at other times.—Therefore do not send him untill I write for him which perhaps may be when I am to ascend the head of the Arkansa River towards the Rocky Mountains sometime next Summer; yet should anything occur which may prove advantageous to him otherwise do not suffer him to let the opportunity escape. I confide altogether in thee my Dearest Friend in all things connected with the Interest of our Dear Boys and think I know full well that thy advice to them will be most excellent—

I am writing by the quire therefore am in a great hurry—it is late—I am fatigued Drawing since daylight and will wish thee and all around thee a blessed good night—

Thine for ever & most affectionately

JOHN J. AUDUBON.

Do not forget to send some few pairs of Socks for me at New Orleans where God willing will be next June—*Fare Thee Well!*—

To MRS. AUDUBON
[No outside address]

St. Augustine Florida Decr 5th 1831

MY DEAREST FRIEND—

At last I have a long letter from thee dated Oct*r* 21*st* Louisville and I dearly thank thee for it.—I am sorry to see the general tenure of its contents so very unpromising.—Not a word doth thou say of thy reception by William and his Wife the whole of which I have a particular desire to have to Judge how far constancy exists in relation's Friendship.—I have this day received a whole parcel of letters from Lord Stanley to the Authorities in Canada.—Several from Havell dated up to the 13*th* of Sep*r* Several from Doc*r* Harlan of Different dates.—One from Rob*t* Gilmore which had been sent back from London—One from M*r* Briggs of London One from Lemuel Godart—One from M*r* Featherstonhaugh.—Two from the Rev*d* John Bachman of Charleston—Two from W*am* Gaston of Savannah, one from young Rob*t* Sully from Petersburgh Virginia and one from Nicholas Berthoud.—Havell was going on *well*!! Do not despond my Lucy, depend upon it we must yet see better days and I think as I believe in God that *he* will grant me Life and health to enable me to finish my tremendous enterprise and grant us a happy Old Life.—I feel as young as ever and I now can undertake and bear as much hardship as I have ever done in my Life.—Industry and perseverance joined to a sound heart will cary me a great ways—indeed *nothing* but an *Accident* can destroy me in this Tedious Journey.—had Victor spoken to me at Baltimore as thy letter now expresses neither thou nor him should have gone to Kentucky—I certainly would have taken him with me and I have no doubt that in twelve months he would have drawn as well as I do and understood as much of Ornithology as would enable him to prosecute in my undertaking in case of emergency—It is now too late for this Journey of the Floridas but should thou coincide in my wishes and Victor also, I wish him to Join me *at New Orleans* on the first of *June next* with a Good Rifle and such Clothings as will answer for the Continuation of my Journey and wait for me there should I not be arrived, then to enter heart and hand in the study of Ornithology and to become able to finish my Labours or to add to them—We have nothing to expect from any one in this World my beloved Friend except appearances many of which are most delusive, but our sons grown under the shade of adversity will be well prepared to stand the rough trails of this Life and to render them able to dispense with supplies from others will always be my Pride.—Meantime should Victor or our Dear John meet with any thing which thou and them think *more Substantial* and sure by all means let them and thee do for the best of your united Knowledge.—

My name is now ranging high and our name will stand still higher should I live through my present travels therefore the name of our sons will be a passport through the World—I have now great Confidence in what I have undertaken and indeed feel so light hearted and willing to follow all my plans to the last that I only pray for your health and comfort untill I have the satisfaction of Joining you all again—Keep up a good heart my Lucy—be gay—be happy—Collect all the Information in thy power to assist me in my future Publications—Urge our children to follow Honest men's conduct and to Interest them selves at all Leisure hours—I feel fully decided that we should all go to Europe together and to work as if an established Partnership for Life consisting of Husband Wife and Children—

I have heard of the arrival of Ann and Mr. Gordon—*Nothing from him* as thou well sayest—Neither do I expect much from N. B. although he writes to me Kindly—

Continue to write to me *here for two months* after this reaches thee and afterwards to Key West care of the *Commanding U. S. Officer*—I have made arrangements to have all letters forwarded after me when I leave this.—

We have drawn 17 Diferent Species since our arrival in Florida but the Species are now exhausted and therefore I will push off to Docr Pochers and McCraigh's Plantation 46 Miles south of this along the coast in about 10 days.—I expect innumerable difficulties afterwards between Indian River and Cape Florida as I am told we will have to walk along the Sea Shore beach for about 150 miles before we meet with an Inhabitant either white or red—but in this country we will not mind this much—My young men are both very willingly enclined and quite well therefore believe me we will proceed on if slowly regularly—I write to thee every Sunday punctually and will do so even in the Wilderness —waiting untill opportunities will offer to send my letters to some distant Post Office Thou wilt not hear from me so often as heretofore, but be assured that I will take all reasonable of my health and of that of my assistants—

My Large trunk has at last arrived and I will have it tomorrow morning—I wish to write by the Packet in answer to all the letters I have received this day which will take me the greater portion of the night, but I wish to go through with it as I may not have other opportunities shortly—tell Victor I thank him for the few lines he has send me but I would have been doubly pleased had I seen a few words in the hand writing of John and of W*am* What did the latter say of the Powder horn and his Wife of a certain shawl—Harlan says that several reviews have appeared of our Work and that on the first day of Jan*y*. one of great Length will come out in the North American Review—I have also received a letter from Col*l* John Abert who forwarded me whilst at Charleston a bill on the U. S. Bank for 219 Dollars—

There is here a M*r* *Hugh Williams* who has coasted this peninsula several times and once in an open skiff with his son when 14 years of age from whom I have derived a great deal of Information—Some Lakes says he exist in the Interior on which are Islands containing *Indian Tribes* who know nothing of the existance of *the Seminoles*—he assures me that Birds are most aboundant and tame—that shells are superb and *Game* most plentiful—he is now unwell but will soon be about and *perhaps* may go with us as he is anxious to publish his own already written observations on this unknown Country after adding new remarks—The man is poor &*c* but possesses knowledge and has the Constitution of a Horse or in other terms much such as I have myself—We have collected some hundreds of Shells and about 100 bird skins all of which will leave this for Philadelphia to Doc*r* Harlan in 2 or 3 days —The Rev*d* John Bachman will also forward those left in his care nearly 300 bird skins and as many shells per first opportunity to Phil*a*—

Keep up a good Correspondence with England—Write to J. B. Kidd, Artist Edinburgh—McGillivray—The Williams—at New Castle to John Adamson—to Miss ——— at Leeds. to the Rathbones at Liverpool and to Thomas Sowler at Manchester.—Havell says that Doc*r* Tooke has been extremely attentive &*c* Havell had procured another Subscriber when he wrote and the 24*th* No was Engraved; the 23*d* delivered.

S*t* Augustine is the poorest hole in the Creation—The living very poor and very high—was it not for the fishes in the bay and a few thousand of oranges that grow immediately around the Village, the people must undoubtedly abandon it or starve for they all are too leazy to work, or if they work at such price as puts it out of the question to employ them. The Country around nothing but bare sand Hills—hot one day cold another &*c* &*c*

A botanist arrived to day who Inquired for me at table in my presence—a man of most comely appearance but one who unfortunately is possesed of Pulmonic Constitution so hoarse and so thin that I doubt if he will surpass this Winter.—yet he speaks of visiting the *Interior*—the Interior [—] God—I will visit it and then will be able to say something on the Subject—

Now my Dearest Friend my Dearly beloved Wife once more *fare thee* well—give my kindest remembrances to W*am* and to his Wife and to thy Brother Thomas when thou seest him—did thou see him at Cincinnati—I am glad to hear how your evenings are spent would to God I could Join you all every night and resume my Labours every morning. I have put Lehman at Drawing Birds and he does them well after I have given such attitudes as are true and natural—I have written to thee before that we have found here a new Species of Vulture—God bless thee and our Dear Sons—and may I have the good fortune to meet you all again in good health on my return—Again and again thine for ever most devotedly attached Friend and husband—

JOHN J. AUDUBON.

Also received my large trunk &*c*
This is the *7th* and merely have to say again God bless Thee
Thy Thine Friend—

J. J. A.

To MRS. AUDUBON

St Augustine Decr 8*th* 1831—

MY DEAREST FRIEND.

Although I wrote a long letter to thee yesterday, I will do so again this morning, the weather being so intolerably bad as to preclude our going after Birds or anything else.—I do so with the more pleasure because I only discovered thy letter of the 21*st* of Oct*r* to be in the post office after I had answered to thine of the 8*th* of November—

I am not sorry of that not remaining at Thomas's house on account of his having such a large Family.—

I am quite of thy opinion respecting our Dear John, I think that it is merely to his great flow of spirits that his carelessness can be attributed to and therefore hope that a very few years will correct all that.—I am not averse to his going on Board a good Steam Boat under a good Commander; far from it I think it will prove to him the necessity of acting for himself altogether when he will feel quite happy I am sure—and as to the Pride of William on that Score care not a Jot.—If I were a King I never would feel it a disgrace to see my Son a Shoe Maker or a Blacksmith provided he was at the head of his trade and was Honest.—What was Franklin?—Newton, Shakespeare and others at first and what have they not done for the World and for themselves?—Should I have the good fortune to finish this Journey with the same success that has attended me in my last visit to my Country I shall fear nothing and think myself pretty certain that we will realize a Suficiency for all of us.—Should William take Victor *in Partnership* well and good, but if not *in Partnership* I strongly advise that he should Join me at New Orleans no later than the first of June *Next.*—On Making enquiries here respecting *Tallahassee* I find that it is a poor place without scarcely any back Country to support any great commerce at any time—indeed I much fear that no portion of this Peninsula is possessed of the rich Lands and advantages represented to exist in it.—Time will however show to me and I will not suffer an opportunity to escape without acquainting you all with my obversations—

I have so far received 3. letters from thee, the one from Wheeling and 2 from Louisville, I shall expect another on Monday next, We have only one mail per week in and out.—I yesterday wrote long letters to Harlan and to Featherstonhaugh, both of which will doubtless be published or probably a compound of both into one article of his monthly Journal, and have requested him to send thee Copies.—F. has written a tremendous Review of my work for the North American Review which will appear on the 1*st* of Jan.*y* next.—I find the News Papers very busy about me and discover with great Satisfaction that the Current of Opinion is greatly changed in my favor by all the great attention paid to me and to my Party wherever we have been—I hope it will continue; this I well can assure thee of that nothing on my part will tend to diminish the Impression now existing.—The Scriblers about Rattlesnake *Stories* will now have to hang their ears and shut their invidious mouths—hast thou read the letter of Colo*l* J. J. Abert to Harlan and published in F.'s Journal? I have a more extraordinary account in store respecting these reptiles.—One was found in this Place, Twisted around the top of a mahogany bed Post in the chamber of a most Venerable Lady, and I have a certificate well attested of that fact.—I have become acquainted here with a M*r* Hugh Williams of whom Major Weir spoke to us at Philadelphia—that man with the enterprise and daring of a Second Columbus circumnavigated the whole of this Peninsula, only accompanied by his Son then 14 years old, in a small open boat, and visited every nook and crook in his way.—he says much to my satisfaction about Birds, Shells and Flowers which we are to see as we proceed South and although many difficulties will be in our way I long to proceed on—This I expect to do in a few days as we drawn all that can be collected near about.—We go 47 Miles off South to Doc*r* Pocher's Plantation by Invitation.—afterwhich to Indian River and afterwards to Cape Florida.—I have written to Government yesterday to send express orders to the Commanders of the Revenue Cutters to assist me on this Coasting Voyage and hope to receive them by return of Mail—if not I will purchase a barge hire 2 Indians and push ahead!—

We collected 280 Skins at Charleston and have collected 103 here.—and have Two boxes of Shells—all these go to Doc*r* Harlan per first opportunity.—I have put Lehman at Drawing *Birds* when pushed by work and he draws them beautifully after they are put in Position by myself.—Henry behaves well and prepares the Skins well.—

I wrote yesterday to Havell, and to Kidd.—to N. Berthoud—to thee, to Harlan, to Featherstonhaugh.—to Col. Abert and to Miss Maria Martin in the absence of her Brother in Law John Bachman—We have here an Irish Doc*r* a Botanist, in consumptive debility and a rare Genius I dare say.—he wears his Locks about him as I used to do, and on sitting at the table at dinner I heard him enquire of the Landlady where M*r* Audubon was in the Floridas—after Dinner he spoke to me, saw our Work and we are now well acquaint.—I fear his days are marked and that he will scarce live the Winter.—

I well know how lonesome thou must feel at time and I assure thee that when I am even one hour without work that I feel wretched also.—I long for thee at every moment it is such a comfort to speak to each other on all subjects and to have immediate answers when together.—but my Sweet Wife try to keep up good Spirits—read & Write and visit such of thy old acquaintances as may yet remain at Louisville or its vicinity.—&*c*—

I have asked thee to knit me some socks, do thee do so. and also a good *Partridge Net* with Long wings—have it all finished with hoops and sticks compleate and sent to New Orleans to M*r* Briggs to be kept until called for by me.—

Do let me If W*am* and his Wife are as kind to thee as thou may wish.

&c—Lehman is at my Elbow finishing a Drawing of a Gull with a beautiful group of Racoon Oysters.—Henry is packing shells in papers *&c* So that rain or no rain we make out to be employed. The thermometer was at 78 yesterday the wind at South.—The musquitoes shocking as well as the sand flies.—this morning the wind is at Northwest pouring rain and the thermometer at 60.—

Our room gives sight to the entrance to the harbor and I can see the Brown Pelicans by hundreds amid clouds of Gulls *&c* but the Rascals are so wary and so shy that there is no coming near them—further South where no gunners are I am told they are as aboundant and quite Gentle.—

I dare say Sister Ann will be with thee when this reaches thee, if so give her my Love—and best regards to both her and her husband and kiss Willie for me.—Dear little fellow I wish I could kiss him and you all myself.—

I write my observations on the Birds every night and I hope will find but little dificulty when I write their Biography.—I find however that to observe the manners of the Water Fowls is much dificult to do than that of the Land Birds.—however my telescope assists me greatly.—When I reach New Orleans I will forward thee all the Drawings on hand for fear of further care of them and begin anew—

Remember me kindly to William and his Wife—and all others who may enquire after the *American Woodsman*—What does Thomas say of our Book?—I understood at Charleston that Thomas Bakewell of Pittsburgh had gone as a delegate from that Place to New York.—

I have not heard a word of Backhouse—I knew him well at York and should I see him will write to Miss Fothergill about him—My best and most affectionate good wishes to our Dear Sons—and to thee dearest sweetest and best of Friends.—I must again bid thee and them adieu—Thyne friend and Husband forever true.

JOHN J. A[———]

To MRS AUDUBON
Louisville, Kentucky

Bulow's Plantation 4*th Jan.y.* 1832—

God bless thee my Dearest Wife and you my Dear Sons!—I have received thy letter dated 30*th* of Nov*r* by which thou didst not know of my arrival at St. Augustine.—

Now my Dearest Friend, do not suffer thy spirits to depress thy Phisical faculties—Keep up thy own Spirits I pray thee.—I am now on my last Journey after Birds in North America and I hope to be so successful as to be able to finish what I need for the Completion of our great enterprise.—Keep up a good heart—Do as I do—have I not had aboundance of mortifications and vexations and yet have not *rather* rose above water? Certainly I have—and so hast thou also.—from thy letter I see that our Dear Sons are exerting themselves also; that being the case I fear nothing for them—The news from England are good up to Sep*r* 30*th* when M*rs* Havell says she had two new names who had paid for the first Volume.—Thou hast also two—I have had 7 since arrived—and I see that the State of Louisiana is likely to take 3 more.—Our names and fame rising fast—The Work must be known throughout the World and by the time we reach Europe again a greater demand is likely to exist.—Do my Beloved Lucy keep up a good Heart.—

I received a beautiful and kind letter from Harlan yesterday dated 14*th* Dec*r*—I wrote to him a few days ago, and also to Featherstonhaugh, Long accounts on my Peregrinations here abouts for Publication—and thou wilt see *in the Papers* more of my progress than through my letters I dare say.—I have no regular opportunity any more to write to thee for some time but I write on all occasions, even a few lines which has been the Case Two or three times lately—

We are all well at the house of a very Wealthy Planter, without ostentation and perfectly well off—have boats and men at Command &*c* the only thing of which I complain is the Scarcity of the Birds of which I am most in need of—I regret not having remained at New York and the Jersey Shore until the 1*t* of this month and then to have sailed for Charleston &*c*—it is too late and I must do my best.—

I have frequently thought that if thou wert to meet me at New Orleans on the first of June it would be good Policy as well as a most happy event for me.—Thou might stay at thy old Friends and I would remain there one week to speak to thee—to kiss thee dearly and to give thee all the Drawings on hand to take care of until my final return—

Should Victor not be busy have him accompany thee.—Let John at his Work until I see Louisville again.—But recollect *not to go* to England without *thy husband* or thy son to take care of thee.—I am forced to close this which will reach thee God knows when as I send it to Charleston by a Cap*n* who does not know when he will leave this River the Alifax—E. Flo*a*—but it will be welcome if it reaches and I send it with all my truest Love to thee and our Dear Children—remembrances all round and again and again

God Bless Thee—

Thine for ever

JOHN. J. AUDUBON.

I will be greatly in want of Socks when I reach New Orleans.—I proceed next Week down to Indian River and the *South Lagoon*—See Map.—*5th Jan.y.* I find that the Captain has forgot my letter having left without my knowing or earlier than expected and continue writing more—On my return from shooting with [———] last evening after having killed some fine Birds, to skin and a tremendous large Alligator about 8 miles from the house, I was handed the New York Papers which give very disagreable accounts of the state of affairs in that country—The Riots are certainly getting to a frightful pitch and I fear a Revolution there unless the Reform Bill is passed—Bristol it seems has been terribly burnt and some lives lost.—do my Sweet Wife try to let me know about Havell as often as possible—I would advise thee not to say much of our own private business by letters unless thou fillest confident of my receiving them in course—yet write me long letters I pray thee.

I am going to write again to Harlan having no Birds to Draw. I will also write to Havell and N. Berthoud.—

Finding an excellent opportunity of going across to the River S*t* John by Land to a Place called *Spring Garden* (on the Map) I will do so on Saturday the 8*th* and will be absent from my Companions de Voyage for 4 days—They Lehman and Henry are going on Sunday morning to the house of a M*r* McCraigh by land only 12 miles by water double that distance and I will meet them there on my return from Spring Garden—I go there to see and Judge of the Interior of the Country, which I am told is curious and Interesting and few opportunities occur.—I go on horse back 45 miles along *an Indian* trail—

Lehman is Drawing at my side and thou wilt see such representations of the Floridas that will bring thee quite in contact with the Floridas—We have now 550 Skins—Two boxes of shells—Some curious seeds and 29 Drawings, eleven of which only are finished for the want of male or female Birds to them—

I see by all the papers that the Winter has been early and severe to the Eastward—here we have had a few cold nights but nothing which can be called Winter—Indeed the trees are all green—There are Butterflies to be seen each fine day and some Flowers in the Swamps.—The Alligators come out of their holes when the sun shines for a few hours &*c*—Snakes are brought to us very often and are said to be most aboundant in the Summer—Harlan says that my Friend Ord has returned to Philadelphia and is as silent as the Tomb about me.—and well he may be!—

The woods here are filled with the *Casava* Root which makes the finest food for the Indians and the best for the whites—I have some of the seeds of it and of splendid Lilly which we found growing 6 feet high in the marshes.—I am fortunate in having brought such strong clothing for nothing else could stand the fan Palmettoes and fan grass of the Marshes through I have to scramble and wade every day—I doubt if ever a man has undergone more fatigues than I now undergo and if I do not succeed I am sure it will not be for want of exertion.—Keep directing thy letters to S*t* Augustine and to Key West until further advised—

Once more my beloved Wife and Friend Adieu—

To MRS. AUDUBON

St Augustine Monday the 16*th Jany*. 1832.—

MY DEAREST FRIEND

I returned to this place the night before last in consequence of my having received the following letter from Government—

"To the officers commanding Revenue Cutters on the Charleston, Key West and Mobile Station.—Treasury Department 23*d* of Dec*r* 1831—M*r* John J. Audubon a distinguished Naturalist at present engaged in a Scientific excursion in the Territory of the Floridas having requested that the commanding officers of the Revenue Cutters employed on that Coast may be permitted to convey him and those associated with him and their baggage to and from certain points within the Limits of their cruising Stations;—and the Department feeling disposed to lend to the cause of Science every aid which may not be incompatible with a just regard to the public Service, I have to request that you will receive M*r* Audubon and his party with their effects on Board the Cutter under your command at any port where they may present themselves and where you may happen to be; and also that you will convey them to such other point within your cruising limits where the duties appertaining to the Revenue [Cut] Service may lead you and where they may wish to go.—I am respect.y. Sir Your Ob*t* Ser*t* Louis McLane Secretary of the Treasury—"

Now it does happen that there are no *Revenue Cutters* at this Port at Present but a *U. S. Schooner of War!* Commanded by a *Lieutenant Pearcy*—The name of the Schooner is *the Spark* sail well and ranges from Charleston to Key West—before my arrival here this last time the Commanding officer heard that I had written to Washington for orders for him and I *am told* expressed himself rather roughly about having the transporting of Audubon and his Party &*c*—however I presented myself to him in Company with Doc*r* Simmons and Lieut*t* Smith of the Army and was received in *a blunt Sailor like manner* and assured that it would give him great pleasure to Convey me and party—he ordered a bottle of Madeira which was drank by us &*c* I afterwards Invited him to come and Spend the evening with me—I also asked about a dozen Gentlemen with whom I am acquainted here—We spent our time agreably and *Soberly* after which My rough Lieut*t* took me by both hands and reassured me that he would do *all in his power* to promote my Wishes—

This now appearing I have determined to go with him first up the S*t* John's River as far as Navigation will permit which in all probability will take 4 or 5 Weeks—after which we return here for a few days, then go to Charleston for 8 or 10 days for a new set of Sails and proceed back to the Floridas coasting it and Making inland excursions at all the places which may be likely to promote my Views Joined to the Service of the United States proceeding as far as Cape Sable after which I will proceed to Mobile and New Orleans still anxious to reach that City on or about the 1*t* of June next.—The Lieut*t* Pearcy has Two officers under him and I have Two assistants and he has proposed that We Should all mess together and divide the expenses which I think quite fair and have promised to do.—These are my present Plans and if the Commandant and I agree I will Stick to the Schooner Spark until I have drawn many a fine Bird—Should he prove unkind or Two rough I will leave him at Charleston and then take the *Revenue Cutter* of that Station to Convey us to Key West—I will however write as often as I can and Keep thee well informed of all my proceedings.—

Dost Know that the legislature of South Carolina has subscribed to our Work?—It is So and was effected through my good Friend Bachman.—I hope that when I reach Charleston again I will be able to send several names.—

Thy last letter received by me is dated 24*th* of November—I am heartily glad that our Dear John has began on his own account and I would advise him to Stick Closely to Business until I See you all—My last letter from M*rs* Havell is of September when Havell was on a Tour at York. —The Mail comes in to night and I hope to hear from Thee, at all events I will not close my letter until the *Spark* is ready to sail which will be as soon as the *Wind* changes.—

I have been on the Head Waters of the S*t* John by Land from the Alifax River across the wildest desolate tract of Pine Barrens, Swamp and Lakes that I ever saw—I remained 2 days at *Spring Garden* (Sea the Map) and went by Water to the S*t* John—had an Island named after me—a Compleat Mass of orange Trees and Live Oaks—Thou must wait for my Journal for Further particulars—I have found Three Species of Heaths—one New Ibis and Some fresh Water Shells and have Skinned 200 Birds—We came from J. J. Bulow's Plantations 40 Miles south of this in a Waggon and 6 Mules with Two Servants who brought us here in one day—This *Bulow* is a wealthy Young Man who was extremely Kind to me and my Lads—

I hope I will possess as much information respecting the Floridas as they now are as any man living and will try to render this information of advantage to us—

I expect that Thou would find Kentucky rather rough after returning from Europe but think of me when I say that Kentucky nay the worst of Kentucky is a Paradise compared with this *Garden* of *the United States*"—

What will my Philadelphia Friends say or think when they read that Audubon is on board of the U. S. Schooner of War the Spark going around the Floridas after *Birds!?* I assure thee my Sweet Girl I begain to be proud of myself when I see that my Industry, perseverance and honesty has thus brought me So high from So Low as I was in 1820 when I could not even procure through my Relations and former Partners the Situation of a Clerk on Board an Ohio Steamer.—now they Prize me—nay wish me well—very good I wish them the same and may God grant them peace and plenty—

I wrote to thee to invite thee to meet me at New Orleans about the first of June—I think it would do thee good and the expense would not be much—M*r* Johnson I hear as a Lady sent through Havell to whom Johnson has written—

Should'st see Anne or Friend Gordon give them my regards and to Dear Willy a Kiss for me.—I will now put this aside as I am obliged to Dress to receive Some Ladies who come boring me by asking to see my Drawings.—it must be done for Politeness sake and to be polite is very necessary and sometimes of great service—God bless Thee—

On receiving this I wish thee to Write adressed Care of the Reverend John Bachman Charleston S. C*a* and he will forward my Letters to Key West whenever an opportunity occurs—I fear that in a Month or six weeks I will have great difficulties in hearing from Thee—Meantime let me engage thee to care of Thy Dear Sweet Self for my own Sake and I will do the same for Thy own Sake.—I will see that the movements of *the Spark* or any Vessel on board of which I may remove the names of Which I will send thee will be announced in the News Papers at Diferent points of the Union—nothing less than the total Loss of the Vessel in great distance from the Shore can Injure me for I can Swim well and far Thou Knowest and my heart and Cause are equally good with my bodily Strength.—

Jany 17*th* I was sadly disapointed last evening at not receiving a Letter from Thee—I received one from N. Berthoud dated Dec*r* 28*th* and one from Co*ll* Abert of Washington City Inclosing me a duplicate of the one which I have copied here from Louis McLane.—

I think that I will sail Tomorrow as this morning is fair and Calm—The 2*d* Lieutenant of the Spark has received a Furlow and goes home—

Thou wilt be surprised to read that I have *abandoned Snuff for ever!* and So has Lehman—I came to that determination on the 1*t* of this Month—I am So tanned and burnt that thou might easily take me for an Indian—My beard has grown unshorn these 5 Weeks—

I will write to Havel to day and to N. Berthoud and Doc*r* Harlan—My Kindest and affectionate love to our Dear Children and W. B. & family—and thou my Sweetest Girl God bless thee—thy *Own Friend*

JOHN J. AUDUBON

18*th* *Wednesday.*—I have Kept my letter as long as possible, but the Mail will close this evening and I must bid thee adieu once more.—The weather is cloudy and very Sultry therefor the Wind may blow from the South tomorrow morning if So we Shall Sail for the S*t* John—I have read Featherstonehaugh's Review it is by no Means equal to that of M*c* and not to compared with Blackwood's.—I am sorry that Such *Noble Subject* Should have been So treated.—God bless Thee My Dearest Lucy, take care of Thy Sweet Self and believe me Thine Friend & Husband forever

J. J. A.

To MRS. AUDUBON

St. Augustine, Feb'y 1st. 1832

I assure thee I was greatly pleased two days ago at receiving the 4 letters which I ought to have had much sooner—but they have come and I kiss them my Sweet Wife until I can do that to thee—The dates of thy letters are Dec*r* 12*th* 18*th* 26*th* and 1*st* of Jan*y*.—I am very much pleased at all the contents but as few parts require an answer I will speak first of what has happened to me since my last.—

We started from this dull place last Wednesday at 12 o'clock with a beautiful prospect—the wind was fair—our Commander *Jolly* and it was expected ere evening's dusk came on we would be moored within the barr at the Entrance of the S*t* John's River—at 4 o'clock the wind hauled round to the Northwest—the sky became suddenly clouded, the breese sprung into a Gale and by 8 o'clock when we made the Light of the S*t* John's Light House it blew a compleat hurricane—Thy poor Friend was dreadfully sea sick—his assistants not much better off—Our Gallant Commander had everything arranged to insure the safety of the Vessel and of our selves—he gave me his own Birth and waited upon me as a Brother would but *he* could not soften the fury of the Gale—It continued to blow tremendously—our light bark danced over the Billows as if quite at her ease until the return of Day—The breese moderated a little but was still so strong and we had gone so far *back* to the South and Eastward that it was thought prudent to return to S*t* Augustine; luckily we did so for in the course of the next night the Gale Increased and the Cold became so intense that everything like a fluid froze on board our *Craft*—Another Vessel that had left at the same time with us for Charleston, returned and reached the Port one hour before us.—

Thus my Initiation to U. S. Schooner Spark has been a severe one—I have been much gratified to see how well everything is managed on Board of a U. S. Vessel of War—the perfect order, silence and promptitude with which every order is obeyed and fullfilled is quite new to me and Impresses the mind with something far above anything I ever saw on board of any vessel in which I have been—the fact is that I am delighted with Lieut Piercy who in fact is a *thorough Goeer* and a brave fellow—I have written to Government to try to have *for him* Leave to go where ever he may think fit and proper during this spring and I sincerely hope that our Government will be pleased to afford us the means of exploring *the within* as well as *the without* of the Floridas.—*Should* this be granted to us depend upon it we will gather something more than *Shells*.—

Do not my Dearest Love be afraid of my being in the South this Spring. I will take all the care I can of myself and will reach New Orleans by the first of June if possible.—*At all events do meet me there* I beg of thee on the first of June and if I am not come *Wait* for me.—I am much pleased at being relieved respecting Havell, and am glad that thou dost keep *an open* correspondence with him.—I have seen nothing of Joseph Backhouse. *I knew him well* at York and should I meet him will easily recognize him.—

I hope the Turkey will reach England safely.—Glad that Miss Chorley has written thee.—do write to *every one in England* who is likely to promote our Interest.—It is about time to receive the Copies of our Work from England.—I will keep a bright eye on *N. B.* and give him no more Latitude than he desires.—present my respects to M*r* Cotby—&*c*—

I write this Laconically because I have reasons for so doing as long as I am at S*t* Augustine; a place which I assure thee is far from being *generally* pleasant.—

Send all thy letters to the care of Rev*d* John Bachman Charleston, S. C*a* he is an excellent man depend upon it—I received a letter from him and one from Harlan when I received thy 4.—Manage to Live quietly comfortably with W. B. whose character I think I know well—where ever there is a good heart at base never mind the roughness of *the Bark!*—

I have not heard a word from M*r* Gordon—*Thou* must not return to England without thy Husband's company.—Cannot very well tell at present if or no I will cross the Continent this Journey.—health and prosperity to our Dear Sons—proud of thy Enconiums about them.—

I have been extremely mortified that *not one Drawing* have we made since one whole month detained by winds &*c* and the scarcity of Specimens—The wind is fair this afternoon and I hope to sail tomorrow morning for the S*t* John—

I fear that after I leave Charleston to go South to the Keys &*c* I will have but few opportunities of writing to thee but depend upon I will lose none and will have Paragraphs Inserted in all News Papers where ever I go—therefore enquire of M*r* Cotby who probably receives the Papers from all parts of the Union—

My young men are well—Henry *does more* than thou art aware of and I think his expenses will be much lighter to us than those of Lehman for whom I have had *nothing to do* for more than a month—

I collect shells from every one whom I meet and have some. Lieut*t* Piercy says that by the time I leave him I will have barrels full of them —Time will prove this—be assured that I will not suffer any opport*y* to be lost.—

I have to write to Harlan and others and must bid thee another Adieu—Then God bless thee my own Sweetest beloved Wife may God grant us the blessing of meeting again and spending our days together —Fare thee well

Thine Friend

J. J. A.

I rec*d* John's letter—my kindest and most affectionate Love to him & to Victor.—

To M*rs* AUDUBON
Louisville, Kentucky

U. S. Schooner Spark St John's River off Jackson's ville E. Fa Feb.y.9th 1832.—

MY DEAREST FRIEND

We have at last changed our Position and I am glad that I can again Inform thee and our Dear Sons of my momental Situation—We left S*t*

Augustine on Sunday last early in the morning and reached the Entrance of this River at an early hour of the night—The weather was so fair and the sea so gentle in her motions that I felt no indisposition whatever.—rather before day Cap*n* Piercy ordered the Firing of our *Great Gun* to Inform the Pilot of our arrival—the report sounded far over the flat shores of the Floridas—Sometime elapsed, no Pilot was there in sight—the breeze freshened and as on this coast not a moment must be lost to ensure the entrance of an harbor a second Gun was fired—We with pleasure saw the return of our Signal at the Light house—; and shortly after, the Light Craft of the Piloter was in view bouncing over the resisted current of the River by the Ocean and approaching us a pace—I assure thee I was glad of it for I must say that I certainly was not Born for a *Sea Man* any more than THOU for the wife of one—

We have ascended thus far gradually when ever the *Tide* and Winds have been fair and we intend or rather say my Cap*n* and Friend Lieut*t* Piercy intends going as far up this Dingy looking River as the draft of the Spark will allow (this is nearly 6 feet) and which I hope may prove to be about 200 Miles and where I further hope that I may find something to Draw—

We have been in compleate Idleness ever since the *25th* of Dec*r* at the Exception of Henry who has more or less to do every day in his own way—

We have had two frolics at Shooting White headed Eagles and killed 5 in 24 hours which is more than most Sportsmen can boast of—

I feel quite comfortable and as Happy as possible when traveling without thy Dear Self at my side—my Cap*n* his officers and his Men all extremely kind to us all—Indeed Lieut*t* Piercy does not suffer a single opportunity to escape which can be appropriated to our benefit to our pleasure or to the advancement of Science—

do not forget to forward all letters to the care of John Bachman (the Reverend) Charleston S. C*a* and to come and meet me at New Orleans on the first of June next—

I offer thee the regards of our Commandant and of Lehman & Henry—my affectionate blessings to our Dear Sons—my good wishes to W*am* his wife and Co Tell brother Thomas when next you meet that I wish him well also—and thou my Dearest Lucy may heaven's pleasures be around thee for ever and for ever I am thy own true Friend and husband

JOHN J. AUDUBON.

Should receive any letters this evening I will mention it on the outside—write to England *to all* who may be concerned about us to keep our names alive in that Land—fare thee well adieu—Thermometer at 12 in the sun 102—in the shade—78—Young Eagles of *this Year* able to fly!!

I have received thine of 8th. [———] Jan.*y*.—Mercy pour celle la!—

To MRS. AUDUBON

U. S. Schooner Spark 100 Miles up the St. John's River, bound upwards—Feb.y 17th—1832

MY BELOVED WIFE—

A dreadful accident gives me an opportunity of writing a few Lines to thee, and I embrace it with as much pleasure as I have felt *sickened* at the occurrence—through which the *chance* of sending this to S*t* Augustine does take place.—One of our Sailors accidentaly *shot* himself through the Hand and forehead, and our Cap*n* is going to convey him at day break tomorrow to S*t* Augustine—

I wrote to thee from *Jacksonville* last week and unfortunately have but little to say as far as the Improvement of our Collection is concerned.—*We have* made out to Draw 2 species of birds and a new species of *Heath*—We are all well; but the stink of the River Water I fear has caused one half of our Crew to be sick—we will probably remain at our present anchorage for 3 or 4 days more after which will proceed up to Lake George and I hope somewhat further—I have been deceived most shamefully about the Floridas—Scarcely a Bird to be seen and these of the most common sort—I look to the leaving of it as an Happy event—

Keep writing to England to every Body as I have no chance of doing so myself—for although little or nothing is to be done with the Pencil a *good deal* is performed by the Pen—God only knows if this will ever reach *thee*, but I write it in hopes it may do so—and pray that God may ever bless thee and our Dear Sons.—I am now truly speaking in a *Wild* and *dreary* and desolate part of the World—No one in the Eastern States has any *true* Idea of this Peninsula—*My account* of what I have or shall see of the Floridas will be far, very far from corroborating of the *flowery sayings* of M*r* Barton the Botanist.—

We are surrounded by thousands of Alligators and I dare not suffer my beautiful and faithful and good Newfoundland Dog *Plato* to go in the River although I have seen him leaped over board and give chase to Porpoises—

Nothing but sand Barrens are about and around us—When now and then an *Impenetrable swamp* is in sight it is hailed with the greatest pleasure for in them only Game or birds of any sort can be procured.—

Once more may God ever bless thee and preserve thee until I can press thee to my own Bosom with the feeling of a devoted Friend and Husband—*affectionate* givings to our Sons and those around who care about thy poor old Friend.—

We are now living *not "on the fat of the Land"* for fat there is none, but on the poorest of "Poor Jobs" oppossums—young alligators &*c* &*c*—Henry caught 5 young alligators at one grasp the other morning, and we have 25 or 30 alive on Board.—

Write to *Harlan* and let him where I am—I will take care of *N. B.!!!*—hast thou heard from *Kidd*? Continue to write care of *John Bachman, Charleston* S. *Ca* untill thou art ready to go *to New Orleans* where God willing I will meet thee *on or about* the first of June—Again and again my Dearest beloved God bless thee—; Thine for ever

JOHN J. AUDUBON.

To MRS. AUDUBON

Charleston S. C. March 13th 1832

MY DEAREST LUCY.—

I have been forced to perform a counter march but it has proved like some performed by Greater Generals than myself a most Honourable and profitable retreat—I wrote thee from S*t* Augustine that I had parted Company from the U. S. Schooner Spark when high up the St. John River and as I think I then told thee the reasons why I will not repeat them.—The Agnes Schooner brought us out of that miserable spot S*t* Augustine on the *5th* Instant with a fair wind and prospect bound to this place.—On the passage we met with the *Spark* from the S*t* John for S*t* Augustine—the Commandant came on board of us, presented me with a most Superb pair of Swans and said *he hoped* I would not say to any one the reasons why I had left his Vessel.—The man may have a good heart, but if his head like an empty box contains not brains enough to enable him to be a *worthy Gentleman*—the man and the head may go a'drift for me.—On the 7*th* when 40 miles of Charleston *we were Struck* with one of those Gales so very prevalent on these Southern Coasts and forced to put back into *Savannah* Georgia—we reached Cock Spurr Island and having obtained a fine Boat and some Sailors from the Commandant of that Post left on the 8*th* and reached Savannah distant 14 miles in 2 hours—I had left my youths on board, (the Cap*n* having equivocated about going up to the town) but a few hours after my arrival there the Agnes arrived also—*I* put up at the City Hotel with a beard and a pair of Mustachios and a dress which at once attracted all attention. I called on W*am* Gaston who received me kindly, took me to his house where I spent the Evening in Company with Major *Le Conte* and a M*r* Myers and Col*l* Keath of this place—I showed my Drawings—*they* were admired but W. Gaston assured me that not a Subscriber could be procured and that himself had so many calls for his money that he could not do so—Thy poor Husband used to disapointment as he is, *merely listened!*—I called the next morning to pay my small a/c to W. Gaston but he refused to receive it.—LeConte was there: The Conversation turned on the Philadelphians—The Major & I spoke of the treatment I had experienced at their hands—Gaston rose whispered to his clerk—The Major went off and in a few minutes *the Merchant* put a check of 200 Dollars in my hands saying "My Dear M*r* A.—*I now* Subscribe to your Work and would were it the last 200 I have"!—he asked me to follow him—we arrived at the Hotel—My Drawings were put in battle array *on the floor of the House* and in about one hour I had 2 more names and 400$ more in my Pocket.

My Seat was taken for this place in the Mail Coach—W*am* Gaston promised more names and more money and I left Savannah well contented.—I arrived here Saturday evening and on *Monday* evening (Yesterday) I received a letter from Gaston inclosing 200$ more and a new name.—to night I send him my Volume to entice others to Subscribe which he thinks he can do—

I found all well at my worthy Friends the Bachman Family—my Youths had not arrived and indeed arrived only this morning—I found a letter from thee to Friend Bachman—One from M*r* Everett containing some from McLane & Woodbury—and Yesterday 2 from Havell—one from N. Berthoud—All well in London Dec*r* 15*th* &*c*—

As *We* have *now* 22 Subscribers in America I think it necessary to send thee an exact list of their names and Residences—They are as follows and thou must transmit it as soon as possible to Havell.—

Miss Douglas and Ed*d* Harris	New York.	2.
Thomas Perkins	Boston.	1
R*d* Harlan M. D. Philo*al* Society Society of Nat*l* Sciences John P. Wetherill	Phil*a*	4
Nath*l* Potter M. D. Rob*t* Gilmor John B. Morris.	Baltimore	3

W*am* Gaston James Potter Alex*r* Telfair Tho*s* Butler King Daniel Blake	Savannah	5
Legislature of S. C*a* Soc'*y* Natural History Charleston 2	South C*a*	3
Legislature of Louisiana	Louisiana	2.
Library of Congress.	Washington C.y.	1.
M*r* Hancock	Louisiana Ky.	1— 22.

15 of these we have obtained since our arrival which is *not Slow!!*—But I am now in need of 10 Copies of the first Volume and there are only 2 in New York—Havell must make a desperate push and have 20 finished and bound as soon as possible and shipped to New York in Parcels of 5 *or* 6 as soon as ready—write so to him and so will I.—I expect to procure more names this and next week—I dine on Thursday with Doc*r* Tidyman &*c* and my Friends are going to *stirr the Wealthy*—

I intend sailing for *Key West as soon as an opportunity will offer* and still contemplate being at New Orleans on the 1*st* of June where & when I do beg of thee to meet me.—do not be afraid respecting my health I will take *all reasonable* care of it.—Send all thy letters to Friend John Bachman and I may receive them—I have many letters to write and will have this copied to be sent Duplicate—J. Bachman will write to thee shortly—Kindest remembrances to our Dear Sons and all about thee.—God preserve and Bless thee

Thine Friend & Husband

JOHN J. AUDUBON.

I have another Subscriber at Savannah through that most extraordinary man W*am* Gaston—the name of whom is Thomas Young Es*qr.*—I have Rec*d* the money for the first Volume.—Should *this run continue Victor Audubon* will have to sail for England instanter *to push the Printing Coloring & Delivery* of the Work to our Subscribers—More of this *when we meet at New Orleans* on the 1*st* of June Next—

16*th March*. I have nothing to add and send this—I will write to thee again in a day or Two—I have seen M*r Poincet* who came with M*r* Gordon—Nothing to be expected from that quarter.—*Fare thee well*

Letters to John Bachman, and One to Lucy, Written During Audubon's Trip to the Gulf of Mexico in the Winter and Spring of 1837

To Reverend John Bachman
Charleston, South Carolina

Mobile Feby 24th 1837—

My Dearest Friends—

We left Charleston on the 17*th* Instant (Ed*d* Harris, John & I) and arrived here last night. Our Journey was performed first by the Railroad to Augusta, a pretty Village in Georgia—the weather was extremely cold; nay the Ice on the morning of the 18*th* was one half Inch deep.—at Augusta we took the Mail, and luckily for us had no others than ourselves in the coach—The roads, in consequence of several previous days & nights of rain were as bad as can be; but we proceeded apace and had no accidents—having crossed Georgia, we entered the State of Alabama after crossing a bridge at Columbus—here the Swamps were shockingly bad, and we feared that our goods & chattels would have been wetted, but thanks to our Yankee drivers (*the very best in the World*) all was kept dry as cocks—the next morning we breakfasted at the Village of   where 100 Creek Warriors were confined in Irons, preparatory to leaving for ever the Land of their births!—Some miles onward we overtook about two thousands of these once free owners of the Forest, marching towards this place under an escort of Rangers, and militia mounted Men, destined for distant lands, unknown to them, and where alas, their future and latter days must be spent in the deepest of Sorrows, afliction and perhaps even phisical want—This view produced on my mind an aflicting series of reflections more powerfuly felt than easy of description—the numerous groups of Warriors, of half clad females and of naked babes, trudging through the mire under the residue of their ever scanty stock of Camp furniture, and household utensiles—The evident regret expressed in the[ir] masked countenances of some and the tears of others—the howlings of their numerous dogs; and the cool demeanour of the chiefs,—all formed such a Picture as I hope I never will again witness in reality—had Victor being with us, ample indeed would have been his means to paint Indians in sorrow—

We reached Montgomery at Night—remained there until 10 of the next day, and on board of a Steamer, made down the River Alabama—a Stream which though much smaller than the Mississippi resembles it very much.—like it, it is muddy, winding, and lined on its shores, by heavy cane brakes, and bluffs of various elevations & formations—

Our Intentions to visit the Families of our Friends the Lees were abandoned, and I wrote to them in stead—We heard from different persons that they were all well Doing and in good health—We saw many Southern Birds, but felt no difference in the climate—Indeed ever *here*, the weather is cool, and the country exhibits no appearance of spring—

Our first enquiry at this place was for Judge Hitchcock, but he is absent—a M*r* Martineau answered in his stead, and introduced us to the Collector of Mobile, who in turn presented us to Cap*n* Foster, who Commands a Cutter; a Jolly old Gentleman, who gave us to understand that he should like a Tour with us, *provided* I would obtain Commodore Dallas' permission to do so.—he gave us some pleasing information of desired birds &c, and we have concluded to go to Pensacola Tomorrow, by Steamer to pay our regards to the Commodore.—our Intention is to spend but one day there; to return here, and await the receipt of answers to letters sent to M*r* Grimshaw and Cap*n* Coste, who we are told is on the New Orleans station, and now at that place—thus far you perceive we are unabled to form our plans; but expect to be able to do so very soon, when I shall not fail to give you all desirable information—Mobile is a small, compact, thriving place, of goodly appearance—there are about 10 Steamers that ply up the Mobile & Alabama Rivers—some to New Orleans *daily*—and also some to Pensacola *daily*—the country around is flat and swampy, and the accounts of the healthiness of this place, so varied that no one can depend on what is said on the subject; at the exception, that the population is about 13,000 people during winter, and that in July & August, it is reduced to about 5,000!—to me this, and what I have seen, is sufficient—My Mind therfor is made up never to seek refuge (much less health) in either the lower parts of Alabama or any of our *Southern States*—

Need I say to you all, how dearly glad we would be, to be enabled suddenly to accompany you to church on Sunday next? I believe not! [———] My spirits are not above par I assure you and this day, I have suffered much from the [———] of Drinking *Alabama Water*—Tomorrow I [———] to be cured, by a dance over the Waters of the Mexican Gulph—and then all will be right again.

John Bachman my friend, the salamanders are still asleep—Hares we have seen none of—Parokeets, by the hundreds, and also Wild Pigeons, and Hutchins' Geese—at Augusta Doc*r* Wray was very kind to us—here we have seen Frank Lee, who looks well, and is Happy—I wish I was as fortunate! M*r* Logan leaves out of Town and we have not had time to call upon him, but will do so on our return—our expenses to this place have amounted to *nearly* 200$—My sweet heart will be so good as to write to My Lucy, and give her the *interest* if any of this letter—I send my love to you all, and thousands of Kisses on the Wing—and Now God bless you all and believe me ever your truly attached & sincere & thankful friend J. J. AUDUBON

MY MARIA, I will write you a long letter on my return from Pensacola and now say with Papa, God bless you all—Most affectionately

J. W. AUDUBON

To REVEREND JOHN BACHMAN,
Charleston, S. Carolina

New Orleans 3d March 1837.—

MY DEAR BACHMAN.—

Having given you an account of our journey as far as Mobile in my last, I now will proceed with one of what has hapened since then.—

The next day we left Mobile for Pensacola by Steamer and reached the latter the same evening late—went to a most rascally house called "Collin's Hotel" May your star never shoot you there!—however morning came, it was Sunday, and poured of Rain—notwithstanding which, we delivered a few letters of introduction, and were taken on Board the U. S. Frigate the Constallation, in Commodore's Dallas' Barge! The Commodore received Friend Harris and I *quite well* (John remained at Mobile) we found him a very aimiable person, and after he had read M*r* Woodbury' letter he assured us that he would do all in his power to serve us & Science, and that in all probability he would put us on board of the Cutter, now commanded by Captain Robert Day! and that he would write to us at Mobile in 5 or 6 days.—he presented us to all his principal officers, shewed us every parts of his superb ship, gave us some first rate wine, and a bottle of Copenhagen *Snuff* that would make your nostrils expand with pleasure, and draw tears from your eyes—the stuff is so very potent.—We took our leave and returned to *Collins* where we sat contemplating the weather to our hearts content.—Pensacola is a small place at present; principally inhabited by Creole Spaniards of the lowest Class, and some few aimiable & talented families of Scotch, and Americans.—The place is said to be *perfectly healthy* The country is deeply sandy, and nothing but Pine Barrens exist for about 80 miles back.—The Bay is grand and of good depth—The Bar at the entrance about 22 feet admits of Vessels of great Burthen—this is guarded by two powerful fortifications.—The Naval Depot or Navy Yard is 9 miles before the Village, we had not time to visit it.—Fish is abundant, and there I saw I think the finest oysters ever observed by me in any portion of the southern country.—Deer, Wild Turkeys and smaller Game is said to be very plentiful.—We saw thousands of Sallamander' Burrows; and here let me assure you that these Animals have an entrance to their burrows resembling that of European Rabbits, but smaller of course.—It is yet too early to procure them.—Rail Roads are in progress, and some projected to communicate with Blakeley (opposite Mobile distant 65 miles) and Montgomery in Alabama distant 175 or thereabouts Major Ingram of the Topographical Department politely shewed us all the plans on *paper*—much of the Iron Carrs, Engines &*c* are already on the spot—a New Town is laid out for sale, and an *Immense* Hotel is now being errected there.—but after all the back country is so poor, and the want of some navigable stream so great in my opinion, that I have great doubts of the ultimate boasted of advancement of either the new or the old town.—The former belongs to a company of New York speculators, and the rage for new Cities in this section is so great, that the lots already sold have brought great sums.—I have forgotten to tell you that Commodore Dallas shewed us the last received dispatches from Gen Jessup in which he gives great hopes of the Florida War being at an end! May this prove true—Harris and I Walked the whole of Monday, and heard of a Bird breeding in that section, called the *Gris* which from the imperfect descriptions we have had, I conclude is My Brown Ibis, but of this we will tell you more another time.—We returned to Mobile on Tuesday—Called on M*r* Logan, but only saw his Wife.—Frank Lee, and John had passed their time pleasantly &—I found 2 letters from my Dear Wife dates 8*th* and 19*th* of Dec*r* and one from Mr Grimshaw informing me that Coste was on the New Orleans station but absent and assisting a wrecked vessel on one of the Keys—that he would be *here* in less than one month—he is not under the control of C*n* Dallas, and we expect to sail with him for the Sabine and intermediate places—We hope to go with Cap*n* Day or Cap*n* Coste as far as Cape Sable and visit all the Keys [

] the *Western* coast of Floridas before we sail for the Westward.—Harris has gone back to Pensacola in the Revenue Cutter the Jackson, Cap*n* Foster, to remain and see the Commodore until something profitable is offered or said, and John & myself will await for news from Harris at this place, where I hope to procure a few subscribers.—We are snug and comfortable at M*r* Grimshaw (James Grimshaw Es*qr*) to whose care please to Write to us.—It pours of rain, and cannot go to Market this morning.—The first fair day we will do so and seak for Squirrels and Rabbits for you—Yesterday I received another letter from London dated 31 of Dec*r*—This latter had rather perplexed me on account of the rapidity with which Victor and Havell have proceeded with the

Work—but Victor will do his best, and I hope that the Drawings made at Charleston will arrive in time to be disposed of accordingly with my late arrangements.—We have found our clothes here, from England, but the things from Charleston have not yet arrived. Why our English letters have been sent here, instead of to you, I cannot guess—I beg of our Dear Sweet heart to write to My Wife and to copy whatever parts of my letters to you or to her, and send these promptly.—and now My Dear Friends God bless you all.—remember us all to every friend—I forgot to pay Friend Kunhardt my last *small* balance pray do so, and excuse me near him for the neglect—I find New Orleans so large, and so much improved in every point of View that I can scarcely recognise one street from another—We have lost however by Death the greater portion of our numerous former acquaintances here.—Ten thousands of Kisses for all the Dear Girls and Mamma too—and "Rabbitt" and "Sweet Meats"—and old friend M*rs* Davies, and the master in Phrenology!

Yours ever truly

JOHN J. AUDUBON

To REV*d* JOHN BACHMAN,
Charleston, South Carolina.

New Orleans March 22d 1837—

MY DEAR BACHMAN—

We will leave this city, tomorrow Morning before day, on board of the Cutter, the Campbell, Commandant *Napoleon L. Coste*, and proceed directly though slowly on our researches—the Vessel is small, yet very roomy—i.e. that she is less incumberded than any of her size I have yet seen.—Coste is full of the expedition, and so is the first Lieu*tt* the other Lieut is I conceive a "Man a War' Man"—full of his duty on the weather side of the quarter Deck during his daily or nightly Watch!—16 Men—3 Boats, and provisions for about 2 Months, one *great Gun*, and Many Pikes, Cutlasses (*Cut-Lasses*) Pistols and Muskets, as can be crammed in so small a Craft.—We Intend Visiting the whole of Galveston Bay, and Islets thereabouts, spite of the Mexican's *Flotilla*—which after all I think is all "My Eye"—We hope for great things but God Knows how many new species will be added to Our Fauna.—We are well provided with ammunition &c but our *apples* have Turned into sour Cider, and I have some doubts whether our butter will not run through our biscuits ere we gobble the latter. John is packing up 4 squirrels and a Wild Cat for you—I hope you never have seen the Like?—I have and think that you will be pleased with them—John or My Nephew Young Berthoud send you a bill of Lading—I am glad, and proud Too; that I have at last been Acknowledged by the public prints as a Native Citizen of Louisianna—

and had it been supposed when first we arrived here that our stay would have been half as long as it has been—I really think that my Country men would have honoured us with a Public *Dinner!* Try to find out the Paragraphs in the New Orleans Courier (French & English) of the begaining of this month.—and above all my Dear Bachman pray attend to the following—

There is coming here another Cutter to take the place of the Campbell, and she may be here before our return, when the Campbell will scarcely be called for on this Coast.—*Coste* is very anxious to have, *in her* (The Campbell) the *Key West Station* (not the Savannah) and tells me that he would be delighted to take us round to Charleston, after having shewed us the different breeding places which he has discovered on the Western Florida Coast.—Now I should like this myself of all things, and the thought has crossed My Mind, that the *Florida War being at an end!!!* the Secretary of the treasury M*r* Levi Woodbury might grant us the privilege of that Vessel for the purpose mentioned above, If some one was at his Elbow, with strength and power enough to urge him to such an act of generosity towards a poor student of Nature, who in all probability is not likely ever afterwards to trouble his Gov*t* again—and Now that M*r* Poinset is the Secretary of War, and you very intimate with him, that were you to write to that Gentleman *at once*, and ask of him to speak to M*r* Woodbury, and ask the request I long for—Woodbury *I think* would hardly refuse *him* (M*r* Poinset!)—all this must however be done at once, and not be put off even for a day if possible, as you Know our time is growing very short, and we are anxious to Make the best we can of it—Ask of M*r* Poinset that in case this last *petition* is granted by Woodbury to urge the latter to forward me a letter to the effect Care of James Grimshaw Esqr New Orleans.—We have a good number of trifling affairs to transact this day, and I now bid you all adieu for a While, and May God bless you all is the fervent wish of yours truly and most faithfully attached friend

JOHN J AUDUBON

Please have an extract of this sent to Lucy—

To M*rs* LUCY AUDUBON
London

New Orleans 23d March 1837—

MY DEAREST BELOVED!—

I have only a little time to say to thee, that we will leave this tomorrow Morning on board the Revenue Cutter, the Campbell, Cap*n* Napoleon Coste, for a Coasting Voyage of about Two Months.—That we *Three* are quite well! that I have received our Dear Victor's letters of the *6th* and *9th* of Jan.y. and that I am now happy and comfortable in the thought that he will Carry the publication according with the lists I have sent him.—I have heard of the arrival at Liverpool of the Mohawk on the 22*d* Jan.y. and hope that the 9 Drawings sent by her were in good time for the Numbers intended for these.—I hope the *Superb* has also reached safely, and if So Victor will have enough until I return to You. —I have felt great uneasiness about your Precious healths since I have read the a/cs of the Influenza in London—May God preserve you both, and May he grant us the happiness of Meeting again all well and Happy. It is not probable that I Shall hear from you now for Two Months but I will be patient and take good Care of John, Harris and Self.—*The Florida War is actually ended!* depend upon this intelligence.—We therefore hope to return by that *Coast* to Charleston after we have been to Galveston Bay &c on the Western Coast of *the Gulph*.—Not a New Subscriber at New Orleans as yet.—*Mr Fortsall* has not even asked me to his house once—I dined at Governor Roman in a large Company—he is a fine Man, and has writen a few Kind things in the Papers here. —My *"Natal City"!*—Remember us to *Every body*, even to Bessy—Oh how glad I shall feel when I Land at No 4 Wimpole Street and Kiss again My best beloved and Dearest Friend & Wife and our Dear Victor.—but now adieu once more—for ever Yours faithfully

JOHN J AUDUBON

To REV*d* JOHN BACHMAN,
Charleston, South Carolina

Mar 29—1837

MY DEAR BACHMAN.—

I have the great satisfaction of receiving your letter of the 15*th* Inst. yesterday, and send you my thanks for it, and a thousand Kisses for all the sweet hearts you and I and Johny have about you!

We are on board of the Cutter the Campbell.—about 2 miles below New Orleans, anchored on the Western side of the great River, and to day is the 29*th* of March of the year of our Lord 1837!—We are only waiting for 5 Sailors, and as our Cap*n* Coste, and the first Lieut*t* are gone to New Orleans in search of the hands we want, we hope to see the remainder of our Crew compleated this day—Cut Stick to night &c &c—Johny is in the swamps outlining Cypress Trees with the Camera for Victor—Harris is gone to town for Letters if any there are and here I am *scribling* this to you.—I thought you would want me pretty soon, but I can echo you at that, and I would willingly give up one year of my Life (*hereafter*) to have you at my side Just Now.—I would first ask what do you say to those *Squirrels?* and again to this Wild Cat? for I hope you have those which we have shipped to you before your eyes just at this very moment.—About one other hundred questions I would ask of you to answer, but we are a pretty good distance asunder now, and must wait for the pleasure of meeting again in *this World!* A World which though Wicked enough in all conscience; is *perhaps* as good as Worlds unknown.

We took Harris on an Alligator Hunt on a *fine* Bayou. We Killed about 20 of these beautiful creatures, and brought only 7 on board.—Harris Killed several. he never had seen any before.—he Likes their flesh too, but no so Johny excepting the latter our *Mess* made a grand Dinner of the "Tail end" of one, and after all, alligators flesh is far from being bad.—God preserve us from ever "Riding" a live one—We had a fine frolic of this, but after all they are not to be fooled with.—Sand Hill Cranes are yet here—blue wings & Green wings.—Few, very few *Herons* have come to this latitude and longitude.—but we have procured here the *Common American* Gull, L. Torhinas.

We have heard through M*r* Grimshaw' English letters that all was well at London at a late date, but have had no letters ourselves.—Bats are plentiful and you shall I hope see some of them.—The Deer here is different from *yours*, and this also I trust you shall see.—in a Word you will be thought of as of a "Worthy Friend" during the whole of our expedition—My former letters will have given you many details which I cannot now repeat. One of your letters (I mean one of our beloved Maria Martin's) has not reached us—God bless her; and D. the Post!—

I have a most Kind Friend here collecting birds in Rum for me during our absence.—I trust that those at Charleston will not forget their promises on that score, and we already thank the latters for Certain "Brown Creepers" that are now snoozing in rum!—Harris Stands the Packets admirably—he is in facto one of the finest Men of Gods Creation—I wish he was my Brother!—

The Steamer *Fancy* was totally destroyed a few evenings ago on her way to Louisville Ky.—She belonged to my youngest brother in Law, Cargo and all. I fear his loss is considerable—The whole of the living on board saved themselves *only* with what they had on their backs—William Bakewell save a Babe from the Waters, but the nurse was drowned. The Child belonged to one of the Passengers.—had this accident taken place at Night, it is more than probable that one half of the People must have been drowned or burnt to Death.

Have you written to My Lucy?—Do not forget this I pray you.—My Beloved Daughter must write also.—and so must our Dear aimiable friend & Sweet heart.—Do not forget to Write to M*r* Poinset for me to ask of M*r* Levi Woodbury to let me have the Campbell, Cap*n* N. L. Coste, to go to Charleston on our return, which I am anxious to make around the Floridas—Write soon, and send Woodbury's answer or Orders (I hope) to this place care of James Grimshaw Esqr.—The failures at New Orleans have dampened the spirits of every one who speculates on Cotton, Land or Dollars.—

God bless you all.—Remember us to all Harris send you his best Wishes & Love to the Ladies—and now My Dear Bachman believe me as ever Your Friend

JOHN J AUDUBON

There is no Grog on board of the Campbell!!—What do say to that?—Snuff is yet partially afloat—but will be dropped astern very soon!—And once More God bless you all.—

To REV*d* JOHN BACHMAN
Charleston, South Carolina

Island of Barataria, Grande Terre, April 6th 1837
U. S. Revenue Cutter Campbell—

MY DEAR BACHMAN—

I wrote a few lines to you from this place by a Schooner bound to New Orleans, but as winds & *Mail carriers* are not always to be depended on, I will try to have this ready for a Gentleman going from here to New Orleans by the Bayous 105 Miles, and who promises to have it put in the Post Office.—

We were detained a few miles below New Orleans for the want of sailors, until raising the wages to 40 Doll*s* we procured a few crew and some stout fellows, after which we sailed down the great stream to its Southwest pass or entrance.—The next morning we sailed (very foolishly) to the Northeast Pass, and sent an officer in a boat in search of a Cap*n* Taylor. also of the Revenue Service, to whom the Collector at New Orleans had sent orders to Join us, and to assist us as a Pilot.—That day was lost.—The next morning we went shooting and Killed *4 Marsh* Terns and some other birds—We had put M*rs* Coste on Shore at a Fishers house to await the return of her husband, and the next morning early we *sailed* on our Expedition. The weather was fair and the sea smooth until we approached the Barr at *this* place, we however crossed it guided by M*r* Tailor whom we towed, on board of his *Crusader*, a small Schooner of about 8 tons, acting as a tender on the Campbell. We anchored safely under the lee of Barataria Island, and have been here ever since—Shooting & fishing at a proper rate.—Johny & I shot 4 White Pelicans—Harris and the two latters a great number of different Tringas, Terns, Gulls &c—and so we have passed our time, at potting species, their habits, and skinning and placing specimens in Rum.—One cask is already filled.—We are all well.—we intend proceeding to Cayo Island 52 Miles West by the first fair wind, and then expect to do well, as it is said to be a great breeding ground.—Not a bat on our Island, and only Racoons, otters, Wild Cats, and a few Rabbitts—we have not seen any thing more than tracts.—Not a New Bird as yet.—have Killed 5 Tringa hymantopus. Marsh Terns abundant. Cayenne and Common D*o*. Larus atricilla D*o*—White & Brown Pelicans—and a good variety of Ducks and the florida Cormorant.—few land Birds. Salt Water Marsh Hens and boat tailed Grackle breeding.—but enough as I have noted every incident worth notice, which you will read from the Journal.—We have now in contemplation to leave the Schooner as soon as we have reached Texas and seen Galveston (Galveston Bay) and return over Land to New Orleans, and there make ready either to go back to you at once, or proceed around the west Coast of Florida—We will however be guided by Circumstances and do all for the best—have this copied and forwarded to My Dear Wife, and if you please have us "reported" in the papers. We have been very Kindly treated by a Planter here who is a Partner of M*r* Forestall of New Orleans, who gave me a few lines of Introduction.—We have had fine vegetables, Milk & Corn Bread and *fresh Butter!*—This Island is about 10 miles long but scarcely a mile broad—it is low, and mostly marsh (hard however) with many ponds, Lagoons &c—it possesses one Sugar plantation and a few dilapidated Government buildings, began by *Jackson* but now abandoned and rotting.—This was "Lafitte's" (The Pirate) Strong hold.—The remains of his fortification, and the ground on which his houses stood are yet discernible.—Some say that much money is deposited there abouts—I wish it was all in the Charleston Bank placed to *our* Credit!—The Island is flat, and in 1830 was overflowed by the waves of the Gulph impelled by a Hurricane to the depth of 4 feet above the highest ground, and Castle &c was sent adrift towards the Main distant some 12 or 15 Miles.—The soil is good enough to produce Cotton or sugar.—and the place healthy and pleasant; and yet I should not like to be imprisoned at large upon it the remainder of my Life—It abounds with *Snakes* not however injurious excepting a very small *ground* Rattle species.—We have placed several in rum for Doc*r* Holbrook, and *Crabs* for yourself! —No Insects of note except *Musquitoes* and sand flies of which we could spare enough God Knows.—I forgot on former occasions to say to you that the *Bird of Washington* is found pretty abundant on the Lakes near New Orleans.—Governor Roman' Cousin assured Harris & I of this fact.—We are promised some in Rum.—M*r* Zaringue (the cousin) has seen it dive after fish frequently and was the man who spoke of it thus. "Connaissez vous le Grand Aigle Brun Pecheur"?—he says that it breeds *on Trees.* he Knows the White headed Well.—and Dear Friend God bless you all.—remember [to] us to all about you. Harris Joins us in best regards &c and I remain as ever Your Friend most truly & sincerely attached

JOHN J AUDUBON

To REV*d* JNO BACHMAN
Charleston, South Carolina

April 18*th* 1837—

MY DEAR BACHMAN

Here we are all safe & well in *Bayou Sallé Bay*, about 18 West of the Mouth of the *Teche*, and in Attakapas.—We are now on board of our Tender Cutter the Crusader, ransacking the shores of this Coast, Most of which is flat & Marshy, and not so abundantly suplied with Birds as either of the (?) might wish it to be. however we have filled 3 casks with Valuables, but not with any new Bird!—We still intend moving Westward as far as Galveston Bay, and may return across the *Land*. I Hope this will reach you all Well, and that you may have received good accounts from My Dear Wife & Victor from England, the result of which I shall expect to find awaiting our Return at New Orleans—but when I cannot pricisely say.—We are all in good spirits and Work very hard I promise you—Kiss all the Dear Ones under your Roof Write to Lucy and to Victor, and believe Me as ever Your Friend, and God bless you all—

JOHN J AUDUBON

MISSOURI RIVER JOURNAL

In March 1843 when Audubon set out on his last long expedition, the "Great Western Journey," as he called it in one letter, he was fifty-eight years old. His major work was behind him. The Birds of America *had been completed in 1838, and in 1839 the fifth and final volume of the* Ornithological Biography *had been published. The smaller octavo edition of* Birds of America *was progressing well, and in 1842 Audubon and his family had moved into their newly built house, Minnie's Land, nine miles from the center of New York City, on the Hudson River.*

The implications of settling down into a permanent home in the civilized East alarmed the old woodsman in Audubon, and helped him make up his mind to see the western territories before age became too much of a handicap. He had dreamed of such a journey for years. There was also the professional necessity of gathering material for his new project, a large work on the mammals of North America that would eventually be finished after his death by his sons and published as the Viviparous Quadrupeds of North America *(1845–54). Audubon arranged for his friend John Bachman to write the text, and by 1843 both Audubon and Bachman were convinced the work could not be completed without the western expedition.*

Audubon was accompanied by his old friend Edward Harris and three other men: John Bell, a taxidermist, Issac Sprague, an artist who would help with backgrounds, and Lewis Squires, a neighbor who signed on as secretary and general factotum. The journey—from Saint Louis up the Missouri in a flat-bottom steamboat deep into Indian and buffalo territory all the way to Fort Union, a federal outpost not far from the confluence of the Missouri and Yellowstone rivers, and back again to Saint Louis after the summer in Fort Union—lasted eight months.

The Missouri Journal *is the most uniformly accomplished of Audubon's American writings. The original manuscript no longer exists, but the journal as printed by Maria Audubon in* Audubon and His Journals *(1897) does not appear to be as heavily edited as some of the other journals she included. For one thing, Audubon wrote it as a sourcebook for the* Quadrupeds, *probably with eventual publication in mind. He sent a copy of it in 1846 to Bachman, who praised it as spirited, instructive, and amusing. For another, Audubon's English had become firmer and more reliable, and he had the advantage of exchanging notes with Edward Harris, who was writing his own journal around the evening campfires.*

I left home at ten o'clock of the morning, on Saturday the 11th of March, 1843, accompanied by my son Victor. I left all well, and I trust in God for the privilege and happiness of rejoining them all some time next autumn, when I hope to return from the Yellowstone River, an expedition undertaken solely for the sake of our work on the Quadrupeds of North America. The day was cold, but the sun was shining, and after having visited a few friends in the city of New York, we departed for Philadelphia in the cars, and reached that place at eleven of the night. As I was about landing, I was touched on the shoulder by a tall, robust-looking man, whom I knew not to be a sheriff, but in fact my good friend Jediah Irish, of the Great Pine Swamp. I also met my friend Edward Harris, who, with old John G. Bell, Isaac Sprague, and young Lewis Squires, are to be my companions for this campaign. We all put up at Mr. Sanderson's. Sunday was spent in visits to Mr. Bowen, Dr. Morton, and others, and we had many calls made upon us at the hotel. On Monday morning we took the cars for Baltimore, and Victor returned home to Minniesland. The weather was rainy, blustery, cold, but we reached Baltimore in time to eat our dinner there, and we there spent the afternoon and the night. I saw Gideon B. Smith and a few other friends, and on the next morning we entered the cars for Cumberland, which we reached the same evening about six. Here we had all our effects weighed, and were charged thirty dollars additional weight—a first-rate piece of robbery. We went on now by coaches, entering the gap, and ascending the Alleghanies amid a storm of snow, which kept us company for about forty hours, when we reached Wheeling, which we left on the 16th of March, and went on board the steamer, that brought us to Cincinnati all safe.

We saw much game on our way, such as Geese, Ducks, etc., but no Turkeys as in times of yore. We left for Louisville in the U. S. mail steamer, and arrived there before daylight on the 19th inst. My companions went to the Scott House, and I to William G. Bakewell's, whose home I reached before the family were up. I remained there four days, and was, of course, most kindly treated; and, indeed, during my whole stay in this city of my youth I did enjoy myself famously well, with dancing, dinner-parties, etc. We left for St. Louis on board the ever-to-be-remembered steamer "Gallant," and after having been struck by a log which did not send us to the bottom, arrived on the 28th of March.

On the 4th of April, Harris went off to Edwardsville, with the rest of my companions, and I went to Nicholas Berthoud, who began housekeeping here that day, though Eliza was not yet arrived from Pittsburgh. My time at St. Louis would have been agreeable to any one fond of company, dinners, and parties; but of these matters I am not, though I did dine at three different houses, *bon gré, mal gré.* In fact, my time was spent procuring, arranging, and superintending the necessary objects for the comfort and utility of the party attached to my undertaking. The Chouteaux supplied us with most things, and, let it be said to their honor, at little or no profit. Captain Sire took me in a light wagon to see old Mr. Chouteau one afternoon, and I found the worthy old gentleman so kind and so full of information about the countries of the Indians that I returned to him a few days afterwards, not only for the sake of the pleasure I enjoyed in his conversation, but also with the view to procure, both dead and alive, a species of Pouched Rat (*Pseudostoma bursarius*) wonderfully abundant in this section of country. One day our friend Harris came back, and brought with him the prepared skins of birds and quadrupeds they had collected, and informed me that they had removed their quarters to B——'s. He left the next day, after we had made an arrangement for the party to return the Friday following, which they did. I drew four figures of Pouched Rats, and outlined two figures of *Sciurus capistratus*, which is here called "Fox Squirrel."

The 25th of April at last made its appearance, the rivers were now opened, the weather was growing warm, and every object in nature proved to us that at last the singularly lingering winter of 1842 and 1843 was over. Having conveyed the whole of our effects on board the steamer, and being supplied with excellent letters, we left St. Louis at 11.30 A.M., with Mr. Sarpy on board, and a hundred and one trappers of all descriptions and nearly a dozen different nationalities, though the greater number were French Canadians, or Creoles of this State. Some were drunk, and many in that stupid mood which follows a state of nervousness produced by drinking and over-excitement. Here is the scene that took place on board the "Omega" at our departure, and what followed when the roll was called.

First the general embarkation, when the men came in pushing and squeezing each other, so as to make the boards they walked upon fairly tremble. The Indians, poor souls, were more quiet, and had already seated or squatted themselves on the highest parts of the steamer, and were tranquil lookers-on. After about three quarters of an hour, the crew and all the trappers (these are called *engagés*) were on board, and we at once pushed off and up the stream, thick and muddy as it was. The whole of the effects and the baggage of the *engagés* was arranged in the main cabin, and presently was seen Mr. Sarpy, book in hand, with the list before him, wherefrom he gave the names of these *attachés*. The men whose names were called nearly filled the fore part of the cabin, where stood Mr. Sarpy, our captain, and one of the clerks. All awaited orders from Mr. Sarpy. As each man was called, and answered to his name, a blanket containing the apparel for the trip was handed to him, and he was ordered at once to retire and make room for the next. The outfit, by the way, was somewhat scanty, and of indifferent quality. Four men were missing, and some appeared rather reluctant; however, the roll was ended, and one hundred and one were found. In many instances their bundles were thrown to them, and they were ordered off as if slaves. I forgot to say that as the boat pushed off from the shore, where stood a crowd of loafers, the men on board had congregated upon the hurricane deck with their rifles and guns of various sorts, all loaded, and began to fire what I should call a very disorganized sort of a salute, which lasted for something like an hour, and which has been renewed at intervals, though in a more desultory manner, at every village we have passed. However, we now find them passably good, quiet, and regularly sobered men. We have of course a motley set, even to Italians. We passed the mouth of the Missouri, and moved very slowly against the current, for it was not less than twenty minutes after four the next morning, when we reached St. Charles, distant forty-two miles. Here we stopped till half-past five, when Mr. Sarpy, to whom I gave my letters home, left us in a wagon.

April 26. A rainy day, and the heat we had experienced yesterday was now all gone. We saw a Wild Goose running on the shore, and it was killed by Bell; but our captain did not stop to pick it up, and I was sorry to see the poor bird dead, uselessly. We now had found out that our berths were too thickly inhabited for us to sleep in; so I rolled myself in my blanket, lay down on deck, and slept very sound.

27th. A fine clear day, cool this morning. Cleaned our boilers last night, landing where the "Emily Christian" is sunk, for a few moments; saw a few Gray Squirrels, and an abundance of our common Partridges in flocks of fifteen to twenty, very gentle indeed. About four this afternoon we passed the mouth of the Gasconade River, a stream coming from the westward, valuable for its yellow-pine lumber. At a woodyard above us we saw a White Pelican that had been captured there, and which, had it been clean, I should have bought. I saw that its legs and feet were red, and not yellow, as they are during autumn and winter. Marmots are quite abundant, and here they perforate their holes in the loose, sandy soil of the river banks, as well as the same soil wherever it is somewhat elevated. We do not know yet if it is *Arctomys monax*, or a new species. The weather being fine, and the night clear, we ran all night and on the morning of the 28th, thermometer 69° to 78° at sunrise, we were in sight of the seat of government, Jefferson. The State House stands prominent, with a view from it up and down the stream of about ten miles; but, with the exception of the State House and the Penitentiary, Jefferson is a poor place, the land round being sterile and broken. This is *said* to be 160 or 170 miles above St. Louis. We saw many Gray Squirrels this morning. Yesterday we passed under long lines of elevated shore, surmounted by stupendous rocks of limestone, with many curious holes in them, where we saw Vultures and Eagles enter towards dusk Harris saw a Peregrine Falcon; the whole of these rocky shores are ornamented with a species of white cedar quite satisfactorily known to us. We took wood at several places; at one I was told that Wild Turkeys were abundant and Squirrels also, but as the squatter observed, "Game is very scarce, especially Bears." Wolves begin to be troublesome to the settlers who have sheep; they are obliged to drive the latter home, and herd them each night.

This evening the weather became cloudy and looked like rain; the weather has been very warm, the thermometer being at 78° at three this afternoon. We saw a pair of Peregrine Falcons, one of them with a bird in its talons; also a few White-fronted Geese, some Blue-winged Teal, and some Cormorants, but none with the head, neck, and breast pure white, as the one I saw two days ago. The strength of the current seemed to increase; in some places our boat merely kept her own, and in one instance fell back nearly half a mile to where we had taken in wood. At about ten this evening we came into such strong water that nothing could be done against it; we laid up for the night at the lower end of a willow island, and then cleaned the boilers and took in 200 fence-rails, which the French Canadians call "perches." Now a *perche* in French means a pole; therefore this must be *patois*.

29TH. We were off at five this rainy morning, and at 9 A.M. reached Booneville, distant from St. Louis about 204 miles. We bought at this place an axe, a saw, three files, and some wafers; also some chickens, at one dollar a dozen. We found here some of the Santa Fé traders with whom we had crossed the Alleghanies. They were awaiting the arrival of their goods, and then would immediately start. I saw a Rabbit sitting under the shelf of a rock, and also a Gray Squirrel. It appears to me that *Sciurus macrourus* of Say relishes the bottom lands in preference to the hilly or rocky portions which alternately present themselves along these shores. On looking along the banks of the river, one cannot help observing the half-drowned young willows, and cotton trees of the same age, trembling and shaking sideways against the current; and methought, as I gazed upon them, of the danger they were in of being immersed over their very tops and thus dying, not through the influence of fire, the natural enemy of wood, but from the force of the mighty stream on the margin of which they grew, and which appeared as if in its wrath it was determined to overwhelm, and undo all that the Creator in His bountifulness had granted us to enjoy. The banks themselves, along with perhaps millions of trees, are ever tumbling, falling, and washing away from the spots where they may have stood and grown for centuries past. If this be not an awful exemplification of the real course of Nature's intention, that all should and must live and die, then, indeed, the philosophy of our learned men cannot be much relied upon!

This afternoon the steamer "John Auld" came up near us, but stopped to put off passengers. She had troops on board and a good number of travellers. We passed the *city* of Glasgow without stopping there, and the black-guards on shore were so greatly disappointed that they actually fired at us with rifles; but whether with balls or not, they did us no harm, for the current proved so strong that we had to make over to the opposite side of the river. We did not run far; the weather was still bad, raining hard, and at ten o'clock, with wood nearly exhausted, we stopped on the west shore, and there remained all the night, cleaning boilers, etc.

Sunday 30th. This morning was cold, and it blew a gale from the north. We started, however, for a wooding-place, but the "John Auld" had the advantage of us, and took what there was; the wind increased so much that the waves were actually running pretty high down-stream, and we stopped until one o'clock. You may depend my party was not sorry for this; and as I had had no exercise since we left St. Louis, as soon as breakfast was over we started—Bell, Harris, Squires, and myself, with our guns—and had quite a frolic of it, for we killed a good deal of game, and lost some. Unfortunately we landed at a place where the water had overflowed the country between the shores and the hills, which are distant about one mile and a half. We started a couple of Deer, which

Bell and I shot at, and a female Turkey flying fast; at my shot it extended its legs downwards as if badly wounded, but it sailed on, and must have fallen across the muddy waters. Bell, Harris, and myself shot running exactly twenty-eight Rabbits, *Lepus sylvaticus*, and two Bachmans, two *Sciurus macrourus* of Say, two *Arctomys monax*, and a pair of *Tetrao* [*Bonasa*] *umbellus*. The woods were alive with the Rabbits, but they were very wild; the Ground-hogs, Marmots, or *Arctomys*, were in great numbers, judging from the innumerable burrows we saw, and had the weather been calm, I have no doubt we would have seen many more. Bell wounded a Turkey hen so badly that the poor thing could not fly; but Harris frightened it, and it was off, and was lost. Harris shot an *Arctomys* without pouches, that had been forced out of its burrow by the water entering it; it stood motionless until he was within ten paces of it; when, ascertaining what it was, he retired a few yards, and shot it with No. 10 shot, and it fell dead on the spot. We found the woods filled with birds—all known, however, to us: Golden-crowned Thrush, Cerulean Warblers, Woodpeckers of various kinds, etc.; but not a Duck in the bayou, to my surprise. At one the wind lulled somewhat, and as we had taken all the fence-rails and a quantity of dry stuff of all sorts, we were ready to attempt our ascent, and did so. It was curious to see sixty or seventy men carrying logs forty or fifty feet long, some well dried and some green, on their shoulders, all of which were wanted by our captain, for some purpose or other. In a great number of instances the squatters, farmers, or planters, as they may be called, are found to abandon their dwellings or make towards higher grounds, which fortunately are here no farther off than from one to three miles. After we left, we met with the strength of the current, but with our stakes, fence-rails, and our dry wood, we made good headway. At one place we passed a couple of houses, with women and children, perfectly surrounded by the flood; these houses stood apparently on the margin of a river coming in from the eastward. The whole farm was under water, and all around was the very perfection of disaster and misfortune. It appeared to us as if the men had gone to procure assistance, and I was grieved that we could not offer them any. We saw several trees falling in, and beautiful, though painful, was the sight. As they fell, the spray which rose along their whole length was exquisite; but alas! these magnificent trees had reached the day of oblivion.

A few miles above New Brunswick we stopped to take in wood, and landed three of our Indians, who, belonging to the Iowa tribe, had to travel up La Grande Rivière. The wind lulled away, and we ran all night, touching, for a few minutes, on a bar in the middle of the river.

MAY 1. This morning was a beautiful one; our run last night was about thirty miles, but as we have just begun this fine day, I will copy here the habits of the Pouched Rats, from my notes on the spot at old Mr. Chouteau's, and again at St. Louis, where I kept several alive for four or five days:—

Plantation of Pierre Chouteau, Sen., four miles west of St. Louis, April 13, 1843. I came here last evening in the company of Mr. Sarpy, for the express purpose of procuring some Pouched Rats, and as I have been fortunate enough to secure several of these strange creatures, and also to have seen and heard much connected with their habits and habitats, I write on the spot, with the wish that no recollection of facts be passed over. The present species is uncommonly abundant throughout this neighborhood, and is even found in the gardens of the city of St. Louis, upon the outskirts. They are extremely pernicious animals to the planter and to the gardener, as they devour every root, grass, or vegetable within their reach, and burrow both day and night in every direction imaginable, wherever they know their insatiable appetites can be recompensed for their labor. They bring forth from five to seven young, about the 25th of March, and these are rather large at birth. The nest, or place of deposit, is usually rounded, and about eight inches in diameter, being globular, and well lined with the hair of the female. This nest is not placed at the end of a burrow, or in any particular one of their long galleries, but oftentimes in the road that may lead to hundreds of yards distant. From immediately around the nest, however, many galleries branch off in divers directions, all tending towards such spots as are well known to the parents to afford an abundance of food. I cannot ascertain how long the young remain under the care of the mother. Having observed several freshly thrown-up mounds in Mr. Chouteau's garden, this excellent gentleman called to some negroes to bring spades, and to dig for the animals with the hope I might procure one alive. All hands went to work with alacrity, in the presence of Dr. Trudeau of St. Louis, my friends the father and son Chouteau, and myself. We observed that the "Muloë" (the name given these animals by the creoles of this country) had worked in two or more opposite directions, and that the main gallery was about a foot beneath the surface of the ground, except where it had crossed the walks, when the burrow was sunk a few inches deeper. The work led the negroes across a large square and two of the walks, on one side of which we found large bunches of carnations, from which the roots had been cut off obliquely, close to the surface of the ground, thereby killing the plants. The roots measured $\frac{7}{8}$ of an inch, and immediately next to them was a rose-bush, where ended the burrow. The other side was now followed, and ended amidst the roots of a fine large peach-tree; these roots were more or less gashed and lacerated, but no animal was there, and on returning on our tracks, we found that several galleries, probably leading outside the garden, existed, and we gave up the chase.

This species throws up the earth in mounds rarely higher than twelve to fifteen inches, and these mounds are thrown up at extremely irregular distances, being at times near to each other, and elsewhere ten to twenty, or even thirty, paces apart, yet generally leading to particular spots, well covered with grapes or vegetables of different kinds. This species remains under ground during the whole winter, inactive, and probably dormant, as they never raise or work the earth at this time. The earth thrown up is as if pulverized, and as soon as the animal has finished his labors, which are for no other purpose than to convey him securely from one spot to another, he closes the aperture, which is sometimes on the top, though more usually on the side towards the sun, leaving a kind of ring nearly one inch in breadth, and about the diameter of the body of the animal. Possessed of an exquisite sense of hearing and of feeling the external pressure of objects travelling on the ground, they stop their labors instantaneously on the least alarm; but if you retire from fifteen to twenty paces to the windward of the hole, and wait for a quarter of an hour or so, you see the "Gopher" (the name given to it by the Missourians—*Americans*) raising the earth with its back and shoulders, and forcing it out forward, leaving the aperture open during the process, and from which it at times issues a few steps, cuts the grasses around, with which it fills its pouches, and then retires to its hole to feed upon its spoils; or it sometimes sits up on its haunches and enjoys the sun, and it may then be shot, provided you are quick. If missed you see it no more, as it will prefer altering the course of its burrow and continuing its labors in quite a different direction. They may be caught in common steel-traps, and two of them were thus procured to-day; but they then injure the foot, the hind one. They are also not uncommonly thrown up by the plough, and one was caught in this manner. They have been known to destroy the roots of hundreds of young fruit-trees in the course of a few days and nights, and will cut roots of grown trees of the most valued kinds, such as apple, pear, peach, plum, etc. They differ greatly in their size and also in their colors, according to age, but not in the sexes. The young are usually gray, the old of a dark chestnut, glossy and shining brown, very difficult to represent in a drawing. The opinion commonly received and entertained, that these Pouched Rats fill their pouches with the earth of their burrows, and empty them when at the entrance, is, I think, quite erroneous; about a dozen which were shot in the act of raising their mounds, and killed at the very mouth of their burrows, had no earth in any of these sacs; the fore feet, teeth, nose, and the anterior portion of the head were found covered with adhesive earth, and most of them had their pouches filled either with blades of grass or roots of different sizes; and I think their being hairy rather corroborates the fact that these pouches are only used for food. In a word, they appear to me to raise the earth precisely in the manner employed by the Mole.

When travelling the tail drags on the ground, and they hobble along with their long front claws drawn underneath; at other times, they move by slow leaping movements, and can travel backwards almost as fast as forwards. When turned over they have much difficulty in replacing themselves in their natural position, and you may see them kicking with their legs and claws for a minute or two before they are right. They bite severely, and do not hesitate to make towards their enemies or assailants with open mouth, squealing like a rat. When they fight among themselves they make great use of the nose in the manner of hogs. They cannot travel faster than the slow walk of a man. They feed frequently while seated on the rump, using their fore paws and long claws somewhat like a squirrel. When sleeping they place the head beneath the breast, and become round, and look like a ball of earth. They clean their whiskers and body in the manner of Rats, Squirrels, etc.

The four which I kept alive never drank anything, though water was given to them. I fed them on potatoes, cabbages, carrots, etc. They tried constantly to make their escape by gnawing at the floor, but in vain. They slept wherever they found clothing, etc., and the rascals cut the lining of my hunting-coat all to bits, so that I was obliged to have it patched and mended. In one instance I had some clothes rolled up for the washerwoman, and, on opening the bundle to count the pieces, one of the fellows caught hold of my right thumb, with fortunately a single one of its upper incisors, and hung on till I shook it off, violently throwing it on the floor, where it lay as if dead; but it recovered, and was as well as ever in less than half an hour. They gnawed the leather straps of my trunks during the night, and although I rose frequently to stop their work, they would begin anew as soon as I was in bed again. I wrote and sent most of the above to John Bachman from St. Louis, after I had finished my drawing of four figures of these most strange and most interesting creatures.

And now to return to this day: When we reached Glasgow, we came in under the stern of the "John Auld." As I saw several officers of the

United States army I bowed to them, and as they all knew that I was bound towards the mighty Rocky Mountains, they not only returned my salutations, but came on board, as well as Father de Smet. They all of them came to my room and saw specimens and skins. Among them was Captain Clark, who married the sister of Major Sandford, whom you all know. They had lost a soldier overboard, two had deserted, and a fourth was missing. We proceeded on until about ten o'clock, and it was not until the 2d of May that we actually reached Independence.

May 2. It stopped raining in the night while I was sound asleep, and at about one o'clock we did arrive at Independence, distant about 379 miles from St. Louis. Here again was the "John Auld," putting out freight for the Santa Fé traders, and we saw many of their wagons. Of course I exchanged a hand-shake with Father de Smet and many of the officers I had seen yesterday. Mr. Meeks, the agent of Colonel Veras, had 148 pounds of tow in readiness for us, and I drew on the Chouteaux for $30.20, for we were charged no less than 12½ to 25 cts. per pound; but this tow might have passed for fine flax, and I was well contented. We left the "Auld," proceeded on our way, and stopped at Madame Chouteau's plantation, where we put out some freight for Sir William Stuart. The water had been two feet deep in her house, but the river has now suddenly fallen about six feet. At Madame Chouteau's I saw a brother of our friend Pierre Chouteau, Senr., now at New York, and he gave me some news respecting the murder of Mr. Jarvis. About twenty picked men of the neighborhood had left in pursuit of the remainder of the marauders, and had sent one of their number back, with the information that they had remained not two miles from the rascally thieves and murderers. I hope they will overtake them all, and shoot them on the spot. We saw a few Squirrels, and Bell killed two Parrakeets.

May 3. We ran all last night and reached Fort Leavenworth at six this morning. We had an early breakfast, as we had intended to walk across the Bend; but we found that the ground was overflowed, and that the bridges across two creeks had been carried away, and reluctantly we gave up our trip. I saw two officers who came on board, also a Mr. Ritchie. The situation of the fort is elevated and fine, and one has a view of the river up and down for some distance. Seeing a great number of Parrakeets, we went after them; Bell killed one. Unfortunately my gun snapped twice, or I should have killed several more. We saw several Turkeys on the ground and in the trees early this morning. On our reaching the landing, a sentinel dragoon came to watch that no one tried to escape.

After leaving this place we fairly entered the Indian country on the west side of the river, for the State of Missouri, by the purchase of the Platte River country, continues for about 250 miles further on the east side, where now we see the only settlements. We saw a good number of Indians in the woods and on the banks, gazing at us as we passed; these are, however, partly civilized, and are miserable enough. Major Mason, who commands here at present, is ill, and I could not see him. We saw several fine horses belonging to different officers. We soon passed Watson, which is considered the head of steam navigation.

In attempting to pass over a shallow, but a short, cut, we grounded on a bar at five o'clock; got off, tried again, and again grounded broadside; and now that it is past six o'clock all hands are busily engaged in trying to get the boat off, but with what success I cannot say. To me the situation is a bad one, as I conceive that as we remain here, the washings of the muddy sands as they float down a powerful current will augment the bar on the weather side (if I may so express myself) of the boat. We have seen another Turkey and many Parrakeets, as well as a great number of burrows formed by the "Siffleurs," as our French Canadians call all and every species of Marmots; Bell and I have concluded that there must be not less than twenty to thirty of these animals for one in any portion of the Atlantic States. We saw them even around the open grounds immediately about Fort Leavenworth.

About half-past seven we fortunately removed our boat into somewhat deeper water, by straightening her bows against the stream, and this was effected by fastening our very long cable to a snag above us, about 200 yards; and now, if we can go backwards and reach the deep waters along shore a few hundred yards below, we shall be able to make fast there for the night. Unfortunately it is now raining hard, the lightning is vivid, and the appearance of the night forbidding.

THURSDAY, MAY 4. We had constant rain, lightning and thunder last night. This morning, at the dawn of day, the captain and all hands were at work, and succeeded in removing the boat several hundred yards below where she had struck; but unfortunately we got fast again before we could reach deep water, and all the exertions to get off were renewed, and at this moment, almost nine, we have a line fastened to the shore and expect to be afloat in a short time. But I fear that we shall lose most of the day before we leave this shallow, intricate, and dangerous channel.

At ten o'clock we found ourselves in deep water, near the shore on the west side. We at once had the men at work cutting wood, which was principally that of ash-trees of moderate size, which wood was brought on board in great quantities and lengths. Thank Heaven, we are off in a few minutes, and I hope will have better luck. I saw on the shore many "Gopher" hills, in all probability the same as I have drawn. Bell shot a Gray Squirrel which I believe to be the same as our *Sciurus carolinensis*. Friend Harris shot two or three birds, which we have not yet fully established, and Bell shot one Lincoln's Finch—strange place for it, when it breeds so very far north as Labrador. Caught a Woodpecker, and killed a Cat-bird, Water-thrush, seventeen Parrakeets, a Yellow Chat, a new Finch, and very curious, two White-throated Finches, one White-crown, a Yellow-rump Warbler, a Gray Squirrel, a Loon, and two Rough-winged Swallows. We saw Cerulean Warblers, Hooded Flycatchers, Kentucky Warblers, Nashville ditto, Blue-winged ditto, Red-eyed and White-eyed Flycatchers, Great-crested and Common Pewees, Redstarts, Towhee Buntings, Ferruginous Thrushes, Wood Thrush, Golden-crowned Thrush, Blue-gray Flycatcher, Blue-eyed Warbler, Blue Yellow-back, Chestnut-sided, Black-and-White Creepers, Nuthatch, Kingbirds, Red Tanagers, Cardinal Grosbeaks, common House Wren, Blue-winged Teals, Swans, large Blue Herons, Crows, Turkey-buzzards, and a Peregrine Falcon, Red-tailed Hawks, Red-headed, Red-bellied, and Golden-winged Woodpeckers, and Partridges. Also, innumerable "Gopher" hills, one Ground-hog, one Rabbit, two Wild Turkeys, one Whippoorwill, one Maryland Yellow-throat, and Swifts. We left the shore with a strong gale of wind, and after having returned to our proper channel, and rounded the island below our troublesome situation of last night, we were forced to come to under the main shore. Here we killed and saw all that is enumerated above, as well as two nests of the White-headed Eagle. We are now for the night at a wooding-place, where we expect to purchase some fresh provisions, if any there are; and as it is nine o'clock I am off to bed.

Friday, May 5. The appearance of the weather this morning was rather bad; it was cloudy and lowering, but instead of rain we have had a strong southwesterly wind to contend with, and on this account our day's work does not amount to much. At this moment, not eight o'clock, we have stopped through its influence.

At half-past twelve we reached the Black Snake Hills settlement, and I was delighted to see this truly beautiful site for a town or city, as will be no doubt some fifty years hence. The hills themselves are about 200 feet above the river, and slope down gently into the beautiful prairie that extends over some thousands of acres, of the richest land imaginable. Five of our trappers did not come on board at the ringing of the bell, and had to walk several miles across a bend to join us and be taken on again. We have not seen much game this day, probably on account of the high wind. We saw, however, a large flock of Willets, two Gulls, one Grebe, many Blue-winged Teals, Wood Ducks, and Coots, and one pair of mated Wild Geese. This afternoon a Black Squirrel was seen. This morning I saw a Marmot; and Sprague, a *Sciurus macrourus* of Say. On examination of the Finch killed by Harris yesterday, I found it to be a new species, and I have taken its measurements across this sheet of paper. It was first seen on the ground, then on low bushes, then on large trees; no note was heard. Two others, that were females to all appearance, could not be procured on account of their extreme shyness. We saw the Indigo-bird, Barn Swallows, Purple Martin, and Greenbacks; also, a Rabbit at the Black Snake Hills. The general aspect of the river is materially altered for the worse; it has become much more crooked or tortuous, in some places very wide with sand-banks naked and dried, so that the wind blows the sand quite high. In one place we came to a narrow and swift chute, four miles above the Black Snake Hills, that in time of extreme high water must be very difficult of ascent. During these high winds it is very hard to steer the boat, and also to land her. The settlers on the Missouri side of the river appear to relish the sight of a steamer greatly, for they all come to look at this one as we pass the different settlements. The thermometer has fallen sixteen degrees since two o'clock, and it feels now very chilly.

Saturday, May 6. High wind all night and cold this morning, with the wind still blowing so hard that at half-past seven we stopped on the western shore, under a range of high hills, but on the weather side of them. We took our guns and went off, but the wind was so high we saw but little; I shot a Wild Pigeon and a Whippoorwill, female, that gave me great trouble, as I never saw one so remarkably wild before. Bell shot two Gray Squirrels and several Vireos, and Sprague, a Kentucky Warbler. Traces of Turkeys and of Deer were seen. We also saw three White Pelicans, but no birds to be added to our previous lot, and I have no wish to keep a strict account of the number of the same species we daily see. It is now half-past twelve; the wind is still very high, but our captain is anxious to try to proceed. We have cut some green wood, and a considerable quantity of hickory for axe-handles. In cutting down a tree we caught two young Gray Squirrels. A Pewee Flycatcher, of some species or other, was caught by the steward, who ran down the poor thing, which was starved on account of the cold and windy weather. Harris shot another of the new Finches, a male also, and I saw what I believe is the female, but it flew upwards of 200 yards without stopping. Bell also shot a small Vireo, which is in all probability a new species (to me at least). We saw a Goshawk, a Marsh Hawk, and a great number of Blackbirds, but could not ascertain the species. The wind was still high when we left our stopping place, but we progressed, and this afternoon came alongside of a beautiful prairie of some thousands of acres, reaching to the hills. Here we stopped to put out our Iowa Indians, and also to land the goods we had for Mr. Richardson, the Indian agent. The goods were landed, but at the wrong place, as the Agent's agent would not receive them there, on account of a creek above, which cannot at present be crossed with wagons. Our Sac Indian chief started at once across the prairie towards the hills, on his way to his wigwam, and we saw Indians on their way towards us, running on foot, and many on horseback, generally riding double on skins or on Spanish saddles. Even the squaws rode, and rode well too! We counted about eighty, amongst whom were a great number of youths of different ages. I was heartily glad that our own squad of them left us here. I observed that though they had been absent from their friends and relatives, they never shook hands, or paid any attention to them. When the freight was taken in we proceeded, and the whole of the Indians followed along the shore at a good round run; those on horseback at times struck into a gallop. I saw more of these poor beings when we approached the landing, perched and seated on the promontories about, and many followed the boat to the landing. Here the goods were received, and Major Richardson came on board, and paid freight. He told us we were now in the country of the Fox Indians as well as that of the Iowas, that the number about him is over 1200, and that his district extends about seventy miles up the river. He appears to be a pleasant man; told us that Hares were very abundant—by the way, Harris saw one to-day. We are now landed on the Missouri side of the river, and taking in wood. We saw a Pigeon Hawk, found Partridges paired, and some also in flocks. When we landed during the high wind we saw a fine sugar camp belonging to Indians. I was pleased to see that many of the troughs they make are formed of bark, and that both ends are puckered and tied so as to resemble a sort of basket or canoe. They had killed many Wild Turkeys, Geese, and Crows, all of which they eat. We also procured a White-eyed and a Warbling Vireo, and shot a male Wild Pigeon. Saw a Gopher throwing out the dirt with his fore feet and not from his pouches. I was within four or five feet of it. Shot a Humming-bird, saw a Mourning Warbler, and Cedar-birds.

May 7, Sunday. Fine weather, but cool. Saw several Gray Squirrels and one Black. I am told by one of our pilots, who has killed seven or eight, that they are much larger than *Sciurus macrourus*, that the hair is coarse, that they are clumsy in their motions, and that they are found from the Black Snake Hills to some distance above the Council Bluffs.

We landed to cut wood at eleven, and we went ashore. Harris killed another of the new Finches, a male also; the scarcity of the females goes on, proving how much earlier the males sally forth on their migrations towards the breeding grounds. We saw five Sand-hill Cranes, some Goldfinches, Yellowshanks, Tell-tale Godwits, Solitary Snipes, and the woods were filled with House Wrens singing their merry songs. The place, however, was a bad one, for it was a piece of bottom land that had overflowed, and was sadly muddy and sticky. At twelve the bell rang for Harris, Bell, and me to return, which we did at once, as dinner was preparing for the table. Talking of dinner makes me think of giving you the hours, usually, of our meals. Breakfast at half-past six, dinner at half-past twelve, tea or supper at seven or later as the case may be. We have not taken much wood here; it is ash, but quite green. We saw Orchard Orioles, Blue-gray Flycatchers, Great-crested and Common Pewees, Mallards, Pileated Woodpeckers, Blue Jays, and Blue-birds; heard a Marsh Wren, saw a Crow, a Wood Thrush, and Water Thrush. Indigo-birds and Parrakeets plentiful. This afternoon we went into the pocket of a sand bar, got aground, and had to back out for almost a mile. We saw an abundance of Ducks, some White Pelicans, and an animal that we guessed was a Skunk. We have run about fifty miles, and therefore have done a good day's journey. We have passed the mouths of several small rivers, and also some very fine prairie land, extending miles towards the hills. It is now nine o'clock, a beautiful night with the moon shining. We have seen several Ravens, and White-headed Eagles on their nests.

May 8, Monday. A beautiful calm day; the country we saw was much the same as that we passed yesterday, and nothing of great importance took place except that at a wooding-place on the very verge of the State of Missouri (the northwest corner) Bell killed a Black Squirrel which friend Bachman has honored with the name of my son John, *Sciurus Audubonii.* We are told that this species is not uncommon here. It was a good-sized adult male, and Sprague drew an outline of it. Harris shot another specimen of the new Finch. We saw Parrakeets and many small birds, but nothing new or very rare. This evening I wrote a long letter to each house, John Bachman, Gideon B. Smith of Baltimore, and

J. W. H. Page of New Bedford, with the hope of having them forwarded from the Council Bluffs.

May 9, Tuesday. Another fine day. After running until eleven o'clock we stopped to cut wood, and two Rose-breasted Grosbeaks were shot, a common Blue-bird, and a common Northern Titmouse. We saw White Pelicans, Geese, Ducks, etc. One of our trappers cut one of his feet dreadfully with his axe, and Harris, who is now the doctor, attended to it as best he could. This afternoon we reached the famous establishment of Belle Vue where resides the brother of Mr. Sarpy of St. Louis, as well as the Indian Agent, or, as he might be more appropriately called, the Custom House officer. Neither were at home, both away on the Platte River, about 300 miles off. We had a famous pack of rascally Indians awaiting our landing—filthy and half-starved. We landed some cargo for the establishment, and I saw a trick of the trade which made me laugh. Eight cords of wood were paid for with five tin cups of sugar and three of coffee—value at St. Louis about twenty-five cents. We have seen a Fish Hawk, Savannah Finch, Green-backed Swallows, Rough-winged Swallows, Martins, Parrakeets, Black-headed Gulls, Blackbirds, and Cowbirds; I will repeat that the woods are fairly alive with House Wrens. Blue Herons, *Emberiza pallida*—Clay-colored Bunting of Swainson—Henslow's Bunting, Crow Blackbirds; and, more strange than all, two large cakes of ice were seen by our pilots and ourselves. I am very much fatigued and will finish the account of this day to-morrow. At Belle Vue we found the brother-in-law of old Provost, who acts as clerk in the absence of Mr. Sarpy. The store is no great affair, and yet I am told that they drive a good trade with Indians on the Platte River, and others, on this side of the Missouri. We unloaded some freight, and pushed off. We saw here the first ploughing of the ground we have observed since we left the lower settlements near St. Louis. We very soon reached the post of Fort Croghan, so called after my old friend of that name with whom I hunted Raccoons on his father's plantation in Kentucky some thirty-eight years ago, and whose father and my own were well acquainted, and fought together in conjunction with George Washington and Lafayette, during the Revolutionary War, against "Merrie England." Here we found only a few soldiers, dragoons; their camp and officers having been forced to move across the prairie to the Bluffs, five miles. After we had put out some freight for the sutler, we proceeded on until we stopped for the night a few miles above, on the same side of the river. The soldiers assured us that their parade ground, and so-called barracks, had been four feet under water, and we saw fair and sufficient evidence of this.

At this place our pilot saw the first Yellow-headed Troupial we have met with. We landed for the night under trees covered by muddy deposits from the great overflow of this season. I slept soundly, and have this morning, May 10, written this.

May 10, Wednesday. The morning was fine, and we were under way at daylight; but a party of dragoons, headed by a lieutenant, had left their camp four miles distant from our anchorage at the same time, and reached the shore before we had proceeded far; they fired a couple of rifle shots ahead of us, and we brought to at once. The young officer came on board, and presented a letter from his commander, Captain Burgwin, from which we found that we had to have our cargo examined. Our captain was glad of it, and so were we all; for, finding that it would take several hours, we at once ate our breakfast, and made ready to go ashore. I showed my credentials and orders from the Government, Major Mitchell of St. Louis, etc., and I was therefore immediately settled comfortably. I desired to go to see the commanding officer, and the lieutenant very politely sent us there on horseback, guided by an old dragoon of considerable respectability. I was mounted on a young white horse, Spanish saddle with holsters, and we proceeded across the prairie towards the Bluffs and the camp. My guide was anxious to take a short cut, and took me across several bayous, one of which was really up to the saddle; but we crossed that, and coming to another we found it so miry, that his horse wheeled after two or three steps, whilst I was looking at him before starting myself; for you all well know that an old traveller is, and must be, prudent. We now had to retrace our steps till we reached the very tracks that the squad sent after us in the morning had taken, and at last we reached the foot of the Bluffs, when my guide asked me if I "could ride at a gallop," to which not answering him, but starting at once at a round run, I neatly passed him ere his horse was well at the pace; on we went, and in a few minutes we entered a beautiful dell or valley, and were in sight of the encampment. We reached this in a trice, and rode between two lines of pitched tents to one at the end, where I dismounted, and met Captain Burgwin, a young man, brought up at West Point, with whom I was on excellent and friendly terms in less time than it has taken me to write this account of our meeting. I showed him my credentials, at which he smiled, and politely assured me that I was too well known throughout our country to need any letters. While seated in front of his tent, I heard the note of a bird new to me, and as it proceeded from a tree above our heads, I looked up and saw the first Yellow-headed Troupial alive that ever came across my own migrations.

The captain thought me probably crazy, as I thought Rafinesque when he was at Henderson; for I suddenly started, shot at the bird, and killed it. Afterwards I shot three more at one shot, but only one female amid hundreds of these Yellow-headed Blackbirds. They are quite abundant here, feeding on the surplus grain that drops from the horses' troughs; they walked under, and around the horses, with as much confidence as if anywhere else. When they rose, they generally flew to the very tops of the tallest trees, and there, swelling their throats, partially spreading their wings and tail, they issue their croaking note, which is a compound, not to be mistaken, between that of the Crow Blackbird and that of the Red-winged Starling. After I had fired at them twice they became quite shy, and all of them flew off to the prairies. I saw then two Magpies in a cage, that had been caught in nooses, by the legs; and their actions, voice, and general looks, assured me as much as ever, that they are the very same species as that found in Europe. Prairie Wolves are extremely abundant hereabouts. They are so daring that they come into the camp both by day and by night; we found their burrows in the banks and in the prairie, and had I come here yesterday I should have had a superb specimen killed here, but which was devoured by the hogs belonging to the establishment. The captain and the doctor—Madison by name—returned with us to the boat, and we saw many more Yellow-headed Troupials. The high Bluffs back of the prairie are destitute of stones. On my way there I saw abundance of Gopher hills, two Geese paired, two Yellow-crowned Herons, Red-winged Starlings, Cowbirds, common Crow Blackbirds, a great number of Baltimore Orioles, a Swallow-tailed Hawk, Yellow Red-poll Warbler, Field Sparrow, and Chipping Sparrow. Sprague killed another of the beautiful Finch. Robins are very scarce, Parrakeets and Wild Turkeys plentiful. The officers came on board, and we treated them as hospitably as we could; they ate their lunch with us, and are themselves almost destitute of provisions. Last July the captain sent twenty dragoons and as many Indians on a hunt for Buffaloes. During the hunt they killed 51 Buffaloes, 104 Deer, and 10 Elks, within 80 miles of the camp. The Sioux Indians are great enemies to the Pötowatamies, and very frequently kill several of the latter in their predatory excursions against them. This kind of warfare has rendered the Potowatamies very cowardly, which is quite a remarkable change from their previous valor and daring. Bell collected six different species of shells, and found a large lump of pumice stone which does float on the water. We left our anchorage (which means tied to the shore) at twelve o'clock, and about sunset we did pass the real Council Bluff. Here, however, the bed of the river is utterly changed, though you may yet see that which is now called the Old Missouri. The Bluffs stand, truly speaking, on a beautiful bank almost forty feet above the water, and run off on a rich prairie, to the hills in the background in a gentle slope, that renders the whole place a fine and very remarkable spot. We tied up for the night about three miles above them, and all hands went ashore to cut wood, which begins to be somewhat scarce, of a good quality. Our captain cut and left several cords of green wood for his return trip, at this place; Harris and Bell went on shore, and saw several Bats, and three Turkeys. This afternoon a Deer was seen scampering across the prairies until quite out of sight. Wild-gooseberry bushes are very abundant, and the fruit is said to be very good.

May 11, Thursday. We had a night of rain, thunder, and heavy wind from the northeast, and we did not start this morning till seven o'clock, therefore had a late breakfast. There was a bright blood-red streak on the horizon at four o'clock that looked forbidding, but the weather changed as we proceeded, with, however, showers of rain at various intervals during the day. We have now come to a portion of the river more crooked than any we have passed; the shores on both sides are evidently lower, the hills that curtain the distance are further from the shores, and the intervening space is mostly prairie, more or less overflowed. We have seen one Wolf on a sand-bar, seeking for food, perhaps dead fish. The actions were precisely those of a cur dog with a long tail, and the bellowing sound of the engine did not seem to disturb him. He trotted on parallel to the boat for about one mile, when we landed to cut drift-wood. Bell, Harris, and I went on shore to try to have a shot at him. He was what is called a brindle-colored Wolf, of the common size. One hundred trappers, however, with their axes at work, in a few moments rather stopped his progress, and when he saw us coming, he turned back on his track, and trotted off, but Bell shot a very small load in the air to see the effect it would produce. The fellow took two or three leaps, stopped, looked at us for a moment, and then started on a gentle gallop. When I overtook his tracks they appeared small, and more rounded than usual. I saw several tracks at the same time, therefore more than one had travelled over this great sandy and muddy bar last night, if not this morning. I lost sight of him behind some large piles of drift-wood, and could see him no more. Turkey-buzzards were on the bar, and I thought that I should have found some dead carcass; but on reaching the spot, nothing was there. A fine large Raven passed at one hundred yards from us, but I did not shoot. Bell found a few small shells, and Harris shot a Yellow-rumped Warbler. We have seen several White Pelicans, Geese, Black-headed Gulls, and Green-backed Swallows, but nothing new. The night is cloudy and intimates more rain. We are fast to a willowed shore, and are preparing lines to try our luck at catching a Catfish or so. I was astonished to find how much stiffened I was this morning, from the exercise I took on horseback yesterday, and think that now it would take me a week, at least, to accustom my body to riding as I was wont to do twenty years ago. The timber is becoming more scarce as we proceed, and I greatly fear that our only opportunities of securing wood will be those afforded us by that drifted on the bars.

May 12, Friday. The morning was foggy, thick, and calm. We passed the river called the *Sioux Pictout*, a small stream formerly abounding with Beavers, Otters, Muskrats, etc., but now quite destitute of any of these creatures. On going along the banks bordering a long and wide prairie, thick with willows and other small brush-wood, we saw four Black-tailed Deer immediately on the bank; they trotted away without appearing to be much alarmed; after a few hundred yards, the two largest, probably males, raised themselves on their hind feet and pawed at each other, after the manner of stallions. They trotted off again, stopping often, but after a while disappeared; we saw them again some hundreds of yards farther on, when, becoming suddenly alarmed, they bounded off until out of sight. They did not trot or run irregularly as our Virginian Deer does, and their color was of a brownish cast, whilst our common Deer at this season is red. Could we have gone ashore, we might in all probability have killed one or two of them. We stopped to cut wood on the opposite side of the river, where we went on shore, and there saw many tracks of Deer, Elk, Wolves, and Turkeys. In attempting to cross a muddy place to shoot at some Yellow-headed Troupials that were abundant, I found myself almost mired, and returned with difficulty. We only shot a Blackburnian Warbler, a Yellow-winged ditto, and a few Finches. We have seen more Geese than usual as well as Mallards and Wood Ducks. This afternoon the weather cleared up, and a while before sunset we passed under Wood's Bluffs, so called because a man of that name fell overboard from his boat while drunk. We saw there many Bank Swallows, and afterwards we came in view of the Blackbird Hill, where the famous Indian chief of that name was buried, at his request, on his horse, whilst the animal was alive. We are now fast to the shore opposite this famed bluff. We cut good ash wood this day, and have made a tolerable run, say forty miles.

Saturday, May 13. This morning was extremely foggy, although I could plainly see the orb of day trying to force its way through the haze.

While this lasted all hands were engaged in cutting wood, and we did not leave our fastening-place till seven, to the great grief of our commander. During the wood cutting, Bell walked to the top of the hills, and shot two Lark Buntings, males, and a Lincoln's Finch. After a while we passed under some beautiful bluffs surmounted by many cedars, and these bluffs were composed of fine white sandstone, of a soft texture, but very beautiful to the eye. In several places along this bluff we saw clusters of nests of Swallows, which we all looked upon as those of the Cliff Swallow, although I saw not one of the birds. We stopped again to cut wood, for our opportunities are not now very convenient. Went out, but only shot a fine large Turkey-hen, which I brought down on the wing at about forty yards. It ran very swiftly, however, and had not Harris's dog come to our assistance, we might have lost it. As it was, however, the dog pointed, and Harris shot it, with my small shot-gun, whilst I was squatted on the ground amid a parcel of low bushes. I was astonished to see how many of the large shot I had put into her body. This hen weighed $11\frac{3}{4}$ pounds. She had a nest, no doubt, but we could not find it. We saw a good number of Geese, though fewer than yesterday; Ducks also. We passed many fine prairies, and in one place I was surprised to see the richness of the bottom lands. We saw this morning eleven Indians of the Omaha tribe. They made signals for us to land, but our captain never heeded them, for he hates the red-skins as most men hate the devil. One of them fired a gun, the group had only one, and some ran along the shore for nearly two miles, particularly one old gentleman who persevered until we came to such bluff shores as calmed down his spirits. In another place we saw one seated on a log, close by the frame of a canoe; but he looked surly, and never altered his position as we passed. The frame of this boat resembled an ordinary canoe. It is formed by both sticks giving a half circle; the upper edges are fastened together by a long stick, as well as the centre of the bottom. Outside of this stretches a Buffalo skin without the hair on; it is said to make a light and safe craft to cross even the turbid, rapid stream—the Missouri. By simply looking at them, one may suppose that they are sufficiently large to carry two or three persons. On a sand-bar afterwards we saw three more Indians, also with a canoe frame, but we only interchanged the common yells usual on such occasions. They looked as destitute and as hungry as if they had not eaten for a week, and no doubt would have given much for a bottle of whiskey. At our last landing for wood-cutting, we also went on shore, but shot nothing, not even took aim at a bird; and there was an Indian with a flint-lock rifle, who came on board and stared about until we left, when he went off with a little tobacco. I pity these poor beings from my heart! This evening we came to the burial-ground bluff of Sergeant Floyd, one of the companions of the never-to-be-forgotten expedition of Lewis and Clark, over the Rocky Mountains, to the Pacific Ocean. A few minutes afterwards, before coming to Floyd's Creek, we started several Turkey-cocks from their roost, and had we been on shore could have accounted for more than one of them. The prairies are becoming more common and more elevated; we have seen more evergreens this day than we have done for two weeks at least. This evening is dark and rainy, with lightning and some distant thunder, and we have entered the mouth of the Big Sioux River, where we are fastened for the night. This is a clear stream and abounds with fish, and on one of the branches of this river is found the famous red clay, of which the precious pipes, or calumets are manufactured. We will try to procure some on our return homeward. It is late; had the weather been clear, and the moon, which is full, shining, it was our intention to go ashore, to try to shoot Wild Turkeys; but as it is pouring down rain, and as dark as pitch, we have thrown our lines overboard and perhaps may catch a fish. We hope to reach Vermilion River day after to-morrow. We saw abundance of the birds which I have before enumerated.

May 14, Sunday. It rained hard and thundered during the night; we started at half-past three, when it had cleared, and the moon shone brightly. The river is crooked as ever, with large bars, and edged with prairies. Saw many Geese, and a Long-billed Curlew. One poor Goose had been wounded in the wing; when approached, it dived for a long distance and came up along the shore. Then we saw a Black Bear, swimming across the river, and it caused a commotion. Some ran for their rifles, and several shots were fired, some of which almost touched Bruin; but he kept on, and swam very fast. Bell shot at it with large shot and must have touched it. When it reached the shore, it tried several times to climb up, but each time fell back. It at last succeeded, almost immediately started off at a gallop, and was soon lost to sight. We stopped to cut wood at twelve o'clock, in one of the vilest places we have yet come to. The rushes were waist-high, and the whole underbrush tangled by grape vines. The Deer and the Elks had beaten paths which we followed for a while, but we saw only their tracks, and those of Turkeys. Harris found a heronry of the common Blue Heron, composed of about thirty nests, but the birds were shy and he did not shoot at any. Early this morning a dead Buffalo floated by us, and after a while the body of a common cow, which had probably belonged to the fort above this. Mr. Sire told us that at this point, two years ago, he overtook three of the deserters of the company, who had left a keel-boat in which they were going down to St. Louis. They had a canoe when overtaken; he took their guns from them, destroyed the canoe, and left them there. On asking him what had become of them, he said they had walked back to the establishment at the mouth of Vermilion River, which by land is only ten miles distant; ten miles, through such woods as we tried in vain to hunt in, is a walk that I should not like at all. We stayed cutting wood for about two hours, when we started again; but a high wind arose, so that we could not make headway, and had to return and make fast again, only a few hundred yards from the previous spot. On such occasions our captain employs his wood-cutters in felling trees, and splitting and piling the wood until his return downwards, in about one month, perhaps, from now. In talking with our captain he tells us that the Black Bear is rarely seen swimming this river, and that one or two of them are about all he observes on going up each trip. I have seen them swimming in great numbers on the lower parts of the Ohio, and on the Mississippi. It is said that at times, when the common Wolves are extremely hard pressed for food, they will eat certain roots which they dig up for the purpose, and the places from which they take this food look as if they had been spaded. When they hunt a Buffalo, and have killed it, they drag it to some distance—about sixty yards or so—and dig a hole large enough to receive and conceal it; they then cover it with earth, and lie down over it until hungry again, when they uncover, and feed upon it. Along the banks of the rivers, when the Buffaloes fall, or cannot ascend, and then die, the Wolves are seen in considerable numbers feeding upon them. Although cunning beyond belief in hiding at the report of a gun, they almost instantly show themselves from different parts around, and if you wish to kill some, you have only to hide yourself, and you will see them coming to the game you have left, when you are not distant more than thirty or forty yards. It is said that though they very frequently hunt their game until the latter take to the river, they seldom, if ever, follow after it. The wind that drove us ashore augmented into a severe gale, and by its present appearance looks as if it would last the whole night. Our fire was comfortable, for, as you know, the thermometer has been very changeable since noon. We have had rain also, though not continuous, but quite enough to wet our men, who, notwithstanding have cut and piled about twelve cords of wood, besides the large quantity we have on board for to-morrow, when we hope the weather will be good and calm.

May 15, Monday. The wind continued an irregular gale the whole of the night, and the frequent logs that struck our weather side kept me awake until nearly daybreak, when I slept about two hours; it unfortunately happened that we were made fast upon the weather shore. This morning the gale kept up, and as we had nothing better to do, it was proposed that we should walk across the bottom lands, and attempt to go to the prairies, distant about two and a half miles. This was accordingly done; Bell, Harris, Mr. La Barge—the first pilot—a mulatto hunter named Michaux, and I, started at nine. We first crossed through tangled brush-wood, and high-grown rushes for a few hundreds of yards, and soon perceived that here, as well as all along the Missouri and Mississippi, the land is highest nearest the shore, and falls off the farther one goes inland. Thus we soon came to mud, and from mud to muddy water, as *pure* as it runs in the Missouri itself; at every step which we took we raised several pounds of mud on our boots. Friend Harris very wisely returned, but the remainder of us proceeded through thick and thin until we came in sight of the prairies. But, alas! between us and them there existed a regular line of willows—and who ever saw willows grow far from water? Here we were of course stopped, and after attempting in many places to cross the water that divided us from the dry land, we were forced back, and had to return as best we could. We were mud up to the very middle, the perspiration ran down us, and at one time I was nearly exhausted; which proves to me pretty clearly that I am no longer as young, or as active, as I was some thirty years ago. When we reached the boat I was glad of it. We washed, changed our clothes, dined, and felt much refreshed. During our excursion out, Bell saw a Virginian Rail, and our sense of smell brought us to a dead Elk, putrid, and largely consumed by Wolves, whose tracks were very numerous about it. After dinner we went to the heronry that Harris had seen yesterday afternoon; for we had moved only one mile above the place of our wooding before we were again forced on shore. Here we killed four fine individuals, all on the wing, and some capital shots they were, besides a Raven. Unfortunately we had many followers, who destroyed our sport; therefore we returned on board, and at half-past four left our landing-place, having cut and piled up between forty and fifty cords of wood for the return of the "Omega." The wind has lulled down considerably, we have run seven or eight miles, and are again fast to the shore. It is reported that the water has risen two feet, but this is somewhat doubtful. We saw abundance of tracks of Elk, Deer, Wolf, and Bear, and had it been anything like tolerably dry ground, we should have had a good deal of sport. Saw this evening another dead Buffalo floating down the river.

May 16, Tuesday. At three o'clock this fair morning we were under way, but the water has actually risen a great deal, say three feet, since

Sunday noon. The current therefore is very strong, and impedes our progress greatly. We found that the Herons we had killed yesterday had not yet laid the whole of their eggs, as we found one in full order, ripe, and well colored and conditioned. I feel assured that the Ravens destroy a great many of their eggs, as I saw one helping itself to two eggs, at two different times, on the same nest. We have seen a great number of Black-headed Gulls, and some Black Terns, some Indians on the east side of the river, and a Prairie Wolf, dead, hung across a prong of a tree. After a while we reached a spot where we saw ten or more Indians who had a large log cabin, and a field under fence. Then we came to the establishment called that of Vermilion River and met Mr. Cerré, called usually Pascal, the agent of the Company at this post, a handsome French gentleman, of good manners. He dined with us. After this we landed, and walked to the fort, if the place may so be called, for we found it only a square, strongly picketed, without portholes. It stands on the immediate bank of the river, opposite a long and narrow island, and is backed by a vast prairie, all of which was inundated during the spring freshet. He told me that game was abundant, such as Elk, Deer, and Bear; but that Ducks, Geese, and Swans were extremely scarce this season. Hares are plenty—no Rabbits. We left as soon as possible, for our captain is a pushing man most truly. We passed some remarkable bluffs of blue and light limestone, towards the top of which we saw an abundance of Cliff-Swallows, and counted upwards of two hundred nests. But, alas! we have finally met with an accident. A plate of one of our boilers was found to be burned out, and we were obliged to stop on the west side of the river, about ten miles below the mouth of the Vermilion River. Here we were told that we might go ashore and hunt to our hearts' content; and so I have, but shot at nothing. Bell, Michaux, and I, walked to the hills full three miles off, saw an extraordinary quantity of Deer, Wolf, and Elk tracks, as well as some of Wild Cats. Bell started a Deer, and after a while I heard him shoot. Michaux took to the top of the hills, Bell about midway, and I followed near the bottom; all in vain, however. I started a Woodcock, and caught one of her young, and I am now sorry for this evil deed. A dead Buffalo cow and calf passed us a few moments ago. Squires has seen one other, during our absence. We took at Mr. Cerré's establishment two *engagés* and four Sioux Indians. We are obliged to keep bright eyes upon them, for they are singularly light-fingered. The woods are filled with wild-gooseberry bushes, and a kind of small locust not yet in bloom, and quite new to me. The honey bee was not found in this country twenty years ago, and now they are abundant. A keel-boat passed, going down, but on the opposite side of the river. Bell and Michaux have returned. Bell wounded a large Wolf, and also a young Deer, but brought none on board, though he saw several of the latter. Harris killed one of the large new Finches, and a Yellow-headed Troupial. Bell intends going hunting to-morrow at daylight, with Michaux; I will try my luck too, but do not intend going till after breakfast, for I find that walking eight or ten miles through the tangled and thorny underbrush, fatigues me considerably, though twenty years ago I should have thought nothing of it.

May 17, Wednesday. This was a most lovely morning. Bell went off with Michaux at four A.M. I breakfasted at five, and started with Mr. La Barge. When we reached the hunting-grounds, about six miles distant, we saw Bell making signs to us to go to him, and I knew from that that they had some fresh meat. When we reached them, we found a very large Deer that Michaux had killed. Squires shot a Woodcock, which I ate for my dinner, in company with the captain. Michaux had brought the Deer—Indian fashion—about two miles. I was anxious to examine some of the intestines, and we all three started on the tracks of Michaux, leaving Squires to keep the Wolves away from the dead Deer. We went at once towards a small stream meandering at the foot of the hills, and as we followed it, Bell shot at a Turkey-cock about eighty yards; his ball cut a streak of feathers from its back, but the gobbler went off. When we approached the spot where Michaux had opened the Deer, we did so cautiously, in the hope of then shooting a Wolf, but none had come; we therefore made our observations, and took up the tongue, which had been forgotten. Bell joined us, and as we were returning to Squires we saw flocks of the Chestnut-collared Lark or Ground-finch, whose exact measurement I have here given, and almost at the same time saw Harris. He and Bell went off after the Finches; we pursued our course to Squires, and waited for their return. Seeing no men to help carry the Deer, Michaux picked it up, Squires took his gun, etc., and we made for the river again. We had the good luck to meet the barge coming, and we reached our boat easily in a few minutes, with our game. I saw upwards of twelve of Harris' new Finch (?) a Marsh Hawk, Henslow's Bunting, *Emberiza pallida*, Robins, Wood Thrushes, Bluebirds, Ravens, the same abundance of House Wrens, and all the birds already enumerated. We have seen floating eight Buffaloes, one Antelope, and one Deer; how great the destruction of these animals must be during high freshets! The cause of their being drowned in such extraordinary numbers might not astonish one acquainted with the habits of these animals, but to one who is not, it may be well enough for me to describe it. Some few hundred miles above us, the river becomes confined between high bluffs or cliffs, many of which are nearly perpendicular, and therefore extremely difficult to ascend. When the Buffaloes have leaped or tumbled down from either side of the stream, they swim with ease across, but on reaching these walls, as it were, the poor animals try in vain to climb them, and becoming exhausted by falling back some dozens of times, give up the ghost, and float down the turbid stream; their bodies have been known to pass, swollen and putrid, the city of St. Louis. The most extraordinary part of the history of these drowned Buffaloes is, that the different tribes of Indians on the shores, are ever on the lookout for them, and no matter how putrid their flesh may be, provided the hump proves at all fat, they swim to them, drag them on shore, and cut them to pieces; after which they cook and eat this loathsome and abominable flesh, even to the marrow found in the bones. In some instances this has been done when the whole of the hair had fallen off, from the rottenness of the Buffalo. Ah! Mr. Catlin, I am now sorry to see and to read your accounts of the Indians *you* saw—how very different they must have been from any that I have seen! Whilst we were on the top of the high hills which we climbed this morning, and looked towards the valley beneath us, including the river, we were undetermined as to whether we saw as much land dry as land overflowed; the immense flat prairie on the east side of the river looked not unlike a lake of great expanse, and immediately beneath us the last freshet had left upwards of perhaps two or three hundred acres covered by water, with numbers of water fowl on it, but so difficult of access as to render our wishes to kill Ducks quite out of the question. From the tops of the hills we saw only a continual succession of other lakes, of the same form and nature; and although the soil was of a fair, or even good, quality, the grass grew in tufts, separated from each other, and as it grows green in one spot, it dies and turns brown in another. We saw here no "carpeted prairies," no "velvety distant landscape;" and if these things are to be seen, why, the sooner we reach them the better. This afternoon I took the old nest of a Vireo, fully three feet above my head, filled with dried mud; it was attached to two small prongs issuing from a branch fully the size of my arm; this proves how high the water must have risen. Again, we saw large trees of which the bark had been torn off by the rubbing or cutting of the ice, as high as my shoulder. This is accounted for as follows: during the first breaking up of the ice, it at times accumulates, so as to form a complete dam across the river; and when this suddenly gives way by the heat of the atmosphere, and the great pressure of the waters above the dam, the whole rushes on suddenly and overflows the country around, hurling the ice against any trees in its course. Sprague has shot two *Emberiza pallida*, two Lincoln's

Finches, and a Black and Yellow Warbler, *Sylvicola* [*Dendrœca*] *maculosa*. One of our trappers, who had gone to the hills, brought on board two Rattlesnakes of a kind which neither Harris nor myself had seen before. The four Indians we have on board are three Puncas and one Sioux; the Puncas were formerly attached to the Omahas; but, having had some difficulties among themselves, they retired further up the river, and assumed this new name. The Omahas reside altogether on the west side of the Missouri. Three of the Puncas have walked off to the establishment of Mr. Cerré to procure moccasins, but will return to-night. They appear to be very poor, and with much greater appetites than friend Catlin describes them to have. Our men are stupid, and very superstitious; they believe the rattles of snakes are a perfect cure for the headache; also, that they never die till after sunset, etc. We have discovered the female of Harris's Finch, which, as well as in the White-crowned Finch, resembles the male almost entirely; it is only a very little paler in its markings. I am truly proud to name it *Fringilla Harrisii*, in honor of one of the best friends I have in this world.

May 18, Thursday. Our good captain called us all up at a quarter before four this fair morning, to tell us that four barges had arrived from Fort Pierre, and that we might write a few letters, which Mr. Laidlow, one of the partners, would take to St. Louis for us. I was introduced to that gentleman and also to Major Dripps, the Indian agent. I wrote four short letters, which I put in an envelope addressed to the Messieurs Chouteau & Co., of St. Louis, who will post them, and we have hopes that some may reach their destination. The names of these four boats are "War Eagle," "White Cloud," "Crow-feather," and "Red-fish." We went on board one of them, and found it comfortable enough. They had ten thousand Buffalo robes on the four boats; the men live entirely on Buffalo meat and pemmican. They told us that about a hundred miles above us the Buffalo were by thousands, that the prairies were covered with dead calves, and the shores lined with dead of all sorts; that Antelopes were there also, and a great number of Wolves, etc.; therefore we shall see them after a while. Mr. Laidlow told me that he would be back at Fort Pierre in two months, and would see us on our return. He is a true Scot, and apparently a clean one. We gave them six bottles of whiskey, for which they were very thankful; they gave us dried Buffalo meat, and three pairs of moccasins. They breakfasted with us, preferring salt meat to fresh venison. They departed soon after six o'clock, and proceeded rapidly down-stream in Indian file. These boats are strong and broad; the tops, or roofs, are supported by bent branches of trees, and these are covered by water-proof Buffalo hides; each has four oarsmen and a steersman, who manages the boat standing on a broad board; the helm is about ten feet long, and the rudder itself is five or six feet long. They row constantly for sixteen hours, and stop regularly at sundown; they, unfortunately for us, spent the night about two miles above us, for had we known of their immediate proximity we should have had the whole of the night granted for writing long, long letters. Our prospect of starting to-day is somewhat doubtful, as the hammering at the boilers still reaches my ears. The day is bright and calm. Mr. Laidlow told us that on the 5th of May the snow fell two feet on the level, and destroyed thousands of Buffalo calves. We felt the same storm whilst we were fast on the bar above Fort Leavenworth. This has been a day of almost pure idleness; our tramps of yesterday and the day previous had tired me, and with the exception of shooting at marks, and Sprague killing one of Bell's Vireo, and a Least Pewee, as well as another female of Harris's Finch, we have done nothing. Bell this evening went off to look for Bats, but saw none.

May 19, Friday. This has been a beautiful, but a very dull day to us all. We started by moonlight at three this morning, and although we have been running constantly, we took the wrong channel twice, and thereby lost much of our precious time; so I look upon this day's travel as a very poor one. The river was in several places inexpressibly wide and shallow. We saw a Deer of the common kind swimming across the stream; but few birds were killed, although we stopped (unfortunately) three times for wood. I forgot to say yesterday two things which I should have related, one of which is of a dismal and very disagreeable nature, being no less than the account given us of the clerks of the Company having killed one of the chiefs of the Blackfeet tribe of Indians, at the upper settlement of the Company, at the foot of the great falls of the Missouri, and therefore at the base of the Rocky Mountains, and Mr. Laidlow assured us that it would be extremely dangerous for us to go that far towards these Indians. The other thing is that Mr. Laidlow brought down a daughter of his, a half-breed of course, whom he is taking to St. Louis to be educated. We saw another Deer crossing the river, and have shot only a few birds, of no consequence.

May 20, Saturday. We have not made much progress this day, for the wind rose early, and rather ahead. We have passed to-day Jacques River, or, as I should call it, La Rivière à Jacques, named after a man who some twenty or more years ago settled upon its banks, and made some money by collecting Beavers, etc., but who is dead and gone. Three White Wolves were seen this morning, and after a while we saw a fourth, of the brindled kind, which was trotting leisurely on, about 150 yards distant from the bank, where he had probably been feeding on some carrion or other. A shot from a rifle was quite enough to make him turn off up the river again, but farther from us, at a full gallop; after a time he stopped again, when the noise of our steam pipe started him, and we soon lost sight of him in the bushes. We saw three Deer in the flat of one of the prairies, and just before our dinner we saw, rather indistinctly, a number of Buffaloes, making their way across the hills about two miles distant; after which, however, we saw their heavy tracks in a well and deep cut line across the said hills. Therefore we are now in what is pronounced to be the "Buffalo country," and may expect to see more of these animals to-morrow. We have stopped for wood no less than three times this day, and are fast for the night. Sprague killed a *Pipilo arcticus*, and Bell three others of the same species. We procured also another Bat, the *Vespertilio subulatus* of Say, and this is all. The country around us has materially changed, and we now see more naked, and to my eyes more completely denuded, hills about us, and less of the rich bottoms of alluvial land, than we passed below our present situation. I will not anticipate the future by all that we hear of the country above, but will continue steadily to accumulate in this, my poor journal, all that may take place from day to day. Three of our Indian rascals left us at our last wooding-ground, and have gone towards their miserable village. We have now only one Sioux with us, who will, the captain says, go to Fort Pierre in our company. They are, all that we have had as yet, a thieving and dirty set, covered with vermin. We still see a great number of Black-headed Gulls, but I think fewer Geese and Ducks than below; this probably on account of the very swampy prairie we have seen, and which appears to become scarce as we are advancing in this strange wilderness.

May 21, Sunday. We have had a great deal that interested us all this day. In the first place we have passed no less than five of what are called rivers, and their names are as follows: Manuel, Basil, L'Eau qui Court, Ponca Creek; and Chouteau's River, all of which are indifferent streams of no magnitude, except the swift-flowing L'Eau qui Court, which in some places is fully as broad as the Missouri itself, fully as muddy, filled with quicksands, and so remarkably shallow that in the autumn its navigation is very difficult indeed. We have seen this day about fifty Buffaloes; two which we saw had taken to the river, with intent to swim across it, but on the approach of our thundering, noisy vessel, turned about and after struggling for a few minutes, did make out to reach the top of the bank, after which they travelled at a moderate gait for some hundreds of yards; then, perhaps smelling or seeing the steamboat, they went off at a good though not very fast gallop, on the prairie by our side, and were soon somewhat ahead of us; they stopped once or twice, again resumed their gallop, and after a few diversions in their course, made to the hill-tops and disappeared altogether. We stopped to wood at a very propitious place indeed, for it was no less than the fort put up some years ago by Monsieur Le Clerc. Finding no one at the spot, we went to work cutting the pickets off his fortifications till we were loaded with the very best of dry wood. After we left that spot, were found several *Pipilo arcticus* which were shot, as well as a Say's Flycatcher. The wind rose pretty high, and after trying our best to stem the current under very high cliffs, we were landed on Poncas Island, where all of us excepting Squires, who was asleep, went on shore to hunt, and to shoot whatever we might find. It happened that this island was well supplied with game; we saw many Deer, and Bell killed a young Doe, which proved good as fresh meat. Some twelve or fourteen of these animals were seen, and Bell saw three Elks which he followed across the island, also a Wolf in its hole, but did not kill it. Sprague saw a Forked-tailed Hawk, too far off to shoot at. We passed several dead Buffaloes near the shore, on which the Ravens were feeding gloriously. The *Pipilo arcticus* is now extremely abundant, and so is the House Wren, Yellow-breasted Chat, etc. We have seen this day Black-headed Gulls, Sandpipers, and Ducks, and now I am going to rest, for after my long walk through the deep mud to reach the ridge on the islands, I feel somewhat wearied and fatigued. Three Antelopes were seen this evening.

May 22, Monday. We started as early as usual, *i.e.*, at half-past three; the weather was fine. We breakfasted before six, and immediately after saw two Wild Cats of the common kind; we saw them running for some hundreds of yards. We also saw several large Wolves, noticing particularly one pure white, that stood and looked at us for some time. Their movements are precisely those of the common cur dog. We have seen five or six this day. We began seeing Buffaloes again in small gangs, but this afternoon and evening we have seen a goodly number, probably more than a hundred. We also saw fifteen or twenty Antelopes. I saw ten at once, and it was beautiful to see them running from the top of a high hill down to its base, after which they went round the same hill, and were lost to us. We have landed three times to cut wood, and are now busy at it on Cedar Island. At both the previous islands we saw an immense number of Buffalo tracks, more, indeed, than I had anticipated. The whole of the prairies as well as the hills have been so trampled by them that I should have considered it quite unsafe for a man to travel on horseback. The ground was literally covered with their tracks, and also with bunches of hair, while the bushes and the trunks of the trees, between which they had passed, were hanging with the latter substance. I collected some, and intend to carry a good deal home. We found here an abundance of what is called the White Apple, but which is anything else but an apple. The fruit grows under the ground about six inches; it is about the size of a hen's egg, covered with a woody, hard pellicle, a sixteenth of an inch thick, from which the fruit can be drawn without much difficulty; this is quite white; the exterior is a dirty, dark brown. The roots are woody. The flowers were not in bloom, but I perceived that the leaves are ovate, and attached in fives. This plant is collected in great quantities by the Indians at this season and during the whole summer, and put to dry, which renders it as hard as wood; it is then pounded fine, and makes an excellent kind of mush, upon which the Indians feed greedily. I will take some home. We found pieces of crystallized gypsum; we saw Meadow Larks whose songs and single notes are quite different from those of the Eastern States; we have not yet been able to kill one to decide if new or not. We have seen the Arkansas Flycatcher, Sparrow-hawks, Geese, etc. The country grows poorer as we ascend; the bluffs exhibit oxide of iron, sulphur, and also magnesia. We have made a good day's run, though the wind blew rather fresh from the northwest. Harris shot a Marsh Hawk, Sprague a Nighthawk, and some small birds, and I saw Martins breeding in Woodpeckers' holes in high and large cotton-trees. We passed the "Grand Town" very early this morning; I did not see it, however. Could we have remained on shore at several places that we passed, we should have made havoc with the Buffaloes, no doubt; but we shall have enough of that sport ere long. They all look extremely poor and shabby; we see them sporting among themselves, butting and tearing up the earth, and when at a gallop they throw up the dust behind them. We saw their tracks all along both shores; where they have landed and are unable to get up the steep cliffs, they follow along the margin till they reach a ravine, and then make their way to the hills, and again to the valleys; they also have roads to return to the river to drink. They appear at this season more on the west side of the Missouri. The Elks, on the contrary, are found on the islands and low bottoms, well covered with timber; the common Deer is found indifferently everywhere. All the Antelopes we have seen were on the west side. After we had left our first landing-place a few miles, we observed some seven or eight Indians looking at us, and again retiring to the woods, as if to cover themselves; when we came nearly opposite them, however, they all came to the shore, and made signs to induce us to land. The boat did not stop for their pleasure, and after we had fairly passed them they began firing at us, not with blank cartridges, but with well-directed rifle-balls, several of which struck the "Omega" in different places. I was standing at that moment by one of the chimneys, and saw a ball strike the water a few feet beyond our bows; and Michaux, the hunter, heard its passing within a few inches of his head. A Scotchman, who was asleep below, was awakened and greatly frightened by hearing a ball pass through the partition, cutting the lower part of his pantaloons, and deadening itself against a trunk. Fortunately no one was hurt. Those rascals were attached to a war party, and belong to the Santee tribes which range across the country from the Mississippi to the Missouri. I will make no comment upon their conduct, but I have two of the balls that struck our boat; it seems to be a wonder that not one person was injured, standing on deck as we were to the number of a hundred or more. We have not seen Parrakeets or Squirrels for several days; Partridges have also deserted us, as well as Rabbits; we have seen Barn Swallows, but no more Rough-winged. We have yet plenty of Red-headed Woodpeckers. Our captain has just sent out four hunters this evening, who are to hunt early to-morrow morning, and will meet the boat some distance above; Squires has gone with them. How I wish I were twenty-five years younger! I should like such a tramp greatly; but I do not think it prudent now for me to sleep on the ground when I can help it, while it is so damp.

May 23, Tuesday. The wind blew from the south this morning and rather stiffly. We rose early, and walked about this famous Cedar Island, where we stopped to cut large red cedars *[Juniperus virginianus]* for one and a half hours; we started at half-past five, breakfasted rather before six, and were on the lookout for our hunters. *Hunters!* Only two of them had ever been on a Buffalo hunt before. One was lost almost in sight of the river. They only walked two or three miles, and camped. Poor Squires' first experience was a very rough one; for, although they made a good fire at first, it never was tended afterwards, and his pillow was formed of a buck's horn accidentally picked up near the place. Our Sioux Indian helped himself to another, and they all felt chilly and damp. They had forgotten to take any spirits with them, and their condition was miserable. As the orb of day rose as red as blood, the party started, each taking a different direction. But the wind was unfavorable; it blew up, not down the river, and the Buffaloes, Wolves, Antelopes, and indeed every animal possessed of the sense of smell, had scent of them in time to avoid them. There happened however to be attached to this party two good and true men, that may be called hunters. One was Michaux; the other a friend of his, whose name I do not know. It happened, by hook or by crook, that these two managed to kill four Buffaloes; but one of them was drowned, as it took to the river after being shot. Only a few pieces from a young bull, and its tongue, were brought on board, most of the men being too lazy, or too far off, to cut out even the tongues of the others; and thus it is that thousands multiplied by thousands of Buffaloes are murdered in senseless play, and their enormous carcasses are suffered to be the prey of the Wolf, the Raven and the Buzzard. However, the hunters all returned safely to the boat, and we took them in, some tired enough, among whom was friend Squires. He had worn out his moccasins, and his feet were sore, blistered, and swollen; he was thirsty enough too, for in taking a drink he had gone to a beautiful clear spring that unfortunately proved to be one of magnesia, which is common enough in this part of our country, and this much increased his thirst. He drank four tumblers of water first, then a glass of grog, ate somewhat of a breakfast, and went to bed, whence I called him a few minutes before dinner. However, he saw some Buffaloes, and had hopes of shooting one, also about twenty Antelopes. Michaux saw two very large White Wolves. At the place where we decided to take the fatigued party in, we stopped to cut down a few dead cedars, and Harris shot a common Rabbit and one Lark Finch. Bell and Sprague saw several Meadow-larks, which I trust will prove new, as these birds have quite different notes and songs from those of our eastern birds. They brought a curious cactus, some handsome well-scented dwarf peas, and several other plants unknown to me. On the island I found abundance of dwarf wild-cherry bushes in full blossom, and we have placed all these plants in press. We had the misfortune to get aground whilst at dinner, and are now fast till to-morrow morning; for all our efforts to get the boat off, and they have been many, have proved ineffectual. It is a bad spot, for we are nearly halfway from either shore. I continued my long letter for home, and wrote the greatest portion of another long one to John Bachman. I intend to write till a late hour this night, as perchance we may reach Fort Pierre early next week.

May 24, Wednesday. We remained on the said bar till four this afternoon. The wind blew hard all day. A boat from Fort Pierre containing two men passed us, bound for Fort Vermilion; one of them was Mr. Charity, one of the Company's associate traders. The boat was somewhat of a curiosity, being built in the form of a scow; but instead of being made of wood, had only a frame, covered with Buffalo skins with the hair on. They had been nine days coming 150 miles, detained every day, more or less, by Indians. Mr. Charity gave me some leather prepared for moccasins—for a consideration, of course. We have seen Buffaloes, etc., but the most important animal to us was one of Townsend's Hare. We shot four Meadow-larks *[Sturnella neglecta]* that have, as I said, other songs and notes than ours, but could not establish them as new. We procured a Red-shafted Woodpecker, two Sparrow-hawks, two Arkansas Flycatchers, a Blue Grosbeak, saw Say's Flycatcher, etc. I went on shore with Harris's small double-barrelled gun, and the first shot I had was pretty near killing me; the cone blew off, and passed so near my ear that I was stunned, and fell down as if shot, and afterwards I was obliged to lie down for several minutes. I returned on board, glad indeed that the accident was no greater. We passed this afternoon bluffs of sulphur, almost pure to look at, and a patch that has burnt for two years in succession. Alum was found strewn on the shores. A toad was brought, supposed to be new by Harris and Bell. We landed for the night on an island so thick with underbrush that it was no easy matter to walk through; perhaps a hundred Buffalo calves were dead in it, and the smell was not pleasant, as you may imagine. The boat of Mr. Charity went off when we reached the shore, after having escaped from the bar. We have seen more White Wolves this day, and few Antelopes. The whole country is trodden down by the heavy Buffaloes, and this renders the walking both fatiguing and somewhat dangerous. The garlic of this country has a red blossom, otherwise it looks much like ours; when Buffalo have fed for some time on this rank weed, their flesh cannot be eaten.

May 25, Thursday. The weather looked cloudy, and promised much rain when we rose this morning at five o'clock; our men kept busy cutting and bringing wood until six, when the "Omega" got under way. It began raining very soon afterwards and it has continued to this present moment. The dampness brought on a chilliness that made us have fires in each of the great cabins. Michaux brought me two specimens of *Neotoma floridana*, so young that their eyes were not open. The nest was found in the hollow of a tree cut down for firewood. Two or three miles above us, we saw three Mackinaw barges on the shore, just such as I have described before; all these belonged to the (so-called) Opposition Company of C. Bolton, Fox, Livingstone & Co., of New York, and therefore we passed them without stopping; but we had to follow their example a few hundred yards above them, for we had to stop also; and then some of the men came on board, to see and talk to their old acquaintances among our extraordinary and motley crew of trappers and *engagés*. On the roofs of the barges lay much Buffalo meat, and on the island we left this morning probably some hundreds of these poor animals, mostly young calves, were found dead at every few steps; and since then we have passed many dead as well as many groups of living. In one place we saw a large gang swimming across the river; they fortunately reached a bank through which they cut their way towards the hills, and marched slowly and steadily on, paying no attention to our boat, as this was far to the lee of them. At another place on the west bank, we saw eight or ten, or perhaps more, Antelopes or Deer of some kind or other, but could not decide whether they were the one or the other. These animals were all lying down, which would be contrary to the general habit of our common Deer, which never lie down during rain, that I am aware of. We have had an extremely dull day of it, as one could hardly venture out of the cabin for pleasure. We met with several difficulties among sand-bars. At three o'clock we passed the entrance into the stream known as White River; half an hour ago we were obliged to land, and send the yawl to try for the channel, but we are now again on our way, and have still the hope of reaching Great Cedar Island this evening, where we must stop to cut wood.—*Later*. Our attempt to reach the island I fear will prove abortive, as we are once more at a standstill for want of deeper water, and the yawl has again gone ahead to feel for a channel. Within the last mile or so, we must have passed upwards of a hundred drowned young Buffalo calves, and many large ones. I will await the moment when we must make fast somewhere, as it is now past eight o'clock. The rain has ceased, and the weather has the appearance of a better day to-morrow, overhead at least. Now it is after nine o'clock; we are fastened to the shore, and I will, for the first time since I left St. Louis, sleep in my cabin, and between sheets.

May 26, Friday. The weather was fine, but we moved extremely slowly, not having made more than ten miles by twelve o'clock. The captain arranged all his papers for Fort Pierre. Three of the best walkers, well acquainted with the road, were picked from among our singularly mixed crew of *engagés*, and were put ashore at Big Bend Creek, on the banks of a high cliff on the western side; they ascended through a ravine, and soon were out of sight. We had stopped previously to cut wood, where our men had to lug it fully a quarter of a mile. We ourselves landed of course, but found the prairie so completely trodden by Buffaloes that it was next to impossible to walk. Notwithstanding this, however, a few birds were procured. The boat continued on with much difficulty, being often stopped for the want of water. At one place we counted over a hundred dead Buffalo calves; we saw a great number, however, that did reach the top of the bank, and proceeded to feeding at once. We saw one animal, quite alone, wading and swimming alternately, till it had nearly crossed the river, when for reasons unknown to us, and when only about fifty yards from the land, it suddenly turned about, and swam and waded back to the western side, whence it had originally come; this fellow moved through the water as represented in this very imperfect sketch, which I have placed here, and with his tail forming nearly half a circle by its erection during the time he swam. It was mired on several occasions while passing from one shoal or sandbar to another. It walked, trotted, or galloped, while on the solid beach, and ultimately, by swimming a few hundred yards, returned to the side from whence it had started, though fully half a mile below the exact spot. There now was heard on board some talk about the *Great Bend*, and the captain asked me whether I would like to go off and camp, and await his arrival on the other side to-morrow. I assured him that nothing would give us more pleasure, and he gave us three stout young men to go with us to carry our blankets, provisions, etc., and to act as guides and hunters. All was ready by about five of the afternoon, when Harris, Bell, Sprague, and I, as well as the three men, were put ashore; and off we went at a brisk walk across a beautiful, level prairie, whereon in sundry directions we could see small groups of Buffaloes, grazing at leisure. Proceeding along, we saw a great number of Cactus, some Bartram Sandpipers, and a Long-billed Curlew. Presently we observed a village of prairie Marmots, *Arctomys [Cynomys] ludovicianus*, and two or three of our party diverged at once to pay them their respects. The mounds which I passed were very low indeed; the holes were opened, but I saw not one of the owners. Harris, Bell, and Michaux, I believe, shot at some of them, but killed none, and we proceeded on, being somewhat anxious to pitch our camp for the night before dark. Presently we reached the hills and were surprised at their composition; the surface looked as if closely covered with small broken particles of coal, whilst the soil was of such greasy or soapy nature, that it was both painful and fatiguing to ascend them. Our guides assured us that such places were never in any other condition, or as they expressed it, were "never dry." Whilst travelling about these remarkable hills, Sprague saw one of Townsend's Hare, and we started the first and only Prairie Hen we have seen since our departure from St. Louis. Gradually we rose on to the very uppermost crest of the hills we had to cross, and whilst reposing ourselves for some minutes we had the gratification of seeing around us one of the great panoramas this remarkable portion of our country affords. There was a vast extent of country beneath and around us. Westward rose the famous Medicine Hill, and in the opposite direction were the wanderings of the Missouri for many miles, and from the distance we were then from it, the river appeared as if a small, very circuitous streamlet. The Great Bend was all in full view, and its course almost resembled that of a chemist's retort, being formed somewhat like the scratch of my pen thus:—

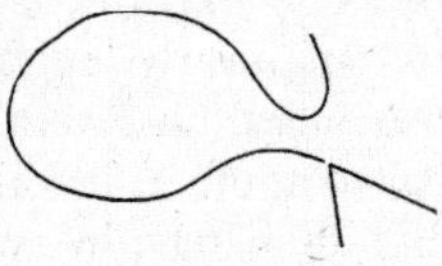

The walk from our landing crossing the prairies was quite four miles, whilst the distance by water is computed to be twenty-six. From the pinnacle we stood on, we could see the movements of our boat quite well, and whilst the men were employed cutting wood for her engines, we could almost count every stroke of their axes, though fully two miles distant, as the crow flies. As we advanced we soon found ourselves on the ridges leading us across the Bend, and plainly saw that we were descending towards the Missouri once more. *Chemin faisant*, we saw four Black-tailed Deer, a shot at which Michaux or Bell, who were in advance, might perhaps have had, had not Harris and Sprague taken a route across the declivity before them, and being observed by these keen-sighted animals, the whole made off at once. I had no fair opportunity of witnessing their movements; but they looked swiftness itself, combined with grace. They were not followed, and we reached the river at a spot which evidently had been previously camped on by Indians; here we made our minds up to stop at once, and arrange for the night, which now promised to be none of the fairest. One man remained with us to prepare the camp, whilst Michaux and the others started in search of game, as if blood-hounds. Meantime we lighted a large and glowing fire, and began preparing some supper. In less than half an hour Michaux was seen to return with a load on his back, which proved to be a fine young buck of the Black-tailed Deer. This produced animation at once. I examined it carefully, and Harris and Sprague returned promptly from the point to which they had gone. The darkness of the night, contrasting with the vivid glare of our fire, which threw a bright light on the skinning of the Deer, and was reflected on the trunks and branches of the cottonwood trees, six of them in one clump, almost arising from the same root, gave such superb effect that I retired some few steps to enjoy the truly fine picture. Some were arranging their rough couches, whilst others were engaged in carrying wood to support our fire through the night; some brought water from the great, muddy stream, and others were busily at work sharpening long sticks for skewers, from which large pieces of venison were soon seen dropping their rich juices upon the brightest of embers. The very sight of this sharpened our appetites, and it must have been laughable to see how all of us fell to, and ate of this first-killed Black-tailed Deer. After a hearty meal we went to sleep, one and all, under the protection of God, and not much afraid of Indians, of whom we have not seen a specimen since we had the pleasure of being fired on by the Santees. We slept very well for a while, till it began to sprinkle rain; but it was only a very slight shower, and I did not even attempt to shelter myself from it. Our fires were mended several times by one or another of the party, and the short night passed on, refreshing us all as only men can be refreshed by sleep under the sky, breathing the purest of air, and happy as only a clear conscience can make one.

May 27, Saturday. At half-past three this morning my ears were saluted by the delightful song of the Red Thrush, who kept on with his strains until we were all up. Harris and Bell went off, and as soon as the two hunters had cleaned their rifles they followed. I remained in camp with Sprague for a while; the best portions of the Deer, *i. e.*, the liver, kidneys, and tongue, were cooked for breakfast, which all enjoyed. No Wolves had disturbed our slumbers, and we now started in search of quadrupeds, birds, and adventures. We found several plants, all new to me, and which are now in press. All the ravines which we inspected were well covered by cedars of the red variety, and whilst ascending several of the hills we found them in many parts partially gliding down as if by the sudden effects of very heavy rain. We saw two very beautiful Avocets *[Recurvirostra americana]* feeding opposite our camp; we saw also a Hawk nearly resembling what is called Cooper's Hawk, but having a white rump. Bell joined the hunters and saw some thousands of Buffalo; and finding a very large bull within some thirty yards of them, they put in his body three large balls. The poor beast went off, however, and is now, in all probability, dead. Many fossil remains have been found on the hills about us, but we saw none. These hills are composed of limestone rocks, covered with much shale. Harris thinks this is a different formation from that of either St. Louis or Belle Vue—but, alas! we are not much of geologists. We shot only one of Say's Flycatcher, and the Finch we have called *Emberiza pallida*, but of which I am by no means certain, for want of more exact descriptions than those of a mere synopsis. Our boat made its appearance at two o'clock; we had observed from the hill-tops that it had been aground twice. At three our camp was broken up, our effects removed, our fire left burning, and our boat having landed for us, and for cutting cedar trees, we got on board, highly pleased with our camping out, especially as we found all well on board. We had not proceeded very far when the difficulties of navigation increased so much that we grounded several times, and presently saw a few Indians on the shore; our yawl was out sounding for a passage amid the many sand-bars in view; the Indians fired, not balls, but a salute, to call us ashore. We neared shore, and talked to them; for, they proving to be Sioux, and our captain being a good scholar in that tongue, there was no difficulty in so doing. He told them to follow us, and that he would come-to. They ran to their horses on the prairie, all of which stood still, and were good-looking, comparatively speaking, leaped on their backs without saddles or stirrups, and followed us with ease at a walk. They fired a second salute as we landed; there were only four of them, and they are all at this moment on board. They are fine-looking fellows; the captain introduced Harris and me to the chief, and we shook hands all round. They are a poor set of beggars after all. The captain gave them supper, sugar and coffee, and about one pound of gunpowder, and the chief coolly said: "What is the use of powder, without balls?" It is quite surprising that these Indians did not see us last night, for I have no doubt our fire could have been seen up and down the river for nearly twenty miles. But we are told their lodges are ten miles inland, and that may answer the question. I shall not be sorry now to go to bed. Our camp of the *Six Trees* is deserted and silent. The captain is almost afraid he may be forced to leave half his cargo somewhere near this, and proceed to Fort Pierre, now distant fifty miles, and return for the goods. The Indians saw nothing of the three men who were sent yesterday to announce our approach to Fort Pierre.

Sunday, May 28. This morning was beautiful, though cool. Our visiting Indians left us at twelve last night, and I was glad enough to be rid of these beggars by trade. Both shores were dotted by groups of Buffaloes as far as the eye could reach, and although many were near the banks they kept on feeding quietly till we nearly approached them; those at the distance of half a mile never ceased their avocations. A Gray Wolf was seen swimming across our bows, and some dozens of shots were sent at the beast, which made it open its mouth and raise its head, but it never stopped swimming away from us, as fast as possible; after a while it reached a sand-bar, and immediately afterwards first trotted, and then galloped off. Three Buffaloes also crossed ahead of us, but at some distance; they all reached the shore, and scrambled up the bank. We have run better this morning than for three or four days, and if fortunate enough may reach Fort Pierre sometime to-morrow. The prairies appear better now, the grass looks green, and probably the poor Buffaloes will soon regain their flesh. We have seen more than 2,000 this morning up to this moment—twelve o'clock.

We reached Fort George at about three this afternoon. This is what is called the "Station of the Opposition line;" some Indians and a few lodges are on the edge of the prairie. Sundry bales of Buffalo robes were brought on board, and Major Hamilton, who is now acting Indian agent here until the return of Major Crisp, came on board also. I knew his father thirty-five years ago. He pointed out to us the cabin on the opposite shore, where a partner of the "Opposition line" shot at and killed two white men and wounded two others, all of whom were remarkable miscreants. We are about thirty miles below Fort Pierre. Indians were seen on both sides the river, ready to trade both here and at Fort Pierre, where I am told there are five hundred lodges standing. The Indian dogs which I saw here so very closely resemble wild Wolves, that I feel assured that if I was to meet with one of them in the woods, I should most assuredly kill it as such. A few minutes after leaving Fort George, we stopped to sound the channel, and could not discover more than three and a half feet of water; our captain told us we would proceed no farther this day, but would camp here. Bell, Harris, and Sprague went off with guns; Squires and I walked to Fort George, and soon met a young Englishman going towards our boat on a "Buffalo Horse" at a swift gallop; but on being hailed he reined up. His name was Illingsworth; he is the present manager of this establishment. He welcomed us, and as he was going to see Captain Sire, we proceeded on. Upon reaching the camp we found a strongly built log cabin, in one end of which we met Mr. Cutting, who told me he had known Victor [Audubon] in Cuba. This young gentleman had been thrown from his horse in a recent Buffalo chase, and had injured one foot so that he could not walk. A Buffalo cow had hooked the horse and thrown the rider about twenty feet, although the animal had not been wounded. We also met here a Mr. Taylor, who showed me the petrified head of a Beaver, which he supposed to be that of a Wolf; but I showed him the difference in the form at once. I saw two young Wolves about six weeks old, of the common kind, alive. They looked well, but their nature was already pretty apparently that of the parents. I saw an abundance of semi-wolf Dogs, and their howlings were distressing to my ear. We entered the lodge of a trader attached to our company, a German, who is a clever man; has considerable knowledge of botany, and draws well. There were about fifteen lodges, and we saw a greater number of squaws and half-breed children than I had expected. But as every clerk and agent belonging to the companies has "a wife," as it is *called*, a spurious population soon exhibits itself around the wigwams. I will not comment upon this here. We returned before dark to our boat, and I am off to bed.

MONDAY, MAY 29. I was up early, and as soon as breakfast was over, Major Hamilton and myself walked to Fort George. We found the three gentlemen to whom I showed the plate of quadrupeds, and afterwards I went to their store to see skins of Wolves and of the Swift Fox. I found a tolerably good Fox skin which was at once given me; I saw what I was assured were two distinct varieties (for I cannot call them species) of Wolves. Both, however, considering the difference in size, were old and young of the same variety. They both had the top of the back dark gray, and the sides, belly, legs, and tail, nearly white. When I have these two sorts in the flesh, I may derive further knowledge. I looked at the Indian Dogs again with much attention, and was assured that there is much cross breeding between these Dogs and Wolves, and that all the varieties actually come from the same root.

Harris now joined us, and found he had met a brother of Mr. Cutting in Europe. The gentlemen from the fort came back to the boat with us; we gave them a luncheon, and later a good substantial dinner, the like of which, so they told us, they had not eaten for many a day. Mr. Illingsworth told us much about Buffaloes; he says the hunting is usually more or less dangerous. The Porcupine is found hereabouts and feeds on the leaves and bark as elsewhere, but not unfrequently retires into the crevices of rocks, whenever no trees of large size are to be found in its vicinity. Elks, at times, assemble in groups of from fifty to two hundred, and their movements are as regular as those of a flock of White Pelicans, so that if the oldest Elk starts in any one direction, all the rest follow at once in his tracks. Where he stops, they all stop, and at times all will suddenly pause, range themselves as if a company of dragoons, ready to charge upon the enemy; which, however, they seldom if ever attempt. After dinner Mr. Illingsworth told me he would go and shoot a Buffalo calf for me—we will see. Bell, Harris, Squires, and myself went off to shoot some Prairie-dogs, as the *Arctomys ludovicianus* is called. After walking over the hills for about one mile, we came to the "village," and soon after heard their cries but not their barkings. The sound they make is simply a "chip, chip, chip," long and shrill enough, and at every cry the animal jerks its tail, without however erecting it upright, as I have seen them represented. Their holes are not perpendicular, but oblique, at an angle of about forty degrees, after which they seem to deviate; but whether sideways or upwards, I cannot yet say. I shot at two of them, which appeared to me to be standing, not across their holes, but in front of them. The first one I never saw after the shot; the second I found dying at the entrance of the burrow, but at my appearance it worked backwards. I drew my ramrod and put the end in its mouth; this it bit hard but kept working backwards, and notwithstanding my efforts, was soon out of sight and touch. Bell saw two enter the same hole, and Harris three. Bell saw some standing quite erect and leaping in the air to see and watch our movements. I found, by lying down within twenty or thirty steps of the hole, that they reappeared in fifteen or twenty minutes. This was the case with me when I shot at the two I have mentioned. Harris saw one that, after coming out of its hole, gave a long and somewhat whistling note, which he thinks was one of invitation to its neighbors, as several came out in a few moments. I have great doubts whether their cries are issued at the appearance of danger or not. I am of opinion that they are a mode of recognition as well as of amusement. I also think they feed more at night than in the day. On my return to the boat, I rounded a small hill and started a Prairie Wolf within a few steps of me. I was unfortunately loaded with No. 3 shot. I pulled one trigger and then the other, but the rascal went off as if unhurt for nearly a hundred yards, when he stopped, shook himself rather violently, and I saw I had hit him; but he ran off again at a very swift rate, his tail down, stopped again, and again shook himself as before, after which he ran out of my sight between the hills. Buffalo cows at this season associate together, with their calves, but if pursued, leave the latter to save themselves. The hides at present are not worth saving, and the Indians as well as the white hunters, when they shoot a Buffalo, tear off the hide, cut out the better portions of the flesh, as well as the tongue, and leave the carcass to the Wolves and Ravens. By the way, Bell saw a Magpie this day, and Harris killed two Black-headed Grosbeaks. Bell also saw several Evening Grosbeaks to-day; therefore there's not much need of crossing the Rocky Mountains for the few precious birds that the talented and truthspeaking Mr. ——— brought or sent to the well-paying Academy of Natural Sciences of Philadelphia! The two men sent to Fort Pierre a few days ago have returned, one this evening, in a canoe, the other this afternoon, by land.

May 30, Tuesday. We had a fine morning, and indeed a very fair day. I was called up long before five to receive a Buffalo calf, and the head of another, which Mr. Illingsworth had the goodness to send me. Sprague has been busy ever since breakfast drawing one of the heads, the size of nature. The other entire calf has been skinned, and will be in strong pickle before I go to bed. Mr. Illingsworth killed two calves, one bull, and one cow. The calves, though not more than about two months old, as soon as the mother was wounded, rushed towards the horse or the man who had struck her. The one bull skinned was so nearly putrid, though so freshly killed, that its carcass was thrown overboard. This gentleman, as well as many others, assured us that the hunting of Buffaloes, for persons unaccustomed to it, was very risky indeed; and said no one should attempt it unless well initiated, even though he may be a first-rate rider. When calves are caught alive, by placing your hands over the eyes and blowing into the nostrils, in the course of a few minutes they will follow the man who performs this simple operation. Indeed if a cow perchance leaves her calf behind during a time of danger, or in the chase, the calf will often await the approach of man and follow him as soon as the operation mentioned is over. Mr. Illingsworth paid us a short visit, and told us that Mr. Cutting was writing to his post near Fort Union to expect us, and to afford us all possible assistance. We made a start at seven, and after laboring over the infernal sand-bars until nearly four this afternoon, we passed them, actually cutting our own channel with the assistance of the wheel. Whilst we were at this, we were suddenly boarded by the yawl of the "Trapper," containing Mr. Picotte, Mr. Chardon, and several others. They had left Fort Pierre this morning, and had come down in one hour and a half. We were all duly presented to the whole group, and I gave to each of these gentlemen the letters I had for them. I found them very kind and affable. They dined after us, being somewhat late, but ate heartily and drank the same. They brought a first-rate hunter with them, of whom I expect to have much to say hereafter. Mr. Picotte promised me the largest pair of Elk horns ever seen in this country, as well as several other curiosities, all of which I will write about when I have them. We have reached Antelope River, a very small creek on the west side. We saw two Wolves crossing the river, and Harris shot a Lark Finch. We have now no difficulties before us, and hope to reach Fort Pierre very early to-morrow morning.

Fort Pierre, May 31, Wednesday. After many difficulties we reached this place at four o'clock this afternoon, having spent the whole previous part of the day, say since half-past three this morning, in coming against the innumerable bars—only *nine miles!* I forgot to say last evening, that where we landed for the night our captain caught a fine specimen of *Neotoma floridana*, a female. We were forced to come-to about a quarter of a mile above Fort Pierre, after having passed the steamer "Trapper" of our Company. Bell, Squires, and myself walked to the Fort as soon as possible, and found Mr. Picotte and Mr. Chardon there. More kindness from strangers I have seldom received. I was presented with the largest pair of Elk horns I ever saw, and also a skin of the animal itself, most beautifully prepared, which I hope to give to my beloved wife. I was also presented with two pairs of moccasins, an Indian riding-whip, one collar of Grizzly Bear's claws, and two long strings of dried white apples, as well as two Indian dresses. I bought the skin of a fine young Grizzly Bear, two Wolf skins, and a parcel of fossil remains. I saw twelve young Buffalo calves, caught a few weeks ago, and yet as wild, apparently, as ever. Sprague will take outlines of them to-morrow morning, and I shall draw them. We have put ashore about one-half of our cargo and left fifty of our *engagés*, so that we shall be able to go much faster, in less water than we have hitherto drawn. We are all engaged in finishing our correspondence, the whole of the letters being about to be forwarded to St. Louis by the steamer "Trapper." I have a letter of seven pages to W. G. Bakewell, James Hall, J. W. H. Page, and Thomas M. Brewer, of Boston, besides those to my family. We are about one and a half miles above the Teton River, or, as it is now called, the Little Missouri, a swift and tortuous stream that finds its source about 250 miles from its union with this great river, in what are called the Bad Lands of Teton River, where it seems, from what we hear, that the country has been at one period greatly convulsed, and is filled with fossil remains. I saw the young Elk belonging to our captain, looking exceedingly shabby, but with the most beautiful eyes I ever beheld in any animal of the Deer kind. We have shot nothing to-day. I have heard all the notes of the Meadow Lark found here and they are utterly different from those of our common species. And now that I am pretty well fatigued with writing letters and this journal, I will go to rest, though I have matter enough in my poor head to write a book. We expect to proceed onwards some time to-morrow.

JUNE 1, THURSDAY. I was up at half-past three, and by four Sprague and I walked to the Fort, for the purpose of taking sketches of young Buffalo calves. These young beasts grunt precisely like a hog, and I would defy any person not seeing the animals to tell one sound from the other. The calves were not out of the stable, and while waiting I measured the Elk horns given me by Mr. Picotte. They are as follows: length, 4 feet $6\frac{1}{2}$ inches; breadth 27 to $27\frac{1}{2}$ inches; circumference at the skull 16 inches, round the knob 12 inches; between the knobs 3 inches. This animal, one of the largest ever seen in this country, was killed in November last. From seventeen to twenty-one poles are necessary to put up a lodge, and the poles when the lodge is up are six or seven feet above the top. The holes at the bottom, all round, suffice to indicate the number of these wanted to tighten the lodge. In time Sprague made several outline sketches of calves, and I drew what I wished. We had breakfast very early, and I ate some good bread and fresh butter. Mr. Picotte presented me with two pipe-stems this morning, quite short, but handsome. At eleven we were on our way, and having crossed the river, came alongside of the "Trapper," of which Mr. John Durack takes the command to St. Louis. The name of our own captain is Joseph A. Sire. Mr. Picotte gave me a letter for Fort Union, as Mr. Culbertson will not be there when we arrive. One of Captain Sire's daughters and her husband are going up with us. She soled three pairs of moccasins for me, as skilfully as an Indian. Bell and Harris shot several rare birds. Mr. Bowie promised to save for me all the curiosities he could procure; he came on board and saw the plates of quadrupeds, and I gave him an almanac, which he much desired.

After we had all returned on board, I was somewhat surprised that Sprague asked me to let him return with the "Omega" to St. Louis. Of course I told him that he was at liberty to do so, though it will keep me grinding about double as much as I expected. Had he said the same at New York, I could have had any number of young and good artists, who would have leaped for joy at the very idea of accompanying such an expedition. Never mind, however.

We have run well this afternoon, for we left Fort Pierre at two o'clock, and we are now more than twenty-five miles above it. We had a rascally Indian on board, who hid himself for the purpose of murdering Mr. Chardon; the latter gave him a thrashing last year for thieving, and Indians never forget such things—he had sworn vengeance, and that was enough. Mr. Chardon discovered him below, armed with a knife; he talked to him pretty freely, and then came up to ask the captain to put the fellow ashore. This request was granted, and he and his bundle were dropped overboard, where the water was waist deep; the fellow scrambled out, and we heard, afterward, made out to return to Fort Pierre. I had a long talk with Sprague, who thought I was displeased with him —a thing that never came into my head—and in all probability he will remain with us. Harris shot a pair of Arkansas Flycatchers, and Squires procured several plants, new to us all. Harris wrote a few lines to Mr. Sarpy at St. Louis, and I have had the pleasure to send the Elk horns, and the great balls from the stomachs of Buffalo given me by our good captain. I am extremely fatigued, for we have been up since before daylight. *At 12 o'clock of the night.* I have got up to scribble this, which it is not strange that after all I saw this day, at this curious place, I should have forgotten. Mr. Picotte took me to the storehouse where the skins procured are kept, and showed me eight or ten packages of White Hare skins, which I feel assured are all of Townsend's Hare of friend Bachman, as no other species are to be met with in this neighborhood during the winter months, when these animals migrate southward, both in search of food and of a milder climate.

June 2, Friday. We made an extremely early start about three A.M. The morning was beautiful and calm. We passed Cheyenne River at half-past seven, and took wood a few miles above it. Saw two White Pelicans, shot a few birds. My hunter, Alexis Bombarde, whom I have engaged, could not go shooting last night on account of the crossing of this river, the Cheyenne, which is quite a large stream. Mr. Chardon gave me full control of Alexis, till we reach the Yellowstone. He is a first-rate hunter, and powerfully built; he wears his hair long about his head and shoulders, as I was wont to do; but being a half-breed, his does not curl as mine did. Whilst we are engaged cutting wood again, many of the men have gone after a Buffalo, shot from the boat. We have seen more Wolves this day than ever previously. We saw where carcasses of Buffaloes had been quite devoured by these animals, and the diversity of their colors and of their size is more wonderful than all that can be said of them. Alexis Bombarde, whom hereafter I shall simply call *Alexis*, says that with a small-bored rifle common size, good shot will kill any Wolf at sixty or eighty yards' distance, as well as bullets. We passed one Wolf that, crossing our bows, went under the wheel and yet escaped, though several shots were fired at it. I had a specimen of *Arvicola pennsylvanicus* brought to me, and I was glad to find this species so very far from New York. These animals in confinement eat each other up, the strongest one remaining, often maimed and covered with blood. This I have seen, and I was glad to have it corroborated by Bell. We are told the Buffalo cows are generally best to eat in the month of July; the young bulls are, however, tough at this season. Our men have just returned with the whole of the Buffalo except its head; it is a young bull, and may prove good. When they reached it, it was standing, and Alexis shot at it twice, to despatch it as soon as possible. It was skinned and cut up in a very few minutes, and the whole of the flesh was brought on board. I am now astonished at the poverty of the bluffs which we pass; no more of the beautiful limestone formations that we saw below. Instead of those, we now run along banks of poor and crumbling clay, dry and hard now, but after a rain soft and soapy. Most of the cedars in the ravines, formerly fine and thrifty, are now, generally speaking, dead and dried up. Whether this may be the effect of the transitions of the weather or not, I cannot pretend to assert. We have seen more Wolves to-day than on any previous occasions. We have made a good day's work of it also, for I dare say that when we stop for the night, we shall have travelled sixty miles. The water is rising somewhat, but not to hurt our progress. We have seen young Gadwall Ducks, and a pair of Geese that had young ones swimming out of our sight.

June 3, Saturday. Alexis went off last night at eleven o'clock, walked about fifteen miles, and returned at ten this morning; he brought three Prairie Dogs, or, as I call them, Prairie Marmots. The wind blew violently till we had run several miles; at one period we were near stopping. We have had many difficulties with the sand-bars, having six or seven times taken the wrong channel, and then having to drop back and try our luck again. The three Marmots had been killed with shot quite too large, and not one of them was fit for drawing, or even skinning. Sprague and I have taken measurements of all their parts, which I give at once. [*Here follow forty-two measurements, all external, of the male and female.*] I received no further intelligence about the habits of this species, except that they are quite numerous in every direction. We passed four rivers to-day; the Little Chayenne, the Moroe, the Grand, and the Rampart. The Moroe is a handsome stream and, I am told, has been formerly a good one for Beaver. It is navigable for barges for a considerable distance. Just before dinner we stopped to cut drift-wood on a sand-bar, and a Wolf was seen upon it. Bell, Harris, and some one else went after it. The wily rascal cut across the bar and, hiding itself under the bank, ran round the point, and again stopped. But Bell had returned towards the very spot, and the fellow was seen swimming off, when Bell pulled the trigger and shot it dead, in or near the head. The captain sent the yawl after it, and it was brought on board. It was tied round the neck and dipped in the river to wash it. It smelled very strong, but I was heartily glad to have it in my power to examine it closely, and to be enabled to take very many measurements of this the first Wolf we have actually procured. It was a male, but rather poor; its general color a grayish yellow; its measurements are as follows [*omitted*]. We saw one Goose with a gosling, several Coots, Grebes, Blue Herons, Doves, Magpies, Red-shafted Woodpeckers, etc. On a sand-bar Bell counted ten

Wolves feeding on some carcass. We also saw three young whelps. This morning we saw a large number of Black-headed Gulls feeding on a dead Buffalo with some Ravens; the Gulls probably were feeding on the worms, or other insects about the carcass. We saw four Elks, and a large gang of Buffaloes. One Wolf was seen crossing the river towards our boat; being fired at, it wheeled round, but turned towards us again, again wheeled round, and returned to where it had started. We ran this evening till our wood was exhausted, and I do not know how we will manage to-morrow. Good-night. God bless you all.

June 4, Sunday. We have run pretty well, though the wind has been tolerably high; the country we have passed this day is somewhat better than what we saw yesterday, which, as I said, was the poorest we have seen. No occurrence of interest has taken place. We passed this morning the old Riccaree Village, where General Ashley was so completely beaten as to lose eighteen of his men, with the very weapons and ammunition that he had trafficked with the Indians of that village, against all the remonstrances of his friends and interpreters; yet he said that it proved fortunate for him, as he turned his steps towards some other spot, where he procured one hundred packs of Beaver skins for a mere song. We stopped to cut wood at an old house put up for winter quarters, and the wood being ash, and quite dry, was excellent. We are now fast for the night at an abandoned post, or fort, of the Company, where, luckily for us, a good deal of wood was found cut. We saw only one Wolf, and a few small gangs of Buffaloes. Bell shot a Bunting which resembles Henslow's, but we have no means of comparing it at present. We have collected a few plants during our landing. The steam is blowing off, and therefore our day's run is ended. When I went to bed last night it was raining smartly, and Alexis did not go off, as he did wish. By the way, I forgot to say that along with the three Prairie Marmots, he brought also four Spoon-billed Ducks, which we ate at dinner to-day, and found delicious. Bell saw many Lazuli Finches this morning. Notwithstanding the tremendous shaking of our boat, Sprague managed to draw four figures of the legs and feet of the Wolf shot by Bell yesterday, and my own pencil was not idle.

June 5, Monday. Alexis went off in the night sometime, and came on board about three o'clock this morning; he had seen nothing whatever, except the traces of Beavers and of Otters, on Beaver Creek, which, by the way, he had to cross on a raft. Speaking of rafts, I am told that one of these, made of two bundles of rushes, about the size of a man's body, and fastened together by a few sticks, is quite sufficient to take two men and two packs of Buffalo robes across this muddy river. In the course of the morning we passed Cannon Ball River, and the very remarkable bluffs about it, of which we cannot well speak until we have stopped there and examined their nature. We saw two Swans alighting on the prairie at a considerable distance. We stopped to take wood at Bowie's settlement, at which place his wife was killed by some of the Riccaree Indians, after some Gros Ventres had assured him that such would be the case if he suffered his wife to go out of the house. She went out, however, on the second day, and was shot with three rifle-balls. The Indians took parts of her hair and went off. She was duly buried; but the Gros Ventres returned some time afterwards, took up the body, and carried off the balance of her hair. They, however, reburied her; and it was not until several months had elapsed that the story came to the ears of Mr. Bowie. We have also passed Apple Creek, but the chief part is yet to be added. At one place where the bluffs were high, we saw five Buffaloes landing a few hundred yards above us on the western side; one of them cantered off immediately, and by some means did reach the top of the hills, and went out of our sight; the four others ran, waded, and swam at different places, always above us, trying to make their escape. At one spot they attempted to climb the bluff, having unconsciously passed the place where their leader had made good his way, and in their attempts to scramble up, tumbled down, and at last became so much affrighted that they took to the river for good, with the intention to swim to the shore they had left. Unfortunately for them, we had been gaining upon them; we had all been anxiously watching them, and the moment they began to swim we were all about the boat with guns and rifles, awaiting the instant when they would be close under our bows. The moment came; I was on the lower deck among several of the people with guns, and the firing was soon heavy; but not one of the Buffaloes was stopped, although every one must have been severely hit and wounded. Bell shot a load of buckshot at the head of one, which disappeared entirely under the water for perhaps a minute. I sent a ball through the neck of the last of the four, but all ineffectually, and off they went, swimming to the opposite shore; one lagged behind the rest, but, having found footing on a sand-bar, it rested awhile, and again swam off to rejoin its companions. They all reached the shore, but were quite as badly off on that side as they had been on the other, and their difficulties must have been great indeed; however, in a short time we had passed them. Mr. Charles Primeau, who is a good shot, and who killed the young Buffalo bull the other day, assured me that it was his opinion the whole of these would die before sundown, but that Buffaloes swimming were a hundred times more difficult to kill than those on shore. I have been told also, that a Buffalo shot by an Indian, in the presence of several whites, exhibited some marks on the inside of the skin that looked like old wounds, and that on close examination they found no less than six balls in its paunch. Sometimes they will run a mile after having been struck through the heart; whilst at other times they will fall dead without such desperate shot. Alexis told me that once he shot one through the thigh, and that it fell dead on the spot. We passed this afternoon a very curious conical mound of earth, about which Harris and I had some curiosity, by which I lost two pounds of snuff, as he was right, and I was wrong. We have seen Geese and Goslings, Ravens, Blue Herons, Bluebirds, Thrushes, Red-headed Woodpeckers and Red-shafted ditto, Martins, an immense number of Rough-winged Swallows about their holes, and Barn Swallows. We heard Killdeers last evening. Small Crested Flycatchers, Summer Yellow-birds, Maryland Yellow-throats, House Wrens are seen as we pass along our route; while the Spotted Sandpiper accompanies us all along the river. Sparrow Hawks, Turkey Buzzards, Arctic Towhee Buntings, Cat-birds, Mallards, Coots, Gadwalls, King-birds, Yellow-breasted Chats, Red Thrushes, all are noted as we pass. We have had a good day's run; it is now half-past ten. The wind has been cold, and this evening we have had a dash of rain. We have seen only one Wolf. We have heard some wonderful stories about Indians and white men, none of which I can well depend upon. We have stopped for the night a few miles above where the "Assiniboin" steamer was burnt with all her cargo uninsured, in the year 1835. I heard that after she had run ashore, the men started to build a scow to unload the cargo; but that through some accident the vessel was set on fire, and that a man and a woman who alone had been left on board, walked off to the island, where they remained some days unable to reach shore.

June 6, Tuesday. This morning was quite cold, and we had a thick white frost on our upper deck. It was also extremely cloudy, the wind from the east, and all about us looked dismal enough. The hands on board seemed to have been busy the whole of the night, for I scarcely slept for the noise they made. We soon came to a very difficult part of the river, and had to stop full three hours. Meanwhile the yawl went off to seek and sound for a channel, whilst the wood-cutters and the carriers—who, by the way, are called "charrettes"—followed their work, and we gathered a good quantity of drift-wood, which burns like straw. Our hopes of reaching the Mandan Village were abandoned, but we at last proceeded on our way and passed the bar; it was nearly dinner-time. Harris and Bell had their guns, and brought two Arctic Towhee Buntings and a Black-billed Cuckoo. They saw two large flocks of Geese making their way westward. The place where we landed showed many signs of Deer, Elk, and Buffaloes. I saw trees where the latter had rubbed their heavy bodies against the bark, till they had completely robbed the tree of its garment. We saw several Red-shafted Woodpeckers, and other birds named before. The Buffalo, when hunted on horseback, does *not* carry its tail erect, as has been represented in books, but close between the legs; but when you see a Buffalo bull work its tail sideways in a twisted rolling fashion, *then* take care of him, as it is a sure sign of his intention to rush against his pursuer's horse, which is very dangerous, both to hunter and steed. As we proceeded I saw two fine White-headed Eagles alighting on their nest, where perhaps they had young—and how remarkably late in the season this species does breed here! We also saw a young Sandhill Crane, and on an open prairie four Antelopes a few hundred yards off. Alexis tells me that at this season this is a rare occurrence, as the females are generally in the brushwood now; but in this instance the male and three females were on open prairie. We have passed what is called the Heart River, and the Square Hills, which, of course, are by no means square, but simply more level than the generality of those we have passed for upwards of three weeks. We now saw four barges belonging to our company, and came to, above them, as usual. A Mr. Kipp, one of the partners, came on board; and Harris, Squires, and myself had time to write each a short letter to our friends at home. Mr. Kipp had a peculiar looking crew who appeared not much better than a set of bandits among the Pyrenees or the Alps; yet they seem to be the very best sort of men for trappers and boatmen. We exchanged four of our men for four of his, as the latter are wanted at the Yellowstone. The country appears to Harris and to myself as if we had outrun the progress of vegetation, as from the boat we observed oaks scarcely in leaflets, whilst two hundred miles below, and indeed at a much less distance, we saw the same timber in nearly full leaf; flowers are also scarce. A single Wolf was seen by some one on deck. Nothing can be possibly keener than the senses of hearing and sight, as well as of smell, in the Antelope. Not one was ever known to jump up close to a hunter; and the very motion of the grasses, as these are wafted by the wind, will keep them awake and on the alert. Immediately upon the breaking up of the ice about the Mandan Village, three Buffaloes were seen floating down on a large cake; they were seen by Mr. Primeau from his post, and again from Fort Pierre. How much further the poor beasts travelled, no one can tell. It happens not infrequently, when the river is entirely closed in with ice, that some hundreds of Buffaloes attempt to cross; their aggregate enormous weight forces the ice to break, and the whole of the gang are drowned, as it is impossible for these animals to climb over the surrounding sharp edges of the ice. We have seen not less than three nests of White-headed Eagles this day. We are fast ashore about sixteen miles below the Mandan Villages, and will, in all probability, reach there to-morrow morning at an early hour. It is raining yet, and the day has been a most unpleasant one.

June 7, Wednesday. We had a vile night of rain, and wind from the northeast, which is still going on, and likely to continue the whole of this blessed day. Yesterday, when we had a white frost, ice was found in the kettles of Mr. Kipp's barges. We reached Fort Clark and the Mandan Villages at half-past seven this morning. Great guns were fired from the fort and from the "Omega," as our captain took the guns from the "Trapper" at Fort Pierre. The site of this fort appears a good one, though it is placed considerably below the Mandan Village. We saw some small spots cultivated, where corn, pumpkins, and beans are grown. The fort and village are situated on the high bank, rising somewhat to the elevation of a hill. The Mandan mud huts are very far from looking poetical, although Mr. Catlin has tried to render them so by placing them in regular rows, and all of the same size and form, which is by no means the case. But different travellers have different eyes! We saw more Indians than at any previous time since leaving St. Louis; and it is possible that there are a hundred huts, made of mud, all looking like so many potato winter-houses in the Eastern States. As soon as we were near the shore, every article that could conveniently be carried off was placed under lock and key, and our division door was made fast, as well as those of our own rooms. Even the axes and poles were put by. Our captain told us that last year they stole his cap and his shot-pouch and horn, and that it was through the interference of the first chief that he recovered his cap and horn; but that a squaw had his leather belt, and would not give it up. The appearance of these poor, miserable devils, as we approached the shore, was wretched enough. There they stood in the pelting rain and keen wind, covered with Buffalo robes, red blankets, and the like, some partially and most curiously besmeared with mud; and as they came on board, and we shook hands with each of them, I felt a clamminess that rendered the ceremony most repulsive. Their legs and naked feet were covered with mud. They looked at me with apparent curiosity, perhaps on account of my beard, which produced the same effect at Fort Pierre. They all looked very poor; and our captain says they are the *ne plus ultra* of thieves. It is said there are nearly three thousand men, women, and children that, during winter, cram themselves into these miserable hovels. Harris and I walked to the fort about nine o'clock. The walking was rascally, passing through mud and water the whole way. The yard of the fort itself was as bad. We entered Mr. Chardon's own room, crawled up a crazy ladder, and in a low garret I had the great pleasure of seeing alive the Swift or Kit Fox which he has given to me. It ran swiftly from one corner to another, and, when approached, growled somewhat in the manner of a common Fox. Mr. Chardon told me that good care would be taken of it until our return, that it would be chained to render it more gentle, and that I would find it an easy matter to take it along. I sincerely hope so. Seeing a remarkably fine skin of a large Cross Fox which I wished to buy, it was handed over to me. After this, Mr. Chardon asked one of the Indians to take us into the village, and particularly to show us the "Medicine Lodge." We followed our guide through mud and mire, even into the Lodge. We found this to be, in general terms, like all the other lodges, only larger, measuring twenty-three yards in diameter, with a large squarish aperture in the centre of the roof, some six or seven feet long by about four wide. We had entered this curiosity shop by pushing aside a wet Elk skin stretched on four sticks. Looking around, I saw a number of calabashes, eight or ten Otter skulls, two very large Buffalo skulls with the horns on, evidently of great age, and some sticks and other magical implements with which none but a "Great Medicine Man" is acquainted. During my survey there sat, crouched down on his haunches, an Indian wrapped in a dirty blanket, with only his filthy head peeping out. Our guide spoke to him; but he stirred not. Again, at the foot of one of the posts that support the central portion of this great room, lay a parcel that I took for a bundle of Buffalo robes; but it moved presently, and from beneath it half arose the emaciated body of a poor blind Indian, whose skin was quite shrivelled; and our guide made us signs that he was about to die. We all shook both hands with him; and he pressed our hands closely and with evident satisfaction. He had his pipe and tobacco pouch by him, and soon lay down again. We left this abode of mysteries, as I was anxious to see the interior of one of the common huts around; and again our guide led us through mud and mire to his own lodge, which we entered in the same way as we had done the other. All these lodges have a sort of portico that leads to the door, and on the tops of most of them I observed Buffalo skulls. This lodge contained the whole family of our guide—several women and children, and another man, perhaps a son-in-law or a brother. All these, except the man, were on the outer edge of the lodge, crouching on the ground, some suckling children; and at nearly equal distances apart were placed berths, raised about two feet above the ground, made of leather, and with square apertures for the sleepers or occupants to enter. The man of whom I have spoken was lying down in one of these, which was all open in front. I walked up to him, and, after disturbing his happy slumbers, shook hands with him; he made signs for me to sit down; and after Harris and I had done so, he rose, squatted himself near us, and, getting out a large spoon made of boiled Buffalo horn, handed it to a young girl, who brought a great rounded wooden bowl filled with pemmican, mixed with corn and some other stuff. I ate a mouthful or so of it, and found it quite palatable; and Harris and the rest then ate of it also. Bell was absent; we had seen nothing of him since we left the boat. This lodge, as well as the other, was dirty with water and mud; but I am told that in dry weather they are kept cleaner, and much cleaning do they need, most truly. A round, shallow hole was dug in the centre for the fire; and from the roof descended over this a chain, by the aid of which they do their cooking, the utensil being attached to the chain when wanted. As we returned towards the fort, I gave our guide a piece of tobacco, and he appeared well pleased. He followed us on board, and as he peeped in my room, and saw the dried and stuffed specimens we have, he evinced a slight degree of curiosity. Our captain, Mr. Chardon, and our men have been busily engaged in putting ashore that portion of the cargo designed for this fort, which in general appearance might be called a poor miniature representation of Fort Pierre. The whole country around was overgrown with "Lamb's quarters" *(Chenopòdium album)*, which I have no doubt, if boiled, would take the place of spinach in this wild and, to my eyes, miserable country, the poetry of which lies in the imagination of those writers who have described the "velvety prairies" and "enchanted castles" (of mud), so common where we now are. We observed a considerable difference in the color of these Indians, who, by the way, are almost all Riccarees; many appeared, and in fact are, redder than others; they are lank, rather tall, and very alert, but, as I have said before, all look poor and dirty. After dinner we went up the muddy bank again to look at the corn-fields, as the small patches that are meanly cultivated are called. We found poor, sickly looking corn about two inches high, that had been represented to us this morning as full six inches high. We followed the prairie, a very extensive one, to the hills, and there found a deep ravine, sufficiently impregnated with saline matter to answer the purpose of salt water for the Indians to boil their corn and pemmican, clear and clean; but they, as well as the whites at the fort, resort to the muddy Missouri for their drinking water, the only fresh water at hand. Not a drop of spirituous liquor has been brought to this place for the last two years; and there can be no doubt that on this account the Indians have become more peaceable than heretofore, though now and then a white man is murdered, and many horses are stolen. As we walked over the plain, we saw heaps of earth thrown up to cover the poor Mandans who died of the small-pox. These mounds in many instances appear to contain the remains of several bodies and, perched on the top, lies, pretty generally, the rotting skull of a Buffalo. Indeed, the skulls of the Buffaloes seem as if a kind of relation to these most absurdly superstitious and ignorant beings. I could not hear a word of the young Grizzly Bear of which Mr. Chardon had spoken to me. He gave me his Buffalo head-dress and other trifles—as he was pleased to call them; all of which will prove more or less interesting and curious to you when they reach Minniesland. He presented Squires with a good hunting shirt and a few other things, and to all of us, presented moccasins. We collected a few round cacti; and I saw several birds that looked much the worse for the cold and wet weather we have had these last few days. Our boat has been thronged with Indians ever since we have tied to the shore; and it is with considerable difficulty and care that we can stop them from intruding into our rooms when we are there. We found many portions of skulls lying on the ground, which, perhaps, did at one period form the circles of them spoken of by Catlin. All around the village is filthy beyond description. Our captain tells us that no matter what weather we may have to-morrow, he will start at daylight, even if he can only go across the river, to get rid of these wolfish-looking vagabonds of Indians. I sincerely hope that we may have a fair day and a long run, so that the air around us may once more be pure and fresh from the hand of Nature. After the Riccarees had taken possession of this Mandan Village, the remains of that once powerful tribe removed about three miles up the river, and there have now fifteen or twenty huts, containing, of course, only that number of families. During the worst periods of the epidemic which swept over this village with such fury, many became maniacs, rushed to the Missouri, leaped into its turbid waters, and were seen no more. Mr. Primeau, wife, and children, as well as another half-breed, have gone to the fort, and are to remain there till further orders. The fort is in a poor condition, roofs leaking, etc. Whilst at the fort this afternoon, I was greatly surprised to see a tall, athletic Indian thrashing the dirty rascals about Mr. Chardon's door most severely; but I found on inquiry that he was called "the soldier," and that he had authority to do so whenever the Indians intruded or congregated in the manner this *canaille* had done. After a while the same tall fellow came on board with his long stick, and immediately began belaboring the fellows on the lower guards; the latter ran off over the planks, and scrambled up the muddy banks as if so many affrighted Buffaloes. Since then we have been comparatively quiet; but I hope they will all go off, as the captain is going to put the boat from the shore, to the full length of our spars. The wind has shifted to the northward, and the atmosphere has been so chilled that a House Swallow was caught, benumbed with cold, and brought to me by our captain. Harris, Bell, and I saw a Cliff Swallow take refuge on board; but this was not caught. We have seen Say's Fly-catcher, the Ground Finch, Cow Buntings, and a few other birds. One of the agents arrived this afternoon from the Gros Ventre, or Minnetaree Village, about twelve miles above us. He is represented as a remarkably brave man, and he relates some strange adventures of his prowess. Several *great warriors* have condescended to shake me by the hand; their very touch is disgusting—it will indeed be a deliverance to get rid of all this "Indian poetry." We are, nevertheless, to take a few to the Yellowstone. Alexis has his wife, who is, in fact, a good-looking young woman; an old patroon, Provost, takes one of his daughters along; and we have, besides, several red-skinned single gentlemen. We were assured that the northern parts of the hills, that form a complete curtain to the vast prairie on which we have walked this afternoon, are still adorned with patches of snow that fell there during last winter. It is now nine o'clock, but before I go to rest I cannot resist giving you a description of the curious exhibition that we have had on board, from a numerous lot of Indians of the first class, say some forty or fifty. They ranged themselves along the sides of the large cabin, squatting on the floor. Coffee had been prepared for the whole party, and hard sea-biscuit likewise. The coffee was first given to each of them, and afterwards the biscuits, and I had the honor of handing the latter to the row on one side of the boat; a box of tobacco was opened and laid on the table. The man who came from the Gros Ventres this afternoon proved to be an excellent interpreter; and after the captain had delivered his speech to him, he spoke loudly to the group, and explained the purport of the captain's speech. They grunted their approbation frequently, and were, no doubt, pleased. Two individuals (Indians) made their appearance highly decorated, with epaulets on the shoulders, red clay on blue uniforms, three cocks' plumes in their head-dress, rich moccasins, leggings, etc. These are men who, though in the employ of the Opposition company, act truly as friends; but who, meantime, being called "Braves," never grunted, bowed, or shook hands with any of us. Supper over and the tobacco distributed, the whole body arose simultaneously, and each and every one of these dirty wretches we had all to shake by the hand. The two braves sat still until all the rest had gone ashore, and then retired as majestically as they had entered, not even shaking hands with our good-humored captain. I am told that this performance takes place once every year, on the passing of the Company's boats. I need not say that the coffee and the two biscuits apiece were gobbled down in less than no time. The tobacco, which averaged about two pounds to each man, was hid in their robes or blankets for future use. Two of the Indians, who must have been of the highest order, and who distributed the "rank weed," were nearly naked; one had on only a breech-clout and one legging, the other was in no better case. They are now all ashore except one or more who are going with us to the Yellowstone; and I will now go to my rest. Though I have said "Good-night," I have arisen almost immediately, and I must write on, for we have other scenes going on both among the trappers below and some of the people above. Many Indians, squaws as well as men, are bartering and trading, and keep up such a babble that Harris and I find sleep impossible; needless to say, the squaws who are on board are of the lowest grade of morality.

June 8, Thursday. This morning was fair and cold, as you see by the range of the thermometer, 37° to 56°. We started at a very early hour, and breakfasted before five, on account of the village of Gros Ventres, where our captain had to stop. We passed a few lodges belonging to the tribe of the poor Mandans, about all that remained. I only counted eight, but am told there are twelve. The village of the Gros Ventres (Minnetarees) has been cut off from the bank of the river by an enormous sand-bar, now overgrown with willows and brush, and we could only see the American flag flying in the cool breeze. Two miles above this, however, we saw an increasing body of Indians, for the prairie was sprinkled with small parties, on horse and on foot. The first who arrived fired a salute of small guns, and we responded with our big gun. They had an abundance of dogs harnessed to take wood back to the village, and their yells and fighting were severe upon our ears. Some forty or more of the distinguished black-guards came on board; and we had to close our doors as we did yesterday. After a short period they were feasted as last evening; and speeches, coffee, and tobacco, as well as some gunpowder, were given them, which they took away in packs, to be divided afterward. We took one more passenger, and lost our interpreter, who is a trader with the Minnetarees. The latter are by no means as fine-looking a set of men as those we have seen before, and I observed none of that whiteness of skin among them. There were numbers of men, women, and children. We saw a crippled and evidently tame Wolf, and two Indians, following us on the top of the hills. We saw two Swans on a bar, and a female Elk, with her young fawn, for a few minutes. I wished that we had been ashore, as I know full well that the mother would not leave her young; and the mother killed, the young one would have been easily caught alive. We are now stopping for the night, and our men are cutting wood. We have done this, I believe, four times to-day, and have run upward of sixty miles. At the last wood-cutting place, a young leveret was started by the men, and after a short race, the poor thing squatted, and was killed by the stroke of a stick. It proved to be the young of *Lepus townsendii* [*L. campestris*], large enough to have left the mother, and weighing rather more than a pound. It is a very beautiful specimen. The eyes are very large, and the iris pure amber color. Its hair is tightly, but beautifully curled. Its measurements are as follows [*omitted*]. Bell will make a fine skin of it to-morrow morning. We have had all sorts of stories related to us; but Mr. Kipp, who has been in the country for twenty-two years, is evidently a person of truth, and I expect a good deal of information from him. Our captain told us that on a previous voyage some Indians asked him if, "when the great Medicine" (meaning the steamer) "was tired, he gave it whiskey." Mr. Sire laughed, and told them he did. "How much?" was the query. "A barrelful, to be sure!" The poor wretches at first actually believed him, and went off contented, but were naturally angry at being undeceived on a later occasion. I have now some hope of finding a young of the Antelope alive at Fort Union, as Mr. Kipp left one there about ten days ago. I am now going to bed, though our axemen and "charettes" are still going; and I hope I may not be called up to-morrow morning, to be ready for breakfast at half-past four. Harris and Bell went off with Alexis. Bell fired at a bird, and a large Wolf immediately made its appearance. This is always the case in this country; when you shoot an animal and hide yourself, you may see, in less than half an hour, from ten to thirty of these hungry rascals around the carcass, and have fine fun shooting at them. We have had a windy day, but a good run on the whole. I hope to-morrow may prove propitious, and that we shall reach Fort Union in five more days.

JUNE 9, FRIDAY. Thermometer 42°, 75°, 66°. We had a heavy white frost last night, but we have had a fine, pleasant day on the whole, and to me a most interesting one. We passed the Little Missouri (the real one) about ten this morning. It is a handsome stream, that runs all the way from the Black Hills, one of the main spurs of the mighty Rocky Mountains. We saw three Elks swimming across it, and the number of this fine species of Deer that are about us now is almost inconceivable. We have heard of burning springs, which we intend to examine on our way down. We started a Goose from the shore that had evidently young ones; she swam off, beating the water with wings half extended, until nearly one hundred yards off. A shot from a rifle was fired at her, and happily missed the poor thing; she afterwards lowered her neck, sank her body, and with the tip of the bill only above water, kept swimming away from us till out of sight. Afterwards one of the trappers shot at two Geese with two young ones. We landed at four o'clock, and Harris and Bell shot some Bay-winged Buntings and *Emberiza pallida*, whilst Sprague and I went up to the top of the hills, bounding the beautiful prairie, by which we had stopped to repair something about the engine. We gathered some handsome lupines, of two different species, and many other curious plants. From this elevated spot we could see the wilderness to an immense distance; the Missouri looked as if only a brook, and our steamer a very small one indeed. At this juncture we saw two men running along the shore upwards, and I supposed they had seen an Elk or something else, of which they were in pursuit. Meantime, gazing around, we saw a large lake, where we are told that Ducks, Geese, and Swans breed in great numbers; this we intend also to visit when we come down. At this moment I heard the report of a gun from the point where the men had been seen, and when we reached the steamboat, we were told that a Buffalo had been killed. From the deck I saw a man swimming round the animal; he got on its side, and floated down the stream with it. The captain sent a parcel of men with a rope; the swimmer fastened this round the neck of the Buffalo, and with his assistance, for he now swam all the way, the poor beast was brought alongside; and as the tackle had been previously fixed, it was hauled up on the fore deck. Sprague took its measurements with me, which are as follows: length from nose to root of tail, 8 feet; height of fore shoulder to hoof, 4 ft. 9½ in.; height at the rump to hoof, 4 ft. 2 in. The head was cut off, as well as one fore and one hind foot. The head is so full of symmetry, and so beautiful, that I shall have a drawing of it to-morrow, as well as careful ones of the feet. Whilst the butchers were at work, I was highly interested to see one of our Indians cutting out the milk-bag of the cow and eating it, quite fresh and raw, in pieces somewhat larger than a hen's egg. One of the stomachs was partially washed in a bucket of water, and an Indian swallowed a large portion of this. Mr. Chardon brought the remainder on the upper deck and ate it uncleaned. I had a piece well cleaned and tasted it; to my utter astonishment, it was very good, but the idea was repulsive to me; besides which, I am not a meat-eater, as you know, except when other provisions fail. The animal was in good condition; and the whole carcass was cut up and dispersed among the men below, reserving the nicer portions for the cabin. This was accomplished with great rapidity; the blood was washed away in a trice, and half an hour afterwards no one would have known that a Buffalo had been dressed on deck. We now met with a somewhat disagreeable accident; in starting and backing off the boat, our yawl was run beneath the boat; this strained it, and sprung one of the planks so much that, when we landed on the opposite side of the river, we had to haul it on shore, and turn it over for examination; it was afterwards taken to the forecastle to undergo repairs to-morrow, as it is often needed. Whilst cutting wood was going on, we went ashore. Bell shot at two Buffaloes out of eight, and killed both; he would also have shot a Wolf, had he had more bullets. Harris saw, and shot at, an Elk; but he knows little about still hunting, and thereby lost a good chance. A negro fire-tender went off with his rifle and shot two of Townsend's Hares. One was cut in two by his ball, and he left it on the ground; the other was shot near the rump, and I have it now hanging before me; and, let me tell you, that I never before saw so beautiful an animal of the same family. My drawing will be a good one; it is a fine specimen, an old male. I have been hearing much of the prevalence of scurvy, from living so constantly on dried flesh, also about the small-pox, which destroyed such numbers of the Indians. Among the Mandans, Riccarées, and Gros Ventres, hundreds died in 1837, only a few surviving; and the Assiniboins were nearly exterminated. Indeed it is said that in the various attacks of this scourge 52,000 Indians have perished. This last visitation of the dread disease has never before been related by a traveller, and I will write more of it when at Fort Union. It is now twenty minutes to midnight; and, with walking and excitement of one kind or another, I am ready for bed. Alexis and another hunter will be off in an hour on a hunt.

June 10, Saturday. I rose at half-past three this morning. It was clear and balmy; our men were cutting wood, and we went off shooting. We saw a female Elk that was loath to leave the neighborhood; and Bell shot a Sharp-tailed Grouse, which we ate at our supper and found pretty good, though sadly out of season. As we were returning to the boat, Alexis and his companion went off after Buffaloes that we saw grazing peaceably on the bank near the river. Whilst they were shooting at the Buffaloes, and almost simultaneously, the fawn of the female Elk was seen lying asleep under the bank. It rose as we approached, and Bell shot at it, but missed; and with its dam it went briskly off. It was quite small, looking almost red, and was beautifully spotted with light marks of the color of the Virginia Deer's fawn. I would have given five dollars for it, as I saw it skipping over the prairie. At this moment Alexis came running, and told the captain they had killed two Buffaloes; and almost all the men went off at once with ropes, to bring the poor animals on board, according to custom. One, however, had been already dressed. The other had its head cut off, and the men were tugging at the rope, hauling the beast along over the grass. Mr. Chardon was seated on it; until, when near the boat, the rope gave way, and the bull rolled over into a shallow ravine. It was soon on board, however, and quickly skinned and cut up. The two hunters had been absent three-quarters of an hour. At the report of the guns, two Wolves made their appearance, and no doubt fed at leisure on the offal left from the first Buffalo. Harris saw a gang of Elks, consisting of between thirty and forty. We have passed a good number of Wild Geese with goslings; the Geese were shot at, notwithstanding my remonstrances on account of the young, but fortunately all escaped. We passed some beautiful scenery when about the middle of the "Bend," and almost opposite had the pleasure of seeing five Mountain Rams, or Bighorns, on the summit of a hill. I looked at them through the telescope; they stood perfectly still for some minutes, then went out of sight, and then again were in view. One of them had very large horns; the rest appeared somewhat smaller. Our captain told us that he had seen them at, or very near by, the same place last season, on his way up. We saw many very curious cliffs, but not one answering the drawings engraved for Catlin's work. We passed Knife River, *Rivière aux Couteaux*, and stopped for a short time to take in wood. Harris killed a Sparrow Hawk, and saw several Red-shafted Woodpeckers. Bell was then engaged in saving the head of the Buffalo cow, of which I made a drawing, and Sprague an outline, notwithstanding the horrible motion of our boat. We passed safely a dangerous chain of rocks extending across the river; we also passed White River; both the streams I have mentioned are insignificant. The weather was warm, and became cloudy, and it is now raining smartly. We have, however, a good quantity of excellent wood, and have made a good run, say sixty miles. We saw what we supposed to be three Grizzly Bears, but could not be sure. We saw on the prairie ahead of us some Indians, and as we neared them, found them to be Assiniboins. There were about ten altogether, men, squaws, and children. The boat was stopped, and a smart-looking, though small-statured man came on board. He had eight plugs of tobacco given him, and was asked to go off; but he talked a vast deal, and wanted powder and ball. He was finally got rid of. During his visit, our Gros Ventre chief and our Sioux were both in my own cabin. The first having killed three of that tribe and scalped them, and the Sioux having a similar record, they had no wish to meet. A few miles above this we stopped to cut wood. Bell and Harris went on shore; and we got a White Wolf, so old and so poor that we threw it overboard. Meantime a fawn Elk was observed crossing the river, coming toward our shore; it was shot at twice, but missed; it swam to the shore, but under such a steep bank that it could not get up. Alexis, who was told of this, ran down the river bank, reached it, and fastened his suspenders around its neck, but could not get it up the bank. Bell had returned, and went to his assistance, but all in vain; the little thing was very strong, and floundered and struggled till it broke the tie, and swam swiftly with the current down the river, and was lost. A slight rope would have secured it to us. This was almost the same spot where the captain caught one alive last season with the yawl; and we could have performed the same feat easily, had not the yawl been on deck undergoing repairs. We pushed off, and very soon saw more Indians on the shore, also Assiniboins. They had crossed the "Bend" below us, and had brought some trifles to trade with us; but our captain passed on, and the poor wretches sat and looked at the "Great Medicine" in astonishment. Shortly after this, we saw a Wolf attempting to climb a very steep bank of clay; he fell down thrice, but at last reached the top and disappeared at once. On the opposite shore another Wolf was lying down on a sand-bar, like a dog, and might readily have been taken for one. We have stopped for the night at nine o'clock; and I now have done my day's putting-up of memoranda and sketches, intending to enlarge upon much after I return home. I forgot to say that last evening we saw a large herd of Buffaloes, with many calves among them; they were grazing quietly on a fine bit of prairie, and we were actually opposite to them and within two hundred yards before they appeared to notice us. They stared, and then started at a handsome canter, suddenly wheeled round, stopped, closed up their ranks, and then passed over a slight knoll, producing a beautiful picturesque view. Another thing I forgot to speak of is a place not far below the Little Missouri, where Mr. Kipp assured us we should find the remains of a petrified forest, which we hope to see later.

June 11, Sunday. This day has been tolerably fine, though windy. We have seen an abundance of game, a great number of Elks, common Virginian Deer, Mountain Rams in two places, and a fine flock of Sharp-tailed Grouse, that, when they flew off from the ground near us, looked very much like large Meadow Larks. They were on a prairie bordering a large patch of Artemisia, which in the distance presents the appearance of acres of cabbages. We have seen many Wolves and some Buffaloes. One young bull stood on the brink of a bluff, looking at the boat steadfastly for full five minutes; and as we neared the spot, he waved his tail, and moved off briskly. On another occasion, a young bull that had just landed at the foot of a very steep bluff was slaughtered without difficulty; two shots were fired at it, and the poor thing was killed by a rifle bullet. I was sorry, for we did not stop for it, and its happy life was needlessly ended. I saw near that spot a large Hawk, and also a very small Tamias, or Ground Squirrel. Harris saw a Spermophile, of what species none of us could tell. We have seen many Elks swimming the river, and they look almost the size of a well-grown mule. They stared at us, were fired at, at an enormous distance, it is true, and yet stood still. These animals are abundant beyond belief hereabouts. We have seen much remarkably handsome scenery, but nothing at all comparing with Catlin's descriptions; his book must, after all, be altogether a humbug. Poor devil! I pity him from the bottom of my soul; had he studied, and kept up to the old French proverb that says, "Bon renommé vaut mieux que ceinture doré," he might have become an "honest man"—the quintessence of God's works. We did hope to have reached L'Eau Bourbeux (the Muddy River) this evening, but we are now fast ashore, about six miles below it, about the same distance that we have been told we were ever since shortly after dinner. We have had one event: our boat caught fire, and burned for a few moments near the stern, the effects of the large, hot cinders coming from the chimney; but it was almost immediately put out, thank God! Any inattention, with about 10,000 lbs. of powder on board, might have resulted in a sad accident. We have decided to write a short letter of thanks to our truly gentlemanly captain, and to present him with a handsome six-barrelled pistol, the only thing we have that may prove of service to him, although I hope he may never need it. Sprague drew four figures of the Buffalo's foot; and Bell and I have packed the whole of our skins. We ran to-day all round the compass, touching every point. The following is a copy of the letter to Captain Sire, signed by all of us.

FORT UNION, MOUTH OF YELLOWSTONE,
UPPER MISSOURI, *June 11th, 1843.*

DEAR SIR,—We cannot part with you previous to your return to St. Louis, without offering to you our best wishes, and our thanks for your great courtesy, assuring you how highly we appreciate, and feel grateful for, your uniform kindness and gentlemanly deportment to each and all of us. We are most happy to add that our passage to the Yellowstone River has been devoid of any material accident, which we can only attribute to the great regularity and constant care with which you have discharged your arduous duties in the difficult navigation of the river.

We regret that it is not in our power, at this moment, to offer you a suitable token of our esteem, but hope you will confer on us the favor of accepting at our hands a six-barrelled, silver-mounted pistol, which we sincerely hope and trust you may never have occasion to use in defence of your person. We beg you to consider us,

Your well-wishers and friends, etc.,

Fort Union, June 12, Monday. We had a cloudy and showery day, and a high wind besides. We saw many Wild Geese and Ducks with their young. We took in wood at two places, but shot nothing. I saw a Wolf giving chase, or driving away four Ravens from a sand-bar; but the finest sight of all took place shortly before we came to the mouth of the Yellowstone, and that was no less than twenty-two Mountain Rams and Ewes mixed, and amid them one young one only. We came in sight of the fort at five o'clock, and reached it at seven. We passed the Opposition fort three miles below this; their flags were hoisted, and ours also. We were saluted from Fort Union, and we fired guns in return, six in number. The moment we had arrived, the gentlemen of the fort came down on horseback, and appeared quite a cavalcade. I was introduced to Mr. Culbertson and others, and, of course, the introduction went the rounds. We walked to the fort and drank some first-rate port wine, and returned to the boat at half-past nine o'clock. Our captain was pleased with the letter and the pistol. Our trip to the this place has been the quickest on record, though our boat is the slowest that ever undertook to reach the Yellowstone. Including all stoppages and detentions, we have made the trip in forty-eight days and seven hours from St. Louis. We left St. Louis April 25th, at noon; reaching Fort Union June 12th, at seven in the evening.

June 13, Tuesday. We had a remarkably busy day on board and on shore, but spent much of our time writing letters. I wrote home at great length to John Bachman, N. Berthoud, and Gideon B. Smith. We walked to the fort once and back again, and dined on board with our captain and the gentlemen of the fort. We took a ride also in an old wagon, somewhat at the risk of our necks, for we travelled too fast for the nature of what I was told was the road. We slept on board the "Omega," probably for the last time.

We have been in a complete state of excitement unloading the boat, reloading her with a new cargo, and we were all packing and arranging our effects, as well as writing letters. After dinner our belongings were taken to the landing of the fort in a large keel-boat, with the last of the cargo. The room which we are to occupy during our stay at this place is rather small and low, with only one window, on the west side. However, we shall manage well enough, I dare say, for the few weeks we are to be here. This afternoon I had a good deal of conversation with Mr. Culbertson, and found him well disposed to do all he can for us; and no one can ask for more politeness than is shown us. Our captain having invited us to remain with him to-night, we have done so, and will breakfast with him to-morrow morning. It is his intention to leave as early as he can settle his business here. All the trappers are gone to the fort, and in a few weeks will be dispersed over different and distant parts of the wilderness. The filth they had left below has been scraped and washed off, as well indeed as the whole boat, of which there was need enough. I have copied this journal and send it to St. Louis by our good captain; also one box of skins, one pair Elk horns, and one bundle of Wolf and other skins.

June 14, Wednesday. At six this morning all hands rose early; the residue of the cargo for St. Louis was placed on board. Our captain told us time was up, and we all started for the fort on foot, quite a short distance. Having deposited our guns there, Bell, Squires, and I walked off to the wooding-place, where our captain was to remain a good while, and it was there we should bid him adieu. We found this walk one of the worst, the very worst, upon which we ever trod; full of wild rose-bushes, tangled and matted with vines, burs, and thorns of all sorts, and encumbered by thousands of pieces of driftwood, some decayed, some sunk in the earth, while others were entangled with the innumerable roots exposed by floods and rains. We saw nothing but a few Ravens. When nearly half way, we heard the trampling of galloping horses, and loud hallooings, which we found to proceed from the wagon of which we have spoken, which, loaded with men, passed us at a speed one would have thought impossible over such ground. Soon after we had a heavy shower of rain, but reached the boat in good order. Harris and Sprague, who had followed us, came afterwards. I was pretty hot, and rather tired. The boat took on wood for half an hour after we arrived; then the captain shook us all by the hand most heartily, and we bade him God speed. I parted from him really with sorrow, for I have found him all I could wish during the whole passage; and his position is no sinecure, to say naught of the rabble under his control. All the wood-cutters who remained walked off by the road; and we went back in the wagon over a bad piece of ground—much easier, however, than returning on foot. As we reached the prairies, we travelled faster, and passed by the late garden of the fort, which had been abandoned on account of the thieving of the men attached to the Opposition Company, at Fort Mortimer. Harris caught a handsome snake, now in spirits. We saw Lazuli Finches and several other sorts of small birds. Upon reaching the fort, from which many great guns were fired as salutes to the steamer, which were loudly returned, I was amused at the terror the firing occasioned to the squaws and their children, who had arrived in great numbers the previous evening; they howled, fell down on the earth, or ran in every direction. All the dogs started off, equally frightened, and made for the distant hills. Dinner not being ready, three of us took a walk, and saw a good number of Tamias holes, many cacti of two sorts, and some plants hitherto uncollected by us. We saw a few Arctic Ground Finches and two Wolves. After dinner Mr. Culbertson told us that if a Wolf made its appearance on the prairie near the fort, he would give it chase on horseback, and bring it to us, alive or dead; and he was as good as his word. It was so handsomely executed, that I will relate the whole affair. When I saw the Wolf (a white one), it was about a quarter of a mile off, alternately standing and trotting; the horses were about one-half the distance off. A man was started to drive these in; and I thought the coursers never would reach the fort, much less become equipped so as to overhaul the Wolf. We were all standing on the platform of the fort, with our heads only above the palisades; and I was so fidgety that I ran down twice to tell the hunters that the Wolf was making off. Mr. Culbertson, however, told me he would see it did not make off; and in a few moments he rode out of the fort, gun in hand, dressed only in shirt and breeches. He threw his cap off within a few yards, and suddenly went off with the swiftness of a jockey bent on winning a race. The Wolf trotted on, and ever and anon stopped to gaze at the rider and the horse; till, finding out the meaning (too late, alas! for him), he galloped off with all his might; but the horse was too swift for the poor cur, as we saw the rider gaining ground rapidly. Mr. Culbertson fired his gun off as a signal, I was told, that the Wolf would be brought in; and the horse, one would think, must have been of the same opinion, for although the Wolf had now reached the hills, and turned into a small ravine, the moment it had entered it, the horse dashed after, the sound of the gun came on the ear, the Wolf was picked up by Mr. Culbertson without dismounting, hardly slackening his pace, and thrown across the saddle. The rider returned as swiftly as he had gone, wet through with a smart shower that had fallen meantime; and the poor Wolf was placed at my disposal. The time taken from the start to the return in the yard did not exceed twenty minutes, possibly something less. Two other men who had started at the same time rode very swiftly also, and skirted the hills to prevent the Wolf's escape; and one of them brought in Mr. C.'s gun, which he had thrown on the ground as he picked up the Wolf to place it on the saddle. The beast was not quite dead when it arrived, and its jaws told of its dying agonies; it scratched one of Mr. C.'s fingers sorely; but we are assured that such things so often occur that nothing is thought of it.

And now a kind of sham Buffalo hunt was proposed, accompanied by a bet of a suit of clothes, to be given to the rider who would load and fire the greatest number of shots in a given distance. The horses were mounted as another Wolf was seen trotting off towards the hills, and Mr. Culbertson again told us he would bring it in. This time, however, he was mistaken; the Wolf was too far off to be overtaken, and it reached the hill-tops, made its way through a deep ravine full of large rocks, and was then given up. Mr. Culbertson was seen coming down without his quarry. He joined the riders, started with his gun empty, loaded in a trice, and fired the first shot; then the three riders came on at full speed, loading and firing first on one side, then on the other of the horse, as if after Buffaloes. Mr. C. fired eleven times before he reached the fort, and within less than half a mile's run; the others fired once less, each. We were all delighted to see these feats. No one was thrown off, though the bridles hung loose, and the horses were under full gallop all the time. Mr. Culbertson's mare, which is of the full Blackfoot Indian breed, is about five years old, and could not be bought for four hundred dollars. I should like to see some of the best English hunting gentlemen hunt in the like manner. We are assured that after dusk, or as soon as the gates of the fort are shut, the Wolves come near enough to be killed from the platform, as these beasts oftentimes come to the trough where the hogs are fed daily. We have seen no less than eight this day from the fort, moving as leisurely as if a hundred miles off. A heavy shower put off running a race; but we are to have a regular Buffalo hunt, where I must act only as a spectator; for, alas! I am now too near seventy to run and load whilst going at full gallop. Two gentlemen arrived this evening from the Crow Indian Nation; they crossed to our side of the river, and were introduced at once. One is Mr. Chouteau, son of Auguste Chouteau, and the other a Scotchman, Mr. James Murray, at whose father's farm, on the Tweed, we all stopped on our return from the Highlands of Scotland. They told us that the snow and ice was yet three feet deep near the mountains, and an abundance over the whole of the mountains themselves. They say they have made a good collection of robes, but that Beavers are very scarce. This day has been spent altogether in talking, sight-seeing, and enjoyment. Our room was small, dark, and dirty, and crammed with our effects. Mr. Culbertson saw this, and told me that to-morrow he would remove us to a larger, quieter, and better one. I was glad to hear this, as it would have been very difficult to draw, write, or work in; and yet it is the very room where the Prince de Neuwied resided for two months, with his secretary and bird-preserver. The evening was cloudy and cold; we had had several showers of rain since our bath in the bushes this morning, and I felt somewhat fatigued. Harris and I made our beds up; Squires fixed some Buffalo robes, of which nine had been given us, on a long old bedstead, never knowing it had been the couch of a foreign prince; Bell and Sprague settled themselves opposite to us on more Buffalo skins, and night closed in. But although we had lain down, it was impossible for us to sleep; for above us was a drunken man affected with a *goître*, and not only was his voice rough and loud, but his words were continuous. His oaths, both in French and English, were better fitted for the Five Points in New York, or St. Giles of London, than anywhere among Christians. He roared, laughed like a maniac, and damned himself and the whole creation. I thought that time would quiet him, but, no! for now clarionets, fiddles, and a drum were heard in the dining-room, where indeed they had been playing at different times during the afternoon, and our friend above began swearing at this as if quite fresh. We had retired for the night; but an invitation was sent us to join the party in the dining-room. Squires was up in a moment, and returned to say that a ball was on foot, and that "all the beauty and fashion" would be skipping about in less than no time. There was no alternative; we all got up, and in a short time were amid the *beau monde* of these parts. Several squaws, attired in their best, were present, with all the guests, *engagés*, clerks, etc. Mr. Culbertson played the fiddle very fairly; Mr. Guèpe the clarionet, and Mr. Chouteau the drum, as if brought up in the army of the great Napoleon. Cotillions and reels were danced with much energy and apparent enjoyment, and the company dispersed about one o'clock. We retired for the second time, and now occurred a dispute between the drunkard and another man; but, notwithstanding this, I was so wearied that I fell asleep.

June 15, Thursday. We all rose late, as one might expect; the weather was quite cool for the season, and it was cloudy besides. We did nothing else than move our effects to an upstairs room. The Mackinaw boats arrived at the fort about noon, and were unloaded in a precious short time; and all hands being called forth, the empty boats themselves were dragged to a ravine, turned over, and prepared for calking previous to their next voyage up or down, as the case might be. The gentlemen from these boats gave me a fine pair of Deer's horns; and to Mr. Culbertson a young Gray Wolf, and also a young Badger, which they had brought in. It snarled and snapped, and sometimes grunted not unlike a small pig, but did not bite. It moved somewhat slowly, and its body looked flattish all the time; the head has all the markings of an adult, though it is a young of the present spring. Bell and Harris hunted a good while, but procured only a Lazuli Finch and a few other birds. Bell skinned the Wolf, and we put its hide in the barrel with the head of the Buffalo cow, etc. I showed the plates of the quadrupeds to many persons, and I hope with success, as they were pleased and promised me much. To-morrow morning a man called Black Harris is to go off after Antelopes for me; and the hunters for the men of the fort and themselves; and perhaps some of the young men may go with one or both parties. I heard many stories about Wolves; particularly I was interested in one told by Mr. Kipp, who assured us he had caught upwards of one hundred with baited fish-hooks. Many other tales were told us; but I shall not forget them, so will not write them down here, but wait till hereafter. After shooting at a mark with a bow made of Elk horn, Mr. Kipp presented it to me. We saw several Wolves, but none close to the fort. Both the common Crow and Raven are found here; Bell killed one of the former.

June 16, Friday. The weather was cool this morning, with the wind due east. I drew the young Gray Wolf, and Sprague made an outline of it. Bell, Provost, Alexis, and Black Harris went over the river to try to procure Antelopes; Bell and Alexis returned to dinner without any game, although they had seen dozens of the animals wanted, and also some Common Deer. The two others, who travelled much farther, returned at dusk with empty stomachs and a young fawn of the Common Deer. Harris and I took a long walk after my drawing was well towards completion, and shot a few birds. The Buffalo, old and young, are fond of rolling on the ground in the manner of horses, and turn quite over; this is done not only to clean themselves, but also to rub off the loose old coat of hair and wool that hangs about their body like so many large, dirty rags. Those about the fort are gentle, but will not allow a person to touch their bodies, not even the young calves of the last spring. Our young Badger is quite fond of lying on his back, and then sleeps. His general appearance and gait remind me of certain species of Armadillo. There was a good deal of talking and jarring about the fort; some five or six men came from the Opposition Company, and would have been roughly handled had they not cleared off at the beginning of trouble. Arrangements were made for loading the Mackinaw barges, and it is intended that they shall depart for St. Louis, leaving on Sunday morning. We shall all be glad when these boats with their men are gone, as we are now full to the brim. Harris has a new batch of patients, and enjoys the work of physician.

June 17, Saturday. Warm and fair, with the river rising fast. The young fawn was hung up, and I drew it. By dinner-time Sprague had well prepared the Gray Wolf, and I put him to work at the fawn. Bell went shooting, and brought five or six good birds. The song of the Lazuli Finch so much resembles that of the Indigo Bird that it would be difficult to distinguish them by the note alone. They keep indifferently among the low bushes and high trees. He also brought a few specimens of *Spermophilus hoodii* of Richardson, of which the measurements were taken. Wolves often retreat into holes made by the sinking of the earth near ravines, burrowing in different directions at the bottoms of these. I sent Provost early this morning to the Opposition fort, to inquire whether Mr. Cutting had written letters about us, and also to see a fine Kit Fox, brought in one of their boats from the Yellowstone. Much has been done in the way of loading the Mackinaw boats. Bell has skinned the young Wolf, and Sprague will perhaps finish preparing the fawn. The hunters who went out yesterday morning have returned, and brought back a quantity of fresh Buffalo meat. Squires brought many fragments of a petrified tree. No Antelopes were shot, and I feel uneasy on this score. Provost returned and told me Mr. Cutting's men with the letters had not arrived, but that they were expected hourly. The Kit Fox had been suffocated to death by some dozens of bundles of Buffalo robes falling on it, while attached to a ladder, and had been thrown out and eaten by the Wolves or the dogs. This evening, quite late, I shot a fine large Gray Wolf. I sincerely hope to see some Antelopes to-morrow, as well as other animals.

June 18, Sunday. This day has been a beautiful, as well as a prosperous one to us. At daylight Provost and Alexis went off hunting across the river. Immediately after an early breakfast, Mr. Murray and three Mackinaw boats started for St. Louis. After the boats were fairly out of sight, and the six-pounders had been twice fired, and the great flag floated in the stiff southwesterly breeze, four other hunters went off over the river, and Squires was one of them. I took a walk with Mr. Culbertson and Mr. Chardon, to look at some old, decaying, and simply constructed coffins, placed on trees about ten feet above ground, for the purpose of finding out in what manner, and when it would be best for us to take away the skulls, some six or seven in number, all Assiniboin Indians. It was decided that we would do so at dusk, or nearly at dark. My two companions assured me that they never had walked so far from the fort unarmed as on this occasion, and said that even a *single* Indian with a gun and a bow might have attacked us; but if several were together, they would pay no attention to us, as that might be construed to mean war. This is a good lesson, however, and one I shall not forget. About ten o'clock Alexis came to me and said that he had killed two male Antelopes, and Provost one Deer, and that he must have a cart to bring the whole in. This was arranged in a few minutes; and Harris and I went across the river on a ferry flat, taking with us a cart and a most excellent mule. Alexis' wife went across also to gather gooseberries. The cart being made ready, we mounted it, I sitting down, and Harris standing up. We took an old abandoned road, filled with fallen timber and bushes innumerable; but Alexis proved to be an excellent driver, and the mule the most active and the strongest I ever saw. We jogged on through thick and thin for about two miles, when we reached a prairie covered with large bushes of Artemisia (called here "Herbe Sainte"), and presently, cutting down a slope, came to where lay our Antelope, a young male, and the skin of the Deer, while its carcass hung on a tree. These were placed in the cart, and we proceeded across the prairie for the other Antelope, which had been tied by the horns to a large bush of Artemisia, being alive when Alexis left it; but it was now dead and stiff. I looked at its eyes at once. This was a fine old male with its coat half shed. I was sorry enough it was dead. We placed it by its relation in the cart, jumped in, and off we went at a good round trot, not returning to the road, but across the prairie and immediately under the clay hills where the Antelope go after they have fed in the prairie below from early dawn until about eight o'clock; there are of course exceptions to the contrary. Part of the way we travelled between ponds made by the melting of the snows, and having on them a few Ducks and a Black Tern, all of which no doubt breed here. After we had passed the last pond, we saw three Antelopes several hundred yards to the lee of us; the moment they perceived us Alexis said they would be off; and so they were, scampering towards the hills until out of sight. We now entered the woods, and almost immediately Harris saw the head of a Deer about fifty yards distant. Alexis, who had only a rifle, would have shot him from the cart, had the mule stood still; but as this was not the case, Alexis jumped down, took a long, deliberate aim, the gun went off, and the Deer fell dead in its tracks. It proved to be a doe with very large milk-bags, and doubtless her fawn or fawns were in the vicinity; but Alexis could not find them in the dense bush. He and Harris dragged her to the cart, where I stood holding the mule. We reached the ferry, where the boat had awaited our return, placed the cart on board without touching the game; and, on landing at the fort, the good mule pulled it up the steep bank into the yard. We now had two Antelopes and two Deer that had been killed before noon. Immediately after dinner, the head of the old male was cut off, and I went to work outlining it; first small, with the camera, and then by squares. Bell was engaged in skinning both the bodies; but I felt vexed that he had carelessly suffered the Gray Wolf to be thrown into the river. I spoke to him on the subject of never losing a specimen till we were quite sure it would not be needed; and I feel well assured he is so honest a man and so good a worker that what I said will last for all time. While looking at the Deer shot this day, Harris and I thought that their tails were very long, and that the animals themselves were very much larger than those we have to the eastward; and we all concluded to have more killed, and examine and measure closely, as this one may be an exception. It was unfortunate we did not speak of this an hour sooner, as two Deer had been killed on this side the river by a hunter belonging to the fort; but Mr. Culbertson assured me that we should have enough of them in a few days. I am told that the Rocky Mountain Rams lost most of their young during the hard frosts of the early spring; for, like those of the common sheep, the lambs are born as early as the 1st of March, and hence their comparative scarcity. Harris and Bell have shot a handsome White Wolf, a female, from the ramparts; having both fired together, it is not known which shot was the fatal one. Bell wounded another in the leg, as there were several marauders about; but the rascal made off.

June 19, Monday. It began raining early this morning; by "early," I mean fully two hours before daylight. The first news I heard was from Mr. Chardon, who told me he had left a Wolf feeding out of the pig's trough, which is immediately under the side of the fort. The next was from Mr. Larpenteur, who opens the gates when the bell rings at sunrise, who told us he saw seven Wolves within thirty yards, or less, of the fort. I have told him since, with Mr. Chardon's permission, to call upon us before he opens these mighty portals, whenever he espies Wolves from the gallery above, and I hope that to-morrow morning we may shoot one or more of these bold marauders. Sprague has been drawing all day, and I a good part of it; and it has been so chilly and cold that we have had fires in several parts of the fort. Bell and Harris have gone shooting this afternoon, and have not yet returned. Bell cleaned the Wolf shot last night, and the two Antelopes; old Provost boiled brine, and the whole of them are now in pickle. There are some notions that two kinds of Deer are found hereabouts, one quite small, the other quite large; but of this I have no proof at present. The weather was too bad for Alexis to go hunting. Young Mr. McKenzie and a companion went across the river, but returned soon afterwards, having seen nothing but one Grizzly Bear. The water is either at a stand, or falling a little.—*Later*. Harris and Bell have returned, and, to my delight and utter astonishment, have brought two new birds: one a Lark, small and beautiful; the other like our common Golden-winged Woodpecker, but with a red mark instead of a black one along the lower mandible running backward. I am quite amazed at the differences of opinion respecting the shedding—or not shedding—of the horns of the Antelope; and this must be looked to with the greatest severity, for if these animals *do* shed their horns, they are no longer *Antelopes*. We are about having quite a ball in honor of Mr. Chardon, who leaves shortly for the Blackfoot Fort.

June 20, Tuesday. It rained nearly all night; and though the ball was given, I saw nothing of it, and heard but little, for I went to bed and to sleep. Sprague finished the drawing of the old male Antelope, and I mine, taking besides the measurements, etc., which I give here. . . . Bell has skinned the head and put it in pickle. The weather was bad, yet old Provost, Alexis, and Mr. Bonaventure, a good hunter and a first-rate shot, went over the river to hunt. They returned, however, without anything, though they saw three or four Deer, and a Wolf almost black, with very long hair, which Provost followed for more than a mile, but uselessly, as the rascal outwitted him after all. Harris and Bell are gone too, and I hope they will bring some more specimens of Sprague's Lark and the new Golden-winged Woodpecker.

To fill the time on this dreary day, I asked Mr. Chardon to come up to our room and give us an account of the small-pox among the Indians, especially among the Mandans and Riccarees, and he related as follows: Early in the month of July, 1837, the steamer "Assiniboin" arrived at Fort Clark with many cases of small-pox on board. Mr. Chardon, having a young son on the boat, went thirty miles to meet her, and took his son away. The pestilence, however, had many victims on the steamboat, and seemed destined to find many more among the helpless tribes of the wilderness. An Indian stole the blanket of one of the steamboat's watchmen (who lay at the point of death, if not already dead), wrapped himself in it, and carried it off, unaware of the disease that was to cost him his life, and that of many of his tribe—thousands, indeed. Mr. Chardon offered a reward immediately for the return of the blanket, as well as a new one in its stead, and promised that no punishment should be inflicted. But the robber was a great chief; through shame, or some other motive, he never came forward, and, before many days, was a corpse. Most of the Riccarees and Mandans were some eighty miles in the prairies, hunting Buffaloes and saving meat for the winter. Mr. Chardon despatched an express to acquaint them all of the awful calamity, enjoining them to keep far off, for that death would await them in their villages. They sent word in return, that their corn was suffering for want of work, that they were not afraid, and would return; the danger to them, poor things, seemed fabulous, and doubtless they thought other reasons existed, for which this was an excuse. Mr. Chardon sent the man back again, and told them their crop of corn was nothing compared to their lives; but Indians are Indians, and, in spite of all entreaties, they moved *en masse*, to confront the awful catastrophe that was about to follow. When they reached the villages, they thought the whites had saved the Riccarees, and put the plague on them alone (they were Mandans). Moreover, they thought, and said, that the whites had a preventive medicine, which the whites would not give them. Again and again it was explained to them that this was not the case, but all to no purpose; the small-pox had taken such a hold upon the poor Indians, and in such malignant form, that they died oftentimes within the rising and setting of a day's sun. They died by hundreds daily; their bodies were thrown down beneath the high bluff, and soon produced a stench beyond description. Men shot their wives and children, and afterwards, driving several balls in their guns, would place the muzzle in their mouths, and, touching the trigger with their feet, blow their brains out. About this time Mr. Chardon was informed that one of the young Mandan chiefs was bent on shooting him, believing he had brought the pestilence upon the Indians. One of Mr. Chardon's clerks heard of this plot, and begged him to remain in the store; at first Mr. Chardon did not place any faith in the tale, but later was compelled to do so, and followed his clerk's advice. The young chief, a short time afterwards, fell a victim to this fearful malady; but probably others would have taken his life had it not been for one of those strange incidents which come, we know not why, nor can we explain them. A number of the chiefs came that day to confer with Mr. Chardon, and while they were talking angrily with him, he sitting with his arms on a table between them, a Dove, being pursued by a Hawk, flew in through the open door, and sat panting and worn out on Mr. Chardon's arm for more than a minute, when it flew off. The Indians, who were quite numerous, clustered about him, and asked him what the bird came to him for? After a moment's thought, he told them that the bird had been sent by the white men, his friends, to see if it was true that the Mandans had killed him, and that it must return with the answer as soon as possible; he added he had told the Dove to say that the Mandans were his friends, and would never kill him, but would do all they could for him. The superstitious redmen believed this story implicitly; thenceforth they looked on Mr. Chardon as one of the Great Spirit's sons, and believed he alone could help them. Little, however, could be done; the small-pox continued its fearful ravages, and the Indians grew fewer and fewer day by day. For a long time the Riccarees did not suffer; the Mandans became more and more astounded at this, and became exasperated against both whites and Indians. The disease was of the most virulent type, so that within a few hours after death the bodies were a mass of rottenness. Men killed themselves, to die a nobler death than that brought by the dreaded plague. One young warrior sent his wife to dig his grave; and she went, of course, for no Indian woman dares disobey her lord. The grave was dug, and the warrior, dressed in his most superb apparel, with lance and shield in hand, walked towards it singing his own death song, and, finding the grave finished, threw down all his garments and arms, and leaped into it, drawing his knife as he did so, and cutting his body almost asunder. This done, the earth was thrown over him, the grave filled up, and the woman returned to her lodge to live with her children, perhaps only another day. A great chief, who had been a constant friend to the whites, having caught the pest, and being almost at the last extremity, dressed himself in his fineries, mounted his war-steed, and, fevered and in agony, rode among the villages, speaking against the whites, urging the young warriors to charge upon them and destroy them all. The harangue over, he went home, and died not many hours afterward. The exposure and exertion brought on great pains, and one of the men from the fort went to him with something that gave him temporary relief; before he died, he acknowledged his error in trying to create trouble between the whites and Indians, and it was his wish to be buried in front of the gate of the fort, with all his trophies around and above his body; the promise was given him that this should be done, and he died in the belief that the white man, as he trod on his grave, would see that he was humbled before him, and would forgive him. Two young men, just sickening with the disease, began to talk of the dreadful death that awaited them, and resolved not to wait for the natural close of the malady, the effects of which they had seen among their friends and relatives. One said the knife was the surest and swiftest weapon to carry into effect their proposed self-destruction; the other contended that placing an arrow in the throat and forcing it into the lungs was preferable. After a long debate they calmly rose, and each adopted his own method; in an instant the knife was driven into the heart of one, the arrow into the throat of the other, and they fell dead almost at the same instant. Another story was of an extremely handsome and powerful Indian who lost an only son, a beautiful boy, upon whom all his hopes and affections were placed. The loss proved too much for him; he called his wife, and, after telling her what a faithful husband he had been, said to her, "Why should we live? all we cared for is taken from us, and why not at once join our child in the land of the Great Spirit?" She consented; in an instant he shot her dead on the spot, reloaded his gun, put the muzzle in his mouth, touched the trigger, and fell back dead. On the same day another curious incident occurred; a young man, covered with the eruption, and apparently on the eve of death, managed to get to a deep puddle of mire or mud, threw himself in it, and rolled over and over as a Buffalo is wont to do. The sun was scorching hot, and the poor fellow got out of the mire covered with a coating of clay fully half an inch thick and laid himself down; the sun's heat soon dried the clay, so as to render it like unburnt bricks, and as he walked or crawled along towards the village, the mud drying and falling from him, taking the skin with it, and leaving the flesh raw and bleeding, he was in agony, and besought those who passed to kill him; but, strange to say, after enduring tortures, the fever left him, he recovered, and is still living, though badly scarred. Many ran to the river, in the delirium of the burning fever, plunged in the stream, and rose no more. The whites in the fort, as well as the Riccarees, took the disease after all. The Indians, with few exceptions, died, and three of the whites. The latter had no food in the way of bread, flour, sugar, or coffee, and they had to go stealthily by night to steal small pumpkins, about the size of a man's fist, to subsist upon—and this amid a large number of wild, raving, mad Indians, who swore revenge against them all the while. This is a mere sketch of the terrible scourge which virtually annihilated two powerful tribes of Indians, and of the trials of the traders attached to the Fur Companies on these wild prairies, and I can tell you of many more equally strange. The mortality, as taken down by Major Mitchell, was estimated by that gentleman at 150,000 Indians, including those from the tribes of the Riccarees, Mandans, Sioux, and Blackfeet. The small-pox was in the very fort from which I am now writing this account, and its ravages here were as awful as elsewhere. Mr. Chardon had the disease, and was left for dead; but one of his clerks saw signs of life, and forced him to drink a quantity of hot whiskey mixed with water and nutmeg; he fell into a sound sleep, and his recovery began from that hour. He says that with him the pains began in the small of the back, and on the back part of his head, and were intense. He concluded by assuring us all that the small-pox had never been known in the civilized world, as it had been among the poor Mandans and other Indians. Only *twenty-seven* Mandans were left to tell the tale; they have now augmented to ten or twelve lodges in the six years that have nearly elapsed since the pestilence.

Harris and Bell came back bringing several small birds, among which three or four proved to be a Blackbird nearly allied to the Rusty Grakle, but with evidently a much shorter and straighter bill. Its measurements will be given, of course. The weather is still lowering and cold, and it rains at intervals. We are now out of specimens of quadrupeds to draw from. Our gentlemen seem to remember the ball of last night, and I doubt not will go early to bed, as I shall.

June 21, Wednesday. Cloudy and lowering weather; however, Provost went off over the river, before daylight, and shot a Deer, of what kind we do not know; he returned about noon, very hungry. The mud was dreadful in the bottoms. Bell and young McKenzie went off after breakfast, but brought nothing but a Sharp-tailed Grouse, though McKenzie shot two Wolves. The one Harris shot last night proved to be an old female not worth keeping; her companions had seamed her jaws, for in this part of the world Wolves feed upon Wolves, and no mistake. This evening I hauled the beast under the ramparts, cut her body open, and had a stake driven quite fast through it, to hold it as a bait. Harris and Bell are this moment on the lookout for the rascals. Wolves here not only eat their own kind, but are the most mischievous animals in the country; they eat the young Buffalo calves, the young Antelopes, and the young of the Bighorn on all occasions, besides Hares of different sorts, etc. Buffaloes never scrape the snow with their feet, but with their noses, notwithstanding all that has been said to the contrary, even by Mr. Catlin. Bell brought home the hind parts, the head, and one forefoot of a new species of small Hare.

We are told these Hares are very plentiful, and yet this is the first specimen we have seen, and sorry am I that it amounts to no specimen at all. Harris and I walked several miles, but killed nothing; we found the nest of a Sparrow-hawk, and Harris, assisted by my shoulders, reached the nest, and drew out two eggs. Sprague went across the hills eastward, and was fortunate enough to shoot a superb specimen of the Arctic Bluebird. This evening, Mr. Culbertson having told me the Rabbits, such as Bell had brought, were plentiful on the road to the steamboat landing, Harris, Bell, and I walked there; but although we were very cautious, we saw none, and only procured a Black-headed Grosbeak, which was shot whilst singing delightfully. To-morrow morning Mr. Chardon leaves us in the keel-boat for the Blackfoot Fort, and Mr. Kipp will leave for the Crows early next week.

June 22, Thursday. We rose very late this morning, with the exception of Provost who went out shooting quite early; but he saw nothing fit for his rifle. All was bustle after breakfast, as Mr. Chardon's boat was loading, the rigging being put in order, the men moving their effects, etc., and a number of squaws, the wives of the men, were moving to and fro for hours before the ultimate departure of the boat, which is called the "Bee." The cargo being arranged, thirty men went on board, including the commander, friend Chardon, thirteen squaws, and a number of children, all more or less half-breeds. The flag of Fort Union was hoisted, the four-pounder run out of the front gate, and by eleven o'clock all was ready. The keel-boat had a brass swivel on her bows, and fired first, then off went the larger gun, and many an Antelope and Deer were doubtless frightened at the report that echoed through the hills far and near. We bid adieu to our good friend Chardon; and his numerous and willing crew, taking the cordelle to their shoulders, moved the boat against a strong current in good style. Harris and Bell had gone shooting and returned with several birds, among which was a female Red-patched Woodpecker, and a Lazuli Finch. Dinner over, I went off with young McKenzie after Hares; found none, but started a Grizzly Bear from her lair. Owen McKenzie followed the Bear and I continued after Hares; he saw no more of Bruin, and I not a Hare, and we both returned to the fort after a tramp of three hours. As I was walking over the prairie, I found an Indian's skull (an Assiniboin) and put it in my game pouch. Provost made a whistle to imitate the noise made by the fawns at this season, which is used to great advantage to decoy the female Deer; shortly afterward Mr. Bonaventure returned, and a cart was sent off at once to bring in a doe which he had killed below. This species of Deer is much larger than the one we have in Virginia, but perhaps no more so than those in Maine; and as yet we cannot tell whether it may, or may not, prove a distinct species. We took all its measurements, and Bell and Provost are now skinning it. Its gross weight is 140 lbs., which I think is heavier than any doe I have seen before. The animal is very poor and evidently has fawns in the woods. The little new Lark that I have named after Sprague has almost all the habits of the Skylark of Europe. Whilst looking anxiously after it, on the ground where we supposed it to be singing, we discovered it was high over our heads, and that sometimes it went too high for us to see it at all. We have not yet been able to discover its nest. Bell is of opinion that the Red-collared Ground Finch has its nest in the deserted holes of the Ground Squirrel, and we intend to investigate this. He also believes that Say's Flycatcher builds in rocky caverns or fissures, as he found the nest of a bird in some such place, after having wounded one of this species, which retired into the fissures of the rock, which he examined in pursuit of the wounded bird. The nest had no eggs; we are going to pay it a visit. Bell was busy most of the day skinning birds, and Sprague drew a beautiful plant. I found a number of wild roses in bloom, quite sweet-scented, though single, and of a very pale rose-color.

June 23, Friday. We have had a fine, warm day. The hunters of Buffaloes started before daylight, and Squires accompanied them; they are not expected back till sometime to-morrow. Provost went across the river with them, and with the assistance of his bleating whistle, brought several does round him, and a good many Wolves. He killed two does, drew them to a tree, and hung his coat near them while he returned for help to bring them to the fort. The hunters have a belief that a garment hung near game freshly killed will keep the Wolves at bay for a time; but there are exceptions to all rules, as when he returned with the cart, a dozen hungry rascals of Wolves had completely devoured one doe and all but one ham of the other; this he brought to the fort. The does at this season, on hearing the "bleat," run to the spot, supposing, no doubt, that the Wolves have attacked their fawns, and in rushing to the rescue, run towards the hunter, who despatches them without much trouble, unless the woods are thickly overgrown with bushes and brush, when more difficulty is experienced in seeing them, although one may hear them close by; but it is a cruel, deceitful, and unsportsmanlike method, of which I can never avail myself, and which I try to discountenance. Bell was busy all day with skins, and Sprague with flowers, which he delineates finely. Mr. Kipp presented me with a complete dress of a Blackfoot warrior, ornamented with many tufts of Indian hair from scalps, and also with a saddle. After dinner, Harris, who felt poorly all morning, was better, and we went to pay a visit at the Opposition fort. We started in a wagon with an old horse called Peter, which stands fire like a stump. In going, we found we could approach the birds with comparative ease, and we had the good fortune to shoot three of the new Larks. I killed two, and Harris one. When this species starts from the ground, they fly in a succession of undulations, which renders aim at them quite difficult; after this, and in the same manner, they elevate themselves to some considerable height, as if about to sing, and presently pitch towards the ground, where they run prettily, and at times stand still and quite erect for a few minutes; we hope to discover their nests soon. Young Meadow Larks, Red-shafted Woodpeckers, and the Red-cheeked ditto, are abundant. We reached Fort Mortimer in due time; passed first between several sulky, half-starved looking Indians, and came to the gate, where we were received by the "bourgeois," a young man by the name of Collins, from Hopkinsville, Ky. We found the place in a most miserable condition, and about to be carried away by the falling in of the banks on account of the great rise of water in the Yellowstone, that has actually dammed the Missouri. The current ran directly across, and the banks gave way at such a rate that the men had been obliged already to tear up the front of the fort and remove it to the rear. To-morrow they are to remove the houses themselves, should they stand the coming night, which appeared to me somewhat dubious. We saw a large athletic man who has crossed the mountains twice to the Pacific; he is a Philadelphian, named Wallis, who had been a cook at Fort Union four years, but who had finally deserted, lived for a time with the Crows, and then joined the Opposition. These persons were very polite to us, and invited us to remain and take supper with them; but as I knew they were short of provisions, I would not impose myself upon them, and so, with thanks for their hospitality, we excused ourselves and returned to Fort Union. As we were in search of birds, we saw a small, whitish-colored Wolf trotting across the prairie, which hereabouts is very extensive and looks well, though the soil is poor. We put Peter to a trot and gained on the Wolf, which did not see us until we were about one hundred yards off; he stopped suddenly, and then went off at a canter. Harris gave the whip to Peter, and off we went, evidently gaining rapidly on the beast, when it saw an Indian in its road; taking fright, it dashed to one side, and was soon lost in a ravine. We congratulated ourselves, on reaching the fort, that we had such good fortune as to be able to sup and sleep here, instead of at Fort Mortimer. Bell had taken a walk and brought in a few birds. The prairie is covered with cacti, and Harris and I suffered by them; my feet were badly pricked by the thorns, which penetrated my boots at the junction of the soles with the upper leathers. I have to-day heard several strange stories about Grizzly Bears, all of which I must have corroborated before I fully accept them. The Otters and Musk-rats of this part of the country are smaller than in the States; the first is the worst enemy that the Beaver has.

June 24, Saturday. Bell killed a small Wolf last night, and Harris wounded another. This morning Provost started at daylight, and Bell followed him; but they returned without game. After breakfast Harris went off on horseback, and brought in a Sharp-tailed Grouse. He saw only one Deer, species not identified. Sprague and I went off last, but brought in nothing new. This afternoon I thought would be a fair opportunity to examine the manners of Sprague's Lark on the wing. Bell drove Peter for me, and I killed four Larks; we then watched the flight of several. The male rises by constant undulations to a great height, say one hundred yards or more; and whilst singing its sweet-sounding notes, beats its wings, poised in the air like a Hawk, without rising at this time; after which, and after each burst of singing, it sails in divers directions, forming three quarters of a circle or thereabouts, then rises again, and again sings; the intervals between the singing are longer than those which the song occupies, and at times the bird remains so long in the air as to render it quite fatiguing to follow it with the eye. Sprague thought one he watched yesterday remained in the air about one hour. Bell and Harris watched one for more than half an hour, and this afternoon I gazed upon one, whilst Bell timed it, for thirty-six minutes. We continued on to Fort Mortimer to see its condition, were received as kindly as yesterday, and saw the same persons. It was four o'clock, and the men were all at dinner, having been obliged to wait until this time because they had no meat in the fort, and their hunters had returned only one hour and a half before. We found that the river had fallen about fourteen inches since last evening, and the men would not remove for the present. On our way homeward Bell shot a fifth Lark, and when we reached the ravine I cut out of a tree-stump the nest of an Arctic Bluebird, with six eggs in it, of almost the same size and color as those of the common Bluebird. Sprague had brought a female of his Lark, and her nest containing five eggs; the measurements of these two species I will write out to-morrow. Our Buffalo hunters are not yet returned, and I think that Squires will feel pretty well fatigued when he reaches the fort. Mr. Culbertson presented me with a pair of stirrups, and a most splendid Blackfoot crupper for my saddle. The day has been warm and clear. We caught seven catfish at the river near the fort, and most excellent eating they are, though quite small when compared with the monsters of this species on the Missouri below.

June 25, Sunday. This day has been warm and the wind high, at first from the south, but this afternoon from the north. Little or nothing has been done in the way of procuring birds or game, except that Harris and Mr. Denig brought in several Arkansas Flycatchers. Not a word from the hunters, and therefore they must have gone far before they met Buffaloes. A few more catfish have been caught, and they are truly excellent.

June 26, Monday. The hunters returned this afternoon about three o'clock; *i.e.*, Squires and McKenzie; but the carts did not reach the fort till after I had gone to bed. They have killed three Antelopes, three bull Buffaloes, and one Townsend's Hare, but the last was lost through carelessness, and I am sorry for it. The men had eaten one of the Antelopes, and the two others are fine males; Bell skinned one, and saved the head and the fore-legs of the other. One of them had the tips of the horns as much crooked inwardly (backwards) as the horns of the European Chamois usually are. This afternoon early Provost brought in a Deer of the large kind, and this also was skinned. After this Harris and Bell went off and brought in several Lazuli Finches, and a black Prairie Lark Finch of the species brought from the Columbia by Townsend and Nuttall. We caught several catfish and a very curious sturgeon, of which Sprague took an outline with the camera, and I here give the measurements. . . . It had run on the shore, and was caught by one of the men. I made a bargain this morning with the hunter Bonaventure Le Brun to procure me ten Bighorns, at $10.00 apiece, or the same price for any number he may get. Mr. Culbertson lent him old Peter, the horse, and I wrote a *petit billet* to Mr. John Collins, to ask him to have them ferried across the river, as our boat was away on a wood-cutting expedition. As Le Brun did not return, of course he was taken across, and may, perhaps, come back this evening, or early to-morrow morning, with something worth having. At this moment Bell has shot a Wolf from the ramparts, and sadly crippled another, but it made off somehow.

June 27, Tuesday. This morning was quite cool, and the wind from the north. After breakfast Bell and Owen McKenzie went off on horseback on this side of the river, to see how far off the Buffaloes are, and they may probably bring home some game. Sprague and I have been drawing all day yesterday and most of to-day. Provost has been making whistles to call the Deer; later he, Harris, and I, walked to the hills to procure the black root plant which is said to be the best antidote for the bite of the rattlesnake. We found the root and dug one up, but the plant is not yet in bloom. The leaves are long and narrow, and the flowers are said to resemble the dwarf sunflower. Harris shot two of what he calls the Small Shore Lark, male and female; but beyond the size being a little smaller than those found at Labrador, I cannot discover any specific difference. From the top of the hills we saw a grand panorama of a most extensive wilderness, with Fort Union beneath us and far away, as well as the Yellowstone River, and the lake across the river. The hills across the Missouri appeared quite low, and we could see the high prairie beyond, forming the background. Bell and McKenzie returned, having shot a Wolf in a curious manner. On reaching the top of a hill they found themselves close to the Wolf. Bell's horse ran quite past it, but young McKenzie shot and broke one fore-leg, and it fell. Bell then gave his horse to McKenzie, jumped off, ran to the Wolf, and took hold of it by the tail, pulling it towards the horses; but it got up and ran rapidly. Bell fired two shots in its back with a pistol without stopping it, then he ran as fast as he could, shot it in the side, and it fell. Bell says its tail was longer than usual, but it was not measured, and the Wolf was left on the prairie, as they had no means of bringing it in. They saw an Antelope, some Magpies, and a Swift Fox, but no Buffaloes, though they were fifteen miles from the fort. They ran a Long-tailed Deer, and describe its movements precisely as do Lewis and Clark. Between every three or four short leaps came the long leap of fully twenty-five feet, if not more. The Kit or Swift Fox which they saw stood by a bunch of wormwood, and whilst looking at the hunters, was seen to brush off the flies with his paws.

I am now going to take this book to Lewis Squires and ask him to write in it his account of the Buffalo hunt.

(The following is in Mr. Squires' handwriting:)

"By Mr. Audubon's desire I will relate the adventures that befell me in my first Buffalo hunt, and I am in hopes that among the rubbish a trifle, at least, may be obtained which may be of use or interest to him. On the morning of Friday, the 23d, before daylight, I was up, and in a short time young McKenzie made his appearance. A few minutes sufficed to saddle our horses, and be in readiness for our contemplated hunt. We were accompanied by Mr. Bonaventure the younger, one of the hunters of the fort, and two carts to bring in whatever kind of meat might be procured. We were ferried across the river in a flatboat, and thence took our departure for the Buffalo country. We passed through a wooded bottom for about one mile, and then over a level prairie for about one mile and a half, when we commenced the ascent of the bluffs that bound the western side of the Missouri valley; our course then lay over an undulating prairie, quite rough, and steep hills with small ravines between, and over dry beds of streams that are made by the spring and fall freshets. Occasionally we were favored with a level prairie never exceeding two miles in extent. When the carts overtook us, we exchanged our horses for them, and sat on Buffalo robes on the bottom, our horses following on behind us. As we neared the place where the Buffaloes had been killed on the previous hunt, Bonaventure rode alone to the top of a hill to discover, if possible, their whereabouts; but to our disappointment nothing living was to be seen. We continued on our way watching closely, ahead, right and left. Three o'clock came and as yet nothing had been killed; as none of us had eaten anything since the night before, our appetites admonished us that it was time to pay attention to them. McKenzie and Bonaventure began to look about for Antelopes; but before any were 'comeatable,' I fell asleep, and was awakened by the report of a gun. Before we, in the carts, arrived at the spot from whence this report proceeded, the hunters had killed, skinned, and nearly cleaned the game, which was a fine male Antelope. I regretted exceedingly I was not awake when it was killed, as I might have saved the skin for Mr. Audubon, as well as the head, but I was too late. It was now about five o'clock, and one may well imagine I was *somewhat* hungry. Owen McKenzie commenced eating the raw liver, and offered me a piece. What others can eat, I felt assured I could at least taste. I accordingly took it and ate quite a piece of it; to my utter astonishment, I found it not only palatable but very good; this experience goes far to convince me that our prejudices make things appear more disgusting than fact proves them to be. Our Antelope cut up and in the cart, we proceeded on our 'winding way,' and scarcely had we left the spot where the entrails of the animal remained, before the Wolves and Ravens commenced coming from all quarters, and from places where a minute before there was not a sign of one. We had not proceeded three hundred yards at the utmost, before eight Wolves were about the spot, and others approaching. On our way, both going and returning, we saw a cactus of a conical shape, having a light straw-colored, double flower, differing materially from the flower of the flat cactus, which is quite common; had I had any means of bringing one in, I would most gladly have done so, but I could not depend on the carts, and as they are rather unpleasant companions, I preferred awaiting another opportunity, which I hope may come in a few days. We shot a young of Townsend's Hare, about seven or eight steps from us, with about a dozen shot; I took good care of it until I left the cart on my return to the fort, but when the carts arrived it had carelessly been lost. This I regretted very much, as Mr. Audubon wanted it. It was nearly sunset when Bonaventure discovered a Buffalo bull, so we concluded to encamp for the night, and run the Buffaloes in the morning. We accordingly selected a spot near a pond of water, which in spring and fall is quite a large lake, and near which there was abundance of good pasture; our horses were soon unsaddled and hoppled, a good fire blazing, and some of the Antelope meat roasting on sticks before it. As soon as a bit was done, we commenced operations, and it was soon gone 'the way of all flesh.' I never before ate meat without salt or pepper, and until then never fully appreciated these two *luxuries,* as they now seemed, nor can any one, until deprived of them, and seated on a prairie as we were, or in some similar situation. On the opposite side of the lake we saw a Grizzly Bear, but he was unapproachable. After smoking our pipes we rolled ourselves in our robes, with our saddles for pillows, and were soon lost in a sound, sweet sleep. During the night I was awakened by a crunching sound; the fire had died down, and I sat up and looking about perceived a Wolf quietly feeding on the remains of our supper. One of the men awoke at the same time and fired at the Wolf, but without effect, and the fellow fled; we neither saw nor heard more of him during the night. By daylight we were all up, and as our horses had not wandered far, it was the work of a few minutes to catch and saddle them. We rode three or four miles before we discovered anything, but at last saw a group of three Buffaloes some miles from us. We pushed on, and soon neared them; before arriving at their feeding-ground, we saw, scattered about, immense quantities of pumice-stone, in detached pieces of all sizes; several of the hills appeared to be composed wholly of it. As we approached within two hundred yards of the Buffaloes they started, and away went the hunters after them. My first intention of being merely a looker-on continued up to this moment, but it was impossible to resist following; almost unconsciously I commenced urging my horse after them, and was soon rushing up hills and through ravines; but my horse gave out, and disappointment and anger followed, as McKenzie and Bonaventure succeeded in killing two, and wounding a third, which escaped. As soon as they had finished them, they commenced skinning and cutting up one, which was soon in the cart, the offal and useless meat being left on the ground. Again the Wolves made their appearance as we were leaving; they seemed shy, but Owen McKenzie succeeded in killing one, which was old and useless. The other

Buffalo was soon skinned and in the cart. In the meantime McKenzie and I started on horseback for water. The man who had charge of the keg had let it all run out, and most fortunately none of us had wanted water until now. We rode to a pond, the water of which was very salt and warm, but we had to drink this or none; we did so, filled our flasks for the rest of the party, and a few minutes afterward rejoined them. We started again for more meat to complete our load. I observed, as we approached the Buffaloes, that they stood gazing at us with their heads erect, lashing their sides with their tails; as soon as they discovered what we were at, with the quickness of thought they wheeled, and with the most surprising speed, for an animal apparently so clumsy and awkward, flew before us. I could hardly imagine that these enormous animals could move so quickly, or realize that their speed was as great as it proved to be; and I doubt if in this country one horse in ten can be found that will keep up with them. We rode five or six miles before we discovered any more. At last we saw a single bull, and while approaching him we started two others; slowly we wended our way towards them until within a hundred yards, when away they went. I had now begun to enter into the spirit of the chase, and off I started, full speed, down a rough hill in swift pursuit; at the bottom of the hill was a ditch about eight feet wide; the horse cleared this safely. I continued, leading the others by some distance, and rapidly approaching the Buffaloes. At this prospect of success my feelings can better be imagined than described. I kept the lead of the others till within thirty or forty yards of the Buffaloes, when I began making preparations to fire as soon as I was sufficiently near; imagine, if possible, my disappointment when I discovered that now, when all my hopes of success were raised to the highest pitch, I was fated to meet a reverse as mortifying as success would have been gratifying. My horse failed, and slackened his pace, despite every effort of mine to urge him on; the other hunters rushed by me at full speed, and my horse stopped altogether. I saw the others fire; the animal swerved a little, but still kept on. After breathing my horse a while, I succeeded in starting him up again, followed after them, and came up in time to fire one shot ere the animal was brought down. I think that I never saw an eye so ferocious in expression as that of the wounded Buffalo; rolling wildly in its socket, inflamed as the eye was, it had the most frightful appearance that can be imagined; and in fact, the picture presented by the Buffalo as a whole is quite beyond my powers of description. The fierce eyes, blood streaming from his sides, mouth, and nostrils, he was the wildest, most unearthly-looking thing it ever fell to my lot to gaze upon. His sufferings were short; he was soon cut up and placed in the cart, and we retraced our steps homeward. Whilst proceeding towards our camping-ground for the night, two Antelopes were killed, and placed on our carts. Whenever we approached these animals they were very curious to see what we were; they would run, first to the right, and then to the left, then suddenly run straight towards us until within gun-shot, or nearly so. The horse attracted their attention more than the rider, and if a slight elevation or bush was between us, they were easily killed. As soon as their curiosity was gratified they would turn and run, but it was not difficult to shoot before this occurred. When they turned they would fly over the prairie for about a mile, when they would again stop and look at us. During the day we suffered very much for want of water, and drank anything that had the appearance of it, and most of the water, in fact all of it, was either impregnated with salt, sulphur, or magnesia—most disgusting stuff at any other time, but drinkable now. The worst of all was some rain-water that we were obliged to drink, first placing our handkerchiefs over the cup to strain it, and keep the worms out of our mouths. I drank it, and right glad was I to get even this. We rode about five miles to where we encamped for the night, near a little pond of water. In a few minutes we had a good fire of Buffalo dung to drive away mosquitoes that were in clouds about us. The water had taken away our appetites completely, and we went to bed without eating any supper. Our horses and beds were arranged as on the previous evening. McKenzie and I intended starting for the fort early in the morning. We saw a great many Magpies, Curlews, Plovers, Doves, and numbers of Antelopes. About daylight I awoke and roused McKenzie; a man had gone for the horses, but after a search of two hours returned without finding them; all the party now went off except one man and myself, and all returned without success except Bonaventure, who found an old horse that had been lost since April last. He was despatched on this to the fort to get other horses, as we had concluded that ours were either lost or stolen. As soon as he had gone, one of the men started again in search of the runaways, and in a short time returned with them. McKenzie and I soon rode off. We saw two Grizzly Bears at the lake again. Our homeward road we made much shorter by cutting off several turns; we overtook Bonaventure about four miles from our encampment, and passed him. We rode forty miles to the fort in a trifle over six hours. We had travelled in all about one hundred and twenty miles. Bonaventure arrived two hours after we did, and the carts came in the evening."

Wednesday, June 28. This is an account of Squires' Buffalo hunt, his first one, which he has kindly written in my journal and which I hope some day to publish. This morning was very cloudy, and we had some rain, but from ten o'clock until this moment the weather has been beautiful. Harris shot a handsome though rather small Wolf; I have made a large drawing, and Sprague a fine diminished one, of the rascal. The first news we had this morning was that the ferry flat had been stolen last night, probably by the deserters from the fort who have had the wish to return to St. Louis. Some person outside of the fort threw a large stone at an Indian woman, and her husband fired in the dark, but no one could be found on searching. There is much trouble and discomfort to the managers of such an establishment as this. Provost went shooting, but saw nothing. Young McKenzie and another man were sent to find the scow, but in vain. On their return they said a hunter from Fort Mortimer had brought a Bighorn, and skinned it, and that he would let me have it if I wished. I sent Bell and Squires, and they brought the skin in. It proves to be that of an old female in the act of shedding her winter coat, and I found that she was covered with abundance of downy wool like the Antelopes under similar circumstances. Mr. Larpenteur caught five small catfish, which we ate at breakfast. After dinner Le Brun returned home, but brought only the skin of a young female of the White-tailed Deer, and I was surprised to see that it had the germ of a horn about one inch long; the skin was quite red, and it is saved. A young Elk was brought in good condition, as the hunters here know how to save skins properly; it was too young, however, to take measurements. The horns were in velvet about six inches long. When one sees the powerful bones and muscles of this young animal, one cannot fail to think of the great strength of the creature when mature, and its ability to bear with ease the enormous antlers with which its head is surmounted. The flesh of the Antelope is not comparable with that of the Deer, being dry and usually tough. It is very rarely indeed that a fat Antelope is killed. Bell has been very busy in skinning small birds and animals. We procured a young Red-shafted Woodpecker, killed by an Indian boy with a bow and arrow. Mr. Kipp's "Mackinaw" was launched this evening, and sent across the river with men to relieve the charcoal-burners; she returned immediately and we expect that Mr. Kipp's crew will go off to-morrow about twelve. I was told a curious anecdote connected with a Grizzly Bear, that I will write down; it is as follows: One of the *engagés* of the Company was forced to run away, having killed an Indian woman, and made his way to the Crow Fort, three hundred miles up the Yellowstone River. When he arrived there he was in sad plight, having his own squaw and one or two children along, who had all suffered greatly with hunger, thirst, and exposure. They were received at the fort, but in a short time, less than a week afterwards, he again ran off with his family, and on foot. The discovery was soon made, and two men were sent after him; but he eluded their vigilance by keeping close in ravines, etc. The men returned, and two others with an Indian were despatched on a second search, and after much travel saw the man and his family on an island, where he had taken refuge from his pursuers. The Buffalo-hide canoe in which he had attempted to cross the river was upset, and it was with difficulty that he saved his wife and children. They were now unable to escape, and when talking as to the best way to secure their return to the fort, the soldiers saw him walk to the body of a dead Buffalo lying on the shore of the island, with the evident intention of procuring some of it for food. As he stooped to cut off a portion, to his utter horror he saw a small Grizzly Bear crawl out from the carcass. It attacked him fiercely, and so suddenly that he was unable to defend himself; the Bear lacerated his face, arms, and the upper part of his body in a frightful manner, and would have killed him, had not the Indian raised his gun and fired at the Bear, wounding him severely, while a second shot killed him. The *engagé* was too much hurt to make further effort to escape, and one of the Company's boats passing soon after, he and his family were taken back to the fort, where he was kept to await his trial.

June 29, Thursday. It rained hard during the night, but at dawn Provost went shooting and returned to dinner, having shot a doe, which was skinned and the meat saved. He saw a Grouse within a few feet of him, but did not shoot, as he had only a rifle. Bell and I took a long walk, and shot several birds. We both were surprised to find a flock of Cliff Swallows endeavoring to build nests beneath the ledges of a clay bank. Watching the moment when several had alighted against the bank, I fired, and killed three. Previous to this, as I was walking along a ravine, a White Wolf ran past within fifteen or twenty paces of me, but I had only very small shot, and did not care to wound where I could not kill. The fellow went off at a limping gallop, and Bell after it, squatting whenever the Wolf stopped to look at him; but at last the rascal lost himself in a deep ravine, and a few minutes after we saw him emerge from the shrubs some distance off, and go across the prairie towards the river. Bell saw two others afterwards, and if ever there was a country where Wolves are surpassingly abundant, it is the one we now are in. Wolves are in the habit of often lying down on the prairies, where they form quite a bed, working at bones the while. We found a nest of the Prairie Lark, with four eggs. We saw Arctic Bluebirds, Say's Flycatcher and Lazuli Finches. Say's Flycatcher has a note almost like the common Pewee. They fly over the prairies like Hawks, looking for grasshoppers, upon which they pounce, and if they lose sight of them, they try again at another place. We returned home to dinner, and after this a discussion arose connected with the Red-shafted Woodpecker. We determined to go and procure one of the young, and finding that these have pale-yellow shafts, instead of deep orange-red, such as the old birds have, the matter was tested and settled according to my statement. Harris and I went off after the doe killed this morning, and killed another, but as I have now skins enough, the measurements only were taken, and the head cut off, which I intend drawing to-morrow. Harris shot also a Grouse, and a Woodpecker that will prove a *Canadensis;* he killed the male also, but could not find it, and we found seven young Red-shafted Woodpeckers in one nest. I killed a female Meadow Lark, the first seen in this country by us. Provost told me (and he is a respectable man) that, during the breeding season of the Mountain Ram, the battering of the horns is often heard as far as a mile away, and that at such times they are approached with comparative ease; and there is no doubt that it is during such encounters that the horns are broken and twisted as I have seen them, and not by leaping from high places and falling on their horns, as poetical travellers have asserted. The fact is that when these animals leap from any height they alight firmly on all their four feet. At this season the young are always very difficult to catch, and I have not yet seen one of them. Harris, Bell, and young McKenzie are going Bighorn hunting to-morrow, and I hope they will be successful; I, alas! am no longer young and alert enough for the expedition. We find the mosquitoes very troublesome, and very numerous.

June 30, Friday. The weather was dark, with the wind at the north-west, and looked so like rain that the hunters did not start as they had proposed. Sprague, Harris, and Bell went out, however, after small game. I began drawing at five this morning, and worked almost without cessation till after three, when, becoming fatigued for want of practice, I took a short walk, regretting I could no longer draw twelve or fourteen hours without a pause or thought of weariness. It is now raining quite hard. Mr. Larpenteur went after a large tree to make a ferry-boat, and the new skiff was begun this morning. I sent Provost to Fort Mortimer to see if any one had arrived from below; he found a man had done so last evening and brought letters to Mr. Collins, requesting him to do all he can for us. He also reported that a party of Sioux had had a battle with the Gros Ventres, and had killed three of the latter and a white man who lived with them as a blacksmith. The Gros Ventres, on the other hand, had killed eight of the Sioux and put them to flight. The blacksmith killed two Sioux, and the enemies cut off one leg and one arm, scalped him, and left the mangled body behind them. It is said there is now no person living who can recollect the manner in which the bitter enmity of these two nations originated. The Yellowstone River is again rising fast, and Mr. Kipp will have tough times before he reaches Fort Alexander, which was built by Mr. Alexander Culbertson, our present host, and the Company had it honored by his name. When a herd of Buffaloes is chased, although the bulls themselves run very swiftly off, their speed is not to be compared to that of the cows and yearlings; for these latter are seen in a few minutes to leave the bulls behind them, and as cows and young Buffaloes are preferable to the old males, when the hunters are well mounted they pursue the cows and young ones invariably. Last winter Buffaloes were extremely abundant close to this fort, so much so that while the people were engaged in bringing hay in carts, the Buffaloes during the night came close in, and picked up every wisp that was dropped. An attempt to secure them alive was made by strewing hay in such a manner as to render the bait more and more plentiful near the old fort, which is distant about two hundred yards, and which was once the property of Mr. Sublette and Co.; but as the hogs and common cattle belonging to the fort are put up there regularly at sunset, the Buffaloes ate the hay to the very gates, but would not enter the enclosure, probably on account of the different smells issuing therefrom. At this period large herds slept in front of the fort, but just before dawn would remove across the hills about one mile distant, and return towards night. An attempt was made to shoot them with a cannon—a four-pounder; three were killed and several wounded. Still the Buffaloes came to their sleeping ground at evening, and many were killed during the season. I saw the head of one Mr. Culbertson shot, and the animal must have been of unusual size.

July 1, Saturday. It was still raining when I got up, but a few minutes later the sun was shining through one of our windows, and the wind being at northwest we anticipated a fine day. The ground was extremely wet and muddy, but Harris and Bell went off on horseback, and returned a few minutes after noon. They brought some birds and had killed a rascally Wolf. Bell found the nest of the Arkansas Flycatcher. The nest and eggs, as well as the manners, of this bird resemble in many ways those of our King-bird. The nest was in an elm, twenty or twenty-five feet above the ground, and he saw another in a similar situation. Mr. Culbertson and I walked to the Pilot Knob with a spy-glass, to look at the present condition of Fort Mortimer. This afternoon Squires, Provost, and I walked there, and were kindly received as usual. We found all the people encamped two hundred yards from the river, as they had been obliged to move from the tumbling fort during the rain of last night. Whilst we were there a trapper came in with a horse and told us the following: This man and four others left that fort on the 1st of April last on an expedition after Beavers. They were captured by a party of about four hundred Sioux, who took them prisoners and kept him one day and a half, after which he was released, but his companions were kept prisoners. He crossed the river and found a horse belonging to the Indians, stole it, and reached the fort at last. He looked miserable indeed, almost without a rag of clothing, long hair, filthy beyond description, and having only one very keen, bright eye, which looked as if he was both proud and brave. He had subsisted for the last eleven days on pomme blanche and the thick leaves of the cactus, which he roasted to get rid of the thorns or spines, and thus had fared most miserably; for, previous to the capture of himself and his companions, he had upset his bull canoe and lost his rifle, which to a trapper is, next to life, his dependence. When he was asked if he would have some dinner, he said that he had forgotten the word, but would try the taste of meat again. Mr. Collins was very polite to me, and promised me a hunter for the whole of next week, expressly to shoot Bighorns. I hope this promise may be better kept than that of Mr. Chardon, who told me that should he have one killed within forty miles he would send Alexis back with it at once. We heard some had been killed, but this may not be true; at any rate, men are men all over the world, and a broken promise is not unheard-of. This evening Mr. Culbertson presented me with a splendid dress, as well as one to Harris and one to Bell, and promised one to Sprague, which I have no doubt he will have. Harris and Sprague went off to procure Woodpeckers' nests, and brought the most curious set of five birds that I ever saw, and which I think will puzzle all the naturalists in the world. The first was found near the nest, of which Sprague shot the female, a light-colored Red-shafted Woodpecker. It proved to be of the same color, but had the rudiments of black stripes on the cheeks. Next, Sprague shot an adult yellow-winged male, with the markings principally such as are found in the Eastern States. Harris then shot a young Red-shafted, just fledged, with a black stripe on the cheek. His next shot was a light-colored Red-shafted male, with black cheeks, and another still, a yellow Red-shafted with a red cheek. After all this Mr. Culbertson proposed to run a sham Buffalo hunt again. He, Harris, and Squires started on good horses, went about a mile, and returned full tilt, firing and cracking.

Squires fired four times and missed once. Harris did not shoot at all; but Mr. Culbertson fired eleven times, starting at the onset with an empty gun, snapped three times, and reached the fort with his gun loaded. A more wonderful rider I never saw.

July 2, Sunday. The weather was cool and pleasant this morning, with no mosquitoes, which indeed—plentiful and troublesome as they are—Provost tells me are more scarce this season than he ever knew them thus far up the Missouri. Sprague finished his drawing of the doe's head about dinner-time, and it looks well. After dinner he went after the puzzling Woodpeckers, and brought three, all different from each other. Mr. Culbertson, his squaw wife, and I rode to Fort Mortimer, accompanied by young McKenzie, and found Mr. Collins quite ill. We saw the hunters of that fort, and they promised to supply me with Bighorns, at ten dollars apiece in the flesh, and also some Black-tailed Deer, and perhaps a Grizzly Bear. This evening they came to the fort for old Peter and a mule, to bring in their game; and may success attend them! When we returned, Harris started off with Mr. Culbertson and his wife to see the condition of Mr. Collins, to whom he administered some remedies. Harris had an accident that was near being of a serious nature; as he was getting into the wagon, thinking that a man had hold of the reins, which was not the case, his foot was caught between the axle-tree and the wagon, he was thrown down on his arm and side, and hurt to some extent; fortunately he escaped without serious injury, and does not complain much this evening, as he has gone on the ramparts to shoot a Wolf. Sprague saw a Wolf in a hole a few yards from the fort, but said not a word of it till after dinner, when Bell and Harris went there and shot it through the head. It was a poor, miserable, crippled old beast, that could not get out of the hole, which is not more than three or four feet deep. After breakfast we had a hunt after Hares or Rabbits, and Harris saw two of them, but was so near he did not care to shoot at them. Whilst Harris and Mr. Culbertson went off to see Mr. Collins, Mr. Denig and I walked off with a bag and instruments, to take off the head of a three-years-dead Indian chief, called the White Cow. Mr. Denig got upon my shoulders and into the branches near the coffin, which stood about ten feet above ground. The coffin was lowered, or rather tumbled, down, and the cover was soon hammered off; to my surprise, the feet were placed on the pillow, instead of the head, which lay at the foot of the coffin—if a long box may so be called. Worms innumerable were all about it; the feet were naked, shrunk, and dried up. The head had still the hair on, but was twisted off in a moment, under jaw and all. The body had been first wrapped up in a Buffalo skin without hair, and then in another robe with the hair on, as usual; after this the dead man had been enveloped in an American flag, and over this a superb scarlet blanket. We left all on the ground but the head. Squires, Mr. Denig and young Owen McKenzie went afterwards to try to replace the coffin and contents in the tree, but in vain; the whole affair fell to the ground, and there it lies; but I intend to-morrow to have it covered with earth. The history of this man is short, and I had it from Mr. Larpenteur, who was in the fort at the time of his decease, or self-committed death. He was a good friend to the whites, and knew how to procure many Buffalo robes for them; he was also a famous orator, and never failed to harangue his people on all occasions. He was, however, consumptive, and finding himself about to die, he sent his squaw for water, took an arrow from his quiver, and thursting it into his heart, expired, and was found dead when his squaw returned to the lodge. He was "buried" in the above-mentioned tree by the orders of Mr. McKenzie, who then commanded this fort. Mr. Culbertson drove me so fast, and Harris so much faster, over this rough ground, that I feel quite stiff. I must not forget to say that we had another sham Buffalo chase over the prairie in front of the fort, the riders being Squires, young McKenzie, and Mr. Culbertson; and I was glad and proud to see that Squires, though so inexperienced a hunter, managed to shoot five shots within the mile, McKenzie eleven, and Mr. Culbertson eight. Harris killed an old Wolf, which he thought was larger and fatter than any killed previously. It was very large, but on examination it was found to be poor and without teeth in the upper jaw.

July 3, Monday. We have had a warm night and day; after breakfast we all six crossed the river in the newly built skiff, and went off in divers directions. Provost and I looked thoroughly through the brushwood, and walked fully six miles from the fort; we saw three Deer, but so far were they that it was useless to shoot. Deer-shooting on the prairies is all hazard; sometimes the animals come tripping along within ten yards of you, and at other times not nearer can you get than one hundred and fifty yards, which was the case this day. The others killed nothing of note, and crossed the river back to the fort two hours at least before us; and we shot and bawled out for nearly an hour, before the skiff was sent for us. I took a swim, found the water very pleasant, and was refreshed by my bath. The Bighorn hunters returned this afternoon with a Bighorn, a female, and also a female Black-tailed Deer. I paid them

$15 for the two, and they are to start again to-morrow evening, or the next day.

July 4, Tuesday. Although we had some fireworks going on last evening, after I had laid myself down for the night, the anniversary of the Independence of the United States has been almost the quietest I have ever spent, as far as my recollection goes. I was drawing the whole day, and Sprague was engaged in the same manner, painting a likeness of Mr. Culbertson. Harris and Bell went off to try and procure a buck of the Long White-tailed Deer, and returned after dinner much fatigued and hungry enough. Bell had shot at a Deer and wounded it very severely; the poor thing ran on, but soon lay down, for the blood and froth were gushing out of its mouth. Bell saw the buck lying down, and not being an experienced hunter, thought it was dead, and instead of shooting it again, went back to call Harris; when they returned, the Deer was gone, and although they saw it again and again, the Deer outwitted them, and, as I have said, they returned weary, with no Deer. After dinner I spoke to Mr. Culbertson on the subject, and he told me that the Deer could probably be found, but that most likely the Wolves would devour it. He prepared to send young McKenzie with both my friends; the horses were soon saddled, and the three were off at a gallop. The poor buck's carcass was found, but several Wolves and Turkey Buzzards had fared well upon it; the vertebræ only were left, with a few bits of skin and portions of the horns in velvet. These trophies were all that they brought home. It was a superb and very large animal, and I am very sorry for the loss of it, as I am anxious to draw the head of one of such a size as they represent this to have been. They ran after a Wolf, which gave them leg bail. Meanwhile Squires and Provost started with the skiff in a cart to go up the river two miles, cross, and camp on the opposite shore. The weather became very gloomy and chill. In talking with Mr. Culbertson he told me that no wise man would ever follow a Buffalo bull immediately in his track, even in a hunt, and that no one well initiated would ever run after Buffaloes between the herd and another hunter, as the latter bears on the former ever and anon, and places him in imminent danger. Buffalo cows rarely, if ever, turn on the assailant, but bulls oftentimes will, and are so dangerous that many a fine hunter has been gored and killed, as well as his horse.

July 5, Wednesday. It rained the whole of last night and the weather has been bad all day. I am at the Bighorn's head, and Sprague at Mr. Culbertson. Provost and Squires returned drenched and hungry, before dinner. They had seen several Deer, and fresh tracks of a large Grizzly Bear. They had waded through mud and water enough for one day, and were well fatigued. Harris and Bell both shot at Wolves from the ramparts, and as these things are of such common occurrence I will say no more about them, unless we are in want of one of these beasts. Harris and I went over to see Mr. Collins, who is much better; his hunters had not returned. We found the men there mostly engaged in playing cards and backgammon. The large patches of rose bushes are now in full bloom, and they are so full of sweet fragrance that the air is perfumed by them. The weather looks clear towards the north, and I expect a fine to-morrow. Old Provost has been telling me much of interest about the Beavers, once so plentiful, but now very scarce. It takes about seventy Beaver skins to make a pack of a hundred pounds; in a good market this pack is worth five hundred dollars, and in fortunate seasons a trapper sometimes made the large sum of four thousand dollars. Formerly, when Beavers were abundant, companies were sent with as many as thirty and forty men, each with from eight to a dozen traps, and two horses. When at a propitious spot, they erected a camp, and every man sought his own game; the skins alone were brought to the camp, where a certain number of men always remained to stretch and dry them.

JULY 6, THURSDAY. The weather has been pleasant, with the wind at northwest, and the prairies will dry a good deal. After breakfast Harris, Bell, and McKenzie went off on horseback. They saw a Red Fox of the country, which is different from those of the States; they chased it, and though it ran slowly at first, the moment it saw the hunters at full gallop, it ran swiftly from them. McKenzie shot with a rifle and missed it. They saw fresh tracks of the small Hare, but not any of the animals themselves. After dinner I worked at Mr. Culbertson's head and dress, and by evening had the portrait nearly finished. At four o'clock Harris, Bell, and Sprague went across the river in the skiff; Sprague to take a view of the fort, the others to hunt. Harris and Bell shot twice at a buck, and killed it, though only one buckshot entered the thigh. Whilst we were sitting at the back gate of the fort, we saw a parcel of Indians coming towards the place, yelling and singing what Mr. Culbertson told me was the song of the scalp dance; we saw through the telescope that they were fourteen in number, with their faces painted black, and that it was a detachment of a war party. When within a hundred yards they all stopped, as if awaiting an invitation; we did not hurry as to this, and they seated themselves on the ground and looked at us, while Mr. Culbertson sent Mr. Denig to ask them to come in by the front gate of the fort, and put them in the Indian house, a sort of camp for the fellows. They all looked miserably poor, filthy beyond description, and their black faces and foully smelling Buffalo robes made them appear to me like so many devils. The leader, who was well known to be a famous rascal, and was painted red, was a tall, well-formed man. The party had only three poor guns, and a few had coarse, common lances; every man had a knife, and the leader was armed with a stick in which were inserted three blades of butcher's-knives; a blow from this weapon would doubtless kill a man. Some of the squaws of the fort, having found that they were Assiniboins, went to meet them; they took one of these, and painted her face black, as a sign of friendship. Most of these mighty warriors had a lump of fresh Buffalo meat slung on his back, which was all traded for by Mr. Larpenteur, who gave them in exchange some dried meat, not worth the notice of Harris's dog, and some tobacco. The report of their expedition is as follows: Their party at first consisted of nearly fifty; they travelled several hundred miles in search of Blackfeet, and having discovered a small troop of them, they hid till the next morning, when at daylight (this is always the time they prefer for an attack) they rushed upon the enemy, surprised them, killed one at the onset, and the rest took to flight, leaving guns, horses, shields, lances, etc., on the ground. The Assiniboins took several guns and seven horses, and the scalp of the dead Indian. It happened that the man they killed had some time ago killed the father of their chief, and he was full of joy. After eating and resting awhile, they followed the trail of the Blackfeet, hoping to again surprise them; but not seeing them, they separated into small parties, and it is one of these parties that is now with us. The chief, to show his pride and delight at killing his enemy, has borrowed a drum; and the company have nearly ever since been yelling, singing, and beating that beastly tambour. Boucherville came to me, and told me that if the swamp over the river was sufficiently dried by to-morrow morning, he would come early with a companion for two horses, and would go after Bighorns. He returned this afternoon from a Buffalo hunt and had killed six. These six animals, all bulls, will suffice for Fort Mortimer only three days. A rascally Indian had stolen his gun and Bighorn bow; the gun he said he could easily replace, but the loss of the bow he regretted exceedingly.

July 7, Friday. This morning the dirty Indians, who could have washed had they so minded, were beating the tambour and singing their miserable scalp song, until Mr. Culbertson ordered the drum taken away, and gave them more tobacco and some vermilion to bedaub their faces.

They were permitted to remain about the fort the remainder of the day, and the night coming they will again be sheltered; but they must depart to-morrow morning. After breakfast Sprague worked on the view of the fort. I went on with the portrait of Mr. Culbertson, who is about as bad a sitter as his wife, whose portrait is very successful, notwithstanding her extreme restlessness. After dinner Harris, Bell, and I started on foot, and walked about four miles from the fort; the day was hot, and horse-flies and mosquitoes pretty abundant, but we trudged on, though we saw nothing; we had gone after Rabbits, the tracks of which had been seen previously. We walked immediately near the foot of the clay hills which run from about a mile from and above the fort to the Lord knows where. We first passed one ravine where we saw some very curious sandstone formations, coming straight out horizontally from the clay banks between which we were passing; others lay loose and detached; they had fallen down, or had been washed out some time or other. All were compressed in such a manner that the usual form was an oval somewhat depressed in the centre; but, to give you some idea of these formations, I will send you a rough sketch. Those in the banks extended from five to seven feet, and the largest one on the ground measured a little less than ten feet. Bell thought they would make good sharpening-stones, but I considered them too soft. They were all smooth, and the grain was alike in all. We passed two much depressed and very broken ravines, and at last reached the Rabbit ground. Whilst looking at the wild scenery around, and the clay hills on the other side of the Missouri opposite the fort, I thought that if all these were granite, the formation and general appearance would resemble the country of Labrador, though the grandeur and sublimity of the latter far surpass anything that I have seen since I left them forever. I must not forget to say that on our way we passed through some grasses with bearded shafts, so sharp that they penetrated our moccasins and entered our feet and ankles, and in the shade of a stumpy ash-tree we took off our moccasins and drew the spines out. The Lazuli Finches and Arctic Bluebirds sang in our view; but though we beat all the clumps of low bushes where the Rabbits must go in, whether during night or day, we did not start one. We saw a Wolf which ran close by, reached the brow of the hill, and kept where he could watch our every motion; this they do on all possible occasions. We were all very warm, so we rested awhile, and ate some service-berries, which I found good; the gooseberries were small and green, and almost choked Harris with their sharp acidity. On our return, as we were descending the first deep ravine, a Raven flew off close by; it was so near Bell that he had no time to shoot. I followed it and although loaded with

No. 6 shot, I drew my trigger and the bird fell dead; only one shot had touched it, but that had passed through the lungs. After we reached the prairie I shot a Meadow Lark, but lost it, as we had unfortunately not taken Bragg (Harris's dog). We saw a patch of wood called in these regions a "Point;" we walked towards it for the purpose of shooting Deer. I was sent to the lower end, Bell took one side, and Harris the other, and the hound we had with us was sent in; no Deer there, however, and we made for the fort, which we reached hot and thirsty enough after our long walk. As soon as I was cooled I took a good swim. I think the Indians hereabouts poor swimmers; they beat the water with their arms, attempting to *"nage à la brasse;"* but, alas! it is too bad to mention. I am told, however, that there are no good specimens to judge from at the fort, so this is not much of an opinion. It is strange how very scarce snakes of every description are, as well as insects, except mosquitoes and horseflies. Young McKenzie had been sent to seek for the lost ferryboat, but returned without success; the new one is expected to be put in the water to-morrow evening. Squires and Provost had the skiff carried overland three miles, and they crossed the river in it with the intention to remain hunting until Sunday night.

July 8, Saturday. Mr. Culbertson told me this morning that last spring early, during a snow-storm, he and Mr. Larpenteur were out in an Indian lodge close by the fort, when they heard the mares which had young colts making much noise; and that on going out they saw a single Wolf that had thrown down one of the colts, and was about doing the same with another. They both made towards the spot with their pistols; and, fearing that the Wolf might kill both the colts, fired before reaching the spot, when too far off to take aim. Master Wolf ran off, but both colts bear evidence of his teeth to this day. When I came down this morning early, I was delighted to see the dirty and rascally Indians walking off to their lodge on the other side of the hills, and before many days they will be at their camp enjoying their merriment (rough and senseless as it seems to me), yelling out their scalp song, and dancing. Now this dance, to commemorate the death of an enemy, is a mere bending and slackening of the body, and patting of the ground with both feet at once, in very tolerable time with their music. Our squaws yesterday joined them in this exemplary ceremony; one was blackened, and all the others painted with vermilion. The art of painting in any color is to mix the color desired with grease of one sort or another; and when well done, it will stick on for a day or two, if not longer. Indians are not equal to the whites in the art of dyeing Porcupine quills; their ingredients are alto-

GREATER FLAMINGO, *Phoenicopterus ruber*

WHIPPOORWILL, *Caprimulgus vociferus*

WOOD DUCK, *Aix sponsa*

PASSENGER PIGEON, *Ectopistes migratorius*

CAROLINA PARAKEET, *Conuropsis carolinensis*

OSPREY,
Pandion haliaetus

NORTHERN RAVEN,
Corvus corax

YELLOW-BREASTED CHAT, *Icteria virens*

SNOWY EGRET, *Egretta thula*

SNOWY OWL, *Nyctea scandiaca*

BROWN PELICAN, *Pelecanus occidentalis*

GYRFALCON,
Falco rusticolus

BARN SWALLOW,
Hirundo rustica

gether too simple and natural to equal the knowledge of chemicals. Mr. Denig dyed a good quantity to-day for Mrs. Culbertson; he boiled water in a tin kettle with the quills put in when the water boiled, to remove the oil attached naturally to them; next they were thoroughly washed, and fresh water boiled, wherein he placed the color wanted, and boiled the whole for a few minutes, when he looked at them to judge of the color, and so continued until all were dyed. Red, yellow, green, and black quills were the result of his labors. A good deal of vegetable acid is necessary for this purpose, as minerals, so they say here, will not answer. I drew at Mr. Culbertson's portrait till he was tired enough; his wife—a pure Indian—is much interested in my work. Bell and Sprague, after some long talk with Harris about geological matters, of which valuable science he knows a good deal, went off to seek a Wolf's hole that Sprague had seen some days before, but of which, with his usual reticence, he had not spoken. Sprague returned with a specimen of rattle-snake root, which he has already drawn. Bell saw a Wolf munching a bone, approached it and shot at it. The Wolf had been wounded before and ran off slowly, and Bell after it. Mr. Culbertson and I saw the race; Bell gained on the Wolf until within thirty steps when he fired again; the Wolf ran some distance further, and then fell; but Bell was now exhausted by the heat, which was intense, and left the animal where it lay without attempting to skin it. Squires and Provost returned this afternoon about three o'clock, but the first alone had killed a doe. It was the first one he had ever shot, and he placed seven buckshot in her body. Owen went off one way, and Harris and Bell another, but brought in nothing. Provost went off to the Opposition camp, and when he returned told me that a Porcupine was there, and would be kept until I saw it; so Harris drove me over, at the usual breakneck pace, and I bought the animal. Mr. Collins is yet poorly, their hunters have not returned, and they are destitute of everything, not having even a medicine chest. We told him to send a man back with us, which he did, and we sent him some medicine, rice, and two bottles of claret. The weather has been much cooler and pleasanter than yesterday.

July 9, Sunday. I drew at a Wolf's head, and Sprague worked at a view of the fort for Mr. Culbertson. I also worked on Mr. Culbertson's portrait about an hour. I then worked at the Porcupine, which is an animal such as I never saw or Bell either. Its measurements are: from nose to anterior canthus of the eye, $1\frac{5}{8}$ in., posterior ditto, $2\frac{1}{8}$; conch of ear, $3\frac{1}{2}$; distances from eyes posteriorly, $2\frac{1}{4}$; fore feet stretched beyond nose, $3\frac{1}{2}$; length of head around, $4\frac{1}{8}$; nose to root of tail, $18\frac{1}{2}$; length of tail vertebræ, $6\frac{3}{8}$; to end of hair, $7\frac{3}{4}$; hind claws when stretched equal to end of tail; greatest breadth of palm, $1\frac{1}{4}$; of sole, $1\frac{3}{8}$; outward width of tail at base, $3\frac{5}{8}$; depth of ditto, $3\frac{1}{8}$; length of palm, $1\frac{1}{2}$; ditto of sole, $1\frac{7}{8}$; height at shoulder, 11; at rump, $10\frac{1}{4}$; longest hair on the back, $8\frac{7}{8}$; breadth between ears, $2\frac{1}{4}$; from nostril to split of upper lip, $\frac{3}{4}$; upper incisors, $\frac{5}{8}$; lower ditto, $\frac{3}{4}$; tongue quite smooth; weight 11 lbs. The habits of this animal are somewhat different from those of the Canadian Porcupine. The one of this country often goes in crevices or holes, and young McKenzie caught one in a Wolf's den, along with the old Wolf and seven young; they climb trees, however.

Provost tells me that Wolves are oftentimes destroyed by wild horses, which he has seen run at the Wolves head down, and when at a proper distance take them by the middle of the back with their teeth, and throw them several feet in the air, after which they stamp upon their bodies with the fore feet until quite dead. I have a bad blister on the heel of my right foot, and cannot walk without considerable pain.

July 10, Monday. Squires, Owen, McKenzie, and Provost, with a mule, a cart, and Peter the horse, went off at seven this morning for Antelopes. Bell did not feel well enough to go with them, and was unable to eat his usual meal, but I made him some good gruel, and he is better now. This afternoon Harris went off on horseback after Rabbits, and he will, I hope, have success. The day has been fine, and cool compared with others. I took a walk, and made a drawing of the beautiful sugar-loaf cactus; it does not open its blossoms until after the middle of the day, and closes immediately on being placed in the shade.

July 11, Tuesday. Harris returned about ten o'clock last night, but saw no Hares; how we are to procure any is more than I can tell. Mr. Culbertson says that it was dangerous for Harris to go so far as he did alone up the country, and he must not try it again. The hunters returned this afternoon, but brought only one buck, which is, however, beautiful, and the horns in velvet so remarkable that I can hardly wait for daylight to begin drawing it. I have taken all the measurements of this perfect animal; it was shot by old Provost. Mr. Culbertson—whose portrait is nearly finished—his wife, and I took a ride to look at some grass for hay, and found it beautiful and plentiful. We saw two Wolves, a common one and a prairie one. Bell is better. Sprague has drawn another cactus; Provost and I have now skinned the buck, and it hangs in the ice-house; the head, however, is untouched.

JULY 12, WEDNESDAY. I rose before three, and began at once to draw the buck's head. Bell assisted me to place it in the position I wanted, and as he felt somewhat better, while I drew, he finished the skin of the Porcupine; so that is saved. Sprague continued his painting of the fort. Just after dinner a Wolf was seen leisurely walking within one hundred yards of the fort. Bell took the repeating rifle, went on the ramparts, fired, and missed it. Mr. Culbertson sent word to young Owen McKenzie to get a horse and give it chase. All was ready in a few minutes, and off went the young fellow after the beast. I left my drawing long enough to see the pursuit, and was surprised to see that the Wolf did not start off on a gallop till his pursuer was within one hundred yards or so of him, and who then gained rapidly. Suddenly the old sinner turned, and the horse went past him some little distance. As soon as he could be turned about McKenzie closed upon him, his gun flashed twice; but now he was almost *à bon touchant*, the gun went off—the Wolf was dead. I walked out to meet Owen with the beast; it was very poor, very old, and good for nothing as a specimen. Harris, who had shot at one last night in the late twilight, had killed it, but was not aware of it till I found the villain this morning. It had evidently been dragged at by its brothers, who, however, had not torn it. Provost went over to the other fort to find out where the Buffaloes are most abundant, and did not return till late, so did no hunting. A young dog of this country's breed ate up all the berries collected by Mrs. Culbertson, and her lord had it killed for our supper this evening. The poor thing was stuck with a knife in the throat, after which it was placed over a hot fire outside of the fort, singed, and the hair scraped off, as I myself have treated Raccoons and Opossums. Then the animal was boiled, and I intend to taste one mouthful of it, for I cannot say that just now I should relish an entire meal from such peculiar fare. There are men, however, who much prefer the flesh to Buffalo meat, or even venison. An ox was broken to work this day, and worked far better than I expected. I finished at last Mr. Culbertson's portrait, and it now hangs in a frame. He and his wife are much pleased with it, and I am heartily glad they are, for in conscience I am not; however, it is all I could do, especially with a man who is never in the same position for one whole minute; so no more can be expected. The dog was duly cooked and brought into Mr. Culbertson's room; he served it out to Squires, Mr. Denig, and myself, and I was astonished when I tasted it. With great care and some repugnance I put a very small piece in my mouth; but no sooner had the taste touched my palate than I changed my dislike to liking, and found this victim of the canine order most excellent, and made a good meal, finding it fully equal to any meat I ever tasted. Old Provost had told me he preferred it to any meat, and his subsequent actions proved the truth of his words. We are having some music this evening, and Harris alone is absent, being at his favorite evening occupation, namely, shooting at Wolves from the ramparts.

July 13, Thursday. This has been a cloudy and a sultry day. Sprague finished his drawing and I mine. After dinner Mr. Culbertson, Squires, and myself went off nine miles over the prairies to look at the "meadows," as they are called, where Mr. Culbertson has heretofore cut his winter crop of hay, but we found it indifferent compared with that above the fort. We saw Sharp-tailed Grouse, and what we thought a new species of Lark, which we shot at no less than ten times before it was killed by Mr. Culbertson, but not found. I caught one of its young, but it proved to be only the Shore Lark. Before we reached the meadows we saw a flock of fifteen or twenty Bob-o-link, *Emberiza orizivora,* and on our return shot one of them (a male) on the wing. It is the first seen since we left St. Louis. We reached the meadows at last, and tied our nag to a tree, with the privilege of feeding. Mr. Culbertson and Squires went in the "meadows," and I walked round the so-called patch. I shot seven Arkansas Flycatchers on the wing. After an hour's walking, my companions returned, but had seen nothing except the fresh tracks of a Grizzly Bear. I shot at one of the White-rumped Hawks, of which I have several times spoken, but although it dropped its quarry and flew very wildly afterwards, it went out of my sight. We found the beds of Elks and their fresh dung, but saw none of these animals. I have forgotten to say that immediately after breakfast this morning I drove with Squires to Fort Mortimer, and asked Mr. Collins to let me have his hunter, Boucherville, to go after Mountain Rams for me, which he promised to do. In the afternoon he sent a man over to ask for some flour, which Mr. Culbertson sent him. They are there in the utmost state of destitution, almost of starvation, awaiting the arrival of the hunters like so many famished Wolves. Harris and Bell went across the river and shot a Wolf under the river bank, and afterwards a Duck, but saw nothing else. But during their absence we have had a fine opportunity of witnessing the agility and extreme strength of a year-old Buffalo bull belonging to the fort. Our cook, who is an old Spaniard, threw his lasso over the Buffalo's horns, and all the men in the fort at the time, hauled and pulled the beast about, trying to get him close to a post. He kicked, pulled, leaped sideways, and up and down, snorting and pawing until he broke loose, and ran, as if quite wild, about the enclosure. He was tied again and again, without any success, and at last got out of the fort, but was soon retaken, the rope being thrown round his horns, and he was brought to the main post of the Buffalo-robe press. There he was brought to a standstill, at the risk of breaking his neck, and the last remnant of his winter coat was removed by main strength, which was the object for which the poor animal had undergone all this trouble. After Harris returned to the fort he saw six Sharp-tailed Grouse. At this season this species have no particular spot where you may rely upon finding them, and at times they fly through the woods, and for a great distance, too, where they alight on trees; when, unless you accidentally see them, you pass by without their moving. After we passed Fort Mortimer on our return we saw coming from the banks of the river no less than eighteen Wolves, which altogether did not cover a space of more than three or four yards, they were so crowded. Among them were two Prairie Wolves. Had we had a good running horse some could have been shot; but old Peter is long past his running days. The Wolves had evidently been feeding on some carcass along the banks, and all moved very slowly. Mr. Culbertson gave me a grand pair of leather breeches and a very handsome knife-case, all manufactured by the Blackfeet Indians.

July 14, Friday. Thermometer 70°–95°. Young McKenzie went off after Antelopes across the river alone, but saw only one, which he could not get near. After breakfast Harris, Squires, and I started after birds of all sorts, with the wagon, and proceeded about six miles on the road we had travelled yesterday. We met the hunter from Fort Mortimer going for Bighorns for me, and Mr. Culbertson lent him a horse and a mule. We caught two young of the Shore Lark, killed seven of Sprague's Lark, but by bad management lost two, either from the wagon, my hat, or Harris's pockets. The weather was exceedingly hot. We hunted for Grouse in the wormwood bushes, and after despairing of finding any, we started up three from the plain, and they flew not many yards to the river. We got out of the wagon and pushed for them; one rose, and Harris shot it, though it flew some yards before he picked it up. He started another, and just as he was about to fire, his gunlock caught on his coat, and off went Mr. Grouse, over and through the woods until out of sight, and we returned slowly home. We saw ten Wolves this morning. After dinner we had a curious sight. Squires put on my Indian dress. McKenzie put on one of Mr. Culbertson's, Mrs. Culbertson put on her own *superb* dress, and the cook's wife put on the one Mrs. Culbertson had given me. Squires and Owen were painted in an awful manner by Mrs. Culbertson, the *Ladies* had their hair loose, and flying in the breeze, and then all mounted on horses with Indian saddles and trappings. Mrs. Culbertson and her maid rode astride like men, and all rode a furious race, under whip the whole way, for more than one mile on the prairie; and how amazed would have been any European lady, or some of our modern belles who boast their equestrian skill, at seeing the magnificent riding of this Indian princess—for that is Mrs. Culbertson's rank—and her servant. Mr. Culbertson rode with them, the horses running as if wild, with these extraordinary Indian riders, Mrs. Culbertson's magnificent black hair floating like a banner behind her. As to the men (for two others had joined Squires and McKenzie), I cannot compare them to anything in the whole creation. They ran like wild creatures of unearthly compound. Hither and thither they dashed, and when the whole party had crossed the ravine below, they saw a fine Wolf and gave the whip to their horses, and though the Wolf cut to right and left Owen shot at him with an arrow and missed, but Mr. Culbertson gave it chase, overtook it, his gun flashed, and the Wolf lay dead. They then ascended the hills and away they went, with our princess and her faithful attendant in the van, and by and by the group returned to the camp, running full speed till they entered the fort, and all this in the intense heat of this July afternoon. Mrs. Culbertson, herself a wonderful rider, possessed of both strength and grace in a marked degree, assured me that Squires was equal to any man in the country as a rider, and I saw for myself that he managed his horse as well as any of the party, and I was pleased to see him in his dress, ornaments, etc., looking, however, I must confess, after Mrs. Culbertson's painting his face, like a being from the infernal regions. Mr. Culbertson presented Harris with a superb dress of the Blackfoot Indians, and also with a Buffalo bull's head, for which Harris had in turn presented him with a gun-barrel of the short kind, and well fitted to shoot Buffaloes. Harris shot a very young one of Townsend's Hare, Mr. Denig gave Bell a Mouse, which, although it resembles *Mus leucopus* greatly, is much larger, and has a short, thick, round tail, somewhat blunted.

July 15, Saturday. We were all up pretty early, for we propose going up the Yellowstone with a wagon, and the skiff on a cart, should we wish to cross. After breakfast all of us except Sprague, who did not wish to go, were ready, and along with two extra men, the wagon, and the cart, we crossed the Missouri at the fort, and at nine were fairly under way—Harris, Bell, Mr. Culbertson, and myself in the wagon, Squires, Provost, and Owen on horseback. We travelled rather slowly, until we had crossed the point, and headed the ponds on the prairie that run at the foot of the hills opposite. We saw one Grouse, but it could not be started, though Harris searched for it. We ran the wagon into a rut, but got out unhurt; however, I decided to walk for a while, and did so for about two miles, to the turning point of the hills. The wheels of our vehicle were very shackling, and had to be somewhat repaired, and though I expected they would fall to pieces, in some manner or other we proceeded on. We saw several Antelopes, some on the prairie which we now travelled on, and many more on the tops of the hills, bounding westward. We stopped to water the horses at a saline spring, where I saw that Buffaloes, Antelopes, and other animals come to allay their thirst, and repose on the grassy margin. The water was too hot for us to drink, and we awaited the arrival of the cart, when we all took a good drink of the river water we had brought with us. After waiting for nearly an hour to allow the horses to bait and cool themselves, for it was very warm, we proceeded on, until we came to another watering-place, a river, in fact, which during spring overflows its banks, but now has only pools of water here and there. We soaked our wheels again, and again drank ourselves. Squires, Provost, and Owen had left sometime before us, but were not out of our sight, when we started, and as we had been, and were yet, travelling a good track, we soon caught up with them. We shot a common Red-winged Starling, and heard the notes of what was supposed to be a new bird by my companions, but which to my ears was nothing more than the Short-billed Marsh Wren of Nuttall. We reached our camping-place, say perhaps twenty miles' distance, by four o'clock, and all things were unloaded, the horses put to grass, and two or three of the party went in "the point" above, to shoot something for supper. I was hungry myself, and taking the Red-wing and the fishing-line, I went to the river close by, and had the good fortune to catch four fine catfish, when, my bait giving out, I was obliged to desist, as I found that these catfish will not take parts of their own kind as food. Provost had taken a bath, and rowed the skiff (which we had brought this whole distance on the cart, dragged by a mule) along with two men, across the river to seek for game on the point opposite our encampment. They returned, however, without having shot anything, and my four catfish were all the fresh provisions that we had, and ten of us partook of them with biscuit, coffee, and claret. Dusk coming on, the tent was pitched, and preparations to rest made. Some chose one spot and some another, and after a while we were settled. Mr. Culbertson and I lay together on the outside of the tent, and all the party were more or less drowsy. About this time we saw a large black cloud rising in the west; it was heavy and lowering, and about ten o'clock, when most of us were pretty nearly sound asleep, the distant thunder was heard, the wind rose to a gale, and the rain began falling in torrents. All were on foot in a few moments, and considerable confusion ensued. Our guns, all loaded with balls, were hurriedly placed under the tent, our beds also, and we all crawled in, in the space of a very few minutes. The wind blew so hard that Harris was obliged to hold the flappers of the tent with both hands, and sat in the water a considerable time to do this. Old Provost alone did not come in, he sat under the shelving bank of the river, and kept dry. After the gale was over, he calmly lay down in front of the tent on the saturated ground, and was soon asleep. During the gale, our fire, which we had built to keep off the myriads of mosquitoes, blew in every direction, and we had to watch the embers to keep them from burning the tent. After all was over, we snugged ourselves the best way we could in our small tent and under the wagon, and slept soundly till daylight. Mr. Culbertson had fixed himself pretty well, but on arising at daylight to smoke his pipe, Squires immediately crept into his comfortable corner, and snored there till the day was well begun. Mr. Culbertson had my knees for a pillow, and also my hat, I believe, for in the morning, although the first were not hurt, the latter was sadly out of shape in all parts. We had nothing for our breakfast except some vile coffee, and about three quarters of a sea-biscuit, which was soon settled among us. The men, poor fellows, had nothing at all. Provost had seen two Deer, but had had no shot, so of course we were in a quandary, but it is now—

July 16, Sunday. The weather pleasant with a fine breeze from the westward, and all eyes were bent upon the hills and prairie, which is here of great breadth, to spy if possible some object that might be killed and eaten. Presently a Wolf was seen, and Owen went after it, and it was not until he had disappeared below the first low range of hills, and Owen also, that the latter came within shot of the rascal, which dodged in all sorts of manners; but Owen would not give up, and after shooting more than once, he killed the beast. A man had followed him to help bring in the Wolf, and when near the river he saw a Buffalo, about two miles off, grazing peaceably, as he perhaps thought, safe in his own dominions; but, alas! white hunters had fixed their eyes upon him, and from that moment his doom was pronounced. Mr. Culbertson threw down his hat, bound his head with a handkerchief, his saddle was on his mare, he was mounted and off and away at a swift gallop, more quickly than I can describe, not towards the Buffalo, but towards the place where Owen had killed the Wolf. The man brought the Wolf on old Peter, and Owen, who was returning to the camp, heard the signal gun fired by Mr. Culbertson, and at once altered his course; his mare was evidently a little heated and blown by the Wolf chase, but both hunters went after the Buffalo, slowly at first, to rest Owen's steed, but soon, when getting within running distance, they gave whip, overhauled the Bison, and shot at it twice with balls; this halted the animal; the hunters had no more balls, and now loaded with pebbles, with which the poor beast was finally killed. The wagon had been sent from the camp. Harris, Bell, and Squires mounted on horseback, and travelled to the scene of action. They met Mr. Culbertson returning to camp, and he told Bell the Buffalo was a superb one, and had better be skinned. A man was sent to assist in the skinning who had been preparing the Wolf which was now cooking, as we had expected to dine upon its flesh; but when Mr. Culbertson returned, covered with blood and looking like a wild Indian, it was decided to throw it away; so I cut out the liver, and old Provost and I went fishing and caught eighteen catfish. I hooked two tortoises, but put them back in the river. I took a good swim, which refreshed me much, and I came to dinner with a fine appetite. This meal consisted wholly of fish, and we were all fairly satisfied. Before long the flesh of the Buffalo reached the camp, as well as the hide. The animal was very fat, and we have meat for some days. It was now decided that Squires, Provost, and Basil (one of the men) should proceed down the river to the Charbonneau, and there try their luck at Otters and Beavers, and the rest of us, with the cart, would make our way back to the fort. All was arranged, and at half-past three this afternoon we were travelling towards Fort Union. But hours previous to this, and before our scanty dinner, Owen had seen another bull, and Harris and Bell joined us in the hunt. The bull was shot at by McKenzie, who stopped its career, but as friend Harris pursued it with two of the hunters and finished it I was about to return, and thought sport over for the day. However, at this stage of the proceedings Owen discovered another bull making his way slowly over the prairie towards us. I was the only one who had balls, and would gladly have claimed the privilege of running him, but fearing I might make out badly on my slower steed, and so lose meat which we really needed, I handed my gun and balls to Owen McKenzie, and Bell and I went to an eminence to view the chase. Owen approached the bull, which continued to advance, and was now less than a quarter of a mile distant; either it did not see, or did not heed him, and they came directly towards each other, until they were about seventy or eighty yards apart, when the Buffalo started at a good run, and Owen's mare, which had already had two hard runs this morning, had great difficulty in preserving her distance. Owen, perceiving this, breathed her a minute, and then applying the whip was soon within shooting distance, and fired a shot which visibly checked the progress of the bull, and enabled Owen to soon be alongside of him, when the contents of the second barrel were discharged into the lungs, passing through the shoulder blade. This brought him to a stand. Bell and I now started at full speed, and as soon as we were within speaking distance, called to Owen not to shoot again. The bull did not appear to be much exhausted, but he was so stiffened by the shot on the shoulder that he could not turn quickly, and taking advantage of this we approached him; as we came near he worked himself slowly round to face us, and then made a lunge at us; we then stopped on one side and commenced discharging our pistols with little or no effect, except to increase his fury with every shot. His appearance was now one to inspire terror had we not felt satisfied of our ability to avoid him. However, even so, I came very near being overtaken by him. Through my own imprudence, I placed myself directly in front of him, and as he advanced I fired at his head, and then ran *ahead* of him, instead of veering to one side, not supposing that he was able to overtake me; but turning my head over my shoulder, I saw to my horror, Mr. Bull within three feet of me, prepared to give me a taste of his horns. The next instant I turned sharply off, and the Buffalo being unable to turn quickly enough to follow me, Bell took the gun from Owen and shot him directly behind the shoulder blade. He tottered for a moment, with an increased jet of blood from the mouth and nostrils, fell forward on his horns, then rolled over on his side, and was dead. He was a very old animal, in poor case, and only part of him was worth taking to the fort. Provost, Squires, and Basil were left at the camp preparing for their departure after Otter and Beaver as decided. We left them eight or nine catfish and a quantity of meat, of which they took care to secure the best, namely the boss or hump. On our homeward way we saw several Antelopes, some quite in the prairie, others far away on the hills, but all of them on the alert. Owen tried unsuccessfully to approach several of them at different times. At one place where two were seen he dismounted, and went round a small hill (for these animals when startled or suddenly alarmed always make to these places), and we hoped would have had a shot; but alas! no! One of the Antelopes ran off to the top of another hill, and the other stood looking at him, and us perhaps, till Owen (who had been re-mounted) galloped off towards us. My surprise was great when I saw the other Antelope following him at a good pace (but not by bounds or leaps, as I had been told by a former traveller they sometimes did), until it either smelt him, or found out he was no friend, and turning round galloped speedily off to join the one on the lookout. We saw seven or eight Grouse, and Bell killed one on the ground. We saw a Sand-hill Crane about two years old, looking quite majestic in a grassy bottom, but it flew away before we were near enough to get a shot. We passed a fine pond or small lake, but no bird was there. We saw several parcels of Ducks in sundry places, all of which no doubt had young near. When we turned the corner of the great prairie we found Owen's mare close by us. She had run away while he was after Antelopes. We tied her to a log to be ready for him when he should reach the spot. He had to walk about three miles before he did this. However, to one as young and alert as Owen, such things are nothing. Once they were not to me. We saw more Antelope at a distance, here called "Cabris," and after a while we reached the wood near the river, and finding abundance of service-berries, we all got out to break branches of these plants, Mr. Culbertson alone remaining in the wagon; he pushed on for the landing. We walked after him munching our berries, which we found very good, and reached the landing as the sun was going down behind the hills. Young McKenzie was already there, having cut across the point. We decided on crossing the river ourselves, and leaving all behind us except our guns. We took to the ferry-boat, cordelled it up the river for a while, then took to the nearest sand-bar, and leaping into the mud and water, hauled the heavy boat, Bell and Harris steering and poling the while. I had pulled off my shoes and socks, and when we reached the shore walked up to the fort barefooted, and made my feet quite sore again; but we have had a rest and a good supper, and I am writing in Mr. Culbertson's room, thinking over all God's blessings on this delightful day.

July 17, Monday. A beautiful day, with a west wind. Sprague, who is very industrious at all times, drew some flowers, and I have been busy both writing and drawing. In the afternoon Bell went after Rabbits, but saw one only, which he could not get, and Sprague walked to the hills about two miles off, but could not see any portion of the Yellowstone River, which Mr. Catlin has given in his view, as if he had been in a balloon some thousands of feet above the earth. Two men arrived last evening by land from Fort Pierre, and brought a letter, but no news of any importance; one is a cook as well as a hunter, the other named Wolff, a German, and a tinsmith by trade, though now a trapper.

July 18, Tuesday. When I went to bed last night the mosquitoes were so numerous downstairs that I took my bed under my arm and went to a room above, where I slept well. On going down this morning,

I found two other persons from Fort Pierre, and Mr. Culbertson very busy reading and writing letters. Immediately after breakfast young McKenzie and another man were despatched on mules, with a letter for Mr. Kipp, and Owen expects to overtake the boat in three or four days. An Indian arrived with a stolen squaw, both Assiniboins; and I am told such things are of frequent occurrence among these sons of nature. Mr. Culbertson proposed that we should take a ride to see the mowers, and Harris and I joined him. We found the men at work, among them one called Bernard Adams, of Charleston, S. C., who knew the Bachmans quite well, and who had read the whole of the "Biographies of Birds." Leaving the men, we entered a ravine in search of plants, etc., and having started an Owl, which I took for the barred one, I left my horse and went in search of it, but could not see it, and hearing a new note soon saw a bird not to be mistaken, and killed it, when it proved, as I expected, to be the Rock Wren; then I shot another sitting by the mouth of a hole. The bird did not fly off; Mr. Culbertson watched it closely, but when the hole was demolished no bird was to be found. Harris saw a Shrike, but of what species he could not tell, and he also found some Rock Wrens in another ravine. We returned to the fort and promised to visit the place this afternoon, which we have done, and procured three more Wrens, and killed the Owl, which proves to be precisely the resemblance of the Northern specimen of the Great Horned Owl, which we published under another name. The Rock Wren, which might as well be called the Ground Wren, builds its nest in holes, and now the young are well able to fly, and we procured one in the act. In two instances we saw these birds enter a hole here, and an investigation showed a passage or communication, and on my pointing out a hole to Bell where one had entered, he pushed his arm in and touched the little fellow, but it escaped by running up his arm and away it flew. Black clouds now arose in the west, and we moved homewards. Harris and Bell went to the mowers to get a drink of water, and we reached home without getting wet, though it rained violently for some time, and the weather is much cooler. Not a word yet from Provost and Squires.

July 19, Wednesday. Squires and Provost returned early this morning, and again I give the former my journal that I may have the account of the hunt in his own words. "As Mr. Audubon has said, he left Provost, Basil, and myself making ready for our voyage down the Yellowstone. The party for the fort were far in the blue distance ere we bid adieu to our camping-ground. We had wished the return party a pleasant ride and safe arrival at the fort as they left us, looking forward to a good supper, and what I *now* call a comfortable bed. We seated ourselves around some boiled Buffalo hump, which, as has been before said, we took good care to appropriate to ourselves according to the established rule of this country, which is, 'When you can, take the best,' and we had done so in this case, more to our satisfaction than to that of the hunters. Our meal finished, we packed everything we had in the skiff, and were soon on our way down the Yellowstone, happy as could be; Provost acting pilot, Basil oarsman, and your humble servant seated on a Buffalo robe, quietly smoking, and looking on the things around. We found the general appearance of the Yellowstone much like the Missouri, but with a stronger current, and the water more muddy. After a voyage of two hours Charbonneau River made its appearance, issuing from a clump of willows; the mouth of this river we found to be about ten feet wide, and so shallow that we were obliged to push our boat over the slippery mud for about forty feet. This passed, we entered a pond formed by the contraction of the mouth and the collection of mud and sticks thereabouts, the pond so formed being six or eight feet deep, and about fifty feet wide, extending about a mile up the river, which is very crooked indeed. For about half a mile from the Yellowstone the shore is lined with willows, beyond which is a level prairie, and on the shores of the stream just beyond the willows are a few scattered trees. About a quarter of a mile from the mouth of the river, we discovered what we were in search of, the Beaver lodge. To measure it was impossible, as it was not perfect, in the first place, in the next it was so muddy that we could not get ashore, but as well as I can I will describe it. The lodge is what is called the summer lodge; it was comprised wholly of brush, willow chiefly, with a single hole for the entrance and exit of the Beaver. The pile resembled, as much as anything to which I can compare it, a brush heap about six feet high, and about ten or fifteen feet base, and standing seven or eight feet from the water. There were a few Beaver tracks about, which gave us some encouragement. We proceeded to our camping-ground on the edge of the prairie; here we landed all our baggage; while Basil made a fire, Provost and I started to set our traps—the two extremes of hunters, the skilful old one, and the ignorant pupil; but I was soon initiated in the art of setting Beaver traps, and to the uninitiated let me say, '*First,* find your game, *then* catch it,' if you can. The first we did, the latter we tried to do. We proceeded to the place where the greatest number of tracks were seen, and commenced operations. At the place where the path enters the water, and about four inches beneath the surface, a level place is made in the mud, upon which the trap is placed, the chain is then fastened to a stake which is firmly driven in the ground under water. The end of a willow twig is then chewed and dipped in the 'Medicine Horn,' which contains the bait; this consists of castoreum mixed with spices; a quantity is collected on the chewed end of the twig, the stick is then placed or stuck in the mud on the edge of the water, leaving the part with the bait about two inches above the surface and in front of the trap; on each side the bait and about six inches from it, two dried twigs are placed in the ground; this done, all's done, and we are ready for the visit of Monsieur Castor. We set two traps, and returned to our camp, where we had supper, then pitched our tent and soon were sound asleep, but before we were asleep we heard a Beaver dive, and slap his tail, which sounded like the falling of a round stone in the water; here was encouragement again. In the morning (Monday) we examined our traps and found—nothing. We did not therefore disturb the traps, but examined farther up the river, where we discovered other tracks and resolved to set our traps there, as Provost concluded that there was but one Beaver, and that a male. We returned to camp and made a good breakfast on Buffalo meat and coffee, *sans* salt, *sans* pepper, *sans* sugar, *sans* anything else of any kind. After breakfast Provost shot a doe. In the afternoon we removed one trap, Basil and I gathered some wild-gooseberries which I stewed for supper, and made a sauce, which, though *rather acid*, was very good with our meat. The next morning, after again examining our traps and finding nothing, we decided to raise camp, which was accordingly done; everything was packed in the skiff, and we proceeded to the mouth of the river. The water had fallen so much since we had entered, as to oblige us to strip, jump in the mud, and haul the skiff over; rich and rare was the job; the mud was about half thigh deep, and a kind of greasy, sticky, black stuff, with a something about it so very peculiar as to be *rather* unpleasant; however, we did not mind much, and at last got into the Yellowstone, scraped and washed the mud off, and encamped on a prairie about one hundred yards below the Charbonneau. It was near sunset; Provost commenced fishing; we joined him, and in half an hour we caught sixteen catfish, quite large ones. During the day Provost started to the Mauvaises Terres to hunt Bighorns, but returned unsuccessful. He baited his traps for the last time. During his absence thunder clouds were observed rising all around us; we stretched our tent, removed everything inside it, ate our supper of meat and coffee, and then went to bed. It rained some part of the night, but not enough to wet through the tent. The next morning (Tuesday) at daylight, Provost started to examine his traps, while we at the camp put everything in the boat, and sat down to await his return, when we proceeded on our voyage down the Yellowstone to

Fort Mortimer, and from thence by land to Fort Union. Nothing of any interest occurred except that we saw two does, one young and one buck of the Bighorns; I fired at the buck which was on a high cliff about a hundred and fifty yards from us; I fired above it to allow for the falling of the ball, but the gun shot so well as to carry where I aimed. The animal was a very large buck; Provost says one of the largest he had seen. As soon as I fired he started and ran along the side of the hill which looked almost perpendicular, and I was much astonished, not only at the feat, but at the surprising quickness with which he moved along, with no apparent foothold. We reached Fort Mortimer about seven o'clock; I left Basil and Provost with the skiff, and I started for Fort Union on foot to send a cart for them. On my way I met Mr. Audubon about to pay a visit to Fort Mortimer; I found all well, despatched the cart, changed my clothes, and feel none the worse for my five days' camping, and quite ready for a dance I hear we are to have to-night."

This morning as I walked to Fort Mortimer, meeting Squires as he has said, well and happy as a Lark, I was surprised to see a good number of horses saddled, and packed in different ways, and I hastened on to find what might be the matter. When I entered the miserable house in which Mr. Collins sleeps and spends his time when not occupied out of doors, he told me thirteen men and seven squaws were about to start for the lakes, thirty-five miles off, to kill Buffaloes and dry their meat, as the last his hunters brought in was already putrid. I saw the cavalcade depart in an E. N. E. direction, remained a while, and then walked back. Mr. Collins promised me half a dozen balls from young animals. Provost was discomfited and crestfallen at the failure of the Beaver hunt; he brought half a doe and about a dozen fine catfish. Mr. Culbertson and I are going to see the mowers, and to-morrow we start on a grand Buffalo hunt, and hope for Antelopes, Wolves, and Foxes.

July 20, Thursday. We were up early, and had our breakfast shortly after four o'clock, and before eight had left the landing of the fort, and were fairly under way for the prairies. Our equipment was much the same as before, except that we had two carts this time. Mr. C. drove Harris, Bell, and myself, and the others rode on the carts and led the hunting horses, or runners, as they are called here. I observed a Rabbit running across the road, and saw some flowers different from any I had ever seen. After we had crossed a bottom prairie, we ascended between the high and rough ravines until we were on the rolling grounds of the plains. The fort showed well from this point, and we also saw a good number of Antelopes, and some young ones. These small things run even faster than the old ones. As we neared the Fox River some one espied four Buffaloes, and Mr. C., taking the telescope, showed them to me, lying on the ground. Our heads and carts were soon turned towards them, and we travelled within half a mile of them, concealed by a ridge or hill which separated them from us. The wind was favorable, and we moved on slowly round the hill, the hunters being now mounted. Harris and Bell had their hats on, but Owen and Mr. Culbertson had their heads bound with handkerchiefs. With the rest of the party I crawled on the ridge, and saw the bulls running away, but in a direction favorable for us to see the chase. On the word of command the horses were let loose, and away went the hunters, who soon were seen to gain on the game; two bulls ran together and Mr. C. and Bell followed after them, and presently one after another of the hunters followed them. Mr. C. shot first, and his bull stopped at the fire, walked towards where I was, and halted about sixty yards from me. His nose was within a few inches of the ground; the blood poured from his mouth, nose, and side, his tail hung down, but his legs looked as firm as ever, but in less than two minutes the poor beast fell on his side, and lay quite dead. Bell and Mr. Culbertson went after the second. Harris took the third, and Squires the fourth. Bell's shot took effect in the buttock, and Mr. Culbertson shot, placing his ball a few inches above or below Bell's; after this Mr. Culbertson ran no more. At this moment Squires's horse threw him over his head, fully ten feet; he fell on his powder-horn and was severely bruised; he cried to Harris to catch his horse, and was on his legs at once, but felt sick for a few minutes. Harris, who was as cool as a cucumber, neared his bull, shot it through the lungs, and it fell dead on the spot. Bell was now seen in full pursuit of his game, and Harris joined Squires, and followed the fourth, which, however, was soon out of my sight. I saw Bell shooting two or three times, and I heard the firing of Squires and perhaps Harris, but the weather was hot, and being afraid of injuring their horses, they let the fourth bull make his escape. Bell's bull fell on his knees, got up again, and rushed on Bell, and was shot again. The animal stood a minute with his tail partially elevated, and then fell dead; through some mishap Bell had no knife with him, so did not bring the tongue, as is customary. Mr. Culbertson walked towards the first bull and I joined him. It was a fine animal about seven years old; Harris's and Bell's were younger. The first was fat, and was soon skinned and cut up for meat. Mr. Culbertson insisted on calling it my bull, so I cut off the brush of the tail and placed it in my hat-band. We then walked towards Harris, who was seated on his bull, and the same ceremony took place, and while they were cutting the animal up for meat, Bell, who said he thought his bull was about three quarters of a mile distant, went off with me to see it; we walked at least a mile and a half, and at last came to it. It was a poor one, and the tongue and tail were all we took away, and we rejoined the party, who had already started the cart with Mr. Pike, who was told to fall to the rear, and reach the fort before sundown; this he could do readily, as we were not more than six miles distant. Mr. Culbertson broke open the head of "my" bull, and ate part of the brains raw, and yet warm, and so did many of the others, even Squires. The very sight of this turned my stomach, but I am told that were I to hunt Buffalo one year, I should like it "even better than dog meat." Mr. Pike did not reach the fort till the next morning about ten, I will say *en passant*. We continued our route, passing over the same road on which we had come, and about midway between the Missouri and Yellowstone Rivers. We saw more Antelopes, but not one Wolf; these rascals are never abundant where game is scarce, but where game is, there too are the Wolves. When we had travelled about ten miles further we saw seven Buffaloes grazing on a hill, but as the sun was about one hour high, we drove to one side of the road where there was a pond of water, and there stopped for the night; while the hunters were soon mounted, and with Squires they went off, leaving the men to arrange the camp. I crossed the pond, and having ascended the opposite bank, saw the bulls grazing as leisurely as usual. The hunters near them, they started down the hill, and the chase immediately began. One broke from the rest and was followed by Mr. C. who shot it, and then abandoned the hunt, his horse being much fatigued. I now counted ten shots, but all was out of my sight, and I seated myself near a Fox hole, longing for him. The hunters returned in time; Bell and Harris had killed one, but Squires had no luck, owing to his being unable to continue the chase on account of the injury he had received from his fall. We had a good supper, having brought abundance of eatables and drinkables. The tent was pitched; I put up my mosquito-bar under the wagon, and there slept very soundly till sunrise. Harris and Bell wedged together under another bar, Mr. C. went into the tent, and Squires, who is tough and likes to rough it with the hunters, slept on a Buffalo hide somewhere with Moncrévier, one of the most skilful of the hunters. The horses were all hoppled and turned to grass; they, however, went off too far, and had to be sent after, but I heard nothing of all this. As there is no wood on the prairies proper, our fire was made of Buffalo dung, which is so abundant that one meets these deposits at every few feet and in all directions.

July 21, Friday. We were up at sunrise, and had our coffee, after which Lafleur a mulatto, Harris, and Bell went off after Antelopes, for we cared no more about bulls; where the cows are, we cannot tell. Cows run faster than bulls, yearlings faster than cows, and calves faster than any of these. Squires felt sore, and his side was very black, so we took our guns and went after Black-breasted Lark Buntings, of which we saw many, but could not near them. I found a nest of them, however, with five eggs. The nest is planted in the ground, deep enough to sink the edges of it. It is formed of dried fine grasses and roots, without any lining of hair or wool. By and by we saw Harris sitting on a high hill about one mile off, and joined him; he said the bulls they had killed last evening were close by, and I offered to go and see the bones, for I expected that the Wolves had devoured it during the night. We travelled on, and Squires returned to the camp. After about two miles of walking against a delightful strong breeze, we reached the animals; Ravens or Buzzards had worked at the eyes, but only one Wolf, apparently, had been there. They were bloated, and smelt quite unpleasant. We returned to the camp and saw a Wolf cross our path, and an Antelope looking at us. We determined to stop and try to bring him to us; I lay on my back and threw my legs up, kicking first one and then the other foot, and sure enough the Antelope walked towards us, slowly and carefully, however. In about twenty minutes he had come two or three hundred yards; he was a superb male, and I looked at him for some minutes; when about sixty yards off I could see his eyes, and being loaded with buck-shot pulled the trigger without rising from my awkward position. Off he went; Harris fired, but he only ran the faster for some hundred yards, when he turned, looked at us again, and was off. When we reached camp we found Bell there; he had shot three times at Antelopes without killing; Lafleur had also returned, and had broken the foreleg of one, but an Antelope can run fast enough with three legs, and he saw no more of it. We now broke camp, arranged the horses and turned our heads towards the Missouri, and in four and three-quarter hours reached the landing. On entering the wood we again broke branches of service-berries, and carried a great quantity over the river. I much enjoyed the trip; we had our supper, and soon to bed in our hot room, where Sprague says the thermometer has been at 99° most of the day. I noticed it was warm when walking. I must not forget to notice some things which happened on our return. First, as we came near Fox River, we thought of the horns of our bulls, and Mr. Culbertson, who knows the country like a book, drove us first to Bell's, who knocked the horns off, then to Harris's, which was served in the same manner; this bull had been eaten entirely except the head, and a good portion of mine had been devoured also; it lay immediately under "Audubon's Bluff" (the name Mr. Culbertson gave the ridge on which I stood to see the chase), and we could see it when nearly a mile distant. Bell's horns were the handsomest and largest, mine next best, and Harris's the smallest, but we are all contented. Mr. Culbertson tells me that Harris and Bell have done wonders, for persons who have never shot at Buffaloes from on horseback. Harris had a fall too, during his second chase, and was bruised in the manner of Squires, but not so badly. I have but little doubt that Squires killed his bull, as he says he shot it three times, and Mr. Culbertson's must have died also. What a terrible destruction of life, as it were for nothing, or next to it, as the tongues only were brought in, and the flesh of these fine animals was left to beasts and birds of prey, or to rot on the spots where they fell. The prairies are literally *covered* with the skulls of the victims, and the roads the Buffalo make in crossing the prairies have all the appearance of heavy wagon tracks. We saw young Golden Eagles, Ravens, and Buzzards. I found the Short-billed Marsh Wren quite abundant, and in such localities as it is found eastward. The Black-breasted Prairie-bunting flies much like a Lark, hovering while singing, and sweeping round and round, over and above its female while she sits on the eggs on the prairie below. I saw only one Gadwall Duck; these birds are found in abundance on the plains where water and rushes are to be found. Alas! alas! eighteen Assiniboins have reached the fort this evening in two groups; they are better-looking than those previously seen by us.

July 22, Saturday. Thermometer 99°–102°. This day has been the hottest of the season, and we all felt the influence of this densely oppressive atmosphere, not a breath of air stirring. Immediately after breakfast Provost and Lafleur went across the river in search of Antelopes, and we remained looking at the Indians, all Assiniboins, and very dirty. When and where Mr. Catlin saw these Indians as he has represented them, dressed in magnificent attire, with all sorts of extravagant accoutrements, is more than I can divine, or Mr. Culbertson tell me. The evening was so hot and sultry that Mr. C. and I went into the river, which is now very low, and remained in the water over an hour. A dozen catfish were caught in the main channel, and we have had a good supper from part of them. Finding the weather so warm I have had my bed brought out on the gallery below, and so has Squires. The Indians are, as usual, shut *out* of the fort, all the horses, young Buffaloes, etc., shut *in;* and much refreshed by my bath, I say God bless you, and good-night.

July 23, Sunday. Thermometer 84°. I had a very pleasant night, and no mosquitoes, as the breeze rose a little before I lay down; and I anticipated a heavy thunder storm, but we had only a few drops of rain.

About one o'clock Harris was called to see one of the Indians, who was bleeding at the nose profusely, and I too went to see the poor devil. He had bled quite enough, and Harris stopped his nostrils with cotton, put cold water on his neck and head—God knows when they had felt it before—and the bleeding stopped. These dirty fellows had made a large fire between the walls of the fort, but outside the inner gates, and it was a wonder that the whole establishment was not destroyed by fire. Before sunrise they were pounding at the gate to be allowed to enter, but, of course, this was not permitted. When the sun had fairly risen, some one came and told me the hilltops were covered with Indians, probably Blackfeet. I walked to the back gate, and the number had dwindled, or the account been greatly exaggerated, for there seemed only fifty or sixty, and when, later, they were counted, there were found to be exactly seventy. They remained a long time on the hill, and sent a youth to ask for whiskey. But whiskey there is none for them, and very little for any one. By and by they came down the hill leading four horses, and armed principally with bows and arrows, spears, tomahawks, and a few guns. They have proved to be a party of Crees from the British dominions on the Saskatchewan River, and have been fifteen days in travelling here. They had seen few Buffaloes, and were hungry and thirsty enough. They assured Mr. Culbertson that the Hudson's Bay Company supplied them all with abundance of spirituous liquors, and as the white traders on the Missouri had none for them, they would hereafter travel with the English. Now ought not this subject to be brought before the press in our country and forwarded to England? If our Congress will not allow our traders to sell whiskey or rum to the Indians, why should not the British follow the same rule? Surely the British, who are so anxious about the emancipation of the blacks, might as well take care of the souls and bodies of the redskins. After a long talk and smoking of pipes, tobacco, flints, powder, gun-screws and vermilion were placed before their great chief (who is tattooed and has a most rascally look), who examined everything minutely, counting over the packets of vermilion; more tobacco was added, a file, and a piece of white cotton with which to adorn his head; then he walked off, followed by his son, and the whole posse left the fort. They passed by the garden, pulled up a few squash vines and some turnips, and tore down a few of the pickets on their way elsewhere. We all turned to, and picked a quantity of peas, which with a fine roast pig, made us a capital dinner. After this, seeing the Assiniboins loitering about the fort, we had some tobacco put up as a target, and many arrows were sent to enter the prize, but I never saw Indians —usually so skilful with their bows—shoot worse in my life. Presently some one cried there were Buffaloes on the hill, and going to see we found that four bulls were on the highest ridge standing still. The horses being got in the yard, the guns were gathered, saddles placed, and the riders mounted, Mr. C., Harris, and Bell; Squires declined going, not having recovered from his fall, Mr. C. led his followers round the hills by the ravines, and approached the bulls quite near, when the affrighted cattle ran down the hills and over the broken grounds, out of our sight, followed by the hunters. When I see game chased by Mr. Culbertson, I feel confident of its being killed, and in less than one hour he had killed two bulls, Harris and Bell each one. Thus these poor animals which two hours before were tranquilly feeding are now dead; short work this. Harris and Bell remained on the hills to watch the Wolves, and carts being ordered, Mr. C. and I went off on horseback to the second one he had killed. We found it entire, and I began to operate upon it at once; after making what measurements and investigations I desired, I saved the head, the tail, and a large piece of the silky skin from the rump. The meat of three of the bulls was brought to the fort, the fourth was left to rot on the ground. Mr. C. cut his finger severely, but paid no attention to that; I, however, tore a strip off my shirt and bound it up for him. It is so hot I am going to sleep on the gallery again; the thermometer this evening is 89°.

July 24, Monday. I had a fine sleep last night, and this morning early a slight sprinkling of rain somewhat refreshed the earth. After breakfast we talked of going to see if Mr. Culbertson's bull had been injured by the Wolves. Mr. C., Harris, and I went off to the spot by a roundabout way, and when we reached the animal it was somewhat swollen, but untouched, but we made up our minds to have it weighed, *coute qui coute*. Harris proposed to remain and watch it, looking for Hares meantime, but saw none. The Wolves must be migratory at this season, or so starved out that they have gone elsewhere, as we now see but few. We returned first to the fort, and mustered three men and Bell, for Sprague would not go, being busy drawing a plant, and finding the heat almost insupportable. We carried all the necessary implements, and found Harris quite ready to drink some claret and water which we took for him. To cut up so large a bull, and one now with so dreadful an odor, was no joke; but with the will follows the success, and in about one hour the poor beast had been measured and weighed, and we were once more *en route* for the fort. This bull measured as follows: from end of nose to root of tail, 131 inches; height at shoulder, 67 inches; at rump, 57 inches; tail vertebræ, 15½ inches, hair in length beyond it 11 inches.

We weighed the whole animal by cutting it in parts and then by addition found that this Buffalo, which was an old bull, weighed 1777 lbs. avoirdupois. The flesh was all tainted, and was therefore left for the beasts of prey. Our road was over high hills, and presented to our searching eyes a great extent of broken ground, and here and there groups of Buffaloes grazing. This afternoon we are going to bring in the skeleton of Mr. Culbertson's second bull. I lost the head of my first bull because I forgot to tell Mrs. Culbertson that I wished to save it, and the princess had its skull broken open to enjoy its brains. Handsome, and really courteous and refined in many ways, I cannot reconcile to myself the fact that she partakes of raw animal food with such evident relish. Before our departure, in came six half-breeds, belonging, or attached to Fort Mortimer; and understanding that they were first-rate hunters, I offered them ten dollars in goods for each Bighorn up to eight or ten in number. They have promised to go to-morrow, but, alas! the half-breeds are so uncertain I cannot tell whether they will move a step or not. Mrs. Culbertson, who has great pride in her pure Indian blood, told me with scorn that "all such no-color fellows are lazy." We were delayed in starting by a very heavy gale of wind and hard rain, which cooled the weather considerably; but we finally got off in the wagon, the cart with three mules following, to bring in the skeleton of the Buffalo which Mr. Culbertson had killed; but we were defeated, for some Wolves had been to it, dragged it about twenty-five feet, and gnawed the ends of the ribs and the backbone. The head of Harris's bull was brought in, but it was smaller; the horns alone were pretty good, and they were given to Sprague. On our return Mrs. Culbertson was good enough to give me six young Mallards, which she had caught by swimming after them in the Missouri; she is a most expert and graceful swimmer, besides being capable of remaining under water a long time; all the Blackfoot Indians excel in swimming and take great pride in the accomplishment. We found three of the Assiniboins had remained, one of whom wanted to carry off a squaw, and probably a couple of horses too. He strutted about the fort in such a manner that we watched him pretty closely. Mr. Culbertson took his gun, and a six-barrelled pistol in his pocket; I, my double-barrelled gun, and we stood at the back gate. The fellow had a spear made of a cut-and-thrust sword, planted in a good stick covered with red cloth, and this he never put down at any time; but no more, indeed, do any Indians, who carry all their goods and chattels forever about their persons. The three gentlemen, however, went off about dusk, and took the road to Fort Mortimer, where six half-breeds from the Northeast brought to Fort Mortimer eleven head of cattle, and came to pay a visit to their friends here. All these men know Provost, and have inquired for him. I feel somewhat uneasy about Provost and La Fleur, who have now been gone four full days. The prairie is wet and damp, so I must sleep indoors. The bull we cut up was not a fat one; I think in good condition it would have weighed 2000 lbs.

July 25, Tuesday. We were all rather lazy this morning, but about dinner-time Owen and his man arrived, and told us they had reached Mr. Kipp and his boat at the crossings within about half a mile of Fort Alexander; that his men were all broken down with drawing the cordelle through mud and water, and that they had lost a white horse, which, however, Owen saw on his way, and on the morning of his start from this fort. About the same time he shot a large Porcupine, and killed four bulls and one cow to feed upon, as well as three rattlesnakes. They saw a large number of Buffalo cows, and we are going after them to-morrow morning bright and early. About two hours later Provost and La Fleur, about whom I had felt some uneasiness, came to the landing, and brought the heads and skins attached to two female Antelopes. Both had been killed by one shot from La Fleur, and his ball broke the leg of a third. Provost was made quite sick by the salt water he had drunk; he killed one doe, on which they fed as well as on the flesh of the "Cabris." Whilst following the Mauvaises Terres (broken lands), they saw about twenty Bighorns, and had not the horse on which Provost rode been frightened at the sight of a monstrous buck of these animals, he would have shot it down within twenty yards. They saw from fifteen to twenty Buffalo cows, and we hope some of the hunters will come up with them to-morrow. I have been drawing the head of one of these beautiful female Antelopes; but their horns puzzle me, and all of us; they seem to me as if they were *new* horns, soft and short; time, however, will prove whether they shed them or not. Our preparations are already made for preserving the skins of the Antelopes, and Sprague is making an outline which I hope will be finished before the muscles of the head begin to soften. Not a word from the six hunters who promised to go after Bighorns on the Yellowstone.

July 26, Wednesday. We were all on foot before daybreak and had our breakfast by an early hour, and left on our trip for Buffalo cows. The wagon was sent across by hauling it through the east channel, which is now quite low, and across the sand-bars, which now reach seven-eighths of the distance across the river. We crossed in the skiff, and walked to the ferry-boat—I barefooted, as well as Mr. Culbertson; others wore boots or moccasins, but my feet have been tender of late, and this is the best cure. Whilst looking about for sticks to support our mosquito bars, I saw a Rabbit standing before me, within a few steps, but I was loaded with balls, and should have torn the poor thing so badly that it would have been useless as a specimen, so let it live. We left the ferry before six, and went on as usual. We saw two Antelopes on entering the bottom prairie, but they had the wind of us, and scampered off to the hills. We saw two Grouse, one of which Bell killed, and we found it very good this evening for our supper. Twelve bulls were seen, but we paid no attention to them. We saw a fine large Hawk, apparently the size of a Red-tailed Hawk, but with the whole head white. It had alighted on a clay hill or bank, but, on being approached, flew off to another, was pursued and again flew away, so that we could not procure it, but I have no doubt that it is a species not yet described. We now crossed Blackfoot River, and saw great numbers of Antelopes. Their play and tricks are curious; I watched many of the groups a long time, and will not soon forget them. At last, seeing we should have no meat for supper, and being a party of nine, it was determined that the first animal seen should be run down and killed. We soon saw a bull, and all agreed to give every chance possible to Squires. Mr. C., Owen, and Squires started, and Harris followed without a gun, to see the chase. The bull was wounded twice by Squires, but no blood came from the mouth, and now all three shot at it, but the bull was not apparently hurt seriously; he became more and more furious, and began charging upon them. Unfortunately, Squires ran between the bull and a ravine quite close to the animal, and it suddenly turned on him; his horse became frightened and jumped into the ravine, the bull followed, and now Squires lost his balance; however, he threw his gun down, and fortunately clung to the mane of his horse and recovered his seat. The horse got away and saved his life, for, from what Mr. C. told me, had he fallen, the bull would have killed him in a few minutes, and no assistance could be afforded him, as Mr. C. and Owen had, at that moment, empty guns. Squires told us all; he had never been so bewildered and terrified before. The bull kept on running, and was shot at perhaps twenty times, for when he fell he had *twelve balls* in his side, and had been shot twice in the head. Another bull was now seen close by us, and Owen killed it after four shots. Whilst we were cutting up this one, La Fleur and some one else went to the other, which was found to be very poor, and, at this season smelling very rank and disagreeable. A few of the best pieces were cut away, and, as usual, the hunters ate the liver and fat quite raw, like Wolves, and we were now on the move again. Presently we saw seven animals coming towards us, and with the glass discovered there were six bulls and one cow. The hunters mounted in quick time, and away after the cow, which Owen killed very soon. To my surprise the bulls did not leave her, but stood about one hundred yards from the hunters, who were cutting her in pieces; the best parts were taken for dried meat. Had we not been so many, the bulls would, in all probability, have charged upon the butchers, but after a time they went off at a slow canter. At this moment Harris and I were going towards the party thus engaged, when a Swift Fox started from a hole under the feet of Harris' horse. I was loaded with balls, and he also; he gave chase and gained upon the beautiful animal with remarkable quickness. Bell saw this, and joined Harris, whilst I walked towards the butchering party. The Fox was overtaken by Harris, who took aim at it several times, but could not get sight on him, and the little fellow doubled and cut about in such a manner that it escaped into a ravine, and was seen no more. Now who will tell me that no animal can compete with this Fox in speed, when Harris, mounted on an Indian horse, overtook it in a few minutes? We were now in sight of a large band of cows and bulls, but the sun was low, and we left them to make our way to the camping-place, which we reached just before the setting of the sun. We found plenty of water, and a delightful spot, where we were all soon at work unsaddling our horses and mules, bringing wood for fires, and picking service-berries, which we found in great quantities and very good. We were thirty miles from Fort Union, close to the three Mamelles, but must have travelled near fifty, searching for and running down the game. All slept well, some outside and others inside the tent, after our good supper. We had a clear, bright day, with the wind from the westward.

JULY 27, THURSDAY. This morning was beautiful, the birds singing all around us, and after our early breakfast, Harris, with La Fleur and Mr. Culbertson, walked to the top of the highest of the three Mamelles; Bell went to skinning the birds shot yesterday, among which was a large Titmouse of the Eastern States, while I walked off a short distance, and made a sketch of the camp and the three Mamelles. I hope to see a fair picture from this, painted by Victor, this next winter, God willing. During the night the bulls were heard bellowing, and the Wolves howling, all around us. Bell had seen evidences of Grizzly Bears close by, but we saw none of the animals. An Antelope was heard snorting early this morning, and seen for a while, but La Fleur could not get it. The snorting of the Antelope is more like a whistling, sneezing sound, than like the long, clear snorting of our common Deer, and it is also very frequently repeated, say every few minutes, when in sight of an object of which the animal does not yet know the nature; for the moment it is assured of danger, it bounds three or four times like a sheep, and then either trots off or gallops like a horse. On the return of the gentlemen from the eminence, from which they had seen nothing but a Hawk, and heard the notes of the Rock Wren, the horses were gathered, and preparations made to go in search of cows. I took my gun and walked off ahead, and on ascending the first hill saw an Antelope, which, at first sight, I thought was an Indian. It stood still, gazing at me about five hundred yards off; I never stirred, and presently it walked towards me; I lay down and lowered my rifle; the animal could not now see my body; I showed it my feet a few times, at intervals. Presently I saw it coming full trot towards me; I cocked my gun, loaded with buck-shot in one barrel and ball in the other. He came within thirty yards of me and stopped suddenly, then turned broadside towards me. I could see his very eyes, his beautiful form, and his fine horns, for it was a buck. I pulled one trigger—it snapped, the animal moved not; I pulled the other, snapped again, and away the Antelope bounded, and ran swiftly from me. I put on fresh caps, and saw it stop after going a few hundred yards, and presently it came towards me again, but not within one hundred and fifty yards, when seeing that it would not come nearer I pulled the trigger with the ball; off it went, and so did the Antelope, which this time went quite out of my sight. I returned to camp and found all ready for a move. Owen went up a hill to reconnoitre for Antelopes and cows; seeing one of the former he crept after it. Bell followed, and at this moment a Hare leaped from the path before us, and stopped within twenty paces. Harris was not loaded with shot, and I only with buck-shot; however, I fired and killed it; it proved to be a large female, and after measuring, we skinned it, and I put on a label "Townsend's Hare, killed a few miles from the three Mamelles, July 27, 1843." After travelling for a good while, Owen, who kept ahead of us, made signs from the top of a high hill that Buffaloes were in sight. This signal is made by walking the rider's horse backwards and forwards several times. We hurried on towards him, and when we reached the place, he pointed to the spot where he had seen them, and said they were travelling fast, being a band of both cows and bulls. The hunters were mounted at once, and on account of Squires' soreness I begged him not to run; so he drove me in the wagon as fast as possible over hills, through plains and ravines of all descriptions, at a pace beyond belief. From time to time we saw the hunters, and once or twice the Buffaloes, which were going towards the fort. At last we reached an eminence from which we saw both the game and the hunters approaching the cattle, preparatory to beginning the chase. It seems there is no etiquette among Buffalo hunters, and this proved a great disappointment to friend Harris, who was as anxious to kill a cow, as he had been to kill a bull. Off went the whole group, but the country was not as advantageous to the pursuers, as to the pursued. The cows separated from the bulls, the latter making their way towards us, and six of them passed within one hundred yards of where I stood; we let them pass, knowing well how savage they are at these times, and turned our eyes again to the hunters. I saw Mr. C. pursuing one cow, Owen another, and Bell a third. Owen shot one and mortally wounded it; it walked up on a hill and stood there for some minutes before falling. Owen killed a second close by the one Mr. C. had now killed, Bell's dropped dead in quite another direction, nearly one mile off. Two bulls we saw coming directly towards us, so La Fleur and I went under cover of the hill to await their approach, and they came within sixty yards of us. I gave La Fleur the choice of shooting first, as he had a rifle; he shot and missed; they turned and ran in an opposite direction, so that I, who had gone some little distance beyond La Fleur, had no chance, and I was sorry enough for my politeness. Owen had shot a third cow, which went part way up a hill, fell, and kicked violently; she, however, rose and again fell, and kept kicking with all her legs in the air. Squires now drove to her, and I walked, followed by Moncrévier, a hunter; seeing Mr. C. and Harris on the bottom below we made signs for them to come up, and they fortunately did, and by galloping to Squires probably saved that young man from more danger; for though I cried to him at the top of my voice, the wind prevented him from hearing me; he now stopped, however, not far from a badly broken piece of ground over which had he driven at his usual speed, which I doubt not he would have attempted, some accident must have befallen him. Harris and Mr. C. rode up to the cow, which expired at that moment. The cow Mr. C. had killed was much the largest, and we left a cart and two men to cut up this, and the first two Owen had killed, and went to the place where the first lay, to have it skinned for me. Bell joined us soon, bringing a tongue with him, and he immediately began operations on the cow, which proved a fine one, and I have the measurements as follows: "Buffalo Cow, killed by Mr. Alexander Culbertson, July 27, 1843. Nose to root of tail, 96 inches. Height at shoulder, 60; at rump, 55½. Length of tail vertebræ, 13; to end of hair, 25; from brisket to bottom of feet, 21½; nose to anterior canthus, 10½; between horns at root, 11⅜; between tops of ditto, 17⅛; between nostrils, 2¼; length of ditto, 2½; height of nose, 3⅛; nose to opening of ear, 20; ear from opening to tip, 5; longest hair on head, 14 inches; from angle of mouth to end of under lip, $3\frac{1}{2}$." Whilst we were at this, Owen and Pike were hacking at their cow. After awhile all was ready for departure, and we made for the "coupe" at two o'clock, and expected to have found water to enable us to water our horses, for we had yet some gallons of the Missouri water for our own use. We found the road to the "coupe," which was seen for many, many miles. The same general appearance of country shows throughout the whole of these dreary prairies; up one hill and down on the other side, then across a plain with ravines of more or less depth. About two miles west of the "coupe," Owen and others went in search of water, but in vain; and we have had to cross the "coupe" and travel fully two miles east of it, when we came to a mere puddle, sufficient however, for the night, and we stopped. The carts with the meat, and our effects, arrived after a while; the meat was spread on the grass, the horses and mules hoppled and let go, to drink and feed. All hands collected Buffalo dung for fuel, for not a bush was in sight, and we soon had a large fire. In the winter season this prairie fuel is too wet to burn, and oftentimes the hunters have to eat their meat raw, or go without their supper. Ours was cooked however; I made mine chiefly from the liver, as did Harris; others ate boiled or roasted meat as they preferred. The tent was pitched, and I made a bed for Mr. C. and myself, and guns, etc., were all under cover; the evening was cool, the wind fresh, and no mosquitoes. We had seen plenty of Antelopes; I shot at one twenty yards from the wagon with small shot. Harris killed a Wolf, but we have seen very few, and now I will wish you all good-night; God bless you!

July 28, Friday. This morning was cold enough for a frost, but we all slept soundly until daylight, and about half-past three we were called for breakfast. The horses had all gone but four, and, as usual, Owen was despatched for them. The horses were brought back, our coffee swallowed, and we were off, Mr. C. and I, in the wagon. We saw few Antelopes, no Buffalo, and reached the ferry opposite the fort at half-past seven. We found all well, and about eleven Assiniboins, all young men, headed by the son of a great chief called "Le mangeur d'hommes" (the man-eater). The poor wretched Indian whom Harris had worked over, died yesterday morning, and was buried at once. I had actually felt chilly riding in the wagon, and much enjoyed a breakfast Mrs. Culbertson had kindly provided for me. We had passed over some very rough roads, and at breakneck speed, but I did not feel stiff as I expected, though somewhat sore, and a good night's rest is all I need. This afternoon the cow's skin and head, and the Hare arrived, and have been preserved. A half-breed well known to Provost has been here to make a bargain with me about Bighorns, Grizzly Bear, etc., and will see what he and his two sons can do; but I have little or no confidence in these gentry. I was told this afternoon that at Mouse River, about two hundred miles north of this, there are eight hundred carts in one gang, and four hundred in another, with an adequate number of half-breeds and Indians, killing Buffalo and drying their meat for winter provisions, and that the animals are there in millions. When Buffalo bulls are shot from a distance of sixty or seventy yards, they rarely charge on the hunter, and Mr. Culbertson has killed as many as nine bulls from the same spot, when unseen by these terrible beasts. Beavers, when shot swimming, and killed, sink at once to the bottom, but their bodies rise again in from twenty to thirty minutes. Hunters, who frequently shoot and kill them by moonlight, return in the morning from their camping-places, and find them on the margins of the shores where they had shot. Otters do the same, but remain under water for an hour or more.

July 29, Saturday. Cool and pleasant. About one hour after daylight Harris, Bell, and two others, crossed the river, and went in search of Rabbits, but all returned without success. Harris, after breakfast, went off on this side, saw none, but killed a young Raven. During the course of the forenoon he and Bell went off again, and brought home an old and young of the Sharp-tailed Grouse. This afternoon they brought in a Loggerhead Shrike and two Rock Wrens. Bell skinned all these. Sprague made a handsome sketch of the five young Buffaloes belonging to the fort. This evening Moncrévier and Owen went on the other side of the river, but saw nothing. We collected berries of the dwarf cherries of this part, and I bottled some service-berries to carry home.

July 30, Sunday. Weather cool and pleasant. After breakfast we despatched La Fleur and Provost after Antelopes and Bighorns. We then went off and had a battue for Rabbits, and although we were nine in number, and all beat the rose bushes and willows for several hundred yards, not one did we see, although their traces were apparent in several places. We saw tracks of a young Grizzly Bear near the river shore. After a good dinner of Buffalo meat, green peas, and a pudding, Mr. C., Owen, Mr. Pike, and I went off to Fort Mortimer. We had an arrival of five squaws, half-breeds, and a gentleman of the same order, who came to see our fort and our ladies. The princess went out to meet them covered with a fine shawl, and the visitors followed her to her own room. These ladies spoke both the French and Cree languages. At Fort Mortimer we found the hunters from the north, who had returned last evening and told me they had seen nothing. I fear that all my former opinions of the half-breeds are likely to be realized, and that they are all more *au fait* at telling lies, than anything else; and I expect now that we shall have to make a regular turn-out ourselves, to kill both Grizzly Bears and Big-horns. As we were riding along not far from this fort, Mr. Culbertson fired off the gun given him by Harris, and it blew off the stock, lock, and breech, and it was a wonder it did not kill him, or me, as I was sitting by his side. After we had been at home about one hour, we were all called out of a sudden by the news that the *Horse Guards* were coming, full gallop, driving the whole of their charge before them. We saw the horses, and the cloud of dust that they raised on the prairies, and presently, when the Guards reached the gates, they told us that they had seen a party of Indians, which occasioned their hurried return. It is now more than one hour since I wrote this, and the Indians are now in sight, and we think they were frightened by three or four squaws who had left the fort in search of "pommes blanches." Sprague has collected a few seeds, but I intend to have some time devoted to this purpose before we leave on our passage downwards. This evening five Indians arrived, among whom is the brother of the man who died a few days ago; he brought a horse, and an Elk skin, which I bought, and he now considers himself a rich man. He reported Buffaloes very near, and to-morrow morning the hunters will be after them. When Buffaloes are about to lie down, they draw all their four feet together slowly, and balancing the body for a moment, bend their fore legs, and fall on their knees first, and the hind ones follow. In young animals, some of which we have here, the effect produced on their tender skin is directly seen, as callous round patches without hair are found; after the animal is about one year old, these are seen no more. I am told that Wolves have not been known to attack men and horses in these parts, but they do attack mules and colts, always making choice of the fattest. We scarcely see one now-a-days about the fort, and yet two miles from here, at Fort Mortimer, Mr. Collins tells me it is impossible to sleep, on account of their howlings at night. When Assiniboin Indians lose a relative by death, they go and cry under the box which contains the body, which is placed in a tree, cut their legs and different parts of the body, and moan miserably for hours at a time. This performance has been gone through with by the brother of the Indian who died here.

July 31, Monday. Weather rather warmer. Mr. Larpenteur went after Rabbits, saw none, but found a horse, which was brought home this afternoon. Mr. C., Harris, Bell, and Owen went after Buffaloes over the hills, saw none, so that all this day has been disappointment to us. Owen caught a *Spermophilus hoodii.* The brother of the dead Indian, who gashed his legs fearfully this morning, went off with his wife and children and six others, who had come here to beg. One of them had for *a letter of recommendation* one of the advertisements of the steamer "Trapper," which will be kept by his chief for time immemorial to serve as a pass for begging. He received from us ammunition and tobacco. Sprague collected seeds this morning, and this afternoon copied my sketch of the three Mamelles. Towards sunset I intend to go myself after Rabbits, along the margins of the bushes and the shore. We have returned from my search after Rabbits; Harris and I each shot one. We saw five Wild Geese. Harris lost his snuff-box, which he valued, and which I fear will never be found. Squires to-day proposed to me to let him remain here this winter to procure birds and quadrupeds, and I would have said "yes" at once, did he understand either or both these subjects, or could draw; but as he does not, it would be useless.

August 1, Tuesday. The weather fine, and warmer than yesterday. We sent off four Indians after Rabbits, but as we foolishly gave them powder and shot, they returned without any very soon, having, of course, hidden the ammunition. After breakfast Mr. C. had a horse put in the cart, and three squaws went off after "pommes blanches," and Sprague and I followed in the wagon, driven by Owen. These women carried sticks pointed at one end, and blunt at the other, and I was perfectly astonished at the dexterity and rapidity with which they worked. They place the pointed end within six inches of the plant, where the stem enters the earth, and bear down upon the other end with all their weight and move about to the right and left of the plant until the point of the stick is thrust in the ground to the depth of about seven inches, when acting upon it in the manner of a lever, the plant is fairly thrown out, and the root procured. Sprague and I, who had taken with us an instrument resembling a very narrow hoe, and a spade, having rather despised the simple instruments of the squaws, soon found out that these damsels could dig six or seven, and in some cases a dozen, to our *one*. We collected some seeds of these plants as well as those of some others, and walked fully six miles, which has rendered my feet quite tender again. Owen told me that he had seen, on his late journey up the Yellowstone, Grouse, both old and young, with a black breast and with a broad tail; they were usually near the margin of a wood. What they are I cannot tell, but he and Bell are going after them to-morrow morning. Just after dinner Provost and La Fleur returned with two male Antelopes, skinned, one of them a remarkably large buck, the other less in size, both skins in capital order. We have taken the measurements of the head of the larger. The timber for our boat has been hauling across the sand-bar ever since daylight, and of course the work will proceed pretty fast. The weather is delightful, and at night, indeed, quite cool enough. I spoke to Sprague last night about remaining here next winter, as he had mentioned his wish to do so to Bell some time ago, but he was very undecided. My regrets that I promised you all so faithfully that I would return this fall are beyond description. I am, as years go, an old man, but I do not feel old, and there is so much of interest here that I forget oftentimes that I am not as young as Owen.

August 2, Wednesday. Bell and Owen started on their tour up the Yellowstone after Cocks of the Plain [Sage Grouse, *Centrocercus urophasianus*]. Provost and Moncrévier went in the timber below after Deer, but saw none. We had an arrival of six Chippeway Indians, and afterwards about a dozen Assiniboins. Both these parties were better dressed, and looked better off than any previous groups that we have seen at this fort. They brought some few robes to barter, and the traffic was carried on by Mr. Larpenteur in his little shop, through a wicket. On the arrival of the Assiniboins, who were headed by an old man, one of the Chippeways discovered a horse, which he at once not only claimed, but tied; he threw down his new blanket on the ground, and was leading off the horse, when the other Indian caught hold of it, and said that he had fairly bought it, etc. The Chippeway now gave him his gun, powder, and ball, as well as his *looking-glass,* the most prized of all his possessions, and the Assiniboin, now apparently satisfied, gave up the horse, which was led away by the new (or old) owner. We thought the matter was ended, but Mr. Culbertson told us that either the horse or the Chippeway would be caught and brought back. The latter had mounted a fine horse which he had brought with him, and was leading the other away, when presently a gun was heard out of the fort, and Mr. C. ran to tell us that the horse of the Chippeway had been shot, and that the rider was running as fast as he could to Fort Mortimer. Upon going out we found the horse standing still, and the man running; we went to the poor animal, and found that the ball had passed through the thigh, and entered the belly. The poor horse was trembling like an aspen; he at last moved, walked about, and went to the river, where he died. Now it is curious that it was not the same Assiniboin who had sold the horse that had shot, but another of their party; and we understand that it was on account of an old grudge against the Chippeway, who, by the way, was a surly-looking rascal. The Assiniboins brought eight or ten horses and colts, and a number of dogs. One of the colts had a necklace of "pommes blanches," at the end of which hung a handful of Buffalo calves' hoofs, not more than $\frac{3}{4}$ inch long, and taken from the calves before birth, when the mothers had been killed. Harris and I took a ride in the wagon over the Mauvaises Terres above the fort, in search of petrified wood, but though we found many specimens, they were of such indifferent quality that we brought home but one. On returning we followed a Wolf path, of which there are hundreds through the surrounding hills, all leading to the fort. It is curious to see how well they understand the best and shortest roads. From what had happened, we anticipated a row among the Indians, but all seemed quiet. Mr. C. gave us a good account of Fort McKenzie. I have been examining the fawn of the Long-tailed Deer of this country, belonging to old Baptiste; the man feeds it regularly, and the fawn follows him everywhere. It will race backwards and forwards over the prairie back of the fort, for a mile or more, running at the very top of its speed; suddenly it will make for the gate, rush through and overwhelm Baptiste with caresses, as if it had actually lost him for some time. If Baptiste lies on the ground pretending to sleep, the fawn pushes with its nose, and licks his face as a dog would, till he awakens.

August 3, Thursday. We observed yesterday that the atmosphere was thick, and indicated the first appearance of the close of summer, which here is brief. The nights and mornings have already become cool, and summer clothes will not be needed much longer, except occasionally. Harris and Sprague went to the hills so much encrusted with shells. We have had some talk about going to meet Bell and Owen, but the distance is too great, and Mr. C. told me he was not acquainted with the road beyond the first twenty-five or thirty miles. We have had a slight shower, and Mr. C. and I walked across the bar to see the progress of the boat. The horse that died near the river was hauled across to the sand-bar, and will make good catfish bate for our fishers. This morning we had another visitation of Indians, seven in number; they were very dirty, wrapped in disgusting Buffalo robes, and were not allowed inside the inner gate, on account of their filthy condition.

August 4, Friday. We were all under way this morning at half-past five, on a Buffalo hunt, that is to say, the residue of *us*, Harris and I, for Bell was away with Owen, and Squires with Provost after Bighorns, and Sprague at Fort Mortimer. Tobacco and matches had been forgotten, and that detained us for half an hour; but at last we started in good order, with only one cart following us, which carried Pike and Moncrévier. We saw, after we had travelled ten miles, some Buffalo bulls; some alone, others in groups of four or five, a few Antelopes, but more shy than ever before. I was surprised to see how careless the bulls were of us, as some actually gave us chances to approach them within a hundred yards, looking steadfastly, as if not caring a bit for us. At last we saw one lying down immediately in our road, and determined to give him a chance for his life. Mr. C. had a white horse, a runaway, in which he placed a good deal of confidence; he mounted it, and we looked after him. The bull did not start till Mr. C. was within a hundred yards, and then at a gentle and slow gallop. The horse galloped too, but only at the same rate. Mr. C. thrashed him until his hands were sore, for he had no whip, the bull went off without even a shot being fired, and the horse is now looked upon as forever disgraced. About two miles farther another bull was observed lying down in our way, and it was concluded to run him with the white horse, accompanied, however, by Harris. The chase took place, and the bull was killed by Harris, but the white horse is now scorned by every one. A few pieces of meat, the tongue, tail, and head, were all that was taken from this very large bull. We soon saw that the weather was becoming cloudy, and we were anxious to reach a camping-place; but we continued to cross ranges of hills, and hoped to see a large herd of Buffaloes. The weather was hot "out of mind," and we continued till, reaching a fine hill, we saw in a beautiful valley below us seventy to eighty head, feeding peacefully in groups and singly, as might happen. The bulls were mixed in with the cows, and we saw one or two calves. Many bulls were at various distances from the main group, but as we advanced towards them they galloped off and joined the others. When the chase began it was curious to see how much swifter the cows were than the bulls, and how soon they divided themselves into parties of seven or eight, exerting themselves to escape from their murderous pursuers. All in vain, however; off went the guns and down went the cows, or stood bleeding through the nose, mouth, or bullet holes. Mr. C. killed three, and Harris one in about half an hour. We had quite enough, and the slaughter was ended. We had driven up to the nearest fallen cow, and approached close to her, and found that she was not dead, but trying to rise to her feet. I cannot bear to see an animal suffer unnecessarily, so begged one of the men to take my knife and stab her to the heart, which was done. The animals were cut up and skinned, with considerable fatigue. To skin bulls and cows and cut up their bodies is no joke, even to such as are constantly in the habit of doing it. Whilst Mr. Culbertson and the rest had gone to cut up another at some distance, I remained on guard to save the meat from the Wolves, but none came before my companions returned. We found the last cow quite dead. As we were busy about her the rain fell in torrents, and I found my blanket *capote* of great service. It was now nearly sundown, and we made up our minds to camp close by, although there was no water for our horses, neither any wood. Harris and I began collecting Buffalo-dung from all around, whilst the others attended to various other affairs. The meat was all unloaded and spread on the ground, the horses made fast, the fire burned freely, pieces of liver were soon cooked and devoured, coffee drunk in abundance, and we went to rest.

August 5, Saturday. It rained in the night; but this morning the weather was cool, wind at northwest, and cloudy, but not menacing rain. We made through the road we had come yesterday, and on our way Harris shot a young of the Swift Fox, which we could have caught alive had we not been afraid of running into some hole. We saw only a few bulls and Antelopes, and some Wolves. The white horse, which had gone out as a *hunter,* returned as a *pack-horse,* loaded with the entire flesh of a Buffalo cow; and our two mules drew three more and the heads of all four. This morning at daylight, when we were called to drink our coffee, there was a Buffalo feeding within twenty steps of our tent, and it moved slowly towards the hills as we busied ourselves making preparations for our departure. We reached the fort at noon; Squires, Provost, and La Fleur had returned; they had wounded a Bighorn, but had lost it. Owen and Bell returned this afternoon; they had seen no Cocks of the plains, but brought the skin of a female Elk, a Porcupine, and a young White-headed Eagle. Provost tells me that Buffaloes become so very poor during hard winters, when the snows cover the ground to the depth of two or three feet, that they lose their hair, become covered with scabs, on which the Magpies feed, and the poor beasts die by hundreds. One can hardly conceive how it happens, notwithstanding these many deaths and the immense numbers that are murdered almost daily on these boundless wastes called prairies, besides the hosts that are drowned in the freshets, and the hundreds of young calves who die in early spring, so many are yet to be found. Daily we see so many that we hardly notice them more than the cattle in our pastures about our homes. But this cannot last; even now there is a perceptible difference in the size of the herds, and before many years the Buffalo, like the Great Auk, will have disappeared; surely this should not be permitted. Bell has been relating his adventures, our boat is going on, and I wish I had a couple of Bighorns. God bless you all.

August 6, Sunday. I very nearly lost the skin of the Swift Fox, for Harris supposed the animal rotten with the great heat, which caused it to have an odor almost insupportable, and threw it on the roof of the gallery. Bell was so tired he did not look at it, so I took it down, skinned it, and with the assistance of Squires put the coat into pickle, where I daresay it will keep well enough. The weather is thick, and looks like a thunderstorm. Bell, having awaked refreshed by his night's rest, has given me the measurements of the Elk and the Porcupine. Provost has put the skin of the former in pickle, and has gone to Fort Mortimer to see Boucherville and others, to try if they would go after Bighorn tomorrow morning. This afternoon we had an arrival of Indians, the same who were here about two weeks ago. They had been to Fort Clark, and report that a battle had taken place between the Crees and Gros Ventres, and that the latter had lost. Antelopes often die from the severity of the winter weather, and are found dead and shockingly poor, even in the immediate vicinity of the forts. These animals are caught in pens in the manner of Buffaloes, and are despatched with clubs, principally by the squaws. In 1840, during the winter, and when the snow was deep on the prairies and in the ravines by having drifted there, Mr. Laidlow, then at Fort Union, caught four Antelopes by following them on horseback and forcing them into these drifts, which were in places ten or twelve feet deep. They were brought home on a sleigh, and let loose about the rooms. They were so very gentle that they permitted the children to handle them, although being loose they could have kept from them. They were removed to the carpenter's shop, and there one broke its neck by leaping over a turning-lathe. The others were all killed in some such way, for they became very wild, and jumped, kicked, etc., till all were dead. Very young Buffaloes have been caught in the same way, by the same gentleman, assisted by Le Brun and four Indians, and thirteen of these he took down the river, when they became somewhat tamed. The Antelopes cannot be tamed except when caught young, and then they can rarely be raised. Mr. Wm. Sublette, of St. Louis, had one however, a female, which grew to maturity, and was so gentle that it would go all over his house, mounting and descending steps, and even going on the roof of the house. It was alive when I first reached St. Louis, but I was not aware of it, and before I left, it was killed by an Elk belonging to the same gentleman. Provost returned, and said that

Boucherville would go with him and La Fleur to-morrow morning early, *but I doubt it.*

August 7, Monday. Provost, Bell, and La Fleur started after breakfast, having waited nearly four hours for Boucherville. They left at seven, and the Indians were curious to know where they were bound, and looked at them with more interest than we all liked. At about nine, we saw Boucherville, accompanied by five men, all mounted, and they were surprised that Provost had not waited for them, or rather that he had left so early. I gave them a bottle of whiskey, and they started under the whip, and must have overtaken the first party in about two hours. To-day has been warmer than any day we have had for two weeks. Sprague has been collecting seeds, and Harris and I searching for stones with impressions of leaves and fern; we found several. Mr. Denig says the Assiniboins killed a Black Bear on White Earth River, about sixty miles from the mouth; they are occasionally killed there, but it is a rare occurrence. Mr. Denig saw the skin of a Bear at their camp last winter, and a Raccoon was also killed on the Cheyenne River by the Sioux, who knew not what to make of it. Mr. Culbertson has given me the following account of a skirmish which took place at Fort McKenzie in the Blackfoot country, which I copy from his manuscript.

"*August 28, 1834.* At the break of day we were aroused from our beds by the report of an enemy being in sight. This unexpected news created naturally a confusion among us all; never was a set of unfortunate beings so surprised as we were. By the time that the alarm had spread through the fort, we were surrounded by the enemy, who proved to be Assiniboins, headed by the chief Gauché (the Antelope). The number, as near as we could judge, was about four hundred. Their first attack was upon a few lodges of Piegans, who were encamped at the fort. They also, being taken by surprise, could not escape. We exerted ourselves, however, to save as many as we could, by getting them into the fort. But the foolish squaws, when they started from their lodges, each took a load of old saddles and skins, which they threw in the door, and stopped it so completely that they could not get in, and here the enemy massacred several. In the mean time our men were firing with muskets and shotguns. Unfortunately for us, we could not use our cannon, as there were a great many Piegans standing between us and the enemy; this prevented us from firing a telling shot on them at once. The engagement continued nearly an hour, when the enemy, finding their men drop very fast, retreated to the bluffs, half a mile distant; there they stood making signs for us to come on, and give them an equal chance on the prairie. Although our force was much weaker than theirs, we determined to give them a trial. At the same time we despatched an expert runner to an encampment of Piegans for a reinforcement. We mounted our horses, and proceeded to the field of battle, which was a perfect level, where there was no chance to get behind a tree, or anything else, to keep off a ball. We commenced our fire at two hundred yards, but soon lessened the distance to one hundred. Here we kept up a constant fire for two hours, when, our horses getting fatigued, we concluded to await the arrival of our reinforcements. As yet none of us were killed or badly wounded, and nothing lost but one horse, which was shot under one of our men named Bourbon. Of the enemy we cannot tell how many were killed, for as fast as they fell they were carried off the field. After the arrival of our reinforcements, which consisted of one hundred and fifty mounted Piegans, we charged and fought again for another two hours, and drove them across the Maria River, where they took another stand; and here Mr. Mitchell's horse was shot under him and he was wounded. In this engagement the enemy had a decided advantage over us, as they were concealed in the bushes, while we were in the open prairie. However, we succeeded in making them retreat from this place back on to a high prairie, but they suddenly rushed upon us and compelled us to retreat across the Maria. Then they had us in their power; but for some reason, either lack of courage or knowledge, they did not avail themselves of their opportunity. They could have killed a great many of us when we rushed into the water, which was almost deep enough to swim our horses; they were close upon us, but we succeeded in crossing before they fired. This foolish move came near being attended with fatal consequences, which we were aware of, but our efforts to stop it were unsuccessful. We, however, did not retreat far before we turned upon them again, with the determination of driving them to the mountains, in which we succeeded. By this time it was so dark that we could see no more, and we concluded to return. During the day we lost seven killed, and twenty wounded. Two of our dead the enemy had scalped. It is impossible to tell how many of the enemy were killed, but their loss must have been much greater than ours, as they had little ammunition, and at the last none. Our Indians took two bodies and burned them, after scalping them. The Indians who were with us in this skirmish deserve but little credit for their bravery, for in every close engagement the whites, who were comparatively few, always were in advance of them. This, however, had one good effect, for it removed the idea they had of our being cowards, and made them believe we were unusually brave. Had it not been for the assistance we gave the Piegans they would have been cut off, for I never saw Indians behave more bravely than the enemy this day; and had they been well supplied with powder and ball they would have done much more execution. But necessity compelled them to spare their ammunition, as they had come a long way, and they must save enough to enable them to return home. And on our side had we been positive they were enemies, even after they had surprised us in the manner they did, we could have killed many of them at first, but thinking that they were a band of Indians coming with this ceremony to trade (which is not uncommon) we did not fire upon them till the balls and arrows came whistling about our heads; then only was the word given, 'Fire!' Had they been bold enough at the onset to have rushed into the fort, we could have done nothing but suffer death under their tomahawks."

Mr. Denig gave me the following "Bear Story," as he heard it from the parties concerned: "In the year 1835 two men set out from a trading-post at the head of the Cheyenne, and in the neighborhood of the Black Hills, to trap Beaver; their names were Michel Carrière and Bernard Le Brun. Carrière was a man about seventy years old, and had passed most of his life in the Indian country, in this dangerous occupation of trapping. One evening as they were setting their traps along the banks of a stream tributary to the Cheyenne, somewhat wooded by bushes and cottonwood trees, their ears were suddenly saluted by a growl, and in a moment a large she Bear rushed upon them. Le Brun, being a young and active man, immediately picked up his gun, and shot the Bear through the bowels. Carrière also fired, but missed. The Bear then pursued them, but as they ran for their lives, their legs did them good service; they escaped through the bushes, and the Bear lost sight of them. They had concluded the Bear had given up the chase, and were again engaged in setting their traps, when Carrière, who was a short distance from Le Brun, went through a small thicket with a trap and came directly in front of the huge, wounded beast, which, with one spring, bounded upon him and tore him in an awful manner. With one stroke of the paw on his face and forehead he cut his nose in two, and one of the claws reached inward nearly to the brain at the root of the nose; the same stroke tore out his right eye and most of the flesh from that side of his face. His arm and side were *literally torn to pieces,* and the Bear, after handling him in this gentle manner for two or three minutes, threw him upwards about six feet, when he lodged, to all appearance dead, in the fork of a tree. Le Brun, hearing the noise, ran to his assistance, and again shot the Bear and killed it. He then brought what he at first thought was the dead body of his friend to the ground. Little appearance of a human being was left to the poor man, but Le Brun found life was not wholly extinct. He made a *travaille* and carried him by short stages to the nearest trading-post, where the wounded man slowly recovered, but was, of course, the most mutilated-looking being imaginable. Carrière, in telling the story, says that he fully believes it to have been the Holy Virgin that lifted him up and placed him in the fork of the tree, and thus preserved his life. The Bear is stated to have been as large as a common ox, and must have weighed, therefore, not far from 1500 lbs." Mr. Denig adds that he saw the man about a year after the accident, and some of the wounds were, even then, not healed. Carrière fully recovered, however, lived a few years, and was killed by the Blackfeet near Fort Union.

When Bell was fixing his traps on his horse this morning, I was amused to see Provost and La Fleur laughing outright at him, as he first put on a Buffalo robe under his saddle, a blanket over it, and over that his mosquito bar and his rain protector. These old hunters could not understand why he needed all these things to be comfortable; then, besides, he took a sack of ship-biscuit. Provost took only an old blanket, a few pounds of dried meat, and his tin cup, and rode off in his shirt and dirty breeches. La Fleur was worse off still, for he took no blanket, and said he could borrow Provost's tin cup; but he, being a most temperate man, carried the bottle of whiskey to mix with the brackish water found in the Mauvaises Terres, among which they have to travel till their return. Harris and I contemplated going to a quarry from which the stones of the powder magazine were brought, but it became too late for us to start in time to see much, and the wrong horses were brought us, being both *runners;* we went, however, across the river after Rabbits. Harris killed a Red-cheeked Woodpecker and shot at a Rabbit, which he missed. We had a sort of show by Moncrévier which was funny, and well performed; he has much versatility, great powers of mimicry, and is a far better actor than many who have made names for themselves in that line. Jean Baptiste told me the following: "About twelve years ago when Mr. McKenzie was the superintendent of this fort, at the season when green peas were plenty and good, Baptiste was sent to the garden about half a mile off, to gather a quantity. He was occupied doing this, when, at the end of a row, to his astonishment, he saw a very large Bear gathering peas also. Baptiste dropped his tin bucket, ran back to the fort as fast as possible, and told Mr. McKenzie, who immediately summoned several other men with guns; they mounted their horses, rode off, and killed the Bear; but, alas! Mr. Bruin had emptied the bucket of peas."

AUGUST 8, TUESDAY. Another sultry day. Immediately after breakfast Mr. Larpenteur drove Harris and myself in search of geological specimens, but we found none worth having. We killed a *Spermophilus hoodii,* which, although fatally wounded, entered its hole, and Harris had to draw it out by the hind legs. We saw a family of Rock Wrens, and killed four of them. I killed two at one shot; one of the others must have gone in a hole, for though we saw it fall we could not find it. Another, after being shot, found its way under a flat stone, and was there picked up, quite dead, Mr. Larpenteur accidentally turning the stone up. We saw signs of Antelopes and of Hares (Townsend), and rolled a large rock from the top of a high hill. The notes of the Rock Wren are a prolonged cree-è-è-è. On our return home we heard that Boucherville and his five hunters had returned with nothing for me, and they had not met Bell and his companions. We were told also that a few minutes after our departure the roarings and bellowings of Buffalo were heard across the river, and that Owen and two men had been despatched with a cart to kill three fat cows but *no more;* so my remonstrances about useless slaughter have not been wholly unheeded. Harris was sorry he had missed going, and so was I, as both of us could have done so. The milk of the Buffalo cow is truly good and finely tasted, but the bag is never large as in our common cattle, and this is probably a provision of nature to render the cows more capable to run off, and escape from their pursuers. Bell, Provost, and La Fleur returned just before dinner; they had seen no Bighorns, and only brought the flesh of two Deer killed by La Fleur, and a young Magpie. This afternoon Provost skinned a calf that was found by one of the cows that Owen killed; it was *very* young, only a few hours old, but large, and I have taken its measurements. It is looked upon as a phenomenon, as no Buffalo cow calves at this season. The calving time is from about the 1st of February to the last of May. Owen went six miles from the fort before he saw the cattle; there were more than three hundred in number, and Harris and I regretted the more we had not gone, but had been fruitlessly hunting for stones. It is curious that while Harris was searching for Rabbits early this morning, he heard the bellowing of the bulls, and thought first it was the growling of a Grizzly Bear, and then that it was the fort bulls, so he mentioned it to no one. To-morrow evening La Fleur and two men will go after Bighorns again, and they are not to return before they have killed one male, at least. This evening we went a-fishing across the river, and caught ten good catfish of the upper Missouri species, the sweetest and best fish of the sort that I have eaten in any part of the country. Our boat is going on well, and looks pretty to boot. Her name will be the "Union," in consequence of the united exertions of my companions to do all that could be done, on this costly expedition. The young Buffaloes now about the fort have begun shedding their red coats, the latter-colored hair dropping off in patches about the size of the palm of my hand, and the new hair is dark brownish black.

AUGUST 9, WEDNESDAY. The weather is cool and we are looking for rain. Squires, Provost, and La Fleur went off this morning after an early breakfast, across the river for Bighorns with orders not to return without some of these wild animals, which reside in the most inaccessible portions of the broken and lofty clay hills and stones that exist in this region of the country; they never resort to the low lands except when moving from one spot to another; they swim rivers well, as do Antelopes. I have scarcely done anything but write this day, and my memorandum books are now crowded with sketches, measurements, and descriptions. We have nine Indians, all Assiniboins, among whom *five* are chiefs. These nine Indians fed for three days on the flesh of only a single Swan; they saw no Buffaloes, though they report large herds about their village, fully two hundred miles from here. This evening I caught about one dozen catfish, and shot a *Spermophilus hoodii,* an old female, which had her pouches distended and filled with the seeds of the wild sunflower of this region. I am going to follow one of their holes and describe the same.

AUGUST 10, THURSDAY. Bell and I took a walk after Rabbits, but saw none. The nine Indians, having received their presents, went off with apparent reluctance, for when you begin to give them, the more they seem to demand. The horseguards brought in another *Spermophilus hoodii;* after dinner we are going to examine one of their burrows. We have been, and have returned; the three burrows which we dug were as follows: straight downward for three or four inches, and gradually becoming deeper in an oblique slant, to the depth of eight or nine inches, but not more, and none of these holes extended more than six or seven feet beyond this. I was disappointed at not finding nests, or rooms for stores. Although I have said much about Buffalo running, and butchering in general, I have not given the particular manner in which the latter is performed by the hunters of this country,—I mean the white hunters,—and I will now try to do so. The moment that the Buffalo is dead, three or four hunters, their faces and hands often covered with gunpowder, and with pipes lighted, place the animal on its belly, and by drawing out each fore and hind leg, fix the body so that it cannot fall down again; an incision is made near the root of the tail, immediately above the root in fact, and the skin cut to the neck, and taken off in the roughest manner imaginable, downwards and on both sides at the same time. The knives are going in all directions, and many wounds occur to the hands and fingers, but are rarely attended to at this time. The pipe of one man has perhaps given out, and with his bloody hands he takes the one of his nearest companion, who has his own hands equally bloody. Now one breaks in the skull of the bull, and with bloody fingers draws out the hot brains and swallows them with peculiar zest; another has now reached the liver, and is gobbling down enormous pieces of it; whilst, perhaps, a third, who has come to the paunch, is feeding luxuriously on some—to me—disgusting-looking offal. But the main business proceeds. The flesh is taken off from the sides of the boss, or hump bones, from where these bones begin to the very neck, and the hump itself is thus destroyed. The hunters give the name of "hump" to the mere bones when slightly covered by flesh; and it is cooked, and very good when fat, young, and well broiled. The pieces of flesh taken from the sides of these bones are called *filets,* and are the best portion of the animal when properly cooked. The forequarters, or shoulders, are taken off, as well as the hind ones, and the sides, covered by a thin portion of flesh called the *depouille,* are taken out. Then the ribs are broken off at the vertebræ, as well as the boss bones. The marrow-bones, which are those of the fore and hind legs only, are cut out last. The feet usually remain attached to these; the paunch is stripped of its covering of layers of fat, the head and the backbone are left to the Wolves, the pipes are all emptied, the hands, faces, and clothes all bloody, and now a glass of grog is often enjoyed, as the stripping off the skins and flesh of three or four animals is truly very hard work. In some cases when no water was near, our supper was cooked without our being washed, and it was not until we had travelled several miles the next morning that we had any opportunity of cleaning ourselves; and yet, despite everything, we are all hungry, eat heartily, and sleep soundly. When the wind is high and the Buffaloes run towards it, the hunter's guns very often snap, and it is during their exertions to replenish their pans, that the powder flies and sticks to the moisture every moment accumulating on their faces; but nothing stops these daring and usually powerful men, who the moment the chase is ended, leap from their horses, let them graze, and begin their butcher-like work.

AUGUST 11, FRIDAY. The weather has been cold and windy, and the day has passed in comparative idleness with me. Squires returned this afternoon alone, having left Provost and La Fleur behind. They have seen only two Bighorns, a female and her young. It was concluded that, if our boat was finished by Tuesday next, we would leave on Wednesday morning, but I am by no means assured of this, and Harris was quite startled at the very idea. Our boat, though forty feet long, is, I fear, too small. *Nous verrons!* Some few preparations for packing have been made, but Owen, Harris, and Bell are going out early to-morrow morning to hunt Buffaloes, and when they return we will talk matters over. The activity of Buffaloes is almost beyond belief; they can climb the steep defiles of the Mauvaises Terres in hundreds of places where men cannot follow them, and it is a fine sight to see a large gang of them proceeding along these defiles four or five hundred feet above the level of the bottoms, and from which pathway if one of the number makes a mis-step or accidentally slips, he goes down rolling over and over, and breaks his neck ere the level ground is reached. Bell and Owen saw a bull about three years old that leaped a ravine filled with mud and water, at least twenty feet wide; it reached the middle at the first bound, and at the second was mounted on the opposite bank, from which it kept on bounding, till it gained the top of quite a high hill. Mr. Culbertson tells me that these animals can endure hunger in a most extraordinary manner. He says that a large bull was seen on a spot half way down a precipice, where it had slid, and from which it could not climb upwards, and either could not or would not descend; at any rate, it did not leave the position in which it found itself. The party who saw it returned to the fort, and, on their way back on the *twenty-fifth* day after, they passed the hill, and saw the bull standing there. The thing that troubles them most is crossing rivers on the ice; their hoofs slip from side to side, they become frightened, and stretch their four legs apart to support the body, and in such situations the Indians and white hunters easily approach, and stab them to the heart, or cut the hamstrings, when they become an easy prey. When in large gangs those in the centre are supported by those on the outposts, and if the stream is not large, reach the shore and readily escape. Indians of different tribes hunt the Buffalo in different ways; some hunt on horseback, and use arrows altogether; they are rarely expert in reloading the gun in the close race. Others hunt on foot, using guns, arrows, or both. Others follow with patient perseverance, and kill them also. But I will give you the manner pursued by the Mandans. Twenty to fifty men start, as the occasion suits, each provided with two horses, one of which is a pack-horse, the other fit for the chase. They have quivers with from twenty to fifty arrows, according to the wealth of the hunter. They ride the pack horse bareback, and travel on, till they see the game, when they leave the pack-horse, and leap on the hunter, and start at full speed and soon find themselves amid the Buffaloes, on the flanks of the herd, and on both sides. When within a few yards the arrow is sent, they shoot at a Buffalo somewhat ahead of them, and send the arrow in an oblique manner, so as to pass through the lights. If the blood rushes out of the nose and mouth the animal is fatally wounded, and they shoot at it no more; if not, a second, and perhaps a third arrow, is sent before this happens. The Buffaloes on starting carry the tail close in between the legs, but when wounded they switch it about, especially if they wish to fight, and then the hunter's horse shies off and lets the mad animal breathe awhile. If shot through the heart, they occasionally fall dead on the instant; sometimes, if not hit in the right place, a dozen arrows will not stop them. When wounded and mad they turn suddenly round upon the hunter, and rush upon him in such a quick and furious manner that if horse and rider are not both on the alert, the former is overtaken, hooked and overthrown, the hunter pitched off, trampled and gored to death. Although the Buffalo is such a large animal, and to all appearance a clumsy one, it can turn with the quickness of thought, and when once enraged, will rarely give up the chase until avenged for the wound it has received. If, however, the hunter is expert, and the horse fleet, they outrun the bull, and it returns to the herd. Usually the greater number of the gang is killed, but it very rarely happens that some of them do not escape. This however is not the case when the animal is pounded, especially by the Gros Ventres, Black Feet, and Assiniboins. These pounds are called "parks," and the Buffaloes are made to enter them in the following manner: The park is sometimes round and sometimes square, this depending much on the ground where it is put up; at the end of the park is what is called a *precipice* of some fifteen feet or less, as may be found. It is approached by a funnel-shaped passage, which like the park itself is strongly built of logs, brushwood, and pickets, and when all is ready a young man, very swift of foot, starts at daylight covered over with a Buffalo robe and wearing a Buffalo head-dress. The moment he sees the herd to be taken, he bellows like a young calf, and makes his way slowly towards the contracted part of the funnel, imitating the cry of the calf, at frequent intervals. The Buffaloes advance after the decoy; about a dozen mounted hunters are yelling and galloping behind them, and along both flanks of the herd, forcing them by these means to enter the mouth of the funnel. Women and children are placed behind the fences of the funnel to frighten the cattle, and as soon as the young man who acts as decoy feels assured that the game is in a fair way to follow to the bank or "precipice," he runs or leaps down the bank, over the barricade, and either rests, or joins in the fray. The poor Buffaloes, usually headed by a large bull, proceed, leap down the bank in haste and confusion, the Indians all yelling and pursuing till every bull, cow, and calf is impounded. Although this is done at all seasons, it is more general in October or November, when the hides are good and salable. Now the warriors are all assembled by the pen, calumets are lighted, and the chief smokes to the Great Spirit, the four points of the compass, and lastly to the Buffaloes. The pipe is passed from mouth to mouth in succession, and as soon as this ceremony is ended, the destruction commences. Guns shoot, arrows fly in all directions, and the hunters being on the outside of the enclosure, destroy the whole gang, before they jump over to clean and skin the murdered herd. Even the children shoot small, short arrows to assist in the destruction. It happens sometimes however, that the leader of the herd will be restless at the sight of the precipices, and if the fence is weak will break through it, and all his fellows follow him, and escape. The same thing sometimes takes place in the pen, for so full does this become occasionally that the animals touch each other, and as they cannot move, the very weight against the fence of the pen is quite enough to break it through; the smallest aperture is sufficient, for in a few minutes it becomes wide, and all the beasts are seen scampering over the prairies, leaving the poor Indians starving and discomfited. Mr. Kipp told me that while travelling from Lake Travers to the Mandans, in the month of August, he rode in a heavily laden cart for six successive days through masses of Buffaloes, which divided for the cart, allowing it to pass without opposition. He has seen the immense prairie back of Fort Clark look black to the tops of the hills, though the ground was covered with snow, so crowded was it with these animals; and the masses probably extended much further. In fact it is *impossible to describe or even conceive* the vast multitudes of these animals that exist even now, and feed on these ocean-like prairies.

August 12, Saturday. Harris, Bell, and Owen went after Buffaloes; killed six cows and brought them home. Weather cloudy, and rainy at times. Provost returned with La Fleur this afternoon, had nothing, but had seen a Grizzly Bear. The "Union" was launched this evening and packing, etc., is going on. I gave a memorandum to Jean Baptiste Moncrévier of the animals I wish him to procure for me.

August 13, Sunday. A most beautiful day. About dinner time I had a young Badger brought to me dead; I bought it, and gave in payment two pounds of sugar. The body of these animals is broader than high, the neck is powerfully strong, as well as the fore-arms, and strongly clawed fore-feet. It weighed 8½ lbs. Its measurements were all taken.

When the pursuer gets between a Badger and its hole, the animal's hair rises, and it at once shows fight. A half-breed hunter told Provost, who has just returned from Fort Mortimer, that he was anxious to go down the river with me, but I know the man and hardly care to have him. If I decide to take him Mr. Culbertson, to whom I spoke of the matter, told me my only plan was to pay him by the piece for what he killed and brought on board, and that in case he did not turn out well between this place and Fort Clark, to leave him there; so I have sent word to him to this effect by Provost this afternoon. Bell is skinning the Badger, Sprague finishing the map of the river made by Squires, and the latter is writing. The half-breed has been here, and the following is our agreement: "It is understood that François Détaillé will go with me, John J. Audubon, and to secure for me the following quadrupeds—if possible —for which he will receive the prices here mentioned, payable at Fort Union, Fort Clark, or Fort Pierre, as may best suit him.

For each Bighorn male	$10.00
For a large Grizzly Bear	20.00
For a large male Elk	6.00
For a Black-tailed Deer, male or female	6.00
For Red Foxes	3.00
For small Gray Foxes	3.00
For Badgers	2.00
For large Porcupine	2.00

Independent of which I agree to furnish him with his passage and food, he to work as a hand on board. Whatever he kills for food will be settled when he leaves us, or, as he says, when he meets the Opposition boat coming up to Fort Mortimer." He will also accompany us in our hunt after Bighorns, which I shall undertake, notwithstanding Mr. Culbertson and Squires, who have been to the Mauvaises Terres, both try to dissuade me from what they fear will prove over-fatiguing; but though my strength is not what it was twenty years ago, I am yet equal to much, and my eyesight far keener than that of many a younger man, though that too tells me I am no longer a youth. . . .

The only idea I can give in *writing* of what are called the "Mauvaises Terres" would be to place some thousands of loaves of sugar of different sizes, from quite small and low, to large and high, all irregularly truncated at top, and placed somewhat apart from each other. No one who has not seen these places can form any idea of these resorts of the Rocky Mountain Rams, or the difficulty of approaching them, putting aside their extreme wildness and their marvellous activity. They form paths around these broken-headed cones (that are from three to fifteen hundred feet high), and run round them at full speed on a track that, to the eye of the hunter, does not appear to be more than a few inches wide, but which is, in fact, from a foot to eighteen inches in width. In some places there are piles of earth from eight to ten feet high, or even more, the tops of which form platforms of a hard and shelly rocky substance, where the Bighorn is often seen looking on the hunter far below, and standing immovable, as if a statue. No one can imagine how they reach these places, and that too with their young, even when the latter are quite small. Hunters say that the young are usually born in such places, the mothers going there to save the helpless little one from the Wolves, which, after men, seem to be their greatest destroyers. The Mauvaises Terres are mostly formed of grayish white clay, very sparsely covered with small patches of thin grass, on which the Bighorns feed, but which, to all appearance, is a very scanty supply, and there, and there only, they feed, as not one has ever been seen on the bottom or prairie land further than the foot of these most extraordinary hills. In wet weather, no man can climb any of them, and at such times they are greasy, muddy, sliding grounds. Oftentimes when a Bighorn is seen on a hill-top, the hunter has to ramble about for three or four miles before he can approach within gunshot of the game, and if the Bighorn ever sees his enemy, pursuit is useless. The tops of some of these hills, and in some cases whole hills about thirty feet high, are composed of a conglomerated mass of stones, sand, and clay, with earth of various sorts, fused together, and having a brick-like appearance. In this mass pumice-stone of various shapes and sizes is to be found. The whole is evidently the effect of volcanic action. The bases of some of these hills cover an area of twenty acres or more, and the hills rise to the height of three or four hundred feet, sometimes even to eight hundred or a thousand; so high can the hunter ascend that the surrounding country is far, far beneath him. The strata are of different colored clays, coal, etc., and an earth impregnated with a salt which appears to have been formed by internal fire or heat, the earth or stones of which I have first spoken in this account, lava, sulphur, salts of various kinds, oxides and sulphates of iron; and in the sand at the tops of some of the highest hills I have found marine shells, but so soft and crumbling as to fall apart the instant they were exposed to the air. I spent some time over various lumps of sand, hoping to find some perfect ones that would be hard enough to carry back to St. Louis; but 't was "love's labor lost," and I regretted exceedingly that only a few fragments could be gathered. I found globular and oval shaped stones, very heavy, apparently composed mostly of iron, weighing from fifteen to twenty pounds; numbers of petrified stumps from one to three feet in diameter; the Mauvaises Terres abound with them; they are to be found in all parts from the valleys to the tops of the hills, and appear to be principally of cedar. On the sides of the hills, at various heights, are shelves of rock or stone projecting out from two to six, eight, or even ten feet, and generally square, or nearly so; these are the favorite resorts of the Bighorns during the heat of the day, and either here or on the tops of the highest hills they are to be found. Between the hills there is generally quite a growth of cedar, but mostly stunted and crowded close together, with very large stumps, and between the stumps quite a good display of grass; on the summits, in some *few* places, there are table-lands, varying from an area of one to ten or fifteen acres; these are covered with a short, dry, wiry grass, and immense quantities of flat leaved cactus, the spines of which often warn the hunter of their proximity, and the hostility existing between them and his feet. These plains are not more easily travelled than the hillsides, as every step may lead the hunter into a bed of these pests of the prairies. In the valleys between the hills are ravines, some of which are not more than ten or fifteen feet wide, while their depth is beyond the reach of the eye. Others vary in depth from ten to fifty feet, while some make one giddy to look in; they are also of various widths, the widest perhaps a hundred feet. The edges, at times, are lined with bushes, mostly wild cherry; occasionally Buffaloes make paths across them, but this is rare. The only safe way to pass is to follow the ravine to the head, which is usually at the foot of some hill, and go round. These ravines are mostly between every two hills, although like every general rule there are variations and occasionally places where three or more hills make only one ravine. These small ravines all connect with some larger one, the size of which is in proportion to its tributaries. The large one runs to the river, or the water is carried off by a subterranean channel. In these valleys, and sometimes on the tops of the hills, are holes, called "sink holes;" these are formed by the water running in a small hole and working away the earth beneath the surface, leaving a crust incapable of supporting the weight of a man; and if an unfortunate steps on this crust, he soon finds himself in rather an unpleasant predicament. This is one of the dangers that attend the hunter in these lands; these holes eventually form a ravine such as I have before spoken of. Through these hills it is almost impossible to travel with a horse, though it is sometimes done by careful management, and a correct knowledge of the country. The sides of the hills are very steep, covered with the earth and stones of which I have spoken, all of which are quite loose on the surface; occasionally a bunch of wormwood here and there seems to assist the daring hunter; for it is no light task to follow the Bighorns through these lands, and the pursuit is attended with much danger, as the least slip at times would send one headlong into the ravines below. On the sides of these high hills the water has washed away the earth, leaving caves of various sizes; and, in fact, in some places all manner of fantastic forms are made by the same process. Occasionally in the valleys are found isolated cones or domes, destitute of vegetation, naked and barren. Throughout the Mauvaises Terres there are springs of water impregnated with salt, sulphur, magnesia, and many other salts of all kinds. Such is the water the hunter is compelled to drink, and were it not that it is as cold as ice it would be almost impossible to swallow it. As it is, many of these waters operate as cathartics or emetics; this is one of the most disagreeable attendants of hunting in these lands. Moreover, venomous snakes of many kinds are also found here. I saw myself only one copperhead, and a common gartersnake. Notwithstanding the rough nature of the country, the Buffaloes have paths running in all directions, and leading from the prairies to the river. The hunter sometimes, after toiling for an hour or two up the side of one of these hills, trying to reach the top in hopes that when there he will have for a short distance at least, either a level place or good path to walk on, finds to his disappointment that he has secured a point that only affords a place scarcely large enough to stand on, and he has the trouble of descending, perhaps to renew his disappointment in the same way, again and again, such is the deceptive character of the country. I was thus deceived time and again, while in search of Bighorns. If the hill does not terminate in a point it is connected with another hill, by a ridge so narrow that nothing but a Bighorn can walk on it. This is the country that the Mountain Ram inhabits, and if, from this imperfect description, any information can be derived, I shall be more than repaid for the trouble I have had in these tiresome hills. Whether my theory be correct or incorrect, it is this: These hills were at first composed of the clays that I have mentioned, mingled with an immense quantity of combustible material, such as coal, sulphur, bitumen, etc.; these have been destroyed by fire, or (at least the greater part) by volcanic action, as to this day, on the Black Hills and in the hills near where I have been, fire still exists; and from the immense quantities of pumice-stone and melted ores found among the hills, even were there no fire now to be seen, no one could doubt that it had, at some date or other, been there; as soon as this process had ceased, the rains washed out the loose material, and carried it to the rivers, leaving the more solid parts as we now find them; the action of water to this day continues. As I have said, the Bighorns are very fond of resorting to the shelves, or ledges, on the sides of the hills, during the heat of the day, when these places are shaded; here they lie, but are aroused instantly upon the least appearance of danger, and, as soon as they have discovered the cause of alarm, away they go, over hill and ravine, occasionally stopping to look round, and when ascending the steepest hill, there is no apparent diminution of their speed. They will ascend and descend places, when thus alarmed, so inaccessible that it is almost impossible to conceive how, and where, they find a foothold. When observed before they see the hunter, or while they are looking about when first alarmed, are the only opportunities the hunter has to shoot them; for, as soon as they start there is no hope, as to follow and find them is a task not easily accomplished, for where or how far they go when thus on the alert, heaven only knows, as but few hunters have ever attempted a chase. At all times they have to be approached with the greatest caution, as the least thing renders them on the *qui vive*. When not found on these shelves, they are seen on the tops of the most inaccessible and highest hills, looking down on the hunters, apparently conscious of their security, or else lying down tranquilly in some sunny spot quite out of reach. As I have observed before, the only times that these animals can be shot are when on these ledges, or when moving from one point to another. Sometimes they move only a few hundred yards, but it will take the hunter several hours to approach near enough for a shot, so long are the *détours* he is compelled to make. I have been thus baffled two or three times. The less difficult hills are found cut up by paths made by these animals; these are generally about eighteen inches wide. These animals appear to be quite as agile as the European Chamois, leaping down precipices, across ravines, and running up and down almost perpendicular hills. The only places I could find that seemed to afford food for them, was between the cedars, as I have before mentioned; but the places where they are most frequently found are barren, and without the least vestige of vegetation. From the character of the lands where these animals are found, their own shyness, watchfulness, and agility, it is readily seen what the hunter must endure, and what difficulties he must undergo to near these "Wild Goats." It is one constant time of toil, anxiety, fatigue, and danger. Such the country! Such the animal! Such the hunting!

August 16. Started from Fort Union at 12 M. in the Mackinaw barge "Union." Shot five young Ducks. Camped at the foot of a high bluff. Good supper of Chickens and Ducks.

THURSDAY, 17TH. Started early. Saw three Bighorns, some Antelopes, and many Deer, fully twenty; one Wolf, twenty-two Swans, many Ducks. Stopped a short time on a bar. Mr. Culbertson shot a female Elk, and I killed two bulls. Camped at Buffalo Bluff, where we found Bear tracks.

FRIDAY, 18TH. Fine. Bell shot a superb male Elk. The two bulls untouched since killed. Stopped to make an oar, when I caught four catfish. "Kayac" is the French Missourian's name for Buffalo Bluffs, original French for Moose; in Assiniboin "Tah-Tah," in Blackfoot "Sick-e-chichoo," in Sioux "Tah-Tah." Fifteen to twenty female Elks drinking, tried to approach them, but they broke and ran off to the willows and disappeared. We landed and pursued them. Bell shot at one, but did not find it, though it was badly wounded. These animals are at times unwary, but at others vigilant, suspicious, and well aware of the coming of their enemies.

SATURDAY, 19TH. Wolves howling, and bulls roaring, just like the long continued roll of a hundred drums. Saw large gangs of Buffaloes walking along the river. Headed Knife River one and a half miles. Fresh signs of Indians, burning wood embers, etc. I knocked a cow down with two balls, and Mr. Culbertson killed her. Abundance of Bear tracks. Saw a great number of bushes bearing the berries of which Mrs. Culbertson has given me a necklace. Herds of Buffaloes on the prairies. Mr. Culbertson killed another cow, and in going to see it I had a severe fall over a partially sunken log. Bell killed a doe and wounded the fawn.

SUNDAY, 20TH. *Tamias quadrivittatus* runs up trees; abundance of them in the ravine, and Harris killed one. Bell wounded an Antelope. Thousands upon thousands of Buffaloes; the roaring of these animals resembles the grunting of hogs, with a rolling sound from the throat. Mr. C. killed two cows, Sprague killed one bull, and I made two sketches of it after death. The men killed a cow, and the bull would not leave her although shot four times. Stopped by the high winds all this day. Suffered much from my fall.

MONDAY, 21ST. Buffaloes all over the bars and prairies, and many swimming; the roaring can be heard for miles. The wind stopped us again at eight o'clock; breakfasted near the tracks of Bears surrounded by hundreds of Buffaloes. We left our safe anchorage and good hunting-grounds too soon; the wind blew high, and we were obliged to land again on the opposite shore, where the gale has proved very annoying. Bear tracks led us to search for those animals, but in vain. Collected seeds. Shot at a Rabbit, but have done nothing. Saw many young and old Ducks,—Black Mallards and Gadwalls. I shot a bull and broke his thigh, and then shot at him thirteen times before killing. Camped at the same place.

Tuesday, 22d. Left early and travelled about twelve miles. Went hunting Elks. Mr. Culbertson killed a Deer, and he and Squires brought the meat in on their backs. I saw nothing, but heard shots which I thought were from Harris. I ran for upwards of a mile to look for him, hallooing the whole distance, but saw nothing of him. Sent three men who hallooed also, but came back without further intelligence. Bell shot a female Elk and brought in part of the meat. We walked to the Little Missouri and shot the fourth bull this trip. We saw many Ducks. In the afternoon we started again, and went below the Little Missouri, returned to the bull and took his horns, etc. Coming back to the boat Sprague saw a Bear; we went towards the spot; the fellow had turned under the high bank and was killed in a few seconds. Mr. Culbertson shot it first through the neck, Bell and I in the body.

Wednesday, 23d. Provost skinned the Bear. No Prairie-Dogs caught. The wind high and cold. Later two Prairie-Dogs were shot; their notes resemble precisely those of the Arkansas Flycatcher. Left this afternoon and travelled about ten miles. Saw another Bear and closely observed its movements. We saw several drowned Buffaloes, and were passed by Wolves and Passenger Pigeons. Camped in a bad place under a sky with every appearance of rain.

Thursday, 24th. A bad night of wind, very cloudy; left early, as the wind lulled and it became calm. Passed "L'Ours qui danse," travelled about twenty miles, when we were again stopped by the wind. Hunted, but found nothing. The fat of our Bear gave us seven bottles of oil. We heard what some thought to be guns, but I believed it to be the falling of the banks. Then the Wolves howled so curiously that it was supposed they were Indian dogs. We went to bed all prepared for action in case of an attack; pistols, knives, etc., but I slept very well, though rather cold.

Friday, 25th. Fair, but foggy, so we did not start early. I found some curious stones with impressions of shells. It was quite calm, and we passed the two Riccaree winter villages. Many Eagles and Peregrine Falcons. Shot another bull. Passed the Gros Ventre village at noon; no game about the place. "La Main Gauche," an Assiniboin chief of great renown, left seventy warriors killed and thirty wounded on the prairie opposite, the year following the small-pox. The Gros Ventres are a courageous tribe. Reached the Mandan village; hundreds of Indians swam to us with handkerchiefs tied on their heads like turbans. Our old friend "Four Bears" met us on the shore; I gave him eight pounds of tobacco. He came on board and went down with us to Fort Clark, which we reached at four o'clock. Mr. Culbertson and Squires rode out to the Gros Ventre village with "Four Bears" after dark, and returned about eleven; they met with another chief who curiously enough was called "The Iron Bear."

Saturday, 26th. Fine, but a cold, penetrating wind. Started early and landed to breakfast. A canoe passed us with two men from the Opposition. We were stopped by the wind for four hours, but started again at three; passed the Butte Quarré at a quarter past five, followed now by the canoe, as the two fellows are afraid of Indians, and want to come on board our boat; we have not room for them, but will let them travel with us. Landed for the night, and walked to the top of one of the buttes from which we had a fine and very extensive view. Saw a herd of Buffaloes, which we approached, but by accident did not kill a cow. Harris, whom we thought far off, shot too soon and Moncrévier and the rest of us lost our chances. We heard Elks whistling, and saw many Swans. The canoe men camped close to us.

Sunday, 27th. Started early in company with the canoe. Saw four Wolves and six bulls, the latter to our sorrow in a compact group and therefore difficult to attack. They are poor at this season, and the meat very rank, but yet are fresh meat. The wind continued high, but we landed in the weeds assisted by the canoe men, as we saw a gang of cows. We lost them almost immediately though we saw their *wet tracks* and followed them for over a mile, but then gave up the chase. On returning to the river we missed the boat, as she had been removed to a better landing below; so we had quite a search for her. Mrs. Culbertson worked at the *parflèche* with Golden Eagle feathers; she had killed the bird herself. Stopped by the wind at noon. Walked off and saw Buffaloes, but the wind was adverse. Bell and Harris, however, killed a cow, a single one, that had been wounded, whether by shot or by an arrow no one can tell. We saw a bull on a sand-bar; the poor fool took to the water and swam so as to meet us. We shot at him about a dozen times, I shot him through one eye, Bell, Harris, and Sprague about the head, and yet the animal made for our boat and came so close that Mr. Culbertson touched him with a pole, when he turned off and swam across the river, but acted as if wild or crazy; he ran on a sand-bar, and at last swam again to the opposite shore, in my opinion to die, but Mr. Culbertson says he may live for a month. We landed in a good harbor on the east side about an hour before sundown. Moncrévier caught a catfish that weighed sixteen pounds, a fine fish, though the smaller ones are better eating.

Monday, 28th. A gale all night and this morning also. We are in a good place for hunting, and I hope to have more to say anon. The men returned and told us of many Bear tracks, and four of us started off. Such a walk I do not remember; it was awful—mire, willows, vines, holes, fallen logs; we returned much fatigued and having seen nothing. The wind blowing fiercely.

Tuesday, 29th. Heavy wind all night. Bad dreams about my own Lucy. Walked some distance along the shores and caught many catfish. Two Deer on the other shore. Cut a cotton-tree to fasten to the boat to break the force of the waves. The weather has become sultry. Beavers during the winter oftentimes come down amid the ice, but enter any small stream they meet with at once. Apple River, or Creek, was formerly a good place for them, as well as Cannon Ball River. Saw a Musk-rat this morning swimming by our barge. Slept on a muddy bar with abundance of mosquitoes.

Wednesday, 30th. Started at daylight. Mr. Culbertson and I went off to the prairies over the most infernal ground I ever saw, but we reached the high prairies by dint of industry, through swamps and mire. We saw two bulls, two calves, and one cow; we killed the cow and the larger calf, a beautiful young bull; returned to the boat through the most abominable swamp I ever travelled through, and reached the boat at one o'clock, thirsty and hungry enough. Bell and all the men went after the meat and the skin of the young bull. I shot the cow, but missed the calf by shooting above it. We started later and made about ten miles before sunset.

Thursday, 31st. Started early; fine and calm. Saw large flocks of Ducks, Geese, and Swans; also four Wolves. Passed Mr. Primeau's winter trading-house; reached Cannon Ball River at half-past twelve. No game; water good-tasted, but warm. Dinner on shore. Saw a Rock Wren on the bluffs here. Saw the prairie on fire, and signs of Indians on both sides. Weather cloudy and hot. Reached Beaver Creek. Provost went after Beavers, but found none. Caught fourteen catfish. Saw a wonderful example of the power of the Buffalo in working through the heavy, miry bottom lands.

Friday, September 1. Hard rain most of the night, and uncomfortably hot. Left our encampment at eight o'clock. Saw Buffaloes and landed, but on approaching them found only bulls; so returned empty-handed to the boat, and started anew. We landed for the night on a large sand-bar connected with the mainland, and saw a large gang of Buffaloes, and Mr. Culbertson and a man went off; they shot at two cows and killed one, but lost her, as she fell in the river and floated down stream, and it was dusk. A heavy cloud arose in the west, thunder was heard, yet the moon and stars shone brightly. After midnight rain came on. The mosquitoes are far too abundant for comfort.

Saturday, September 2. Fine but windy. Went about ten miles and stopped, for the gale was so severe. No fresh meat on board. Saw eight Wolves, four white ones. Walked six miles on the prairies, but saw only three bulls. The wind has risen to a gale. Saw abundance of Black-breasted Prairie Larks, and a pond with Black Ducks. Returned to the pond after dinner and killed four Ducks.

Sunday, 3d. Beautiful, calm, and cold. Left early and at noon put ashore to kill a bull, having no fresh meat on board. He took the wind and ran off. Touched on a bar, and I went overboard to assist in pushing off and found the water very pleasant, for our cold morning had turned into a hot day. Harris shot a Prairie Wolf. At half-past four saw ten or twelve Buffaloes. Mr. Culbertson, Bell, a canoe man, and I, went after them; the cattle took to the river, and we went in pursuit; the other canoe man landed, and ran along the shore, but could not head them. He shot, however, and as the cattle reached the bank we gave them a volley, but uselessly, and are again under way. Bell and Mr. C. were well mired and greatly exhausted in consequence. No meat for another day. Stopped for the night at the mouth of the Moreau River. Wild Pigeons, Sandpipers, but no fish.

Monday, 4th. Cool night. Wind rose early, but a fine morning. Stopped by the wind at eleven. Mr. Culbertson, Bell, and Moncrévier gone shooting. Many signs of Elk, etc., and flocks of Wild Pigeons. A bad place for hunting, but good for safety. Found Beaver tracks, and small trees cut down by them. Provost followed the bank and found their lodge, which he says is an old one. It is at present a mass of sticks of different sizes matted together, and fresh tracks are all around it. To dig them out would have proved impossible, and we hope to catch them in traps to-night. Beavers often feed on berries when they can reach them, especially Buffalo berries. Mr. Culbertson killed a buck, and we have sent men to bring it entire. The Beavers in this lodge are not residents, but vagrant Beavers. The buck was brought in; it is of the same kind as at Fort Union, having a longer tail, we think, than the kind found East. Its horns were very small, but it is skinned and in brine. We removed our camp about a hundred yards lower down, but the place as regards wood is very bad. Provost and I went to set traps for Beaver; he first cut two dry sticks eight or nine feet long; we reached the river by passing through the tangled woods; he then pulled off his breeches and waded about with a pole to find the depth of the water, and having found a fit spot he dug away the mud in the shape of a half circle, placed a bit of willow branch at the bottom and put the trap on that. He had two small willow sticks in his mouth; he split an end of one, dipped it in his horn of castoreum, or "medicine," as he calls his stuff, and left on the end of it a good mass of it, which was placed in front of the jaws of the trap next the shore; he then made the chain of the trap secure, stuck in a few untrimmed branches on each side, and there the business ended. The second one was arranged in the same way, except that there was no bit of willow under it. Beavers when caught in shallow water are often attacked by the Otter, and in doing this the latter sometimes lose their own lives, as they are very frequently caught in the other trap placed close by. Mr. Culbertson and Bell returned without having shot, although we heard one report whilst setting the traps. Elks are very numerous here, but the bushes crack and make so much noise that they hear the hunters and fly before them. Bell shot five Pigeons at once. Harris and Squires are both poorly, having eaten too indulgently of Buffalo brains. We are going to move six or seven hundred yards lower down, to spend the night in a more sheltered place. I hope I may have a large Beaver to-morrow.

Tuesday, 5th. At daylight, after some discussion about Beaver lodges, Harris, Bell, Provost, and I, with two men, went to the traps—nothing caught. We now had the lodge demolished outwardly, namely, all the sticks removed, under which was found a hole about two and a half feet in diameter, through which Harris, Bell, and Moncrévier (who had followed us) entered, but found nothing within, as the Beaver had gone to the river. Harris saw it, and also the people at the boat. I secured some large specimens of the cuttings used to build the lodge, and a pocketful of the chips. Before Beavers fell the tree they long for, they cut down all the small twigs and saplings around. The chips are cut above and below, and then split off by the animal; the felled trees lay about us in every direction. We left our camp at half-past five; I again examined the lodge, which was not finished, though about six feet in diameter. We saw a Pigeon Hawk giving chase to a Spotted Sandpiper on the wing. When the Hawk was about to seize the little fellow it dove under water and escaped. This was repeated five or six times; to my great surprise and pleasure, the Hawk was obliged to relinquish the prey. As the wind blew high, we landed to take breakfast, on a fine beach, portions of which appeared as if paved by the hand of man. The canoe men killed a very poor cow, which had been wounded, and so left alone. The wind fell suddenly, and we proceeded on our route till noon, when it rose, and we stopped again. Mr. Culbertson went hunting, and returned having killed a young buck Elk. Dined, and walked after the meat and skin, and took the measurements. Returning, saw two Elks driven to the hills by Mr. Culbertson and Bell. Met Harris, and started a monstrous buck Elk from its couch in a bunch of willows; shot at it while running about eighty yards off, but it was not touched. Meantime Provost had heard us from our dinner camp; loading his rifle he came within ten paces, when his gun snapped. We yet hope to get this fine animal. Harris found a Dove's nest with one young one, and an egg just cracked by the bird inside; the nest was on the ground. Curious all this at this late late season, and in a woody part of the country. Saw a Bat.

Wednesday, 6th. Wind blowing harder. Ransacked the point and banks both below and above, but saw only two Wolves; one a dark gray, the largest I have yet seen. Harris shot a young of the Sharp-tailed Grouse; Bell, three Pigeons; Provost went off to the second point below, about four miles, after Elks; Sprague found another nest of Doves on the ground, with very small young. The common Bluebird was seen, also a Whip-poor-will and a Night-Hawk. Wind high and from the south.

Thursday, 7th. About eleven o'clock last night the wind shifted *suddenly* to northwest, and blew so violently that we all left the boat in a hurry. Mrs. Culbertson, with her child in her arms, made for the willows, and had a shelter for her babe in a few minutes. Our guns and ammunition were brought on shore, as we were afraid of our boat sinking. We returned on board after a while; but I could not sleep, the motion making me very sea-sick; I went back to the shore and lay down after mending our fire. It rained hard for about two hours; the sky then became clear, and the wind wholly subsided, so I went again to the boat and slept till eight o'clock. A second gale now arose; the sky grew dark; we removed our boat to a more secure position, but I fear we are here for another day. Bell shot a *Caprimulgus,* so small that I have no doubt it is the one found on the Rocky Mountains by Nuttall, after whom I have named it. These birds are now travelling south. Mr. Culbertson and I walked up the highest hills of the prairie, but saw nothing. The river has suddenly risen two feet, the water rises now at the rate of eight inches in two and a half hours, and the wind has somewhat moderated. The little Whip-poor-will proves an old male, but it is now in moult. Left our camp at five, and went down rapidly to an island four miles below. Mr. Culbertson, Bell, Harris, and Provost went off to look for Elks, but I fear fruitlessly, as I see no tracks, nor do I find any of their beds. About ten o'clock Harris called me to hear the notes of the new Whip-poor-will; we heard two at once, and the sound was thus: "Oh-will, oh-will," repeated often and quickly, as in our common species. The night was beautiful, but cold.

FRIDAY, 8TH. Cloudy and remarkably cold; the river has risen $6\frac{1}{2}$ feet since yesterday, and the water is muddy and thick. Started early. The effect of sudden rises in this river is wonderful upon the sand-bars, which are no sooner covered by a foot or so of water than they at once break up, causing very high waves to run, through which no small boat could pass without imminent danger. The swells are felt for many feet as if small waves at sea. Appearances of rain. The current very strong; but we reached Fort Pierre at half-past five, and found all well.

SATURDAY, 9TH. Rain all night. Breakfasted at the fort. Exchanged our boat for a larger one. Orders found here obliged Mr. Culbertson to leave us and go to the Platte River establishment, much to my regret.

SUNDAY, 10TH. Very cloudy. Mr. Culbertson gave me a *parflèche* which had been presented to him by "L'Ours de Fer," the Sioux chief. It is very curiously painted, and is a record of a victory of the Sioux over their enemies, the Gros Ventres. Two rows of horses with Indians dressed in full war rig are rushing onwards; small black marks everywhere represent the horse tracks; round green marks are shields thrown away by the enemy in their flight, and red spots on the horses, like wafers, denote wounds.

Monday, 11th. Cloudy; the men at work fitting up our new boat. Rained nearly all day, and the wind shifted to every point of the compass. Nothing done.

Tuesday, 12th. Partially clear this morning early, but rained by ten o'clock. Nothing done.

Wednesday, 13th. Rainy again. Many birds were seen moving southwest. Our boat is getting into travelling shape. I did several drawings of objects in and about the fort.

Thursday, 14th. Cloudy and threatening. Mr. Laidlow making ready to leave for Fort Union, and ourselves for our trip down the river. Mr. Laidlow left at half-past eleven, and we started at two this afternoon; landed at the farm belonging to the fort, and procured a few potatoes, some corn, and a pig.

Friday, 15th. A foggy morning. Reached Fort George. Mr. Illingsworth left at half-past ten. Wind ahead, and we were obliged to stop on this account at two. Fresh signs of both Indians and Buffaloes, but nothing killed.

Saturday, 16th. Windy till near daylight. Started early; passed Ebbett's new island. Bell heard Parrakeets. The day was perfectly calm. Found *Arvicola pennsylvanica*. Landed at the Great Bend for Black-tailed Deer and wood. Have seen nothing worthy our attention. Squires put up a board at our old camp the "Six Trees," which I hope to see again. The Deer are lying down, and we shall not go out to hunt again till near sunset. The note of the Meadow Lark here is now unheard. I saw fully two hundred flying due south. Collected a good deal of the Yucca plant.

Sunday, 17th. We had a hard gale last night with rain for about an hour. This morning was beautiful; we started early, but only ran for two hours, when we were forced to stop by the wind, which blew a gale. Provost saw fresh signs of Indians, and we were told that there were a few lodges at the bottom of the Bend, about two miles below us. The wind is north and quite cold, and the contrast between to-day and yesterday is great. Went shooting, and killed three Sharp-tailed Grouse. Left our camp about three o'clock as the wind abated. Saw ten or twelve Antelopes on the prairie where the Grouse were. We camped about a mile from the spot where we landed in May last, at the end of the Great Bend. The evening calm and beautiful.

Monday, 18th. The weather cloudy and somewhat windy. Started early; saw a Fish Hawk, two Gulls, two White-headed Eagles and abundance of Golden Plovers. The Sharp-tailed Grouse feeds on rose-berries and the seeds of the wild sunflower and grasshoppers. Stopped at twenty minutes past nine, the wind was so high, and warmed some coffee. Many dead Buffaloes are in the ravines and on the prairies. Harris, Bell, and Sprague went hunting, but had no show with such a wind. Sprague outlined a curious hill. The wind finally shifted, and then lulled down. Saw Say's Flycatcher, with a Grosbeak. Saw two of the common Titlark. Left again at two, with a better prospect. Landed at sunset on the west side. Signs of Indians. Wolves howling, and found one dead on the shore, but too far gone to be skinned; I was sorry, as it was a beautiful gray one. These animals feed on wild plums in great quantities. Tried to shoot some Doves for my Fox and Badger, but without success. Pea-vines very scarce.

Tuesday, 19th. Dark and drizzly. Did not start until six. Reached Cedar Island, and landed for wood to use on the boat. Bell went off hunting. Wind north. Found no fit trees and left. Passed the burning cliffs and got on a bar. The weather fine, and wind behind us. Wolves will even eat the frogs found along the shores of this river. Saw five, all gray. At three o'clock we were obliged to stop on account of the wind, under a poor point. No game.

Wednesday, 20th. Wind very high. Tracks of Wild Cats along the shore. The motion of the boat is so great it makes me sea-sick. Sprague saw a Sharp-tailed Grouse. We left at half-past twelve. Saw immense numbers of Pin-tailed Ducks, but could not get near them. Stopped on an island to procure pea-vines for my young Deer, and found plenty. Our camp of last night was only two miles and a half below White River. Ran on a bar and were delayed nearly half an hour. Shot two Blue-winged Teal. Camped opposite Bijou's Hill.

Thursday, 21st. Wind and rain most of the night. Started early. Weather cloudy and cold. Landed to examine Burnt Hills, and again on an island for pea-vines. Fresh signs of Indians. Saw many Antelopes and

Mule Deer. At twelve saw a bull on one side of the river, and in a few moments after a herd of ten cattle on the other side. Landed, and Squires, Harris, Bell, and Provost have gone to try to procure fresh meat; these are the first Buffaloes seen since we left Fort Pierre. The hunters only killed one bull; no cows among eleven bulls, and this is strange at this season. Saw three more bulls in a ravine. Stopped to camp at the lower end of great Cedar Island at five o'clock. Fresh signs of Buffaloes and Deer. We cut some timber for oars. Rain set in early in the evening, and it rained hard all night.

Friday, 22d. Raining; left at a quarter past eight, with the wind ahead. Distant thunder. Everything wet and dirty after a very uncomfortable night. We went down the river about a mile, when we were forced to come to on the opposite side by the wind and the rain. Played cards for a couple of hours. No chance to cook or get hot coffee, on account of the heavy storm. We dropped down a few miles and finally camped till next day in the mud, but managed to make a roaring fire. Wolves in numbers howling all about us, and Owls hooting also. Still raining heavily. We played cards till nine o'clock to kill time. Our boat a quagmire.

Saturday, 23d. A cloudy morning; we left at six o'clock. Five Wolves were on a sand-bar very near us. Saw Red-shafted Woodpeckers, and two House Swallows. Have made a good run of about sixty miles. At four this afternoon we took in three men of the steamer "New Haven" belonging to the Opposition, which was fast on the bar, eight miles below. We reached Ponca Island and landed for the night. At dusk the steamer came up, and landed above us, and we found Messrs. Cutting and Taylor, and I had the gratification of a letter from Victor and Johnny, of July 22d.

Sunday, 24th. Cloudy, windy, and cold. Both the steamer and ourselves left as soon as we could see. Saw a Wolf on a bar, and a large flock of White Pelicans, which we took at first for a keel-boat. Passed the Poncas, L'Eau qui Court, Manuel, and Basil rivers by ten o'clock. Landed just below Basil River, stopped by wind. Hunted and shot one Raven, one Turkey Buzzard, and four Wood-ducks. Ripe plums abound, and there are garfish in the creek. Found feathers of the Wild Turkey. Signs of Indians, Elks, and Deer. Provost and the men made four new oars. Went to bed early.

Monday, 25th. Blowing hard all night, and began raining before day. Cold, wet, and misty. Started at a quarter past ten, passed Bonhomme Island at four, and landed for the night at five, fifteen miles below.

Tuesday, 26th. Cold and cloudy; started early. Shot a Pelican. Passed Jack's River at eleven. Abundance of Wild Geese. Bell killed a young White Pelican. Weather fairer but coldish. Sprague killed a Goose, but it was lost. Camped a few miles above the Vermilion River. Harris saw Raccoon tracks on Basil River.

Wednesday, 27th. Cloudy but calm. Many Wood-ducks, and saw Raccoon tracks again this morning. Passed the Vermilion River at half-past seven. My Badger got out of his cage last night, and we had to light a candle to secure it. We reached the Fort of Vermilion at twelve, and met with a kind reception from Mr. Pascal. Previous to this we met a barge going up, owned and commanded by Mr. Tybell, and found our good hunter Michaux. He asked me to take him down, and I promised him $20 per month to St. Louis. We bought two barrels of superb potatoes, two of corn, and a good fat cow. For the corn and potatoes I paid no less than $16.00.

Thursday, 28th. A beautiful morning, and we left at eight. The young man who brought me the calf at Fort George has married a squaw, a handsome girl, and she is here with him. Antelopes are found about twenty-five miles from this fort, but not frequently. Landed fifteen miles below on Elk Point. Cut up and salted the cow. Provost and I went hunting, and saw three female Elks, but the order was to shoot only bucks; a large one started below us, jumped into the river, and swam across, carrying his horns flat down and spread on each side of his back; the neck looked to me about the size of a flour-barrel. Harris killed a hen Turkey, and Bell and the others saw plenty but did not shoot, as Elks were the order of the day. I cannot eat beef after being fed on Buffaloes. I am getting an old man, for this evening I missed my footing on getting into the boat, and bruised my knee and my elbow, but at seventy and over I cannot have the spring of seventeen.

Friday, 29th. Rained most of the night, and it is raining and blowing at present. Crossed the river and have encamped at the mouth of the Iowa River the boundary line of the Sioux and Omahas. Harris shot a Wolf. My knee too sore to allow me to walk. Stormy all day.

Saturday, 30th. Hard rain all night, the water rose four inches. Found a new species of large bean in the Wild Turkey. Mosquitoes rather troublesome. The sun shining by eight o'clock, and we hope for a good dry day. Whip-poor-wills heard last night, and Night-hawks seen flying. Saw a Long-tailed Squirrel that ran on the shore at the cry of our Badger. Michaux had the boat landed to bring on a superb set of Elk-horns that he secured last week. Abundance of Geese and Ducks. Weather clouding over again, and at two we were struck by a heavy gale of wind, and were obliged to land on the weather shore; the wind continued heavy, and the motion of the boat was too much for me, so I slipped on shore and with Michaux made a good camp, where we rolled ourselves in our blankets and slept soundly.

Sunday, October 1. The wind changed, and lulled before morning, so we left at a quarter past six. The skies looked rather better, nevertheless we had several showers. Passed the [Big] Sioux River at twenty minutes past eleven. Heard a Pileated Woodpecker, and saw Fish Crows. Geese very abundant. Landed below the Sioux River to shoot Turkeys, having seen a large male on the bluffs. Bell killed a hen, and Harris two young birds; these will keep us going some days. Stopped again by the wind opposite Floyd's grave; started again and ran about four miles, when we were obliged to land in a rascally place at twelve o'clock. Had hail and rain at intervals. Camped at the mouth of the Omaha River, six miles from the village. The wild Geese are innumerable. The wind has ceased and stars are shining.

Monday, 2d. Beautiful but *cold*. The water has risen nine inches, and we travel well. Started early. Stopped at eight by the wind at a vile place, but plenty of Jerusalem artichokes, which we tried and found very good. Started again at three, and made a good run till sundown, when we found a fair camping-place and made our supper from excellent young Geese.

Tuesday, 3d. A beautiful, calm morning; we started early. Saw three Deer on the bank. A Prairie Wolf travelled on the shore beside us for a long time before he found a place to get up on the prairie. Plenty of Sand-hill Cranes were seen as we passed the Little Sioux River. Saw three more Deer, another Wolf, two Swans, several Pelicans, and abundance of Geese and Ducks. Passed Soldier River at two o'clock. We were caught by a snag that scraped and tore us a little. Had we been two feet nearer, it would have ruined our barge. We passed through a very swift cut-off, most difficult of entrance. We have run eighty-two miles and encamped at the mouth of the cut-off, near the old bluffs. Killed two Mallards; the Geese and Ducks are abundant beyond description. Brag, Harris' dog, stole and hid all the meat that had been cooked for our supper.

WEDNESDAY, 4TH. Cloudy and coldish. Left early and can't find my pocket knife, which I fear I have lost. We were stopped by the wind at Cabané Bluffs, about twenty miles above Fort Croghan; we all hunted, with only fair results. Saw some hazel bushes, and some black walnuts. Wind-bound till night, and nothing done.

THURSDAY, 5TH. Blew hard all night, but a clear and beautiful sunrise. Started early, but stopped by the wind at eight. Bell, Harris, and Squires have started off for Fort Croghan. As there was every appearance of rain we left at three and reached the fort about half-past four. Found all well, and were most kindly received. We were presented with some green corn, and had a quantity of bread made, also bought thirteen eggs from an Indian for twenty-five cents. Honey bees are found here, and do well, but none are seen above this place. I had an unexpected slide on the bank, as it had rained this afternoon; and Squires had also one at twelve in the night, when he and Harris with Sprague came to the boat after having played whist up to that hour.

FRIDAY, 6TH. Some rain and thunder last night. A tolerable day. Breakfast at the camp, and left at half-past eight. Our man Michaux was passed over to the officer's boat, to steer them down to Fort Leavenworth, where they are ordered, but we are to keep in company, and he is to cook for us at night. The whole station here is broken up, and Captain Burgwin leaves in a few hours by land with the dragoons, horses, etc. Stopped at Belle Vue at nine, and had a kind reception; bought 6 lbs. coffee, 13 eggs, 2 lbs. butter, and some black pepper. Abundance of Indians, of four different nations. Major Miller, the agent, is a good man for this place. Left again at eleven. A fine day. Passed the Platte and its hundreds of snags, at a quarter past one, and stopped for the men to dine. The stream quite full, and we saw some squaws on the bar, the village was in sight. Killed two Pelicans, but only got one. Encamped about thirty miles below Fort Croghan. Lieutenant Carleton supped with us, and we had a rubber of whist.

SATURDAY, 7TH. Fine night, and fine morning. Started too early, while yet dark, and got on a bar. Passed McPherson's, the first house in the

State of Missouri, at eight o'clock. Bell skinned the young of *Fringilla harrisi*. Lieutenant Carleton came on board to breakfast with us—a fine companion and a perfect gentleman. Indian war-whoops were heard by him and his men whilst embarking this morning after we left. We encamped at the mouth of Nishnebottana, a fine, clear stream. Went to the house of Mr. Beaumont, who has a pretty wife. We made a fine run of sixty or seventy miles.

SUNDAY, 8TH. Cloudy, started early, and had rain by eight o'clock. Stopped twice by the storm, and played cards to relieve the dulness. Started at noon, and ran till half-past four. The wind blowing hard we stopped at a good place for our encampment. Presented a plate of the quadrupeds to Lieut. James Henry Carleton, and he gave me a fine Black Bear skin, and has promised me a set of Elk horns. Stopped on the east side of the river in the evening. Saw a remarkably large flock of Geese passing southward.

MONDAY, 9TH. Beautiful and calm; started early. Bell shot a Gray Squirrel, which was divided and given to my Fox and my Badger. Squires, Carleton, Harris, Bell, and Sprague walked across the Bend to the Black Snake Hills, and killed six Gray Squirrels, four Parrakeets, and two Partridges. Bought butter, eggs, and some whiskey for the men; exchanged knives with the lieutenant. Started and ran twelve miles to a good camp on the Indian side.

TUESDAY, 10TH. Beautiful morning, rather windy; started early. Great flocks of Geese and Pelicans; killed two of the latter. Reached Fort Leavenworth at four, and, as usual everywhere, received most kindly treatment and reception from Major Morton. Lieutenant Carleton gave me the Elk horns. Wrote to John Bachman, Gideon B. Smith, and a long letter home.

WEDNESDAY, 11TH. Received a most welcome present of melons, chickens, bread, and butter from the generous major. Lieutenant Carleton came to see me off, and we parted reluctantly. Left at half-past six; weather calm and beautiful. Game scarce, paw-paws plentiful. Stopped at Madame Chouteau's, where I bought three pumpkins. Stopped at Liberty Landing and delivered the letters of Laidlow to Black Harris. Reached Independence Landing at sundown; have run sixty miles. Found no letters. Steamer "Lebanon" passed upwards at half-past eight.

Thursday, 12th. Beautiful and calm; stopped and bought eggs, etc., at a Mr. Shivers', from Kentucky. Ran well to Lexington, where we again stopped for provisions; ran sixty miles to-day.

Friday, 13th. Heavy white frost, and very foggy. Started early and ran well. Tried to buy butter at several places, but in vain. At Greenville bought coffee. Abundance of Geese and White Pelicans; many Sand-hill Cranes. Harris killed a Wood-duck. Passed Grand River; stopped at New Brunswick, where we bought excellent beef at 2½ cents a pound, but very inferior to Buffalo. Camped at a deserted wood yard, after running between sixty and seventy miles.

Saturday, 14th. A windy night, and after eight days' good run, I fear we shall be delayed to-day. Stopped by a high wind at twelve o'clock. We ran ashore, and I undertook to push the boat afloat, and undressing for the purpose got so deep in the mud that I had to spend a much longer time than I desired in very cold water. Visited two farm houses, and bought chickens, eggs, and butter; very little of this last. At one place we procured corn bread. The squatter visited our boat, and we camped near him. He seemed a good man; was from North Carolina, and had a fine family. Michaux killed two Hutchins' Geese, the first I ever saw in the flesh. Ran about twenty miles; steamer "Lebanon" passed us going downwards, one hour before sunset. Turkeys and Long-tailed Squirrels very abundant.

Sunday, 15th. Cold, foggy, and cloudy; started early. Passed Chariton River and village, and Glasgow; bought bread, and oats for my Deer. Abundance of Geese and Ducks. Passed Arrow Rock at eleven. Passed Boonesville, the finest country on this river; Rocheport, with high, rocky cliffs; six miles below which we encamped, having run sixty miles.

Monday, 16th. Beautiful autumnal morning, a heavy white frost and no wind. Started early, before six. The current very strong. Passed Nashville, Marion, and steamer "Lexington" going up. Jefferson City at twelve. Passed the Osage River and saw twenty-four Deer opposite Smith Landing; camped at sundown, and found Giraud, the "strong man." Ran sixty-one miles. Met the steamer "Satan," badly steered. Abundance of Geese and Ducks everywhere.

Tuesday, 17th. Calm and very foggy. Started early and floated a good deal with the strong current. Saw two Deer. The fog cleared off by nine o'clock. Passed the Gasconade River at half-past nine. Landed at Pinckney to buy bread, etc. Buffaloes have been seen mired, and unable to defend themselves, and the Wolves actually eating their noses while they struggled, but were eventually killed by the Wolves. Passed Washington and encamped below it at sundown; a good run.

Wednesday, 18th. Fine and calm; started very early. Passed Mount Pleasant. Landed at St. Charles to purchase bread, etc. Provost became extremely drunk, and went off by land to St. Louis. Passed the Charbonnière River, and encamped about one mile below. The steamer "Tobacco Plant" landed on the shore opposite. Bell and Harris killed a number of Gray Squirrels.

Thursday, 19th. A heavy white frost, foggy, but calm. We started early, the steamer after us. Forced by the fog to stop on a bar, but reached St. Louis at three in the afternoon. Unloaded and sent all the things to Nicholas Berthoud's warehouse. Wrote home.

Left St. Louis October 22, in steamer "Nautilus" for Cincinnati.

Reached home at 3 P.M., November 6th, 1843, and thank God, found all my family quite well.

EPISODES
("DELINEATIONS OF AMERICAN SCENERY AND CHARACTER")

These short personal essays, or "episodes," with the exception of the autobiographical piece Audubon wrote in 1831 ("My Style of Drawing Birds"), were all included by Audubon in the first three volumes of his five-volume Ornithological Biography *(1831–39). The main purpose of the* Biography, *of course, was to collect the "bird biographies," individual texts written by Audubon to provide information on the various species of birds contained in the* Birds of America *(1827–38). He inserted the episodes (there was a total of sixty) at regular intervals among the biographies. Audubon was always careful to distinguish the highly colored descriptions in the episodes (referred to collectively in the* Biography *as "delineations of American scenery and character") from the more serious and scientific bird biographies.*

When he eventually republished the revised bird biographies in the octavo edition of the Birds of America *(1840–44), combining both monumental works in a single definitive (and more affordable) testament, the episodes were deleted. The decision was deliberate but should not be thought of as a repudiation. Audubon, highly sensitive to his lack of a formal university education, wanted above all to be respected as a legitimate naturalist. The episodes were important to Audubon, but he realized they gave his critics and enemies just the ammunition they needed to ambush his presumptions as a scientist. Yet the episodes contain some of Audubon's most memorable writing and a wealth of vivid narrative portraits. In many ways, they are more vital expressions of Audubon the instinctive artist and untamed frontier spirit than the somewhat more studious descriptions of birds in the biographies.*

In writing the episodes, Audubon shifted back and forth between the frontier sketch (then much in vogue) and the informal travel essay, sometimes combining the two in original hybrids of his own invention. A large number of the episodes were taken directly from the journals he kept during his scouting expeditions for new birds in Florida, Labrador, and other remote regions. Others are remembrances from his early days in Kentucky and Louisiana wandering the primeval forests of the South. Of these, "The Prairie" is the most powerful, a hypnotic tale of evil outwitted, and one of the great narratives of the entire overdramatic frontier experience. And a few, including the unforgettable "Death of a Pirate," Audubon recast from stories he had heard from friends and other travelers. This collection includes forty episodes, all taken from Maria Audubon's edition of Audubon and His Journals *(1897). Her rough chronological order of the episodes has been respected, though it should be noted that she was able to assign dates only up through the "Bay of Fundy" episode. Several of the episodes following "The Bay of Fundy" obviously refer to the early periods of Audubon's life on the frontier.*

Louisville in Kentucky

Louisville in Kentucky has always been a favorite place of mine. The beauty of its situation on the banks of *La Belle Rivière,* just at the commencement of the famed rapids, commonly called the Falls of the Ohio, had attracted my notice, and when I removed to it, immediately after my marriage, I found it more agreeable than ever. The prospect from the town is such that it would please even the eye of a Swiss. It extends along the river for seven or eight miles, and is bounded on the opposite side by a fine range of low mountains, known by the name of the Silver Hills. The rumbling sound of the waters as they tumble over the rock-paved bed of the rapids is at all times soothing to the ear. Fish and game are abundant. But, above all, the generous hospitality of the inhabitants, and the urbanity of their manners, had induced me to fix upon it as a place of residence; and I did so with the more pleasure when I found that my wife was as much gratified as myself by the kind attentions which were shown to us, utter strangers as we were, on our arrival.

No sooner had we landed, and made known our intention of remaining, than we were introduced to the principal inhabitants of the place and its vicinity, although we had not brought a single letter of introduction, and could not but see, from their unremitting kindness, that the Virginian spirit of hospitality displayed itself in all the words and actions of our newly formed friends. I wish here to name those persons who so unexpectedly came forward to render our stay among them agreeable, but feel at a loss with whom to begin, so equally deserving are they of our gratitude. The Croghans, the Clarks (our great traveller included), the Berthouds, the Galts, the Maupins, the Tarascons, the Beals, and the Booths, form but a small portion of the long list which I could give. The matrons acted like mothers to my wife, the daughters proved agreeable associates, and the husbands and sons were friends and companions to me. If I absented myself on business, or otherwise, for any length of time, my wife was removed to the hospitable abode of some friend in the neighborhood until my return, and then, kind reader, I was several times obliged to spend a week or more with these good people before they could be prevailed upon to let us return to our own residence. We lived for two years at Louisville, where we enjoyed many of the best pleasures which this life can afford; and whenever we have since chanced to pass that way, we have found the kindness of our former friends unimpaired.

During my residence at Louisville, much of my time was employed in my ever favorite pursuits. I drew and noted the habits of everything which I procured, and my collection was daily augmenting, as every individual who carried a gun always sent me such birds or quadrupeds as he thought might prove useful to me. My portfolios already contained upwards of two hundred drawings. Dr. W. C. Galt being a botanist, was often consulted by me, as well as his friend, Dr. Ferguson. Mr. Gilly drew beautifully, and was fond of my pursuits. So was my friend, and now relative, N. Berthoud. As I have already said, our time was spent in the most agreeable manner, through the hospitable friendship of our acquaintance.

One fair morning I was surprised by the sudden entrance into our counting-room of Mr. Alexander Wilson, the celebrated author of the "American Ornithology," of whose existence I had never until that moment been apprised. This happened in March, 1810. How well do I remember him, as he walked up to me! His long, rather hooked nose, the keenness of his eyes, and his prominent cheek bones, stamped his countenance with a peculiar character. His dress, too, was of a kind not usually seen in that part of the country,—a short coat, trousers, and a waistcoat of gray cloth. His stature was not above the middle size. He had two volumes under his arm, and as he approached the table at which I was working, I thought I discovered something like astonishment in his countenance. He, however, immediately proceeded to disclose the object of his visit, which was to procure subscriptions for his work. He opened his books, explained the nature of his occupations, and requested my patronage.

I felt surprised and gratified at the sight of his volumes, turned over a few of the plates, and had already taken a pen to write my name in his favor, when my partner, rather abruptly, said to me in French, "My dear Audubon, what induces you to subscribe to this work? Your drawings are certainly far better, and again, you must know as much of the habits of American birds as this gentlemen." Whether Mr. Wilson understood French or not, or if the suddenness with which I paused disappointed him, I cannot tell; but I clearly perceived he was not pleased. Vanity and the encomiums of my friend prevented me from subscribing. Mr. Wilson asked me if I had many drawings of birds. I rose, took down a large portfolio, laid it on the table, and showed him, as I would show you, kind reader, or any other person fond of such subjects, the whole of the contents, with the same patience with which he had shown me his own engravings.

His surprise appeared great, as he told me he never had the most distant idea that any other individual than himself had been engaged in forming such a collection. He asked me if it was my intention to publish, and when I answered in the negative, his surprise seemed to increase. And, truly, such was not my intention; for until long after, when I met the Prince of Musignano in Philadelphia, I had not the least idea of presenting the fruits of my labors to the world. Mr. Wilson now examined my drawings with care, asked if I should have any objections to lending him a few during his stay, to which I replied that I had none; he then bade me good-morning, not, however, until I had made an arrangement to explore the woods in the vicinity with him, and had promised to procure for him some birds of which I had drawings in my collection, but which he had never seen.

It happened that he lodged in the same house with us, but his retired habits, I thought, exhibited either a strong feeling of discontent or a decided melancholy. The Scotch airs which he played sweetly on his flute made me melancholy too, and I felt for him. I presented him to my wife and friends, and seeing that he was all enthusiasm, exerted myself as much as was in my power to procure for him the specimens which he wanted. We hunted together, and obtained birds which he had never before seen; but, reader, I did not subscribe to his work, for, even at that time, my collection was greater than his. Thinking that perhaps he might be pleased to publish the results of my researches, I offered them to him, merely on condition that what I had drawn, or might afterwards draw and send to him, should be mentioned in his work as coming from my pencil. I, at the same time, offered to open a correspondence with him, which I thought might prove beneficial to us both. He made no reply to either proposal, and before many days had elapsed, left Louisville, on his way to New Orleans, little knowing how much his talents were appreciated in our little town, at least by myself and my friends.

Some time elapsed, during which I never heard of him, or of his work. At length, having occasion to go to Philadelphia, I, immediately after my arrival there, inquired for him, and paid him a visit. He was then drawing a White-headed Eagle. He received me with civility, and took me to the exhibition rooms of Rembrandt Peale, the artist, who had then portrayed Napoleon crossing the Alps. Mr. Wilson spoke not of birds nor drawings. Feeling, as I was forced to do, that my company was not agreeable, I parted from him; and after that I never saw him again. But judge of my astonishment sometime after, when, on reading the thirty-ninth page of the ninth volume of "American Ornithology," I found in it the following paragraph:—

"*March 23, 1810.* I bade adieu to Louisville, to which place I had four letters of recommendation, and was taught to expect much of everything there; but neither received one act of civility from those to whom I was recommended, one subscriber nor one new bird; though I delivered my letters, ransacked the woods repeatedly, and visited all the characters likely to subscribe. Science or literature has not one friend in this place."

A Wild Horse

While residing at Henderson in Kentucky, I became acquainted with a gentleman who had just returned from the country in the neighborhood of the head-waters of the Arkansas River, where he had purchased a newly caught "Wild Horse," a descendant of some of the horses originally brought from Spain, and set at liberty in the vast prairies of the Mexican lands. The animal was by no means handsome; he had a large head, with a considerable prominence in its frontal region, his thick and unkempt mane hung along his neck to the breast, and his tail, too scanty to be called flowing, almost reached the ground. But his chest was broad, his legs clean and sinewy, and his eyes and nostrils indicated spirit, vigor, and endurance. He had never been shod, and although he had been ridden hard, and had performed a long journey, his black hoofs had suffered no damage. His color inclined to bay, the legs of a deeper tint, and gradually darkening below until they became nearly black. I inquired what might be the value of such an animal among the Osage Indians, and was answered that, the horse being only four years old, he had given for him, with the tree and the buffalo-tug fastened to his head, articles equivalent to about thirty-five dollars. The gentleman added that he had never mounted a better horse, and had very little doubt that, if well fed, he could carry a man of ordinary weight from thirty-five to forty miles a day for a month, as he had travelled at that rate upon him, without giving him any other food than the grass of the prairies, or the canes of the bottom lands, until he had crossed the Mississippi at Natchez, when he fed him with corn. Having no farther use for him, now that he had ended his journey, he said he was anxious to sell him, and thought he might prove a good hunting-horse for me, as his gaits were easy, and he stood fire as well as any charger he had seen. Having some need of a horse possessed of qualities similar to those represented as belonging to the one in question, I asked if I might be allowed to try him. "Try him, sir, and welcome; nay, if you will agree to feed him and take care of him, you may keep him for a month if you choose." So I had the horse taken to the stable and fed.

About two hours afterwards, I took my gun, mounted the prairie nag, and went to the woods. I was not long in finding him very sensible to the spur, and as I observed that he moved with great ease, both to himself and his rider, I thought of leaping over a log several feet in diameter, to judge how far he might prove serviceable in deer-driving or bear-hunting. So I gave him the reins, and pressed my legs to his belly without using the spur, on which, as if aware that I wished to try his mettle, he bounded off, and cleared the log as lightly as an elk. I turned him, and made him leap the same log several times, which he did with equal ease, so that I was satisfied of his ability to clear any impediment in the woods. I next determined to try his strength, for which purpose I took him to a swamp, which I knew was muddy and tough. He entered it with his nose close to the water, as if to judge of its depth, at which I was well pleased, as he thus evinced due caution. I then rode through the swamp in different directions, and found him prompt, decided, and unflinching. Can he swim well? thought I,—for there are horses, which, although excellent, cannot swim at all, but will now and then lie on their side, as if contented to float with the current, when the rider must either swim and drag them to the shore, or abandon them. To the Ohio then I went, and rode into the water. He made off obliquely against the current, his head well raised above the surface, his nostrils expanded, his breathing free, and without any of the grunting noise emitted by many horses on such occasions. I turned him down the stream, then directly against it, and finding him quite to my mind, I returned to the shore, on reaching which he stopped of his own accord, spread his legs, and almost shook me off my seat. After this, I put him to a gallop, and returning home through the woods, shot from the saddle a Turkey-cock, which he afterwards approached as if he had been trained to the sport, and enabled me to take it up without dismounting.

As soon as I reached the house of Dr. Rankin, where I then resided, I sent word to the owner of the horse that I should be glad to see him. When he came, I asked him what price he would take; he said, fifty dollars in silver was the lowest. So I paid the money, took a bill of sale, and became master of the horse. The doctor, who was an excellent judge, said smiling to me, "Mr. Audubon, when you are tired of him, I will refund you the fifty dollars, for depend upon it he is a capital horse." The mane was trimmed, but the tail left untouched; the doctor had him shod "all round," and for several weeks he was ridden by my wife, who was highly pleased with him.

Business requiring that I should go to Philadelphia, Barro (he was so named after his former owner) was put up for ten days, and well tended. The time of my departure having arrived, I mounted him, and set off at the rate of four miles an hour—but here I must give you the line of my journey, that you may, if you please, follow my course on some such map as that of Tanner's. From Henderson through Russellville, Nashville, and Knoxville, Abingdon in Virginia, the Natural Bridge, Harrisonburg, Winchester, and Harper's Ferry, Frederick, and Lancaster, to Philadelphia. There I remained four days, after which I returned by way of Pittsburgh, Wheeling, Zanesville, Chillicothe, Lexington, and Louisville, to Henderson. But the nature of my business was such as to make me deviate considerably from the main roads, and I computed the whole distance at nearly two thousand miles, the post roads being rather more than sixteen hundred. I travelled not less than forty miles a day, and it was allowed by the doctor that my horse was in as good condition on my return as when I set out. Such a journey on a single horse may seem somewhat marvellous in the eyes of a European; but in these days almost every merchant had to perform the like, some from all parts of the western country, even from St. Louis on the Missouri, although the travellers not unfrequently, on their return, sold their horses at Baltimore, Philadelphia, or Pittsburg, at which latter place they took boat. My wife rode on a single horse from Henderson to Philadelphia, travelling at the same rate. The country was then comparatively new; few coaches travelled, and in fact the roads were scarcely fit for carriages. About twenty days were considered necessary for performing a journey on horseback from Louisville to Philadelphia, whereas now the same distance may be travelled in six or seven days, or even sometimes less, this depending on the height of the water in the Ohio.

It may not be uninteresting to you to know the treatment which the horse received on those journeys. I rose every morning before day, cleaned my horse, pressed his back with my hand, to see if it had been galled, and placed on it a small blanket folded double, in such a manner that when the saddle was put on, half of the cloth was turned over it. The surcingle, beneath which the saddle-bags were placed, confined the blanket to the seat, and to the pad behind was fastened the great coat or cloak, tightly rolled up. The bridle had a snaffle bit; a breast-plate was buckled in front to each skirt, to render the seat secure during an ascent; but my horse required no crupper, his shoulders being high and well-formed. On starting he trotted off at the rate of four miles an hour, which he continued. I usually travelled from fifteen to twenty miles before breakfast, and after the first hour allowed my horse to drink as much as he would. When I halted for breakfast, I generally stopped two hours, cleaned the horse, and gave him as much corn-blades as he could eat. I then rode on until within half an hour of sunset, when I watered him well, poured a bucket of cold water over his back, had his skin well rubbed, his feet examined and cleaned. The rack was filled with blades, the trough with corn, a good-sized pumpkin or some hen's-eggs, whenever they could be procured, were thrown in, and if oats were to be had, half a bushel of them was given in preference to corn, which is apt to heat some horses. In the morning, the nearly empty trough and rack afforded sufficient evidence of the state of his health.

I had not ridden him many days before he became so attached to me that on coming to some limpid stream in which I had a mind to bathe, I could leave him at liberty to graze, and he would not drink if told not to do so. He was ever sure-footed, and in such continual good spirits that now and then, when a Turkey happened to rise from a dusting-place before me, the mere inclination of my body forward was enough to bring him to a smart canter, which he would continue until the bird left the road for the woods, when he never failed to resume his usual trot. On my way homeward I met at the crossings of the Juniata River a gentleman from New Orleans, whose name is Vincent Nolte. He was mounted on a superb horse, for which he had paid three hundred dollars, and a servant on horseback led another as a change. I was then an utter stranger to him, and as I approached and praised his horse, he not very courteously observed that he wished I had as good a one. Finding that he was going to Bedford to spend the night, I asked him at what hour he would get there. "Just soon enough to have some trout ready for our supper, provided you will join when you get there." I almost imagined that Barro understood our conversation; he pricked up his ears, and lengthened his pace, on which Mr. Nolte caracoled his horse, and then put him to a quick trot; but all in vain, for I reached the hotel nearly a quarter of an hour before him, ordered the trout, saw to the putting away of my good horse, and stood at the door ready to welcome my companion. From that day Vincent Nolte has been a friend to me. It was from him I received letters of introduction to the Rathbones of Liverpool, for which I shall ever be grateful to him. We rode together as far as Shippingport, where my worthy friend Nicholas Berthoud, Esq., resided, and on parting with me he repeated what he had many times said before, that he never had seen so serviceable a creature as Barro.

If I recollect rightly, I gave a short verbal account of this journey, and of the good qualities of my horse, to my learned friend J. Skinner, Esq., of Baltimore, who, I believe, has noticed them in his excellent Sporting

Magazine. We agreed that the importation of horses of this kind from the Western prairies might improve our breeds generally; and judging from those which I have seen, I am inclined to think that some of them may prove fit for the course. A few days after reaching Henderson, I parted with Barro, not without regret, for a hundred and twenty dollars.

The Prairie

On my return from the Upper Mississippi I found myself obliged to cross one of the wide prairies which, in that portion of the United States, vary the appearance of the country. The weather was fine; all around me was as fresh and blooming as if it had just issued from the bosom of Nature. My knapsack, my gun, and my dog were all I had for baggage and company. But, although well moccasined, I moved slowly along, attracted by the brilliancy of the flowers, and the gambols of the fawns around their dams, to all appearance as thoughtless of danger as I felt myself.

My march was of long duration; I saw the sun sinking below the horizon long before I could perceive any appearance of woodland, and nothing in the shape of man had I met with that day. The track which I followed was only an old Indian trace, and as darkness over-shadowed the prairie I felt some desire to reach at least a copse, in which I might lie down to rest. The Night Hawks were skimming over and around me, attracted by the buzzing wings of the beetles which form their food, and the distant howling of wolves gave me some hope that I should soon arrive at the skirts of some woodlands.

I did so, and almost at the same instant, a firelight attracting my eye, I moved towards it, full of confidence that it proceeded from the camp of some wandering Indians. I was mistaken: I discovered by its glare that it was from the hearth of a small log cabin, and that a tall figure passed and repassed between it and me, as if busily engaged in household arrangements.

I reached the spot, and presenting myself at the door, asked the tall figure, which proved to be a woman, if I might take shelter under her roof for the night. Her voice was gruff, and her attire negligently thrown about her. She answered in the affirmative. I walked in, took a wooden stool, and quietly seated myself by the fire. The next object that attracted my notice was a finely formed young Indian, resting his head between his hands, with his elbows on his knees. A long bow rested against the log wall near him, while a quantity of arrows and two or three Raccoon skins lay at his feet. He moved not; he apparently breathed not. Accustomed to the habits of Indians, and knowing that they pay little attention to the approach of civilized strangers (a circumstance which in some countries is considered as evincing the apathy of their character), I addressed him in French, a language not infrequently partially known to the people in that neighborhood. He raised his head, pointed to one of his eyes with his finger, and gave me a significant glance with the other. His face was covered with blood. The fact was that an hour before this, as he was in the act of discharging an arrow at a Raccoon in the top of a tree, the arrow had split upon the cord, and sprung back with such violence into his right eye as to destroy it forever.

Feeling hungry, I inquired what sort of fare I might expect. Such a thing as a bed was not to be seen, but many large untanned Bear and Buffalo hides lay piled in a corner. I drew a fine time-piece from my breast, and told the woman that it was late, and that I was fatigued. She had espied my watch, the richness of which seemed to operate upon her feelings with electric quickness. She told me there was plenty of venison and jerked buffalo meat, and that on removing the ashes I should find a cake. But my watch had struck her fancy, and her curiosity had to be gratified by an immediate sight of it. I took off the gold chain that secured it, from around my neck, and presented it to her; she was all ecstasy, spoke of its beauty, asked me its value, and put the chain round her brawny neck, saying how happy the possession of such a watch would make her. Thoughtless, and as I fancied myself in so retired a spot secure, I paid little attention to her talk or her movements. I helped my dog to a good supper of venison, and was not long in satisfying the demands of my own appetite.

The Indian rose from his seat, as if in extreme suffering. He passed and repassed me several times, and once pinched me on the side so violently that the pain nearly brought forth an exclamation of anger. I looked at him. His eye met mine, but his look was so forbidding that it struck a chill into the more nervous part of my system. He again seated himself, drew his butcher-knife from its greasy scabbard, examined its edge, as I would do that of a razor suspected dull, replaced it, and again taking his tomahawk from his back, filled the pipe of it with tobacco, and sent me expressive glances, whenever our hostess chanced to have her back towards us.

Never until that moment had my senses been awakened to the danger which I now suspected to be about me. I returned glance for glance to my companion, and rested well assured that, whatever enemies I might have, he was not of their number.

I asked the woman for my watch, wound it up, and under pretence of wishing to see how the weather might probably be on the morrow, took up my gun, and walked out of the cabin. I slipped a ball into each barrel, scraped the edges of my flints, renewed the primings, and returning to the hut gave a favorable report of my observations. I took a few Bear skins, made a pallet of them, and calling my faithful dog to my side, lay down, with my gun close to my body, and in a few minutes was, to all appearance, fast asleep.

A short time had elapsed when some voices were heard, and from the corner of my eye I saw two athletic youths making their entrance, bearing a dead stag on a pole. They disposed of their burden, and asking for whiskey, helped themselves freely to it. Observing me and the wounded Indian, they asked who I was, and why the devil that rascal (meaning the Indian, who, they knew, understood not a word of English) was in the house. The mother—for so she proved to be—bade them speak less loudly, made mention of my watch, and took them to a corner, where a conversation took place, the purport of which it required little shrewdness in me to guess. I tapped my dog gently. He moved his tail, and with indescribable pleasure I saw his fine eyes alternately fixed on me, and raised towards the trio in the corner. I felt that he perceived danger in my situation. The Indian exchanged a last glance with me.

The lads had eaten and drunk themselves into such a condition that I already looked upon them as *hors de combat*; and the frequent visits of the whiskey bottle to the ugly mouth of their dam, I hoped would soon reduce her to a like state. Judge of my astonishment, reader, when I saw this incarnate fiend take a large carving-knife, and go to the grindstone to whet its edge; I saw her pour the water on the turning machine, and watched her working away with the dangerous instrument, until the cold sweat covered every part of my body, in despite of my determination to defend myself to the last. Her task finished, she walked to her reeling sons, and said: "There, that'll soon settle him! Boys, kill yon —— ——, and then for the watch."

I turned, cocked my gun-locks silently, touched my faithful companion, and lay ready to start up and shoot the first who might attempt my life. The moment was fast approaching, and that night might have been my last in this world, had not Providence made preparations for my rescue. All was ready. The infernal hag was advancing slowly, probably contemplating the best way of despatching me, whilst her sons should be engaged with the Indian. I was several times on the eve of rising and shooting her on the spot; but she was not to be punished thus. The door was suddenly opened, and there entered two stout travellers, each with a long rifle on his shoulder. I bounced up on my feet, and making them most heartily welcome, told them how well it was for me that they should have arrived at that moment. The tale was told in a minute. The drunken sons were secured, and the woman, in spite of her defence and vociferations, shared the same fate. The Indian fairly danced with joy, and gave us to understand that, as he could not sleep for pain, he would watch over us. You may suppose we slept much less than we talked. The two strangers gave me an account of their once having been themselves in a somewhat similar situation. Day came, fair and rosy, and with it the punishment of our captives.

They were now quite sobered. Their feet were unbound, but their arms were still securely tied. We marched them into the woods off the road, and having used them as Regulators were wont to use such delinquents, we set fire to the cabin, gave all the skins and implements to the young Indian warrior, and proceeded, well pleased, towards the settlements.

During upwards of twenty-five years, when my wanderings extended to all parts of our country, this was the only time at which my life was in danger from my fellow-creatures. Indeed, so little risk do travellers run in the United States that no one born there ever dreams of any to be encountered on the road; and I can only account for this occurrence by supposing that the inhabitants of the cabin were not Americans.

Will you believe, good-natured reader, that not many miles from the place where this adventure happened, and where fifteen years ago, no habitation belonging to civilized man was expected, and very few ever seen, large roads are now laid out, cultivation has converted the woods into fertile fields, taverns have been erected, and much of what we Americans call comfort is to be met with? So fast does improvement proceed in our abundant and free country.

The Earthquake

Travelling through the Barrens of Kentucky (of which I shall give you an account elsewhere) in the month of November, I was jogging on one afternoon, when I remarked a sudden and strange darkness rising from the western horizon. Accustomed to our heavy storms of thunder and rain I took no more notice of it, as I thought the speed of my horse might enable me to get under shelter of the roof of an acquaintance, who lived not far distant, before it should come up. I had proceeded about a mile, when I heard what I imagined to be the distant rumbling of a violent tornado, on which I spurred my steed, with a wish to gallop as fast as possible to a place of shelter; but it would not do, the animal knew better than I what was forthcoming, and instead of going faster, so nearly stopped that I remarked he placed one foot after another on the ground, with as much precaution as if walking on a smooth sheet of ice. I thought he had suddenly foundered, and, speaking to him, was on the point of dismounting and leading him, when he all of a sudden fell a-groaning piteously, hung his head, spread out his four legs, as if to save himself from falling, and stood stock still, continuing to groan. I thought my horse was about to die, and would have sprung from his back had a minute more elapsed, but at that instant all the shrubs and trees began to move from their very roots, the ground rose and fell in successive furrows, like the ruffled waters of a lake, and I became bewildered in my ideas, as I too plainly discovered that all this awful commotion in nature was the result of an earthquake.

I had never witnessed anything of the kind before, although, like every other person, I knew of earthquakes by description. But what is description compared with the reality? Who can tell of the sensations which I experienced when I found myself rocking as it were on my horse, and with him moved to and fro like a child in a cradle, with the most imminent danger around, and expecting the ground every moment to open and present to my eye such an abyss as might engulf myself and all around me? The fearful convulsion, however, lasted only a few minutes, and the heavens again brightened as quickly as they had become obscured; my horse brought his feet to their natural position, raised his head, and galloped off as if loose and frolicking without a rider.

I was not, however, without great apprehension respecting my family, from which I was yet many miles distant, fearful that where they were the shock might have caused greater havoc than I had witnessed. I gave the bridle to my steed, and was glad to see him appear as anxious to get home as myself. The pace at which he galloped accomplished this sooner than I had expected, and I found with much pleasure that hardly any greater harm had taken place than the apprehension excited for my own safety.

Shock succeeded shock almost every day or night for several weeks, diminishing, however, so gradually as to dwindle away into mere vibrations of the earth. Strange to say, I for one became so accustomed to the feeling as rather to enjoy the fears manifested by others. I never can forget the effects of one of the slighter shocks which took place when I was at a friend's house, where I had gone to enjoy the merriment that, in our Western country, attends a wedding. The ceremony being performed, supper over, and the fiddles tuned, dancing became the order of the moment. This was merrily followed up to a late hour, when the party retired to rest. We were in what is called, with great propriety, a *log-house*, one of large dimensions, and solidly constructed. The owner was a physician, and in one corner were not only his lancets, tourniquets, amputating knives, and other sanguinary apparatus, but all the drugs which he employed for the relief of his patients, arranged in jars and phials of different sizes. These had some days before had a narrow escape from destruction, but had been fortunately preserved by closing the doors of the cases in which they were contained.

As I have said, we had all retired to rest, some to dream of sighs or smiles, some to sink into oblivion. Morning was fast approaching, when the rumbling noise that precedes the earthquake, began so loudly as to waken and alarm the whole party, and drive them out of bed in the greatest consternation. The scene which ensued it is impossible for me to describe, and it would require the humorous pencil of Cruikshank to do justice to it. Fear knows no restraint. Every person, young and old, filled with alarm at the creaking of the log-house, and apprehending instant destruction, rushed wildly out to the grass enclosure fronting the building. The full moon was slowly descending from her throne, covered at times by clouds that rolled heavily along, as if to conceal from her view the scenes of terror which prevailed on the earth below. On the grass-plat we all met, in such condition as rendered it next to impossible to discriminate any of the party, all huddled together in a state of great dishabille. The earth waved like a field of corn before the breeze; the birds left their perches, and flew about, not knowing whither; and the doctor, recollecting the danger of his gallipots, ran to his shop room, to prevent their dancing off the shelves to the floor. Never for a moment did he think of closing the doors, but, spreading his arms, jumped about the front of the cases, pushing back here and there the falling jars; with so little success, however, that before the shock was over he had lost nearly all he possessed.

The shock at length ceased, and the frightened women now sensible of their undress, fled to their several apartments. The earthquake produced more serious consequences in other places. Near New Madrid and for some distance on the Mississippi, the earth was rent asunder in several places, one or two islands sunk forever, and the inhabitants fled in dismay towards the eastern shore.

The Hurricane

Various portions of our country have at different periods suffered severely from the influence of violent storms of wind, some of which have been known to traverse nearly the whole extent of the United States, and to leave such deep impressions in their wake as will not easily be forgotten. Having witnessed one of these awful phenomena, in all its grandeur, I shall attempt to describe it for your sake, kind reader, and for your sake only; the recollection of that astonishing revolution of the ethereal element even now bringing with it so disagreeable a sensation that I feel as if about to be affected by a sudden stoppage of the circulation of my blood.

I had left the village of Shawanee, situated on the banks of the Ohio, on my return from Henderson, which is also situated on the banks of the same beautiful stream. The weather was pleasant, and I thought not warmer than usual at that season. My horse was jogging quietly along, and my thoughts were, for once at least in the course of my life, entirely engaged in commercial speculations. I had forded Highland Creek, and was on the eve of entering a tract of bottom land or valley that lay between it and Canoe Creek, when on a sudden I remarked a great difference in the aspect of the heavens. A hazy thickness had overspread the country, and I for some time expected an earthquake; but my horse exhibited no propensity to stop and prepare for such an occurrence. I had nearly arrived at the verge of the valley, when I thought fit to stop near a brook, and dismounted to quench the thirst which had come upon me.

I was leaning on my knees, with my lips about to touch the water, when, from my proximity to the earth, I heard a distant murmuring sound of an extraordinary nature. I drank, however, and as I rose on my feet, looked towards the southwest, where I observed a yellowish oval spot, the appearance of which was quite new to me. Little time was left me for consideration, as the next moment a smart breeze began to agitate the taller trees. It increased to an unexpected height, and already the smaller branches and twigs were seen falling in a slanting direction towards the ground. Two minutes had scarcely elapsed, when the whole forest before me was in fearful motion. Here and there, where one tree pressed against another, a creaking noise was produced, similar to that occasioned by the violent gusts which sometimes sweep over the country. Turning instinctively towards the direction from which the wind blew, I saw to my great astonishment that the noblest trees of the forest bent their lofty heads for a while, and, unable to stand against the blast, were falling into pieces. First the branches were broken off with a crackling noise; then went the upper parts of the massy trunks; and in many places whole trees of gigantic size were falling entire to the ground. So rapid was the progress of the storm that before I could think of taking measures to insure my safety the hurricane was passing opposite the place where I stood. Never can I forget the scene which at that moment presented itself. The tops of the trees were seen moving in the strangest manner, in the central current of the tempest, which carried along with it a mingled mass of twigs and foliage that completely obscured the view. Some of the largest trees were seen bending and writhing under the gale; others suddenly snapped across; and many, after a momentary resistance, fell uprooted to the earth. The mass of branches, twigs, foliage, and dust that moved through the air was whirled onwards like a cloud of feathers, and on passing disclosed a wide space filled with fallen trees, naked stumps, and heaps of shapeless ruins which marked the path of the tempest. This space was about a fourth of a mile in breadth, and to my imagination resembled the dried up bed of the Mississippi, with its thousands of planters and sawyers strewed in the sand and inclined in various degrees. The horrible noise resembled that of the great cataracts of Niagara, and, as it howled along in the track of the desolating tempest, produced a feeling in my mind which it were impossible to describe.

The principal force of the hurricane was now over, although millions of twigs and small branches that had been brought from a great distance were seen following the blast, as if drawn onwards by some mysterious power. They even floated in the air for some hours after, as if supported by the thick mass of dust that rose high above the ground. The sky had now a greenish lurid hue, and an extremely disagreeable sulphurous odor was diffused in the atmosphere. I waited in amazement, having sustained no material injury, until nature at length resumed her wonted aspect. For some moments I felt undetermined whether I should return to Morgantown, or attempt to force my way through the wrecks of the tempest. My business, however, being of an urgent nature, I ventured into the path of the storm, and after encountering innumerable difficulties, succeeded in crossing it. I was obliged to lead my horse by the bridle, to enable him to leap over the fallen trees, whilst I scrambled over or under them in the best way I could, at times so hemmed in by the broken tops and tangled branches as almost to become desperate. On arriving at my house, I gave an account of what I had seen, when, to my astonishment, I was told there had been very little wind in the neighborhood, although in the streets and gardens many branches and twigs had fallen in a manner which excited great surprise.

Many wondrous accounts of the devastating effects of this hurricane were circulated in the country after its occurrence. Some log houses, we were told, had been overturned and their inmates destroyed. One person informed me that a wire sifter had been conveyed by the gust to a distance of many miles. Another had found a cow lodged in the fork of a large half-broken tree. But, as I am disposed to relate only what I have myself seen, I shall not lead you into the region of romance, but shall content myself with saying that much damage was done by this awful visitation. The valley is yet a desolate place, overgrown with briers and bushes, thickly entangled amidst the tops and trunks of the fallen trees, and is the resort of ravenous animals, to which they betake themselves when pursued by man, or after they have committed their depredations on the farms of the surrounding district. I have crossed the path of the storm at a distance of a hundred miles from the spot where I witnessed its fury, and again, four hundred miles farther off, in the State of Ohio. Lastly, I observed traces of its ravages on the summits of the mountains connected with the Great Pine Forest of Pennsylvania, three hundred miles beyond the place last mentioned. In all these different parts it appeared to me not to have exceeded a quarter of a mile in breadth.

Colonel Boone

Daniel Boone, or, as he was usually called in the Western country, Colonel Boone, happened to spend a night with me under the same roof, more than twenty years ago. We had returned from a shooting excursion, in the course of which his extraordinary skill in the management of the rifle had been fully displayed. On retiring to the room appropriated to that remarkable individual and myself for the night, I felt anxious to know more of his exploits and adventures than I did, and accordingly took the liberty of proposing numerous questions to him. The stature and general appearance of this wanderer of the western forests approached the gigantic. His chest was broad and prominent; his muscular powers displayed themselves in every limb; his countenance gave indication of his great courage, enterprise, and perseverance; and when he spoke, the very motion of his lips brought the impression that whatever he uttered could not be otherwise than strictly true. I undressed, whilst he merely took off his hunting shirt, and arranged a few folds of blankets on the floor, choosing rather to lie there, as he observed, than on the softest bed. When we had both disposed of ourselves, each after his own fashion, he related to me the following account of his powers of memory, which I lay before you, kind reader, in his own words, hoping that the simplicity of his style may prove interesting to you.

"I was once," said he, "on a hunting expedition on the banks of the Green River, when the lower parts of this State (Kentucky) were still in the hands of nature, and none but the sons of the soil were looked upon as its lawful proprietors. We Virginians had for some time been waging a war of intrusion upon them, and I, amongst the rest, rambled through the woods in pursuit of their race as I now would follow the tracks of any ravenous animal. The Indians outwitted me one dark night, and I was as unexpectedly as suddenly made a prisoner by them. The trick had been managed with great skill; for no sooner had I extinguished the fire of my camp, and laid me down to rest, in full security as I thought, than I felt myself seized by an indistinguishable number of hands, and was immediately pinioned, as if about to be led to the scaffold for execution. To have attempted to be refractory would have proved useless and dangerous to my life; and I suffered myself to be removed from my camp to theirs, a few miles distant, without uttering even a word of complaint. You are aware, I dare say, that to act in this manner was the best policy, as you understand that, by so doing, I proved to the Indians at once that I was born and bred as fearless of death as any of themselves.

"When we reached the camp, great rejoicings were exhibited. Two squaws and a few pappooses appeared particularly delighted at the sight of me, and I was assured, by very unequivocal gestures and words, that, on the morrow, the mortal enemy of the Red-skins would cease to live. I never opened my lips, but was busy contriving some scheme which might enable me to give the rascals the slip before dawn. The women immediately fell a-searching about my hunting-shirt for whatever they might think valuable, and, fortunately for me, soon found my flask filled with *monongahela* (that is, reader, strong whiskey). A terrific grin was exhibited on their murderous countenances, while my heart throbbed with joy at the anticipation of their intoxication. The crew immediately began to beat their bellies and sing, as they passed the bottle from mouth to mouth. How often did I wish the flask ten times its size, and filled with aqua-fortis! I observed that the squaws drank more freely than the warriors, and again my spirits were about to be depressed, when the report of a gun was heard at a distance. The Indians all jumped on their feet. The singing and drinking were both brought to a stand, and I saw, with inexpressible joy, the men walk off to some distance and talk to the squaws. I knew that they were consulting about me, and I foresaw that in a few moments the warriors would go to discover the cause of the gun having been fired so near their camp. I expected that the squaws would be left to guard me. Well, sir, it was just so. They returned; the men took up their guns and walked away. The squaws sat down again, and in less than five minutes had my bottle up to their dirty mouths, gurgling down their throats the remains of the whiskey.

"With what pleasure did I see them becoming more and more drunk, until the liquor took such hold of them that it was quite impossible for these women to be of any service. They tumbled down, rolled about, and began to snore: when I, having no other chance of freeing myself from the cords that fastened me, rolled over and over towards the fire, and, after a short time, burned them asunder. I rose on my feet, stretched my stiffened sinews, snatched up my rifle, and, for once in my life, spared that of Indians. I now recollect how desirous I once or twice felt to lay open the skulls of the wretches with my tomahawk; but when I again thought upon killing beings unprepared and unable to defend themselves, it looked like murder without need, and I gave up the idea.

"But, sir, I felt determined to mark the spot, and walking to a thrifty ash sapling, I cut out of it three large chips, and ran off. I soon reached the river, soon crossed it, and threw myself deep into the cane-brakes, imitating the tracks of an Indian with my feet, so that no chance might be left for those from whom I had escaped to overtake me.

"It is now nearly twenty years since this happened, and more than five since I left the Whites' settlements, which I might probably never have visited again had I not been called on as a witness in a law-suit that was pending in Kentucky, and which I really believe would never have been settled had I not come forward and established the beginning of a certain boundary line. This is the story, sir.

"Mr. —— moved from Old Virginia into Kentucky, and having a large tract granted to him in the new State, laid claim to a certain parcel of land adjoining Green River, and, as chance would have it, took for one of his corners the very ash-tree on which I had made my mark, and finished his survey of some thousands of acres, beginning, as it is expressed in the deed, 'at an Ash marked by three distinct notches of the tomahawk of a white man.'

"The tree had grown much, and the bark had covered the marks; but, somehow or other, Mr. —— heard from some one all that I have already said to you, and thinking that I might remember the spot alluded to in the deed, but which was no longer discoverable, wrote for me to come and try at least to find the place or the tree. His letter mentioned that all my expenses should be paid, and not caring much about once more going back to Kentucky, I started and met Mr. ——. After some conversation, the affair with the Indians came to my recollection. I considered for a while, and began to think that after all I could find the very spot, as well as the tree, if it was yet standing.

"Mr. —— and I mounted our horses, and off we went to the Green River Bottoms. After some difficulties, for you must be aware, sir, that great changes have taken place in those woods, I found at last the spot where I had crossed the river, and, waiting for the moon to rise, made for the course in which I thought the ash-tree grew. On approaching the place, I felt as if the Indians were there still, and as if I was still a prisoner among them. Mr. —— and I camped near what I conceived the spot, and waited until the return of day.

"At the rising of the sun I was on foot, and, after a good deal of musing, thought that an ash-tree then in sight must be the very one on which I had made my mark. I felt as if there could be no doubt of it, and mentioned my thought to Mr. ——. 'Well, Colonel Boone,' said he, 'if you think so, I hope it may prove true, but we must have some witnesses; do you stay here about, and I will go and bring some of the settlers whom I know.' I agreed. Mr. —— trotted off, and I, to pass the time, rambled about to see if a Deer was still living in the land. But ah! sir, what a wonderful difference thirty years makes in the country! Why, at the time when I was caught by the Indians, you would not have walked out in any direction for more than a mile without shooting a buck or a Bear. There were then thousands of Buffaloes on the hills in Kentucky; the land looked as if it never would become poor; and to hunt in those days was a pleasure indeed. But when I was left to myself on the banks of Green River, I dare say for the last time in my life, a few *signs* only of Deer were to be seen, and as to a Deer itself, I saw none.

"Mr. —— returned, accompanied by three gentlemen. They looked upon me as if I had been Washington himself, and walked to the ash-tree, which I now called my own, as if in quest of a long-lost treasure. I took an axe from one of them, and cut a few chips off the bark. Still no signs were to be seen. So I cut again until I thought it was time to be cautious, and I scraped and worked away with my butcher knife until I *did* come to where my tomahawk had left an impression in the wood. We now went regularly to work, and scraped at the tree with care, until three hacks as plain as any three notches ever were, could be seen. Mr. —— and the other gentlemen were astonished, and, I must allow, I was as much surprised as pleased myself. I made affidavit of this remarkable occurrence in presence of these gentlemen. Mr. —— gained his cause. I left Green River forever, and came to where we now are; and, sir, I wish you a good night."

I trust, kind reader, that when I again make my appearance with another volume of Ornithological Biography, I shall not have to search in vain for the impression which I have made, but shall have the satisfaction of finding its traces still unobliterated. I now withdraw, and, in the words of the noted wanderer of the Western wilds, "wish you a good night."

Natchez in 1820

One clear, frosty morning in December I approached in my flatboat the city of Natchez. The shores were crowded with boats of various kinds, laden with the produce of the Western country; and there was a bustle about them such as you might see at a general fair, each person being intent on securing the advantage of a good market. Yet the scene was far from being altogether pleasing, for I was yet "under the hill;" but on removing from the Lower Town I beheld the cliffs on which the city, properly so called, has been built. Vultures unnumbered flew close along the ground on expanded pinions, searching for food; large pines and superb magnolias here and there raised their evergreen tops towards the skies; while on the opposite shores of the Mississippi vast alluvial beds stretched along, and the view terminated with the dense forest. Steamers moved rapidly on the broad waters of the great stream; the sunbeams fell with a peculiarly pleasant effect on the distant objects; and as I watched the motions of the White-headed Eagle while pursuing the Fishing Hawk, I thought of the wonderful ways of that Power to whom I too owe my existence.

Before reaching the land I had observed that several saw-mills were placed on ditches or narrow canals, along which the water rushed from the inner swamps towards the river, and by which the timber is conveyed to the shore; and, on inquiring afterwards, I found that one of those temporary establishments had produced a net profit of upwards of six thousand dollars in a single season.

There is much romantic scenery about Natchez. The Lower Town forms a most remarkable contrast with the Upper; for in the former the houses were not regularly built, being generally dwellings formed of the abandoned flatboats, placed in rows, as if with the view of forming a long street. The inhabitants formed a medley which it is beyond my power to describe; hundreds of laden carts and other vehicles jogged along the declivity between the two towns; but when, by a very rude causeway, I gained the summit, I was relieved by the sight of an avenue of those beautiful trees called here the Pride of China. In the Upper Town I found the streets all laid off at right angles to each other, and tolerably well lined with buildings constructed with painted bricks or boards.

The agricultural richness of the surrounding country was shown by the heaps of cotton bales and other produce that encumbered the streets. The churches, however, did not please me; but as if to make up for this, I found myself unexpectedly accosted by my relative, Mr. Berthoud, who presented me with letters from my wife and sons. These circumstances put me in high spirits, and we proceeded towards the best hotel in the place, that of Mr. Garnier. The house, which was built on the Spanish plan, and of great size, was surrounded by large verandas overlooking a fine garden, and stood at a considerable distance from any other. At this period the city of Natchez had a population not exceeding three thousand individuals. I have not visited it often since, but I have no doubt that, like all the other towns in the western district of our country, it has greatly increased. It possessed a bank, and the mail arrived there thrice in the week from all parts of the Union.

The first circumstance that strikes a stranger is the mildness of the temperature. Several vegetables as pleasing to the eye as agreeable to the palate, and which are seldom seen in our Eastern markets before May, were here already in perfection. The Pewee Fly-catcher had chosen the neighborhood of the city for its winter quarters, and our deservedly famed Mocking-bird sang and danced gratis to every passer by. I was surprised to see the immense number of Vultures that strode along the streets or slumbered on the roofs. The country for many miles inland is gently undulated. Cotton is produced abundantly, and wealth and happiness have taken up their abode under most of the planters' roofs, beneath which the wearied traveller or the poor wanderer in search of a resting-place is sure to meet with comfort and relief. Game is abundant, and the free Indians were wont in those days to furnish the markets with ample supplies of venison and Wild Turkey. The Mississippi, which bathes the foot of the hill some hundred feet below the town, supplies the inhabitants with fish of various kinds. The greatest deficiency is that of water, which for common purposes is dragged on sledges or wheels from the river, while that used for drinking is collected in tanks from the roofs, and becomes very scarce during protracted droughts. Until of late years the orange-tree bore fruit in the open air; but, owing to the great change that has taken place in the temperature, severe though transient frosts occasionally occur, which now prevent this plant from coming to perfection in the open air.

The remains of an old Spanish fort are still to be seen at a short distance from the city. If I am correctly informed, about two years previous to this visit of mine a large portion of the hill near it gave way, sank about a hundred feet, and carried many of the houses of the Lower Town into the river. This, it would appear, was occasioned by the quicksand running springs that flow beneath the strata of mixed pebbles and clay of which the hill is composed. The part that has subsided presents the appearance of a basin or bowl, and is used as a depot for the refuse of the town, on which the Vultures feed when they can get nothing better. There it was that I saw a White-headed Eagle chase one of those filthy birds, knock it down, and feast on the entrails of a horse which the Carrion Crow had partly swallowed.

I did not meet at Natchez many individuals fond of ornithological pursuits, but the hospitality with which I was received was such as I am not likely to forget. Mr. Garnier subsequently proved an excellent friend to me, as you may find elsewhere recorded. Of another individual, whose kindness to me is indelibly impressed on my heart, I would say a few words, although he was such a man as Fénelon alone could describe. Charles Carré was of French origin, the son of a nobleman of the old régime. His acquirements and the benevolence of his disposition were such that when I first met him I could not help looking upon him as another Mentor. Although his few remaining locks were gray, his countenance still expressed the gayety and buoyant feelings of youth. He had the best religious principles; for his heart and his purse were ever open to the poor. Under his guidance it was that I visited the whole neighborhood of Natchez; for he was acquainted with all its history, from the period at which it had first come under the power of the Spaniards to that of their expulsion from the country, its possession by the French, and subsequently by ourselves. He was also well versed in the Indian languages, spoke French with the greatest purity, and was a religious poet. Many a pleasant hour have I spent in his company; but alas! he has gone the way of all the earth!

The Lost Portfolio

While I was at Natchez, on the 31st of December, 1820, my kind friend, Nicholas Berthoud, Esq., proposed to me to accompany him in his keel-boat to New Orleans. At one o'clock the steam-boat "Columbus" hauled off from the landing and took our bark in tow. The steamer was soon ploughing along at full speed, and little else engaged our minds than the thought of our soon arriving at the emporium of the commerce of the Mississippi. Towards evening, however, several inquiries were made respecting particular portions of the luggage, among which ought to have been one of my portfolios, containing a number of drawings made by me while gliding down the Ohio and Mississippi from Cincinnati to Natchez, and of which some were to me peculiarly valuable, being of birds previously unfigured, and perhaps undescribed. The portfolio was nowhere to be found, and I recollected that I had brought it under my arm to the margin of the stream, and there left it to the care of one of my friend's servants, who, in the hurry of our departure, had neglected to take it on board. Besides the drawings of birds, there was in this collection a sketch in black chalk to which I always felt greatly attached while from home. It is true the features which it represented were indelibly engraved in my heart; but the portrait of her to whom I owe so much of the happiness that I have enjoyed was not the less dear to me. When I thought during the following night of the loss I had sustained in consequence of my own negligence, imagined the possible fate of the collection, and saw it in the hands of one of the numerous boatmen lounging along the shores, who might paste the drawings to the walls of his cabin, nail them to the steering-oars of his flatboat, or distribute them among his fellows, I felt little less vexed than I did some years before when the rats, as you know, devoured a much larger collection.

It was useless to fret myself, and so I began to devise a scheme for recovering the drawings. I wrote to Mr. Garnier and my venerable friend Charles Carré. Mr. Berthoud also wrote to a mercantile acquaintance. The letters were forwarded to Natchez from the first landing-place at which we stopped, and in the course of time we reached the great eddy running by the levee, or artificial embankment, at New Orleans. But before I present you with the answers to the letters sent to our acquaintances at Natchez, allow me to offer a statement of our adventures upon the Mississippi.

After leaving the eddy at Natchez, we passed a long file of exquisitely beautiful bluffs. At the end of twenty hours we reached Bayou Sara, where we found two brigs at anchor, several steamers, and a number of flatboats, the place being of considerable mercantile importance. Here the "Columbus" left us to shift for ourselves, her commander being anxious to get to Baton Rouge by a certain hour, in order to secure a good cargo of cotton. We now proceeded along the great stream, sometimes floating and sometimes rowing. The shores gradually became lower and flatter, orange-trees began to make their appearance around the dwellings of the wealthy planters, and the verdure along the banks assumed a brighter tint. The thermometer stood at 68° in the shade at noon; Butterflies fluttered among the flowers, of which many were in full blow; and we expected to have seen Alligators half awake floating on the numberless logs that accompanied us in our slow progress. The eddies were covered with Ducks of various kinds, more especially with the beautiful species that breeds by preference on the great sycamores that every now and then present themselves along our southern waters. Baton Rouge is a very handsome place, but at present I have no time to describe it. Levees now began to stretch along the river, and wherever there was a sharp point on the shore, negroes were there amusing themselves by raising shrimps, and now and then a catfish, with scooping-nets.

The river increased in breadth and depth, and the sawyers and planters, logs so called, diminished in number the nearer we drew towards the famed city. At every bend we found the plantations increased, and now the whole country on both sides became so level and destitute of trees along the water's edge that we could see over the points before us, and observe the great stream stretching along for miles. Within the levees the land is much lower than the surface of the river when the water is high; but at this time we could see over the levee from the deck of our boat only the upper windows of the planters' houses, or the tops of the trees about them, and the melancholy-looking cypresses covered with Spanish moss forming the background. Persons rode along the levees at full speed; Pelicans, Gulls, Vultures, and Carrion Crows sailed over the stream, and at times there came from the shore a breeze laden with the delicious perfume of the orange-trees, which were covered with blossoms and golden fruits.

Having passed Bayou Lafourche, our boat was brought to on account of the wind, which blew with violence. We landed, and presently made our way to the swamps, where we shot a number of those beautiful birds called Boat-tailed Grakles. The Mocking-birds on the fence stakes saluted us with so much courtesy and with such delightful strains that we could not think of injuring them; but we thought it no harm to shoot a whole covey of Partridges. In the swamps we met with warblers of various kinds, lively and beautiful, waiting in these their winter retreats for the moment when Boreas should retire to his icy home, and the gentle gales of the South should waft them toward their breeding-places in the North. Thousands of Swallows flew about us, the Cat-birds mewed in answer to their chatterings, the Cardinal Grosbeak elevated his glowing crest as he stood perched on the magnolia branch, the soft notes of the

Doves echoed among the woods, nature smiled upon us, and we were happy.

On the fourth of January we stopped at Bonnet Carré, where I entered a house to ask some questions about birds. I was received by a venerable French gentleman, whom I found in charge of about a dozen children of both sexes, and who was delighted to hear that I was a student of nature. He was well acquainted with my old friend Charles Carré, and must, I thought, be a good man, for he said he never suffered any of his pupils to rob a bird of her eggs or young, although, said he with a smile, "they are welcome to peep at them and love them." The boys at once surrounded me, and from them I received satisfactory answers to most of my queries respecting birds.

The 6th of January was so cold that the thermometer fell to 30°, and we had seen ice on the running-boards of our keel-boat. This was quite unlooked for, and we felt uncomfortable; but before the middle of the day, all nature was again in full play. Several beautiful steamers passed us. The vegetation seemed not to have suffered from the frost; green peas, artichokes, and other vegetables were in prime condition. This reminds me that on one of my late journeys I ate green peas in December in the Floridas, and had them once a week at least in my course over the whole of the Union, until I found myself and my family feeding on the same vegetable more than a hundred miles to the north of the St. John's River in New Brunswick.

Early on the 7th, thousands of tall spars, called masts by the mariners, came in sight; and as we drew nearer, we saw the port filled with ships of many nations, each bearing the flag of its country. At length we reached the levee, and found ourselves once more at New Orleans. In a short time my companions dispersed, and I commenced a search for something that might tend to compensate me for the loss of my drawings.

On the 16th of March following, I had the gratification of receiving a letter from Mr. A. P. Bodley, of Natchez, informing me that my portfolio had been found and deposited at the office of the "Mississippi Republican," whence an order from me would liberate it. Through the kindness of Mr. Garnier, I received it on the 5th of April. So very generous had been the finder of it, that when I carefully examined the drawings in succession, I found them all present and uninjured, save one, which had probably been kept by way of commission.

The Cougar

There is an extensive swamp in the section of the State of Mississippi which lies partly in the Choctaw territory. It commences at the borders of the Mississippi, at no great distance from a Chickasaw village situated near the mouth of a creek known by the name of Vanconnah, and partly inundated by the swellings of several large bayous, the principal of which, crossing the swamp in its whole extent, discharges its waters not far from the mouth of the Yazoo River. This famous bayou is called False River. The swamp of which I am speaking follows the windings of the Yazoo, until the latter branches off to the northeast, and at this point forms the stream named Cold Water River, below which the Yazoo receives the draining of another bayou inclining towards the northwest and intersecting that known by the name of False River at a short distance from the place where the latter receives the waters of the Mississippi. This tedious account of the situation of the swamp is given with the view of pointing it out to all students of nature who may happen to go that way, and whom I would earnestly urge to visit its interior, as it abounds in rare and interesting productions,—birds, quadrupeds, and reptiles, as well as molluscous animals, many of which, I am persuaded, have never been described.

In the course of one of my rambles, I chanced to meet with a squatter's cabin on the banks of the Cold Water River. In the owner of this hut, like most of those adventurous settlers in the uncultivated tracts of our frontier districts, I found a person well versed in the chase, and acquainted with the habits of some of the larger species of quadrupeds and birds. As he who is desirous of instruction ought not to disdain listening to any one who has knowledge to communicate, however humble may be his lot, or however limited his talents, I entered the squatter's cabin, and immediately opened a conversation with him respecting the situation of the swamp, and its natural productions. He told me he thought it the very place I ought to visit, spoke of the game which it contained, and pointed to some Bear and Deer skins, adding that the individuals to which they had belonged formed but a small portion of the number of those animals which he had shot within it. My heart swelled with delight, and on asking if he would accompany me through the great morass, and allow me to become an inmate of his humble but hospitable mansion, I was gratified to find that he cordially assented to all my proposals. So I immediately unstrapped my drawing materials, laid up my gun, and sat down to partake of the homely but wholesome fare intended for the supper of the squatter, his wife, and his two sons.

The quietness of the evening seemed in perfect accordance with the gentle demeanor of the family. The wife and children, I more than once thought, seemed to look upon me as a strange sort of person, going about, as I told them I was, in search of birds and plants; and were I here to relate the many questions which they put to me in return for those I addressed to them, the catalogue would occupy several pages. The husband, a native of Connecticut, had heard of the existence of such men as myself, both in our own country and abroad, and seemed greatly pleased to have me under his roof. Supper over, I asked my kind host what had induced him to remove to this wild and solitary spot. "The people are growing too numerous now to thrive in New England," was his answer. I thought of the state of some parts of Europe, and calculating the denseness of their population compared with that of New England, exclaimed to myself, "How much more difficult must it be for men to thrive in those populous countries!" The conversation then changed, and the squatter, his sons and myself, spoke of hunting and fishing until at length, tired, we laid ourselves down on pallets of Bear skins, and reposed in peace on the floor of the only apartment of which the hut consisted.

Day dawned, and the squatter's call to his hogs, which, being almost in a wild state, were suffered to seek the greater portion of their food in the woods, awakened me. Being ready dressed I was not long in joining him. The hogs and their young came grunting at the well known call of their owner, who threw them a few ears of corn, and counted them, but told me that for some weeks their number had been greatly diminished by the ravages committed upon them by a large *Panther*, by which name the Cougar is designated in America, and that the ravenous animal did not content himself with the flesh of his pigs, but now and then carried off one of his calves, notwithstanding the many attempts he had made to shoot it. The *Painter*, as he sometimes called it, had on several occasions robbed him of a dead Deer; and to these exploits the squatter added several remarkable feats of audacity which it had performed, to give me an idea of the formidable character of the beast. Delighted by his description, I offered to assist him in destroying the enemy, at which he was highly pleased, but assured me that unless some of his neighbors should join us with their dogs and his own, the attempt would prove fruitless. Soon after, mounting a horse, he went off to his neighbors several of whom lived at a distance of some miles, and appointed a day of meeting.

The hunters, accordingly, made their appearance, one fine morning, at the door of the cabin, just as the sun was emerging from beneath the horizon. They were five in number, and fully equipped for the chase, being mounted on horses which in some parts of Europe might appear sorry nags, but which in strength, speed, and bottom, are better fitted for pursuing a Cougar or a Bear through woods and morasses than any in that country. A pack of large, ugly curs were already engaged in making acquaintance with those of the squatter. He and myself mounted his two best horses, whilst his sons were bestriding others of inferior quality.

Few words were uttered by the party until we had reached the edge of the swamp, where it was agreed that all should disperse and seek for the fresh track of the Painter, it being previously settled that the discoverer should blow his horn, and remain on the spot, until the rest should join him. In less than an hour, the sound of the horn was clearly heard, and, sticking close to the squatter, off we went through the thick woods, guided only by the now and then repeated call of the distant huntsmen. We soon reached the spot, and in a short time the rest of the party came up. The best dog was sent forward to track the Cougar, and in a few moments the whole pack were observed diligently trailing, and bearing in their course for the interior of the Swamp. The rifles were immediately put in trim, and the party followed the dogs, at separate distances, but in sight of each other, determined to shoot at no other game than the Panther.

The dogs soon began to mouth, and suddenly quickened their pace. My companion concluded that the beast was on the ground, and putting our horses to a gentle gallop, we followed the curs, guided by their voices. The noise of the dogs increased, when, all of a sudden their mode of barking became altered, and the squatter, urging me to push on, told me that the beast was *treed*, by which he meant that it had got upon some low branch of a large tree to rest for a few moments, and that should we not succeed in shooting him when thus situated, we might expect a long chase of it. As we approached the spot, we all by degrees united into a body, but on seeing the dogs at the foot of a large tree, separated again, and galloped off to surround it.

Each hunter now moved with caution, holding his gun ready, and allowing the bridle to dangle on the neck of his horse, as it advanced slowly towards the dogs. A shot from one of the party was heard, on which the Cougar was seen to leap to the ground, and bound off with such velocity as to show that he was very unwilling to stand our fire longer. The dogs set off in pursuit with great eagerness and a deafening cry. The hunter who had fired came up and said that his ball had hit the monster, and had probably broken one of his fore-legs near the shoulder, the only place at which he could aim. A slight trail of blood was discovered on the ground, but the curs proceeded at such a rate that we merely noticed this, and put spurs to our horses, which galloped on towards the centre of the Swamp. One bayou was crossed, then another still larger and more muddy; but the dogs were brushing forward, and as the horses began to pant at a furious rate, we judged it expedient to leave them and advance on foot. These determined hunters knew that the Cougar being wounded, would shortly ascend another tree, where in all probability he would remain for a considerable time, and that it would be easy to follow the track of the dogs. We dismounted, took off the saddles and bridles, set the bells attached to the horses' necks at liberty to jingle, hoppled the animals, and left them to shift for themselves.

Now, kind reader, follow the group marching through the swamp, crossing muddy pools, and making the best of their way over fallen trees and amongst the tangled rushes that now and then covered acres of ground. If you are a hunter yourself, all this will appear nothing to you; but if crowded assemblies of "beauty and fashion," or the quiet enjoyment of your "pleasure grounds" alone delight you, I must mend my pen before I attempt to give you an idea of the pleasure felt on such an expedition.

After marching for a couple of hours, we again heard the dogs. Each of us pressed forward, elated at the thought of terminating the career of the Cougar. Some of the dogs were heard whining, although the greater number barked vehemently. We felt assured that the Cougar was treed, and that he would rest for some time to recover from his fatigue. As we came up to the dogs, we discovered the ferocious animal lying across a large branch, close to the trunk of a cotton-wood tree. His broad breast lay towards us; his eyes were at one time bent on us and again on the dogs beneath and around him; one of his fore-legs hung loosely by his side, and he lay crouched, with his ears lowered close to his head, as if he thought he might remain undiscovered. Three balls were fired at him, at a given signal, on which he sprang a few feet from the branch, and tumbled headlong to the ground. Attacked on all sides by the enraged curs, the infuriated Cougar fought with desperate valor; but the squatter, advancing in front of the party, and almost in the midst of the dogs, shot him immediately behind and beneath the left shoulder. The Cougar writhed for a moment in agony, and in another lay dead.

The sun was now sinking in the west. Two of the hunters separated from the rest to procure venison, whilst the squatter's sons were ordered to make the best of their way home, to be ready to feed the hogs in the morning. The rest of the party agreed to camp on the spot. The Cougar was despoiled of its skin, and its carcass left to the hungry dogs. Whilst engaged in preparing our camp, we heard the report of a gun, and soon after one of our hunters returned with a small Deer. A fire was lighted, and each hunter displayed his *pone* of bread, along with a flask of whiskey. The deer was skinned in a trice, and slices placed on sticks before the fire. These materials afforded us an excellent meal, and as the night grew darker, stories and songs went round, until my companions, fatigued, laid themselves down, close under the smoke of the fire, and soon fell asleep.

I walked for some minutes round the camp, to contemplate the beauties of that nature from which I have certainly derived my greatest pleasures. I thought of the occurrences of the day, and glancing my eye around, remarked the singular effects produced by the phosphorescent qualities of the large decayed trunks which lay in all directions around me. How easy, I thought, would it be for the confused and agitated mind of a person bewildered in a swamp like this, to imagine in each of these luminous masses some wondrous and fearful being, the very sight of which might make the hair stand erect on his head. The thought of being myself placed in such a predicament burst over my mind, and I hastened to join my companions, beside whom I laid me down and slept, assured that no enemy could approach us without first rousing the dogs, which were growling in fierce dispute over the remains of the Cougar.

At daybreak we left our camp, the squatter bearing on his shoulder the skin of the late destroyer of his stock, and retraced our steps until we found our horses, which had not strayed far from the place where we had left them. These we soon saddled, and jogging along, in a direct course, guided by the sun, congratulating each other on the destruction of so formidable a neighbor as the Panther had been, we soon arrived at my host's cabin. The five neighbors partook of such refreshment as the house could afford, and dispersing, returned to their homes, leaving me to follow my favorite pursuits.

The Runaway

Never shall I forget the impression made on my mind by the *rencontre* which forms the subject of this article, and I even doubt if the relation of it will not excite in that of my reader emotions of varied character.

Late in the afternoon of one of those sultry days which render the atmosphere of the Louisiana swamps pregnant with baneful effluvia, I directed my course towards my distant home, laden with a pack, consisting of five or six Wood Ibises, and a heavy gun, the weight of which, even in those days, when my natural powers were unimpaired, prevented me from moving with much speed. Reaching the banks of a miry bayou, only a few yards in breadth, but of which I could not ascertain the depth, on account of the muddiness of its waters, I thought it might be dangerous to wade through it with my burden, for which reason, throwing to the opposite side each of my heavy birds in succession, together with my gun, powder-flask, and shot-bag, and drawing my hunting-knife from its scabbard, to defend myself, if need should be, against Alligators, I entered the water, followed by my faithful dog. As I advanced carefully, and slowly, "Plato" swam around me, enjoying the refreshing influence of the liquid element that cooled his fatigued and heated frame. The water deepened, as did the mire of its bed; but with a stroke or two I gained the shore.

Scarcely had I stood erect on the opposite bank, when my dog ran to me, exhibiting marks of terror; his eyes seeming ready to burst from their sockets, and his mouth grinning with the expression of hatred, while his feelings found vent in a stifled growl. Thinking that all this was produced by the scent of a Wolf or Bear, I stooped to take up my gun, when a stentorian voice commanded me to "stand still, or die!" Such a *qui vive* in these woods was as unexpected as it was rare. I instantly raised and cocked my gun; and although I did not yet perceive the individual who had thus issued so peremptory a mandate, I felt determined to combat with him for the free passage of the grounds. Presently a tall, firmly built negro emerged from the bushy underwood, where until that moment he must have been crouched, and in a louder voice repeated his injunction. Had I pressed a trigger, his life would have instantly terminated; but observing that the gun which he aimed at my breast, was a wretched, rusty piece, from which fire could not readily be produced, I felt little fear, and therefore did not judge it necessary to proceed at once to extremities. I laid my gun at my side, tapped my dog quietly, and asked the man what he wanted.

My forbearance, and the stranger's long habit of submission, produced the most powerful effect on his mind. "Master," said he, "I am a runaway; I might perhaps shoot you down; but God forbids it, for I feel just now as if I saw him ready to pass his judgment against me for such a foul deed, and I ask mercy at your hands. For God's sake, do not kill me, master!" "And why," answered I, "have you left your quarters, where certainly you must have fared better than in these unwholesome swamps?" "Master, my story is a short, but a sorrowful one. My camp is close by, and, as I know you cannot reach home this night, if you will follow me there, depend upon *my honor* you shall be safe until the morning, when I will carry your birds, if you choose, to the great road."

The large, intelligent eyes of the negro, the complacency of his manners, and the tones of his voice, I thought invited me to venture; and as I felt that I was at least his equal, while moreover, I had my dog to second me, I answered that I would *follow him*. He observed the emphasis laid on the words, the meaning of which he seemed to understand so thoroughly that, turning to me, he said, "There, master, take my butcher's knife, while I throw away the flint and priming from my gun!" Reader, I felt confounded: this was too much for me: I refused the knife, and told him to keep his piece ready, in case we might accidentally meet a Cougar or a Bear.

Generosity exists everywhere. The greatest monarch acknowledges its impulse, and all around him, from the lowliest menial to the proud nobles that encircle his throne, at times experience that overpowering sentiment. I offered to shake hands with the runaway. "Master," said he, "I beg you thanks," and with this he gave me a squeeze that alike impressed me with the goodness of his heart and his great physical strength. From that moment we proceeded through the woods together. My dog smelt at him several times, but as he heard me speak in my usual tone of voice, he soon left us and rambled around as long as my whistle was unused. As we proceeded, I observed that he was guiding me towards the setting of the sun, and quite contrary to my homeward course. I remarked this to him, when he with the greatest simplicity replied, "Merely for our security."

After trudging along for some distance, and crossing several bayous, at all of which he threw his gun and knife to the opposite bank, and stood still until I had got over, we came to the borders of an immense cane-brake, from which I had, on former occasions, driven and killed several Deer. We entered, as I had frequently done before, now erect, then on "all fours." He regularly led the way, divided here and there the tangled stalks, and, whenever we reached a fallen tree, assisted me in getting over it, with all possible care. I saw that he was a perfect Indian in his knowledge of the woods, for he kept a direct course as precisely as any "Red-skin" I ever travelled with. All of a sudden he emitted a loud shriek, not unlike that of an Owl, which so surprised me, that I once more instantly levelled my gun. "No harm, master, I only give notice to my wife and children I am coming." A tremulous answer of the same nature gently echoed through the tree tops. The runaway's lips separated with an expression of gentleness and delight, when his beautiful set of ivory teeth seemed to smile through the dusk of evening that was thickening around us. "Master," said he, "my wife, though black, is as beautiful to me as the President's wife is to him; she is my queen, and I look on our young ones as so many princes; but you shall see them all, for here they are, thank God."

There, in the heart of the cane-brake, I found a regular camp. A small fire was lighted, and on its embers lay gridling some large slices of venison. A lad nine or ten years old was blowing the ashes from some fine sweet potatoes. Various articles of household furniture were carefully disposed around, and a large pallet of Bear and Deer skins, seemed to be the resting-place of the whole family. The wife raised not her eyes towards mine, and the little ones, three in number, retired into a corner, like so many discomfited Raccoons; but the Runaway, bold, and apparently happy, spoke to them in such cheering words, that at once one and all seemed to regard me as one sent by Providence to relieve them from all their troubles. My clothes were hung up by them to dry, and the negro asked if he might clean and grease my gun, which I permitted him to do, while the wife threw a large piece of Deer's flesh to my dog, which the children were already caressing.

Only think of my situation, reader! Here I was, ten miles at least from home, and four or five from the nearest plantation, in the camp of runaway slaves, and quite at their mercy. My eyes involuntarily followed their motions, but as I thought I perceived in them a strong desire to make me their confidant and friend, I gradually relinquished all suspicions. The venison and potatoes looked quite tempting, and by this time I was in a condition to relish much less savory fare; so, on being humbly asked to divide the viands before us, I partook of as hearty a meal as I had ever done in my life.

Supper over, the fire was completely extinguished, and a small lighted pine-knot placed in a hollowed calabash. Seeing that both the husband and the wife were desirous of communicating something to me, I at once and fearlessly desired them to unburden their minds, when the Runaway told me a tale of which the following is the substance.

About eighteen months before, a planter, residing not very far off, having met with some losses, was obliged to expose his slaves at a public sale. The value of his negroes was well known, and on the appointed day the auctioneer laid them out in small lots, or offered them singly, in the manner which he judged most advantageous to their owner. The Runaway, who was well known as being the most valuable next to his wife, was put up by himself for sale, and brought an immoderate price.

For his wife, who came next, and alone, eight hundred dollars were bidden and paid down. Then the children were exposed, and, on account of their breed, brought high prices. The rest of the slaves went off at rates corresponding to their qualifications.

The Runaway chanced to be bought by the overseer of the plantation; the wife was bought by an individual residing about a hundred miles off, and the children went to different places along the river. The heart of the husband and father failed him under this dire calamity. For a while he pined in sorrow under his new master; but having marked down in his memory the names of the different persons who had purchased each dear portion of his family, he feigned illness, if indeed, he whose affections had been so grievously blasted could be said to feign it, refrained from food for several days, and was little regarded by the overseer, who felt himself disappointed in what he had considered a bargain.

On a stormy night, when the elements raged with all the fury of a hurricane, the poor negro made his escape, and being well acquainted with all the neighboring swamps, at once made directly for the canebrake in the centre of which I found his camp. A few nights afterwards he gained the abode of his wife, and the very next after their meeting, he led her away. The children, one after another, he succeeded in stealing, until at last the whole of the objects of his love were under his care.

To provide for five individuals was no easy task in those wilds, which after the first notice was given of the wonderful disappearance of this extraordinary family, were daily ransacked by armed planters. Necessity, it is said, will bring the Wolf from the forest. The Runaway seems to have well understood the maxim, for under the cover of night he approached his first master's plantation, where he had ever been treated with the greatest kindness. The house-servants knew him too well not to aid him to the best of their power, and at the approach of each morning he returned to his camp with an ample supply of provisions. One day, while in search of wild fruits, he found a Bear dead before the muzzle of a gun that had been set for the purpose. Both articles he carried to his home. His friends at the plantation managed to supply him with some ammunition, and on damp and cloudy days he first ventured to hunt around his camp. Possessed of courage and activity, he gradually became more careless, and rambled farther in search of game. It was on one of his excursions that I met him, and he assured me the noise which I made in passing the bayou had caused him to lose the chance of killing a fine Deer, "although," said he, "my old musket misses fire sadly too often."

The Runaways, after disclosing their secret to me, both rose from their seat, with eyes full of tears. "Good master, for God's sake, do something for us and our children," they sobbed forth with one accord. Their little ones lay sound asleep in the fearlessness of their innocence. Who could have heard such a tale without emotion? I promised them my most cordial assistance. They both sat up that night to watch my repose, and I slept close to their urchins, as if on a bed of the softest down.

Day broke so fair, so pure, and so gladdening that I told them such heavenly appearances were ominous of good, and that I scarcely doubted of obtaining their full pardon. I desired them to take their children with them, and promised to accompany them to the plantation of their first master. They gladly obeyed. My Ibises were hung round their camp, and, as a memento of my having been there, I notched several trees; after which I bade adieu, perhaps for the last time, to that cane-brake. We soon reached the plantation, the owner of which, with whom I was well acquainted, received me with all the generous kindness of a Louisiana planter. Ere an hour had elapsed, the Runaway and his family were looked upon as his own. He afterwards repurchased them from their owners, and treated them with his former kindness; so that they were rendered as happy as slaves generally are in that country, and continued to cherish that attachment to each other which had led to their adventures. Since this event happened, it has, I have been informed, become illegal to separate slave families without their consent.

A Long Calm at Sea

On the 17th of May, 1826, I left New Orleans on board the ship "Delos," commanded by Joseph Hatch, Esq., of Kennebunk, bound for Liverpool. The steamer "Hercules," which towed the ship, left us several miles outside of the Balize, about ten hours after our departure; but there was not a breath of wind, the waters were smoother than the prairies of the Opelousas, and notwithstanding our great display of canvas, we lay like a dead whale, floating at the mercy of the currents. The weather was uncommonly fair, and the heat excessive; and in this helpless state we continued for many days. About the end of a week we had lost sight of the Balize, although I was assured by the commander that all this while the ship had rarely answered the helm. The sailors whistled for wind, and raised their hands in all directions, anxious as they were to feel some motion in the air; but all to no purpose; it was a dead calm, and we concluded that "Æolus" had agreed with "Neptune" to detain us, until our patience should be fairly tried, or our sport exhausted; for sport we certainly had, both on board and around the ship. I doubt if I can better contribute to your amusement at present than by giving you a short account of the occurrences that took place during this sleepy fit of the being on whom we depended for our progress toward merry England.

Vast numbers of beautiful Dolphins glided by the side of the vessel, glancing like burnished gold through the day, and gleaming like meteors by night. The captain and his mates were expert at alluring them with baited hooks, and not less so at piercing them with five-pronged instruments, which they called grains; and I was delighted with the sport, because it afforded me an opportunity of observing and noting some of the habits of this beautiful fish, as well as several other kinds.

On being hooked, the Dolphin flounces vigorously, shoots off with great impetuosity to the very end of the line, when, being suddenly checked, it often rises perpendicularly several feet out of the water, shakes itself violently in the air, gets disentangled, and thus escapes. But when well secured, it is held in play for a while by the experienced fisher, soon becomes exhausted, and is hauled on board. Some persons prefer pulling them in at once, but they seldom succeed, as the force with which the fish shakes itself on being raised out of the water is generally sufficient to enable it to extricate itself. Dolphins move in shoals, varying from four or five to twenty or more, hunting in packs in the waters, as Wolves pursue their prey on land. The object of their pursuit is generally the Flying-fish, now and then the Bonita; and when nothing better can be had, they will follow the little Rudder-fish, and seize it immediately under the stern of the ship. The Flying-fishes after having escaped for a while by dint of their great velocity, on being again approached by the Dolphin, emerge from the waters, and spreading their broad wing-like fins, sail through the air and disperse in all directions, like a covey of timid Partridges before the rapacious Falcon. Some pursue a direct course, others diverge on either side; but in a short time they all drop into their natural element. While they are travelling in the air, their keen and hungry pursuer, like a greyhound, follows in their wake, and performing a succession of leaps, many feet in extent, rapidly gains upon the quarry, which is often seized just as it falls into the sea.

Dolphins manifest a very remarkable sympathy with each other. The moment one of them is hooked or grained, those in company make up to it, and remain around until the unfortunate fish is pulled on board, when they generally move off together, seldom biting at anything thrown out to them. This, however, is the case only with the larger individuals, which keep apart from the young, in the same manner as is observed in several species of birds; for when the smaller Dolphins are in large shoals, they all remain under the bows of a ship, and bite in succession at any sort of line, as if determined to see what has become of their lost companions, in consequence of which they are often all caught.

You must not suppose that the Dolphin is without its enemies. Who, in this world, man or fish, has not enough of them? Often it conceives itself on the very eve of swallowing a fish, which, after all, is nothing but a piece of lead, with a few feathers fastened to it, to make it look like a Flying-fish, when it is seized and severed in two by the insidious Balacouda, which I have once seen to carry off by means of its sharp teeth, the better part of a Dolphin that was hooked, and already hoisted to the surface of the water.

The Dolphins caught in the Gulf of Mexico during this calm were suspected to be poisonous; and to ascertain whether this was really the case, our cook, who was an African negro, never boiled or fried one without placing beside it a dollar. If the silver was not tarnished by the time the Dolphin was ready for the table, the fish was presented to the passengers, with an assurance that it was perfectly good. But as not a single individual of the hundred that we caught had the property of converting silver into copper, I suspect that our African sage was no magician.

One morning, that of the 22d of June, the weather sultry, I was surprised on getting out of my hammock, which was slung on deck, to find the water all around swarming with Dolphins, which were sporting in great glee. The sailors assured me that this was a certain "token of wind," and, as they watched the movements of the fishes, added, "ay, and of a fair breeze too." I caught several Dolphins in the course of an hour, after which scarcely any remained about the ship. Not a breath of air came to our relief all that day, no, nor even the next. The sailors were in despair, and I should probably have become despondent also, had not my spirits been excited by finding a very large Dolphin on my hook. When I had hauled it on board, I found it to be the largest I had ever caught. It was a magnificent creature. See how it quivers in the agonies of death! its tail flaps the hard deck, producing a sound like the rapid roll of a drum. How beautiful the changes of its colors! Now it is blue, now green, silvery, golden, and burnished copper! Now it presents a blaze of all the hues of the rainbow intermingled; but, alack! it is dead, and the play of its colors is no longer seen. It has settled into the deep calm that has paralyzed the energies of the blustering winds, and smoothed down the proud waves of the ocean.

The best bait for the Dolphin is a long strip of Shark's flesh. I think it generally prefers this to the semblance of the Flying-fish, which indeed it does not often seize unless when the ship is under way, and it is made to rise to the surface. There are times, however, when hunger and the absence of their usual food will induce the Dolphins to dash at any sort of bait; and I have seen some caught by means of a piece of white linen fastened to a hook. Their appetite is as keen as that of the Vulture, and whenever a good opportunity occurs, they gorge themselves to such a degree that they become an easy prey to their enemies the Balacouda and the Bottle-nosed Porpoise. One that had been grained while lazily swimming immediately under the stern of our ship, was found to have its stomach completely crammed with Flying-fish, all regularly disposed side by side, with their tails downwards—by which I mean to say that the Dolphin always *swallows its prey tail-foremost.* They looked in fact like so many salted Herrings packed in a box, and were to the number of twenty-two, each six or seven inches in length.

The usual length of the Dolphins caught in the Gulf of Mexico is about three feet, and I saw none that exceeded four feet two inches. The weight of one of the latter size was only eighteen pounds; for this fish is extremely narrow in proportion to its length, although rather deep in its form. When just caught, the upper fin, which reaches from the forehead to within a short distance of the tail, is of a fine dark blue. The upper part of the body in its whole length is azure, and the lower parts are of a golden hue, mottled irregularly with deep-blue spots. It seems that they at times enter very shallow water, as in the course of my last voyage along the Florida coast, some were caught in a seine, along with their kinsman the "Cavalier," of which I shall speak elsewhere.

The flesh of the Dolphin is rather firm, very white, and lies in flakes when cooked. The first caught are generally eaten with great pleasure, but when served many days in succession, they become insipid. It is not, as an article of food, equal to the Balacouda, which is perhaps as good as any fish caught in the waters of the Gulf of Mexico.

Still Becalmed

On the 4th of June, we were still in the same plight, although the currents of the Gulf had borne us to a great distance from the place where, as I have informed you, we had amused ourselves with catching Dolphins. These currents are certainly very singular, for they carried us hither and thither, at one time rendering us apprehensive of drifting on the coast of Florida, at another threatening to send us to Cuba. Sometimes a slight motion in the air revived our hopes, swelled our sails a little, and carried us through the smooth waters like a skater gliding on ice; but in a few hours it was again a dead calm.

One day several small birds, after alighting on the spars, betook themselves to the deck. One of them, a female Rice Bunting, drew our attention more particularly, for, a few moments after her arrival, there came down, as if in her wake, a beautiful Peregrine Falcon. The plunderer hovered about for a while, then stationed himself on the end of one of the yard-arms, and suddenly pouncing on the little gleaner of the meadows, clutched her and carried her off in exultation. But, reader, mark the date, and judge besides of my astonishment when I saw the Falcon feeding on the Finch while on wing, precisely with the same ease and composure as the Mississippi Kite might show while devouring high in air a Red-throated Lizard, swept from one of the magnificent trees of the Louisiana woods.

There was a favorite pet on board belonging to our captain, and which was nothing more nor less than the female companion of a cock—in other words, a common hen. Some liked her because she now and then dropped a fresh egg—a rare article at sea, even on board the "Delos;" others, because she exhibited a pleasing simplicity of character; others again, because, when they had pushed her overboard, it gave them pleasure to see the poor thing in terror strike with her feet, and strive to reach her floating home, which she would never have accomplished, however, had it not been for the humane interference of our captain, Mr. Joseph Hatch, of Kennebunk. Kind, good-hearted man! when, several weeks after, the same pet hen accidentally flew overboard, as we were scudding along at a furious rate, I thought I saw a tear stand in his eye, as she floated panting in our wake. But as yet we are becalmed, and heartily displeased at old "Æolus" for overlooking us.

One afternoon we caught two Sharks. In one of them, a female, about seven feet long, we found ten young ones, all alive, and quite capable of swimming, as we proved by experiment; for, on casting one of them into the sea, it immediately made off, as if it had been accustomed to shift for itself. Of another, that had been cut in two, the head half swam off out of our sight. The rest were cut in pieces, as was the old shark, as bait for the Dolphins, which I have already said are fond of such food.

Our captain, who was much intent on amusing me, informed me that the Rudder-fishes were plentiful astern, and immediately set to dressing hooks for the purpose of catching them. There was now some air above us, the cotton sheets aloft bulged out, the ship moved through the water, and the captain and I repaired to the cabin window. I was furnished with a fine hook, a thread line, and some small bits of bacon, as was the captain, and we dropped our bait among the myriads of delicate little fishes below. Up they came, one after another, so fast in succession that, according to my journal, we caught three hundred and seventy in about two hours. What a mess! and how delicious when roasted! If ever I am again becalmed in the Gulf of Mexico, I shall not forget the Rudder-fish. The little things scarcely measured three inches in length; they were thin and deep in form, and afforded excellent eating. It was curious to see them keep to the lee of the rudder in a compact body; and so voracious were they that they actually leaped out of the water at the sight of the bait, as "sunnies" are occasionally wont to do in our rivers. But the very instant that the ship became still, they dispersed around her sides, and would no longer bite. I made a figure of one of them, as indeed I tried to do of every other species that occurred during this deathlike calm. Not one of these fishes did I ever see when crossing the Atlantic, although many kinds at times come close to the stern of any vessel in the great sea, and are called by the same name.

Another time we caught a fine Porpoise, which measured about two yards in length. This took place at night, when the light of the moon afforded me a clear view of the spot. The fish, contrary to custom, was grained, instead of being harpooned; but in such a way and so effectually, through the forehead, that it was thus held fast, and allowed to flounce and beat about the bows of the ship, until the person who had struck it gave the line holding the grains to the captain, slid down upon the bobstays with a rope, and after a while managed to secure it by the tail. Some of the crew then hoisted it on board. When it arrived on deck, it gave a deep groan, flapped with great force, and soon expired. On opening it next morning, eight hours after death, we found its intestines still warm. They were arranged in the same manner as those of a pig; the paunch contained several cuttle-fishes partially digested. The lower jaw extended beyond the upper about three-fourths of an inch, and both were furnished with a single row of conical teeth, about half an inch long, and just so far separated as to admit those of one jaw between the corresponding ones of the other. The animal might weigh about four hundred pounds; its eyes were extremely small, its flesh was considered delicate by some on board; but in my opinion, if it be good, that of a large Alligator is equally so; and on neither do I intend to feast for some time. The captain told me that he had seen these Porpoises leap at times perpendicularly out of the water to the height of several feet, and that small boats have now and then been sunk by their falling into them when engaged with their sports.

During all this time flocks of Pigeons were crossing the Gulf, between Cuba and the Floridas; many a Rose-breasted Gull played around by day; Noddies alighted on the rigging by night; and now and then the Frigate bird was observed ranging high over head in the azure of the cloudless sky.

The directions of the currents were tried, and our captain, who had an extraordinary genius for mechanics, was frequently employed in turning powder-horns and other articles. So calm and sultry was the weather that we had a large awning spread, under which we took our meals and spent the night. At length we got so wearied of it that the very sailors, I thought, seemed disposed to leap overboard and swim to land. But at length, on the thirty-seventh day after our departure, a smart breeze overtook us. Presently there was an extraordinary bustle on board; about twelve the Tortugas light-house bore north of us, and in a few hours more we gained the Atlantic. Æolus had indeed awakened from his long sleep; and on the nineteenth day after leaving the Capes of Florida, I was landed at Liverpool.

Great Egg Harbor

Some years ago, after having spent the spring in observing the habits of the migratory Warblers and other land birds, which arrived in vast numbers in the vicinity of Camden in New Jersey, I prepared to visit the sea shores of that State, for the purpose of making myself acquainted with their feathered inhabitants. June had commenced, the weather was pleasant, and the country seemed to smile in the prospect of bright days and gentle gales. Fishermen-gunners passed daily between Philadelphia and the various small seaports, with Jersey wagons, laden with fish, fowls, and other provisions, or with such articles as were required by the families of those hardy boatmen; and I bargained with one of them to take myself and my baggage to Great Egg Harbor.

One afternoon, about sunset, the vehicle halted at my lodgings, and the conductor intimated that he was anxious to proceed as quickly as possible. A trunk, a couple of guns, and such other articles as are found necessary by persons whose pursuits are similar to mine, were immediately thrust into the wagon, and were followed by their owner. The conductor whistled to his steeds, and off we went at a round pace over the loose and deep sand that in almost every part of this State forms the basis of the roads. After a while we overtook a whole caravan of similar vehicles, moving in the same direction, and when we got near them our horses slackened their pace to a regular walk, the driver leaped from his seat, I followed his example, and we presently found ourselves in the midst of a group of merry wagoners, relating their adventures of the week, it being now Saturday night. One gave intimation of the number of "Sheep-heads" he had taken to town, another spoke of the Curlews which yet remained on the sands, and a third boasted of having gathered so many dozens of Marsh Hens' eggs. I inquired if the Fish Hawks were plentiful near Great Egg Harbor, and was answered by an elderly man, who with a laugh asked if I had ever seen the "Weak fish" along the coast without the bird in question. Not knowing the animal he had named, I confessed my ignorance, when the whole party burst into a loud laugh, in which, there being nothing better for it, I joined.

About midnight the caravan reached a half-way house, where we rested a while. Several roads diverged from this spot, and the wagons separated, one only keeping us company. The night was dark and gloomy, but the sand of the road indicated our course very distinctly. Suddenly the galloping of horses struck my ear, and on looking back we perceived that our wagon must in an instant be in imminent danger. The driver leaped off, and drew his steeds aside, barely in time to allow the runaways to pass without injuring us. Off they went at full speed, and not long after their owner came up panting, and informed us that they had suddenly taken fright at some noise proceeding from the woods, but hoped they would soon stop. Immediately after we heard a crack; then for a few moments all was silent; but the neighing of horses presently assured us that they had broken loose. On reaching the spot we found the wagon upset, and a few yards farther on were the horses, quietly browsing by the roadside.

The first dawn of morn in the Jerseys in the month of June is worthy of a better description than I can furnish, and therefore I shall only say that the moment the sunbeams blazed over the horizon, the loud and mellow notes of the Meadow Lark saluted our ears. On each side of the road were open woods, on the tallest trees of which I observed at intervals the nest of a Fish Hawk, far above which the white-breasted bird slowly winged its way, as it commenced its early journey to the sea, the odor of which filled me with delight. In half an hour more we were in the centre of Great Egg Harbor.

There I had the good fortune to be received into the house of a thoroughbred fisherman-gunner, who, besides owning a comfortable cot only a few hundred yards from the shore, had an excellent woman for a wife, and a little daughter as playful as a kitten, though as wild as a Sea-Gull. In less than half an hour I was quite at home, and the rest of the day was spent in devotion.

Oysters, though reckoned out of season at this period, are as good as ever when fresh from their beds, and my first meal was of some as large and white as any I have eaten. The sight of them placed before me on a clean table, with an honest and industrious family in my company, never failed to afford more pleasure than the most sumptuous fare under different circumstances; and our conversation being simple and harmless, gayety shone in every face. As we became better acquainted, I had to answer several questions relative to the object of my visit. The good man rubbed his hands with joy, as I spoke of shooting and fishing, and of long excursions through the swamps and marshes around.

My host was then, and I hope still is, a tall, strong-boned, muscular man, of dark complexion, with eyes as keen as those of the Sea-Eagle. He was a tough walker, laughed at difficulties, and could pull an oar with any man. As to shooting, I have often doubted whether he or Mr. Egan, the worthy pilot of Indian Isle, was best; and rarely indeed have I seen either of them miss a shot.

At daybreak on Monday, I shouldered my double-barrelled gun, and my host carried with him a long fowling-piece, a pair of oars, and a pair of oyster-tongs, while the wife and daughter brought along a seine. The boat was good, the breeze gentle, and along the inlets we sailed for parts well known to my companions. To such naturalists as are qualified to observe many different objects at the same time, Great Egg Harbor would probably afford as ample a field as any part of our coast, excepting the Florida Keys. Birds of many kinds are abundant, as are fishes and testaceous animals. The forests shelter many beautiful plants, and even on the driest sand-bar you may see insects of the most brilliant tints. Our principal object, however, was to procure certain birds known there by the name of Lawyers, and to accomplish this we entered and followed for several miles a winding inlet or bayou, which led us to the interior of a vast marsh, where after some search we found the birds and their nests. Our seine had been placed across the channel, and when we returned to it the tide had run out, and left in it a number of fine fish, some of which we cooked and ate on the spot. One, which I considered as a curiosity, was saved, and transmitted to Baron Cuvier. Our repast ended, the seine was spread out to dry, and we again betook ourselves to the marshes to pursue our researches until the return of the tide. Having collected enough to satisfy us, we took up our oars, and returned to the shore in front of the fisherman's house, where we dragged the seine several times with success.

In this manner I passed several weeks along those delightful and healthy shores, one day going to the woods, to search the swamps in which the Herons bred, passing another amid the joyous cries of the Marsh Hens, and on a third carrying slaughter among the White-breasted Sea-Gulls; by way of amusement sometimes hauling the fish called the Sheep's-head from an eddy along the shore, or watching the gay Terns as they danced in the air, or plunged into the waters to seize the tiny fry. Many a drawing I made at Great Egg Harbor, many a pleasant day I spent along its shores; and much pleasure would it give me once more to visit the good and happy family in whose house I resided there.

The Great Pine Swamp

I left Philadelphia, at four of the morning, by the coach, with no other accoutrements than I knew to be absolutely necessary for the jaunt which I intended to make. These consisted of a wooden box, containing a small stock of linen, drawing-paper, my journal, colors, and pencils, together with twenty-five pounds of shot, some flints, the due quantum of cash, my gun *Tear-jacket*, and a heart as true to Nature as ever.

Our coaches are none of the best, nor do they move with the velocity of those of some other countries. It was eight, and a dark night, when I reached Mauch Chunk, now so celebrated in the Union for its rich coal-mines, and eighty-eight miles distant from Philadelphia. I had passed through a very diversified country, part of which was highly cultivated, while the rest was yet in a state of nature, and consequently much more agreeable to me. On alighting, I was shown to the traveller's room, and on asking for the landlord, saw coming towards me a fine-looking young man, to whom I made known my wishes. He spoke kindly, and offered to lodge and board me at a much lower rate than travellers who go there for the very simple pleasure of being dragged on the railway. In a word, I was fixed in four minutes, and that most comfortably.

No sooner had the approach of day been announced by the cocks of the little village, than I marched out with my gun and note-book, to judge for myself of the wealth of the country. After traversing much ground, and crossing many steep hills, I returned, if not wearied, at least much disappointed at the extraordinary scarcity of birds. So I bargained to be carried in a cart to the central parts of the Great Pine Swamp, and, although a heavy storm was rising, ordered my conductor to proceed. We winded round many a mountain and at last crossed the highest. The storm had become tremendous, and we were thoroughly drenched, but, my resolution being fixed, the boy was obliged to continue his driving. Having already travelled about fifteen miles or so, we left the turnpike, and struck up a narrow and bad road, that seemed merely cut out to enable the people of the Swamp to receive the necessary supplies from the village which I had left. Some mistakes were made, and it was almost dark when a post directed us to the habitation of a Mr. Jediah Irish, to whom I had been recommended. We now rattled down a steep declivity, edged on one side by almost perpendicular rocks, and on the other by a noisy stream, which seemed grumbling at the approach of strangers. The ground was so overgrown by laurels and tall pines of different kinds that the whole presented only a mass of darkness.

At length we reached the house, the door of which was already opened, the sight of strangers being nothing uncommon in our woods, even in the most remote parts. On entering, I was presented with a chair, while my conductor was shown the way to the stable, and on expressing a wish that I should be permitted to remain in the house for some weeks, I was gratified by receiving the sanction of the good woman to my proposal, although her husband was then from home. As I immediately began to talk about the nature of the country, and inquired if birds were numerous in the neighborhood, Mrs. Irish, more *au fait* in household affairs than ornithology, sent for a nephew of her husband's, who soon made his appearance, and in whose favor I became at once prepossessed. He conversed like an educated person, saw that I was comfortably disposed of, and finally bade me good-night in such a tone as made me quite happy.

The storm had rolled away before the first beams of the morning sun shone brightly on the wet foliage, displaying all its richness and beauty. My ears were greeted by the notes, always sweet and mellow, of the Wood Thrush and other songsters. Before I had gone many steps, the woods echoed to the report of my gun, and I picked from among the leaves a lovely Sylvia, long sought for, but until then sought for in vain. I needed no more, and standing still for a while, I was soon convinced that the Great Pine Swamp harbored many other objects as valuable to me.

The young man joined me, bearing his rifle, and offered to accompany me through the woods, all of which he well knew. But I was anxious to transfer to paper the form and beauty of the little bird I had in my hand;

and requesting him to break a twig of blooming laurel, we returned to the house, speaking of nothing else than the picturesque beauty of the country around.

A few days passed, during which I became acquainted with my hostess and her sweet children, and made occasional rambles, but spent the greater portion of my time in drawing. One morning, as I stood near the window of my room, I remarked a tall and powerful man alight from his horse, loose the girth of the saddle, raise the latter with one hand, pass the bridle over the head of the animal with the other, and move towards the house, while the horse betook himself to the little brook to drink. I heard some movements in the room below, and again the same tall person walked towards the mill and stores, a few hundred yards from the house. In America business is the first object in view at all times, and right it is that it should be so. Soon after my hostess entered my room, accompanied by the fine-looking woodsman, to whom, as Mr. Jediah Irish, I was introduced. Reader, to describe to you the qualities of that excellent man were vain; you should know him, as I do, to estimate the value of such men in our sequestered forests. He not only made me welcome, but promised all his assistance in forwarding my views.

The long walks and long talks we have had together I can never forget, nor the many beautiful birds which we pursued, shot, and admired. The juicy venison, excellent Bear flesh, and delightful trout that daily formed my food, methinks I can still enjoy. And then, what pleasure I had in listening to him as he read his favorite poems of Burns, while my pencil was occupied in smoothing and softening the drawing of the bird before me! Was not this enough to recall to my mind the early impressions that had been made upon it by the description of the golden age, which I here found realized?

The Lehigh about this place forms numerous short turns between the mountains, and affords frequent falls, as well as below the falls deep pools, which render this stream a most valuable one for mills of any kind. Not many years before this date, my host was chosen by the agent of the Lehigh Coal Company, as their mill-wright, and manager for cutting down the fine trees which covered the mountains around. He was young, robust, active, industrious, and persevering. He marched to the spot where his abode now is, with some workmen, and by dint of hard labor first cleared the road mentioned above, and reached the river at the centre of a bend, where he fixed on erecting various mills. The pass here is so narrow that it looks as if formed by the bursting asunder of the mountain, both sides ascending abruptly, so that the place where the settlement was made is in many parts difficult of access, and the road then newly cut was only sufficient to permit men and horses to come to the spot where Jediah and his men were at work. So great, in fact, were the difficulties of access that, as he told me, pointing to a spot about one hundred and fifty feet above us, they for many months slipped from it their barrelled provisions, assisted by ropes, to their camp below. But no sooner was the first saw-mill erected than the axe-men began their devastations. Trees, one after another, were, and are yet, constantly heard falling during the days; and in calm nights, the greedy mills told the sad tale that in a century the noble forests around should exist no more. Many mills were erected, many dams raised, in defiance of the impetuous Lehigh. One full third of the trees have already been culled, turned into boards, and floated as far as Philadelphia.

In such an undertaking the cutting of the trees is not all. They have afterwards to be hauled to the edge of the mountains bordering the river, launched into the stream, and led to the mills over many shallows and difficult places. Whilst I was in the Great Pine Swamp, I frequently visited one of the principal places for the launching of logs. To see them tumbling from such a height, touching here and there the rough angle of a projecting rock, bouncing from it with the elasticity of a foot-ball, and at last falling with an awful crash into the river, forms a sight interesting in the highest degree, but impossible for me to describe. Shall I tell you that I have seen masses of these logs heaped above each other to the number of five thousand? I may so tell you, for such I have seen. My friend Irish assured me that at some seasons, these piles consisted of a much greater number, the river becoming in those places completely choked up.

When *freshets* (or floods) take place, then is the time chosen for forwarding the logs to the different mills. This is called a *Frolic*. Jediah Irish, who is generally the leader, proceeds to the upper leap with his men, each provided with a strong wooden handspike, and a short-handled axe. They all take to the water, be it summer or winter, like so many Newfoundland spaniels. The logs are gradually detached, and, after a time, are seen floating down the dancing stream, here striking against a rock and whirling many times round, there suddenly checked in dozens by a shallow, over which they have to be forced with the handspikes. Now they arrive at the edge of a dam, and are again pushed over. Certain numbers are left in each dam, and when the party has arrived at the last, which lies just where my friend Irish's camp was first formed, the drenched leader and his men, about sixty in number, make their way home, find there a healthful repast, and spend the evening and a portion of the night in dancing and frolicking, in their own simple manner, in the most perfect amity, seldom troubling themselves with the idea of the labor prepared for them on the morrow.

That morrow now come, one sounds a horn from the door of the store-house, at the call of which each returns to his work. The sawyers, the millers, the rafters, and raftsmen are all immediately busy. The mills are all going, and the logs, which a few months before were the supporters of broad and leafy tops, are now in the act of being split asunder. The boards are then launched into the stream, and rafts are formed of them for market.

During the months of summer and autumn, the Lehigh, a small river of itself, soon becomes extremely shallow, and to float the rafts would prove impossible, had not art managed to provide a supply of water for this express purpose. At the breast of the lower dam is a curiously constructed lock, which is opened at the approach of the rafts. They pass through this lock with the rapidity of lightning, propelled by the water that had been accumulated in the dam, and which is of itself generally sufficient to float them to Mauch Chunk, after which, entering regular canals, they find no other impediments, but are conveyed to their ultimate destination.

Before population had greatly advanced in this part of Pennsylvania, game of all description found within that range was extremely abundant. The Elk itself did not disdain to browse on the shoulders of the mountains near the Lehigh. Bears and the common Deer must have been plentiful, as, at the moment when I write, many of both are seen and killed by the resident hunters. The Wild Turkey, the Pheasant, and the Grouse, are also tolerably abundant, and as to trout in the streams—ah, reader, if you are an angler, do go there and try for yourself. For my part, I can only say that I have been made weary with pulling up from the rivulets the sparkling fish, allured by the struggles of the common grasshopper.

A comical affair happened with the Bears, which I shall relate to you, good reader. A party of my friend Irish's raftsmen, returning from Mauch Chunk one afternoon, through sundry short-cuts over the mountains, at the season when the huckleberries are ripe and plentiful, were suddenly apprised of the proximity of some of these animals by their snuffing the air. No sooner was this perceived than, to the astonishment of the party, not fewer than eight Bears, I was told, made their appearance. Each man, being provided with his short-handled axe, faced about, and willingly came to the scratch; but the assailed soon proved the assailants, and with claw and tooth drove the men off in a twinkling. Down they all rushed from the mountain; the noise spread quickly; rifles were soon procured and shouldered; but when the spot was reached, no Bears were to be found; night forced the hunters back to their homes, and a laugh concluded the affair.

I spent six weeks in the Great Pine Forest—Swamp it cannot be called—where I made many a drawing. Wishing to leave Pennsylvania, and to follow the migratory flocks of our birds to the South, I bade adieu to the excellent wife and rosy children of my friend, and to his kind nephew. Jediah Irish, shouldering his heavy rifle, accompanied me, and trudging directly across the mountains, we arrived at Mauch Chunk in good time for dinner. Shall I ever have the pleasure of seeing that good, that generous man again?

At Mauch Chunk, where we both spent the night, Mr. White, the civil engineer, visited me, and looked at the drawings which I had made in the Great Pine Forest. The news he gave me of my sons, then in Kentucky, made me still more anxious to move in their direction; and long before daybreak, I shook hands with the good man of the forest, and found myself moving towards the capital of Pennsylvania,* having as my sole companion a sharp, frosty breeze. Left to my thoughts, I felt amazed that such a place as the Great Pine Forest should be so little known to the Philadelphians, scarcely any of whom could direct me towards it. How much it is to be regretted, thought I, that the many young gentlemen who are there, so much at a loss how to employ their leisure days, should not visit these wild retreats, valuable as they are to the student of nature. How differently would they feel, if, instead of spending weeks in smoothing a useless bow, and walking out in full dress, intent on displaying the make of their legs, to some rendezvous where they may enjoy their wines, they were to occupy themselves in contemplating the rich profusion which nature has poured around them, or even in procuring some desiderated specimen for their Peale's Museum, once so valuable, and so finely arranged! But, alas, no! they are none of them aware of the richness of the Great Pine Swamp, nor are they likely to share the hospitality to be found there.

The Lost One

A "live-oaker" employed on the St. John's River, in East Florida, left his cabin, situated on the banks of that stream, and, with his axe on his shoulder, proceeded towards the swamp in which he had several times

* Then Philadelphia.

before plied his trade of felling and squaring the giant trees that afford the most valuable timber for naval architecture and other purposes.

At the season which is the best for this kind of labor, heavy fogs not unfrequently cover the country, so as to render it difficult for one to see farther than thirty or forty yards in any direction. The woods, too, present so little variety that every tree seems the mere counterpart of every other; and the grass, when it has not been burnt, is so tall that a man of ordinary stature cannot see over it, whence it is necessary for him to proceed with great caution, lest he should unwittingly deviate from the ill-defined trail which he follows. To increase the difficulty, several trails often meet, in which case, unless the explorer be perfectly acquainted with the neighborhood, it would be well for him to lie down, and wait until the fog should disperse. Under such circumstances, the best woodsmen are not unfrequently bewildered for a while; and I well remember that such an occurrence happened to myself, at a time when I had imprudently ventured to pursue a wounded quadruped, which led me some distance from the track.

The live-oaker had been jogging onwards for several hours, and became aware that he must have travelled considerably more than the distance between his cabin and the "hummock" which he desired to reach. To his alarm, at the moment when the fog dispersed, he saw the sun at its meridian height, and could not recognize a single object around him.

Young, healthy, and active, he imagined he had walked with more than usual speed, and had passed the place to which he was bound. He accordingly turned his back upon the sun, and pursued a different route, guided by a small trail. Time passed, and the sun headed his course; he saw it gradually descend in the west; but all around him continued as if enveloped with mystery. The huge gray trees spread their giant boughs over him, the rank grass extended on all sides, not a living being crossed his path; all was silent and still, and the scene was like a dull and dreary dream of the land of oblivion. He wandered like a forgotten ghost that had passed into the land of spirits, without yet meeting one of his kind with whom to hold converse.

The condition of a man lost in the woods is one of the most perplexing that could be imagined by a person who has not himself been in a like predicament. Every object he sees, he at first thinks he recognizes, and while his whole mind is bent on searching for more that may gradually lead to his extrication, he goes on committing greater errors the farther he proceeds. This was the case with the live-oaker. The sun was now setting with a fiery aspect, and by degrees it sunk in its full circular form, as if giving warning of a sultry morrow. Myriads of insects, delighted at its departure, now filled the air on buzzing wings. Each piping frog arose from the muddy pool in which it had concealed itself; the Squirrel retired to its hole, the Crow to its roost, and, far above, the harsh, croaking voice of the Heron announced that, full of anxiety, it was wending its way towards the miry interior of some distant swamp. Now the woods began to resound to the shrill cries of the Owl; and the breeze, as it swept among the columnar stems of the forest trees, came laden with heavy and chilling dews. Alas! no moon with her silvery light shone on the dreary scene, and the Lost One, wearied and vexed, laid himself down on the damp ground. Prayer is always consolatory to man in every difficulty or danger, and the woodsman fervently prayed to his Maker, wished his family a happier night than it was his lot to experience, and with a feverish anxiety waited the return of day.

You may imagine the length of that dull, cold, moonless night. With the dawn of day came the usual fogs of those latitudes. The poor man started on his feet, and with a sorrowful heart, pursued a course which he thought might lead him to some familiar object, although, indeed, he scarcely knew what he was doing. No longer had he the trace of a track to guide him, and yet, as the sun rose, he calculated the many hours of daylight he had before him, and the farther he went, the faster he walked. But vain were all his hopes; that day was spent in fruitless endeavors to regain the path that led to his home, and when night again approached, the terror that had been gradually spreading over his mind, together with the nervous debility produced by fatigue, anxiety, and hunger, rendered him almost frantic. He told me that at this moment he beat his breast, tore his hair, and, had it not been for the piety with which his parents had in early life imbued his mind, and which had become habitual, would have cursed his existence. Famished as he now was, he laid himself on the ground, and fed on the weeds and grasses that grew around him. That night was spent in the greatest agony and terror. "I knew my situation," he said to me. "I was fully aware that unless Almighty God came to my assistance, I must perish in those uninhabited woods. I knew that I had walked more than fifty miles, although I had not met with a brook, from which I could quench my thirst, or even allay the burning heat of my parched lips and bloodshot eyes. I knew that if I should not meet with some stream I must die, for my axe was my only weapon, and although Deer and Bears now and then started within a few yards, or even feet of me, not one of them could I kill; and although I was in the midst of abundance, not a mouthful did I expect to procure, to satisfy the cravings of my empty stomach. Sir, may God preserve you from ever feeling as I did the whole of that day."

For several days after, no one can imagine the condition in which he was, for when he related to me this painful adventure, he assured me that he had lost all recollection of what had happened. "God," he continued, "must have taken pity on me one day, for, as I ran wildly through those dreadful pine barrens, I met with a tortoise. I gazed upon it with amazement and delight, and, although I knew that were I to follow it undisturbed, it would lead me to some water, my hunger and thirst would not allow me to refrain from satisfying both, by eating its flesh, and drinking its blood. With one stroke of my axe the beast was cut in two, and in a few moments I had despatched all but the shell. Oh, sir, how much I thanked God, whose kindness had put the Tortoise in my way! I felt greatly renewed. I sat down at the foot of a pine, gazed on the heavens, thought of my poor wife and children, and again and again thanked my God for my life; for now I felt less distracted in mind, and more assured that before long I must recover my way, and get back to my home."

The Lost One remained and passed the night, at the foot of the same tree under which his repast had been made. Refreshed by a sound sleep, he started at dawn to resume his weary march. The sun rose bright, and he followed the direction of the shadows. Still the dreariness of the woods was the same, and he was on the point of giving up in despair, when he observed a Raccoon lying squatted in the grass. Raising his axe, he drove it with such violence through the helpless animal that it expired without a struggle. What he had done with the tortoise, he now did with the Raccoon, the greater part of which he actually devoured at one meal. With more comfortable feelings he then resumed his wanderings—his journey, I cannot say—for although in the possession of all his faculties, and in broad daylight, he was worse off than a lame man groping his way in the dark out of a dungeon, of which he knew not where the doors stood.

Days, one after another, passed—nay, weeks in succession. He fed now on cabbage-trees, then on frogs and snakes. All that fell in his way was welcome and savory. Yet he became daily more emaciated, until at length he could scarcely crawl. Forty days had elapsed, by his own reckoning, when he at last reached the banks of the river. His clothes in tatters, his once bright axe dimmed with rust, his face begrimed with beard, his hair matted, and his feeble frame little better than a skeleton covered with parchment, there he laid himself down to die. Amid the perturbed dreams of his fevered fancy, he thought he heard the noise of oars far away on the silent river. He listened, but the sounds died away on his ear. It was, indeed, a dream, the last glimmer of expiring hope, and now the light of life was about to be quenched forever. But again the sound of oars woke him from his lethargy. He listened so eagerly that the hum of a fly could not have escaped his ear. They were, indeed, the measured beats of oars. And now, joy to the forlorn soul! the sound of human voices thrilled to his heart, and awoke the tumultuous pulses of returning hope. On his knees did the eye of God see that poor man by the broad, still stream that glittered in the sunbeams, and human eyes soon saw him too, for round that headland covered with tangled brushwood, boldly advances the little boat, propelled by its lusty rowers. The Lost One raises his feeble voice on high; it was a loud, shrill scream of joy and fear. The rowers pause, and look around. Another, but feebler scream, and they observe him. It comes, his heart flutters, his sight is dimmed, his brain reels, he gasps for breath. It comes—it has run upon the beach, and the Lost One is found.

This is no tale of fiction, but the relation of an actual occurrence, which might be embellished, no doubt, but which is better in the plain garb of truth. The notes by which I recorded it were written in the cabin of the once lost live-oaker, about four years after the painful incident occurred. His amiable wife, and loving children, were present at the recital, and never shall I forget the tears that flowed from their eyes as they listened to it, albeit it had long been more familiar to them than a tale thrice told. Sincerely do I wish, good reader, that neither you nor I may ever elicit such sympathy by having undergone such sufferings, although no doubt, such sympathy would be a rich recompense for them.

It only remains for me to say that the distance between the cabin and the live-oak hummock to which the woodsman was bound, scarcely exceeded eight miles, while the part of the river where he was found was thirty-eight miles from his house. Calculating his daily wanderings at ten miles, we may believe they amounted in all to four hundred. He must therefore have rambled in a circuitous direction, which people generally do in such circumstances. Nothing but the great strength of his constitution, and the merciful aid of his Maker, could have supported him for so long a time.

The Live-Oakers

The greater part of the forests of East Florida consist principally of what in that country are called "pine barrens." In these districts, the woods are rather thin, and the only trees that are seen in them are tall pines of indifferent quality, beneath which is a growth of rank grass, here and there mixed with low bushes, and sword-palmettoes. The soil is of a sandy nature, mostly flat, and consequently either covered with water during the rainy season, or parched in the summer or autumn, although you meet at times with ponds of stagnant water, where the cattle, which are abundant, allay their thirst, and around which resort the various kinds of game found in these wilds.

The traveller, who has pursued his course for many miles over the barrens, is suddenly delighted to see in the distance the appearance of a dark "hummock" of live-oaks and other trees, seeming as if they had been planted in the wilderness. As he approaches, the air feels cooler and more salubrious, the song of numerous birds delights his ear, the herbage assumes a more luxuriant appearance, the flowers become larger and brighter, and a grateful fragrance is diffused around. These objects contribute to refresh his mind, as much as the sight of the waters of some clear spring gliding among the undergrowth seems already to allay his thirst. Overhead festoons of innumerable vines, jessamines, and bignonias, link each tree with those around it, their slender stems being interlaced as if in mutual affection. No sooner, in the shade of these beautiful woods, has the traveller finished his mid-day repast than he perceives small parties of men lightly accoutred, and each bearing an axe, approaching towards his resting-place. They exchange the usual civilities, and immediately commence their labors, for they too have just finished their meal.

I think I see them proceeding to their work. Here two have stationed themselves on the opposite sides of the trunk of a noble and venerable live-oak. Their keen-edged and well-tempered axes seem to make no impression on it, so small are the chips that drop at each blow around the mossy and wide-spreading roots. There, one is ascending the stem of another, of which, in its fall, the arms have stuck among the tangled tops of the neighboring trees. See how cautiously he proceeds, barefooted, and with a handkerchief around his head. Now he has climbed to the height of about forty feet from the ground; he stops, and squaring himself with the trunk on which he so boldly stands, he wields with sinewy arms his trusty blade, the repeated blows of which, although the tree be as tough as it is large, will soon sever it in two. He has changed sides, and his back is turned to you. The trunk now remains connected only by a thin strip of wood. He places his feet on the part which is lodged, and shakes it with all his might. Now swings the huge log under his leaps, now it suddenly gives way, and as it strikes upon the ground its echoes are repeated through the hummock, and every Wild Turkey within hearing utters his gobble of recognition. The wood-cutter however, remains collected and composed; but the next moment, he throws his axe to the ground, and, assisted by the nearest grapevine, slides down and reaches the earth in an instant.

Several men approach and examine the prostrate trunk. They cut at both its extremities, and sound the whole of its bark, to enable them to judge if the tree has been attacked by the white rot. If such has unfortunately been the case, there, for a century or more, this huge log will remain until it gradually crumbles; but if not, and if it is free of injury or "wind-shakes," while there is no appearance of the sap having already ascended, and its pores are altogether sound, they proceed to take its measurement. Its shape ascertained, and the timber that is fit for use laid out by the aid of models, which, like fragments of the skeleton of a ship, show the forms and sizes required, the "hewers" commence their labors. Thus, reader, perhaps every known hummock in the Floridas is annually attacked, and so often does it happen that the white rot or some other disease has deteriorated the quality of the timber, that the woods may be seen strewn with trunks that have been found worthless, so that every year these valuable oaks are becoming scarcer. The destruction of the young trees of this species caused by the fall of the great trunks is of course immense, and as there are no artificial plantations of these trees in our country, before long a good-sized live-oak will be so valuable that its owner will exact an enormous price for it, even while it yet stands in the wood. In my opinion, formed on personal observation, live-oak hummocks are *not quite* so plentiful as they are represented to be, and of this I will give you *one* illustration.

On the 25th of February, 1832, I happened to be far up the St. John's River in East Florida, in the company of a person employed by our government in protecting the live-oaks of that section of the country, and who received a good salary for his trouble. While we were proceeding along one of the banks of that most singular stream, my companion pointed out some large hummocks of dark-leaved trees on the opposite side, which he said were entirely formed of live-oaks. I thought differently, and as our controversy on the subject became a little warm, I proposed that our men should row us to the place, where we might examine the leaves and timber, and so decide the point. We soon landed, but after inspecting the woods, not a single tree of the species did we find, although there were thousands of large "swamp-oaks." My companion acknowledged his mistake, and I continued to search for birds.

One dark evening as I was seated on the banks of this same river, considering what arrangements I should make for the night, as it began to rain in torrents, a man who happened to see me, came up and invited me to go to his cabin, which he said was not far off. I accepted his kind offer, and followed him to his humble dwelling. There I found his wife, several children, and a number of men, who, as my host told me, were, like himself, live-oakers. Supper was placed on a large table, and on being desired to join the party, I willingly assented, doing my best to diminish the contents of the tin pans and dishes set before the company by the active and agreeable housewife. We then talked of the country, its climate and productions, until a late hour, when we laid ourselves down on Bears' skins, and reposed till daybreak.

I longed to accompany these hardy woodcutters to the hummock where they were engaged in preparing live-oak timber for a man-of-war. Provided with axes and guns, we left the house to the care of the wife and children, and proceeded for several miles through a pine-barren, such as I have attempted to describe. One fine Wild Turkey was shot, and when we arrived at the *shanty* put up near the hummock, we found another party of wood-cutters waiting our arrival, before eating their breakfast, already prepared by a negro man, to whom the Turkey was consigned to be roasted for part of that day's dinner.

Our repast was an excellent one, and vied with a Kentucky breakfast; beef, fish, potatoes, and other vegetables, were served up, with coffee in tin cups, and plenty of biscuit. Every man seemed hungry and happy, and the conversation assumed the most humorous character. The sun now rose above the trees, and all, excepting the cook, proceeded to the hummock, on which I had been gazing with great delight, as it promised rare sport. My host, I found, was the chief of the party; and although he also had an axe, he made no other use of it than for stripping here and there pieces of bark from certain trees which he considered of doubtful soundness. He was not only well versed in his profession, but generally intelligent, and from him I received the following account, which I noted at the time.

The men who are employed in cutting the live-oak, after having discovered a good hummock, build shanties of small logs, to retire to at night, and feed in by day. Their provisions consist of beef, pork, potatoes, biscuit, flour, rice and fish, together with excellent whiskey. They are mostly hale, strong, and active men, from the eastern parts of the Union, and receive excellent wages, according to their different abilities. Their labors are only of a few months' duration. Such hummocks as are found near navigable streams are first chosen, and when it is absolutely necessary, the timber is sometimes hauled five or six miles to the nearest water-course, where, although it sinks, it can with comparative ease, be shipped to its destination. The best time for cutting the live-oak is considered to be from the first of December to the beginning of March, or while the sap is completely down. When the sap is flowing, the tree is "bloom," and more apt to be "shaken." The white-rot, which occurs so frequently in the live-oak, and is perceptible only by the best judges, consists of round spots, about an inch and a half in diameter, on the outside of the bark, through which, at that spot, a hard stick may be driven several inches, and generally follows the heart up or down the trunk of the tree. So deceiving are these spots and trees to persons unacquainted with this defect, that thousands of trees are cut, and afterwards abandoned. The great number of trees of this sort strewn in the woods would tend to make a stranger believe that there is much more good oak in the country than there really is; and perhaps, in reality, not more than one-fourth of the quantity usually reported, is to be procured.

The live-oakers generally revisit their distant homes in the Middle and Eastern Districts, where they spend the summer, returning to the Floridas at the approach of winter. Some, however, who have gone there with their families, remain for years in succession; although they suffer much from the climate, by which their once good constitutions are often greatly impaired. This was the case with the individual above mentioned, from whom I subsequently received much friendly assistance in my pursuits.

Spring Garden

Having heard many wonderful accounts of a certain spring near the sources of the St. John's River in East Florida, I resolved to visit it, in order to judge for myself. On the 6th of January, 1832, I left the plantation of my friend John Bulow, accompanied by an amiable and accomplished Scotch gentleman, an engineer employed by the planters of those districts in erecting their sugar-house establishments. We were mounted on horses of the Indian breed, remarkable for their activity and strength, and were provided with guns and some provisions. The weather was pleasant, but not so our way, for no sooner had we left the "King's Road," which had been cut by the Spanish government for a goodly distance, than we entered a thicket of scrubby oaks, succeeded by a still denser mass of low palmettoes, which extended about three miles, and among the roots of which our nags had great difficulty in making good their footing. After this we entered the pine barrens, so extensively distributed in this portion of the Floridas. The sand seemed to be all sand and nothing but sand, and the palmettoes at times so covered the narrow Indian trail which we followed, that it required all the instinct or sagacity of ourselves and our horses to keep it. It seemed to us as if we were approaching the end of the world. The country was perfectly flat, and, so far as we could survey it, presented the same wild and scraggy aspect. My companion, who had travelled there before, assured me that, at particular seasons of the year, he had crossed the barrens when they were covered with water fully knee-deep, when, according to his expression, they "looked most awful;" and I readily believed him, as we now and then passed through muddy pools, which reached the saddle-girths of our horses. Here and there large tracts covered with tall grasses, and resembling the prairies of the western wilds, opened to our view. Wherever the country happened to be sunk a little beneath the general level, it was covered with cypress trees, whose spreading arms were hung with a profusion of Spanish moss. The soil in such cases consisted of black mud, and was densely covered with bushes, chiefly of the Magnolia family.

We crossed in succession the heads of three branches of Haw Creek, of which the waters spread from a quarter to half a mile in breadth, and through which we made our way with extreme difficulty. While in the middle of one, my companion told me that once, when in the very spot where we then stood, his horse chanced to place his fore-feet on the back of a large alligator, which, not well pleased at being disturbed in his repose, suddenly raised his head, opened his monstrous jaws, and snapped off part of the lips of the affrighted pony. You may imagine the terror of the poor beast, which, however, after a few plunges, resumed its course, and succeeded in carrying its rider through in safety. As a reward for this achievement, it was ever after honored with the appellation of "Alligator."

We had now travelled about twenty miles, and, the sun having reached the zenith, we dismounted to partake of some refreshment. From a muddy pool we contrived to obtain enough of tolerably clear water to mix with the contents of a bottle, the like of which I would strongly recommend to every traveller in these swampy regions; our horses, too, found something to grind among the herbage that surrounded the little pool; but as little time was to be lost, we quickly remounted, and resumed our disagreeable journey, during which we had at no time proceeded at a rate exceeding two miles and a half in the hour.

All at once, however, a wonderful change took place:—the country became more elevated and undulating; the timber was of a different nature, and consisted of red and live-oaks, magnolias, and several kinds of pine. Thousands of "Mole-hills," or the habitations of an animal here called "the Salamander," and "Gopher's burrows" presented themselves to the eye, and greatly annoyed our horses, which now and then sank to the depth of a foot, and stumbled at the risk of breaking their legs, and what we considered fully as valuable, our necks. We now saw beautiful lakes of the purest water, and passed along a green space, having a series of them on each side of us. These sheets of water became larger and more numerous the farther we advanced—some of them extending to a length of several miles, and having a depth of from two to twenty feet of clear water; but their shores being destitute of vegetation, we observed no birds near them. Many tortoises, however, were seen basking in the sun, and all, as we approached, plunged into the water. Not a trace of man did we observe during our journey, scarcely a bird, and not a single quadruped, not even a Rat; nor can one imagine a poorer and more desolate country than that which lies between the Halifax River, which we had left in the morning, and the undulating grounds at which we had now arrived.

But at length we perceived the tracks of living beings, and soon after saw the huts of Colonel Rees's negroes. Scarcely could ever African traveller have approached the city of Timbuctoo with more excited curiosity than we felt in approaching this plantation. Our Indian horses seemed to participate in our joy, and trotted at a smart rate towards the principal building, at the door of which we leaped from our saddles, just as the sun was withdrawing his ruddy light. Colonel Rees was at home, and received us with great kindness. Refreshments were immediately placed before us, and we spent the evening in agreeable conversation.

The next day I walked over the plantation, and examining the country around, found the soil of good quality, it having been reclaimed from swampy ground of a black color, rich, and very productive. The greater part of the cultivated land was on the borders of a lake, which communicates with others, leading to the St. John's River, distant about seven miles, and navigable so far by vessels not exceeding fifty or sixty tons. After breakfast, our amiable host showed us the way to the celebrated spring, the sight of which afforded me pleasure sufficient to counterbalance the tediousness of my journey.

This spring presents a circular basin, having a diameter of about sixty feet, from the centre of which the water is thrown up with great force, although it does not rise to a height of more than a few inches above the general level. A kind of whirlpool is formed, on the edges of which are deposited vast quantities of shells, with pieces of wood, gravel, and other substances, which have coalesced into solid masses, having a very curious appearance. The water is quite transparent, although of a dark color, but so impregnated with sulphur that it emits an odor which to me was highly nauseous. Its surface lies fifteen or twenty feet below the level of the woodland lakes in the neighborhood, and its depth, in the autumnal months, is about seventeen feet, when the water is lowest. In all the lakes, the same species of shell as those thrown up by the spring, occur in abundance, and it seems more than probable that it is formed of the water collected from them by infiltration, or forms the subterranean outlet of some of them. The lakes themselves are merely reservoirs, containing the residue of the waters which fall during the rainy seasons, and contributing to supply the waters of the St. John's River, with which they all seem to communicate by similar means. This spring pours its waters into "Rees's Lake," through a deep and broad channel called Spring Garden Creek. This channel is said to be in some places fully sixty feet deep, but it becomes more shallow as you advance towards the entrance of the lake, at which you are surprised to find yourself on a mud-flat covered only by about fifteen inches of water, under which the depositions from the spring lie to a depth of four or five feet in the form of the softest mud, while under this again is a bed of fine white sand. When this mud is stirred up by the oars of your boat or otherwise, it appears of a dark-green color, and smells strongly of sulphur. At all times it sends up numerous bubbles of air, which probably consist of suphuretted hydrogen gas.

The mouth of this curious spring is calculated to be two and a half feet square; and the velocity of its water, during the rainy season, is three feet per second. This would render the discharge per hour about 499,500 gallons. Colonel Rees showed us the remains of another spring of the same kind, which had dried up from some natural cause.

My companion, the engineer, having occupation for another day, I requested Colonel Rees to accompany me in his boat towards the river St. John's, which I was desirous of seeing, as well as the curious country in its neighborhood. He readily agreed, and after an early breakfast next morning, we set out, accompanied by two servants to manage the boat. As we crossed Rees's Lake, I observed that its northeastern shores were bounded by a deep swamp, covered by a rich growth of tall cypresses, while the opposite side presented large marshes and islands ornamented by pines, live-oaks, and orange-trees. With the exception of a very narrow channel, the creek was covered with nympheæ, and in its waters swam numerous Alligators, while Ibises, Gallinules, Anhingas, Coots, and Cormorants were seen pursuing their avocations on its surface or along its margins. Over our heads the Fish Hawks were sailing, and on the broken trees around we saw many of their nests.

We followed Spring Garden Creek for about two miles and a half, and passed a mud bar, before we entered "Dexter's Lake." The bar was stuck full of unios, in such profusion that each time the negroes thrust their hands into the mud they took up several. According to their report these shell-fish are quite unfit for food. In this lake the water had changed its hue, and assumed a dark chestnut color, although it was still transparent. The depth was very uniformly five feet, and the extent of the lake was about eight miles by three. Having crossed it we followed the creek, and soon saw the entrance of Woodruff's Lake, which empties its still darker waters into the St. John's River.

I here shot a pair of curious Ibises, which you will find described in my fourth volume, and landed on a small island covered with wild orange trees, the luxuriance and freshness of which were not less pleasing to the sight than the perfume of their flowers was to the smell. The group seemed to me like a rich bouquet formed by nature to afford consolation to the weary traveller, cast down by the dismal scenery of swamps and pools and rank grass around him. Under the shade of these beautiful evergreens, and amidst the golden fruits that covered the ground, while the Humming-birds fluttered over our heads, we spread our cloth on the grass, and with a happy and thankful heart, I refreshed myself with the bountiful gifts of an ever-careful Providence. Colonel Rees informed me that this charming retreat was one of the numerous *terræ incognitæ* of this region of lakes, and that it should henceforth bear the name of "Audubon's Isle."

In conclusion, let me inform you that the spring has been turned to good account by my generous host, Colonel Rees, who, aided by my amiable companion, the engineer, has directed its current so as to turn a mill, which suffices to grind the whole of his sugar-cane.

Death of a Pirate

In the calm of a fine moonlight night, as I was admiring the beauty of the clear heavens, and the broad glare of light that glanced from the trembling surface of the waters around, the officer on watch came up and entered into conversation with me. He had been a turtler in other years, and a great hunter to boot, and although of humble birth and pretensions, energy and talent, aided by education, had raised him to a higher station. Such a man could not fail to be an agreeable companion, and we talked on various subjects, principally, you may be sure, birds and other natural productions. He told me he once had a disagreeable adventure, when looking out for game, in a certain cove on the shores of the Gulf of Mexico; and, on my expressing a desire to hear it, he willingly related to me the following particulars, which I give you, not, perhaps, precisely in his own words, but as nearly so as I can remember.

"Towards evening, one quiet summer day, I chanced to be paddling along a sandy shore, which I thought well fitted for my repose, being covered with tall grass, and as the sun was not many degrees above the horizon, I felt anxious to pitch my mosquito bar or net, and spend the night in this wilderness. The bellowing notes of thousands of bull-frogs in a neighboring swamp might lull me to rest, and I looked upon the flocks of Blackbirds that were assembling as sure companions in this secluded retreat.

"I proceeded up a little stream, to insure the safety of my canoe from any sudden storm, when, as I gladly advanced, a beautiful yawl came unexpectedly in view. Surprised at such a sight in a part of the country then scarcely known, I felt a sudden check in the circulation of my blood. My paddle dropped from my hands, and fearfully indeed, as I picked it up, did I look towards the unknown boat. On reaching it, I saw its sides marked with stains of blood, and looking with anxiety over the gunwale, I perceived, to my horror, two human bodies covered with gore. Pirates or hostile Indians, I was persuaded, had perpetrated the foul deed, and my alarm naturally increased; my heart fluttered, stopped, and heaved with unusual tremors, and I looked towards the setting sun in consternation and despair. How long my reveries lasted I cannot tell; I can only recollect that I was roused from them by the distant groans of one apparently in mortal agony. I felt as if refreshed by the cold perspiration that oozed from every pore, and I reflected that though alone, I was well armed, and might hope for the protection of the Almighty.

"Humanity whispered to me that, if not surprised and disabled, I might render assistance to some sufferer, or even be the means of saving a useful life. Buoyed up by this thought, I urged my canoe on shore, and seizing it by the bow, pulled it at one spring high among the grass.

"The groans of the unfortunate person fell heavy on my ear as I cocked and reprimed my gun, and I felt determined to shoot the first that should rise from the grass. As I cautiously proceeded, a hand was raised over the weeds, and waved in the air in the most supplicating manner. I levelled my gun about a foot below it, when the next moment the head and breast of a man covered with blood were convulsively raised, and a faint hoarse voice asked me for mercy and help! A deathlike silence followed his fall to the ground. I surveyed every object around with eyes intent, and ears impressible by the slightest sound, for my situation that moment I thought as critical as any I had ever been in. The croaking of the frogs, and the last Blackbirds alighting on their roosts, were the only sounds or sights; and I now proceeded towards the object of my mingled alarm and commiseration.

"Alas! the poor being who lay prostrate at my feet was so weakened by loss of blood that I had nothing to fear from him. My first impulse was to run back to the water, and having done so, I returned with my cap filled to the brim. I felt at his heart, washed his face and breast, and rubbed his temples with the contents of a phial which I kept about me as an antidote for the bites of snakes. His features, seamed by the ravages of time, looked frightful and disgusting; but he had been a powerful man, as the breadth of his chest plainly showed. He groaned in the most appalling manner, as his breath struggled through the mass of blood that seemed to fill his throat. His dress plainly disclosed his occupation. A large pistol he had thrust into his bosom, a naked cutlass lay near him on the ground, a red silk handkerchief was bound over his projecting brows, and over a pair of loose trousers he wore fisherman's boots. He was, in short, a pirate.

"My exertions were not in vain, for as I continued to bathe his temples he revived, his pulse resumed some strength, and I began to hope that he might perhaps survive the deep wounds he had received. Darkness, deep darkness, now enveloped us. I spoke of making a fire. 'Oh! for mercy's sake,' he exclaimed, 'don't.' Knowing, however, that under existing circumstances it was expedient for me to do so, I left him, went to his boat, and brought the rudder, the benches, and the oars, which with my hatchet I soon splintered. I then struck a light, and presently stood in the glare of a blazing fire. The pirate seemed struggling between terror and gratitude for my assistance; he desired me several times in half English and Spanish to put out the flames; but after I had given him a draught of strong spirits, he at length became more composed. I tried to stanch the blood that flowed from the deep gashes in his shoulders and side. I expressed my regret that I had no food about me, but when I spoke of eating he sullenly waved his head.

"My situation was one of the most extraordinary that I have ever been placed in. I naturally turned my talk towards religious subjects, but, alas, the dying man hardly believed in the existence of a God. 'Friend,' said he, 'for friend you seem to be, I have never studied the ways of Him of whom you talk. I am an outlaw, perhaps you will say a wretch—I have been for many years a pirate. The instructions of my parents were of no avail to me, for I have always believed that I was born to be a most cruel man. I now lie here, about to die in the weeds, because I long ago refused to listen to their many admonitions. Do not shudder when I tell you—these now useless hands murdered the mother whom they had embraced. I feel that I have deserved the pangs of the wretched death that hovers over me; and I am thankful that one of my kind will alone witness my last gaspings.'

"A fond but feeble hope that I might save his life, and perhaps assist in procuring his pardon, induced me to speak to him on the subject. 'It is all in vain, friend—I have no objection to die—I am glad that the villains who wounded me were not my conquerors—I want no pardon from *any one*. Give me some water, and let me die alone.' With the hope that I might learn from his conversation something that might lead to the capture of his guilty associates, I returned from the creek with another capful of water, nearly the whole of which I managed to introduce into his parched mouth, and begged him, for the sake of his future peace, to disclose his history to me. 'It is impossible,' said he; 'there will not be time, the beatings of my heart tell me so. Long before day these sinewy limbs will be motionless. Nay, there will hardly be a drop of blood in my body; and that blood will only serve to make the grass grow. My wounds are mortal, and I must and will die without what you call confession.'

"The moon rose in the east. The majesty of her placid beauty impressed me with reverence. I pointed towards her, and asked the pirate if he could not recognize God's features there. 'Friend, I see what you are driving at,' was his answer; 'you, like the rest of our enemies, feel the desire of murdering us all. Well—be it so. To die is, after all, nothing more than a jest; and were it not for the pain, no one, in my opinion, need care a jot about it. But, as you really have befriended me, I will tell you all that is proper.'

"Hoping his mind might take a useful turn, I again bathed his temples, and washed his lips with spirits. His sunk eyes seemed to dart fire at mine; a heavy and deep sigh swelled his chest, and struggled through his blood-choked throat, and he asked me to raise him for a little. I did so, when he addressed me somewhat as follows; for, as I have told you, his speech was a mixture of Spanish, French, and English, forming a jargon the like of which I had never heard before, and which I am utterly unable to imitate. However, I shall give you the substance of his declaration.

" 'First, tell me how many bodies you found in the boat, and what sort of dresses they had on.' I mentioned their number and described their apparel. 'That's right,' said he; 'they are the bodies of the scoundrels who followed me in that infernal Yankee barge. Bold rascals they were, for when they found the water too shallow for their craft, they took to it, and waded after me. All my companions had been shot, and to lighten my own boat I flung them overboard; but as I lost time in this, the two ruffians caught hold of my gunwale, and struck on my head and body in such a manner that after I had disabled and killed them both in the boat, I was scarce able to move. The other villains carried off our schooner and one of our boats, and perhaps ere now have hung all my companions whom they did not kill at the time. I have commanded my beautiful vessel many years, captured many ships, and sent many rascals to the devil. I always hated the Yankees, and only regret that I have not killed more of them.—I sailed from Matanzas.—I have often been in concert with others. I have money without counting, but it is buried where it will never be found, and it would be useless to tell you of it.' His throat filled with blood, his voice failed, the cold hand of death was laid on his brow; feebly and hurriedly he muttered, 'I am a dying man. Farewell!'

"Alas! it is painful to see death in any shape; in this it was horrible, for there was no hope. The rattling of his throat announced the moment of dissolution, and already did the body fall on my arms with a weight that was insupportable. I laid him on the ground. A mass of dark blood poured from his mouth; then came a frightful groan, the last breathing of that foul spirit; and what now lay at my feet in the wild desert?—a mangled mass of clay!

"The remainder of that night was passed in no enviable mood; but my feelings cannot be described. At dawn I dug a hole with the paddle of my canoe, rolled the body into it, and covered it. On reaching the boat I found several buzzards feeding on the bodies, which I in vain attempted to drag to the shore. I therefore covered them with mud and weeds, and launching my canoe, paddled from the cove with a secret joy for my escape, overshadowed with the gloom of mingled dread and abhorrence."

The Wreckers of Florida

Long before I reached the lovely islets that border the southeastern shores of the Floridas, the accounts I had heard of "The Wreckers" had deeply prejudiced me against them. Often had I been informed of the cruel and cowardly methods which it was alleged they employed to allure vessels of all nations to the dreaded reefs, that they might plunder their cargoes, and rob their crews and passengers of their effects. I therefore could have little desire to meet with such men under any circumstances, much less to become liable to receive their aid; and with the name of Wreckers there were associated in my mind ideas of piratical depredations, barbarous usage, and even murder.

One fair afternoon, while I was standing on the polished deck of the United States revenue cutter, the "Marion," a sail hove in sight, bearing in an opposite course, and close-hauled to the wind. The gentle rake of her masts, as she rocked to and fro in the breeze, brought to my mind the wavings of the reeds on the fertile banks of the Mississippi. By and by the vessel, altering her course, approached us. The "Marion," like a sea-bird with extended wings, swept through the waters, gently inclining to either side, while the unknown vessel leaped as it were, from wave to wave, like the dolphin in eager pursuit of his prey. In a short time we were gliding side by side, and the commander of the strange schooner saluted our captain, who promptly returned the compliment. What a beautiful vessel! we all thought; how trim, how clean rigged, and how well manned! She swims like a duck; and now with a broad sheer, off she makes for the reefs a few miles under our lee. There, in that narrow passage, well known to her commander, she rolls, tumbles, and dances, like a giddy thing, her copper sheathing now gleaming and again disappearing under the waves. But the passage is thridded, and now, hauling on the wind, she resumes her former course, and gradually recedes from the view. Reader, it was a Florida Wrecker.

When at the Tortugas, I paid a visit to several vessels of this kind, in company with my excellent friend Robert Day, Esq. We had observed the regularity and quickness of the men then employed at their arduous tasks, and as we approached the largest schooner, I admired her form, so well adapted to her occupation, her great breadth of beam, her light draught, the correctness of her water-line, the neatness of her painted sides, the smoothness of her well-greased masts, and the beauty of her rigging. We were welcomed on board with all the frankness of our native tars. Silence and order prevailed on her decks. The commander and the second officer led us into a spacious cabin, well-lighted, and furnished with every convenience for fifteen or more passengers. The former brought me his collection of marine shells, and whenever I pointed to one that I had not seen before, offered it with so much kindness that I found it necessary to be careful in expressing my admiration of any particular shell. He had also many eggs of rare birds, which were all handed over to me, with an assurance that before the month should expire, a new set could easily be procured; "for," said he, "we have much idle time on the reefs at this season." Dinner was served, and we partook of their fare, which consisted of fish, fowl, and other materials. These rovers, who were both from "down east," were stout, active men, cleanly and smart in their attire. In a short time we were all extremely social and merry. They thought my visit to the Tortugas, in quest of birds, was rather a "curious fancy;" but, notwithstanding, they expressed their pleasure while looking at some of my drawings, and offered their services in procuring specimens. Expeditions far and near were proposed, and on settling that one of them was to take place on the morrow, we parted friends.

Early next morning, several of these kind men accompanied me to a small Key called Booby Island, about ten miles distant from the lighthouse. Their boats were well-manned, and rowed with long and steady strokes, such as whalers and men-of-war's men are wont to draw. The captain sang, and at times, by way of frolic, ran a race with our own beautiful bark. The Booby Isle was soon reached, and our sport there was equal to any we had elsewhere. They were capital shots, had excellent guns, and knew more about Boobies and Noddies than nine-tenths of the best naturalists in the world. But what will you say when I tell you the Florida Wreckers are excellent at a Deer hunt, and that at certain seasons, "when business is slack," they are wont to land on some extensive Key, and in a few hours procure a supply of delicious venison.

Some days afterwards, the same party took me on an expedition in quest of sea shells. There we were all in water, at times to the waist, and now and then much deeper. Now they would dip, like ducks, and on emerging would hold up a beautiful shell. This occupation they seemed to enjoy above all others.

The duties of the "Marion," having been performed, intimation of our intended departure reached the Wreckers. An invitation was sent to me to go and see them on board their vessels, which I accepted. Their object on this occasion was to present me with some superb corals, shells, live Turtles of the Hawk-bill species, and a great quantity of eggs. Not a "picayune" would they receive in return, but putting some letters in my hands, requested me "to be so good as to put them in the mail at Charleston," adding that they were for their wives "down east." So anxious did they appear to be to do all they could for me, that they proposed to sail before the "Marion," and meet her under way, to give me some birds that were rare on the coast, and of which they knew the haunts.

Circumstances connected with "the service" prevented this, however, and with sincere regret, and a good portion of friendship, I bade these excellent fellows adieu. How different, thought I, is often the knowledge of things acquired by personal observation from that obtained by report!

I had never before seen Florida Wreckers, nor has it since been my fortune to fall in with any; but my good friend Dr. Benjamin Strobel, having furnished me with a graphic account of a few days which he spent with them, I shall present you with it in his own words:—

"On the 12th day of September, while lying in harbor at Indian Key, we were joined by five wrecking vessels. Their licenses having expired, it was necessary to go to Key West to renew them. We determined to accompany them the next morning; and here it will not be amiss for me to say a few words respecting these far-famed Wreckers, their captains and crews. From all that I had heard, I expected to see a parcel of dirty, pirate-looking vessels, officered and manned by a set of black-whiskered fellows, who carried murder in their very looks. I was agreeably surprised on discovering the vessels were fine large sloops and schooners, regular clippers, kept in first-rate order. The captains generally were jovial, good-natured sons of Neptune who manifested a disposition to be polite and hospitable, and to afford every facility to persons passing up and down the Reef. The crews were hearty, well-dressed and honest-looking men.

"On the 13th, at the appointed hour, we all set sail together; that is, the five Wreckers and the schooner 'Jane.' As our vessel was not noted for fast sailing, we accepted an invitation to go on board of a Wrecker. The fleet got under way about eight o'clock in the morning, the wind light but fair, the water smooth, the day fine. I can scarcely find words to express the pleasure and gratification which I this day experienced. The sea was of a beautiful, soft, pea-green color, smooth as a sheet of glass, and as transparent, its surface agitated only by our vessels as they parted its bosom, or by the Pelican in pursuit of his prey, which rising for a considerable distance in the air, would suddenly plunge down with distended mandibles, and secure his food. The vessels of our little fleet with every sail set that could catch a breeze, and the white foam curling round the prows, glided silently along, like islands of flitting shadows, on an immovable sea of light. Several fathoms below the surface of the water, and under us, we saw great quantities of fish diving and sporting among the sea-grass, sponges, sea-feathers, and corals, with which the bottom was covered. On our right hand were the Florida Keys, which, as we made them in the distance, looked like specks upon the surface of the water, but as we neared them, rose to view as if by enchantment, clad in the richest livery of spring, each variety of color and hue rendered soft and delicate by a clear sky and a brilliant sun overhead. All was like a fairy scene; my heart leaped up in delighted admiration, and I could not but exclaim, in the language of Scott,—

Those seas behold
Round thrice an hundred islands rolled.

The trade wind played round us with balmy and refreshing sweetness; and, to give life and animation to the scene, we had a contest for the mastery between all the vessels of the fleet, while a deep interest was excited in favor of this or that vessel, as she shot ahead, or fell astern.

"About three o'clock in the afternoon, we arrived off the Bay of Honda. The wind being light and no prospect of reaching Key West that night, it was agreed that we should make a harbor here. We entered a beautiful basin, and came to anchor about four o'clock. Boats were got out, and several hunting parties formed. We landed, and were soon on the scent, some going in search of shells, others of birds. An Indian, who had been picked up somewhere along the coast by a Wrecker, and who was employed as a hunter, was sent ashore in search of venison. Previous to his leaving the vessel, a rifle was loaded with a single ball and put into his hands. After an absence of several hours, he returned with two Deer, which he had killed at a single shot. He watched until they were both in range of his gun, side by side, when he fired and brought them down.

"All hands having returned, and the fruits of our excursion being collected, we had wherewithal to make an abundant supper. Most of the game was sent on board the largest vessel, where we proposed supping. Our vessels were all lying within hail of each other, and as soon as the moon arose, boats were seen passing from vessel to vessel, and all were busily and happily engaged in exchanging civilities. One could never have supposed that these men were professional rivals, so apparent was the good feeling that prevailed among them. About nine o'clock we started for supper; a number of persons had already collected, and as soon as we arrived on board the vessel, a German sailor, who played remarkably well on the violin, was summoned on the quarter-deck, when all hands, with a good will, cheerily danced to lively airs until supper was ready. The table was laid in the cabin, and groaned under its load of venison, Wild Ducks, Pigeons, Curlews, and fish. Toasting and singing succeeded the supper, and among other curious matters introduced, the following song was sung by the German fiddler, who accompanied his voice with his instrument. He is said to be the author of the song. I say nothing of the poetry, but merely give it as it came on my ear. It is certainly very characteristic:—

THE WRECKERS' SONG.

Come, ye good people, one and all,
Come listen to my song;
A few remarks I have to make,
Which won't be very long.

'T is of our vessel, stout and good
As ever yet was built of wood,
Along the reef where the breakers roar,
The Wreckers on the Florida shore!

Key Tavernier's our rendezvous;
At anchor there we lie,
And see the vessels in the Gulf,
Carelessly passing by.
When night comes on we dance and sing,
Whilst the current some vessel is floating in;
When daylight comes, a ship 's on shore,
Among the rocks where the breakers roar.

When daylight dawns we 're under way,
And every sail is set,
And if the wind it should prove light,
Why, then our sails we wet.
To gain her first each eager strives,
To save the cargo and the people's lives,
Amongst the rocks where the breakers roar,
The Wreckers on the Florida shore.

When we get 'longside we find she's bilged;
We know well what to do,
Save the cargo that we can,
The sails and rigging too;
Then down to Key West we soon will go,
When quickly our salvage we shall know;
When everything it is fairly sold,
Our money down to us it is told.

Then one week's cruise *we'll have on shore,*
Before we do sail again,
And drink success to the sailor lads
That are ploughing of the main.

And when you are passing by this way,
On the Florida reef should you chance to stray,
Why we will come to you on the shore,
Amongst the rocks where the breakers roar.

Great emphasis was laid upon particular words by the singer, who had a broad German accent. Between the verses he played an interlude, remarking, 'Gentlemen, I makes dat myself.' The chorus was trolled by twenty or thirty voices, which, in the stillness of the night, produced no unpleasant effect."

St. John's River in Florida

Soon after landing at St. Augustine, in East Florida, I formed acquaintance with Dr. Simmons, Dr. Porcher, Judge Smith, the Misses Johnson, and other individuals, my intercourse with whom was as agreeable as beneficial to me. Lieutenant Constantine Smith, of the United States army, I found of a congenial spirit, as was the case with my amiable but since deceased friend, Dr. Bell of Dublin. Among the planters who extended their hospitality to me, I must particularly mention General Hernandez, and my esteemed friend John Bulow, Esq. To all these estimable individuals I offer my sincere thanks.

While in this part of the peninsula I followed my usual avocation, although with little success, it then being winter. I had letters from the Secretaries of the Navy and Treasury of the United States, to the commanding officers of vessels of war of the revenue service, directing them to afford me any assistance in their power; and the schooner "Spark" having come to St. Augustine, on her way to the St. John's River, I presented my credentials to her commander Lieutenant Piercy, who readily and with politeness received me and my assistants on board. We soon after set sail with a fair breeze. The strict attention to duty on board even this small vessel of war, afforded matter of surprise to me. Everything went on with the regularity of a chronometer: orders were given, answered to, and accomplished, before they had ceased to vibrate on the ear. The neatness of the crew equalled the cleanliness of the white planks of the deck; the sails were in perfect condition; and, built as the "Spark" was, for swift sailing, on she went, gambolling from wave to wave.

I thought that, while thus sailing, no feeling but that of pleasure could exist in our breasts; but, alas! how fleeting are our enjoyments. When we were almost at the entrance of the river, the wind changed, the sky became clouded, and, before many minutes had elapsed, the little bark was lying to "like a Duck," as her commander expressed himself. It blew a hurricane—let it blow, reader. At break of day we were again at anchor within the bar of St. Augustine.

Our next attempt was successful. Not many hours after we had crossed the bar, we perceived the star-like glimmer of the light in the great lantern at the entrance of the St. John's River. This was before daylight; and, as the crossing of the sand-banks or bars, which occur at the mouths of all the streams of this peninsula is difficult, and can be accomplished only when the tide is up, one of the guns was fired as a signal for the government pilot. The good man, it seemed, was unwilling to leave his couch, but a second gun brought him in his canoe alongside. The depth of the channel was barely sufficient. My eyes, however, were not directed towards the waters, but on high, where flew some thousands of snowy Pelicans, which had fled affrighted from their resting-grounds. How beautifully they performed their broad gyrations, and how matchless, after a while, was the marshalling of their files, as they flew past us.

On the tide we proceeded apace. Myriads of Cormorants covered the face of the waters, and over it Fish-Crows innumerable were already arriving from their distant roosts. We landed at one place to search for the birds whose charming melodies had engaged our attention, and here and there some young Eagles we shot, to add to our store of fresh provisions. The river did not seem to me equal in beauty to the fair Ohio; the shores were in many places low and swampy, to the great delight of the numberless Herons that moved along in gracefulness, and the grim Alligators that swam in sluggish sullenness. In going up a bayou, we caught a great number of the young of the latter for the purpose of making experiments upon them.

After sailing a considerable way, during which our commander and officers took the soundings, as well as the angles and bearings of every nook and crook of the sinuous stream, we anchored one evening at a distance of fully one hundred miles from the mouth of the river. The weather, although it was the 12th of February, was quite warm, the thermometer on board standing at 75°, and on shore at 90°. The fog was so thick that neither of the shores could be seen, and yet the river was not a mile in breadth. The "blind mosquitoes" covered every object, even in the cabin, and so wonderfully abundant were these tormentors that they more than once fairly extinguished the candles whilst I was writing my journal, which I closed in despair, crushing between the leaves more than a hundred of the little wretches. Bad as they are, however, these blind mosquitoes do not bite. As if purposely to render our situation doubly uncomfortable, there was an establishment for jerking beef on the nearer shores, to the windward of our vessel, from which the breeze came laden with no sweet odors.

In the morning when I arose, the country was still covered with thick fogs, so that although I could plainly hear the notes of the birds on shore, not an object could I see beyond the bowsprit, and the air was as close and sultry as on the previous evening. Guided by the scent of the jerkers' works we went on shore, where we found the vegetation already far advanced. The blossoms of the jessamine, ever pleasing, lay steeped in dew, the humming bee was collecting her winter's store from the snowy flowers of the native orange; and the little warblers frisked along the twigs of the smilax. Now, amid the tall pines of the forest, the sun's rays began to force their way, and as the dense mists dissolved in the atmosphere, the bright luminary at length shone forth. We explored the woods around, guided by some friendly live-oakers who had pitched their camp in the vicinity. After a while the "Spark" again displayed her sails, and as she silently glided along, we spied a Seminole Indian approaching us in his canoe. The poor, dejected son of the woods, endowed with talents of the highest order, although rarely acknowledged by the proud usurpers of his native soil, has spent the night in fishing, and the morning in procuring the superb feathered game of the swampy thickets; and with both he comes to offer them for our acceptance. Alas! thou fallen one, descendant of an ancient line of freeborn hunters, would that I could restore to thee thy birthright, thy natural independence, the generous feelings that were once fostered in thy brave bosom. But the irrevocable deed is done, and I can merely admire the perfect symmetry of his frame, as he dexterously throws on our deck the Trout and Turkeys which he has captured. He receives a recompense, and without smile or bow, or acknowledgment of any kind, off he starts with the speed of an arrow from his own bow.

Alligators were extremely abundant, and the heads of the fishes which they had snapped off, lay floating around on the dark waters. A rifle bullet was now and then sent through the eye of one of the largest, which, with a tremendous splash of its tail, expired. One morning we saw a monstrous fellow lying on the shore. I was desirous of obtaining him to make an accurate drawing of his head, and accompanied by my assistant and two of the sailors, proceeded cautiously towards him. When within a few yards, one of us fired, and sent through his side an ounce ball which tore open a hole large enough to receive a man's hand.

He slowly raised his head, bent himself upwards, opened his huge jaws, swung his tail to and fro, rose on his legs, blew in a frightful manner, and fell to the earth. My assistant leaped on shore, and, contrary to my injunctions, caught hold of the animal's tail, when the alligator, awakening from its trance, with a last effort crawled slowly towards the water, and plunged heavily into it. Had he thought of once flourishing his tremendous weapon, there might have been an end of his assailant's life, but he fortunately went in peace to his grave, where we left him, as the water was too deep. The same morning, another of equal size was observed swimming directly for the bows of our vessel, attracted by the gentle rippling of the water there. One of the officers, who had watched him, fired, and scattered his brain through the air, when he tumbled and rolled at a fearful rate, blowing all the while most furiously. The river was bloody for yards around, but although the monster passed close by the vessel, we could not secure him, and after a while he sunk to the bottom.

Early one morning, I hired a boat and two men, with the view of returning to St. Augustine by a short-cut. Our baggage being placed on board, I bade adieu to the officers, and off we started. About four in the afternoon we arrived at the short-cut, forty miles distant from our point of departure, and where we had expected to procure a wagon, but were disappointed. So we laid our things on the bank, and leaving one of my assistants to look after them, I set out accompanied by the other and my Newfoundland dog. We had eighteen miles to go; and as the sun was only two hours high, we struck off at a good rate. Presently we entered a pine-barren. The country was as level as a floor; our path, although narrow, was well-beaten, having been used by the Seminole Indians for ages, and the weather was calm and beautiful. Now and then a rivulet occurred, from which we quenched our thirst, while the magnolias and other flowering plants on its banks relieved the dull uniformity of the woods. When the path separated into two branches, both seemingly leading the same way, I would follow one, while my companion took the other, and unless we met again in a short time, one of us would go across the intervening forest.

The sun went down behind a cloud, and the southeast breeze that sprung up at this moment, sounded dolefully among the tall pines. Along the eastern horizon lay a bed of black vapor, which gradually rose, and soon covered the heavens. The air felt hot and oppressive, and we knew that a tempest was approaching. Plato was now our guide, the white spots on his coat being the only objects that we could discern amid the darkness, and as if aware of his utility in this respect, he kept a short way before us on the trail. Had we imagined ourselves more than a few miles from the town, we should have made a camp, and remained under its shelter for the night; but conceiving that the distance could not be great, we resolved to trudge along.

Large drops began to fall from the murky mass overhead; thick impenetrable darkness surrounded us, and to my dismay, the dog refused to proceed. Groping with my hands on the ground, I discovered that several trails branched out at the spot where he lay down; and when I had selected one, he went on. Vivid flashes of lightning streamed across the heavens, the wind increased to a gale, and the rain poured down upon us like a torrent. The water soon rose on the level ground so as almost to cover our feet, and we slowly advanced, fronting the tempest. Here and there a tall pine on fire presented a magnificent spectacle, illumining the trees around it, and surrounding them with a halo of dim light, abruptly bordered with the deep black of the night. At one time we passed through a tangled thicket of low trees, at another crossed a stream flushed by the heavy rain, and again proceeded over the open barrens.

How long we thus, half lost, groped our way is more than I can tell you; but at length the tempest passed over, and suddenly the clear sky became spangled with stars. Soon after, we smelt the salt marshes, and walking directly towards them, like pointers advancing on a covey of partridges, we at last to our great joy descried the light of the beacon near St. Augustine. My dog began to run briskly around, having met with ground on which he had hunted before, and taking a direct course, led us to the great causeway that crosses the marshes at the back of the town. We refreshed ourselves with the produce of the first orange-tree that we met with, and in half an hour more arrived at our hotel. Drenched with rain, steaming with perspiration, and covered to the knees with mud, you may imagine what figures we cut in the eyes of the good people whom we found snugly enjoying themselves in the sitting-room. Next morning, Major Gates, who had received me with much kindness, sent a wagon with mules and two trusty soldiers for my companion and luggage.

The Florida Keys

I

As the "Marion" neared the Inlet called "Indian Key," which is situated on the eastern coast of the peninsula of Florida, my heart swelled with uncontrollable delight. Our vessel once over the coral reef that everywhere stretches along the shore like a great wall reared by an army of giants, we found ourselves in safe anchoring grounds, within a few furlongs of the land. The next moment saw the oars of a boat propelling us towards the shore, and in brief time we stood on the desired beach. With what delightful feelings did we gaze on the objects around us!—the gorgeous flowers, the singular and beautiful plants, the luxuriant trees. The balmy air which we breathed filled us with animation, so pure and salubrious did it seem to be. The birds which we saw were almost all new to us; their lovely forms appeared to be arrayed in more brilliant apparel than I had ever seen before, and as they fluttered in happy playfulness among the bushes, or glided over the light green waters, we longed to form a more intimate acquaintance with them.

Students of nature spend little time in introductions, especially when they present themselves to persons who feel an interest in their pursuits. This was the case with Mr. Thruston, the deputy collector of the island, who shook us all heartily by the hand, and in a trice had a boat manned, and at our service. Accompanied by him, his pilot and fishermen, off we went, and after a short pull landed on a large key. Few minutes had elapsed when shot after shot might be heard, and down came whirling through the air the objects of our desire. One thrust himself into the tangled groves that covered all but the beautiful coral beach that in a continued line bordered the island, while others gazed on the glowing and diversified hues of the curious inhabitants of the deep. I saw one of my party rush into the limpid element to seize on a crab, that, with claws extended upward, awaited his approach, as if determined not to give way. A loud voice called him back to the land, for sharks are as abundant along these shores as pebbles, and the hungry prowlers could not have found a more savory dinner.

The pilot, besides being a first-rate shot, possessed a most intimate acquaintance with the country. He had been a "conch diver," and no matter what number of fathoms measured the distance between the surface of the water and its craggy bottom, to seek for curious shells in their retreat seemed to him more pastime than toil. Not a Cormorant or Pelican, a Flamingo, an Ibis, or Heron had ever in his days formed its nest without his having marked the spot; and as to the Keys to which the Doves are wont to resort, he was better acquainted with them than many fops are with the contents of their pockets. In a word, he positively knew every channel that led to these islands, and every cranny along their shores. For years his employment had been to hunt those singular animals called Sea-cows or Manatees, and he had conquered hundreds of them, "merely," as he said, because the flesh and hide bring "a fair price" at Havana. He never went anywhere to land without "Long Tom," which proved indeed to be a wonderful gun, and which made smart havoc when charged with "groceries" a term by which he designated the large shot he used. In like manner, he never paddled his light canoe without having by his side the trusty javelin with which he unerringly transfixed such fishes as he thought fit either for market or for his own use. In attacking Turtles, netting, or overturning them, I doubt if his equal ever lived on the Florida coast. No sooner was he made acquainted with my errand, than he freely offered his best services, and from that moment until I left Key West he was seldom out of my hearing.

While the young gentlemen who accompanied us were engaged in procuring plants, shells, and small birds, he tapped me on the shoulder, and with a smile said to me, "Come along, I'll show you something better worth your while." To the boat we betook ourselves, with the captain and only a pair of tars, for more he said would not answer. The yawl for a while was urged at a great rate, but as we approached a point, the oars were taken in, and the pilot alone sculling desired us to make ready, for in a few minutes we should have "rare sport." As we advanced, the more slowly did we move, and the most profound silence was maintained, until suddenly coming almost in contact with a thick shrubbery of mangroves, we beheld, right before us, a multitude of Pelicans. A discharge of artillery seldom produced more effect; the dead, the dying, and the wounded, fell from the trees upon the water, while those unscathed flew screaming through the air in terror and dismay. "There," said he, "did not I tell you so; is it not rare sport?" The birds, one after another, were lodged under the gunwales, when the pilot desired the captain to order the lads to pull away. Within about half a mile we reached the extremity of the Key. "Pull away," cried the pilot, "never mind them on the wing, for those black rascals don't mind a little firing—now, boys, lay her close under the nests." And there we were with four hundred Cormorant's nests over our heads. The birds were sitting, and when we fired, the number that dropped as if dead, and plunged into the water was such, that I thought by some unaccountable means or other we had killed the whole colony. You would have smiled at the loud laugh and curious gestures of the pilot. "Gentlemen," said he, "almost a blank shot!" And so it was, for, on following the birds as one after another peeped up from the water, we found only a few unable to take to wing. "Now," said the pilot, "had you waited until *I had spoken* to the black villains, you might have killed a score or more of them." On inspection, we found that our shots had lodged in the tough dry twigs of which these birds form their nests, and that we had lost the more favorable opportunity of hitting them, by not waiting until they rose. "Never mind," said the pilot, "if you wish it, you may load *The Lady of the Green Mantle** with them in less than a week. Stand still, my lads; and now, gentlemen, in ten minutes you and I will bring down a score of them." And so we did. As we rounded the island, a beautiful bird of the species called Peale's Egret came up, and was shot. We now landed, took in the rest of our party, and returned to Indian Key, where we arrived three hours before sunset.

The sailors and other individuals to whom my name and pursuits had become known, carried our birds to the pilot's house. His good wife had a room ready for me to draw in, and my assistant might have been seen busily engaged in skinning, while George Lehman was making a sketch of the lovely isle.

Time is ever precious to the student of nature. I placed several birds in their natural attitudes, and began to outline them. A dance had been prepared also, and no sooner was the sun lost to our eye, than males and females, including our captain and others from the vessel, were seen advancing gayly towards the house in full apparel. The birds were skinned, the sketch was on paper, and I told my young men to amuse themselves. As to myself, I could not join in the merriment, for, full of the remembrance of you, reader, and of the patrons of my work both in America and in Europe, I went on "grinding"—not on an organ, like the Lady of Bras d'Or, but on paper, to the finishing not merely of my outlines, but of my notes respecting the objects seen this day.

The room adjoining that in which I worked was soon filled. Two miserable fiddlers screwed their screeching, silken strings,—not an inch of catgut graced their instruments,—and the bouncing of brave lads and fair lasses shook the premises to the foundation. One with a slip came down heavily on the floor, and the burst of laughter that followed echoed over the isle. Diluted claret was handed round to cool the ladies, while a beverage of more potent energies warmed their partners. After supper our captain returned to the "Marion," and I, with my young men, slept in light swinging hammocks under the eaves of the piazza.

It was the end of April, when the nights were short, and the days therefore long. Anxious to turn every moment to account, we were on board Mr. Thruston's boat at three next morning. Pursuing our way through the deep and tortuous channels that everywhere traverse the immense muddy soap-like flats that stretch from the outward Keys to the Main, we proceeded on our voyage of discovery. Here and there we

* The name given by the wreckers and smugglers to the "Marion."

met with great beds of floating seaweeds, which showed us that Turtles were abundant there, these masses being the refuse of their feeding. On talking to Mr. Thruston of the nature of these muddy flats, he mentioned that he had once been lost amongst their narrow channels for several days and nights, when in pursuit of some smugglers' boat, the owners of which were better acquainted with the place than the men who were along with him. Although in full sight of several of the Keys, as well as of the main land, he was unable to reach either until a heavy gale raised the water, when he sailed directly over the flats, and returned home almost exhausted with fatigue and hunger. His present pilot often alluded to the circumstance afterwards, ending with a great laugh, and asserting that had he "been there, the rascals would not have escaped."

Coming under a Key on which multitudes of Frigate Pelicans had begun to form their nests, we shot a good number of them, and observed their habits. The boastings of our pilot were here confirmed by the exploits which he performed with his long gun, and on several occasions he brought down a bird from a height of fully a hundred yards. The poor bird, unaware of the range of our artillery, sailed calmly along, so that it was not difficult for "Long Tom," or rather for his owner, to furnish us with as many as we required. The day was spent in this manner, and towards night we returned, laden with booty, to the hospitable home of the pilot.

The next morning was delightful. The gentle sea-breeze glided over the flowery isle, the horizon was clear, and all was silent, save the long breakers that rushed over the distant reefs. As we were proceeding towards some Keys seldom visited by men, the sun rose from the bosom of the waters with a burst of glory that flashed on my soul the idea of that power which called into existence so magnificent an object. The moon, thin and pale, as if ashamed to show her feeble light, concealed herself in the dim west. The surface of the waters shone in its tremulous smoothness, and the deep blue of the clear heavens was pure as the world that lies beyond them. The Heron heavily flew towards the land, like a glutton retiring at daybreak, with well lined paunch, from the house of some wealthy patron of good cheer. The Night Heron and the Owl, fearful of day, with hurried flight sought safety in the recesses of the deepest swamps; while the Gulls and Terns, ever cheerful, gambolled over the water, exulting in the prospect of abundance. I also exulted in hope, my whole frame seemed to expand; and our sturdy crew showed by their merry faces that nature had charms for them too. How much of beauty and joy is lost to them who never view the rising sun, and of whose waking existence, the best half is nocturnal.

Twenty miles our men had to row before we reached "Sandy Island," and as on its level shores we all leaped, we plainly saw the southernmost cape of the Foridas. The flocks of birds that covered the shelly beaches, and those hovering overhead, so astonished us that we could for a while scarcely believe our eyes. The first volley procured a supply of food sufficient for two days' consumption. Such tales, you have already been told, are well enough at a distance from the place to which they refer; but you will doubtless be still more surprised when I tell you that our first fire among a crowd of the Great Godwits laid prostrate sixty-five of these birds. Rose-colored Curlews stalked gracefully beneath the mangroves. Purple Herons rose at almost every step we took, and each cactus supported the nest of a White Ibis. The air was darkened by whistling wings, while, on the waters, floated Gallinules and other interesting birds. We formed a kind of shed with sticks and grass, the sailor cook commenced his labors, and ere long we supplied the deficiencies of our fatigued frames. The business of the day over, we secured ourselves from insects by means of mosquito-nets, and were lulled to rest by the cacklings of the beautiful Purple Gallinules!

In the morning we rose from our sandy beds, and—

The Florida Keys

II

I left you abruptly, perhaps uncivilly, reader, at the dawn of day, on Sandy Island, which lies just six miles from the extreme point of South Florida. I did so because I was amazed at the appearance of things around me, which in fact looked so different then from what they seemed at night, that it took some minutes' reflection to account for the change. When we laid ourselves down in the sand to sleep, the waters almost bathed our feet; when we opened our eyes in the morning, they were at an immense distance. Our boat lay on her side, looking not unlike a whale reposing on a mud bank. The birds in myriads were probing their exposed pasture-ground. There great flocks of Ibises fed apart from equally large collections of Godwits, and thousands of Herons gracefully paced along, ever and anon thrusting their javelin bills into the body of some unfortunate fish confined in a small pool of water. Of Fish-Crows, I could not estimate the number, but from the havoc they made among the crabs, I conjecture that these animals must have been scarce by the time of next ebb. Frigate Pelicans chased the Jager, which himself had just robbed a poor Gull of its prize, and all the Gallinules, ran with spread wings from the mud-banks to the thickets of the island, so timorous had they become when they perceived us.

Surrounded as we were by so many objects that allured us, not one could we yet attain, so dangerous would it have been to venture on the mud; and our pilot, having assured us that nothing could be lost by waiting, spoke of our eating, and on this hint told us that he would take us to a part of the island where "our breakfast would be abundant although uncooked." Off we went, some of the sailors carrying baskets, others large tin pans and wooden vessels, such as they use for eating their meals in. Entering a thicket of about an acre in extent, we found on every bush several nests of the Ibis, each containing three large and beautiful eggs, and all hands fell to gathering. The birds gave way to us, and ere long we had a heap of eggs that promised delicious food. Nor did we stand long in expectation, for, kindling a fire, we soon prepared in one way or other enough to satisfy the cravings of our hungry maws. Breakfast ended, the pilot, looking at the gorgeous sunrise, said: "Gentlemen, prepare yourselves for fun; the tide is coming."

Over these enormous mud-flats, a foot or two of water is quite sufficient to drive all the birds ashore, even the tallest Heron or Flamingo, and the tide seems to flow at once over the whole expanse. Each of us, provided with a gun, posted himself behind a bush, and no sooner had the water forced the winged creatures to approach the shore than the work of destruction commenced. When it at length ceased, the collected mass of birds of different kinds looked not unlike a small haycock. Who could not with a little industry have helped himself to a few of their skins? Why, reader, surely no one as fond of these things as I am. Every one assisted in this, and even the sailors themselves tried their hand at the work.

Our pilot, good man, told us he was no hand at such occupations and would go after something else. So taking "Long Tom" and his fishing-tackle, he marched off quietly along the shores. About an hour afterwards we saw him returning, when he looked quite exhausted, and on our inquiring the cause said, "There is a dewfish yonder, and a few balacoudas, but I am not able to bring them, or even to haul them here; please send the sailors after them." The fishes were accordingly brought, and as I had never seen a dewfish, I examined it closely, and took an outline of its form, which some days hence you may perhaps see. It exceeded a hundred pounds in weight, and afforded excellent eating. The balacouda is also a good fish, but at times a dangerous one, for, according to the pilot, on more than one occasion "some of these gentry" had followed him when waist-deep in the water, in pursuit of a more valuable prize, until in self-defence, he had to spear them, fearing that "the gentlemen" might at one dart cut off his legs, or some other nice bit, with which he was unwilling to part.

Having filled our cask from a fine well, long since dug in the sand of Cape Sable, either by Seminole Indians or pirates, no matter which, we left Sandy Isle about full tide, and proceeded homeward, giving a call here and there at different Keys, with the view of procuring rare birds, and also their nests and eggs. We had twenty miles to go, "as the birds fly," but the tortuosity of the channels rendered our course fully a third longer. The sun was descending fast, when a black cloud suddenly obscured the majestic orb. Our sails swelled by a breeze that was scarcely felt by us; and the pilot, requesting us to sit on the weather gunwale, told us that we were "going to get it." One sail was hauled in and secured, and the other was reefed, although the wind had not increased. A low murmuring noise was heard, and across the cloud that now rolled along in tumultuous masses shot vivid flashes of lightning. Our experienced guide steered directly across a flat towards the nearest land. The sailors passed their quids from one cheek to the other, and our pilot having covered himself with his oil jacket, we followed his example. "Blow, sweet breeze," cried he at the tiller, and "we'll reach the land before the blast overtakes us, for, gentlemen, it is a furious cloud yon."

A furious cloud indeed was the one which now, like an eagle on outstretched wings, approached so swiftly that one might have deemed it in haste to destroy us. We were not more than a cable's length from the shore, when, with an imperative voice, the pilot calmly said to us, "Sit quite still, gentlemen, for I should not like to lose you overboard just now; the boat can't upset, my word for that, if you will but sit still—Here we have it!"

Reader, persons who have never witnessed a hurricane, such as not unfrequently desolates the sultry climates of the South, can scarcely form an idea of their terrific grandeur. One would think that, not content with laying waste all on land, it must needs sweep the waters of the shallows quite dry, to quench its thirst. No respite for an instant does it afford to the objects within the reach of its furious current. Like the scythe of the destroying angel, it cuts everything by the roots, as it were, with the careless ease of the experienced mower. Each of its revolving sweeps collects a heap that might be likened to the full-sheaf which the husbandman flings by his side. On it goes with a wildness and fury that are indescribable, and when at last its frightful blasts have ceased, Nature, weeping and disconsolate, is left bereaved of her beauteous offspring. In some instances, even a full century is required before, with all her powerful energies, she can repair her loss. The planter has not only lost his mansion, his crops, and his flocks, but he has to clear his lands anew, covered and entangled as they are with the trunks and branches of trees that are everywhere strewn. The bark, overtaken by the storm, is cast on the lee-shore, and if any are left to witness the fatal results, they are the "wreckers" alone, who, with inward delight, gaze upon the melancholy spectacle.

Our light bark shivered like a leaf the instant the blast reached her sides. We thought she had gone over; but the next instant she was on the shore. And now in contemplation of the sublime and awful storm, I gazed around me. The waters drifted like snow; the tough mangroves hid their tops amid their roots, and the loud roaring of the waves driven among them blended with the howl of the tempest. It was not rain that fell; the masses of water flew in a horizontal direction, and where a part of my body was exposed I felt as if a smart blow had been given me on it. But enough—in half an hour it was over. The pure blue sky once more embellished the heavens, and although it was now quite night, we considered our situation a good one.

The crew and some of the party spent the night in the boat. The pilot, myself, and one of my assistants took to the heart of the mangroves, and having found high land, we made a fire as well as we could, spread a tarpauling, and fixing our insect bars over us, soon forgot in sleep the horrors that had surrounded us.

Next day the "Marion" proceeded on her cruise, and in a few more days, having anchored in another safe harbor, we visited other Keys, of which I will, with your leave, give you a short account.

The deputy-collector of Indian Isle gave me the use of his pilot for a few weeks, and I was the more gratified by this, that besides knowing him to be a good man, and a perfect sailor, I was now convinced that he possessed a great knowledge of the habits of birds, and could without loss of time lead me to their haunts. We were a hundred miles or so farther to the south. Gay May; like a playful babe, gambolled on the bosom of his mother Nature, and everything was replete with life and joy. The pilot had spoken to me of some birds which I was very desirous of obtaining. One morning, therefore, we went in two boats to some distant isle, where they were said to breed. Our difficulties in reaching that Key might to some seem more imaginary than real, were I faithfully to describe them. Suffice it for me to tell you that after hauling our boats and pushing them with our hands, for upwards of nine miles, over the flats, we at last reached the deep channel that usually surrounds each of the mangrove islands. We were much exhausted by the labor and excessive heat, but we were now floating on deep water, and by resting a short while under the shade of some mangroves, we were soon refreshed by the breeze that gently blew from the Gulf. We further repaired our strength by taking some food; and I may as well tell you here that, during all the time I spent in that part of the Floridas, my party restricted themselves to fish and soaked biscuit, while our only and constant beverage was molasses and water. I found that in these warm latitudes, exposed as we constantly were to alternate heat and moisture, ardent spirits and more substantial food would prove dangerous to us. The officers, and those persons who from time to time kindly accompanied us, adopted the same regimen, and not an individual of us had ever to complain of so much as a headache.

But we were under the mangroves; at a great distance on one of the flats, the Heron which I have named *Ardea occidentalis* was seen moving majestically in great numbers. The tide rose and drove them away, and as they came towards us, to alight and rest for a time on the tallest trees, we shot as many as I wished. I also took under my charge several of their young alive.

At another time we visited the "Mule Keys." There the prospect was in many respects dismal in the extreme. As I followed their shores, I saw bales of cotton floating in all the coves, while spars of every description lay on the beach, and far off on the reefs I could see the last remains of a lost ship, her dismantled hulk. Several schooners were around her; they were wreckers. I turned me from the sight with a heavy heart. Indeed, as I slowly proceeded, I dreaded to meet the floating or cast-ashore bodies of some of the unfortunate crew. Our visit to the Mule Keys was in no way profitable, for besides meeting with but a few birds, in two or three instances I was, whilst swimming in the deep channel of a mangrove isle, much nearer a large shark than I wish ever to be again.

"The service" requiring all the attention, prudence, and activity of Captain Day and his gallant officers, another cruise took place, of which you will find some account in the sequel; and while I rest a little on the deck of the "Lady of the Green Mantle," let me offer my humble thanks to the Being who has allowed me the pleasure of thus relating to you, kind reader, a small part of my adventures.

The Turtlers

The Tortugas are a group of islands lying about eighty miles from Key West, and the last of those that seem to defend the peninsula of the Floridas. They consist of five or six extremely low, uninhabitable banks, formed of shelly sand, and are resorted to principally by that class of men called wreckers and turtlers. Between these islands are deep channels, which, although extremely intricate, are well known to those adventurers, as well as to the commanders of the revenue cutters, whose duties call them to that dangerous coast. The great coral reef, or wall, lies about eight miles from these inhospitable isles, in the direction of the Gulf, and on it many an ignorant or careless navigator has suffered shipwreck. The whole ground around them is densely covered with corals, seafans, and other productions of the deep, amid which crawl innumerable testaceous animals, while shoals of curious and beautiful fishes fill the limpid waters above them. Turtles of different species resort to these banks, to deposit their eggs in the burning sand, and clouds of seafowl arrive every spring for the same purpose. These are followed by persons called "eggers," who, when their cargoes are completed, sail to distant markets, to exchange their ill-gotten ware for a portion of that gold on the acquisition of which all men seem bent.

The "Marion" having occasion to visit the Tortugas, I gladly embraced the opportunity of seeing those celebrated islets. A few hours before sunset the joyful cry of "Land!" announced our approach to them; but as the breeze was fresh, and the pilot was well acquainted with all the windings of the channels, we held on, and dropped anchor before twilight. If you have never seen the sun setting in those latitudes, I would recommend to you to make a voyage for the purpose, for I much doubt if, in any other portion of the world, the departure of the orb of day is accompanied with such gorgeous appearances. Look at the great red disk, increased to triple its ordinary dimensions! Now it has partially sunk beneath the distant line of waters, and with its still remaining half irradiates the whole heavens with a flood of golden light, purpling the far-off clouds that hover over the western horizon. A blaze of refulgent glory streams through the portals of the west, and the masses of vapor assume the semblance of mountains of molten gold. But the sun has now disappeared, and from the east slowly advances the gray curtain which night draws over the world.

The Night-hawk is flapping its noiseless wings in the gentle sea-breeze; the Terns, safely landed, have settled on their nests; the Frigate Pelicans are seen wending their way to distant mangroves; and the Brown Gannet, in search of a resting-place, has perched on the yard of the vessel. Slowly advancing landward, their heads alone above the water, are observed the heavily laden Turtles, anxious to deposit their eggs in the well-known sands. On the surface of the gently rippling stream, I dimly see their broad forms, as they toil along, while at intervals may be heard their hurried breathings, indicative of suspicion and fear. The moon with her silvery light now illumines the scene, and the Turtle, having landed, slowly and laboriously drags her heavy body over the sand, her "flippers" being better adapted for motion in the water than on shore. Up the slope, however, she works her way; and see how industriously she removes the sand beneath her, casting it out on either side. Layer after layer she deposits her eggs, arranging them in the most careful manner, and with her hind paddles brings the sand over them. The business is accomplished, the spot is covered over, and with a joyful heart the Turtle swiftly retires towards the shore, and launches into the deep.

But the Tortugas are not the only breeding places of the Turtles; these animals, on the contrary, frequent many other Keys, as well as various parts of the coast of the mainland. There are four different species, which are known by the names of the *Green* Turtle, the *Hawk-billed* Turtle, the *Logger-head* Turtle, and the *Trunk* Turtle. The first is considered the best as an article of food, in which capacity it is well known to most epicures. It approaches the shores, and enters the bays, inlets, and rivers, early in the month of April, after having spent the winter in the deep waters. It deposits its eggs in convenient places, at two different times in May, and once again in June. The first deposit is the largest, and the last the least, the total quantity being, at an average, about two hundred and forty. The Hawk-billed Turtle, whose shell is so valuable as an article of commerce, being used for various purposes in the arts, is the next with respect to the quality of its flesh. It resorts to the outer Keys only, where it deposits its eggs in two sets, first in July, and again in August, although it "crawls" the beaches of these Keys much earlier in the season, as if to look for a safe place. The average number of its eggs is about three hundred. The Logger-head visits the Tortugas in April, and lays from that period until late in June three sets of eggs, each set averaging one hundred and seventy. The Trunk Turtle, which is sometimes of an enormous size, and which has a pouch like a Pelican, reaches the shores latest. The shell and flesh are so soft that one may push his finger into them, almost as into a lump of butter. This species is therefore considered as the least valuable, and, indeed, is seldom eaten, unless by the Indians, who, ever alert when the Turtle season commences, first carry off the eggs, and afterwards catch the Turtles themselves. The average number of eggs which it lays in the season, in two sets, may be three hundred and fifty.

The Logger-head and the Trunk Turtles are the least cautious in choosing the places in which to deposit their eggs, whereas the two other species select the wildest and most secluded spots. The Green Turtle resorts either to the shores of the Main, between Cape Sable and Cape Florida, or enters Indian, Halifax, and other large rivers or inlets, from which it makes its retreat as speedily as possible, and betakes itself to the open sea. Great numbers, however, are killed by the turtlers and Indians, as well as by various species of carnivorous animals, as Cougars, Lynxes, Bears, and Wolves. The Hawk-bill, which is still more wary, and is always the most difficult to surprise, keeps to the sea-islands. All the species employ nearly the same method in depositing their eggs in the sand, and as I have several times observed them in the act, I am enabled to present you with a circumstantial account of it.

On first nearing the shores, and mostly on fine, calm, moonlight nights, the Turtle raises her head above the water, being still distant thirty or forty yards from the beach, looks around her, and attentively examines the objects on the shore. Should she observe nothing likely to disturb her intended operations, she emits a loud hissing sound, by which such of her many enemies as are unaccustomed to it are startled, and so are apt to remove to another place, although unseen by her. Should she hear any noise, or perceive indications of danger, she instantly sinks, and goes off to a considerable distance; but should everything be quiet, she advances slowly towards the beach, crawls over it, her head raised to the full stretch of her neck, and when she has reached a place fitted for her purpose, she gazes all round in silence. Finding "all well" she proceeds to form a hole in the sand, which she effects by removing it from *under* her body with her *hind* flippers, scooping it out with so much dexterity that the sides seldom if ever fall in. The sand is raised alternately with each flipper, as with a large ladle, until it has accumulated behind her, when, supporting herself with her head and fore part on the ground fronting her body, she, with a spring from each flipper, sends the sand around her, scattering it to the distance of several feet. In this manner the hole is dug to the depth of eighteen inches, or sometimes more than two feet. This labor I have seen performed in the short period of nine minutes. The eggs are then dropped one by one, and disposed in regular layers, to the number of a hundred and fifty, or sometimes nearly two hundred. The whole time spent in this part of the operation may be about twenty minutes. She now scrapes the loose sand back over the eggs, and so levels and smooths the surface that few persons on seeing the spot could imagine anything had been done to it. This accomplished to her mind, she retreats to the water with all possible despatch, leaving the hatching of the eggs to the heat of the sand. When a Turtle, a Loggerhead for example, is in the act of dropping her eggs, she will not move, although one should go up to her, or even seat himself on her back, for it seems that at this moment she finds it necessary to proceed at all events, and is unable to intermit her labor. The moment it is finished, however, off she starts; nor would it then be possible for one, unless he were as strong as a Hercules, to turn her over and secure her.

To upset a Turtle on the shore, one is obliged to fall on his knees, and placing his shoulder behind her fore-arm, gradually raise her up by pushing with great force, and then with a jerk throw her over. Sometimes it requires the united strength of several men to accomplish this; and, if the Turtle should be of very great size, as often happens on that coast, even handspikes are employed. Some turtlers are so daring as to swim up to them while lying asleep on the surface of the water, and turn them over in their own element, when, however, a boat must be at hand, to enable them to secure their prize. Few Turtles can bite beyond the reach of their fore-legs, and few, when once turned over, can, without assistance, regain their natural position; but, notwithstanding this, their flippers are generally secured by ropes so as to render their escape impossible.

Persons who search for Turtles' eggs, are provided with a light stiff cane or a gun-rod, with which they go along the shores probing the sand near the tracks of the animals, which, however, cannot always be seen, on account of the winds and heavy rains that often obliterate them. The nests are discovered not only by men, but also by beasts of prey, and the eggs are collected, or destroyed on the spot, in great numbers, as on certain parts of the shores hundreds of Turtles are known to deposit their eggs within the space of a mile. They form a new hole each time they lay, and the second is generally dug near the first, as if the animal were quite unconscious of what had befallen it. It will readily be understood that the numerous eggs seen in a Turtle on cutting it up, could not be all laid the same season. The whole number deposited by an individual in one summer may amount to four hundred, whereas, if the animal is caught on or near her nest, as I have witnessed, the remaining eggs, all small, without shells, and as it were threaded like so many large beads, exceed three thousand. In an instance where I found that number, the Turtle weighed nearly four hundred pounds. The young, soon after being hatched, and when yet scarcely larger than a dollar, scratch their way through their sandy covering, and immediately betake themselves to the water.

The food of the Green Turtle consists chiefly of marine plants, more especially the Grasswrack (*Zostera marina*) which they cut near the roots to procure the most tender and succulent parts. Their feeding-grounds, as I have elsewhere said, are easily discovered by floating masses of these plants on the flats, or along the shores to which they resort. The Hawk-billed species feeds on sea-weeds, crabs, various kinds of shell-fish and fishes; the Logger-head mostly on the fish of conch-shells of large size, which they are enabled, by means of their powerful beak, to crush to pieces with apparently as much ease as a man cracks a walnut. One which was brought on board the "Marion," and placed near the fluke of one of her anchors, made a deep indentation in that hammered piece of iron, which quite surprised me. The Trunk Turtle feeds on mollusca, fish, crustacea, sea urchins, and various marine plants.

All the species move through the water with surprising speed; but the Green and Hawk-billed, in particular, remind you, by their celerity and the ease of their motions, of the progress of a bird in the air. It is, therefore, no easy matter to strike one with a spear, and yet this is often done by an accomplished turtler.

While at Key West, and other islands on the coast, where I made the observations here presented to you, I chanced to have need to purchase some Turtles, to feed my friends on board "The Lady of the Green Mantle"—not my friends her gallant officers, or the brave tars who formed her crew, for all of them had already been satiated with Turtle soup, but my friends the Herons, of which I had a goodly number alive in coops, intending to carry them to John Bachman of Charleston, and other persons for whom I ever feel a sincere regard. So I went to a "crawl" accompanied by Dr. Benjamin Strobel, to inquire about prices, when, to my surprise, I found that the smaller the Turtles above ten-pounds weight, the dearer they were, and that I could have purchased one of the Logger-head kind that weighed more than seven hundred pounds, for little more money than another of only thirty pounds. While I gazed on the large one, I thought of the soups the contents of its shell would have furnished for a "Lord Mayor's dinner," of the numerous eggs which its swollen body contained, and of the curious carriage which might be made of its shell—a car in which Venus herself might sail over the Caribbean Sea, provided her tender Doves lent their aid in drawing the divinity, and provided no shark or hurricane came to upset it. The turtler assured me that although the "great monster" was, in fact, better meat than any other of a less size, there was no disposing of it, unless, indeed, it had been in his power to have sent it to some very distant market. I would willingly have purchased it, but I knew that if killed, its flesh could not keep much longer than a day, and on that account I bought eight or ten small ones, which "my friends" really relished exceedingly, and which served to support them for a long time.

Turtles, such as I have spoken of, are caught in various ways on the coasts of the Floridas, or in estuaries and rivers. Some turtlers are in the habit of setting great nets across the entrance of streams, so as to answer the purpose either at the flow or at the ebb of the waters. These nets are formed of very large meshes, into which the Turtles partially enter, when, the more they attempt to extricate themselves, the more they get entangled. Others harpoon them in the usual manner; but in my estimation no method is equal to that employed by Mr. Egan, the pilot of Indian Isle.

That extraordinary turtler had an iron instrument which he called a *peg*, and which at each end had a point not unlike what nail-makers call a brad, it being four-cornered but flattish, and of a shape somewhat resembling the beak of an Ivory-billed Woodpecker, together with a neck and shoulder. Between the two shoulders of this instrument a fine tough-line, fifty or more fathoms in length, was fastened by one end being passed through a hole in the centre of the peg and the line itself was carefully coiled up, and placed in a convenient part of the canoe. One extremity of this peg enters a sheath of iron that loosely attaches it to a long wooden spear, until a Turtle has been pierced through the shell by the other extremity. He of the canoe paddles away as silently as possible whenever he spies a Turtle basking on the water, until he gets within a distance of ten or twelve yards, when he throws the spear so as to hit the animal about the place which an entomologist would choose, were it a large insect, for pinning it to a piece of cork. As soon as the Turtle is struck, the wooden handle separates from the peg, in consequence of the looseness of its attachment. The smart of the wound urges on the animal as if distracted, and it appears that the longer the peg remains in its shell, the more firmly fastened it is, so great a pressure is exercised upon it by the shell of the Turtle, which, being suffered to run like a whale, soon becomes fatigued, and is secured by hauling in the line with great care. In this manner, as the pilot informed me, eight hundred Green Turtles were caught by one man in twelve months.

Each turtler has his *crawl*, which is a square wooden building or pen formed of logs, which are so far separated as to allow the tide to pass freely through, and stand erect in the mud. The Turtles are placed in this enclosure, fed and kept there until sold. If the animals thus confined have not laid their eggs previous to their seizure, they drop them in the water, so that they are lost. The price of Green Turtles, when I was at Key West, was from four to six cents per pound.

The loves of the Turtles are conducted in the most extraordinary manner; but as the recital of them must prove out of place here, I shall pass them over. There is, however, a circumstance relating to their habits which I cannot omit, although I have it not from my own ocular evidence, but from report. When I was in the Floridas several of the turtlers assured me that any Turtle taken from the depositing ground, and carried on the deck of a vessel several hundred miles, would, if then let loose, certainly be met with at the same spot, either immediately after, or in the following breeding season. Should this prove true, and it certainly may, how much will be enhanced the belief of the student in the uniformity and solidity of Nature's arrangements, when he finds that the Turtle, like a migratory bird, returns to the same locality, with perhaps a delight similar to that experienced by the traveller, who, after visiting distant countries, once more returns to the bosom of his cherished family.

Labrador

When I look back upon the many pleasant hours that I spent with the young gentlemen who composed my party, during our excursions along the coast of sterile and stormy Labrador, I think that a brief account of our employments may prove not altogether uninteresting to my readers.

We had purchased our stores at Boston, with the aid of my generous friend, Dr. Parkman of that city; but unfortunately many things necessary on an expedition like ours were omitted. At Eastport in Maine we therefore laid in these requisites. No traveller, let me say, ought to neglect anything that is calculated to insure the success of his undertaking, or to contribute to his personal comfort, when about to set out on a long and perhaps hazardous voyage. Very few opportunities of replenishing stores of provisions, clothing, or ammunition, occur in such a country as Labrador; and yet, we all placed too much confidence in the zeal and foresight of our purveyors at Eastport. We had abundance of ammunition, excellent bread, meat, and potatoes; but the butter was quite rancid, the oil only fit to grease our guns, the vinegar too liberally diluted with cider, the mustard and pepper deficient in due pungency. All this, however, was not discovered until it was too late to be remedied. Several of the young men were not clothed as hunters should be, and some of the guns were not so good as we could have wished. We were, however, fortunate with respect to our vessel, which was a notable sailer, did not leak, had a good crew, and was directed by a capital seaman.

The hold of the schooner was floored, and an entrance made to it from the cabin, so that in it we had a very good parlor, dining-room, drawing-room, library, etc., all those apartments, however, being comprised in one. An extravagantly elongated deal table ranged along the centre; one of the party had slung his hammock at one end, and in its vicinity slept the cook and a lad who acted as armorer. The cabin was small; but being fitted in the usual manner with side berths, was used for a dormitory. It contained a small table and a stove, the latter of diminutive size, but smoky enough to discomfit a host. We had adopted in a great measure the clothing worn by the American fishermen on that coast, namely, thick blue cloth trousers, a comfortable waistcoat, and a pea-jacket of blanket. Our boots were large, round-toed, strong, and well studded with large nails to prevent sliding on the rocks. Worsted comforters, thick mittens, and round broad-brimmed hats, completed our dress, which was more picturesque than fashionable. As soon as we had an opportunity, the boots were exchanged for Esquimaux mounted moccasins of Seal-skin, impermeable to water, light, easy, and fastening at top about the middle of the thigh to straps, which when buckled over the hips secured them well. To complete our equipment, we had several good boats, one of which was extremely light and adapted for shallow water.

No sooner had we reached the coast and got into harbor, than we agreed to follow certain regulations intended for the general benefit. Every morning the cook was called before three o'clock. At half-past three, breakfast was on the table, and everybody equipped. The guns, ammunition, botanical boxes, and baskets for eggs or minerals were all in readiness. Our breakfast consisted of coffee, bread, and various other materials. At four, all except the cook, and one seaman, went off in different directions, not forgetting to carry with them a store of cooked provisions. Some betook themselves to the islands, others to the deep bays; the latter on landing wandered over the country till noon, when laying themselves down on the rich moss, or sitting on the granite rock, they would rest for an hour, eat their dinner, and talk of their successes or disappointments. I often regret that I did not take sketches of the curious groups formed by my young friends on such occasions, and when, after returning at night, all were engaged in measuring, weighing, comparing, and dissecting the birds we had procured; operations which were carried on with the aid of a number of candles thrust into the necks of bottles. Here one examined the flowers and leaves of a plant, there another explored the recesses of a Diver's gullet, while a third skinned a Gull or a Grouse. Nor was one journal forgotten. Arrangements were made for the morrow, and at twelve we left matters to the management of the cook, and retired to our roosts.

If the wind blew hard, all went on shore, and, excepting on a few remarkably rainy days, we continued our pursuits, much in the same manner during our stay in the country. The physical powers of the young men were considered in making our arrangements. Shattuck and Ingalls went together; the captain and Coolidge were fond of each other, the latter having also been an officer; Lincoln and my son being the strongest and most determined hunters, generally marched by themselves; and I went with one or other of the parties, according to circumstances, although it was by no means my custom to do so regularly, as I had abundance of work on hand in the vessel.

The return of my young companions and the sailors was always looked for with anxiety. On getting on board, they opened their budgets, and laid their contents on the deck, amid much merriment, those who had procured most specimens being laughed at by those who had obtained the rarest, and the former joking the latter in return. A substantial meal always awaited them, and fortunate we were in having a capital cook, although he was a little too fond of the bottle.

Our "Fourth of July" was kept sacred, and every Saturday night the toast of "wives and sweethearts" was the first given, "parents and friends" the last. Never was there a more merry set. Some with the violin and flute accompanied the voices of the rest, and few moments were spent in idleness. Before a month had elapsed, the spoils of many a fine bird hung around the hold; shrubs and flowers were in the press, and I had several drawings finished, some of which you have seen, and of which I hope you will ere long see the remainder. Large jars were filling apace with the bodies of rare birds, fishes, quadrupeds and reptiles, as well as molluscous animals. We had several pets too, Gulls, Cormorants, Guillemots, Puffins, Hawks, and a Raven. In some of the harbors, curious fishes were hooked in our sight, so clear was the water.

We found that camping out at night was extremely uncomfortable, on account of the annoyance caused by flies and mosquitoes, which attacked the hunters in swarms at all times, but more especially when they lay down, unless they enveloped themselves in thick smoke, which is not much more pleasant. Once when camping the weather became very bad, and the party was twenty miles distant from Whapatigan as night threw her mantle over the earth. The rain fell in torrents, the northeast wind blew furiously, and the air was extremely cold. The oars of the boats were fixed so as to support some blankets, and a small fire was with difficulty kindled, on the embers of which a scanty meal was cooked. How different from a camp on the shores of the Mississippi, where wood is abundant, and the air generally not lacking heat, where mosquitoes, although plentiful enough, are not accompanied by Caribou flies, and where the barkings of a joyful Squirrel, or the notes of the Barred Owl, that grave buffoon of our western woods, never fail to gladden the camper as he cuts to the right and left such branches and canes as most easily supply materials for forming a lodging for the night. On the coast of Labrador there are no such things; granite and green moss are spread around, silence like that of the grave envelops all, and when night has closed the dreary scene from your sight, the Wolves, attracted by the scent of the remains of your scanty repast, gather around you. Cowards as they are they dare not venture on a charge; but their howlings effectually banish sleep. You must almost roast your feet to keep them warm, while your head and shoulders are chilled by the blast. When morning comes, she smiles not on you with rosy cheeks, but appears muffled in a gray mantle of cold mist, which shows you that there is no prospect of a fine day. The object of the expedition, which was to procure some Owls that had been observed there by day, was entirely frustrated. At early dawn the party rose stiffened and dispirited, and glad were they to betake themselves to their boats, and return to their floating home.

Before we left Labrador, several of my young friends began to feel the want of suitable clothing. The sailor's ever-tailoring system, was, believe me, fairly put to the test. Patches of various colors ornamented knees and elbows; our boots were worn out; our greasy garments and battered hats were in harmony with our tanned and weather-beaten faces; and, had you met with us, you might have taken us for a squad of wretched vagrants; but we were joyous in the expectation of a speedy return, and exulted at the thoughts of our success.

As the chill blast that precedes the winter's tempest thickened the fogs on the hills and ruffled the dark waters, each successive day saw us more anxious to leave the dreary wilderness of grim rocks and desolate moss-clad valleys. Unfavorable winds prevented us for a while from spreading our white sails; but at last one fair morning smiled on the wintry world, the "Ripley" was towed from the harbor, her tackle trimmed, and as we bounded over the billows, we turned our eyes towards the wilds of Labrador, and heartily bade them farewell forever!

The Eggers of Labrador

The distinctive appellation of "eggers" is given to certain persons who follow, principally or exclusively, the avocation of procuring the eggs of wild birds, with the view of disposing of them at some distant port. Their great object is to plunder every nest, wherever they can find it, no matter where, and at whatever risk. They are the pest of the feathered tribes, and their brutal propensity to destroy the poor creatures after they have robbed them, is abundantly gratified whenever an opportunity presents itself.

Much had been said to me respecting these destructive pirates before I visited the coast of Labrador, but I could not entirely credit all their cruelties until I had actually witnessed their proceedings, which were such as to inspire no small degree of horror. But you shall judge for yourself.

See yon shallop, shyly sailing along; she sneaks like a thief wishing, as it were, to shun the very light of heaven. Under the lee of every rocky isle some one at the tiller steers her course. Were his trade an honest one, he would not think of hiding his back behind the terrific rocks that seem to have been placed there as a resort to the myriads of birds that annually visit this desolate region of the earth, for the purpose of rearing their young at a distance from all disturbers of their peace. How unlike the open, the bold, the honest mariner, whose face needs no mask, who scorns to skulk under any circumstances. The vessel herself is a shabby thing; her sails are patched with stolen pieces of better canvas, the owners of which have probably been stranded on some inhospitable coast, and have been plundered, perhaps murdered, by the wretches before us. Look at her again! Her sides are neither painted, nor even pitched; no, they are daubed over, plastered and patched with strips of Seal-skins laid along the seams. Her deck has never been washed or sanded; her hold —for no cabin has she—though at present empty, sends forth an odor pestilential as that of a charnel house. The crew, eight in number, lie sleeping at the foot of their tottering mast, regardless of the repairs needed in every part of her rigging. But see! she scuds along, and as I suspect her crew to be bent on the commission of some evil deed, let us follow her to the first harbor.

There rides the filthy thing! The afternoon is half over. Her crew have thrown their boat overboard, they enter and seat themselves, each with a rusty gun. One of them sculls the skiff towards an island for a century past the breeding-place of myriads of Guillemots, which are now to be laid under contribution. At the approach of the vile thieves, clouds of birds rise from the rock and fill the air around, wheeling and screaming over their enemies. Yet thousands remain in an erect posture, each covering its single egg, the hope of both parents. The reports of several muskets loaded with heavy shot are now heard, while several dead and wounded birds fall heavily on the rock, or into the water. Instantly all the sitting birds rise and fly off affrighted to their companions above, and hover in dismay over their assassins, who walk forward exultingly, and with their shouts mingling oaths and execrations. Look at them! See how they crush the chick within its shell, how they trample on every egg in their way with their huge and clumsy boots. Onward they go, and when they leave the isle, not an egg that they can find is left entire. The dead birds they collect and carry to their boat. Now they have regained their filthy shallop; they strip the birds by a single jerk, of their feathery apparel while the flesh is yet warm, and throw them on some coals, where in a short time they are broiled. The rum is produced when the Guillemots are fit for eating, and after stuffing themselves with this oily fare, and enjoying the pleasure of beastly intoxication, over they tumble on the deck of their crazed craft, where they pass the short hours of night in turbid slumber.

The sun now rises above the snow-clad summit of the eastern mount. "Sweet is the breath of morn," even in this desolate land. The gay Bunting erects his white crest, and gives utterance to the joy he feels in the presence of his brooding mate. The Willow Grouse on the rock crows his challenge aloud. Each floweret chilled by the night air expands its pure petals. The gentle breeze shakes from the blades of grass the heavy dew-drops. On the Guillemot isle the birds have again settled, and now renew their loves. Startled by the light of day, one of the eggers springs to his feet and rouses his companions, who stare around them for a while, endeavoring to collect their senses. Mark them, as with clumsy fingers they clear their drowsy eyes! Slowly they rise on their feet. See how the filthy lubbers stretch out their arms, and yawn; you shrink back, for verily "that throat might frighten a shark."

But the master soon recollecting that so many eggs are worth a dollar or a crown, casts his eye towards the rock, marks the day in his memory and gives orders to depart. The light breeze enables them to reach another harbor a few miles distant, one which, like the last, lies concealed from the ocean by some other rocky isle. Arrived there, they re-act the scene of yesterday, crushing every egg they can find. For a week each night is passed in drunkenness and brawls, until, having reached the last breeding-place on the coast, they return, touch at every isle in succession, shoot as many birds as they need, collect the fresh eggs, and lay in a cargo. At every step each ruffian picks up an egg so beautiful that any man with a feeling heart would pause to consider the motive which could induce him to carry it off. But nothing of this sort occurs to the egger, who gathers and gathers until he has swept the rock bare. The dollars alone chink in his sordid mind, and he assiduously plies the trade which no man would ply who had the talents and industry to procure subsistence by honorable means.

With a bark nearly half filled with fresh eggs they proceed to the principal rock, that on which they first landed. But what is their surprise when they find others there helping themselves as industriously as they can! In boiling rage they charge their guns and ply their oars. Landing on the rock they run up to the eggers, who, like themselves, are desperadoes. The first question is a discharge of musketry, the answer another. Now, man to man, they fight like tigers. One is carried to his boat with a fractured skull, another limps with a shot in his leg, and a third feels how many of his teeth have been driven through the hole in his cheek. At last, however, the quarrel is settled; the booty is to be equally divided; and now see them all drinking together. Oaths and curses and filthy jokes are all that you hear; but see, stuffed with food, and reeling with drink, down they drop one by one; groans and execrations from the wounded mingle with the snoring of the heavy sleepers. There let the brutes lie.

Again it is dawn, but no one stirs. The sun is high; one by one they open their heavy eyes, stretch their limbs, yawn, and raise themselves from the deck. But see, here comes a goodly company. A hundred honest fishermen, who for months past have fed on salt meat, have felt a desire to procure some eggs. Gallantly their boats advance, impelled by the regular pull of their long oars. Each buoyant bark displays the flag of its nation. No weapons do they bring, nor anything that can be used as such save their oars and their fists. Cleanly clad in Sunday attire, they arrive at the desired spot, and at once prepare to ascend the rock. The eggers, now numbering a dozen, all armed with guns and bludgeons, bid defiance to the fishermen. A few angry words pass between the parties. One of the eggers, still under the influence of drink, pulls his trigger, and an unfortunate sailor is seen to reel in agony. Three loud cheers fill the air. All at once rush on the malefactors; a horrid fight ensues, the result of which is that every egger is left on the rock beaten and bruised. Too frequently the fishermen man their boats, row to the shallops, and break every egg in the hold.

The eggers of Labrador not only rob the birds in this cruel manner, but also the fishermen, whenever they can find an opportunity; and the quarrels they excite are numberless. While we were on the coast, none of our party ever ventured on any of the islands which these wretches call their own, without being well provided with means of defence. On one occasion, when I was present, we found two eggers at their work of destruction. I spoke to them respecting my visit, and offered them premiums for rare birds and some of their eggs; but although they made fair promises, not one of the gang ever came near the "Ripley."

These people gather all the eider-down they can find; yet so inconsiderate are they, that they kill every bird which comes in their way. The eggs of Gulls, Guillemots, and Ducks are searched for with care; and the Puffins and some other birds they massacre in vast numbers for the sake of their feathers. So constant and persevering are their depredations that these species, which, according to the accounts of the few settlers I saw in the country, were exceedingly abundant twenty years ago, have abandoned their ancient breeding places, and removed much farther north in search of peaceful security. Scarcely, in fact, could I procure a young Guillemot before the eggers left the coast, nor was it until late in July that I succeeded, after the birds had laid three or four eggs each, instead of one, and when, nature having been exhausted, and the season nearly spent, thousands of these birds left the country without having accomplished the purpose for which they had visited it. This war of extermination cannot last many years more. The eggers themselves will be the first to repent the entire disappearance of the myriads of birds that made the coast of Labrador their summer residence, and unless they follow the persecuted tribes to the northward, they must renounce their trade.

The Squatters of Labrador

Go where you will, if a shilling can there be procured, you may expect to meet with individuals in search of it.

In the course of last summer, I met with several persons, as well as families, whom I could not compare to anything else than what in America we understand by the appellation of "squatters." The methods they employed to accumulate property form the subject of the observations which I now lay before you.

Our schooner lay at anchor in a beautiful basin on the coast of Labrador, surrounded by uncouth granitic rocks, partially covered with stunted vegetation. While searching for birds and other objects I chanced one morning to direct my eye towards the pinnacle of a small island, separated from the mainland by a very narrow channel, and presently commenced inspecting it with my telescope. There I saw a man on his knees with clasped hands, and face inclined heavenwards. Before him was a small monument of unhewn stones, supporting a wooden cross. In a word, reader, the person whom I thus unexpectedly discovered was engaged in prayer. Such an incident in that desolate land was affecting, for there one seldom finds traces of human beings; and the aid of the Almighty, although necessary everywhere, seems there peculiarly required to enable them to procure the means of subsistence. My curiosity having been raised, I betook myself to my boat, landed on the rock, and scrambled to the place, where I found the man still on his knees. When his devotions were concluded, he bowed to me, and addressed me in very indifferent French. I asked him why he had chosen so dreary a spot for his prayers. "Because," answered he, "the sea lies before me, and from it I receive my spring and summer sustenance. When winter approaches, I pray fronting the mountains on the main, as at that period the Caribous come towards the shore, and I kill them, feed on their flesh, and form my bedding of their skins." I thought the answer reasonable, and as I longed to know more of him, followed him to his hut. It was low, and very small, formed of stones plastered with mud to a considerable thickness. The roof was composed of a sort of thatching made of weeds and moss. A large Dutch stove filled nearly one half the place; a small port-hole then stuffed with old rags, served at times instead of a window; the bed was a pile of Deerskins; a bowl, a jug, and an iron pot were placed on a rude shelf; three old and rusty muskets, their locks fastened by thongs, stood in a corner; and his buckshot, powder, and flints, were tied up in bags of skin. Eight Esquimaux dogs yelled and leaped about us. The strong smell that emanated from them, together with the smoke and filth of the apartment, rendered my stay in it extremely disagreeable.

Being a native of France, the good man showed much politeness, and invited me to take some refreshment, when, without waiting for my assent, he took up his bowl, and went off I knew not whither. No sooner had he and his strange dogs disappeared than I went out also, to breathe the pure air, and gaze on the wild and majestic scenery around. I was struck with the extraordinary luxuriance of the plants and grasses that had sprung up on the scanty soil in the little valley which the squatter had chosen for his home. Their stalks and broad blades reached my waist. June had come, and the flies, mosquitoes, and other insects filled the air, and were as troublesome to me as if I had been in a Florida swamp.

The squatter returned, but he was chop-fallen; nay, I thought his visage had assumed a cadaverous hue. Tears ran down his cheeks, and he told me that his barrel of *rum* had been stolen by the "eggers" or some fishermen. He said that he had been in the habit of hiding it in the bushes, to prevent its being carried away by those merciless thieves, who must have watched him in some of his frequent walks to the spot. "Now," said he, "I can expect none till next spring, and God knows what will become of me in the winter."

Pierre Jean Baptiste Michaux had resided in that part of the world for upwards of ten years. He had run away from the fishing-smack that had brought him from his fair native land, and expected to become rich some day by the sale of the furs, Seal-skins, eider-down, and other articles, which he collected yearly, and sold to the traders who regularly visited his dreary abode. He was of moderate stature, firmly framed, and as active as a Wild Cat. He told me that excepting the loss of his rum, he had never experienced any other cause of sorrow, and that he felt as "happy as a lord."

Before parting with this fortunate mortal, I inquired how his dogs managed to find sufficient food. "Why, sir, during spring and summer they ramble along the shores, where they meet with abundance of dead fish, and in winter they eat the flesh of the Seals which I kill late in autumn, when these animals return from the north. As to myself, everything eatable is good, and when hard pushed, I relish the fare of my dogs, I assure you, as much as they do themselves."

Proceeding along the rugged indentations of the bay with my companions, I reached the settlement of another person, who, like the first, had come to Labrador with the view of making his fortune. We found him after many difficulties; but as our boats turned a long point jutting out into the bay, we were pleased to see several small schooners at anchor, and one lying near a sort of wharf. Several neat-looking houses enlivened the view, and on landing, we were kindly greeted with a polite welcome from a man who proved to be the owner of the establishment. For the rude simplicity of him of the rum-cask, we found here the manners and dress of a man of the world. A handsome fur cap covered his dark brow, his clothes were similar to our own, and his demeanor was that of a gentleman. On my giving my name to him, he shook me heartily by the hand, and on introducing each of my companions to him, he extended the like courtesy to them also. Then, to my astonishment, he addressed me as follows: "My dear sir, I have been expecting you these three weeks, having read *in the papers* your intention to visit Labrador; and some fishermen told me of your arrival at Little Natasquam. Gentlemen, walk in."

Having followed him to his neat and comfortable mansion, he introduced us to his wife and children. Of the latter there were six, all robust and rosy. The lady, although a native of the country, was of French extraction, handsome, and sufficiently accomplished to make an excellent companion to a gentleman. A smart girl brought us a luncheon, consisting of bread, cheese, and good port wine, to which, having rowed fourteen or fifteen miles that morning, we helped ourselves in a manner that seemed satisfactory to all parties. Our host gave us newspapers from different parts of the world, and showed us his small, but choice collection of books. He inquired after the health of the amiable Captain Bayfield of the Royal Navy, and the officers under him, and hoped they would give him a call.

Having refreshed ourselves, we walked out with him, when he pointed to a very small garden, where a few vegetables sprouted out, anxious to see the sun. Gazing on the desolate country around, I asked him how *he* had thus secluded himself from the world. For it he had no relish, and although he had received a liberal education, and had mixed with society, he never intended to return to it. "The country around," said he, "is all my own, much farther than you can see. No fees, no lawyers, no taxes are *here*. I do pretty much as I choose. My means are ample through my own industry. These vessels come here for Seal-skins, Seal-oil, and salmon, and give me in return all the necessaries, and indeed comforts, of the life I love to follow; and what else could *the world* afford me?" I spoke of the education of his children. "My wife and I teach them all that is *useful* for them to know, and is not that enough? My girls will marry their countrymen, my sons the daughters of my neighbors, and I hope all of them will live and die in the country!" I said no more, but by way of compensation for the trouble I had given him, purchased from his eldest child a beautiful Fox's skin.

Few birds, he said, came round him in summer, but in winter thousands of Ptarmigans were killed, as well as great numbers of Gulls. He had a great dislike to all fishermen and eggers, and I really believe was always glad to see the departure even of the hardy navigators who annually visited him for the sake of his salmon, Seal-skins, and oil. He had more than forty Esquimaux dogs; and as I was caressing one of them he said, "Tell my brother-in-law at Bras d'Or, that we are all well here, and that, after visiting my wife's father, I will give him a call."

Now, reader, his wife's father resided at the distance of seventy miles down the coast, and, like himself, was a recluse. He of Bras d'Or, was at double that distance; but, when the snows of winter have thickly covered the country, the whole family, in sledges drawn by dogs, travel with ease, and pay their visits, or leave their cards. This good gentleman had already resided there more than twenty years. Should he ever read this article, I desire him to believe that I shall always be grateful to him and his wife for their hospitable welcome.

When our schooner, the "Ripley," arrived at Bras d'Or, I paid a visit to Mr. ——, the brother-in-law, who lived in a house imported from Quebec, which fronted the strait of Belle Isle, and overlooked a small island, over which the eye reached the coast of Newfoundland, whenever it was the wind's pleasure to drive away the fogs that usually lay over both coasts. The gentleman and his wife, we were told, were both out on a walk, but would return in a very short time, which they in fact did, when we followed them into the house, which was yet unfinished. The usual immense Dutch stove formed a principal feature of the interior. The lady had once visited the metropolis of Canada, and seemed desirous of acting the part of a blue-stocking. Understanding that I knew something of the fine arts, she pointed to several of the vile prints hung on the bare walls, which she said were *elegant* Italian pictures, and continued her encomiums upon them, assuring me that she had purchased them from an Italian, who had come there with a trunk full of them. She had paid a shilling sterling for each, frame included. I could give no answer to the good lady on this subject, but I felt glad to find that she possessed a feeling heart, for one of her children had caught a Siskin, and was tormenting the poor bird, when she rose from her seat, took the little fluttering thing from the boy, kissed it, and gently launched it into the air. This made me quite forget the tattle about the fine arts.

Some excellent milk was poured out for us in clean glasses. It was a pleasing sight, for not a cow had we yet seen in the country. The lady turned the conversation on music, and asked me if I played on any instrument. I answered that I did, but very indifferently. Her forte, she said, was music, of which she was indeed immoderately fond. Her instrument had been sent to Europe to be repaired, but would return that season, when the whole of her children would again perform many beautiful airs; for in fact anybody could use it with ease, as when she or the children felt fatigued, the servant played on it for them. Rather surprised at the extraordinary powers of this family of musicians, I asked what sort of an instrument it was, when she described it as follows: "Gentlemen, my instrument is large, longer than broad, and stands on four legs, like a table. At one end is a crooked handle, by turning which round, either fast or slow, I do assure you we make most excellent music." The lips of my young friends and companions instantly curled, but a glance from me as instantly recomposed their features. Telling the fair one that it must be a hand-organ she used, she laughingly said, "Ah, that is it; it is a hand-organ, but I had forgot the name, and for the life of me could not recollect it."

The husband had gone out to work, and was in the harbor calking an old schooner. He dined with me on board the "Ripley," and proved to be also an excellent fellow. Like his brother-in-law, he had seen much of the world, having sailed nearly round it; and, although no scholar like him, too, he was disgusted with it. He held his land on the same footing as his neighbors, caught Seals without number, lived comfortably and happily, visited his father-in-law and the scholar, by the aid of his dogs, of which he kept a great pack, bartered or sold his commodities, as his relations did, and cared about nothing else in the world. Whenever the weather was fair, he walked with his dame over the moss-covered rocks of the neighborhood; and during winter killed Ptarmigans and Caribous, while his eldest son attended to the traps, and skinned the animals caught in them. He had the only horse that was to be found in that part of the country, as well as several cows; but, above all, he was kind to every one, and every one spoke well of him. The only disagreeable thing about his plantation or settlement, was a heap of fifteen hundred carcasses of skinned Seals, which, at the time when we visited the place, in the month of August, notwithstanding the coolness of the atmosphere, sent forth a stench that, according to the ideas of some naturalists, might have sufficed to attract all the Vultures in the United States.

During our stay at Bras d'Or, the kind-hearted and good Mrs. —— daily sent us fresh milk and butter, for which we were denied the pleasure of making any return.

A Ball in Newfoundland

On our return from the singularly wild and interesting country of Labrador, the "Ripley" sailed close along the northern coast of Newfoundland. The weather was mild and clear, and, while my young companions amused themselves on the deck with the music of various instruments, I gazed on the romantic scenery spread along the bold and often magnificent shores. Portions of the wilds appeared covered with a luxuriance of vegetable growth, far surpassing that of the regions which we had just left, and in some of the valleys I thought I saw trees of moderate size. The number of habitations increased apace, and many small vessels and boats danced on the waves of the coves which we passed. Here a precipitous shore looked like the section of a great mountain, of which the lost half had sunk into the depths of the sea, and the dashing of the waters along its base was such as to alarm the most daring seaman. The huge masses of broken rock impressed my mind with awe and reverence, as I thought of the power that still gave support to the gigantic fragments which everywhere hung, as if by magic, over the sea, awaiting, as it were, the proper moment to fall upon and crush the impious crew of some piratical vessel. There, again, gently swelling hills reared their heads towards the sky, as if desirous of existing within the influence of its azure purity; and I thought the bleatings of Reindeer came on my ear. Dark clouds of Curlews were seen winging their way towards the south, and thousands of Larks and Warblers were flitting through the air. The sight of these birds excited in me a wish that I also had wings to fly back to my country and friends.

Early one morning our vessel doubled the northern cape of the Bay of St. George, and, as the wind was light, the sight of that magnificent expanse of water, which extends inward to the length of eighteen leagues, with a breadth of thirteen, gladdened the hearts of all on board. A long range of bold shores bordered it on one side, throwing a deep shadow over the water, which added greatly to the beauty of the scene. On the other side, the mild beams of the autumnal sun glittered on the water, and whitened the sails of the little barks that were sailing to and fro, like so many silvery Gulls. The welcome sight of cattle feeding in cultivated meadows, and of people at their avocations, consoled us for the labors which we had undergone, and the privations which we had suffered; and, as the "Ripley" steered her course into a snug harbor that suddenly opened to our view, the number of vessels that were anchored there, and a pretty village that presented itself increased our delight.

Although the sun was fast approaching the western horizon when our anchor was dropped, no sooner were the sails furled than we all went ashore. There appeared a kind of curious bustle among the people, as if they were anxious to know who we were; for our appearance, and that of our warlike looking schooner showed that we were not fishermen. As we bore our usual arms and hunting accoutrements, which were half Indian and half civilized, the individuals we met on shore manifested considerable suspicion, which our captain observing, he instantly made a signal, when the star-spangled banner glided to the mast-head, and saluted the flags of France and Britain in kindly greeting. We were welcomed and supplied with abundance of fresh provisions. Glad at once more standing on something like soil, we passed through the village, and walked round it, but as night was falling were quickly obliged to return to our floating home, where, after a hearty supper, we serenaded with repeated glees the peaceful inhabitants of the village.

At early dawn I was on deck admiring the scene of industry that presented itself. The harbor was already covered with fishing-boats employed in procuring mackerel, some of which we appropriated to ourselves. Signs of cultivation were observed on the slopes of the hills, the trees seemed of goodly size, a river made its way between two ranges of steep rocks, and here and there a group of Micmac Indians were searching along the shores for lobsters, crabs, and eels, all of which we found abundant and delicious. A canoe laden with Reindeer meat came alongside, paddled by a pair of athletic Indians, who exchanged their cargo for some of our stores. You would have been amused to see the manner in which these men, and their families on shore cooked the lobsters; they threw them alive into a great wood fire, and as soon as they were broiled devoured them, while yet so hot that none of us could have touched them. When properly cooled, I tasted these roasted lobsters, and found them infinitely better flavored than boiled ones. The country was represented as abounding in game. The temperature was higher by twenty degrees than that of Labrador, and yet I was told that the ice in the bay seldom broke up before the middle of May, and that few vessels attempted to go to Labrador before the 10th of June, when the codfishery at once commences.

One afternoon we were visited by a deputation from the inhabitants of the village, inviting our whole party to a ball which was to take place that night, and requesting us to take with us our musical instruments. We unanimously accepted the invitation, which had been made from friendly feelings; and finding that the deputies had a relish for "old Jamaica" we helped them pretty freely to some, which soon showed that it had lost nothing of its energies by having visited Labrador. At ten o'clock, the appointed hour, we landed, and were lighted to the dancing-hall by paper lanterns, one of us carrying a flute, another a violin, and I with a flageolet stuck into my waistcoat pocket.

The hall proved nothing else than the ground-floor of a fisherman's house. We were presented to his wife, who, like her neighbors, was an adept in the piscatory art. She courtesied, not *à la* Taglioni, it is true, but with a modest assurance, which to me was quite as pleasing as the airiness with which the admired performer just mentioned might have paid her respects. The good woman was rather unprepared, and quite *en negligée*, as was the apartment, but full of activity, and anxious to arrange things in becoming style. In one hand she held a bunch of candles, in the other a lighted torch, and distributing the former at proper intervals along the walls, she applied the latter to them in succession. This done, she emptied the contents of a large tin vessel into a number of glasses, which were placed on a tea-tray on the only table in the room.

The chimney, black and capacious, was embellished with coffee-pots, milk-jugs, cups and saucers, knives and forks, and all the paraphernalia necessary on so important an occasion. A set of primitive wooden stools and benches was placed around, for the reception of the belles of the village, some of whom now dropped in, flourishing in all the rosy fatness produced by an invigorating northern climate, and in decoration vying with the noblest Indian queen of the West. Their stays seemed ready to burst open, and their shoes were equally pressed. Around their necks, brilliant beads mingled with ebony tresses, and their naked arms might have inspired apprehension had they not been constantly employed in arranging flowing ribbons, gaudy flowers, and muslin flounces.

Now arrived one of the beaux, just returned from the fishing, who, knowing all, and being equally known, leaped without ceremony on the loose boards that formed a kind of loft overhead, where he soon exchanged his dripping apparel for a dress suited to the occasion, when he dropped upon the floor, and strutting up and down, bowed and scraped to the ladies, with as much ease, if not elegance, as a Bond Street highly scented exquisite. Others came in by degrees, ready dressed, and music was called for. My son, by way of overture, played "Hail Columbia, happy land," then went on with "La Marseillaise," and ended with "God save the King." Being merely a spectator, I ensconced myself in a corner, by the side of an old European gentleman, whom I found an agreeable and well informed companion, to admire the decorum of the motley assemblage.

The dancers stood in array, little time having been spent in choosing partners, and a Canadian accompanying my son on his Cremona, mirth and joy soon abounded. Dancing is certainly one of the most healthful and innocent amusements; I have loved it a vast deal more than watching for the nibble of a trout, and I have sometimes thought the enjoyment of it softened my nature as much as the pale, pure light of the moon softens and beautifies a winter night. A maiden lady who sat at my side, and who was the only daughter of my talkative companion, relished my remarks on the subject so much that the next set saw her gracing the floor with her tutored feet.

At each pause of the musicians refreshments were handed round by the hostess and her son, and I was not a little surprised to see all the ladies, maids and matrons, swallow, like their sweethearts and husbands, a full glass of pure rum, with evident pleasure. I should perhaps have recollected that, in cold climates, a glass of ardent spirits is not productive of the same effects as in burning latitudes, and that refinement had not yet induced these healthy and robust dames to affect a delicacy foreign to their nature.

It was now late, and knowing how much I had to accomplish next day, I left the party and proceeded to the shore. My men were sound asleep in the boat, but in a few moments I was on board the "Ripley." My young friends arrived towards daylight, but many of the fishermen's sons and daughters kept up the dance, to the music of the Canadian, until after our breakfast was over.

The Bay of Fundy

It was in the month of May that I sailed in the United States revenue cutter, the "Swiftsure," engaged in a cruise in the Bay of Fundy. Our sails were quickly unfurled and spread out to the breeze. The vessel seemed to fly over the surface of the liquid element, as the sun rose in full splendor, while the clouds that floated here and there formed, with their glowing hues, a rich contrast with the pure azure of the heavens above us. We approached apace the island of Grand Menan, of which the stupendous cliffs gradually emerged from the deep with the majestic boldness of her noblest native chief. Soon our bark passed beneath its craggy head, covered with trees, which, on account of the height, seemed scarcely larger than shrubs. The prudent Raven spread her pinions, launched from the cliff, and flew away before us; the Golden Eagle, soaring aloft, moved majestically along in wide circles; the Guillemots sat on their eggs upon the shelving precipices, or plunging into the water, dived, and rose again at a great distance; the broad-breasted Eider Duck covered her eggs among the grassy tufts; on a naked rock the Seal lazily basked, its sleek sides glistening in the sunshine; while shoals of porpoises were swiftly gliding through the waters around us, showing by their gambols that, although doomed to the deep, their life was not devoid of pleasure. Far away stood the bold shores of Nova Scotia, gradually fading in the distance, of which the gray tints beautifully relieved the wing-like sails of many a fishing bark.

Cape after cape, forming eddies and counter currents far too terrific to be described by a landsman, we passed in succession, until we reached a deep cove, near the shores of White Head Island, which is divided from Grand Menan by a narrow strait, where we anchored secure from every blast that could blow. In a short time we found ourselves under the roof of Captain Frankland, the sole owner of the isle, of which the surface contains about fifteen hundred acres. He received us all with politeness and gave us permission to seek out its treasures, which we immediately set about doing, for I was anxious to study the habits of certain Gulls that breed there in great numbers. As Captain Coolidge, our worthy commander, had assured me, we found them on their nests on almost every *tree* of a wood that covered several acres. What a treat, reader, was it to find birds of this kind lodged on fir-trees, and sitting comfortably on their eggs! Their loud cackling notes led us to their place of resort, and ere long we had satisfactorily observed their habits, and collected as many of themselves and their eggs as we considered sufficient. In our walks we noticed a Rat, the only quadruped found on the island, and observed abundance of gooseberries, currants, raspberries, strawberries, and huckleberries. Seating ourselves on the summit of the rocks, in view of the vast Atlantic, we spread out our stores, and refreshed ourselves with our simple fare.

Now we followed the objects of our pursuit through the tangled woods, now carefully picked our steps over the spongy grounds. The air was filled with the melodious concerts of birds, and all Nature seemed to smile in quiet enjoyment. We wandered about until the setting sun warned us to depart, when, returning to the house of the proprietor, we sat down to an excellent repast, and amused ourselves with relating anecdotes and forming arrangements for the morrow. Our captain complimented us on our success, when we reached the "Swiftsure," and in due time we betook ourselves to our hammocks.

The next morning, a strange sail appearing in the distance, preparations were instantly made to pay her commander a visit. The signal staff of White Head Island displayed the British flag, while Captain Frankland and his men stood on the shore, and as we gave our sails to the wind, three hearty cheers filled the air, and were instantly responded to by us. The vessel was soon approached, but all was found right with her, and squaring our yards, onward we sped, cheerily bounding over the gay billows, until our captain sent us ashore at Eastport.

At another time my party was received on board the revenue cutter's tender, the "Fancy,"—a charming name for so beautiful a craft. We set sail towards evening. The cackling of the "old wives" that covered the bay filled me with delight, and thousands of Gulls and Cormorants seemed as if anxious to pilot us into Head Harbor Bay, where we anchored for the night. Leaping on the rugged shore, we made our way to the lighthouse, where we found Mr. Snelling, a good and honest Englishman from Devonshire. His family consisted of three wild-looking lasses, beautiful, like the most finished productions of nature. In his lighthouse snugly ensconced, he spent his days in peaceful forgetfulness of the world, subsisting principally on the fish of the bay.

When day broke, how delightful it was to see fair Nature open her graceful eyelids, and present herself arrayed in all that was richest and purest before her Creator. Ah, reader, how indelibly are such moments engraved on my soul! With what ardor have I at such times gazed around me, full of the desire of being enabled to comprehend all that I saw! How often have I longed to converse with the feathered inhabitants of the forest, all of which seemed then intent on offering up their thanks to the object of my own adoration! But the wish could not be gratified, although I now feel satisfied that I have enjoyed as much of the wonders and beauties of nature as it was proper for me to enjoy. The delightful trills of the Winter Wren rolled through the underwood, the Red Squirrel smacked time with his chops, the loud notes of the Robin sounded clearly from the tops of the trees, the rosy Grosbeak nipped the tender blossoms of the maples, and high overhead the Loons passed in pairs, rapidly wending their way towards far distant shores. Would that I could have followed in their wake! The hour of our departure had come; and, as we sailed up the bay, our pilot, who had been fishing for cod, was taken on board. A few of his fish were roasted on a plank before the embers, and formed the principal part of our breakfast. The breeze was light, and it was not until afternoon that we arrived at Point Lepreaux Harbor, where every one, making choice of his course, went in search of curiosities and provender.

Now, reader, the little harbor in which, if you wish it, we shall suppose we still are, is renowned for a circumstance which I feel much inclined to endeavor to explain to you. Several species of Ducks, that in myriads cover the waters of the Bay of Fundy, are at times destroyed in this particular spot in a very singular manner. When July has come, all the water birds that are no longer capable of reproducing, remain like so many forlorn bachelors and old maids, to renew their plumage along the shores. At the period when these poor birds are unfit for flight, troops of Indians make their appearance in light bark canoes, paddled by their squaws and papooses. They form their flotilla into an extended curve, and drive before them the birds, not in silence, but with simultaneous horrific yells, at the same time beating the surface of the water with long poles and paddles. Terrified by the noise, the birds swim a long way before them, endeavoring to escape with all their might. The tide is high, every cove is filled, and into the one where we now are, thousands of Ducks are seen entering. The Indians have ceased to shout, and the canoes advance side by side. Time passes on, the tide swiftly recedes as it rose, and there are the birds left on the beach. See with what pleasure each wild inhabitant of the forest seizes his stick, the squaws and younglings following with similar weapons! Look at them rushing on their prey, falling on the disabled birds, and smashing them with their cudgels, until all are destroyed! In this manner upwards of five hundred wild fowls have often been procured in a few hours.

Three pleasant days were spent at Point Lepreaux, when the "Fancy" spread her wings to the breeze. In one harbor we fished for shells with a capital dredge, and in another searched along the shore for eggs. The Passamaquoddy chief is seen gliding swiftly over the deep in his fragile bark. He has observed a porpoise breathing. Watch him, for now he is close upon the unsuspecting dolphin. He rises erect, aims his musket; smoke rises curling from the pan, and rushes from the iron tube, when soon after the report comes on the ear. Meantime the porpoise has suddenly turned back downwards,—it is dead. The body weighs a hundred pounds or more, but this to the tough-fibred son of the woods is nothing; he reaches it with his muscular arms, and at a single jerk, while with his legs he dexterously steadies the canoe, he throws it lengthwise at his feet. Amidst the highest waves of the Bay of Fundy, these feats are performed by the Indians during the whole of the season when the porpoises resort thither.

You have often, no doubt, heard of the extraordinary tides of this bay; so had I, but, like others, I was loath to believe the reports were strictly true. So I went to the pretty town of Windsor in Nova Scotia, to judge for myself. But let us leave the "Fancy" for a while, and imagine ourselves at Windsor. Late one day in August my companions and I were seated on the grassy and elevated bank of the river, about eighty feet or so above its bed, which was almost dry, and extended for nine miles below like a sandy wilderness. Many vessels lay on the high banks taking in their lading of gypsum. We thought the appearance very singular, but we were too late to watch the tide that evening. Next morning we resumed our station, and soon perceived the water flowing towards us, and rising with a rapidity of which we had previously seen no example. We planted along the steep declivity of the bank a number of sticks, each three feet long, the base of one being placed on a level with the top of that below it, and when about half flow the tide reached their tops, one after another, rising three feet in ten minutes, or eighteen in the hour; and, at high water the surface was sixty-five feet above the bed of the river! On looking for the vessels which we had seen the preceding evening, we were told most of them were gone with the night tide.

But now we are again on board the "Fancy;" Mr. Claredge stands near the pilot, who sits next to the man at the helm. On we move swiftly for the breeze has freshened; many islands we pass in succession; the wind increases to a gale; with reefed sails we dash along, and now rapidly pass a heavily laden sloop gallantly running across our course with undiminished sail; when suddenly we see her upset. Staves and spars are floating around, and presently we observe three men scrambling up her sides, and seating themselves on the keel, where they make signals of distress to us. By this time we have run to a great distance; but Claredge, cool and prudent, as every seaman ought to be, has already issued his orders to the helmsman and crew, and now near the wind we gradually approach the sufferers. A line is thrown to them, and the next moment we are alongside the vessel. A fisher's boat, too, has noticed the disaster; and, with long strokes of her oars, advances, now rising on the curling wave, and now sinking out of sight. By our mutual efforts the men are brought on board, and the sloop is slowly towed into a safe harbor. An hour later my party was safely landed at Eastport, where, on looking over the waters, and observing the dense masses of vapor that veiled the shores, we congratulated ourselves at having escaped from the Bay of Fundy.

A Flood

Many of our larger streams, such as the Mississippi, the Ohio, the Illinois, the Arkansas, and the Red River, exhibit at certain seasons the most extensive overflowings of their waters, to which the name of *floods* is more appropriate than the term *freshets*, usually applied to the sudden risings of smaller streams. If we consider the vast extent of country through which an inland navigation is afforded by the never-failing supply of water furnished by these wonderful rivers, we cannot suppose them exceeded in magnitude by any other in the known world. It will easily be imagined what a wonderful spectacle must present itself to the eye of the traveller who for the first time views the enormous mass of waters, collected from the vast central regions of our continent, booming along, turbid and swollen to overflowing, in the broad channels of the Mississippi and Ohio, the latter of which has a course of more than a thousand miles, and the former of several thousands.

To give you some idea of a *Booming Flood* of these gigantic streams, it is necessary to state the causes which give rise to it. These are, the sudden melting of the snows on the mountains, and heavy rains continued for several weeks. When it happens that, during a severe winter, the Alleghany Mountains have been covered with snow to the depth of several feet, and the accumulated mass has remained unmelted for a length of time, the materials of a flood are thus prepared. It now and then happens that the winter is hurried off by a sudden increase of temperature, when the accumulated snows melt away simultaneously over the whole country, and the southeasterly wind, which then usually blows, brings along with it a continued fall of heavy rain, which, mingling with the dissolving snow, deluges the alluvial portions of the western country, filling up the rivulets, ravines, creeks, and small rivers. These delivering their waters to the great streams, cause the latter not merely to rise to a surprising height, but to overflow their banks, wherever the land is low. On such occasions the Ohio itself presents a splendid, and at the same time, an appalling spectacle; but when its waters mingle with those of the Mississippi, then, kind reader, is the time to view an American flood in all its astonishing magnificence.

At the foot of the Falls of the Ohio, the water has been known to rise upwards of sixty feet above its lowest level. The river, at this point, has already run a course of nearly seven hundred miles from its origin at Pittsburgh in Pennsylvania, during which it has received the waters of its numberless tributaries, and overflowing all the bottom lands or valleys, has swept along the fences and dwellings which have been unable to resist its violence. I could relate hundreds of incidents which might prove to you the dreadful effects of such an inundation, and which have been witnessed by thousands besides myself. I have known, for example, of a cow swimming through a window, elevated at least seven feet from the ground, and sixty-two feet above low-water mark. The house was then surrounded by water from the Ohio, which runs in front of it, while the neighboring country was overflowed; yet, the family did not remove from it, but remained in its upper portion, having previously taken off the sashes of the lower windows, and opened the doors. But let us return to the Mississippi.

There the overflow is astonishing, for no sooner has the water reached the upper part of the banks than it rushes out and overspreads the whole of the neighboring swamps, presenting an ocean overgrown with stupendous forest-trees. So sudden is the calamity that every individual, whether man or beast, has to exert his utmost ingenuity to enable him to escape from the dreaded element. The Indian quickly removes to the hills of the interior, the cattle and game swim to the different strips of land that remain uncovered in the midst of the flood, or attempt to force their way through the waters until they perish from fatigue. Along the banks of the river, the inhabitants have rafts ready made, on which they remove themselves, their cattle, and their provisions, and which they then fasten with ropes or grape-vines to the larger trees, while they contemplate the melancholy spectacle presented by the current, as it carries off their houses and wood-yards piece by piece. Some who have nothing to lose, and are usually known by the name of *squatters*, take this opportunity of traversing the woods in canoes, for the purpose of procuring game, and particularly the skins of animals, such as the Deer and Bear, which may be converted into money. They resort to the low ridges surrounded by the waters, and destroy thousands of Deer, merely for their skins, leaving the flesh to putrefy.

The river itself, rolling its swollen waters along, presents a spectacle of the most imposing nature. Although no large vessel, unless propelled by steam, can now make its way against the current, it is seen covered by boats, laden with produce, which, running out from all the smaller streams, float silently towards the city of New Orleans, their owners meanwhile not very well assured of finding a landing-place even there. The water is covered with yellow foam and pumice, the latter having floated from the Rocky Mountains of the Northwest. The eddies are larger and more powerful than ever. Here and there tracts of forest are observed undermined, the trees gradually giving way, and falling into the stream. Cattle, horses, Bears, and Deer are seen at times attempting to swim across the impetuous mass of foaming and boiling water; whilst here and there a Vulture or an Eagle is observed perched on a bloated carcass, tearing it up in pieces, as regardless of the flood as on former occasions it would have been of the numerous sawyers and planters with which the surface of the river is covered when the water is low. Even the steamer is frequently distressed. The numberless trees and logs that float along break its paddles, and retard its progress. Besides, it is on such occasions difficult to procure fuel to maintain its fires; and it is only at very distant intervals that a wood-yard can be found which the water has not carried off.

Following the river in your canoe, you reach those parts of the shores that are protected against the overflowings of the waters, and are called *levees*. There you find the whole population of the district at work repairing and augmenting those artificial barriers, which are several feet above the level of the fields. Every person appears to dread the opening of a *crevasse*, by which the waters may rush into his fields. In spite of all exertions, however, the crevasse opens, the water bursts impetuously over the plantations, and lays waste the crops which so lately were blooming in all the luxuriance of spring. It opens up a new channel, which, for aught I know to the contrary, may carry its waters even to the Mexican Gulf.

I have floated on the Mississippi and Ohio when thus swollen, and have in different places visited the submersed lands of the interior, propelling a light canoe by the aid of a paddle. In this manner I have traversed immense portions of the country overflowed by the waters of these rivers, and particularly when floating over the Mississippi bottom-lands I have been struck with awe at the sight. Little or no current is met with, unless when the canoe passes over the bed of a bayou. All is silent and melancholy, unless when the mournful bleating of the hemmed-in Deer reaches your ear, or the dismal scream of an Eagle or a Raven is heard, as the foul bird rises, disturbed by your approach, from the carcass on which it was allaying its craving appetite. Bears, Cougars, Lynxes, and all other quadrupeds that can ascend the trees are observed crouched among their top branches. Hungry in the midst of abundance, although they see floating around them the animals on which they usually prey, they dare not venture to swim to them. Fatigued by the exertions which they have made to reach the dry land, they will there stand the hunter's fire, as if to die by a ball were better than to perish amid the waste of waters. On occasions like this, all these animals are shot by hundreds.

Opposite the city of Natchez, which stands on a bluff bank of considerable elevation, the extent of inundated land is immense, the greater portion of the tract lying between the Mississippi and the Red River, which is more than thirty miles in breadth, being under water. The mail-bag has often been carried through the immersed forests, in a canoe, for even a greater distance, in order to be forwarded to Natchitochez.

But now, kind reader, observe this great flood gradually subsiding, and again see the mighty changes which it has effected. The waters have now been carried into the distant ocean. The earth is everywhere covered by a deep deposit of muddy loam, which in drying splits into deep and narrow chasms, presenting a reticulated appearance, and from which, as the weather becomes warmer, disagreeable, and at times noxious, exhalations arise, and fill the lower stratum of the atmosphere as with a dense fog. The banks of the river have almost everywhere been broken down in a greater or less degree. Large streams are now found to exist, where none were formerly to be seen, having forced their way in direct lines from the upper parts of the bends. These are by the navigator called *short-cuts*. Some of them have proved large enough to produce a change in the navigation of the Mississippi. If I mistake not, one of these, known by the name of the *Grand Cut-off*, and only a few miles in length, has diverted the river from its natural course, and has shortened it by fifty miles. The upper parts of the islands present a bulwark consisting of an enormous mass of floated trees of all kinds, which have lodged there.

Large sand-banks have been completely removed by the impetuous whirls of the waters, and have been deposited in other places. Some appear quite new to the eye of the navigator, who has to mark their situation and bearings in his log-book. The trees on the margins of the banks have in many parts given way. They are seen bending over the stream, like the grounded arms of an overwhelmed army of giants. Everywhere are heard the lamentations of the farmer and planter, whilst their servants and themselves are busily employed in repairing the damages occasioned by the floods. At one crevasse an old ship or two, dismantled for the purpose, are sunk, to obstruct the passage opened by the still rushing waters, while new earth is brought to fill up the chasms. The squatter is seen shouldering his rifle, and making his way through the morass, in search of his lost stock, to drive the survivors home, and save the skins of the drowned. New fences have everywhere to be formed; even new houses must be erected, to save which from a like disaster, the settler places them on an elevated platform supported by pillars made by the trunks of trees. The land must be ploughed anew, and if the season is not too far advanced, a crop of corn and potatoes may yet be raised. But the rich prospects of the planter are blasted. The traveller is impeded in his journey, the creeks and smaller streams having broken up their banks in a degree proportionate to their size. A bank of sand, which seems firm and secure, suddenly gives way beneath the traveller's horse, and the next moment the animal has sunk in the quicksand, either to the chest in front, or over the crupper behind, leaving its master in a situation not to be envied.

Unlike the mountain torrents and small rivers of other parts of the world, the Mississippi rises but slowly during these floods, continuing for several weeks to increase at the rate of about an inch a day. When at its height, it undergoes little fluctuation for some days, and after this, subsides as slowly as it rose. The usual duration of a flood is from four to six weeks, although, on some occasions, it is protracted to two months.

Every one knows how largely the idea of floods and cataclysms enters into the speculations of the geologist. If the streamlets of the European continent afford illustrations of the formation of strata, how much more must the Mississippi, with its ever-shifting sand-banks, its crumbling shores, its enormous masses of drift timber, the source of future beds of coal, its extensive and varied alluvial deposits, and its mighty mass of waters rolling sullenly along, like the flood of eternity.

The Squatters of the Mississippi

Although every European traveller who has glided down the Mississippi, at the rate of ten miles an hour, has told his tale of the squatters, yet none has given any other account of them, than that they are "a sallow, sickly looking sort of miserable beings," living in swamps, and subsisting on pig-nuts, Indian-corn, and Bear's-flesh. It is obvious, however, that none but a person acquainted with their history, manners, and condition, can give any real information respecting them.

The individuals who become squatters, choose that sort of life of their own free will. They mostly remove from other parts of the United States, after finding that land has become too high in price, and they are persons who, having a family of strong and hardy children, are anxious to enable them to provide for themselves. They have heard from good authorities that the country extending along the great streams of the West, is of all parts of the Union, the richest in its soil, the growth of its timber, and the abundance of its game; that, besides, the Mississippi is the great road to and from all the markets in the world; and that every vessel borne by its waters affords to settlers some chance of selling their commodities, or of exchanging them for others. To these recommendations is added another, of even greater weight with persons of the above denomination, namely, the prospect of being able to settle on land, and perhaps to hold it for a number of years, without purchase, rent or tax of any kind. How many thousands of individuals in all parts of the globe would gladly try their fortune with such prospects, I leave to you, reader, to determine.

As I am not disposed too highly to color the picture which I am about to submit to your inspection, instead of pitching on individuals who have removed from our eastern boundaries, and of whom certainly there are a good number, I shall introduce to you the members of a family from Virginia, first giving you an idea of their condition in that country, previous to their migration to the west. The land which they and their ancestors have possessed for a hundred years, having been constantly forced to produce crops of one kind or another, is now completely worn out. It exhibits only a superficial layer of red clay, cut up by deep ravines, through which much of the soil has been conveyed to some more fortunate neighbor, residing in a yet rich and beautiful valley. Their strenuous efforts to render it productive have failed. They dispose of everything too cumbrous or expensive for them to remove, retaining only a few horses, a servant or two, and such implements of husbandry and other articles as may be necessary on their journey, or useful when they arrive at the spot of their choice.

I think I see them at this moment harnessing their horses, and attaching them to their wagons, which are already filled with bedding, provisions, and the younger children, while on their outside are fastened spinning-wheels and looms, and a bucket filled with tar and tallow swings between the hind wheels. Several axes are secured to the bolster, and the feeding-trough of the horses contains pots, kettles, and pans. The servant, now become a driver, rides the near saddled horse, the wife is mounted on another, the worthy husband shoulders his gun, and his sons, clad in plain substantial homespun, drive the cattle ahead, and lead the procession, followed by the hounds and other dogs. Their day's journey is short, and not agreeable; the cattle, stubborn or wild, frequently leave the road for the woods, giving the travellers much trouble; the harness of the horses here and there gives way, and needs immediate repair; a basket, which has accidentally dropped, must be gone after, for nothing that they have can be spared; the roads are bad, and now and then all hands are called to push on the wagon, or prevent it from upsetting. Yet by sunset they have proceeded perhaps twenty miles. Rather fatigued, all assemble round the fire, which has been lighted, supper is prepared, and a camp being erected, there they pass the night.

Days and weeks, nay months, of unremitting toil, pass before they gain the end of their journey. They have crossed both the Carolinas, Georgia, and Alabama. They have been travelling from the beginning of May to that of September, and with heavy hearts they traverse the State of Mississippi. But now, arrived on the banks of the broad stream, they gaze in amazement on the dark deep woods around them. Boats of various kinds they see gliding downwards with the current, while others slowly ascend against it. A few inquiries are made at the nearest dwelling, and assisted by the inhabitants with their boats, and canoes, they at once cross the Mississippi, and select their place of habitation.

The exhalations arising from the swamps and morasses around them have a powerful effect on these new settlers, but all are intent on preparing for the winter. A small patch of ground is cleared by the axe and the fire, a temporary cabin is erected, to each of the cattle is attached a jingling bell before it is let loose into the neighboring cane-brake, and the horses remain about the house, where they find sufficient food at that season. The first trading-boat that stops at their landing, enables them to provide themselves with some flour, fish-hooks, and ammunition, as well as other commodities. The looms are mounted, the spinning-wheels soon furnish some yarn, and in a few weeks the family throw off their ragged clothes, and array themselves in suits adapted to the climate. The father and sons meanwhile have sown turnips and other vegetables; and from some Kentucky flatboat, a supply of live poultry has been procured.

October tinges the leaves of the forest, the morning dews are heavy, the days hot, the nights chill, and the unacclimated family in a few days are attacked with ague. The lingering disease almost prostrates their whole faculties, and one seeing them at such a period might well call them sallow and sickly. Fortunately the unhealthy season soon passes over, and the hoar-frosts make their appearance. Gradually each individual recovers strength. The largest ash-trees are felled; their trunks are cut, split, and corded in front of the building; a large fire is lighted at night on the edge of the water, and soon a steamer calls to purchase the wood, and thus add to their comforts during the winter.

The first fruit of their industry imparts new courage to them; their exertions multiply, and when spring returns, the place has a cheerful look. Venison, Bear's-flesh, Wild Turkeys, Ducks and Geese, with now and then some fish, have served to keep up their strength, and now their enlarged field is planted with corn, potatoes, and pumpkins. Their stock of cattle, too, has augmented; the steamer, which now stops there as if by preference, buys a calf or a pig, together with the whole of their wood. Their store of provisions is renewed, and brighter rays of hope enliven their spirits.

Who is he of the settlers on the Mississippi that cannot realize some profit? Truly none who is industrious. When the autumnal months return, all are better prepared to encounter the ague which then prevails. Substantial food, suitable clothing, and abundant firing, repel its attacks; and before another twelvemonth has elapsed the family is naturalized. The sons have by this time discovered a swamp covered with excellent timber, and as they have seen many great rafts of saw logs, bound for the mills of New Orleans, floating past their dwelling, they resolve to try the success of a little enterprise. Their industry and prudence have already enhanced their credit. A few cross-saws are purchased, and some broad-wheeled "carry-logs" are made by themselves. Log after log, is hauled to the bank of the river, and in a short time their first raft is made on the shore, and loaded with cord-wood. When the next freshet sets it afloat, it is secured by long grape-vines or cables, until the proper time being arrived, the husband and sons embark on it, and float down the mighty stream.

After encountering many difficulties, they arrive in safety at New Orleans, where they dispose of their stock, the money obtained for which may be said to be all profit, supply themselves with such articles as may add to their convenience or comfort, and with light hearts procure a passage on the upper deck of a steamer, at a very cheap rate, on account of the benefit of their labor in taking in wood or otherwise.

And now the vessel approaches their home. See the joyous mother and daughters as they stand on the bank! A store of vegetables lies around them, a large tub of fresh milk is at their feet, and in their hands are plates, filled with rolls of butter. As the steamer stops, three broad straw hats are waved from the upper deck, and soon husband and wife, brothers and sisters, are in each other's embrace. The boat carries off the provisions for which value has been left, and as the captain issues his orders for putting on the steam, the happy family enter their humble dwelling. The husband gives his bag of dollars to the wife, while the sons present some token of affection to the sisters. Surely, at such a moment, the squatters are richly repaid for all their labors.

Every successive year has increased their savings. They now possess a large stock of horses, cows, and hogs, with abundance of provisions, and domestic comfort of every kind. The daughters have been married to the sons of neighboring squatters, and have gained sisters to themselves by the marriage of their brothers. The government secures to the family the lands on which, twenty years before, they settled in poverty and sickness. Larger buildings are erected on piles, secure from the inundations; where a single cabin once stood, a neat village is now to be seen; warehouses, stores, and workshops increase the importance of the place. The squatters live respected, and in due time die regretted by all who knew them.

Thus are the vast frontiers of our country peopled, and thus does cultivation, year after year, extend over the western wilds. Time will no doubt be, when the great valley of the Mississippi, still covered with primeval forests interspersed with swamps, will smile with corn-fields and orchards, while crowded cities will rise at intervals along its banks, and enlightened nations will rejoice in the bounties of Providence.

Kentucky Sports

It may not be amiss, kind reader, before I attempt to give you some idea of the pleasures experienced by the sportsmen of Kentucky, to introduce the subject with a slight description of that State.

Kentucky was formerly attached to Virginia, but in those days the

Indians looked upon that portion of the western wilds as their own, and abandoned the district only when forced to do so, moving with disconsolate hearts farther into the recesses of the unexplored forests. Doubtless the richness of its soil, and the beauty of its borders, situated as they are along one of the most beautiful rivers in the world, contributed as much to attract the Old Virginians as the desire, so generally experienced in America, of spreading over the uncultivated tracts, and bringing into cultivation lands that have for unknown ages teemed with the wild luxuriance of untamed nature. The conquest of Kentucky was not performed without many difficulties. The warfare that long existed between the intruders and the Redskins was sanguinary and protracted; but the former at length made good their footing, and the latter drew off their shattered bands, dismayed by the mental superiority and indomitable courage of the white men.

This region was probably discovered by a daring hunter, the renowned Daniel Boone. The richness of its soil, its magnificent forests, its numberless navigable streams, its salt springs and licks, its saltpetre caves, its coal strata, and the vast herds of Buffaloes and Deer that browsed on its hills and amidst its charming valleys, afforded ample inducements to the new settler, who pushed forward with a spirit far above that of the most undaunted tribes which for ages had been the sole possessors of the soil.

The Virginians thronged towards the Ohio. An axe, a couple of horses, and a heavy rifle, with store of ammunition, were all that were considered necessary for the equipments of the man, who, with his family, removed to the new State, assured that, in that land of exuberant fertility, he could not fail to provide amply for all his wants. To have witnessed the industry and perseverance of these emigrants must at once have proved the vigor of their minds. Regardless of the fatigue attending every movement which they made, they pushed through an unexplored region of dark and tangled forests, guiding themselves by the sun alone, and reposing at night on the bare ground. Numberless streams they had to cross on rafts, with their wives and children, their cattle and their luggage, often drifting to considerable distances before they could effect a landing on the opposite shores. Their cattle would often stray amid the rice pasturage of these shores, and occasion a delay of several days. To these troubles add the constantly impending danger of being murdered, while asleep in their encampments, by the prowling and ruthless Indians; while they had before them a distance of hundreds of miles to be traversed, before they could reach certain places of rendezvous called *Stations*. To encounter difficulties like these must have required energies of no ordinary kind; and the reward which these veteran settlers enjoy was doubtless well merited.

Some removed from the Atlantic shores to those of the Ohio in more comfort and security. They had their wagons, their negroes, and their families. Their way was cut through the woods by their own axemen, the day before their advance, and when night overtook them, the hunters attached to the party came to the place pitched upon for encamping, loaded with the dainties of which the forest yielded an abundant supply, the blazing light of a huge fire guiding their steps as they approached, and the sounds of merriment that saluted their ears assuring them that all was well. The flesh of the Buffalo, the Bear, and the Deer soon hung, in large and delicious steaks, in front of the embers; the cakes already prepared were deposited in their proper places, and under the rich drippings of the juicy roasts were quickly baked. The wagons contained the bedding, and whilst the horses which had drawn them were turned loose to feed on the luxuriant undergrowth of the woods—some perhaps hoppled, but the greater number merely with a light bell hung to their neck, to guide their owners in the morning to the spot where they might have rambled—the party were enjoying themselves after the fatigues of the day.

In anticipation all is pleasure; and these migrating bands feasted in joyous sociality, unapprehensive of any greater difficulties than those to be encountered in forcing their way through the pathless woods to the land of abundance; and although it took months to accomplish the journey, and a skirmish now and then took place between them and the Indians, who sometimes crept unperceived into their very camp, still did the Virginians cheerfully proceed towards the western horizon, until the various groups all reached the Ohio, when, struck with the beauty of that magnificent stream, they at once commenced the task of clearing land, for the purpose of establishing a permanent residence.

Others, perhaps encumbered with too much luggage, preferred descending the stream. They prepared *arks* pierced with port-holes, and glided on the gentle current, more annoyed, however, than those who marched by land by the attacks of the Indians who watched their motions. Many travellers have described these boats, formerly called *arks*, but now named *flatboats*. But have they told you, kind reader, that in those times a boat thirty or forty feet in length, by ten or twelve in breadth, was considered a stupendous fabric; that this boat contained men, women and children, huddled together, with horses, cattle, hogs and poultry for their companions, while the remaining portion was crammed with vegetables and packages of seeds? The roof or deck of the boat was not unlike a farm-yard, being covered with hay, ploughs, carts, wagons, and various agricultural implements, together with numerous others, among which the spinning-wheels of the matrons were conspicuous. Even the sides of the floating-mass were loaded with the wheels of the different vehicles, which themselves lay on the roof. Have they told you that these boats contained the little all of each family of venturous emigrants, who, fearful of being discovered by the Indians under night moved in darkness, groping their way from one part to another of these floating habitations, denying themselves the comfort of fire or light, lest the foe that watched them from the shore should rush upon them and destroy them? Have they told you that this boat was used, after the tedious voyage was ended, as the first dwelling of these new settlers? No, kind reader, such things have not been related to you before. The travellers who have visited our country have had other objects in view.

I shall not describe the many massacres which took place among the different parties of white and red men, as the former moved down the Ohio; because I have never been very fond of battles, and indeed have always wished that the world were more peaceably inclined than it is; and shall merely add that, in one way or other, Kentucky was wrested from the original owners of the soil. Let us, therefore, turn our attention to the sports still enjoyed in that now happy portion of the United States.

We have individuals in Kentucky, kind reader, that even there are considered wonderful adepts in the management of the rifle. To *drive a nail* is a common feat, not more thought off by the Kentuckians than to cut off a Wild Turkey's head, at a distance of a hundred yards. Others will *bark* off Squirrels one after another, until satisfied with the number procured. Some, less intent on destroying game, may be seen under night *snuffing a candle* at the distance of fifty yards, off-hand, without extinguishing it. I have been told that some have proved so expert and cool as to make choice of the eye of a foe at a wonderful distance, boasting beforehand of the sureness of their piece, which has afterwards been fully proved when the enemy's head has been examined!

Having resided some years in Kentucky, and having more than once been witness of rifle sport, I shall present you with the results of my observation, leaving you to judge how far rifle-shooting is understood in that State.

Several individuals who conceive themselves expert in the management of the gun are often seen to meet for the purpose of displaying their skill, and betting a trifling sum, put up a target, in the centre of which a common-sized nail is hammered for about two-thirds of its length. The marksmen make choice of what they consider a proper distance, which may be forty paces. Each man cleans the interior of his tube, which is called *wiping* it, places a ball in the palm of his hand, pouring as much powder from his horn upon it as will cover it. This quantity is supposed to be sufficient for any distance within a hundred yards. A shot which comes very close to the nail is considered as that of an indifferent marksman; the bending of the nail is, of course, somewhat better; but nothing less than hitting it right on the head is satisfactory. Well, kind reader, one out of three shots generally hits the nail, and should the shooters amount to half a dozen, two nails are frequently needed before each can have a shot. Those who drive the nail have a further trial amongst themselves, and the two best shots out of these generally settle the affair, when all the sportsmen adjourn to some house, and spend an hour or two in friendly intercourse, appointing, before they part, a day for another trial. This is technically termed *driving the nail.*

Barking off Squirrels is delightful sport, and in my opinion requires a greater degree of accuracy than any other. I first witnessed this manner of procuring Squirrels whilst near the town of Frankfort. The performer was the celebrated Daniel Boone. We walked out together, and followed the rocky margins of the Kentucky River, until we reached a piece of flat land thickly covered with black walnuts, oaks, and hickories. As the general mast was a good one that year, Squirrels were seen gambolling on every tree around us. My companion, a stout, hale, and athletic man, dressed in a homespun hunting-shirt, bare-legged and moccasined, carried a long and heavy rifle, which, as he was loading it, he said had proved efficient in all his former undertakings, and which he hoped would not fail on this occasion, as he felt proud to show me his skill. The gun was wiped, the powder measured, the ball patched with six-hundred-thread linen, and the charge sent home with a hickory rod. We moved not a step from the place, for the Squirrels were so numerous that it was unnecessary to go after them. Boone pointed to one of these animals which had observed us, and was crouched on a branch about fifty paces distant, and bade me mark well the spot where the ball should hit. He raised his piece gradually, until the *bead* (that being the name given by the Kentuckians to the *sight*) of the barrel was brought to a line with the spot which he intended to hit. The whip-like report resounded through the woods and along the hills, in repeated echoes. Judge of my surprise when I perceived that the ball had hit the piece of the bark immediately beneath the Squirrel, and shivered it into splinters, the concussion produced by which had killed the animal, and sent it whirling through the air, as if it had been blown up by the explosion of a powder magazine. Boone kept up his firing, and, before many hours had elapsed, we had procured as many Squirrels as we wished; for you must know, kind reader, that to load a rifle requires only a moment, and that if it is wiped once after each shot, it will do duty for hours. Since that first interview with our veteran Boone I have seen many other individuals perform the same feat.

The *snuffing of a candle* with a ball, I first had an opportunity of seeing near the banks of Green River, not far from a large Pigeon-roost to which I had previously made a visit. I heard many reports of guns during the early part of a dark night, and knowing them to be those of rifles, I went towards the spot to ascertain the cause. On reaching the place, I was welcomed by a dozen of tall stout men, who told me they were exercising, for the purpose of enabling them to shoot under night at the reflected light from the eyes of a Deer or Wolf, by torchlight, of which I shall give you an account somewhere else. A fire was blazing near, the smoke of which rose curling among the thick foliage of the trees. At a distance which rendered it scarcely distinguishable, stood a burning candle, as if intended for an offering to the goddess of night, but which in reality was only fifty yards from the spot on which we all stood. One man was within a few yards of it, to watch the effects of the shots, as well as to light the candle should it chance to go out, or to replace it should the shot cut it across. Each marksman shot in his turn. Some never hit either the snuff or the candle, and were congratulated with a loud laugh; while others actually snuffed the candle without putting it out, and were recompensed for their dexterity by numerous hurrahs. One of them, who was particularly expert, was very fortunate, and snuffed the candle three times out of seven, whilst all the other shots either put out the candle or cut it immediately under the light.

Of the feats performed by the Kentuckians with the rifle, I could say more than might be expedient on the present occasion. In every thinly peopled portion of the State, it is rare to meet one without a gun of that description, as well as a tomahawk. By way of recreation, they often cut off a piece of the bark of a tree, make a target of it, using a little powder wetted with water or saliva, for the bull's-eye, and shoot into the mark all the balls they have about them, picking them out of the wood again.

After what I have said, you may easily imagine with what ease a Kentuckian procures game, or despatches an enemy, more especially when I tell you that every one in the State is accustomed to handle the rifle from the time when he is first able to shoulder it until near the close of his career. That murderous weapon is the means of procuring them subsistence during all their wild and extensive rambles, and is the source of their principal sports and pleasures.

The Traveller and the Pole-Cat

On a journey from Louisville to Henderson in Kentucky, performed during very severe winter weather, in company with a foreigner, the initials of whose name are D. T., my companion, spying a beautiful animal, marked with black and pale yellow, and having a long and bushy tail, exclaimed, "Mr. Audubon, is not that a beautiful Squirrel?" "Yes," I answered, "and of a kind that will suffer you to approach it and lay hold of it, if you are well gloved." Mr. D. T., dismounting, took up a dry stick, and advanced towards the pretty animal, with his large cloak floating in the breeze. I think I see him approach, and laying the stick gently across the body of the animal, try to secure it; and I can yet laugh almost as heartily as I did then, when I plainly saw the discomfiture of the traveller. The Pole-cat (for a true Pole-cat it was, the *Mephitis americana* of zoölogists) raised its fine bushy tail, and showered such a discharge of the fluid given him by nature as a defence that my friend, dismayed and infuriated, began to belabor the poor animal. The swiftness and good management of the Pole-cat, however, saved its bones, and as it made its retreat towards its hole, it kept up at every step a continued ejectment, which fully convinced the gentleman that the pursuit of such Squirrels as these was at the best an unprofitable employment.

This was not all, however. I could not suffer his approach, nor could my horse; it was with difficulty he mounted his own; and we were forced to continue our journey far asunder, and he much to leeward. Nor did the matter end here. We could not proceed much farther that night; as, in the first place, it was nearly dark when we saw the Pole-cat, and as, in the second place, a heavy snow-storm began, and almost impeded our progress. We were forced to make for the first cabin we saw. Having asked and obtained permission to rest for the night, we dismounted and found ourselves amongst a crowd of men and women who had met for the purpose of *corn-shucking*.

To a European who has not visited the western parts of the United States, an explanation of this corn-shucking may not be unacceptable. Corn (or you may prefer calling it maize) is gathered in the husk, that is, by breaking each large ear from the stem. These ears are first thrown into heaps in the field, and afterwards carried in carts to the barn, or, as in this instance, and in such portions of Kentucky, to a shed made of the blades or long leaves that hang in graceful curves from the stalk, and which, when plucked and dried, are used instead of hay as food for horses and cattle. The husk consists of several thick leaves rather longer than the corn-ear itself, and which secure it from the weather. It is quite a labor to detach these leaves from the ear when thousands of bushels of the corn are gathered and heaped together. For this purpose, however, and in the western country more especially, several neighboring families join alternately at each other's plantations, and assist in clearing away the husks, thus preparing the maize for the market or for domestic use.

The good people whom we met with at this hospitable house were on the point of going to the barn (the farmer here being in rather good condition) to work until towards the middle of the night. When we had stood the few stares to which strangers must accustom themselves, no matter where, even in a drawing-room, we approached the fire. What a shock for the whole party! The scent of the Pole-cat, that had been almost stifled on my companion's vestments by the cold of the evening air, now recovered its primitive strength. The cloak was put out of the house, but its owner could not well be used in the same way. The company, however, took to their heels, and there only remained a single black servant, who waited on us till supper was served.

I felt vexed with myself, as I saw the good traveller displeased. But he had so much good-breeding as to treat this important affair with great forbearance, and merely said he was sorry for his want of knowledge in zoölogy. The good gentleman, however, was not only deficient in zoölogical lore, but, fresh as he was from Europe, felt more than uneasy in this out-of-the-way house, and would have proceeded towards my own home that night, had I not at length succeeded in persuading him that he was in perfect security.

We were shown to bed. As I was almost a stranger to him, and he to me, he thought it a very awkward thing to be obliged to lie in the same bed with me, but afterwards spoke of it as a happy circumstance, and requested that I should suffer him to be placed next the logs, thinking, no doubt, that there he should run no risk.

We started by break of day, taking with us the frozen cloak, and after passing a pleasant night in my own house, we parted. Some years after, I met my Kentucky companion in a far distant land, when he assured me that whenever the sun shone on his cloak or it was brought near a fire, the scent of the Pole-cat became so perceptible that he at last gave it to a poor monk in Italy.

The animal commonly known in America by the name of the Pole-cat is about a foot and a half in length, with a large bushy tail, nearly as long as the body. The color is generally brownish-black, with a large white patch on the back of the head; but there are many varieties of coloring, in some of which the broad white bands of the back are very conspicuous. The Pole-cat burrows, or forms a subterranean habitation among the roots of trees, or in rocky places. It feeds on birds, young Hares, Rats, Mice, and other animals, and commits great depredations on poultry. The most remarkable peculiarity of this animal is the power, alluded to above, of squirting for its defence a most nauseously scented fluid contained in a receptacle situated under the tail, which it can do to a distance of several yards. It does not, however, for this purpose sprinkle its tail with the fluid, as some allege, unless when extremely harassed by its enemies. The Pole-cat is frequently domesticated. The removal of the glands prevents the secretion of the nauseous fluid, and when thus improved, the animal becomes a great favorite, and performs the offices of the common cat with great dexterity.

Deer Hunting

The different modes of Deer hunting are probably too well understood, and too successfully practised in the United States; for, notwithstanding the almost incredible abundance of these beautiful animals in our forests and prairies, such havoc is carried on amongst them that, in a few centuries, they will probably be as scarce in America as the Great Bustard now is in Britain.

We have three modes of hunting Deer, each varying in some slight degree in the different States and districts. The first is termed *still hunting*, and is by far the most destructive. The second is called *fire-light hunting*, and is next in its exterminating effects. The third, which may be looked upon as a mere amusement, is named *driving*. Although many Deer are destroyed by this latter method, it is not by any means so pernicious as the others. These methods I shall describe separately.

Still hunting is followed as a kind of trade by most of our frontiermen. To be practised with success it requires great activity, an expert management of the rifle, and a thorough knowledge of the forest, together with an intimate acquaintance with the habits of the Deer, not only at different seasons of the year, but also at every hour of the day, as the hunters must be aware of the situations which the game prefers, and in which it is most likely to be found at any particular time. I might here present you with a full account of the habits of our Deer, were it not my intention to lay before you, at some future period, in the form of a distinct work, the observations which I have made on the various quadrupeds of our extensive territories.

Illustrations of any kind require to be presented in the best possible light. We shall therefore suppose that we are now about to follow the *true hunter*, as the "still hunter" is also called, through the interior of the tangled woods, across morasses, ravines, and such places, where the game may prove more or less plentiful, even should none be found there in the first instance. We shall allow our hunter all the agility, patience, and care which his occupation requires, and will march in his rear, as if we were spies, watching all his motions.

His dress, you observe, consists of a leather hunting-shirt, and a pair of trousers of the same material. His feet are well moccasined; he wears a belt round his waist; his heavy rifle is resting on his brawny shoulder; on one side hangs his ball pouch, surmounted by the horn of an ancient Buffalo, once the terror of the herd, but now containing a pound of the best gunpowder; his butcher knife is scabbarded in the same strap; and behind is a tomahawk, the handle of which has been thrust through his girdle. He walks with so rapid a step that probably few men, beside ourselves, that is, myself and my kind reader, could follow him, unless for a short distance, in their anxiety to witness his ruthless deeds. He stops, looks to the flint of his gun, its priming, and the leather cover of the lock, then glances his eye towards the sky, to judge of the course most likely to lead him to the game.

The heavens are clear, the red glare of the morning sun gleams through the lower branches of the lofty trees, the dew hangs in pearly drops at the top of every leaf. Already has the emerald hue of the foliage been converted into the more glowing tints of our autumnal months. A slight frost appears on the fence-rails of his little cornfield. As he proceeds he looks to the dead foliage under his feet, in search of the well-known traces of a buck's hoof. Now he bends towards the ground, on which something has attracted his attention. See! he alters his course, increases his speed, and will soon reach the opposite hill. Now he moves with caution, stops at almost every tree, and peeps forward, as if already within shooting distance of the game. He advances again, but how very slowly! He has reached the declivity, upon which the sun shines in all its growing splendor; but mark him! he takes the gun from his shoulder, has already thrown aside the leathern cover of the lock, and is wiping the edge of the flint with his tongue. Now he stands like a monumental figure, perhaps measuring the distance that lies between him and the game which he has in view. His rifle is slowly raised, the report follows, and he runs. Let us run also. Shall I speak to him, and ask him the result of this first essay? Assuredly, reader, for I know him well.

"Pray, friend, what have you killed?" for to say, "What have you shot at?" might imply the possibility of having missed, and so might hurt his feelings. "Nothing but a buck." "And where is it?" "Oh, it has taken a jump or so, but I settled it, and will soon be with it. My ball struck, and must have gone through his heart." We arrive at the spot where the animal had laid itself down among the grass in a thicket of grape-vines, sumach, and spruce bushes, where it intended to repose during the middle of the day. The place is covered with blood, the hoofs of the Deer have left deep prints in the ground, as it bounced in the agonies produced by its wound; but the blood that has gushed from its side discloses the course which it has taken. We soon reach the spot. There lies the buck, its tongue out, its eye dim, its breath exhausted; it is dead. The hunter draws his knife, cuts the buck's throat almost asunder, and prepares to skin it. For this purpose he hangs it upon the branch of a tree. When the skin is removed, he cuts off the hams, and abandoning the rest of the carcass to the Wolves and Vultures, reloads his gun, flings the venison, enclosed by the skin, upon his back, secures it with a strap, and walks off in search of more game, well knowing that, in the immediate neighborhood, another at least is to be found.

Had the weather been warmer, the hunter would have sought for the buck along the *shadowy* side of the hills. Had it been the spring season, he would have led us through some thick cane-brake, to the margin of some remote lake, where you would have seen the Deer immersed to his head in the water, to save his body from the tormenting attacks of mosquitoes. Had winter overspread the earth with a covering of snow, he would have searched the low, damp woods, where the mosses and lichens, on which at that period the Deer feeds, abound; the trees being generally crusted with them for several feet from the ground. At one time he might have marked the places where the Deer clears the velvet from his horns by rubbing them against the low stems of bushes, and where he frequently scrapes the earth with his fore-hoofs; at another he would have betaken himself to places where persimmons and crab-apples abound, as beneath these trees the Deer frequently stops to munch their fruits. During early spring our hunter would imitate the bleating of the doe, and thus frequently obtain both her and the fawn, or, like some tribes of Indians, he would prepare a Deer's head, placed on a stick, and creeping with it amongst the tall grass of the prairies, would decoy Deer in reach of his rifle. But, kind reader, you have seen enough of the *still hunter*. Let it suffice for me to add that by the mode pursued by him thousands of Deer are annually killed, many individuals shooting these animals merely for the skin, not caring for even the most valuable portions of the flesh, unless hunger, or a near market, induce them to carry off the hams.

The mode of destroying deer by *fire-light*, or, as it is named in some parts of the country, *forest-light*, never fails to produce a very singular feeling in him who witnesses it for the first time. There is something in it which at times appears awfully grand. At other times a certain degree of fear creeps over the mind, and even affects the physical powers of him who follows the hunter through the thick undergrowth of our woods, having to leap his horse over hundreds of huge fallen trunks, at one time impeded by a straggling grape-vine crossing his path, at another squeezed between two stubborn saplings, whilst their twigs come smack in his face, as his companion has forced his way through them. Again, he now and then runs the risk of breaking his neck, by being suddenly pitched headlong on the ground, as his horse sinks into a hole covered over with moss. But I must proceed in a more regular manner, and leave you, kind reader, to judge whether such a mode of hunting would suit your taste or not.

The hunter has returned to his camp or his house, has rested and eaten of his game. He waits impatiently for the return of night. He has procured a quantity of pine knots filled with resinous matter, and has an old frying-pan, that, for aught I know to the contrary, may have been used by his great-grandmother, in which the pine-knots are to be placed when lighted. The horses stand saddled at the door. The hunter comes forth, his rifle slung on his shoulder, and springs upon one of them, while his son, or a servant, mounts the other with the frying-pan and the pine-knots. Thus accoutred, they proceed towards the interior of the forest. When they have arrived at the spot where the hunt is to begin, they strike fire with a flint and steel, and kindle the resinous wood. The person who carries the fire moves in the direction judged to be the best. The blaze illuminates the near objects, but the distant parts seem involved in deepest obscurity. The hunter who bears the gun keeps immediately in front, and after a while discovers before him two feeble lights, which are produced by the reflection of the pine-fire from the eyes of an animal of the Deer or Wolf kind. The animal stands quite still. To one unacquainted with this strange mode of hunting, the glare from its eyes might bring to his imagination some lost hobgoblin that had strayed from its usual haunts. The hunter, however, nowise intimidated, approaches the object, sometimes so near as to discern its form, when, raising the rifle to his shoulder, he fires and kills it on the spot. He then dismounts, secures the skin and such portions of the flesh as he may want, in the manner already described, and continues his search through the greater part of the night, sometimes until the dawn of day, shooting from five to ten Deer, should these animals be plentiful. This kind of hunting proves fatal, not to the Deer alone, but also sometimes to Wolves, and now and then to a horse or cow, which may have straggled far into the woods.

Now, kind reader, prepare to mount a generous, full-blood Virginian hunter. See that your gun is in complete order, for hark to the sound of the bugle and horn, and the mingled clamor of a pack of harriers! Your friends are waiting for you, under the shade of the wood, and we must together go *driving* the light-footed Deer. The distance over which one has to travel is seldom felt when pleasure is anticipated as the result; so galloping we go pell-mell through the woods, to some well-known place where many a fine buck has drooped its antlers under the ball of the hunter's rifle. The servants, who are called the drivers, have already begun their search. Their voices are heard exciting the hounds, and unless we put spurs to our steeds, we may be too late at our stand, and thus lose the first opportunity of shooting the fleeting game as it passes by. Hark again! The dogs are in chase, the horn sounds louder and more clearly. Hurry, hurry on, or we shall be sadly behind!

Here we are at last! Dismount, fasten your horse to this tree, place yourself by the side of that large yellow poplar, and mind you do not shoot me! The Deer is fast approaching; I will to my own stand, and he who shoots him dead wins the prize.

The Deer is heard coming. It has inadvertently cracked a dead stick with its hoof, and the dogs are now so near that it will pass in a moment. There it comes! How beautifully it bounds over the ground! What a splendid head of horns! How easy its attitudes, depending, as it seems to do, on its own swiftness for safety! All is in vain, however; a gun is fired, the animal plunges and doubles with incomparable speed. There he goes! He passes another stand, from which a second shot, better directed than the first, brings him to the ground. The dogs, the servants, the sportsmen are now rushing forward to the spot. The hunter who has shot it is congratulated on his skill or good luck, and the chase begins again in some other part of the woods.

A few lines of explanation may be required to convey a clear idea of this mode of hunting. Deer are fond of following and retracing paths which they have formerly pursued, and continue to do so even after they have been shot at more than once. These tracks are discovered by persons on horseback in the woods, or a Deer is observed crossing a road, a field, or a small stream. When this has been noticed twice, the deer may be shot from the places called *stands* by the sportsman, who is stationed there, and waits for it, a line of stands being generally formed so as to cross the path which the game will follow. The person who ascertains the usual pass of the game, or discovers the parts where the animal feeds or lies down during the day, gives intimation to his friends, who then prepare for the chase. The servants start the Deer with the hounds, and by good management generally succeed in making it run the course that will soonest bring it to its death. But, should the Deer be cautious, and take another course, the hunters, mounted on swift horses, gallop through the woods to intercept it, guided by the sound of the horns and the cry of the dogs, and frequently succeed in shooting it. This sport is extremely agreeable, and proves successful on almost every occasion.

Hoping that this account will be sufficient to induce you, kind reader, to go *driving* in our western and southern woods, I now conclude my chapter on Deer Hunting by informing you that the species referred to above is the Virginia Deer, *Cervus virginianus*; and that, until I be able to present you with a full account of its habits and history, you may consult for information respecting it the excellent "Fauna Americana" of my esteemed friend Dr. Harlan, of Philadelphia.

The Eccentric Naturalist

"What an odd-looking fellow!" said I to myself, as, while walking by the river, I observed a man landing from a boat, with what I thought a bundle of dried clover on his back; "how the boatmen stare at him! sure he must be an original!" He ascended with a rapid step, and approaching me asked if I could point out the house in which Mr. Audubon resided. "Why, I am the man," said I, "and will gladly lead you to my dwelling."

The traveller rubbed his hands together with delight, and drawing a letter from his pocket handed it to me without any remark. I broke the seal and read as follows: "My dear Audubon, I send you an odd fish, which you may prove to be undescribed, and hope you will do so in your next letter. Believe, me always your friend B." With all the simplicity of a woodsman I asked the bearer where the odd fish was, when M. de T. (for, kind reader, the individual in my presence was none else than that renowned naturalist) smiled, rubbed his hands, and with the greatest good-humor said, "I am that odd fish I presume, Mr. Audubon." I felt confounded and blushed, but contrived to stammer an apology.

We soon reached the house, when I presented my learned guest to my family, and was ordering a servant to go to the boat for M. de T.'s luggage, when he told me he had none but what he brought on his back. He then loosened the pack of weeds which had first drawn my attention. The ladies were a little surprised, but I checked their critical glances for the moment. The naturalist pulled off his shoes, and while engaged in drawing his stockings, not up, but down, in order to cover the holes about the heels, told us in the gayest mood imaginable that he had walked a great distance, and had only taken a passage on board the *ark*, to be put on this shore, and that he was sorry his apparel had suffered so much from his late journey. Clean clothes were offered, but he would not accept them, and it was with evident reluctance that he performed the lavations usual on such occasions before he sat down to dinner.

At table, however, his agreeable conversation made us all forget his singular appearance; and, indeed, it was only as we strolled together in the garden that his attire struck me as exceedingly remarkable. A long loose coat of yellow nankeen, much the worse for the many rubs it had got in its time, and stained all over with the juice of plants, hung loosely about him like a sac. A waistcoat of the same, with enormous pockets, and buttoned up to his chin, reached below over a pair of tight pantaloons, the lower parts of which were buttoned down to the ankles. His beard was as long as I have known my own to be during some of my peregrinations, and his lank black hair hung loosely over his shoulders. His forehead was so broad and prominent that any tyro in phrenology would instantly have pronounced it the residence of a mind of strong powers. His words impressed an assurance of rigid truth, and as he directed the conversation to the study of the natural sciences, I listened to him with as much delight as Telemachus could have listened to Mentor. He had come to visit me, he said, expressly for the purpose of seeing my drawings, having been told that my representations of birds were accompanied with those of shrubs and plants, and he was desirous of knowing whether I might chance to have in my collection any with which he was unacquainted. I observed some degree of impatience in his request to be allowed at once to see what I had. We returned to the house, when I opened my portfolios and laid them before him.

He chanced to turn over the drawing of a plant quite new to him. After inspecting it closely, he shook his head, and told me no such plant existed in nature; for, kind reader, M. de T., although a highly scientific man, was suspicious to a fault, and believed such plants only to exist as he had himself seen, or such as, having been discovered of old, had, according to Father Malebranche's expression, acquired a "venerable beard." I told my guest that the plant was common in the immediate neighborhood, and that I should show it him on the morrow. "And why to-morrow, Mr. Audubon? Let us go now." We did so, and on reaching the bank of the river I pointed to the plant. M. de T., I thought, had gone mad. He plucked the plants one after another, danced, hugged me in his arms, and exultingly told me that he had got not merely a new species, but a new genus. When we returned home, the naturalist opened the bundle which he had brought on his back, and took out a journal rendered water-proof by means of a leather case, together with a small parcel of linen, examined the new plant, and wrote its description. The examination of my drawings then went on. You would be pleased, kind reader, to hear his criticisms, which were of the greatest advantage to me, for, being well acquainted with books as well as with nature, he was well fitted to give me advice.

It was summer, and the heat was so great that the windows were all open. The light of the candles attracted many insects, among which was observed a large species of Scarabæus. I caught one, and, aware of his inclination to believe only what he should himself see, I showed him the insect, and assured him it was so strong that it would crawl on the table with the candlestick on its back. "I should like to see the experiment made, Mr. Audubon," he replied. It was accordingly made, and the insect moved about, dragging its burden so as to make the candlestick change its position as if by magic, until coming upon the edge of the table, it dropped on the floor, took to wing, and made its escape.

When it waxed late, I showed him to the apartment intended for him during his stay, and endeavored to render him comfortable, leaving him writing materials in abundance. I was indeed heartily glad to have a naturalist under my roof. We had all retired to rest. Every person I imagined was in deep slumber save myself, when of a sudden I heard a great uproar in the naturalist's room. I got up, reached the place in a few moments, and opened the door, when to my astonishment, I saw my guest running about the room naked, holding the handle of my favorite violin, the body of which he had battered to pieces against the walls in attempting to kill the bats which had entered by the open window, probably attracted by the insects flying around his candle. I stood amazed, but he continued jumping and running round and round, until he was fairly exhausted, when he begged me to procure one of the animals for him, as he felt convinced they belonged to "a new species." Although I was convinced of the contrary, I took up the bow of my demolished

Cremona, and administering a smart tap to each of the bats as it came up, soon got specimens enough. The war ended, I again bade him good-night, but could not help observing the state of the room. It was strewed with plants, which it would seem he had arranged into groups, but which were now scattered about in confusion. "Never mind, Mr. Audubon," quoth the eccentric naturalist, "never mind, I'll soon arrange them again. I have the bats, and that's enough."

Some days passed, during which we followed our several occupations. M. de T. searched the woods for plants, and I for birds. He also followed the margins of the Ohio, and picked up many shells, which he greatly extolled. With us, I told him, they were gathered into heaps to be converted into lime. "Lime! Mr. Audubon; why, they are worth a guinea apiece in any part of Europe." One day, as I was returning from a hunt in a cane-brake, he observed that I was wet and spattered with mud, and desired me to show him the interior of one of these places, which he said he had never visited.

The cane, kind reader, formerly grew spontaneously over the greater portions of the State of Kentucky and other western districts of our Union, as well as in many farther south. Now, however, cultivation, the introduction of cattle and horses, and other circumstances connected with the progress of civilization, have greatly altered the face of the country, and reduced the cane within comparatively small limits. It attains a height of from twelve to thirty feet, and a diameter of from one to two inches, and grows in great patches resembling osier-holts, in which occur plants of all sizes. The plants frequently grow so close together, and in course of time become so tangled, as to present an almost impenetrable thicket. A portion of ground thus covered with canes is called a *cane-brake.*

If you picture to yourself one of these cane-brakes growing beneath the gigantic trees that form our western forests, interspersed with vines of many species, and numberless plants of every description, you may conceive how difficult it is for one to make his way through it, especially after a heavy shower of rain or a fall of sleet, when the traveller, in forcing his way through, shakes down upon himself such quantities of water as soon reduce him to a state of the utmost discomfort. The hunters often cut little paths through the thickets with their knives, but the usual mode of passing through them is by pushing one's self backward, and wedging a way between the stems. To follow a Bear or a Cougar pursued by dogs through these brakes is a task the accomplishment of which may be imagined, but of the difficulties and dangers accompanying which I cannot easily give an adequate representation.

The canes generally grow on the richest soil, and are particularly plentiful along the margins of the great western rivers. Many of our new settlers are fond of forming farms in their immediate vicinity, as the plant is much relished by all kinds of cattle and horses, which feed upon it at all seasons, and again because these brakes are plentifully stocked with game of various kinds. It sometimes happens that the farmer clears a portion of the brake. This is done by cutting the stems—which are fistular and knotted, like those of other grasses—with a large knife or cutlass. They are afterwards placed in heaps, and when partially dried set fire to. The moisture contained between the joints is converted into steam, which causes the cane to burst with a smart report, and when a whole mass is crackling, the sounds resemble discharges of musketry. Indeed, I have been told that travellers floating down the rivers, and unacquainted with these circumstances, have been induced to pull their oars with redoubled vigor, apprehending the attack of a host of savages, ready to scalp every one of the party.

A day being fixed, we left home after an early breakfast, crossed the Ohio, and entered the woods. I had determined that my companion should view a cane-brake in all its perfection, and after leading him several miles in a direct course, came upon as fine a sample as existed in that part of the country. We entered, and for some time proceeded without much difficulty, as I led the way, and cut down the canes which were most likely to incommode him. The difficulties gradually increased, so that we were presently obliged to turn our backs to the foe, and push ourselves on the best way we could. My companion stopped here and there to pick up a plant and examine it. After a while we chanced to come upon the top of a fallen tree, which so obstructed our passage that we were on the eve of going round, instead of thrusting ourselves through amongst the branches, when, from its bed in the centre of the tangled mass, forth rushed a Bear, with such force, and snuffing the air in so frightful a manner, that M. de T. became suddenly terror-struck, and, in his haste to escape, made a desperate attempt to run, but fell amongst the canes in such a way that he looked as if pinioned. Perceiving him jammed in between the stalks, and thoroughly frightened, I could not refrain from laughing at the ridiculous exhibition which he made. My gayety, however, was not very pleasing to the *savant*, who called out for aid, which was at once administered. Gladly would he have retraced his steps, but I was desirous that he should be able to describe a cane-brake, and enticed him to follow me by telling him that our worst difficulties were nearly over. We proceeded, for by this time the Bear was out of hearing.

The way became more and more tangled. I saw with delight that a heavy cloud, portentous of a thunder gust, was approaching. In the mean time, I kept my companion in such constant difficulties that he now panted, perspired, and seemed almost overcome by fatigue. The thunder began to rumble, and soon after a dash of heavy rain drenched us in a few minutes. The withered particles of leaves and bark attached to the canes stuck to our clothes. We received many scratches from briers, and now and then a switch from a nettle. M. de T. seriously inquired if we should ever get alive out of the horrible situation in which we were. I spoke of courage and patience, and told him I hoped we should soon get to the margin of the brake, which, however, I knew to be two miles distant. I made him rest, and gave him a mouthful of brandy from my flask; after which, we proceeded on our slow and painful march. He threw away all his plants, emptied his pockets of the fungi, lichens, and mosses which he had thrust into them, and finding himself much lightened, went on for thirty or forty yards with a better grace. But, kind reader, enough—I led the naturalist first one way, then another, until I had nearly lost myself in the brake, although I was well acquainted with it, kept him tumbling and crawling on his hands and knees until long after mid-day, when we at length reached the edge of the river. I blew my horn, and soon showed my companion a boat coming to our rescue. We were ferried over, and on reaching the house, found more agreeable occupation in replenishing our empty coffers.

M. de T. remained with us for three weeks, and collected multitudes of plants, shells, bats, and fishes, but never again expressed a desire of visiting a cane-brake. We were perfectly reconciled to his oddities, and, finding him a most agreeable and intelligent companion, hoped that his sojourn might be of long duration. But, one evening when tea was prepared, and we expected him to join the family, he was nowhere to be found. His grasses and other valuables were all removed from his room. The night was spent in searching for him in the neighborhood. No eccentric naturalist could be discovered. Whether he had perished in a swamp, or had been devoured by a Bear or a Gar-fish, or had taken to his heels, were matters of conjecture; nor was it until some weeks after that a letter from him, thanking us for our attention, assured me of his safety.

Scipio and the Bear

The Black Bear (*Ursus americanus*), however clumsy in appearance, is active, vigilant, and persevering; possesses great strength, courage, and address; and undergoes with little injury the greatest fatigues and hardships in avoiding the pursuit of the hunter. Like the Deer, it changes its haunts with the seasons, and for the same reason, namely, the desire of obtaining suitable food, or of retiring to the more inaccessible parts, where it can pass the time in security, unobserved by man, the most dangerous of its enemies. During the spring months, it searches for food in the low rich alluvial lands that border the rivers, or by the margins of such inland lakes as, on account of their small size, are called by us ponds. There it procures abundance of succulent roots, and of the tender juicy stems of plants, upon which it chiefly feeds at that season. During the summer heat, it enters the gloomy swamps, passes much of its time in wallowing in the mud, like a hog, and contents itself with crayfish, roots, and nettles, now and then, when hard pressed by hunger, seizing on a young pig, or perhaps a sow, or even a calf. As soon as the different kinds of berries which grow on the mountains begin to ripen, the Bears betake themselves to the high grounds, followed by their cubs. In such retired parts of the country where there are no hilly grounds, it pays visits to the maize fields, which it ravages for a while. After this, the various species of nuts, acorns, grapes, and other forest fruits, that form what in the western country is called *mast*, attract its attention. The Bear is then seen rambling singly through the woods to gather this harvest, not forgetting meanwhile to rob every *Bee-tree* it meets with, Bears being, as you well know, expert at this operation. You also know that they are good climbers, and may have been told, or at least may now be told, that the Black Bear now and then *houses* itself in the hollow trunks of the larger trees for weeks together, when it is said to suck its paws. You are probably not aware of a habit in which it indulges, and which, being curious, must be interesting to you.

At one season, the Black Bear may be seen examining the lower part of the trunk of a tree for several minutes with much attention, at the same time looking around, and snuffing the air, to assure itself that no enemy is near. It then raises itself on its hind-legs, approaches the trunk, embraces it with its fore-legs, and scratches the bark with its teeth and claws for several minutes in continuance. Its jaws clash against each other, until a mass of foam runs down on both sides of the mouth. After this it continues its rambles.

In various portions of our country, many of our woodsmen and hunters who have seen the Bear performing the singular operation just described, imagine that it does so for the purpose of leaving behind it an indication of its size and power. They measure the height at which the scratches are made, and in this manner can, in fact, form an estimate of the magnitude of the individual. My own opinion, however, is different. It seems to me that the Bear scratches the trees, not for the purpose of shewing its size or its strength, but merely for that of sharpening its teeth and claws, to enable it better to encounter a rival of its own species during the amatory season. The Wild Boar of Europe clashes its tusks and scrapes the earth with its feet, and the Deer rubs its antlers against the lower part of the stems of young trees or bushes, for the same purpose.

Being one night sleeping in the house of a friend, I was wakened by a negro servant bearing a light, who gave me a note, which he said his master had just received. I ran my eye over the paper, and found it to be a communication from a neighbor, requesting my friend and myself to join him as soon as possible, and assist in killing some Bears at that moment engaged in destroying his corn. I was not long in dressing, you may be assured, and, on entering the parlor, found my friend equipped and only waiting for some bullets, which a negro was employed in casting. The overseer's horn was heard calling up the negroes from their different cabins. Some were already engaged in saddling our horses, whilst others were gathering all the cur-dogs of the plantation. All was bustle. Before half an hour had elapsed, four stout negro men, armed with axes and knives, and mounted on strong nags of their own (for you must know, kind reader, that many of our slaves rear horses, cattle, pigs, and poultry, which are exclusively their own property), were following us at a round gallop through the woods, as we made directly for the neighbor's plantation, a little more than five miles off.

The night was none of the most favorable, a drizzling rain rendering the atmosphere thick and rather sultry; but as we were well acquainted with the course, we soon reached the house, where the owner was waiting our arrival. There were now three of us armed with guns, half a dozen servants, and a good pack of dogs of all kinds. We jogged on towards the detached field in which the Bears were at work. The owner told us that for some days several of these animals had visited his corn, and that a negro who was sent every afternoon to see at what part of the enclosure they entered, had assured him there were at least five in the field that night. A plan of attack was formed: the bars at the usual gap of the fence were to be put down without noise; the men and dogs were to divide, and afterwards proceed so as to surround the Bears, when, at the sounding of our horns, every one was to charge towards the centre of the field, and shout as loudly as possible, which it was judged would so intimidate the animals as to induce them to seek refuge upon the dead trees with which the field was still partially covered.

The plan succeeded. The horns sounded, the horses galloped forward, the men shouted, the dogs barked and howled. The shrieks of the negroes were enough to frighten a legion of Bears, and those in the field took to flight, so that by the time we reached the centre they were heard hurrying towards the tops of the trees. Fires were immediately lighted by the negroes. The drizzling rain had ceased, the sky cleared, and the glare of the crackling fires proved of great assistance to us. The Bears had been so terrified that we now saw several of them crouched at the junction of the larger boughs with the trunks. Two were immediately shot down. They were cubs of no great size, and being already half dead, we left them to the dogs, which quickly despatched them.

We were anxious to procure as much sport as possible, and having observed one of the Bears, which from its size we conjectured to be the mother, ordered the negroes to cut down the tree on which it was perched, when it was intended the dogs should have a tug with it, while we should support them, and assist in preventing the Bear from escaping by wounding it in one of the hind-legs. The surrounding woods now echoed to the blows of the axemen. The tree was large and tough, having been girded more than two years, and the operation of felling it seemed extremely tedious. However, it began to vibrate at each stroke; a few inches alone now supported it; and in a short time it came crashing to the ground, in so awful a manner that Bruin must doubtless have felt the shock as severe as we should feel a shake of the globe produced by the sudden collision of a comet.

The dogs rushed to the charge, and harassed the Bear on all sides. We had remounted, and now surrounded the poor animal. As its life depended upon its courage and strength, it exercised both in the most energetic manner. Now and then it seized a dog, and killed him by a single stroke. At another time, a well administered blow of one of its fore-legs sent an assailant off yelping so piteously that he might be looked upon as *hors de combat.* A cur had daringly ventured to seize the Bear by the snout, and was seen hanging to it, covered with blood, whilst a dozen or more scrambled over its back. Now and then the infuriated animal was seen to cast a revengeful glance at some of the party, and we had already determined to despatch it, when, to our astonishment, it suddenly shook off all the dogs, and, before we could fire, charged upon one of the negroes, who was mounted on a pied horse. The Bear seized the steed with teeth and claws, and clung to its breast. The terrified horse snorted and plunged. The rider, an athletic young man, and a capital horseman, kept his seat, although only saddled on a sheep's-skin tightly girthed, and requested his master not to fire at the

Bear. Notwithstanding his coolness and courage, our anxiety for his safety was raised to the highest pitch, especially when in a moment we saw rider and horse come to the ground together; but we were instantly relieved on witnessing the masterly manner in which Scipio despatched his adversary, by laying open his skull with a single well-directed blow of his axe, when a deep growl announced the death of the Bear, and the valorous negro sprung to his feet unhurt.

Day dawned, and we renewed our search. Two of the remaining Bears were soon discovered, lodged in a tree about a hundred yards from the spot where the last one had been overpowered. On approaching them in a circle, we found that they manifested no desire to come down, and we resolved to try *smoking*. We surrounded the tree with a pile of brushwood and large branches. The flames ascended and caught hold of the dry bark. At length the tree assumed the appearance of a pillar of flame. The Bears mounted to the top branches. When they had reached the uppermost, they were seen to totter, and soon after, the branch cracking and snapping across, they came to the ground, bringing with them a mass of broken twigs. They were cubs, and the dogs soon worried them to death.

The party returned to the house in triumph. Scipio's horse, being severely wounded, was let loose in the field, to repair his strength by eating the corn. A cart was afterwards sent for the game. But before we had left the field, the horses, dogs, and Bears, together with the fires, had destroyed more corn within a few hours than the poor Bear and her cubs had during the whole of their visits.

A Kentucky Barbecue

Beargrass Creek, which is one of the many beautiful streams of the highly cultivated and happy State of Kentucky, meanders through a deeply shaded growth of majestic beechwoods, in which are interspersed various species of walnut, oak, elm, ash, and other trees, extending on either side of its course. The spot on which I witnessed the celebration of an anniversary of the glorious proclamation of our independence is situated on its banks near the city of Louisville. The woods spread their dense tufts towards the shores of the fair Ohio on the west, and over the gently rising grounds to the south and east. Every open spot forming a plantation was smiling in the luxuriance of a summer harvest. The farmer seemed to stand in admiration of the spectacle; the trees of his orchards bowed their branches, as if anxious to restore to their mother earth the fruit with which they were laden; the flocks leisurely ruminated as they lay on their grassy beds; and the genial warmth of the season seemed inclined to favor their repose.

The free, single-hearted Kentuckian, bold, erect, and proud of his Virginian descent, had, as usual, made arrangements for celebrating the day of his country's independence. The whole neighborhood joined with one consent. No personal invitation was required where every one was welcomed by his neighbor, and from the governor to the guider of the plough, all met with light hearts and merry faces.

It was indeed a beautiful day; the bright sun rode in the clear blue heavens; the gentle breezes wafted around the odors of the gorgeous flowers; the little birds sang their sweetest songs in the woods, and the fluttering insects danced in the sunbeams. Columbia's sons and daughters seemed to have grown younger that morning. For a whole week or more many servants and some masters had been busily engaged in clearing an area. The undergrowth had been carefully cut down, the low boughs lopped off, and the grass alone, verdant and gay, remained to carpet the sylvan pavilion. Now the wagons were seen slowly moving along under their load of provisions which had been prepared for the common benefit. Each denizen had freely given his ox, his ham, his venison, his Turkeys and other fowls. Here were to be seen flagons of every beverage used in the country; "la belle rivière" had opened her finny stores, the melons of all sorts, peaches, plums, and pears, would have sufficed to stock a market. In a word, Kentucky, the land of abundance, had supplied a feast for her children. A purling stream gave its waters freely, while the grateful breezes cooled the air. Columns of smoke from the newly kindled fires rose above the trees; fifty cooks or more moved to and fro as they plied their trade; waiters of all qualities were disposing the dishes, the glasses and the punch-bowls, amid vases filled with rich wines. "Old Monongahela" filled many a barrel for the crowd. And now the roasting viands perfume the air, and all appearances conspire to predict the speedy commencement of a banquet such as may suit the vigorous appetite of American woodsmen. Every steward is at his post ready to receive the joyous groups that at this moment begin to emerge from the dark recesses of the woods.

Each comely fair one, clad in pure white, is seen advancing under the protection of her sturdy lover, the neighing of their prancing steeds proclaiming how proud they are of their burden. The youthful riders leap from their seats, and the horses are speedily secured by twisting their bridles round a branch. As the youth of Kentucky lightly and gayly advanced towards the barbecue, they resembled a procession of nymphs and disguised divinities. Fathers and mothers smiled upon them as they followed the brilliant cortége. In a short time the ground was alive with merriment. A great wooden cannon bound with iron hoops was now crammed with home-made powder; fire was conveyed to it by means of a train, and as the explosion burst forth, thousands of hearty huzzas mingled with its echoes. From the most learned a good oration fell in proud and gladdening words on every ear, and although it probably did not equal the eloquence of a Clay, an Everett, a Webster, or a Preston, it served to remind every Kentuckian present of the glorious name, the patriotism, the courage, and the virtue of our immortal Washington. Fifes and drums sounded the march which had ever led him to glory; and as they changed to our celebrated "Yankee-Doodle," the air again rang with acclamations.

Now the stewards invited the assembled throngs to the feast. The fair led the van, and were first placed around the tables, which groaned under the profusion of the best productions of the country that had been heaped upon them. On each lovely nymph attended her gay beau, who in her chance or sidelong glances ever watched an opportunity of reading his happiness. How the viands diminished under the action of so many agents of destruction, I need not say, nor is it necessary that you should listen to the long recital. Many a national toast was offered and accepted, many speeches were delivered, and many essayed in amicable reply. The ladies then retired to booths that had been erected at a little distance, to which they were conducted by their partners, who returned to the table, and having thus cleared for action, recommenced a series of hearty rounds. However, as Kentuckians are neither slow nor long at their meals, all were in a few minutes replenished, and after a few more draughts from the bowl, they rejoined the ladies and prepared for the dance.

Double lines of a hundred fair ones extended along the ground in the most shady part of the woods, while here and there smaller groups awaited the merry trills of reels and cotillons. A burst of music from violins, clarionets, and bugles gave the welcome notice, and presently the whole assemblage seemed to be gracefully moving through the air. The "hunting-shirts" now joined in the dance, their fringed skirts keeping time with the gowns of the ladies, and the married people of either sex stepped in and mixed with their children. Every countenance beamed with joy, every heart leaped with gladness; no pride, no pomp, no affectation were there; their spirits brightened as they continued their exhilarating exercise, and care and sorrow were flung to the winds. During each interval of rest refreshments of all sorts were handed round, and while the fair one cooled her lips with the grateful juice of the melon, the hunter of Kentucky quenched his thirst with ample draughts of well-tempered punch.

I know, reader, that had you been with me on that day you would have richly enjoyed the sight of this national *fête champêtre.* You would have listened with pleasure to the ingenuous tale of the lover, the wise talk of the elder on the affairs of the State, the accounts of improvement in stock and utensils, and the hopes of continued prosperity to the country at large, and to Kentucky in particular. You would have been pleased to see those who did not join in the dance shooting at distant marks with their heavy rifles, or watched how they showed off the superior speed of their high bred "Old Virginia" horses, while others recounted their hunting exploits, and at intervals made the woods ring with their bursts of laughter. With me the time sped like an arrow in its flight, and although more than twenty years have elapsed since I joined a Kentucky barbecue, my spirit is refreshed every Fourth of July by the recollection of that day's merriment.

But now the sun has declined, and the shades of evening creep over the scene. Large fires are lighted in the woods, casting the long shadows of the live columns far along the trodden ground, and flaring on the happy groups loath to separate. In the still, clear sky, begin to sparkle the distant lamps of heaven. One might have thought that Nature herself smiled on the joy of her children. Supper now appeared on the tables, and after all had again refreshed themselves, preparations were made for departure. The lover hurried for the steed of his fair one, the hunter seized the arm of his friend, families gathered into loving groups, and all returned in peace to their happy homes.

And now, reader, allow me also to take my leave, and wish you good-night, trusting that when I again appear with another volume, you will be ready to welcome me with a cordial greeting.

A Raccoon Hunt in Kentucky

The Raccoon, which is a cunning and crafty animal, is found in all our woods, so that its name is familiar to every child in the Union. The propensity which it evinces to capture all kinds of birds accessible to it in its nightly prowlings, for the purpose of feasting on their flesh, induces me to endeavor to afford you some idea of the pleasure which our western hunters feel in procuring it. With your leave, then, reader, I will take you to a "Coon Hunt."

A few hours ago the sun went down far beyond the "far west." The woodland choristers have disappeared, the matron has cradled her babe, and betaken herself to the spinning-wheel; the woodsman, his sons, and "the stranger," are chatting before a blazing fire, making wise reflections on past events, and anticipating those that are to come. Autumn, sallow and sad, prepares to bow her head to the keen blast of approaching winter; the corn, though still on its stalk, has lost its blades; the woodpile is as large as the woodsman's cabin; the nights have become chill, and each new morn has effected a gradual change in the dews, which now crust the withered herbage with a coat of glittering white. The sky is still cloudless; a thousand twinkling stars reflect their light from the tranquil waters; all is silent and calm in the forest, save the nightly prowlers that roam in its recesses. In the cheerful cabin all is happiness; its inmates generously strive to contribute to the comfort of the stranger who has chanced to visit them; and, as Raccoons are abundant in the neighborhood, they propose a hunt. The offer is gladly accepted. The industrious woman leaves her wheel, for she has listened to her husband's talk; now she approaches the fire, takes up the board shovel, stirs the embers, produces a basket filled with sweet potatoes, arranges its contents side by side in front of the hearth, and covers them with hot ashes and glowing coals. All this she does because she "guesses" that hungry stomachs will be calling for food when the sport is over. Ah! reader, what "homely joys" there are in such scenes, and how you would enjoy them! The rich may produce a better, or a more sumptuous meal, but his feelings can never be like those of the poor woodsman. Poor, I ought not to call him, for nature and industry bountifully supply all his wants; the woods and rivers produce his chief dainties, and his toils are his pleasures.

Now mark him! the bold Kentuckian is on his feet; his sons and the stranger prepare for the march. Horns and rifles are in requisition. The good man opens the wooden-hinged door, and sends forth a blast loud enough to scare a Wolf. The Raccoons scamper away from the cornfields, break through the fences, and hie to the woods. The hunter has taken an axe from the wood-pile, and returning, assures us that the night is fine, and that we shall have rare sport. He blows through his rifle to ascertain that it is clear, examines his flint, and thrusts a feather into the touch-hole. To a leathern bag swung at his side is attached a powder-horn; his sheath-knife is there also; below hangs a narrow strip of homespun linen. He takes from his bag a bullet, pulls with his teeth the wooden stopper from his powder-horn, lays the ball on one hand, and with the other pours the powder upon it until it is just overtopped. Raising the horn to his mouth, he again closes it with the stopper, and restores it to its place. He introduces the powder into the tube; springs the box of his gun, greases the "patch" over with some melted tallow, or damps it; then places it on the honey-combed muzzle of his piece. The bullet is placed on the patch over the bore, and pressed with the handle of the knife, which now trims the edge of the linen. The elastic hickory rod, held with both hands, smoothly pushes the ball to its bed; once, twice, thrice has it rebounded. The rifle leaps as it were into the hunter's arms, the feather is drawn from the touch-hole, the powder fills the pan, which is closed. "Now I'm ready," cries the woodsman. His companions say the same. Hardly more than a minute has elapsed. I wish, reader, you had seen this fine fellow—but hark! the dogs are barking.

All is now bustle within and without; a servant lights a torch, and off we march to the woods. "Don't mind the boys, my dear sir," says the woodsman, "follow me close, for the ground is covered with logs, and the grapevines hang everywhere across. Toby, hold up the light, man, or we'll never see the gullies. Trail your gun, sir, as General Clark used to say—not so, but this way—that's it; now then, no danger, you see; no fear of snakes, poor things! They are stiff enough, I'll be bound. The dogs have treed one. Toby, you old fool, why don't you turn to the right?—not so much; there—go ahead, and give us light. What's that? Who's there? Ah, you young rascals! you've played us a trick, have you? It's all well enough, but now just keep behind, or I'll—" And, in fact, the boys, with eyes good enough to see in the dark, although not quite so well as an Owl's, had cut directly across the dogs, which had surprised a Raccoon on the ground, and bayed it until the lads knocked it on the head. "Seek him, boys!" cried the hunter. The dogs, putting their noses to the ground, pushed off at a good rate. "Master, they're making for the creek," says old Toby. On towards it therefore we push. What woods, to be sure! No gentleman's park this, I assure you, reader. We are now in a low flat; the soil thinly covers the hard clay; nothing but beech-trees hereabouts, unless now and then a maple. Hang the limbs! say I—hang the supple-jacks too—here I am, fast by the neck; cut it with your knife. My knee has had a tremendous rub against a log; now my foot is jammed between two roots; and here I stick. "Toby, come back; don't you know the stranger is not up to the woods? Halloo, Toby, Toby!" There I stood perfectly shackled, the hunter laughing heartily, and the lads glad of an opportunity of slipping off. Toby arrived, and held the torch near the ground, on which the hunter, cutting one of the roots with his hatchet, set me free. "Are you hurt, sir?"—"No, not in the least." Off we start again. The boys had got up with the dogs, which were baying a Raccoon in a small puddle. We soon joined them with the light. "Now, stranger, watch and see!" The Raccoon was all but swimming, and yet had hold of the bottom of the pool with his feet. The glare of the lighted torch was doubtless distressing to him; his coat was ruffled, and his rounded tail seemed thrice its ordinary size; his eyes shone like emeralds; with foaming jaws he watched the dogs, ready to seize each by the snout if it came within reach. They kept him busy for several minutes; the water became thick with mud; his coat now hung dripping, and his draggled tail lay floating on the surface. His guttural growlings, in place of intimidating his assailants excited them the more; and they very unceremoniously closed upon him, curs as they were, and without the breeding of gentle dogs. One seized him by the rump, and tugged, but was soon forced to let go; another stuck to his side, but soon taking a better directed bite of his muzzle than another dog had just done of his tail, Coon made him yelp; and pitiful were the cries of luckless Tyke. The Raccoon would not let go, but in the mean time the other dogs seized him fast, and worried him to death, yet to the last he held by his antagonist's snout. Knocked on the head by an axe, he lay gasping his last breath, and the heaving of his chest was painful to see. The hunters stood gazing at him in the pool, while all around was by the flare of the torch rendered trebly dark and dismal. It was a good scene for a skilful painter.

We had now two Coons, whose furs were worth two quarters of a dollar, and whose bodies, which I must not forget, as Toby informed us, were worth two more. "What now?" I asked. "What now?" quoth the father; "why, go after more, to be sure." So we did, the dogs ahead, and I far behind. In a short time the curs treed another, and when we came up, we found them seated on their haunches, looking upwards, and barking. The hunters now employed their axes, and sent the chips about at such a rate that one of them coming in contact with my cheek, marked it so that a week after several of my friends asked me where, in the name of wonder, I had got that black eye. At length the tree began to crack, and slowly leaning to one side, the heavy mass swung rustling through the air, and fell to the earth with a crash. It was not one Coon that was surprised here, but three—ay, three of them, one of which, more crafty than the rest, leaped fairly from the main top while the tree was staggering. The other two stuck to the hollow of a branch, from which they were soon driven by one of the dogs. Tyke and Lion, having nosed the cunning old one, scampered after him, not mouthing like the well-trained hounds of our southern Fox-hunters, but yelling like furies. The hunter's sons attacked those on the tree, while the woodsman and I, preceded by Toby, made after the other; and busy enough we all were. Our animal was of extraordinary size, and after some parley, a rifle-ball was sent through his brain. He reeled once only; next moment he lay dead. The rest were despatched by the axe and the club, for a shot in those days was too valuable to be spent when it could be saved. It could procure a Deer, and therefore was worth more than a Coon's skin.

Now, look at the moon! how full and clear has she risen on the Raccoon hunters! Now is the time for sport! Onward we go, one following the long shadow of his precursor. The twigs are no impediment, and we move at a brisker pace, as we return to the hills. What a hue and cry! here are the dogs. Overhead and all around, on the forks of each tree, the hunter's keen eye searches for something round, which is likely to prove a coiled-up Raccoon. There's one! Between me and the moon I spied the cunning thing crouched in silence. After taking aim, I raise my barrel ever so little, the trigger is pressed; down falls the Raccoon to the ground. Another and another are on the same tree. Off goes a bullet, then a second; and we secure the prey. "Let us go home, stranger," says the woodsman; and contented with our sport, towards his cabin we trudge. On arriving there, we find a cheerful fire. Toby stays without, prepares the game, stretches the skins on a frame of cane, and washes the bodies. The table is already set; the cake and the potatoes are all well done; four bowls of buttermilk are ranged in order, and now the hunters fall to.

The Raccoon is a cunning animal, and makes a pleasant pet. Monkey-like, it is quite dexterous in the use of its fore-feet, and it will amble after its master, in the manner of a Bear, and even follow him into the street. It is fond of eggs, but prefers them raw, and it matters not whether it be morning, noon, or night when it finds a dozen in the pheasant's nest, or one placed in your pocket to please him. He knows the habits of mussels better than most conchologists. Being an expert climber he ascends to the hole of the Woodpecker, and devours the young birds. He knows, too, how to watch the soft-shelled Turtle's crawl, and, better still, how to dig up her eggs. Now, by the edge of the pond, grimalkin-like, he lies seemingly asleep, until the Summer-Duck comes within reach. No negro knows better when the corn is juicy and pleasant to eat; and although Squirrels and Woodpeckers know this too, the Raccoon is found in the corn-field longer in the season than any of them, the havoc he commits there amounting to a tithe. His fur is good in winter, and many think his flesh good also; but for my part, I prefer a live Raccoon to a dead one; and should find more pleasure in hunting one than in eating him.

Pitting of Wolves

There seems to be a universal feeling of hostility among men against the Wolf, whose strength, agility, and cunning, which latter is scarcely inferior to that of his relative, Master Reynard, tend to render him an object of hatred, especially to the husbandman, on whose flocks he is ever apt to commit depredations. In America, where this animal was formerly abundant, and in many parts of which it still occurs in considerable numbers, it is not more mercifully dealt with than in other parts of the world. Traps and snares of all sorts are set for catching it, while dogs and horses are trained for hunting the Fox. The Wolf, however, unless in some way injured, being more powerful and perhaps better winded than the Fox, is rarely pursued with hounds or any other dogs in open chase; but as his depredations are at times extensive and highly injurious to the farmer, the greatest exertions have been used to exterminate his race. Few instances have occurred among us of any attack made by Wolves on man, and only one has come under my own notice.

Two young negroes who resided near the banks of the Ohio, in the lower part of the state of Kentucky, about twenty-three years ago, had sweethearts living on a plantation ten miles distant. After the labors of the day were over, they frequently visited the fair ladies of their choice, the nearest way to whose dwelling lay directly across a great cane-brake. As to the lover every moment is precious, they usually took this route to save time. Winter had commenced, cold, dark, and forbidding, and after sunset scarcely a glimpse of light or glow of warmth, one might imagine, could be found in that dreary swamp, excepting in the eyes and bosoms of the ardent youths, or the hungry Wolves that prowled about. The snow covered the earth, and rendered them more easy to be scented from a distance by the famished beasts. Prudent in a certain degree, the young lovers carried their axes on their shoulders, and walked as briskly as the narrow path would allow. Some transient glimpses of light now and then met their eyes, but so faint were they that they believed them to be caused by their faces coming in contact with the slender reeds covered with snow. Suddenly, however, a long and frightful howl burst upon them, and they instantly knew that it proceeded from a troop of hungry, perhaps desperate Wolves. They stopped, and putting themselves in an attitude of defence, awaited the result. All around was dark, save a few feet of snow, and the silence of night was dismal. Nothing could be done to better their situation, and after standing a few minutes in expectation of an attack, they judged it best to resume their march; but no sooner had they replaced their axes on their shoulders and begun to move, than the foremost found himself assailed by several foes. His legs were held fast as if pressed by a powerful screw, and the torture inflicted by the fangs of the ravenous animal was for a moment excruciating. Several Wolves in the meantime sprung upon the breast of the other negro, and dragged him to the ground. Both struggled manfully against their foes; but in a short time one of them ceased to move, and the other, reduced in strength, and perhaps despairing of maintaining his ground, still more of aiding his unfortunate companion, sprung to the branch of a tree, and speedily gained a place of safety near the top. The next morning the mangled remains of his comrade lay scattered around on the snow, which was stained with blood. Three dead Wolves lay around, but the rest of the pack had disappeared, and Scipio, sliding to the ground, took up the axes, and made the best of his way home, to relate the sad adventure.

About two years after this occurrence, as I was travelling between Henderson and Vincennes, I chanced to stop for the night at a farmer's house by the side of the road. After putting up my horse and refreshing myself, I entered into conversation with mine host, who asked if I should like to pay a visit to the Wolf-pits, which were about half a mile distant. Glad of the opportunity I accompanied him across the fields to the neighborhood of a deep wood, and soon saw the engines of destruction. He had three pits, within a few hundred yards of each other. They were about eight feet deep and broader at bottom, so as to render it impossible for the most active animal to escape from them. The aperture was covered with a revolving platform of twigs attached to a central axis. On either surface of the platform was fastened a large piece of putrid venison, with other matters by no means pleasing to my olfactory nerves, although no doubt attractive to the Wolves. My companion wished to visit them that evening, merely as he was in the habit of doing so daily, for the purpose of seeing that all was right. He said that Wolves were very abundant that autumn, and had killed nearly the whole of his sheep and one of his colts, but that he was now "paying them off in full;" and added that if I would tarry a few hours with him next morning, he would beyond a doubt show me some sport rarely seen in those parts. We retired to rest in due time, and were up with the dawn.

"I think," said my host, "that all's right, for I see the dogs are anxious to get away to the pits, and although they are nothing but curs, their noses are none the worse for that." As he took up his gun, an axe, and a large knife, the dogs began to howl and bark, and whisked around us, as if full of joy. When we reached the first pit, we found the bait all gone, and the platform much injured; but the animal that had been entrapped had scraped a subterranean passage for himself, and so escaped. On peeping into the next, he assured me that "three famous fellows were safe enough" in it. I also peeped in and saw the Wolves, two black, and the other brindled, all of goodly size, sure enough. They lay flat on the earth, their ears laid close over the head, their eyes indicating fear more than anger. "But how are we to get them out?" "How, sir?" said the farmer; "why, by going down, to be sure, and hamstringing them." Being a novice in these matters, I begged to be merely a looker-on. "With all my heart," quoth the farmer; "stand here and look at me through the brush." Whereupon he glided down, taking with him his axe and knife, and leaving his rifle to my care. I was not a little surprised to see the cowardice of the Wolves. He pulled out successively their hind legs, and with a side stroke of the knife cut the principal tendon above the joint, exhibiting as little fear as if he had been marking lambs.

"Lo!" exclaimed the farmer, when he had got out, "we have forgotten the rope; I'll go after it." Off he went accordingly, with as much alacrity as any youngster could show. In a short time he returned out of breath, and wiping his forehead with the back of his hand—"Now for it." I was desired to raise and hold the platform on its central balance, whilst he, with all the dexterity of an Indian, threw a noose over the neck of one of the Wolves. We hauled it up motionless with fright, as if dead, its disabled legs swinging to and fro, its jaws wide open, and the gurgle in its throat alone indicating that it was alive. Letting him drop on the ground, the farmer loosened the rope by means of a stick, and left him to the dogs, all of which set upon him with great fury and soon worried him to death. The second was dealt with in the same manner; but the third, which was probably the oldest, as it was the blackest, showed some spirit the moment it was left loose to the mercy of the curs. This Wolf, which we afterwards found to be a female, scuffled along on its fore-legs at a surprising rate, giving a snap every now and then to the nearest dog, which went off howling dismally, with a mouthful of skin torn from its side. And so well did the furious beast defend itself, that apprehensive of its escape, the farmer levelled his rifle at it, and shot it through the heart, on which the curs rushed upon it, and satiated their vengeance on the destroyer of their master's flock.

The Opossum

This singular animal is found more or less abundant in most parts of the Southern, Western, and Middle States of the Union. It is the *Didelphis virginiana* of Pennant, Harlan, and other authors who have given some accounts of its habits; but as none of them, so far as I know, have illustrated its propensity to dissimulate, and as I have had opportunities of observing its manners, I trust that a few particulars of its biography will prove amusing.

The Opossum is fond of secluding itself during the day, although it by no means confines its predatory rangings to the night. Like many other quadrupeds which feed principally on flesh, it is also both frugivorous and herbivorous, and, when very hard pressed by hunger, it seizes various kinds of insects and reptiles. Its gait, while travelling, and at a time when it supposes itself unobserved, is altogether ambling; in other words, it, like a young foal, moves the two legs of one side forward at once. The Newfoundland dog manifests a similar propensity. Having a constitution as hardy as that of the most northern animals, it stands the coldest weather, and does not hibernate, although its covering of fur and hair may be said to be comparatively scanty even during winter. The defect, however, seems to be compensated by a skin of considerable thickness, and a general subcutaneous layer of fat. Its movements are usually rather slow, and as it walks or ambles along, its curious prehensile tail is carried just above the ground, its rounded ears are directed forward, and at almost every step its pointed nose is applied to the objects beneath it, in order to discover what sort of creatures may have crossed its path. Methinks I see one at this moment slowly and cautiously trudging over the melting snows by the side of an unfrequented pond, nosing as it goes for the fare its ravenous appetite prefers. Now it has come upon the fresh track of a Grouse or Hare, and it raises its snout and snuffs the keen air. At length it has decided on its course, and it speeds onward at the rate of a man's ordinary walk. It stops and seems at a loss in what direction to go, for the object of its pursuit has either taken a considerable leap or has cut backwards before the Opossum entered its track. It raises itself up, stands for a while on its hind feet, looks around, snuffs the air again, and then proceeds; but now, at the foot of a noble tree, it comes to a full stand. It walks round the base of the huge trunk, over the snow-covered roots, and among them finds an aperture which it at once enters. Several minutes elapse, when it reappears, dragging along a Squirrel already deprived of life, with which in its mouth it begins to ascend the tree. Slowly it climbs. The first fork does not seem to suit it, for perhaps it thinks it might there be too openly exposed to the view of some wily foe; and so it proceeds, until it gains a cluster of branches intertwined with grapevines, and there composing itself, it twists its tail round one of the twigs, and with its sharp teeth demolishes the unlucky Squirrel, which it holds all the while with its fore-paws.

The pleasant days of spring have arrived, and the trees vigorously shoot forth their buds; but the Opossum is almost bare, and seems nearly exhausted by hunger. It visits the margins of creeks, and is pleased to see the young frogs, which afford it a tolerable repast. Gradually the poke-berry and the nettle shoot up, and on their tender and juicy stems it gladly feeds. The matin calls of the Wild Turkey Cock delight the ear of the cunning creature, for it well knows that it will soon hear the female and trace her to her nest, when it will suck the eggs with delight. Travelling through the woods, perhaps on the ground, perhaps aloft, from tree to tree, it hears a cock crow, and its heart swells as it remembers the savory food on which it regaled itself last summer in the neighboring farm-yard. With great care, however, it advances, and at last conceals itself in the very hen-house.

Honest farmer! why did you kill so many Crows last winter? ay and Ravens too? Well, you have had your own way of it; but now hie to the village and procure a store of ammunition, clean your rusty gun, set your traps, and teach your lazy curs to watch the Opossum. There it comes. The sun is scarcely down, but the appetite of the prowler is keen; hear the screams of one of your best chickens that has been seized by him! The cunning beast is off with it, and nothing can now be done, unless you stand there to watch the Fox or the Owl, now exulting in the thought that you have killed their enemy and your own friend, the poor Crow. That precious hen under which you last week placed a dozen eggs or so is now deprived of them. The Opossum, notwithstanding her angry outcries and rufflings of feathers, has removed them one by one, and now look at the poor bird as she moves across your yard; if not mad, she is at least stupid, for she scratches here and there, calling to her chickens all the while. All this comes from your shooting Crows. Had you been more merciful or more prudent, the Opossum might have been kept within the woods, where it would have been satisfied with a Squirrel, a young Hare, the eggs of a Turkey, or the grapes that so profusely adorn the boughs of our forest trees. But I talk to you in vain.

There cannot be a better exemplification of maternal tenderness than the female Opossum. Just peep into that curious sack in which the young are concealed, each attached to a teat. The kind mother not only nourishes them with care, but preserves them from their enemies; she moves with them as the shark does with its progeny, and now, aloft on the tulip-tree, she hides among the thick foliage. By the end of two months they begin to shift for themselves; each has been taught its particular lesson, and must now practise it.

But suppose the farmer has surprised an Opossum in the act of killing one of his best fowls. His angry feelings urge him to kick the poor beast, which, conscious of its inability to resist, rolls off l ke a ball. The more the farmer rages, the more reluctant is the animal to manifest resentment; at last there it lies, not dead, but exhausted, its jaws open, its tongue extended, its eye dimmed; and there it would lie until the bottle-fly should come to deposit its eggs, did not its tormentor at length walk off. "Surely," says he to himself, "the beast must be dead." But no, reader, it is only " 'possuming," and no sooner has its enemy withdrawn than it gradually gets on its legs, and once more makes for the woods.

Once, while descending the Mississippi, in a sluggish flat-bottomed boat, expressly for the purpose of studying those objects of nature more nearly connected with my favorite pursuits, I chanced to meet with two well-grown Opossums, and brought them alive to the "ark." The poor things were placed on the roof or deck, and were immediately assailed by the crew, when, following their natural instinct, they lay as if quite dead. An experiment was suggested, and both were thrown overboard. On striking the water, and for a few moments after, neither evinced the least disposition to move; but finding their situation desperate, they began to swim towards our uncouth rudder, which was formed of a long slender tree, extending from the middle of the boat thirty feet beyond its stern. They both got upon it, were taken up, and afterwards let loose in their native woods.

In the year 1829, I was in a portion of lower Louisiana, where the Opossum abounds at all seasons, and having been asked by the President and the Secretary of the Zoölogical Society of London, to forward live animals of this species to them, I offered a price a little above the common, and soon found myself plentifully supplied, twenty-five having been brought to me. I found them excessively voracious, and not less cowardly. They were put into a large box, with a great quantity of food, and conveyed to a steamer bound for New Orleans. Two days afterwards, I went to that city, to see about sending them off to Europe; but, to my surprise, I found that the old males had destroyed the younger ones, and eaten off their heads, and that only sixteen remained alive. A separate box was purchased for each, and some time after they reached my friends, the Rathbones of Liverpool, who, with their usual attention, sent them off to London, where, on my return, I saw a good number of them in the Zoölogical Gardens.

This animal is fond of grapes, of which a species now bears its name. Persimmons are greedily eaten by it, and in severe weather I have observed it eating lichens. Fowls of every kind, and quadrupeds less powerful than itself, are also its habitual prey.

The flesh of the Opossum resembles that of a young pig, and would perhaps be as highly prized, were it not for the prejudice generally entertained against it. Some "very particular" persons, to my knowledge, have pronounced it excellent eating. After cleaning its body, suspend it for a whole week in the frosty air, for it is not eaten in summer; then place it on a heap of hot wood embers; sprinkle it when cooked with gunpowder; and now tell me, good reader, does it not equal the famed Canvas-back Duck? Should you visit any of our markets, you may see it there in company with the best game.

My Style of Drawing Birds

When, as a little lad, I first began my attempts at representing birds on paper, I was far from possessing much knowledge of their nature, and, like hundreds of others, when I had laid the effort aside, I was under the impression that it was a finished picture of a bird because it possessed some sort of a head and tail, and two sticks in lieu of legs; I never troubled myself with the thought that abutments were requisite to prevent it from falling either backward or forward, and oh! what bills and claws I did draw, to say nothing of a perfectly straight line for a back, and a tail stuck in anyhow, like an unshipped rudder.

Many persons besides my father saw my miserable attempts, and so many praised them to the skies that perhaps no one was ever nearer being completely wrecked than I by these mistaken, though affectionate words. My father, however, spoke very differently to me; he constantly impressed upon me that nothing in the world possessing life and animation was easy to imitate, and that as I grew older he hoped I would become more and more alive to this. He was so kind to me, and so deeply interested in my improvement that to have listened carelessly to his serious words would have been highly ungrateful. I listened less to others, more to him, and his words became my law.

The first collection of drawings I made were from European specimens, procured by my father or myself, and I still have them in my possession. They were all represented *strictly ornithologically,* which means neither more nor less than in stiff, unmeaning profiles, such as are found in most works published to the present day. My next set was begun in America, and there, without my honored mentor, I betook myself to the drawing of specimens hung by a string tied to one foot, having a desire to show every portion, as the wings lay loosely spread, as well as the tail. In this manner I made some pretty fair signs for poulterers.

One day, while watching the habits of a pair of Pewees at Mill Grove, I looked so intently at their graceful attitudes that a thought struck my mind like a flash of light, that nothing, after all, could ever answer my enthusiastic desires to represent nature, except to copy her in her own way, alive and moving! Then I began again. On I went, forming, literally, hundreds of outlines of my favorites, the Pewees; how good or bad I cannot tell, but I fancied I had mounted a step on the high pinnacle before me. I continued for months together, simply outlining birds as I observed them, either alighted or on the wing, but could finish none of my sketches. I procured many individuals of different species, and laying them on the table or on the ground, tried to place them in such attitudes as I had sketched. But, alas! they were *dead,* to all intents and purposes, and neither wing, leg, nor tail could I place according to my wishes. A second thought came to my assistance; by means of threads I raised or lowered a head, wing, or tail, and by fastening the threads securely, I had something like life before me; yet much was wanting. When I saw the living birds, I felt the blood rush to my temples, and almost in despair spent about a month without drawing, but in deep thought, and daily in the company of the feathered inhabitants of dear Mill Grove.

I had drawn from the "manikin" whilst under David, and had obtained tolerable figures of our species through this means, so I cogitated how far a manikin of a bird would answer. I labored with wood, cork, and wires, and formed a grotesque figure, which I cannot describe in any other words than by saying that when set up it was a tolerable-looking Dodo. A friend roused my ire by laughing at it immoderately, and assuring me that if I wished to represent a tame gander it might do. I gave it a kick, broke it to atoms, walked off, and thought again.

Young as I was, my impatience to obtain my desire filled my brains with many plans. I not infrequently dreamed that I had made a new discovery; and long before day, one morning, I leaped out of bed fully persuaded that I had obtained my object. I ordered a horse to be saddled, mounted, and went off at a gallop towards the little village of Norristown, distant about five miles. When I arrived there not a door was open, for it was not yet daylight. Therefore I went to the river, took a bath, and, returning to the town, entered the first opened shop, inquired for wire of different sizes, bought some, leaped on my steed, and was soon again at Mill Grove. The wife of my tenant, I really believe, thought that I was mad, as, on offering me breakfast, I told her I only wanted my gun. I was off to the creek, and shot the first Kingfisher I met. I picked the bird up, carried it home by the bill, sent for the miller, and bade him bring me a piece of board of soft wood. When he returned he found me filing sharp points to some pieces of wire, and I proceeded to show him what I meant to do. I pierced the body of the fishing bird, and fixed it on the board; another wire passed above his upper mandible held the head in a pretty fair attitude, smaller ones fixed the feet according to my notions, and even common pins came to my assistance. The last wire proved a delightful elevator to the bird's tail, and at last—there stood before me the *real* Kingfisher.

Think not that my lack of breakfast was at all in my way. No, indeed! I outlined the bird, aided by compasses and my eyes, colored it, finished it, without a thought of hunger. My honest miller stood by the while, and was delighted to see me pleased. This was what I shall call my first drawing actually from nature, for even the eye of the Kingfisher was as if full of life whenever I pressed the lids aside with my finger.

In those happy days of my youth I was extremely fond of reading what I still call the delightful fables of La Fontaine. I had frequently perused the one entitled "*L'hirondelle et les petits oiseaux,*" and thought much of the meaning imparted in the first line, which, if I now recollect rightly, goes on to say that "*Quiconque a beaucoup vu, peut avoir beaucoup retenu.*" To me this meant that to study Nature was to ramble through her domains late and early, and if I observed all as I should, that the memory of what I saw would at least be of service to me.

"Early to bed, and early to rise," was another adage which I thought, and still think, of much value; 't is a pity that instead of being merely an adage it has not become a general law; I have followed it ever since I was a child, and am ever grateful for the hint it conveyed.

As I wandered, mostly bent on the study of birds, and with a wish to represent all those found in our woods, to the best of my powers, I gradually became acquainted with their forms and habits, and the use of my wires was improved by constant practice. Whenever I produced a better representation of any species the preceding one was destroyed, and after a time I laid down what I was pleased to call a constitution of my manner of drawing birds, formed upon natural principles, which I will try to put briefly before you.

The gradual knowledge of the forms and habits of the birds of our country impressed me with the idea that each part of a family must possess a certain degree of affinity, distinguishable at sight in any one of them. The Pewees, which I knew by experience were positively Flycatchers, led me to the discovery that every bird truly of that genus, when standing, was usually in a passive attitude; that they sat uprightly, now and then glancing their eyes upwards or sideways, to watch the approach of their insect prey; that if in pursuit of this prey their movements through the air were, in each and all of that tribe, the same, etc., etc.

Gallinaceous birds I saw were possessed of movements and positions peculiar to them. Amongst the waterbirds also I found characteristic manners. I observed that the Herons walked with elegance and stateliness, that, in fact, every family had some mark by which it could be known; and, after having collected many ideas and much material of this kind, I fairly began, in greater earnest than ever, the very collection of Birds of America, which is now being published.

The better I understood my subjects, the better I became able to represent them in what I hoped were natural positions. The bird once fixed with wires on squares, I studied as a lay figure before me, its nature, previously known to me as far as habits went, and its general form having been frequently observed. Now I could examine more thoroughly the bill, nostrils, eyes, legs, and claws, as well as the structure of the wings and tail; the very tongue was of importance to me, and I thought the more I understood all these particulars, the better representations I made of the originals.

My drawings at first were made altogether in watercolors, but they wanted softness and a great deal of finish. For a long time I was much dispirited at this, particularly when vainly endeavoring to imitate birds of soft and downy plumage, such as that of most Owls, Pigeons, Hawks, and Herons. How this could be remedied required a new train of thought, or some so-called accident, and the latter came to my aid.

One day, after having finished a miniature portrait of the one dearest to me in all the world, a portion of the face was injured by a drop of water, which dried where it fell; and although I labored a great deal to repair the damage, the blur still remained. Recollecting that, when a pupil of David, I had drawn heads and figures in different colored chalks, I resorted to a piece of that material of the tint required for the part, applied the pigment, rubbed the place with a cork stump, and at once produced the desired effect.

My drawings of Owls and other birds of similar plumage were much improved by such applications; indeed, after a few years of patience, some of my attempts began almost to please me, and I have continued the same style ever since, and that now is for more than thirty years.

Whilst travelling in Europe as well as America, many persons have evinced the desire to draw birds in my manner, and I have always felt much pleasure in showing it to any one by whom I hoped ornithological delineations or portraitures would be improved.

BIRD BIOGRAPHIES

In 1830 Audubon decided to publish the Ornithological Biography *as a series of companion volumes to the* Birds of America *folio, still in the process of being issued to subscribers in "numbers" of five plates apiece. He was assisted by his wife, Lucy, and by William MacGillivray, a young Scottish scientist and teacher he had found in Edinburgh. MacGillivray helped identify and filter out "asperities" in the text, provided some of the measurements, and did the anatomical drawings at the end of each biography. Working intensely, often ten to twelve hours a day, they finished the first volume (published in April 1831) within four months. The completed* Biography *would eventually comprise five dense volumes; the final one appeared in 1839, a year after the last number of the great double-elephant folio* Birds of America *(1827–38) had been printed and sent to subscribers, and a year before the first volume of the smaller octavo version of* Birds of America *(1840–44) was published.*

Very little escaped Audubon during the long years he had spent tracking his birds up and down the Mississippi Valley. The natural world of the solitary walker of the woods had been his university. Audubon knew his academic training in the official sciences was limited, but he prided himself on writing directly from his own observations and experiences. "I know that I am not a scholar, but meantime I am aware that no man living knows better than I do the habits of our birds; no man living has studied them as much as I have done, and with the assistance of my old journals and memorandum-books which were written on the spot, I can at least put down plain truths. . . ."

Accuracy was Audubon's primary consideration in writing the bird biographies; as for style, despite the strict scientific guidelines he set for himself, and, it must be said, despite the occasional effusion and straining after effect (standard liabilities of conventional Victorian prose), Audubon was nevertheless capable of finding the exact poetic equivalent whenever he wanted to convey the shock of a spontaneous perception or an odd situation. He could describe the muffled sound of young puffins moving about unseen in their underground burrows as "voices from the grave," and his account in "The Whooping Crane" of being chased by a mad crane is a small masterpiece of ornithological humor. Many readers will recognize certain classic passages in "The Passenger Pigeon" and "The Chimney Swallow, or American Swift," which have long since taken their place in the great nature writing of the nineteenth century. The bird biographies included in this collection are taken from Audubon's final versions in the octavo seven-volume edition of the Birds of America *(1840–44). I have deleted the anatomical measurements and drawings.*

The Great White Heron

ARDEA OCCIDENTALIS, *AUD.*

I am now about to present you with an account of the habits of the largest species of the Heron tribe hitherto found in the United States, and which is indeed remarkable not only for its great size, but also for the pure white of its plumage at every period of its life. Writers who have subdivided the family, and stated that none of the true Herons are white, will doubtless be startled when they, for the first time, look at my plate of this bird. I think, however, that our endeavours to discover the natural arrangement of things cannot be uniformly successful, and it is clear that he only who has studied *all* can have much chance of disposing all according to their relations.

On the 24th of April, 1832, I landed on Indian Key in Florida, and immediately after formed an acquaintance with Mr. EGAN. He it was who first gave me notice of the species which forms the subject of this article, and of which I cannot find any description. The next day after that of my arrival, when I was prevented from accompanying him by my anxiety to finish a drawing, he came in with two young birds alive, and another lying dead in a nest, which he had cut off from a mangrove. You may imagine how delighted I was, when at the very first glance I felt assured that they were different from any that I had previously seen. The two living birds were of a beautiful white, slightly tinged with cream-colour, remarkably fat and strong for their age, which the worthy pilot said could not be more than three weeks. The dead bird was quite putrid and much smaller. It looked as if it had accidentally been trampled to death by the parent birds ten or twelve days before, the body being almost flat and covered with filth. The nest with the two live birds was placed in the yard. The young Herons seemed quite unconcerned when a person approached them, although on displaying one's hand to them, they at once endeavoured to strike it with their bill. My Newfoundland dog, a well-trained and most sagacious animal, was whistled for and came up; on which the birds rose partially on their legs, ruffled all their feathers, spread their wings, opened their bills, and clicked their mandibles in great anger, but without attempting to leave the nest. I ordered the dog to go near them, but not to hurt them. They waited until he went within striking distance, when the largest suddenly hit him with its bill, and hung to his nose. Plato, however, took it all in good part, and merely brought the bird towards me, when I seized it by the wings, which made it let go its hold. It walked off as proudly as any of its tribe, and I was delighted to find it possessed of so much courage. These birds were left under the charge of Mrs. EGAN, until I returned from my various excursions to the different islands along the coast.

On the 26th of the same month, Mr. THRUSTON took me and my companions in his beautiful barge to some keys on which the Florida Cormorants were breeding in great numbers. As we were on the way we observed two tall White Herons standing on their nests; but although I was anxious to procure them alive, an unfortunate shot from one of the party brought them to the water. They were, I was told, able to fly, but probably had never seen a man before. While searching that day for the nests of the Zenaida Dove, we observed a young Heron of this species stalking among the mangroves that bordered the key on which we were, and immediately pursued it. Had you been looking on, good reader, you might have enjoyed a hearty laugh, although few of us could have joined you. Seven or eight persons were engaged in the pursuit of this single bird, which, with extended neck, wings, and legs, made off among the tangled trees at such a rate, that, anxious as I was to obtain it alive, I several times thought of shooting it. At length, however, it was caught, its bill was securely tied, its legs were drawn up, and fastened by a strong cord, and the poor thing was thus conveyed to Indian Key, and placed along with its kinsfolk. On seeing it, the latter immediately ran towards it with open bills, and greeted it with a most friendly welcome, passing their heads over and under its own in the most curious and indeed ludicrous manner. A bucketful of fish was thrown to them, which they swallowed in a few minutes. After a few days, they also ate pieces of pork-rhind, cheese, and other substances.

While sailing along the numerous islands that occur between Indian Key and Key West, I saw many birds of this species, some in pairs, some single, and others in flocks; but on no occasion did I succeed in getting within shot of one. Mr. EGAN consoled me by saying that he knew some places beyond Key West where I certainly should obtain several, were we to spend a day and a night there for the purpose. Dr. BENJAMIN STROBEL afterwards gave me a similar assurance. In the course of a week after reaching Key West, I in fact procured more than a dozen birds of different ages, as well as nests and eggs, and their habits were carefully examined by several of my party.

At three o'clock one morning, you might have seen Mr. EGAN and myself, about eight miles from our harbour, paddling as silently as possible over some narrow and tortuous inlets, formed by the tides through a large flat and partially submersed key. There we expected to find many White Herons; but our labour was for a long time almost hopeless, for, although other birds occurred, we had determined to shoot nothing but the Great White Heron, and none of that species came near us. At length, after six or seven hours of hard labour, a Heron flew right over our heads, and to make sure of it, we both fired at once. The bird came down dead. It proved to be a female, which had either been sitting on her eggs or had lately hatched her young, her belly being bare, and her plumage considerably worn. We now rested awhile, and breakfasted on some biscuit soaked in molasses and water, reposing under the shade of the mangroves, where the mosquitoes had a good opportunity of breaking their fast also. We went about from one key to another, saw a great number of White Herons, and at length, towards night, reached the Marion, rather exhausted, and having a solitary bird. Mr. EGAN and I had been most of the time devising schemes for procuring others with less trouble, a task which might easily have been accomplished a month before, when, as he said, the birds were "sitting hard." He asked if I would return that night at twelve o'clock to the last key which we had visited. I mentioned the proposal to our worthy Captain, who, ever willing to do all in his power to oblige me, when the service did not require constant attendance on board, said that if I would go, he would accompany us in the gig. Our guns were soon cleaned, provisions and ammunition placed in the boats, and after supping we talked and laughed until the appointed time.

"Eight Bells" made us bound on our feet, and off we pushed for the islands. The moon shone bright in the clear sky; but as the breeze had died away, we betook ourselves to our oars. The state of the tide was against us, and we had to drag our boats several miles over the soapy shallows; but at last we found ourselves in a deep channel beneath the hanging mangroves of a large key, where we had observed the Herons retiring to roost the previous evening. There we lay quietly until daybreak. But the musquitoes and sandflies! Reader, if you have not been in such a place, you cannot easily conceive the torments we endured for a whole hour, when it was absolutely necessary for us to remain perfectly motionless. At length day dawned, and the boats parted, to meet on the other side of the key. Slowly and silently each advanced. A Heron sprung from its perch almost directly over our heads. Three barrels were discharged,—in vain; the bird flew on unscathed; the pilot and I had probably been too anxious. As the bird sped away, it croaked loudly, and the noise, together with the report of our guns, roused some hundreds of these Herons, which flew from the mangroves, and in the grey light appeared to sail over and around us like so many spectres. I almost despaired of procuring any more. The tide was now rising, and when we met with the other boat we were told, that if we had waited until we could have shot at them while perched, we might have killed several; but that now we must remain until full tide, for the birds had gone to their feeding grounds.

The boats parted again, and it was now arranged that whenever a Heron was killed, another shot should be fired exactly one minute after, by which each party would be made aware of the success of the other. Mr. EGAN, pointing to a nest on which stood two small young birds, desired to be landed near it. I proceeded into a narrow bayou, where we remained quiet for about half an hour, when a Heron flew over us and was shot. It was a very fine old male. Before firing my signal shot, I heard a report from afar, and a little after mine was discharged I heard another shot, so I felt assured that two birds had been killed. When I reached the Captain's boat I found that he had in fact obtained two; but Mr. EGAN had waited two hours in vain near the nest, for none of the old birds came up. We took him from his hiding place, and brought the Herons along with us. It was now nearly high water. About a mile from us, more than a hundred Herons stood on a mud-bar up to their bellies. The pilot said that now was our best chance, as the tide would soon force them to fly, when they would come to rest on the trees. So we divided, each choosing his own place, and I went to the lowest end of the key, where it was separated from another by a channel. I soon had the pleasure of observing all the Herons take to wing, one after another, in quick succession. I then heard my companions' guns, but no signal of success. Obtaining a good chance as I thought, I fired at a remarkably large bird, and distinctly heard the shot strike it. The Heron merely croaked, and pursued its course. Not another bird came near enough to be shot at, although many had alighted on the neighbouring key, and stood perched like so many newly finished statues of the purest alabaster, forming a fine contrast to the deep blue sky. The boats joined us. Mr. EGAN had one bird, the Captain another, and both looked at me with surprise. We now started for the next key, where we expected to see more. When we had advanced several hundred yards along its low banks, we found the bird at which I had shot lying with extended wings in the agonies of death. It was from this specimen that the drawing was made. I was satisfied with the fruits of this day's excursion. On other occasions I procured fifteen more birds, and judging that number sufficient, I left the Herons to their occupations.

This species is extremely shy. Sometimes they would rise when at the distance of half a mile from us, and fly quite out of sight. If pursued, they would return to the very keys or mud-flats from which they had risen, and it was almost impossible to approach one while perched or standing in the water. Indeed, I have no doubt that half a dozen specimens of *Ardea Herodias* could be procured for one of the present, in the same time and under similar circumstances.

The Great White Heron is a constant resident on the Florida Keys, where it is found more abundant during the breeding season than anywhere else. They rarely go as far eastward as Cape Florida, and are not seen on the Tortugas, probably because these islands are destitute of mangroves. They begin to pair early in March, but many do not lay their eggs until the middle of April. Their courtships were represented to me as similar to those of the Great Blue Heron. Their nests are at times met with at considerable distances from each other, and although many are found on the same keys, they are placed farther apart than those of the species just mentioned. They are seldom more than a few feet above high water-mark, which in the Floridas is so low, that they look as if only a yard or two above the roots of the trees. From twenty to thirty nests which I examined were thus placed. They were large, about three feet in diameter, formed of sticks of different sizes, but without any appearance of lining, and quite flat, being several inches thick. The eggs are always three, measure two inches and three quarters in length, one inch and eight-twelfths in breadth, and have a rather thick shell, of a uniform plain light bluish-green colour. Mr. EGAN told me that incubation continues about thirty days, that both birds sit, (the female, however, being most assiduous,) and with their legs stretched out before them, in the same manner as the young when two or three weeks old. The latter, of which I saw several from ten days to a month old, were pure white, slightly tinged with cream colour, and had no indications of a crest. Those which I carried to Charleston, and which were kept for more than a year, exhibited nothing of the kind. I am unable to say how long it is before they attain their full plumage as represented in the plate, when, as you see, the head is broadly but loosely and shortly tufted, the feathers of the breast pendent, but not remarkably long, and there are none of the narrow feathers seen in other species over the rump or wings.

These Herons are sedate, quiet, and perhaps even less animated than the *A. Herodias*. They walk majestically, with firmness and great elegance. Unlike the species just named, they *flock* at their feeding grounds, sometimes a hundred or more being seen together; and what is still more remarkable is, that they betake themselves to the mud-flats or sand-bars at a distance from the keys on which they roost and breed. They seem, in so far as I could judge, to be diurnal, an opinion corroborated by the testimony of Mr. EGAN, a person of great judgment, sagacity and integrity. While on these banks, they stand motionless, rarely moving towards their prey, but waiting until it comes near, when they strike it and swallow it alive, or when large beat it on the water, or shake it violently, biting it severely all the while. They never leave their feeding grounds until driven off by the tide, remaining until the water reaches their body. So wary are they, that although they may return to roost on the same keys, they rarely alight on trees to which they have resorted before, and if repeatedly disturbed they do not return, for many weeks at least. When roosting, they generally stand on one foot, the other being drawn up, and, unlike the Ibises, are never seen lying flat on trees, where, however, they draw in their long neck, and place their head under their wing.

I was often surprised to see that while a flock was resting by day in the position just described, one or more stood with outstretched necks, keenly eyeing all around, now and then suddenly starting at the sight of a Porpoise or Shark in chase of some fish. The appearance of a man or a boat, seemed to distract them; and yet I was told that nobody ever goes in pursuit of them. If surprised, they leave their perch with a rough croaking sound, and fly directly to a great distance, but never inland.

The flight of the Great White Heron is firm, regular, and greatly protracted. They propel themselves by regular slow flaps, the head being drawn in after they have proceeded a few yards, and their legs extended behind, as is the case with all other Herons. They also now and then rise high in the air, where they sail in wide circles, and they never alight without performing this circling flight, unless when going to feeding grounds on which other individuals have already settled. It is truly surprising that a bird of so powerful a flight never visits Georgia or the Carolinas, nor goes to the mainland. When you see them about the middle of the day on their feeding grounds they "loom" to about double their size, and present a singular appearance. It is difficult to kill them unless with buck-shot, which we found ourselves obliged to use.

When I left Key West, on our return towards Charleston, I took with me two young birds that had been consigned to the care of my friend Dr. B. STROBEL, who assured me that they devoured more than their weight of food per day. I had also two young birds of the *Ardea Herodias* alive. After bringing them on board, I placed them all together in a very large coop; but was soon obliged to separate the two species, for the white birds would not be reconciled to the blue, which they would have killed. While the former had the privilege of the deck for a few minutes, they struck at the smaller species, such as the young of *Ardea rufescens* and *A. Ludoviciana*, some of which they instantly killed and swallowed entire, although they were abundantly fed on the flesh of green turtles. None of the sailors succeeded in making friends with them.

On reaching Indian Key, I found those which had been left with Mrs. EGAN, in excellent health and much increased in size, but to my surprise observed that their bills were much broken, which she assured me had been caused by the great force with which they struck at the fishes thrown to them on the rocks of their enclosure,—a statement which I found confirmed by my own observation in the course of the day. It was almost as difficult to catch them in the yard, as if they had never seen a man before, and we were obliged to tie their bills fast, to avoid being wounded by them while carrying them on board. They thrived well, and never manifested the least animosity towards each other. One of them which accidentally walked before the coop in which the Blue Herons were, thrust its bill between the bars, and transfixed the head of one of these birds, so that it was instantaneously killed.

When we arrived at Charleston, four of them were still alive. They were taken to my friend JOHN BACHMAN, who was glad to see them. He kept a pair, and offered the other to our mutual friend Dr. SAMUEL WILSON, who accepted them, but soon afterwards gave them to Dr. GIBBES of Columbia College, merely because they had killed a number of Ducks. My friend BACHMAN kept two of these birds for many months; but it was difficult for him to procure fish enough for them, as they swallowed a bucketful of mullets in a few minutes, each devouring about a gallon of these fishes. They betook themselves to roosting in a beautiful arbour in his garden; where at night they looked with their pure white plumage like beings of another world. It is a curious fact, that the points of their bills, of which an inch at least had been broken, grew again, and were as regularly shaped at the end of six months as if nothing had happened to them. In the evening or early in the morning, they would frequently set, like pointer dogs, at moths which hovered over the flowers, and with a well-directed stroke of their bill seize the fluttering insect and instantly swallow it. On many occasions, they also struck at chickens, grown fowls and ducks, which they would tear up and devour. Once a cat which was asleep in the sunshine, on the wooden steps of the viranda, was pinned through the body to the boards and killed by one of them. At last they began to pursue the younger children of my worthy friend, who therefore ordered them to be killed. One of them was beautifully mounted by my assistant Mr. HENRY WARD, and is now in the Museum of Charleston. Dr. GIBBES was obliged to treat his in the same manner; and I afterwards saw one of them in his collection.

Mr. EGAN kept for about a year one of these birds, which he raised from the nest, and which, when well grown, was allowed to ramble along the shores of Indian Key in quest of food. One of the wings had been cut, and the bird was known to all the resident inhabitants, but was at last shot by some Indian hunter, who had gone there to dispose of a collection of sea shells.

Some of the Herons feed on the berries of certain trees during the latter part of autumn and the beginning of winter. Dr. B. STROBEL observed the Night Heron eating those of the "Gobolimbo," late in September at Key West.

Among the varied and contradictory descriptions of Herons, you will find it alleged that these birds seize fish while on wing by plunging the head and neck into the water; but this seems to me extremely doubtful. Nor, I believe, do they watch for their prey while perched on trees. Another opinion is, that Herons are always thin, and unfit for food. This, however, is by no means generally the case in America, and I have thought these birds very good eating when not too old.

The Great Blue Heron

ARDEA HERODIAS, *LINN.*

The State of Louisiana has always been my favourite portion of the Union, although Kentucky and some other States have divided my affections; but as we are on the banks of the fair Ohio, let us pause awhile, good reader, and watch the Heron. In my estimation, few of our waders are more interesting than the birds of this family. Their contours and movements are always graceful, if not elegant. Look on the one that stands near the margin of the pure stream:—see his reflection dipping as it were into the smooth water, the bottom of which it might reach had it not to contend with the numerous boughs of those magnificent trees. How calm, how silent, how grand is the scene! The tread of the tall bird himself no one hears, so carefully does he place his foot on the moist ground, cautiously suspending it for awhile at each step of his progress. Now his golden eye glances over the surrounding objects, in surveying which he takes advantage of the full stretch of his graceful neck. Satisfied that no danger is near, he lays his head on his shoulders, allows the feathers of his breast to droop, and patiently awaits the approach of his finned prey. You might imagine what you see to be the statue of a bird, so motionless is it. But now, he moves; he has taken a silent step, and with great care he advances; slowly does he raise his head from his shoulders, and now, what a sudden start! his formidable bill has transfixed a perch, which he beats to death on the ground. See with what difficulty he gulps it down his capacious throat! and now his broad wings open, and away he slowly flies to another station, or perhaps to avoid his unwelcome observers.

The "Blue Crane" (by which name this species is generally known in the United States) is met with in every part of the Union. Although more abundant in the low lands of our Atlantic coast, it is not uncommon in the countries west of the Alleghany Mountains. I have found it in every State in which I have travelled, as well as in all our "Territories." It is well known from Louisiana to Maine, but seldom occurs farther east than Prince Edward's Island in the Gulf of St. Lawrence, and not a Heron of any kind did I see or hear of in Newfoundland or Labrador. Westward, I believe, it reaches to the very bases of the Rocky Mountains. It is a hardy bird, and bears the extremes of temperature surprisingly, being in its tribe what the Passenger Pigeon is in the family of Doves. During the coldest part of winter the Blue Heron is observed in the State of Massachusetts and in Maine, spending its time in search of prey about the warm springs and ponds which occur there in certain districts. They are not rare in the Middle States, but more plentiful to the west and south of Pennsylvania, which perhaps arises from the incessant war waged against them.

Extremely suspicious and shy, this bird is ever on the look-out. Its sight is as acute as that of any Falcon, and it can hear at a considerable distance, so that it is enabled to mark with precision the different objects it sees, and to judge with accuracy of the sounds which it hears. Unless under very favourable circumstances, it is almost hopeless to attempt to approach it. You may now and then surprise one feeding under the bank of a deep creek or bayou, or obtain a shot as he passes unawares over you on wing; but to walk up towards one would be a fruitless adventure. I have seen many so wary, that, on seeing a man at any distance within half a mile, they would take to wing; and the report of a gun forces one off his grounds from a distance at which you would think he could not be alarmed. When in close woods, however, and perched on a tree, they can be approached with a good chance of success.

The Blue Heron feeds at all hours of the day, as well as in the dark and dawn, and even under night, when the weather is clear, his appetite alone determining his actions in this respect; but I am certain that when disturbed during dark nights it feels bewildered, and alights as soon as possible. When passing from one part of the country to another at a distance, the case is different, and on such occasions they fly under night at a considerable height above the trees, continuing their movements in a regular manner.

The commencement of the breeding season varies, according to the latitude, from the beginning of March to the middle of June. In the Floridas it takes place about the first of these periods, in the Middle Districts about the 15th of May, and in Maine a month later. It is at the approach of this period only that these birds associate in pairs, they being generally quite solitary at all other times; nay, excepting during the breeding season, each individual seems to secure for itself a certain district as a feeding ground, giving chase to every intruder of its own species. At such times they also repose singly, for the most part roosting on trees, although sometimes taking their station on the ground, in the midst of a wide marsh, so that they may be secure from the approach of man. This unsocial temper probably arises from the desire of securing a certain abundance of food, of which each individual in fact requires a large quantity.

The manners of this Heron are exceedingly interesting at the approach of the breeding season, when the males begin to look for partners. About sunrise you see a number arrive and alight either on the margin of a broad sand-bar or on a savannah. They come from different quarters, one after another, for several hours; and when you see forty or fifty before you, it is difficult for you to imagine that half the number could have resided in the same district. Yet in the Floridas I have seen hundreds thus collected in the course of a morning. They are now in their full beauty, and no young birds seem to be among them. The males walk about with an air of great dignity, bidding defiance to their rivals, and the females croak to invite the males to pay their addresses to them. The females utter their coaxing notes all at once, and as each male evinces an equal desire to please the object of his affection, he has to encounter the enmity of many an adversary, who, with little attention to politeness, opens his powerful bill, throws out his wings, and rushes with fury on his foe. Each attack is carefully guarded against, blows are exchanged for blows; one would think that a single well-aimed thrust might suffice to inflict death, but the strokes are parried with as much art as an expert swordsman would employ; and, although I have watched these birds for half an hour at a time as they fought on the ground, I never saw one killed on such an occasion; but I have often seen one felled and trampled upon, even after incubation had commenced. These combats over, the males and females leave the place in pairs. They are now mated for the season, at least I am inclined to think so, as I never saw them assemble twice on the same ground, and they become comparatively peaceable after pairing.

It is by no means a constant practice with this species to breed in communities, whether large or small; for although I have seen many such associations, I have also found many pairs breeding apart. Nor do they at all times make choice of the trees placed in the interior of a swamp, for I have found heronries in the pine-barrens of the Floridas, more than ten miles from any marsh, pond, or river. I have also observed nests on the tops of the tallest trees, while others were only a few feet above the ground: some also I have seen on the ground itself, and many on cactuses. In the Carolinas, where Herons of all sorts are extremely abundant, perhaps as much so as in the lower parts of Louisiana or the Floridas, on account of the numerous reservoirs connected with the rice plantations, and the still more numerous ditches which intersect the rice-fields, all of which contain fish of various sorts, these birds find it easy to procure food in great abundance. There the Blue Herons breed in considerable numbers, and if the place they have chosen be over a swamp, few situations can be conceived more likely to ensure their safety, for one seldom ventures into those dismal retreats at the time when these birds breed, the effluvia being extremely injurious to health, besides the difficulties to be overcome in making one's way to them.

Imagine, if you can, an area of some hundred acres, overgrown with huge cypress trees, the trunks of which, rising to a height of perhaps fifty feet before they send off a branch, spring from the midst of the dark muddy waters. Their broad tops, placed close together with interlaced branches, seem intent on separating the heavens from the earth. Beneath their dark canopy scarcely a single sunbeam ever makes its way; the mire is covered with fallen logs, on which grow matted grasses and lichens, and the deeper parts with nympheæ and other aquatic plants. The congo snake and watermoccasin glide before you as they seek to elude your sight, hundreds of turtles drop, as if shot, from the floating trunks of the fallen trees, from which also the sullen alligator plunges into the dismal pool. The air is pregnant with pestilence, but alive with musquitoes and other insects. The croaking of the frogs, joined with the hoarse cries of the Anhingas and the screams of the Herons, forms fit music for such a scene. Standing knee-deep in the mire, you discharge your gun at one of the numerous birds that are breeding high over head, when immediately such a deafening noise arises, that, if you have a companion with you, it were quite useless to speak to him. The frightened birds cross each other confusedly in their flight; the young attempting to secure themselves, some of them lose their hold, and fall into the water with a splash; a shower of leaflets whirls downwards from the tree-tops, and you are glad to make your retreat from such a place. Should you wish to shoot Herons, you may stand, fire, and pick up your game as long as you please; you may obtain several species, too, for not only does the Great Blue Heron breed there, but the White, and sometimes the Night Heron, as well as the Anhinga, and to such places they return year after year, unless they have been cruelly disturbed.

The nest of the Blue Heron, in whatever situation it may be placed, is large and flat, externally composed of dry sticks, and matted with weeds and mosses to a considerable thickness. When the trees are large and convenient, you may see several nests on the same tree. The full complement of eggs which these birds lay is three, and in no instance have I found more. Indeed, this is constantly the case with all the large species with which I am acquainted, from *Ardea cœrulea* to *Ardea occidentalis;* but the smaller species lay more as they diminish in size, the Louisiana Heron having frequently four, and the Green Heron five, and even sometimes six. Those of the Great Blue Heron are very small compared with the size of the bird, measuring only two and a half inches by one and seven-twelfths; they are of a dull bluish-white, without spots, rather rough, and of a regular oval form.

The male and the female sit alternately, receiving food from each other, their mutual affection being as great as it is towards their young, which they provide for so abundantly, that it is not uncommon to find the nest containing a quantity of fish and other food, some fresh, and some in various stages of putrefaction. As the young advance they are less frequently fed, although still as copiously supplied whenever opportunity offers; but now and then I have observed them, when the nests were low, standing on their haunches, with their legs spread widely before them, and calling for food in vain. The quantity which they require is now so great that all the exertions of the old birds appear at times to be insufficient to satisfy their voracious appetite; and they do not provide for themselves until fully able to fly, when their parents chase them off, and force them to shift as they can. They are generally in good condition when they leave the nest; but from want of experience they find it difficult to procure as much food as they have been accustomed to, and soon become poor. Young birds from the nest afford tolerable eating; but the flesh of the old birds is by no means to my taste, nor so good as some epicures would have us to believe, and I would at any time prefer that of a Crow or young Eagle.

The principal food of the Great Blue Heron is fish of all kinds; but it also devours frogs, lizards, snakes, and birds, as well as small quadrupeds, such as shrews, meadow-mice, and young rats, all of which I have found in its stomach. Aquatic insects are equally welcome to it, and it is an expert flycatcher, striking at moths, butterflies, and libellulæ, whether on the wing or when alighted. It destroys a great number of young Marsh-Hens, Rails, and other birds; but I never saw one catch a fiddler or a crab; and the only seeds that I have found in its stomach were those of the great water-lily of the Southern States. It always strikes its prey through the body, and as near the head as possible. When the animal is strong and active, it kills it by beating it against the ground or a rock, after which it swallows it entire. While on the St. John's river in East Florida, I shot one of these birds, and on opening it on board, found in its stomach a fine perch quite fresh, but of which the head had been cut off. The fish, when cooked, I found excellent, as did Lieutenant PIERCY and my assistant Mr. WARD. When on a visit to my friend JOHN BULOW, I was informed by him, that although he had several times imported gold fishes from New York, with the view of breeding them in a pond, through which ran a fine streamlet, and which was surrounded by a wall, they all disappeared in a few days after they were let loose. Suspecting the Heron to be the depredator, I desired him to watch the place carefully with a gun; which was done, and the result was, that he shot a superb specimen of the present species, in which was found the last gold fish that remained.

In the wild state it never, I believe, eats dead fish of any sort, or indeed any other food than that killed by itself. Now and then it strikes at a fish so large and strong as to endanger its own life; and I once saw one on the Florida coast, that, after striking a fish, when standing in the water to the full length of its legs, was dragged along for several yards, now on the surface, and again beneath. When, after a severe struggle, the Heron disengaged itself, it appeared quite overcome, and stood still near the shore, his head turned from the sea, as if afraid to try another such experiment. The number of fishes, measuring five or six inches, which one of these birds devours in a day, is surprising. Some which I kept on board the Marion would swallow, in the space of half an hour, a bucketful of young mullets; and when fed on the flesh of green turtles, they would eat several pounds at a meal. I have no doubt that, in favourable circumstances, one of them could devour several hundreds of small fishes in a day. A Heron that was caught alive on one of the Florida keys, near Key West, looked so emaciated when it came on board, that I had it killed to discover the cause of its miserable condition. It was an adult female that had bred that spring; her belly was in a state of mortification, and on opening her, we found the head of a fish measuring several inches, which, in an undigested state, had lodged among the entrails of the poor bird. How long it had suffered could only be guessed, but this undoubtedly was the cause of the miserable state in which it was found.

I took a pair of young Herons of this species to Charleston. They were nearly able to fly when caught, and were standing erect a few yards from the nest, in which lay a putrid one that seemed to have been trampled to death by the rest. They offered little resistance, but grunted with a rough uncouth voice. I had them placed in a large coop, containing four individuals of the *Ardea occidentalis*, who immediately attacked the newcomers in the most violent manner, so that I was obliged to turn them loose on the deck. I had frequently observed the great antipathy evinced by the majestic white species towards the blue in the wild state, but was surprised to find it equally strong in young birds which had never seen one, and were at that period smaller than the others. All my endeavours to remove their dislike were unavailing, for when placed in a large yard, the White Herons attacked the Blue, and kept them completely under. The latter became much tamer, and were more attached to each other. Whenever a piece of turtle was thrown to them, it was dexterously caught in the air and gobbled up in an instant, and as they became more familiar, they ate bits of biscuit, cheese, and even rhinds of bacon.

When wounded, the Great Blue Heron immediately prepares for defence, and woe to the man or dog who incautiously comes within reach of its powerful bill, for that instant he is sure to receive a severe wound, and the risk is so much the greater that birds of this species commonly aim at the eye. If beaten with a pole or long stick, they throw themselves on their back, cry aloud, and strike with their bill and claws with great force. I have shot some on trees, which, although quite dead, clung by their claws for a considerable time before they fell. I have also seen the Blue Heron giving chase to a Fish Hawk, whilst the latter was pursuing its way through the air towards a place where it could feed on the fish which it bore in its talons. The Heron soon overtook the Hawk, and at the very first lounge made by it, the latter dropped its quarry, when the Heron sailed slowly towards the ground, where it no doubt found the fish. On one occasion of this kind, the Hawk dropped the fish in the water, when the Heron, as if vexed that it was lost to him, continued to harass the Hawk, and forced it into the woods.

The flight of the Great Blue Heron is even, powerful, and capable of being protracted to a great distance. On rising from the ground or on leaving its perch, it goes off in silence with extended neck and dangling legs, for eight or ten yards, after which it draws back its neck, extends its feet in a straight line behind, and with easy and measured flappings continues its course, at times flying low over the marshes, and again, as if suspecting danger, at a considerable height over the land or the forest. It removes from one pond or creek, or even from one marsh to another, in a direct manner, deviating only on apprehending danger. When about to alight, it now and then sails in a circular direction, and when near the spot it extends its legs, and keeps its wings stretched out until it has effected a footing. The same method is employed when it alights on a tree, where, however, it does not appear to be as much at its ease as on the ground. When suddenly surprised by an enemy, it utters several loud discordant notes, and mutes the moment it flies off.

This species takes three years in attaining maturity, and even after that period it still increases in size and weight. When just hatched they have a very uncouth appearance, the legs and neck being very long, as well as the bill. By the end of a week the head and neck are sparingly covered with long tufts of silky down, of a dark grey colour, and the body exhibits young feathers, the quills large, with soft blue sheaths. The tibio-tarsal joints appear monstrous, and at this period the bones of the leg are so soft, that one may bend them to a considerable extent without breaking them. At the end of four weeks, the body and wings are well covered with feathers of a dark slate-colour, broadly margined with ferruginous, the latter colour shewing plainly on the thighs and the flexure of the wing; the bill has grown wonderfully, the legs would not now easily break, and the birds are able to stand erect on the nest or on the objects near it. They are now seldom fed oftener than once a day, as if their parents were intent on teaching them that abstinence without which it would often be difficult for them to subsist in their after life. At the age of six or seven weeks they fly off, and at once go in search of food, each by itself.

In the following spring, at which time they have grown much, the elongated feathers of the breast and shoulders are seen, the males shew the commencement of the pendent crest, and the top of the head has become white. None breed at this age, in so far as I have been able to observe. The second spring, they have a handsome appearance, the upper parts have become light, the black and white marks are much purer, and some have the crest three or four inches in length. Some breed at this age. The third spring, the Great Blue Heron is as represented in the plate.

The males are somewhat larger than the females, but there is very little difference between the sexes in external appearance. This species moults in the Southern States about the beginning of May, or as soon as the young are hatched, and one month after the pendent crest is dropped, and much of the beauty of the bird is gone for the season. The weight of a full grown Heron of this kind, when it is in good condition, is about eight pounds; but this varies very much according to circumstances, and I have found some having all the appearance of old birds that did not exceed six pounds. The stomach consists of a long bag, thinly covered by a muscular coat, and is capable of containing several fishes at a time. The intestine is not thicker than the quill of a Swan, and measures from eight and a half to nine feet in length.

The Passenger Pigeon

ECTOPISTES MIGRATORIA, *LINN.*

The Passenger Pigeon, or, as it is usually named in America, the Wild Pigeon, moves with extreme rapidity, propelling itself by quickly repeated flaps of the wings, which it brings more or less near to the body, according to the degree of velocity which is required. Like the Domestic Pigeon, it often flies, during the love season, in a circling manner, supporting itself with both wings angularly elevated, in which position it keeps them until it is about to alight. Now and then, during these circular flights, the tips of the primary quills of each wing are made to strike against each other, producing a smart rap, which may be heard at a distance of thirty or forty yards. Before alighting, the Wild Pigeon, like the Carolina Parrot and a few other species of birds, breaks the force of its flight by repeated flappings, as if apprehensive of receiving injury from coming too suddenly into contact with the branch or the spot of ground on which it intends to settle.

I have commenced my description of this species with the above account of its flight, because the most important facts connected with its habits relate to its migrations. These are entirely owing to the necessity of procuring food, and are not performed with the view of escaping the severity of a northern latitude, or of seeking a southern one for the purpose of breeding. They consequently do not take place at any fixed period or season of the year. Indeed, it sometimes happens that a continuance of a sufficient supply of food in one district will keep these birds absent from another for years. I know, at least, to a certainty, that in Kentucky they remained for several years constantly, and were nowhere else to be found. They all suddenly disappeared one season when the mast was exhausted, and did not return for a long period. Similar facts have been observed in other States.

Their great power of flight enables them to survey and pass over an astonishing extent of country in a very short time. This is proved by facts well known. Thus, Pigeons have been killed in the neighbourhood of New York, with their crops full of rice, which they must have collected in the fields of Georgia and Carolina, these districts being the nearest in which they could possibly have procured a supply of that kind of food. As their power of digestion is so great that they will decompose food entirely in twelve hours, they must in this case have travelled between three and four hundred miles in six hours, which shews their speed to be at an average of about one mile in a minute. A velocity such as this would enable one of these birds, were it so inclined, to visit the European continent in less than three days.

This great power of flight is seconded by as great a power of vision, which enables them, as they travel at that swift rate, to inspect the country below, discover their food with facility, and thus attain the object for which their journey has been undertaken. This I have also proved to be the case, by having observed them, when passing over a sterile part of the country, or one scantily furnished with food suited to them, keep high in the air, flying with an extended front, so as to enable them to survey hundreds of acres at once. On the contrary, when the land is richly covered with food, or the trees abundantly hung with mast, they fly low, in order to discover the part most plentifully supplied.

Their body is of an elongated oval form, steered by a long well-plumed tail, and propelled by well-set wings, the muscles of which are very large and powerful for the size of the bird. When an individual is seen gliding through the woods and close to the observer, it passes like a thought, and on trying to see it again, the eye searches in vain; the bird is gone.

The multitudes of Wild Pigeons in our woods are astonishing. Indeed, after having viewed them so often, and under so many circumstances, I even now feel inclined to pause, and assure myself that what I am going to relate is fact. Yet I have seen it all, and that too in the company of persons who, like myself, were struck with amazement.

In the autumn of 1813, I left my house at Henderson, on the banks of the Ohio, on my way to Louisville. In passing over the Barrens a few miles beyond Hardensburgh, I observed the Pigeons flying from north-east to south-west, in greater numbers than I thought I had ever seen them before, and feeling an inclination to count the flocks that might pass within the reach of my eye in one hour, I dismounted, seated myself on an eminence, and began to mark with my pencil, making a dot for every flock that passed. In a short time finding the task which I had undertaken impracticable, as the birds poured in in countless multitudes, I rose, and counting the dots then put down, found that 163 had been made in twenty-one minutes. I travelled on, and still met more the farther I proceeded. The air was literally filled with Pigeons; the light of noon-day was obscured as by an eclipse; the dung fell in spots, not unlike melting flakes of snow; and the continued buzz of wings had a tendency to lull my senses to repose.

Whilst waiting for dinner at YOUNG's inn at the confluence of Salt river with the Ohio, I saw, at my leisure, immense legions still going by, with a front reaching far beyond the Ohio on the west, and the beech-wood forests directly on the east of me. Not a single bird alighted; for not a nut or acorn was that year to be seen in the neighbourhood. They consequently flew so high, that different trials to reach them with a capital rifle proved ineffectual; nor did the reports disturb them in the least. I cannot describe to you the extreme beauty of their aerial evolutions, when a Hawk chanced to press upon the rear of a flock. At once, like a torrent, and with a noise like thunder, they rushed into a compact mass, pressing upon each other towards the centre. In these almost solid masses, they darted forward in undulating and angular lines, descended and swept close over the earth with inconceivable velocity, mounted perpendicularly so as to resemble a vast column, and, when high, were seen wheeling and twisting within their continued lines, which then resembled the coils of a gigantic serpent.

Before sunset I reached Louisville, distant from Hardensburgh fifty-five miles. The Pigeons were still passing in undiminished numbers, and continued to do so for three days in succession. The people were all in arms. The banks of the Ohio were crowded with men and boys, incessantly shooting at the pilgrims, which there flew lower as they passed the river. Multitudes were thus destroyed. For a week or more, the population fed on no other flesh than that of Pigeons, and talked of nothing but Pigeons.

It is extremely interesting to see flock after flock performing exactly the same evolutions which had been traced as it were in the air by a preceding flock. Thus, should a Hawk have charged on a group at a certain spot, the angles, curves, and undulations that have been described by the birds, in their efforts to escape from the dreaded talons of the plunderer, are undeviatingly followed by the next group that comes up. Should the bystander happen to witness one of these affrays, and, struck with the rapidity and elegance of the motions exhibited, feel desirous of seeing them repeated, his wishes will be gratified if he only remain in the place until the next group comes up.

As soon as the Pigeons discover a sufficiency of food to entice them to alight, they fly around in circles, reviewing the country below. During their evolutions, on such occasions, the dense mass which they form exhibits a beautiful appearance, as it changes its direction, now displaying a glistening sheet of azure, when the backs of the birds come simultaneously into view, and anon, suddenly presenting a mass of rich deep purple. They then pass lower, over the woods, and for a moment are lost among the foliage, but again emerge, and are seen gliding aloft. They now alight, but the next moment, as if suddenly alarmed, they take to wing, producing by the flappings of their wing a noise like the roar of distant thunder, and sweep through the forests to see if danger is near. Hunger, however, soon brings them to the ground. When alighted, they are seen industriously throwing up the withered leaves in quest of the fallen mast. The rear ranks are continually rising, passing over the main-body, and alighting in front, in such rapid succession, that the whole flock seems still on wing. The quantity of ground thus swept is astonishing, and so completely has it been cleared, that the gleaner who might follow in their rear would find his labour completely lost. Whilst feeding, their avidity is at times so great that in attempting to swallow a large acorn or nut, they are seen gasping for a long while, as if in the agonies of suffocation.

On such occasions, when the woods are filled with these Pigeons, they are killed in immense numbers, although no apparent diminution ensues. About the middle of the day, after their repast is finished, they settle on the trees, to enjoy rest, and digest their food. On the ground they walk with ease, as well as on the branches, frequently jerking their beautiful tail, and moving the neck backwards and forwards in the most graceful manner. As the sun begins to sink beneath the horizon, they depart *en masse* for the roosting-place, which not unfrequently is hundreds of miles distant, as has been ascertained by persons who have kept an account of their arrivals and departures.

Let us now, kind reader, inspect their place of nightly rendezvous. One of these curious roosting-places, on the banks of the Green river in Kentucky, I repeatedly visited. It was, as is always the case, in a portion of the forest where the trees were of great magnitude, and where there was little underwood. I rode through it upwards of forty miles, and, crossing it in different parts, found its average breadth to be rather more than three miles. My first view of it was about a fortnight subsequent to the period when they had made choice of it, and I arrived there nearly two hours before sunset. Few Pigeons were then to be seen, but a great number of persons, with horses and wagons, guns and ammunition, had already established encampments on the borders. Two farmers from the vicinity of Russelsville, distant more than a hundred miles, had driven upwards of three hundred hogs to be fattened on the pigeons which were to be slaughtered. Here and there, the people employed in plucking and salting what had already been procured, were seen sitting in the midst of large piles of these birds. The dung lay several inches deep, covering the whole extent of the roosting-place. Many trees two feet in diameter, I observed, were broken off at no great distance from the ground; and the branches of many of the largest and tallest had given way, as if the forest had been swept by a tornado. Every thing proved to me that the number of birds resorting to this part of the forest must be immense beyond conception. As the period of their arrival approached, their foes anxiously prepared to receive them. Some were furnished with iron-pots containing sulphur, others with torches of pine-knots, many with poles, and the rest with guns. The sun was lost to our view, yet not a Pigeon had arrived. Every thing was ready, and all eyes were gazing on the clear sky, which appeared in glimpses amidst the tall trees. Suddenly there burst forth a general cry of "Here they come!" The noise which they made, though yet distant, reminded me of a hard gale at sea, passing through the rigging of a close-reefed vessel. As the birds arrived and passed over me, I felt a current of air that surprised me. Thousands were soon knocked down by the pole-men. The birds continued to pour in. The fires were lighted, and a magnificent, as well as wonderful and almost terrifying, sight presented itself. The Pigeons, arriving by thousands, alighted everywhere, one above another, until solid masses were formed on the branches all round. Here and there the perches gave way under the weight with a crash, and, falling to the ground, destroyed hundreds of the birds beneath, forcing down the dense groups with which every stick was loaded. It was a scene of uproar and confusion. I found it quite useless to speak, or even to shout to those persons who were nearest to me. Even the reports of the guns were seldom heard, and I was made aware of the firing only by seeing the shooters reloading.

No one dared venture within the line of devastation. The hogs had been penned up in due time, the picking up of the dead and wounded being left for the next morning's employment. The Pigeons were constantly coming, and it was past midnight before I perceived a decrease in the number of those that arrived. The uproar continued the whole night; and as I was anxious to know to what distance the sound reached,

I sent off a man, accustomed to perambulate the forest, who, returning two hours afterwards, informed me he had heard it distinctly when three miles distant from the spot. Towards the approach of day, the noise in some measure subsided: long before objects were distinguishable, the Pigeons began to move off in a direction quite different from that in which they had arrived the evening before, and at sunrise all that were able to fly had disappeared. The howlings of the wolves now reached our ears, and the foxes, lynxes, cougars, bears, racoons, opossums and pole-cats were seen sneaking off, whilst eagles and hawks of different species, accompanied by a crowd of vultures, came to supplant them, and enjoy their share of the spoil.

It was then that the authors of all this devastation began their entry amongst the dead, the dying, and the mangled. The Pigeons were picked up and piled in heaps, until each had as many as he could possibly dispose of, when the hogs were let loose to feed on the remainder.

Persons unacquainted with these birds might naturally conclude that such dreadful havoc would soon put an end to the species. But I have satisfied myself, by long observation, that nothing but the gradual diminution of our forests can accomplish their decrease, as they not unfrequently quadruple their numbers yearly, and always at least double it. In 1805 I saw schooners loaded in bulk with Pigeons caught up the Hudson river, coming in to the wharf at New York, when the birds sold for a cent a piece. I knew a man in Pennsylvania, who caught and killed upwards of 500 dozens in a clap-net in one day, sweeping sometimes twenty dozens or more at a single haul. In the month of March 1830, they were so abundant in the markets of New York, that piles of them met the eye in every direction. I have seen the Negroes at the United States' Salines or Saltworks of Shawanee Town, wearied with killing Pigeons, as they alighted to drink the water issuing from the leading pipes, for weeks at a time; and yet in 1826, in Louisiana, I saw congregated flocks of these birds as numerous as ever I had seen them before, during a residence of nearly thirty years in the United States.

The breeding of the Wild Pigeons, and the places chosen for that purpose, are points of great interest. The time is not much influenced by season, and the place selected is where food is most plentiful and most attainable, and always at a convenient distance from water. Forest-trees of great height are those in which the Pigeons form their nests. Thither the countless myriads resort, and prepare to fulfil one of the great laws of nature. At this period the note of the Pigeon is a soft *coo-coo-coo-coo*, much shorter than that of the domestic species. The common notes resemble the monosyllables *kee-kee-kee-kee*, the first being the loudest, the others gradually diminishing in power. The male assumes a pompous demeanour, and follows the female, whether on the ground or on the branches, with spread tail and drooping wings, which it rubs against the part over which it is moving. The body is elevated, the throat swells, the eyes sparkle. He continues his notes, and now and then rises on the wing, and flies a few yards to approach the fugitive and timorous female. Like the domestic Pigeon and other species, they caress each other by billing, in which action, the bill of the one is introduced transversely into that of the other, and both parties alternately disgorge the contents of their crop by repeated efforts. These preliminary affairs are soon settled, and the Pigeons commence their nests in general peace and harmony. They are composed of a few dry twigs, crossing each other, and are supported by forks of the branches. On the same tree from fifty to a hundred nests may frequently be seen:—I might say a much greater number, were I not anxious, kind reader, that however wonderful my account of the Wild Pigeon is, you may not feel disposed to refer it to the marvellous. The eggs are two in number, of a broadly elliptical form, and pure white. During incubation, the male supplies the female with food. Indeed, the tenderness and affection displayed by these birds towards their mates, are in the highest degree striking. It is a remarkable fact, that each brood generally consists of a male and a female.

Here again, the tyrant of the creation, man, interferes, disturbing the harmony of this peaceful scene. As the young birds grow up, their enemies, armed with axes, reach the spot, to seize and destroy all they can. The trees are felled, and made to fall in such a way that the cutting of one causes the overthrow of another, or shakes the neighbouring trees so much, that the young Pigeons, or *squabs*, as they are named, are violently hurried to the ground. In this manner also, immense quantities are destroyed.

The young are fed by the parents in the manner described above; in other words, the old bird introduces its bill into the mouth of the young one in a transverse manner, or with the back of each mandible opposite the separations of the mandibles of the young bird, and disgorges the contents of its crop. As soon as the young birds are able to shift for themselves, they leave their parents, and continue separate until they attain maturity. By the end of six months they are capable of reproducing their species.

The flesh of the Wild Pigeon is of a dark colour, but affords tolerable eating. That of young birds from the nest is much esteemed. The skin is covered with small white filmy scales. The feathers fall off at the least touch, as has been remarked to be the case in the Carolina Turtle-dove.

I have only to add, that this species, like others of the same genus, immerses its head up to the eyes while drinking.

In March 1830, I bought about 350 of these birds in the market of New York, at four cents a piece. Most of these I carried alive to England, and distributed them amongst several noblemen, presenting some at the same time to the Zoological Society.

This celebrated bird is mentioned by Dr. RICHARDSON as "annually reaching the 62nd degree of latitude, in the warm central districts of the Fur Countries, and attaining the 58th parallel on the coast of Hudson's Bay in very fine summers only. Mr. HUTCHINS mentions a flock which visited York Factory and remained there two days, in 1775, as a very remarkable occurrence. A few hordes of Indians that frequent the low flooded tracts at the south end of Lake Winnipeg, subsist principally on the Pigeons, during a part of the summer, when the sturgeon-fishery is unproductive, and the *Zizania aquatica* has not yet ripened; but farther north, these birds are too few in number to furnish a material article of diet." Mr. TOWNSEND states that this species is found on the Rocky Mountains, but not on the Columbia river, where the Band-tailed Pigeon, *Columba fasciata* of Say, is abundant. Whilst in the Texas, I was assured that the Passenger Pigeon was plentiful there, although at irregular intervals. In the neighbourhood of Boston it arrives, as Dr. T. M. BREWER informs me, in small scattered flocks, much less numerous than in the interior of that State.

My friend Dr. BACHMAN says, in a note sent to me, "In the more cultivated parts of the United States, these birds now no longer breed in communities. I have secured many nests scattered throughout the woods, seldom near each other. Four years ago, I saw several on the mountains east of Lansinburgh, in the State of New York. They were built close to the stems of thin but tall pine trees (*Pinus strobus*), and were composed of a few sticks; the eggs invariably two, and white. There is frequently but one young bird in the nest, probably from the loose manner in which it has been constructed, so that either a young bird or an egg drops out. Indeed, I have found both at the foot of the tree. This is no doubt accidental, and not to be attributed to a habit which the bird may be supposed to have of throwing out an egg or one of its young. I have frequently taken two of the latter from the same nest and reared them. The Wild Pigeons appear in Carolina during winter at irregular periods, sometimes in cold, but often in warm weather, driven here no doubt, as you have mentioned, not by the cold, but by a failure of mast in the western forests."

A curious change of habits has taken place in England in those Pigeons which I presented to the Earl of Derby in 1830, that nobleman having assured me that ever since they began breeding in his aviaries, they have laid only one egg. My noble friend has raised a great number of these birds, and has distributed them freely. It is not therefore very surprising that some which have escaped from confinement have been shot; but that this species should naturally have a claim to be admitted into the British Fauna appears to me very doubtful. The eggs measure one inch five-eighths in length, one inch one-eighth and a half in breadth, and are nearly equally rounded at both ends.

The Chimney Swallow, or American Swift

CHÆTURA PELASGIA, *TEMM.*

Since the progress of civilization in our country has furnished thousands of convenient places for this Swallow to breed in, safe from storms, snakes, or quadrupeds, it has abandoned, with a judgment worthy of remark, its former abodes in the hollows of trees, and taken possession of the chimneys which emit no smoke in the summer season. For this reason, no doubt, it has obtained the name by which it is generally known. I well remember the time when, in Lower Kentucky, Indiana, and Illinois, many resorted to excavated branches and trunks, for the purpose of breeding; nay, so strong is the influence of original habit, that not a few still betake themselves to such places, not only to roost, but also to breed, especially in those wild portions of our country that can scarcely be said to be inhabited. In such instances, they appear to be as nice in the choice of a tree, as they generally are in our cities in the choice of a chimney, wherein to roost. Sycamores of gigantic growth, and having a mere shell of bark and wood to support them, seem to suit them best, and wherever I have met with one of those patriarchs of the forest rendered habitable by decay, there I have found the Swallows breeding in spring and summer, and afterwards roosting until the time of their departure. I had a tree of this kind cut down, which contained about thirty of their nests in its trunk, and one in each of the hollow branches.

The nest, whether placed in a tree or chimney, consists of small dry twigs, which are procured by the birds in a singular manner. While on wing, the Chimney Swallows are seen in great numbers whirling round the tops of some decayed or dead tree, as if in pursuit of their insect prey. Their movements at this time are extremely rapid; they throw their body suddenly against the twig, grapple it with their feet, and by an instantaneous jerk, snap it off short, and proceed with it to the place intended for the nest. The Frigate Pelican sometimes employs the same method for a similar purpose, carrying away the stick in its bill, in place of holding it with its feet.

The Swallow fixes the first sticks on the wood, the rock, or the chimney wall, by means of its saliva, arranging them in a semicircular form, crossing and interweaving them, so as to extend the framework outwards. The whole is afterwards glued together with saliva, which is spread around it for an inch or more, to fasten it securely. When the nest is in a chimney, it is generally placed on the east side, and is from five to eight feet from the entrance; but in the hollow of a tree, where only they breed in communities, it is placed high or low according to convenience. The fabric, which is very frail, now and then gives way, either under the pressure of the parents and young, or during sudden bursts of heavy rain, when the whole is dashed to the ground. The eggs are from four to six, and of a pure white colour. Two broods are raised in the season.

The flight of this species is performed somewhat in the manner of the European Swift, but in a more hurried although continued style, and generally by repeated flappings, unless when courtship is going on, on which occasion it is frequently seen sailing with its wings fixed as it were; both sexes as they glide through the air issuing a shrill rattling twitter, and the female receiving the caresses of the male. At other times it is seen ranging far and wide at a considerable elevation over the forests and cities; again, in wet weather, it flies close over the ground; and anon it skims the water, to drink and bathe. When about to descend into a hollow tree or a chimney, its flight, always rapid, is suddenly interrupted as if by magic, for down it goes in an instant, whirling in a peculiar manner, and whirring with its wings, so as to produce a sound in the chimney like the rumbling of very distant thunder. They never alight on trees or on the ground. If one is caught and placed on the latter, it can only move in a very awkward fashion. I believe that the old birds sometimes fly at night, and have reason to think that the young are fed at such times, as I have heard the whirring sound of the former, and the acknowledging cries of the latter, during calm and clear nights.

When the young accidentally fall, which sometimes happens, although the nest should remain, they scramble up again, by means of their sharp claws, lifting one foot after another, in the manner of young Wood Ducks, and supporting themselves with their tail. Some days before the young are able to fly, they scramble up the walls to near the mouth of the chimney, where they are fed. Any observer may discover this, as he sees the parents passing close over them, without entering the funnel. The same occurrence takes place when they are bred in a tree.

In the cities, these birds make choice of a particular chimney for their roosting place, where, early in spring, before they have begun building, both sexes resort in multitudes, from an hour or more before sunset, until long after dark. Before entering the aperture, they fly round and over it many times, but finally go in one at a time, until hurried by the lateness of the hour, several drop in together. They cling to the wall with their claws, supporting themselves also by their sharp tail, until the dawn, when, with a roaring sound, the whole pass out almost at once. Whilst at St. Francisville in Louisiana, I took the trouble of counting how many entered one chimney before dark. I sat at a window not far from the spot, and reckoned upwards of a thousand, having missed a considerable number. The place at that time contained about a hundred houses, and no doubt existed in my mind that the greater number of these birds were on their way southward, and had merely stopped there for the night.

Immediately after my arrival at Louisville, in the State of Kentucky, I became acquainted with the late hospitable and amiable Major WILLIAM CROGHAN and his family. While talking one day about birds, he asked me if I had seen the trees in which the Swallows were supposed to spend the winter, but which they only entered, he said, for the purpose of roosting. Answering in the affirmative, I was informed that on my way back to town, there was a tree remarkable on account of the immense numbers that resorted to it, and the place in which it stood was described to me. I found it to be a sycamore, nearly destitute of branches, sixty or seventy feet high, between seven and eight feet in diameter at the base, and about five for the distance of forty feet up, where the stump of a broken hollowed branch, about two feet in diameter, made out from the main stem. This was the place at which the Swallows entered. On closely examining the tree, I found it hard, but hollow to near the roots. It was now about four o'clock after noon, in the month of July. Swallows were flying over Jeffersonville, Louisville, and the woods around, but there were none near the tree. I proceeded home, and shortly after returned on foot. The sun was going down behind the Silver Hills; the evening was beautiful; thousands of Swallows were flying closely above me, and three or four at a time were pitching into the hole, like bees hurrying into their hive. I remained, my head leaning on the tree, listening to the roaring noise made within by the birds as they settled and arranged themselves, until it was quite dark, when I left the place, although I was convinced that many more had to enter. I did not pretend to count them, for the number was too great, and the birds rushed to the entrance so thick as to baffle the attempt. I had scarcely returned to Louisville, when a violent thunder-storm passed suddenly over the town, and its appearance made me think that the hurry of the Swallows to enter the tree was caused by their anxiety to avoid it. I thought of the Swallows almost the whole night, so anxious had I become to ascertain their number, before the time of their departure should arrive.

Next morning I rose early enough to reach the place long before the least appearance of daylight, and placed my head against the tree. All was silent within. I remained in that posture probably twenty minutes, when suddenly I thought the great tree was giving way, and coming down upon me. Instinctively I sprung from it, but when I looked up to it again, what was my astonishment to see it standing as firm as ever. The Swallows were now pouring out in a black continued stream. I ran back to my post, and listened in amazement to the noise within, which I could compare to nothing else than the sound of a large wheel revolving under a powerful stream. It was yet dusky, so that I could hardly see the hour on my watch, but I estimated the time which they took in getting out at more than thirty minutes. After their departure, no noise was heard within, and they dispersed in every direction with the quickness of thought.

I immediately formed the project of examining the interior of the tree, which, as my kind friend, Major CROGHAN, had told me, proved the most remarkable I had ever met with. This I did, in company with a hunting associate. We went provided with a strong line and a rope, the first of which we, after several trials, succeeded in throwing across the broken branch. Fastening the rope to the line we drew it up, and pulled it over until it reached the ground again. Provided with the longest cane we could find, I mounted the tree by the rope, without accident, and at length seated myself at ease on the broken branch; but my labour was fruitless, for I could see nothing through the hole, and the cane, which was about fifteen feet long, touched nothing on the sides of the tree within that could give any information. I came down fatigued and disappointed.

The next day I hired a man, who cut a hole at the base of the tree. The shell was only eight or nine inches thick, and the axe soon brought the inside to view, disclosing a matted mass of exuviæ, with rotten feathers reduced to a kind of mould, in which, however, I could perceive fragments of insects and quills. I had a passage cleared, or rather bored through this mass, for nearly six feet. This operation took up a good deal of time, and knowing by experience that if the birds should notice the hole below, they would abandon the tree, I had it carefully closed. The Swallows came as usual that night, and I did not disturb them for several days. At last, provided with a dark lantern, I went with my companion about nine in the evening, determined to have a full view of the interior of the tree. The hole was opened with caution. I scrambled up the sides of the mass of exuviæ, and my friend followed. All was perfectly silent. Slowly and gradually I brought the light of the lantern to bear on the sides of the hole above us, when we saw the Swallows clinging side by side, covering the whole surface of the excavation. In no instance did I see one above another. Satisfied with the sight, I closed the lantern. We then caught and killed with as much care as possible more than a hundred, stowing them away in our pockets and bosoms, and slid down into the open air. We observed that, while on this visit, not a bird had dropped its dung upon us. Closing the entrance, we marched towards Louisville perfectly elated. On examining the birds which we had procured, a hundred and fifteen in number, we found only six females. Eighty-seven were adult males; of the remaining twenty-two the sex could not be ascertained, and I had no doubt that they were the young of that year's first brood, the flesh and quill-feathers being tender and soft.

Let us now make a rough calculation of the number that clung to the tree. The space beginning at the pile of feathers and moulded exuviæ, and ending at the entrance of the hole above, might be fully 25 feet in height, with a breadth of 15 feet, supposing the tree to be 5 feet in diameter at an average. There would thus be 375 feet square of surface. Each square foot, allowing a bird to cover a space of 3 inches by $1\frac{1}{2}$, which is more than enough, judging from the manner in which they were packed, would contain 32 birds. The number of Swallows, therefore, that roosted in this single tree was 9000.

I watched the motions of the Swallows, and when the young birds that had been reared in the chimneys of Louisville, Jeffersonville, and the houses of the neighbourhood, or the trees suited for the purpose, had left their native recesses, I visited the tree on the 2nd day of August. I concluded that the numbers resorting to it had not increased; but I found many more females and young than males, among upwards of fifty, which were caught and opened. Day after day I watched the tree. On the 13th of August, not more than two or three hundred came there to roost. On the 18th of the same month, not one did I see near it, and only a few scattered individuals were passing, as if moving southward.

In September I entered the tree at night, but not a bird was in it. Once more I went to it in February, when the weather was very cold; and perfectly satisfied that all these Swallows had left our country, I finally closed the entrance, and left off visiting it.

May arrived, bringing with its vernal warmth the wanderers of the air, and I saw their number daily augmenting, as they resorted to the tree to roost. About the beginning of June, I took it in my head to close the aperture above, with a bundle of straw, which with a string I could draw off whenever I might choose. The result was curious enough; the birds as usual came to the tree towards night; they assembled, passed and repassed, with apparent discomfort, until I perceived many flying off to a great distance, on which I removed the straw, when many entered the hole, and continued to do so until I could no longer see them from the ground.

I left Louisville, having removed my residence to Henderson, and did not see the tree until five years after, when I still found the Swallows resorting to it. The pieces of wood with which I had closed the entrance had rotted, or had been carried off, and the hole was again completely filled with exuviæ and mould. During a severe storm, their ancient tenement at length gave way, and came to the ground.

General WILLIAM CLARK assured me that he saw this species on the whole of his route to the Pacific, and there can be no doubt that in those wilds it still breeds in trees or rocky caverns.

Its food consists entirely of insects, the pellets composed of the indigestible parts of which it disgorges. It is furnished with glands which supply the unctuous matter with which it fastens its nest.

This species does not appear to extend its migrations farther east than the British provinces of New Brunswick and Nova Scotia. It is unknown in Newfoundland and Labrador; nor was it until the 29th of May that I saw some at Eastport in Maine, where a few breed.

The Raven

CORVUS CORAX, *LINN.*

Leaving to compilers the task of repeating the mass of fabulous and unedifying matter that has been accumulated in the course of ages, respecting this and other remarkable species of birds, and arranging the materials which I obtained during years of laborious but gratifying observation, I will now attempt to delineate the manners of this species which I have noted in the course of a life chiefly spent in studying the birds of my native land, where I have had abundant opportunities of contemplating their manners, and of admiring the manifestations of the glorious perfections of their Omnipotent Creator.

There, amid the tall grass of the far-extended prairies of the West, in the solemn forests of the North, on the heights of the midland mountains, by the shores of the boundless ocean, and on the bosom of the vast lakes and magnificent rivers, have I sought to search out the things which have been hidden since the creation of this wondrous world, or seen only by the naked Indian, who has, for unknown ages, dwelt in the gorgeous but melancholy wilderness. Who is the stranger to my own dear country that can form an adequate conception of the extent of its primeval woods,—of the glory of those columnar trunks, that for centuries have waved in the breeze, and resisted the shock of the tempest, —of the vast bays of our Atlantic coasts, replenished by thousands of streams, differing in magnitude, as differ the stars that sparkle in the expanse of the pure heavens,—of the diversity of aspect in our western plains, our sandy southern shores interspersed with reedy swamps, and the cliffs that protect our eastern coasts,—of the rapid currents of the Mexican Gulf, and the rushing tide streams of the Bay of Fundy,—of our ocean-lakes, our mighty rivers, our thundering cataracts, our majestic mountains, rearing their snowy heads into the calm regions of the clear cold sky?

In the United States, the Raven is in some measure a migratory bird, individuals retiring to the extreme south during severe winters, but returning towards the Middle, Western, and Northern Districts at the first indications of milder weather. A few are known to breed in the mountainous portions of South Carolina, but instances of this kind are rare, and are occasioned merely by the security afforded by inaccessible precipices, in which they may rear their young. Their usual places of resort are the mountains, the abrupt banks of rivers, the rocky shores of lakes, and the cliffs of thinly-peopled or deserted islands. It is in such places that these birds must be watched and examined, before one can judge of their natural habits, as manifested amid their freedom from the dread of their most dangerous enemy, the lord of the creation.

There, through the clear and rarified atmosphere, the Raven spreads his glossy wings and tail, and, as he onward sails, rises higher and higher each bold sweep that he makes, as if conscious that the nearer he approaches the sun, the more splendent will become the tints of his plumage. Intent on convincing his mate of the fervour and constancy of his love, he now gently glides beneath her, floats in the buoyant air, or sails by her side. Would that I could describe to you, reader, the many musical inflections by means of which they hold converse during these amatory excursions! These sounds doubtless express their pure conjugal feelings, confirmed and rendered more intense by long years of happiness in each other's society. In this manner they may recall the pleasing remembrance of their youthful days, recount the events of their life, and express the pleasure they enjoy.

Now, their matins are over; the happy pair are seen to glide towards the earth in spiral lines; they alight on the boldest summit of a rock, so high that you can scarcely judge of their actual size; they approach each other, their bills meet, and caresses are exchanged as tender as those of the gentle Turtle Dove. Far beneath, wave after wave dashes in foam against the impregnable sides of the rocky tower, the very aspect of which would be terrific to almost any other creatures than the sable pair, which for years have resorted to it, to rear the dearly-cherished fruits of their connubial love. Midway between them and the boiling waters, some shelving ledge conceals their eyry. To it they now betake themselves, to see what damage it has sustained from the peltings of the winter tempests. Off they fly to the distant woods for fresh materials with which to repair the breach; or on the plain they collect the hair and fur of quadrupeds; or from the sandy beach pick up the weeds that have been washed there. By degrees, the nest is enlarged and trimmed, and when every thing has been rendered clean and comfortable, the female deposits her eggs, and begins to sit upon them, while her brave and affectionate mate protects and feeds her, and at intervals takes her place.

All around is now silent, save the hoarse murmur of the waves, or the whistling sounds produced by the flight of the waterfowl travelling towards the northern regions. At length the young burst the shell, when the careful parents, after congratulating each other on the happy event, disgorge some half-macerated food, which they deposit in their tender mouths. Should the most daring adventurer of the air approach, he is attacked with fury and repelled. As the young grow up, they are urged to be careful and silent:—a single false movement might precipitate them into the abyss below; a single cry during the absence of their parents might bring upon them the remorseless claws of the swift Peregrine or Jerfalcon. The old birds themselves seem to improve in care, diligence, and activity, varying their course when returning to their home, and often entering it when unexpected. The young are now seen to stand on the edge of the nest; they flap their wings, and at length take courage and fly to some more commodious and not distant lodgment. Gradually they become able to follow their parents abroad, and at length search for maintenance in their company, and that of others, until the period of breeding arrives, when they separate in pairs, and disperse.

Notwithstanding all the care of the Raven, his nest is invaded wherever it is found. His usefulness is forgotten, his faults are remembered and multiplied by imagination; and whenever he presents himself he is shot at, because from time immemorial ignorance, prejudice, and destructiveness have operated on the mind of man to his detriment. Men will peril their lives to reach his nest, assisted by ropes and poles, alleging merely that he has killed one of their numerous sheep or lambs. Some say they destroy the Raven because he is black; others, because his croaking is unpleasant and ominous! Unfortunate truly are the young ones that are carried home to become the wretched pets of some ill-brought-up child! For my part, I admire the Raven, because I see much in him calculated to excite our wonder. It is true that he may sometimes hasten the death of a half-starved sheep, or destroy a weakly lamb; he may eat the eggs of other birds, or occasionally steal from the farmer some of those which he calls his own; young fowls also afford precious morsels to himself and his progeny;—but how many sheep, lambs, and fowls, are saved through his agency! The more intelligent of our farmers are well aware that the Raven destroys numberless insects, grubs, and worms; that he kills mice, moles, and rats, whenever he can find them; that he will seize the weasel, the young opossum, and the skunk; that, with the perseverance of a cat, he will watch the burrows of foxes, and pounce on the cubs; our farmers also are fully aware that he apprises them of the wolf's prowlings around their yard, and that he never intrudes on their corn-fields except to benefit them;—yes, good reader, the farmer knows all this well, but he also knows his power, and, interfere as you may, with tale of pity or of truth, the bird is a Raven, and, as LAFONTAINE has aptly and most truly said, *"La loi du plus fort est toujours la meilleure!"*

The flight of the Raven is powerful, even, and at certain periods greatly protracted. During calm and fair weather it often ascends to an immense height, sailing there for hours at a time; and although it cannot be called swift, it propels itself with sufficient power to enable it to contend with different species of Hawks, and even with Eagles when attacked by them. It manages to guide its course through the thickest fogs of the countries of the north, and is able to travel over immense tracts of land or water without rest.

The Raven is omnivorous, its food consisting of small animals of every kind, eggs, dead fish, carrion, shell-fish, insects, worms, nuts, berries, and other kinds of fruit. I have never seen one attack a large living animal, as the Turkey Buzzard and Carrion Crow are wont to do; but I have known it follow hunters when without dogs, to feed on the offals of the game, and carry off salted fish when placed in a spring to freshen. It often rises in the air with a shell-fish for the purpose of breaking it by letting it fall on a rock. Its sight is exceedingly acute, but its smell, if it possesses the sense, is weak. In this respect, it bears a great resemblance to our Vultures.

The breeding season of this bird varies, according to the latitude, from the beginning of January to that of June. I have found young Ravens on the banks of the Lehigh and the Susquehanna rivers on the 1st of May; about ten days later on those of the majestic Hudson; in the beginning of June on the island of Grand Manan off the Bay of Fundy; and at Labrador, as late as the middle of July. The nest is always placed in the most inaccessible parts of rocks that can be found, never, I believe, on trees, at least in America. It is composed of sticks, coarse weeds, wool, and bunches of hair of different animals. The eggs are from four to six, of a rather elongated oval shape, fully two inches in length, having a ground colour of light greenish-blue, sprinkled all over with small irregular blotches of light purple and yellowish-brown, so numerous on the larger end, as almost entirely to cover it. The period of incubation extends to nineteen or twenty days. Only one brood is raised in a year, unless the eggs or young be removed or destroyed. The young remain in the nest many weeks before they are able to fly. The old birds return to the same nest for years in succession; and should one of them be destroyed, the other will lead a new partner to the same abode. Even after the young have made their appearance, should one of the parents be killed, the survivor usually manages to find a mate, who undertakes the task of assisting in feeding them.

The Raven may be said to be of a social disposition, for, after the breeding season, flocks of forty, fifty, or more, may sometimes be seen, as I observed on the coast of Labrador, and on the Missouri. When domesticated, and treated with kindness, it becomes attached to its owner, and will follow him about with all the familiarity of a confiding friend. It is capable of imitating the human voice, so that individuals have sometimes been taught to enunciate a few words with great distinctness.

On the ground the Raven walks in a stately manner, its motions exhibiting a kind of thoughtful consideration, almost amounting to gravity. While walking it frequently moves up its wings as if to keep their muscles in action. I never knew an instance of their roosting in the woods, although they frequently alight on trees, to which they sometimes resort for the purpose of procuring nuts and other fruits. They usually betake themselves at night to high rocks, in situations protected from the northerly winds. Possessing to all appearance the faculty of judging of the coming weather, they remove from the higher, wild and dreary districts where they breed, into the low lands, at the approach of winter, when they are frequently seen along the shores of the sea, collecting the garbage that has been cast to land, or picking up the shell-fish as the tide retires. They are vigilant, industrious, and, when the safety of their young or nest is at stake, courageous, driving away Hawks and Eagles whenever they happen to come near, although in no case do they venture to attack man. Indeed, it is extremely difficult to get within shot of an old Raven. I have more than once been only a few yards from one while it was sitting on its eggs, having attained this proximity by creeping cautiously to the overhanging edge of a precipice; but the moment the bird perceived me, it would fly off apparently in much confusion. They are so cunning and wary, that they can seldom be caught in a trap; and they will watch one intended for a fox, a wolf, or a bear, until one of these animals comes up, and is taken, when they will go to it and eat the alluring bait.

While at Little Macatina Harbour, on the coast of Labrador, in July 1833, I saw a Raven's nest placed under the shelvings of the rugged and fearful rocks that form one side of that singular place. The young were nearly fledged, and now and then called loudly to their parents, as if to inquire why our vessel had come there. One of them in attempting to fly away fell into the water. It was secured, when I trimmed one of its wings, and turned it loose on the deck along with some other birds. The mother, however, kept sailing high over the schooner, repeating some notes, which it seems the young one understood, for it walked carefully to the end of the bowsprit, opened its wings, and tried to fly, but being unable, fell into the water and was drowned. In a few days the rest of the family left the place, and we saw no more of them. Some of the sailors who had come to the harbour eight years in succession, assured me that they had always observed the Ravens breeding there. My whole party found it impossible to shoot one of the old ones, who went to the nest and left it with so much caution, that the task of watching them became irksome. One afternoon I concealed myself under a pile of detached rocks for more than two hours. The young frequently croaked as I was waiting there, but no parent came; so I left the place, but the next moment the female was seen from the deck of the Ripley. She alighted in the nest, fed her young, and was off again before I could reach within shooting distance. It was at this place that I observed how singularly well those birds could travel to and from their nest, at a time when I could not, on account of the fog, see them on wing at a greater distance than twenty or thirty yards. On the 29th of the same month, young Ravens were seen in flocks with their parents; but they were already very shy.

I found a nest of this bird at a narrow part of the Lehigh in Pennsylvania, in a deep fissure of the rocks, not more than twenty feet above the water, the security afforded by which had probably been considered as equivalent to that which might have been gained by a greater height of rock. The nest, in fact, hung over the stream, so that it was impossible to reach it either from above or from below. Many years ago, I saw another placed immediately beneath the arch of the Rock Bridge in Virginia. It was situated on a small projecting stone scarcely a foot square; yet the Raven appeared quite satisfied as to the security of her brood on that narrow bed. This extraordinary production of Nature is placed on the ascent of a hill, which appears to have been rent asunder by some convulsion of the earth. The fissure is about 200 feet deep, and above 80 in width under the arch, narrowing to 40 or so at the bottom. The thickness of the arch probably exceeds 30 feet, and increases at either end. At the bottom is seen the water of what is called Cedar Creek, gently meandering in its rocky channel. The place, when I saw it, was graced by handsome trees, and in some positions there was a pleasing view of the "Blue Ridge" and the "North Mountain." Tradition reports that General WASHINGTON threw a dollar over the bridge from the creek below.

I have already stated that some Ravens breed as far south as the Carolinas. The place to which they resort for this purpose is called the Table Mountain, which is situated in the district of Pendleton, and of which I extract an account from DRAYTON's Views of South Carolina. "The Table Mountain is the most distinguished of all the eminences of the State. Its height exceeds 3000 feet, and thirty farms may be discerned at any one view from its top by the unaided eye. Its side is an abrupt precipice of solid rock, 300 feet deep, and nearly perpendicular. The valley underneath appears to be as much below the level as the top of the mountain towers above it. This precipice is called the Lover's Leap. To those who are in the valley, it looks like an immense wall stretching up to heaven, and the awe which it inspires is considerably increased by the quantities of bones which lie whitening at its base,—the remains of various animals which had incautiously approached too near its edge. Its summit is often enveloped in clouds. The gradual ascent of the country from the sea-coast to this western extremity of the State, added to the height of this mountain, must place its top more than 4000 feet above the level of the Atlantic Ocean; an eminence from which vessels crossing the bar of Charleston might be seen with the aid of such improved glasses as are now in use. Large masses of snow tumble from the side of this mountain in the winter season, the fall of which has been heard seven miles. Its summit is the resort of deer and bears. The woods produce mast in abundance; Wild Pigeons resort to it in such numbers as sometimes to break the limbs of trees on which they alight."

A friend of mine, who is an excellent observer of the habits of birds, has told me that he saw a Raven's nest in the high lands of New York placed in a deep fissure of a rock, in the immediate vicinity of that of a Golden Eagle. I chanced one day, while in the Great Pine Forest of Pennsylvania, to stop, for the purpose of resting and refreshing myself, at a camp with JEDIAH IRISH. We had seen some Ravens that day, and our conversation returning to them, the person employed in preparing the food of the woodcutters told us, that whenever she chanced to place a salt mackerel or other fish in the brook running from the spring near the camp, "the Raven was sure to carry it away in less than an hour." She firmly believed that it had the power of smelling the fish as she carried it from the hut to the water. We went to the spot with her, and, leaving a fish there, returned to our homely meal, but on visiting the place several hours after, we found it untouched. "The Raven perhaps smelt the powder in our guns!" At all events, it did not choose to come that day.

The flesh of this bird is tough and unfit for food, but this indicates its great strength. When wounded, it bites severely, and scratches with its claws as fiercely as a Hawk. Like the latter also, it disgorges indigestible substances, as bones, hair, and feathers.

This species is plentiful on the Rocky Mountains and along the Columbia river, and also abounds in the Fur Countries, and, according to Dr. RICHARDSON, visits the remotest islands of the Polar seas. It frequents the Barren Grounds even in the most intense winter colds, its movements being directed in a great measure by those of the herds of Rein Deer, Musk Oxen, and Bison, which it follows, ready to assist in devouring such as are killed by beasts of prey or by accident. He relates a curious instance of the propensity it shews to appropriate to itself any metallic substance. "Mr. KENDAL, in crossing the heights of land which divide the waters that flow towards Hudson's Bay, from those which fall into the Arctic Sea, saw a Raven flying off with something in his claws, pursued by a number of his clamorous companions. The bird being fired at dropped the object of contention, which proved to be the lock of a chest!" Mr. TOWNSEND informs me that on the Columbia river the Ravens constantly attend on the salmon fisheries, and that during winter they are very expert at discovering the small tents raised by the Indians for the purpose of saving their fish. They are in all those districts constant attendants upon the hunters, for the purpose of devouring the offal of all such game as may be slaughtered.

Although I have found eggs of this species which measured rather more than two inches in length, by an inch and three-eighths, others did not measure more than one inch and seven-eighths by an inch and four-twelfths. They also differ considerably in the tint of their ground-colour, as well as in their markings.